"Contemporary Orthodox theology is like a spring flower that has budded after a harsh winter's thaw. This book signals the blossoming of Orthodox theology in the English-speaking world after centuries of inhospitable historical conditions under Islam and Communism. Previously confined to traditional Orthodox countries such as Russia, Romania, Greece and Serbia, Orthodox theology today is emerging with striking advances in Western Europe and North America. With vast erudition, this stunningly well-conceived book traces the influence of the spiritual classic, the *Philokalia*, on leading Orthodox thinkers, lay theologians and monastics in the nineteenth and twentieth centuries. This original work provides an unparalleled resource for understanding the theological vision of Orthodox thinkers over the last two centuries. It is a landmark achievement that validates the thesis that the Orthodox Church is on the cusp of a major theological renaissance in the twenty-first century."

Bradley Nassif, professor of biblical and theological studies, North Park University, coeditor of *The Philokalia: A Classic Text of Orthodox Spirituality*

"Through the lives and thought of a score of Orthodox theologians, Andrew Louth shows the distinctiveness of their theology, grounded not in academic concepts and constructs but rather in prayer, paths toward holiness and the experience of the living church. A thoroughly engaging introduction to the ways of modern Orthodox theology."

Vigen Guroian, author of *The Melody of Faith*

"Fr. Andrew Louth, who is himself one of the foremost Orthodox theologians of our time, offers us in this volume much more than a survey of 'modern Orthodox thinkers,' despite the humble simplicity of the title. The wonderfully surprising grace of this work is that it succeeds in communicating not only the thought of the major figures in modern Orthodox theology but the spiritual wellsprings of that thought in Orthodox prayer and liturgy. An equally inspired feat is his presentation of the rich diversity of modern Orthodoxy, comprising clerical and lay theologians, both men and women, hailing from a great variety of backgrounds and perspectives. This is a work of scholarship that is imbued with a Eucharistic spirit. The reader will feel both nourished by its erudition and deeply grateful for its illumination of the manifold manifestations of the Spirit in modern Orthodoxy."

Khaled Anatolios, University of Notre Dame

"This is sure to become the standard handbook on the ways of Orthodox theology in the nineteenth and twentieth century inspired by, and inspiring, the love of the good and beautiful."

V. Rev. Dr. John Behr, St Vladimir's Seminary, New York

"Rewarding and timely, *Modern Orthodox Thinkers* is both an informative introduction to a gallery of individual thinkers and a coherent meditation on the significance of Orthodox thought in the modern world."

Avril Pyman, FBA, reader emerita in Russian literature, University of Durham

"By following the trajectory of Orthodox thought wherever it has blossomed across the world, this revelatory book charts a whole new constellation in the cosmos of Eastern Christianity. Andrew Louth's warm and lucid exposition, combined with his deep learning, makes him the ideal ambassador of the religious ideals he explores."

Rosamund Bartlett, author of *Tolstoy: A Russian Life*

"We have needed this book for a long time. Praise to Andrew Louth for his extraordinary breadth and depth in painting a multicolored portrait of the many faces of Orthodox theology since the late eighteenth century."

Sarah Hinlicky Wilson, Institute for Ecumenical Research, Strasbourg, consultant, International Lutheran–Orthodox Joint Commission

"Father Andrew Louth offers us an account of Eastern Christianity made up of men and women, flesh and blood, engaged on the extraordinary project of the kingdom of God on earth. The celebrated English Orthodox theologian gives us the chance to meet the living icons for whom Orthodoxy was an existential, rather than confessional, guide. It is an anthology with the secret project of pursuing a tradition of thought that refuses to separate the good, the just and the beautiful. A book to read and re-read."

Antoine Arjakovsky, founding director of the institute of ecumenical studies, Lviv, Ukraine, research director, Collège des Bernardins, Paris

MODERN ORTHODOX THINKERS

From the *Philokalia* to the Present

ANDREW LOUTH

IVP Academic

An imprint of InterVarsity Press
Downers Grove, Illinois

InterVarsity Press
P.O. Box 1400, Downers Grove, IL 60515-1426
ivpress.com
email@ivpress.com

InterVarsity Press® is the book-publishing division of InterVarsity Christian Fellowship/USA®, a movement of students and faculty active on campus at hundreds of universities, colleges and schools of nursing in the United States of America, and a member movement of the International Fellowship of Evangelical Students. For information about local and regional activities, visit intervarsity.org.

Cover design: Cindy Kiple
Images: ©druvo/iStockphoto

ISBN 978-0-8308-5121-8 (print)
ISBN 978-0-8308-9962-3 (digital)

Printed in the United States of America ∞

Library of Congress Cataloging-in-Publication Data

Louth, Andrew, author.
 Modern Orthodox thinkers : from the Philokalia to the present day / Andrew Louth.
  pages cm
 Includes bibliographical references and index.
 ISBN 978-0-8308-5121-8 (paperback)
 1. Orthodox Eastern Church--Doctrines. 2. Orthodox Eastern Church--History. I. Title.
 BX320.3.L6872 2015
 230'.190922--dc23

                                                                                                2015027318

| P | 19 | 18 | 17 | 16 | 15 | 14 | 13 | 12 | 11 | 10 | 9 | 8 | 7 | 6 | 5 | 4 | 3 | 2 | 1 |
| Y | 31 | 30 | 29 | 28 | 27 | 26 | 25 | 24 | 23 | 22 | 21 | 20 | 19 | 18 | 17 | 16 | 15 |

For Anna

Contents

Contents

Illustrations

Preface

This book is a revised version of public lectures given in the academic years 2012/13, 2013/14, at the Amsterdam Centre for Eastern Orthodox Studies (ACEOT), during which time I was Visiting Professor for Eastern Orthodox Theology at the Vrije Universiteit, Amsterdam: ACEOT belongs to its Faculty of Theology. The final book owes a great deal to the encouragement of those who attended and their questions and observations. Many other people helped me form my ideas: Deacon Michael Bakker, the director of ACEOT, Fr John Behr, with whom I have had many discussions of issues connected with the book, likewise Brandon Gallaher. I was helped (and encouraged) on particular chapters by Avril Pyman-Sokolova (especially on Fr Pavel Florensky), Vladimir Cvetković (on St Justin Popović), Denise Harvey (on Philip Sherrard), Marilyn Wood (on Mother Thekla), Fr Serafim Aldea (aka Leonard Aldea: especially on Fr Sophrony, but on others, too). On matters Greek, I have been helped (though they may not be aware of this) by Niki Tsironi, Fr Andreas Andreopoulos, Sotiris Mitralexis, and my research student at ACEOT, Fr Alexandros Chouliaras (who has also helped with books from Greece). There are other debts that go back much further, not least to Metropolitan Kallistos. One person in particular read all the lectures, asking annoyingly pertinent questions, and then all the chapters, removing asperities and unclarities: my friend, Anna Zaranko, to whom the book is dedicated.

A word should perhaps be said about transliteration of Greek and Russian words and names: it is inconsistent, as everyone always confesses. I think I have mostly used forms that would not look too outlandish in English, but have indulged my pet hates.

Andrew Louth
Feast of St Anastasia, Curer of Wounds

Abbreviations

Conf.	Augustine, *Confessions*
ECR	*Eastern Churches Review*
ep.	epistle
ET	English translation
GOTR	*Greek Orthodox Theological Review*
Haer.	Irenaeus, *Against Heresies*
Hist. eccl.	Eusebius, *History of the Church*
Hom. Exod.	Origen, *Homily on Exodus*
Ign. *Eph.*	Ignatios of Antioch, *To the Ephesians*
Ign. *Smyrn.*	Ignatios of Antioch, *To the Smyrnaeans*
IJSCC	*International Journal for the Study of the Christian Church*
Irén.	*Irénikon*
ITQ	*Irish Theological Quarterly*
JECS	*Journal of Eastern Christian Studies*
LXX	Septuagint
Or. Bas.	Gregory the Theologian, *Oratio in laudem Basilii*
PG	Patrologica graeca, ed. J.-P. Migne; 162 vols (Paris, 1857–86)
RHR	*Revue d'histoire des religions*
RSPT	*Revue des sciences philosophiques et théologiques*
SC	Sources Chrétiennes (Paris, 1943–)
SSTS	Studies Supplementary to *Sobornost*
SVTQ	*St Vladimir's Theological Quarterly*
WCC	World Council of Churches

Introduction

Various presuppositions or intuitions lie behind this book. The first, which affects the scope of the work, is that the publication of the *Philokalia* in Venice in 1782 can be seen, at least in retrospect, to mark a kind of watershed in the history of modern Orthodox theology. Not all Orthodox theology after that date is marked by the *Philokalia*; indeed most academic theology in Greece and Russia seems to have been quite unaffected by it (at least until very recently). In what way was the *Philokalia* a watershed? Very briefly, because it suggested a way of approaching theology that had at its heart an experience of God, an experience mediated by prayer, that demanded the transformation of the seeker after God; it is an approach that shuns any idea of turning God into a concept, a philosophical hypothesis, or some sort of ultimate moral guarantor. Furthermore, it sought to return the living of the Christian life (primarily, but not exclusively, the monastic life) to its roots in the Fathers; it was, it claimed, an anthology gathered together from 'our Holy and God-bearing Fathers, in which through ethical philosophy, in accordance with action and contemplation, the intellect is purified, illumined, and perfected' (as asserted on the title page of the original Greek edition): so a theology rooted in the Christian experience of prayer, and all that that entails by way of ascetic struggle and deepening insight – nourished by the Fathers (and Mothers) of the Church.

My second intuition is rather different (though maybe not unrelated). This is a book about people: it is a history of Orthodox *thinkers*, rather than a history of Orthodox *thought*, or theology. For thoughts – or theology – do not float through some intellectual ether, but are thought by thinkers. I am wary of ways of presenting the history of thought as if it were in some way detached from the thinkers who had these thoughts, thinkers who were men and women – human beings of flesh and blood, who belonged to specific places and faced particular problems – in the world in which they lived, in the relationships in which they were caught up, and (most important, though often quite hidden) in the depths of their souls.

After some account of the immediate influence of the *Philokalia* in Russia in the first chapter, we shall turn to the colourful character of Vladimir Solov'ev, a thinker and poet who had an immense influence in Russia at the end of the nineteenth and the beginning of the twentieth century – on people such as Dostoevsky (though Dostoevsky was much older, and the influence most likely was the other way about), poets like Andrei Bely and Aleksandr Blok, and thinkers, including those whom I shall go on to discuss in the chapters immediately following: Fr Pavel Florensky, Fr Sergii Bulgakov, Nikolai Berdyaev (it is an influence that continues, as we shall discover). Of those three men, two were among the intellectuals expelled from Russia by Trotsky in 1922, ending up eventually in Paris: Bulgakov and Berdyaev. We shall continue by looking at some other exiles in Paris: Myrrha Lot-Borodine (who had arrived in Paris as a student in 1906), Fr Georges Florovsky, Vladimir Lossky, and Mother Maria Skobtsova, now St Maria of Paris, who died a martyr in Ravensbrück. There follow two other Orthodox thinkers, affected in different ways by Russian theology in the diaspora – Fr Dumitru Stăniloae of Romania and Fr (now St) Justin Popović of Serbia – as well as by their native traditions.

Our series of thinkers then continues with the next generation of Russians in Paris: Paul Evdokimov, as well as Fr John Meyendorff and Fr Alexander Schmemann, the latter two of whom left Paris for the USA, where they were instrumental in founding the Orthodox Church of America and establishing the reputation of St Vladimir's Orthodox Seminary, though it can be argued that their theological influence, at least among Orthodox, was greater in Greece.

The focus of our account will then turn to Greece: first of all, those influenced by Meyendorff's neo-Palamism and Schmemann's liturgical theology. Then there are other Greeks influenced by the Russian émigré theologians: Fr John Romanides and John Zizioulas, now Metropolitan John of Pergamon, both of whom studied under Florovsky, and lay thinkers such as Christos Yannaras (himself much influenced by Vladimir Lossky, though not at first hand) and Stelios Ramfos. Other lay theologians we shall consider include the Englishman Philip Sherrard, and the French thinkers Olivier Clément and Elisabeth Behr-Sigel.

A feature of Orthodox theology down the ages has been the importance of spiritual elders, the revival of which in modern times was one of the effects of the *Philokalia*. This could be the subject of a whole book, and I have illustrated the importance of monastic theology by taking as examples two monastics whom I knew, at least a little: Mother Thekla of Normanby and Fr Sophrony of Essex (and his monastic mentor, St Silouan the Athonite).

The penultimate chapter returns to Russia, the theological contribution of which has mostly been pursued in this book through émigré thinkers, looking at a few of those who kept the faith alive in academic circles, before turning to the priest, thinker and martyr, Fr Aleksandr Men'. The book reaches its conclusion with Metropolitan Kallistos of Diokleia, Timothy Ware, whose influence in the English-speaking Orthodox world has been unparalleled, and who is also closely associated with the *Philokalia*, both by spearheading the translation of the *Philokalia* from Greek into English and by presenting in his own theological reflections what might well be called a 'philokalic' vision of theology.

As will become clearer in the course of the book, this is more than just a random list of thinkers: there is a sense of development from the immediate influence of the *Philokalia* on Russian Orthodox life and thought in the nineteenth century, through the development from this of various approaches to theology in the diaspora, especially, to begin with, in Paris, and their further development throughout the Orthodox world – Romania, Serbia, Greece and the Orthodox diaspora in Western Europe and North America.

I have presented a selection of Orthodox thinkers from the nineteenth and twentieth centuries, although, as I have just remarked, it is not a random selection, but reflects the spread of Orthodox theology in the modern world from being confined to traditionally Orthodox countries to having a growing impact throughout Western Europe and North America – and beyond. There are many other people I might have talked about; some of them will come into the book in a minor role: the great Metropolitan Philaret of Moscow in the nineteenth century and some other Russians – Losev and Averintsev – come to mind. I have been very selective of the thinkers of the so-called Paris School; many others could have been discussed, such as Sem'en Frank, Fr Nikolai Afanasiev, and even Lev Shestov who was not a Christian (nor, however, was he a practising Jew), not to mention Nicolas Zernov. There are other Greeks I might have talked about – Nikos Nissiotis, Nikos Matsoukas, Constantine Scouteris, or St Nektarios of Aegina or even the poet Odysseus Elytis – and other people closer to home, such as Metropolitan Anthony Bloom and Fr Lev Gillet. Moreover, there are Orthodox theologians, my contemporaries or younger, such as Fr John Behr or Fr Nikolaos Loudovikos, who will play a major part in any history of Orthodox theology in the twenty-first century, but to whom I feel too close to be comfortable in discussing them. And then there are surely many others of whom I have simply not heard, or whose works I have not read. I don't think, however, that my selection is particularly arbitrary – I hope not – and I like to think that it will give some sense of theological thinking among the Orthodox over the last two centuries.

Even missing out so many possible thinkers, this book covers a host of people. In each chapter I have made no attempt to be comprehensive; I have filled in the historical background necessary to understand each of our thinkers and, furthermore, I have selected a topic or issue that I think is central to that individual. I hope that in this way each thinker comes over with his or her distinctive character.

There are, however, some features of my selection that demand explanation or at least comment. Not very many of my thinkers belong to the ranks of professional theologians; I have largely (almost entirely) passed over the professors in the spiritual academies of Russia before the Communist Revolution or in the theological faculties of Greece. This is deliberate, and may well be seen as a weakness, but professional Orthodox theology has been, and often still is, constrained by theological categories derived from the West. It is not that I am anti-Western – or I hope not – but I do not think that an unthinking acquiescence in, or indeed opposition to, the theological categories of historical Western academic theology is at all helpful for Orthodox theology. In fact, these categories have been criticized by Western theologians themselves, and with good reason. If we are to engage with Western theology, it should be with its living manifestations, not the dead categories of the past, already more than half abandoned in the West.

Two other matters I want to comment on. They are both, in different ways, related to the point just made. Many of my thinkers are neither priests nor bishops, but laymen, and some of these laymen have been very influential: Solov'ev and Lossky among the Russians, Koutroubis and Yannaras among the Greeks. Even among the clergy, few of them can be said to have had a professional theological formation: Florovsky was a historian and philosopher, Bulgakov a philosopher and economist, by their academic training. I can't help thinking that this has been a strength, rather than a weakness, in modern Orthodox theology. Also, my cast does not consist only of men: my thinkers are indeed mostly dead white males, but there are exceptions – Myrrha Lot-Borodine, St Maria of Paris, Elisabeth Behr-Sigel and Mother Thekla.

A final point: this is an Introduction to a book which is itself an introduction. On almost everyone I have discussed there could have been a book written. Sometimes, there has been: Solov'ev has not been short of commentators, there have been recently both a biography of Elisabeth Behr-Sigel and also a monograph, as well as, very recently, a brilliant book on Fr Georges Florovsky, based on a careful reading of his texts (not always available in the most obvious form) and extensive searching in the archives; there have been several studies of Fr Stăniloae, and doctoral theses and shorter introductions to several others.[1] There are a few books that look at the thinkers of the Russian Religious Renaissance, and one pioneering book on modern Greek Orthodox theology which covers ground that I have simply passed over.[2] I have made use of what I could find, but this is a very provisional book. I hope, however, it will be found useful as a broad, though theologically focused, survey.

---

[1] For details see 'Further reading'.
[2] Yannis Spiteris, *La teologia ortodossa neo-greca* (Bologna: Edizioni Dehoniane, 1992).

1

The *Philokalia* and its influence

This first chapter is called 'The *Philokalia* and its influence', because I want to suggest, and indeed argue, that the *Philokalia* has a kind of emblematic significance for modern Orthodox theology, marking a watershed in the history of Orthodox theology. It was published in 1782 in Venice – at that date printing was not allowed in the Ottoman Empire.[1] It is an anthology – which is what the Greek title, *Philokalia*, means – of Byzantine ascetic and mystical texts from the fourth or fifth to the fourteenth century: a collection of diverse texts spanning nearly a millennium. It was compiled by two monks who belonged to the monastic communities of the Holy Mountain of Athos: St Makarios, by then bishop of Corinth, and St Nikodimos of the Holy Mountain. It was but one aspect of a movement of renewal among the Athonite monks, in which St Nikodimos played a leading part, a renewal that had many different dimensions.

For the publication of the *Philokalia* was not an isolated event; it was part of a movement of renewal in the Orthodox Church that stemmed from the monastic community of Athos, the Holy Mountain.[2] It was a movement of renewal that was deeply traditional – though, in some ways, more traditional in ideal than in reality. The name given to the group of monks was the *Kollyvades*, named after *kollyva*, the food made of wheat grains eaten at memorial services for the departed. The *Kollyvades* were concerned to restore the traditional practice of holding such services on Saturdays, not Sundays. It might seem a small point, but concern with tradition often focuses on details. More generally they were concerned with the restoration of the traditions of Byzantine monasticism: a return to the Fathers, a return to an understanding of monasticism that focused on prayer, both communal and private, and in the latter case particularly the Jesus Prayer. The controversy on Mount Athos in the fourteenth century – the hesychast controversy – and in particular the role St Gregory Palamas played in it was for these monks emblematic of Orthodoxy. The focus on the prolonged and serious practice of prayer went along with another feature: the importance of

---

[1] English translation (ET): *The Philokalia: The Complete Text Compiled by St Nikodimos of the Holy Mountain and St Makarios of Corinth*, translated from the Greek by G. E. H. Palmer, Philip Sherrard, Kallistos Ware, 4 vols (so far, out of 5) (London: Faber & Faber, 1979–95).

[2] See *The* Philokalia: *A Classic Text of Orthodox Spirituality*, ed. Brock Bingaman and Bradley Nassif (New York: Oxford University Press, 2012). Also the classical article by Metropolitan Kallistos, 'Philocalie', in *Dictionnaire de spiritualité*, tome XII, première partie (Paris: Beauchesne, 1984), 1336–52.

spiritual fatherhood, or spiritual eldership. It was bound up, too, with a stress laid on frequent communion.

Some sense of the concerns of this movement of renewal can be gained from looking at the enormous activity of St Nikodimos of the Holy Mountain, one of the editors of the *Philokalia*.[3] As well as the *Philokalia*, he edited together with Makarios of Corinth the vast collection of monastic wisdom drawn from the Fathers, collected by Paul Evergetinos in the eleventh century, called the *Synagoge*, or just the *Evergetinos*.[4] Nikodimos also edited the *Rudder*, or the *Pidalion*, a collection, with commentary, of the canons of the Orthodox Church.[5] He prepared editions of St Symeon the New Theologian (together with Dionysios Zagoraios, though most of the work seems to have been Nikodimos') – the standard edition, though difficult to find, until the edition in Sources Chrétiennes in the last century – of the Gaza ascetics, Saints Varsanouphios and John, and of St Gregory Palamas, though this edition was lost as a result of the arrest of Nikodimos' printer in Vienna; it would be another 150 years before an edition of Palamas began to appear.

St Nikodimos also composed works of spiritual guidance and direction. It is striking that these works betray dependence on works of Counter-Reformation Roman Catholic spirituality: his work, *Unseen Warfare*, is a translation of Lorenzo Scupoli's *Combattimento Spirituale*,[6] he produced a translation of Ignatius Loyola's *Spiritual Exercises*, and his works on confession and frequent communion are also based on Catholic sources. His *Handbook of Spiritual Counsel* is his own,[7] as is his invaluable commentary on the canons for the Great Feasts, his *Eortodromion*.[8]

Nikodimos, then, was concerned with renewal in all aspects of the life of the Church: its canonical structures, its liturgical and sacramental life, the nature of spiritual guidance, as well as providing resources for a return to the springs of Orthodox theology that he found in the spiritual writers of the Church. His enthusiasm for contemporary Catholic devotional writing is notable; it must express genuine appreciation for Catholic spirituality, as he had no lack of access to patristic material. This appreciation of post-Reformation Western spirituality, both Catholic and Protestant, remains a feature of the spirituality inspired by the *Philokalia*, though many Orthodox seem rather embarrassed by it.

---

[3] On St Nikodimos, see Constantine Cavarnos, *St Nikodemos the Hagiorite* (Belmont, MA: The Institute for Byzantine and Modern Greek Studies, 1974), and Metropolitan Kallistos, 'St Nikodimos and the *Philokalia*', in *The* Philokalia, ed. Bingaman–Nassif, 9–35, and *Mount Athos the Sacred Bridge: The Spirituality of the Holy Mountain*, ed. Dimitri Conomos and Graham Speake (Oxford: Peter Lang, 2005), 69–121.

[4] Venice, 1783; reprinted with modern Greek translation, Athens, 6th edn, 1993.

[5] Leipzig, 1800; frequently reprinted: reprint with modern Greek translation, Thessaloniki, 2003.

[6] Venice, 1796. ET of St Theophan the Recluse's Russian version: E. Kadloubovsky and G. E. H. Palmer (London: Faber & Faber, 1952).

[7] ET: Peter A. Chamberas (Mahwah, NY: Paulist Press, 1989).

[8] Venice, 1836. Reprint, 3 vols, Thessaloniki, 1987.

If we are to see the *Philokalia* as a turning point in the history of Orthodox theology, then there seem to me to be various entailments, both negative and positive. First of all, it suggests a break from the route down which Orthodox theology had gone since the fall of Constantinople in the fifteenth century, if not from the beginnings of the union movement in the thirteenth century. For, in the wake of the Reformation disputes, Orthodox theology had found itself caught up in those disputes as it tried to explain itself to Protestants and Catholics, both of whom sought the support of the Orthodox in their disputes with each other. The history, beginning with Cyril Loukaris' endorsement of a rather Calvinist theology, and its opposition by Patriarch Dositheos of Jerusalem and Peter Moghila, we can't go into here, but it led to Orthodox theology being expressed in the terms and categories of Western theology. The return to the Fathers, part of the Philokalic revival, entailed a rejection of such an approach to theology.

Something similar happened in the Russian world, only there it became institutionalized. Early in the seventeenth century, Peter Moghila founded the spiritual academy in Kiev, and introduced teaching based on Latin, Catholic textbooks. This became the model for the spiritual academies set up by Peter the Great as part of his reforms in the Church, and remained so well into the nineteenth century. The Philokalic return to the Fathers can be seen as a repudiation of the way theology was conceived and taught, both among the Greeks in the Ottoman Empire and in the Orthodox Russian Empire. But theology as inspired by the *Philokalia* was not just negatively opposed to the developments in the teaching of theology in the Orthodox world; such inspiration had a positive dimension, though it was one that remained implicit, and needed working out in practice.

As already mentioned in the Introduction, the *Philokalia* presents itself as a volume of writings 'in which, through ethical philosophy, in accordance with action and contemplation, the intellect is purified, illumined and perfected' (title page). This implies an approach to theology, not as a set of doctrines, as set forth in the creeds or the councils, but an approach to knowing God in which the intellect is prepared for union with God by purification, illumination and perfection. This suggests several things. First of all, this is the language of prayer in the Christian tradition: prayer understood not just as petition, asking God for things, but prayer as engagement with God, an engagement that takes place through the 'three ways' of purification, illumination, and perfection or deification. Furthermore, it suggests an understanding of knowledge in theology, which is not a collection of information, but rather knowledge of God that involves some kind of participation in him. It suggests, in short, an understanding of theology much closer to what we find in the Fathers, where there is no real separation between the object of knowledge and the process of knowing, where to come to know God is to be assimilated to God in some way, where knowledge of God entails what came to be called, especially in the Greek tradition, deification or *theosis*.

A sketch of the influence of the *Philokalia*, mostly in Russia

The *Philokalia* was published in 1782 in Venice. It represents the recovery of a tradition, the tradition that found confirmation in various church synods in the course of the hesychast controversy in the fourteenth century. Evidence as to how far the *Philokalia* marks a new starting point or a signal publication representing a more widespread movement is somewhat contradictory. On the one hand, Nikodimos himself says of the works he has gathered together in the *Philokalia* that they 'have never in earlier times been published, or if they have, lie in obscurity, in darkness, in a corner, uncherished and moth-eaten, and from there dispersed and squandered'.[9] On the other hand, there is manuscript evidence for what might be called 'proto-Philokalias',[10] and from the history of Païssy Velichkovsky it would appear that he had already been engaged on the translation of the texts that were eventually published as the Slavonic *Philokalia* or *Dobrotolubiye* for some years before the *Philokalia* was published in Venice by St Nikodimos. Perhaps the truth is that the revival of the tradition of which the *Philokalia* is the signal example was the revival of a tradition that had been reduced to a trickle, observed by a small minority of monks on the Holy Mountain, but that this revival was somewhat more widespread than Nikodimos suggests in the Introduction to the *Philokalia*, from which the remark quoted is taken.

As we have already mentioned, while Sts Makarios and Nikodimos were compiling the *Philokalia*, St Païssy Velichkovsky was already translating into Slavonic some of the works that came to be included in the *Philokalia*. When this collection was published in 1793, it was called the *Dobrotolubiye*, the word being a calque of the Greek *philokalia*, with no independent meaning as a Slavonic word (and thus simply suggesting to the Slav ear the meaning 'love of beauty'), making clear that Païssy thought of it as a rendering of St Makarios and Nikodimos' collection. St Païssy had, however, come to the Holy Mountain already aware of a living tradition of hesychast spirituality. This may ultimately be traceable to the hesychast tradition of St Nil Sorsky and the Non-possessing monks,[11] some of whom may have migrated to the Romanian princedoms of Wallachia and Moldavia during the time of Peter the Great and Catherine the Great. More immediately he owed his knowledge of Philokalic spirituality to a Romanian elder, St Basil of Poiana Mărului, whom he had met during his period in the monasteries of Moldavia in 1742–6, after his studies at the Moghila Academy in Kiev, and who tonsured him as a monk in 1750 on Mount Athos.[12]

It used to be thought that St Païssy had simply selected from the Greek

---

[9] *Philokalia* (Venice, 1782), 6.

[10] See John Anthony McGuckin, 'The Making of the *Philokalia*: A Tale of Monks and Manuscripts', in *The* Philokalia, ed. Bingaman–Nassif, 36–49.

[11] On which see George A. Maloney SJ, *Russian Hesychasm: The Spirituality of Nil Sorsky* (The Hague–Paris: Mouton, 1973).

[12] Kallistos Ware, 'St Nikodimos and the *Philokalia*', in *Mount Athos the Sacred Bridge*, 69–121, here 104–5; see also Placide Deseille, *La Spiritualité orthodoxe et la Philocalie* (Paris: Albin Michel, 2011), 61–4.

Philokalia in making his translation, but it now looks rather as if his selection derived from similar sources to the Greek anthology, while having close parallels with it (for it may, before publication, have been checked against the Greek text); as Metropolitan Kallistos has put it, 'during 1746–75 Paisy, working independently, translated into Slavonic nearly four-fifths of the material [I think that must mean authors] subsequently included in the Greek *Philokalia* of 1782'.[13]

For the purposes of our story, it is the publication of the Slavonic *Dobrotolubiye*, 11 years after the Greek *Philokalia*, that is important. For while the Greek *Philokalia* seems to have had little immediate influence, no doubt because of the prolonged struggle throughout the nineteenth century for liberation on the part of the Greeks from the Ottoman yoke, that is not true of the Slavonic *Dobrotolubiye*. The *Dobrotolubiye* in its Slavonic form was destined to have a remarkable influence. One of the intentions of St Nikodimos, as he makes clear in his Introduction, was to make the riches of the tradition represented by it available to all Orthodox Christians, married as well as monastics. Many have detected in this a contradiction, for many of the texts included insist on the importance of personal guidance from an experienced spiritual father (or mother), and where, outside a monastery, is such a guide likely to be found?[14] St Nikodimos was willing to take the risk of these writings being misinterpreted, for the sake of the benefits they would bring, which he felt would outweigh any such danger.[15] St Païssy was more inclined to avoid any such contradiction by keeping his *Dobrotolubiye* strictly for monastic eyes; it was only at the insistence of Gabriel, Metropolitan of Novgorod and St Petersburg, a friend of the great spiritual master St Tikhon of Zadonsk, that the *Dobrotolubiye* was published at all.[16]

It certainly seems to be the case that the advance of the *Dobrotolubiye* among the Slavs went hand in hand with an emphasis on the importance of spiritual fatherhood, *starchestvo*. Disciples of St Païssy brought the *Dobrotolubiye* and its spirituality to Russia. One of the monks involved, at Metropolitan Gabriel's behest, in preparing the 1793 edition of the *Dobrotolubiye*, the monk Nazar, originally from Sarov and then refounder of the monastery of Valaam on Lake Ladoga, retired to Sarov in 1801, taking a copy of the *Dobrotolubiye* with him; through him St Seraphim became acquainted with the *Dobrotolubiye*, though his spirituality was already indebted to the authentic tradition of St Nil Sorsky.[17] It was, however, the monastery of Optino, just under 200 miles to the south-west of Moscow, that rapidly became a centre for this movement of renewal. We catch a glimpse of this in the early chapters of Dostoevsky's novel *The Brothers Karamazov*, in the figure of the *starets* Zossima, given central importance, but viewed with suspicion by many of his fellow monks. Because of its accessibility from Moscow, Optina Pustyn' attracted

---

[13] Ware, 'St Nikodimos', 101.
[14] See, e.g., Ware, 'St Nikodimos', 106–9.
[15] See the last two pages of St Nikodimos' Introduction: *Philokalia* (Venice, 1782), 7–8.
[16] See Ware, 'St Nikodimos', 108; Deseille, *La Spiritualité orthodoxe*, 64.
[17] Deseille, *La Spiritualité orthodoxe*, 235–6.

many of the intelligentsia, especially among the Slavophils.

The Slavophils

These Slavophils, notably Alexei Khomiakov and Ivan Kireevsky, play an important role in the story of Orthodox theology I am seeking to unfold. They were, both of them, laymen, not academics – cultured gentlemen, philosophers rather than theologians – but it is their way of thinking that proved to be seminal in the development of Russian religious thought in the nineteenth century. As the name suggests, the Slavophils prided themselves on their Slav identity. At this stage, such Slav identity meant pride in what they thought of as the way of understanding the world – the *Weltanschauung* – characteristic of the Russian Slavs; only later did the tradition come to have the political overtones of a 'panslavism', according to which the Russian Empire took upon itself the task of defending and promoting the cause of their Slav brothers and sisters in southern Europe. It means a self-conscious pride in the tradition of the Slavs as distinct from the West; it involved some kind of anti-Westernism.

Khomiakov sometimes argued that, while Western Christianity was heir to three traditions – of Hebrew religion, Greek philosophy and Roman law – Slav Christianity, or Orthodox Christianity, was heir only to two of these

Alexei Khomiakov

6

traditions – Hebrew religion and Greek philosophy (a very questionable position, given the importance of law in the Justinianic reform).[18] This meant, in particular, that the Slavs had no real grasp of the notion of an individual, which Khomiakov saw as embedded in Roman law, and it was the notion of the individual, cut off from the organic community to which human beings should properly belong, that for Khomiakov was the root cause of the problems of the West: problems that had been introduced into Russian society by the reforms of Peter the Great and strengthened during the reign of Catherine the Great.

In truth, it seems to me that Khomiakov and his Slavophilism were not as unique to Slav experience as he thought. Many thinkers throughout the Western world were alarmed at the corrosive effects on human society of industrialization and urbanization, which they felt destroyed natural communities, and reduced human beings to interchangeable units – individuals, identified by a factory number or by their place of residence in some faceless flat. Andrzej Walicki calls Slavophils 'conservative romanticists'.[19] 'Conservative Romanticism' was something that could be found throughout Europe in the nineteenth century; an English example would be Coleridge, with whom it would be profitable, I think, to compare Khomiakov. Khomiakov looked back to the Russian village, with its church, the great house and its lands, ruled by a village council, in which all members of the village participated. Such a society was an organic community; it was not made up of independent individuals, but was a society in which its members found their identity by belonging. It was an example of the 'one and the many': the one and the many balancing each other, neither reducible to the other.

The 'one and the many' was a central issue in the movements in German philosophy that followed in the wake of Kant, and sought to restore the sense of organic unity of knower and known that Kant had severed: movements characterized as 'Idealism'. For all the anti-Westernism implicit in Slavophil thought, it was, in truth, deeply in debt to the currents of German Idealist philosophy, especially the thought of Schelling.[20] This is not, however, something that I want to pursue in any detail here. What was important for Slavophils like Khomiakov and Kireevsky was that the reconciliation of the one and the many was rooted in God the Holy Trinity, in which unity and the manifold are already united, and that this complementarity of the one and the many was characteristic of the cosmos created by God, and in particular of the Church, at least the Eastern Orthodox Church.

Khomiakov used the Slavonic word that translated the Greek *katholikos* in the creed – *soborny* – to characterize the way in which the Church held together the one and the many. The word *soborny* is derived from the verb *sobrat'*, to gather together, and seems to have been a careful attempt to render

---

[18] See Nicolas Zernov, *Three Russian Prophets* (London: SCM Press, 1944), 71.

[19] Andrzej Walicki, *The Slavophile Controversy* (Oxford: Clarendon Press, 1975).

[20] See Walicki, *Slavophile Controversy*, 316–17.

the root meaning of *katholikos*, which is derived from the expression *kath' holon*, meaning something like 'to take as a whole'. For what is characteristic of the Orthodox Church, according to Khomiakov, is precisely that the whole body of believers is gathered into a single whole; together they form a unity without having their freedom suppressed. Reconciling freedom and unity was a problem that Schelling had wrestled with, as part of the problem of the One and the Many, which is perhaps why Schelling – of all the German Idealists – was so attractive to the Slavophils. The *soborny* nature of the Orthodox Church, which later Slavophils came to call by the abstract noun *sobornost'*, was something that Khomiakov contrasted with what he found in the Western Churches; in his view, Catholicism found unity at the price of freedom, whereas the Protestant Church sacrificed unity in the interests of freedom. Only in the Orthodox Church and her *sobornost'* could be found both unity and freedom: a union freely embraced and a freedom that did not itch to tear apart unity.

This sense of an organic unity, rooted in Christ and his body the Church, in which believers found their identity through faith in the One Christ and belonging to the One Church – a belonging expressed in the sacramental life of the Church and the mutual concern for each other of all its members, living and departed, human and angelic – reaches back behind the clash of authority and freedom that marked the Reformation to an understanding of the Church more characteristic of patristic thought. Much of Khomiakov's thought found expression through his acquaintance with William Palmer, an Englishman, an Anglican deacon, who made his way to Russia in his quest to promote the unity of the Church. Palmer and Khomiakov exchanged letters, and Khomiakov wrote for him a short ecclesiological treatise, *The Church Is One*. In that treatise he expresses very beautifully the meaning of *sobornost'*, the way in which the individual finds his or her true reality in union with others in the Church, in contrast to the destructive solitude that characterizes reliance on one's self:

> We know that when any one of us falls, he falls alone; but no one is saved alone. He who is saved is saved in the Church, as a member of her, and in unity with all her other members. If anyone believes, he is in the communion of faith; if he loves, he is in the communion of love; if he prays, he is in the communion of prayer. Wherefore no one can rest his hope on his own prayers, and every one who prays asks the whole Church for intercession, not as if he had any doubts of the intercession of Christ, the one Advocate, but in the assurance that the whole Church ever prays for all her members. All the angels pray for us, the apostles, martyrs, and patriarchs, and above all, the Mother of our Lord, and this holy unity is the true life of the Church. But if the Church, visible and invisible, prays without ceasing, why do we ask for her prayers? Do we not entreat mercy of God and Christ, although his mercy precedes our prayer? The very reason that we ask the Church for her prayers is that we know that she gives the assistance of her intercession even to him who does not ask for it, and to him that asks she gives it in far greater measure than he

asks: for in her is the fulness of the Spirit of God.[21]

This is one of the points at which the Slavophils found themselves at one with the fundamentals of the Philokalic revival. This link between Slavophilism and the *Philokalia* was more than a simple convergence of ideas; it had practical, or even institutional, expression through the monastery of Optino, which, we have already noted, had become a place visited by the Russian intellectuals. Later Dostoevsky, Solov'ev, and even Tolstoy would visit Optina Pustyn'. Another Slavophil, Ivan Kireevsky, had early on close links with the monastery, and encouraged the publication of translations of the works of the Fathers sponsored by the monastery.[22] Ivan Kireevsky's sense of the paramount value of the witness of the Fathers can be seen as reflecting the influence of the *Philokalia*. For him, 'The Holy Fathers speak of a country they have been to'; in their writings the Fathers bear 'testimony as eyewitnesses'.[23] As we have seen, the Philokalic revival had several strands: return to the Fathers, emphasis on inner prayer, as practised in the hesychast tradition of monasticism, especially the Jesus Prayer, and the role of spiritual fatherhood, or eldership, *starchestvo*. All of these were found in Optina Pustyn', which nurtured a succession of spiritual fathers, most notably Elder Amvrosy, whom Dostoevsky met, and who became one of the models for the figure of Starets Zossima in *The Brothers Karamazov*.

The *Philokalia* and growing interest in the Fathers

A key figure in the history of the Russian Church in the nineteenth century was St Philaret, Archbishop and then Metropolitan of Moscow from 1821 until his death in 1867. He had been a monk at the Trinity-St Sergii Monastery outside Moscow, where a very similar revival of Philokalic spirituality to that at Optina Pustyn' took place. As Metropolitan of Moscow, and therefore the senior hierarch of the Russian Orthodox Church, he both encouraged the renewal of monasticism and fostered renewal in the spiritual academies. One project to which Philaret gave his blessing was a comprehensive programme of translation of patristic writings into Russian that was undertaken in the course of the nineteenth century. The Spiritual Academy of Moscow undertook the translation of the works of the Fathers of the Golden Age of Greek Patristic Literature, as Quasten called it:[24] the writings of the Greek Fathers of the fourth to the seventh century (Athanasios to Maximos the

---

[21] Alexey Stepanovich Khomiakov, *The Church Is One*, with an Introduction by Nicolas Zernov (London: Fellowship of St Alban and St Sergius, 1968), 38–9. (There is also a translation of this treatise in *On Spiritual Unity: A Slavophile Reader*, ed. and trans. Boris Jakim and Robert Bird (Hudson, NY: Lindisfarne, 1998), 31–53.)

[22] On Kireevsky and Optino, see Hélène Slezkine (Mother Olga of Bussy-en-Othe), *Kireievski et Optino Poustyne* (Lavardac: Éditions Saint-Jean le Roumain, 2001).

[23] From Kireevsky's 'Fragments': translation in *On Spiritual Unity*, 248, 243.

[24] The title of the third volume of J. Quasten's *Patrology* (Utrecht–Antwerp: Spectrum, 1966), though Quasten was thinking only of the Greek Fathers of the fourth century and the first half of the fifth.

Confessor and John Damascene). The Spiritual Academy of St Petersburg provided translations of the Church Histories and the Byzantine Chronicles, also of the collections of ancient liturgical texts, both Eastern and Western, as well as the complete works of St John Chrysostom and St Theodore of Stoudios. The Spiritual Academy of Kiev undertook the translation of the Latin Fathers: of Tertullian, St Cyprian, Arnobius, St Ambrose, St Jerome and St Augustine. Finally, the Spiritual Academy of Kazan translated the Acts of the Councils, both Œcumenical and Local.

With such a comprehensive translation of patristic literature, it was no exaggeration for Olivier Clément to say that 'at the end of the nineteenth century, Russia had at its disposal, in its own language, the best patristic library in Europe':[25] not even the parallel translation of the Fathers into English, initiated by the leaders of the Oxford Movement, in the *Library of the Fathers*, and taken further in the *Ante-Nicene Christian Library* and the two series of *Nicene and Post-Nicene Fathers*, could match the Russian enterprise in breadth of coverage. This work of translation did not stand alone; in the period from the mid-nineteenth century to the Revolution there were major works of scholarship on several of the Fathers of the Church, such as Gregory of Nyssa, Maximos the Confessor (Epifanovich) and Theodore of Stoudios (Dobroklonsky), at that time little studied in the West; Augustine was not neglected, either.[26]

The *Philokalia* as a watershed in Orthodox theology

It is my contention that the publication of the *Philokalia* in 1782 can be seen as marking a turning point in Orthodox theology, a move away from the defensiveness of early modern Orthodox theology – the theology of the so-called 'Symbolic Books' – to a more confident style of theology, based on the authentic sources of Orthodox theology, namely the Fathers of the Church. This movement of renewal had deep roots and led the Orthodox Churches out of the problems that dogged them at the end of the eighteenth century. It is difficult not to see St Nikodimos as preparing the Greek Church under the Ottoman Empire for the independence it was to achieve in the course of the nineteenth century, providing it with what was needed for its spiritual, liturgical and canonical or structural well-being. The path before it was to be long and hard, and there is still much to be done, as we shall see.

The Philokalic revival took root most quickly in the Russian Church,

---

[25] Olivier Clément, 'Les Pères de l'Église dans l'Église orthodoxe', *Connaissance des Pères de l'Église* 52 (December 1993), 25–6, quoted by Boris Bobrinskoy in 'Le Renouveau actuel de la patristique dans l'Orthodoxie', in *Les Pères de l'Église au XXe siècle: Histoire – Littérature – Théologie* (Paris: Cerf, 1997), 437–44, at 440. Most of the information in this paragraph is taken from Bobrinskoy, 'Le Renouveau actuel', 440.

[26] This is clear from two recent books, though both are mostly concerned with the twentieth century: Michael Aksionov Meerson, *The Trinity of Love in Modern Russian Theology* (Quincy, IL: Franciscan Press, 1998); Myroslaw I. Tataryn, *Augustine and Russian Orthodoxy* (Lanham, MD: International Scholars, 2000).

where the problems were different. The Russian Orthodox Church was not under the yoke of a conqueror of a different religion; the Russians had, in the fourteenth and fifteenth centuries, successfully turned back the oppression of the Golden Horde, and emerged with their temporal and spiritual centre in Moscow, where eventually a tsar and a patriarch of 'Moscow and all the Russias' were established. But as the Church entered the eighteenth century, it brought with it the self-inflicted wounds of the schism – the 'Old Believer' schism – that resulted from Patriarch Nikon's attempt to renew the Church, only to be encountered by Peter the Great and his attempts to make the Russian nation a nation on a par with the nations of Western Europe, which weakened the true traditions of Eastern Orthodoxy and subordinated the Church to the state in an uncompromising way. The nineteenth century saw the awakening of attempts to restore the true traditions of Orthodoxy, not least the traditions of monasticism which Peter the Great and Catherine the Great had tried to weaken, if not destroy, as irrelevant to their plans for a modern Western Russia. The Philokalic movement provided a powerful resource for such return to Orthodox principles, as it had at its heart a programme for a renewed personal spirituality, based on the Jesus Prayer, and an emphasis on the importance of *starchestvo*, spiritual eldership, that, at its best, made sure that the spiritual revival remained sound and healthy.

There is another marker of the influence of the *Philokalia* in nineteenth-century Russia – and indeed beyond – that I want to mention, though it could be said that it has little to do with theology. It is a small work known in English as *The Way of a Pilgrim*, in Russian *Candid Tales of a Pilgrim to His Spiritual Father*. The story is extremely well known (that is a measure of its influence) – about a 'pilgrim', perhaps better a wanderer, or *strannik*, familiar even to non-Russian readers from Tolstoy's novels and stories, who travelled from place to place, as many did in Imperial Russia. Our *strannik*, who did once try to make a pilgrimage to Jerusalem, is presented as anxious to fulfil the apostle's command to 'pray without ceasing'. After receiving several explanations of this command, which he finds unsatisfactory, he learns about, and then learns to practise, the Jesus Prayer. He also acquires a copy of the *Dobrotolubiye* – a worn and battered one, for which he pays two roubles – which he pores over every day, and carries in his knapsack. The Jesus Prayer is for him a revelation, and a source of joy:

> And when with all this in mind I prayed with my heart, everything around me seemed delightful and marvellous. The trees, the grass, the birds, the earth, the air, the light seemed to be telling me that they existed for man's sake, that they witnessed to the love of God for man, that everything proved the love of God for man, that all things prayed to God and sang his praise.[27]

This apparently artless work has had a tremendous influence, both within

---

[27] *The Way of a Pilgrim* and *The Pilgrim Continues His Way*, trans. R. M. French (London: SPCK, 1954), 31.

11

and outside the Orthodox world. It famously appeared as a 'pea-green book' in J. D. Salinger's *Franny and Zooey*. Recent research has revealed something of its background.[28] The familiar, and indeed classic, version is a later version, edited by St Theophan the Recluse – himself the Russian translator of the *Dobrotolubiye* – who made the figure of the spiritual father, the *starets*, central. It is based on earlier material that has its context in the missionary work of an Orthodox priest, a former Old Believer, Fr Mikhail Kozlov, among the Old Believers with whom the *stranniki* were popular. It illustrates the paradox of the issue of the accessibility of the Jesus Prayer, for St Theophan's version, edited to bring the spiritual father into prominence, has introduced the practice of the Jesus Prayer well beyond circles in which a spiritual father could be found – even beyond the boundaries of Orthodoxy, or indeed any traditional form of Christianity.

---

[28] See the Introduction to *The Pilgrim's Tale*, trans. Aleksei Pentkovsky (Mahwah, NJ: Paulist Press, 1999), and the articles on which it is based in *Simvol* 27 (Paris, 1992).

2

Vladimir Solov′ev and Sophia

Vladimir Solov′ev was an utterly remarkable figure in the intellectual life of late nineteenth-century Russia. He bridged many of the divides of that society and consequently often appears a contradictory figure: he was an intellectual, and yet returned to the priestly tradition of his family, at least to the extent of study-ing in a seminary and writing extensively on theology, even though he was never ordained; he was a Slavophil – that is, one who opposed the Westernizing tendencies in Russian society, and sought out what he believed to be a pecu-liarly Russian (and Orthodox) tradition – and yet he believed deeply in the unity of the Church, and came to see, at least for a time, Rome as a necessary safeguard of that unity.[1] He was a friend of Dostoevsky – and indeed quite as bizarre as any of the characters in his novels; Alesha in *The Brothers Karamazov* is said to be based on him, as is Ivan Karamazov! – and like the novelist was influ-enced by the revival of monasticism in the nineteenth-century Russian Church.

Early life

He was born on 16 June 1853, his father a professor, but his grandfather a priest, so he belonged to one of the 'levitical families' of Russia, from which the priests were drawn. He lost his faith in his teens, but soon regained it. At the University of Moscow, he began studying physics and mathematics. After two years he changed to history and philosophy, and at the same time took courses in theology at the Moscow Spiritual Academy at Sergiev Posad, then quite an unusual thing to do. During these years he read voraciously: among the philosophers Schelling made a great impression, as did Plato; he also read a good deal of the Church Fathers, and also extensively in the early modern mystics, such as Jakob Boehme. He graduated in 1873, and published his first article: 'The Mythological Progress of Ancient Paganism'. His next work, 'The Crisis of Western Philosophy', he presented as his master's thesis, and in 1874 was appointed a Fellow of the University of Moscow in the Faculty of Philosophy.

Meetings with Sophia

Soon after, he went to England to study Indian and Gnostic philosophy, and worked in the British Museum. There, under the great dome of the Reading

---

[1] For a discussion of Solov′ev's relationship with Rome, see Mark Everitt, 'Vladimir Solov′ev: A Russian Newman?', *Sobornost/ECR* 1:1 (1979), 23–38.

Room, he had a vision of Sophia, as a young woman. This was the second such vision. The first had occurred some ten years earlier, when he was 12, in church: standing there, he felt himself penetrated by the colour azure, and began to discern before him a figure, also suffused with golden azure – Sophia, as a young girl, holding a flower from unearthly lands, who smiled and nodded . . . and vanished! On the second occasion, in the Reading Room, Sophia appeared again, suffused once more with golden azure; this time he saw her face and she told him to go to Egypt. Obediently he set off, without delay, not even stopping in Paris. Once in Egypt he went out into the desert, where, wandering around in his black overcoat and top hat, he was taken for a demon by some Bedouins, who attacked him and tied him up, and then later, realizing their mistake, released him. But by this time it was night, and alone in the desert, Solov'ev had his third and final vision of Sophia. Again, there was the azure and the sense of being absorbed by eternity:

> I saw it all, and all I saw was one.
> A single image of all female beauty . . .
> The immeasurable encompassing its sum.
> You stand alone before me, and within me.[2]

All this we learn from a poem called 'Three Meetings', which Solov'ev wrote over 20 years later. By this time, he had become a vastly influential and controversial figure, the author of several substantial theological and philosophical works.

From this brief account of the early part of Solov'ev's life, there are a few things to notice. First of all, there is the role of experience. The story just related from his account in 'Three Meetings' is important from several points of view. It is an experience, and we shall find that an appeal to personal experience is a characteristic of the tradition that can be traced back to (or through) Solov'ev. But, as Avril Pyman observes, the poem relates the story in a deliberately bathetic way: bathos used to deflect rationalist analysis (and dismissal) of his account, so that it would be recognized that 'his chivalrous cult of Sophia the Divine Wisdom was based on some kind of real experience, which had had real consequences for him; that he was, as it were, consecrated by his love of Sophia to the salvation of the world'[3] – an experience that was defiant of the intellectual currents dominant in Western thought since the Enlightenment. This chimed in with his Slavophil mistrust of the West and sense of the special destiny of the Russians.

It also chimed in with a tradition in the West that, equally alarmed and fascinated by the rapid change in the intellectual climate in the nineteenth century, sought desperately for the sense of the unity of knowledge and of the ultimate mystery of reality that seemed to be fragmented by the analytic rationalism that characterized the methods of modern science. This tradition

---

[2] Translation from Judith Deutsch Kornblatt, *Divine Sophia: The Wisdom Writings of Vladimir Soloyov* (Ithaca–London: Cornell University Press, 2009), 271.

[3] Avril Pyman, *A History of Russian Symbolism* (Cambridge: Cambridge University Press, 1994), 228–9.

ran, in the West, parallel with the Enlightenment and the advance of modern science, and was in reaction against it; the intellectual advances of Western culture were mistrusted, and there was a sense that the West had taken a wrong turn, leading to a belief, or a hope, that it was to the East that we should look for a solution to the problems of the West: *Ex oriente lux!*

Although such ideas grew apace during the eighteenth and nineteenth centuries – the names of Emanuel Swedenborg and, for the English, at least, William Blake, come to mind – this tradition has a long prehistory, stretching at least back to the Renaissance and the rediscovery of Neoplatonism and Hermetic philosophy (taken at face value, as derived from Egyptian learning), and attempts to discover a *pristina theologia* hidden behind the increasingly fragmented theologies of Western Christendom, which were justifying the divisions that lay behind the wars of religion and the terrible human suffering that went with them.[4] Out of these concerns one can trace a tradition, associated with names like Jakob Boehme, Angelus Silesius, John Pordage, Thomas Taylor (the 'English Platonist'), Franz von Baader – and Meister Eckhart (who occurs at this point in the list, quite unfairly, as it was only in the nineteenth century that his German works had been discovered, and

Vladimir Solov'ev

4 See D. P. Walker, *The Ancient Theology* (London: Duckworth, 1972).

he burst upon the intellectual scene with all the meretricious splendour of a condemned heretic): a tradition that influenced more respectable (or at least more mainstream) names like Hegel, Schelling and Schopenhauer. This is a tradition marked by a resistance to the analytic fragmentation of the sciences, together with a longing for a sense of ultimate unity, and a sense that ultimately all is – or may be – gathered up into the One.

Furthermore, in this tradition, the idea, even the figure, of Wisdom, or Sophia, comes to play a role. It represents, in this context, the idea of something deeper than mere knowledge, in which the increasingly alienated specialized branches of the sciences might coinhere to form a unified whole. Wisdom also represents an approach that secures the human person – increasingly excluded from a mechanically conceived universe – a central role, for Wisdom is conceived in terms inseparable from the person, in whom she dwells.

> Eternal Wisdom builds:
> I shall the palace be
> When I in wisdom rest
> and wisdom rests in me.[5]

What might be thought of as an alternative – maybe even esoteric – tradition in Western thought, which in the nineteenth century becomes part of the mainstream through German Idealism, is clearly of enormous importance for Solov'ev. It takes a special form in him through the notion – or rather experience – of Sophia, experienced by Solov'ev in the dream figure of a young girl, and in his later life sought by him through his relationships with various women. He is a complex and strange figure, who was dismissed by the generation that followed him (Merezhkovsky, Rozanov, for example) as bizarre and unstable, but to the next generation (Blok, Bely, Ivanov) a source of fascination. As Avril Pyman put it:

> To the first generation, therefore, Solov'ev was a father-figure to be cast down. To the second he was a benevolent ancestor to be sanctified, a visionary, a fallen warrior in the struggle for spiritual renewal, misunderstood and despised (just as they felt themselves to be) by a complacent society.[6]

Pyman was talking about Solov'ev's reception among writers and poets; we are concerned with theology, where much the same pattern can be discerned, especially the fascination he exercised over the generation of theologians contemporary with Blok and Bely, the generation that experienced the Communist Revolution.

Intellectual background

Before we go any further, we need to dwell a little more on the intellectual tradition, just sketched, to which Solov'ev was indebted. Solov'ev was

---

[5] Angelus Silesius, *The Cherubinic Wanderer* I. 178; translation from the selection by Willard R. Trask (New York: Pantheon Books, 1953), 27.
[6] Pyman, *Russian Symbolism*, 228.

enormously widely read and found himself trying to think through in a Russian context concepts and ideas that had been around in the West for a long time. It is as if Solov'ev and some of his contemporaries were trying to catch up with centuries of intellectual development in the West in a matter of decades; they are thinkers in a hurry.

This sense of haste is manifest in the way Solov'ev tries to draw together an immense range of learning and a host of concepts and images. Something that might have happened piece by piece happened almost all at once. Another problem with Solov'ev is that his enormous learning and the speed with which he put his ideas together make it easy to mistake his historical context, for it is often the case that what looks like his historical context is not something he assumed, but rather something that he created.

An example could be found in his relationship to Gnosticism. He denied that his notion of the eternal feminine was Gnostic, and certainly its most obvious source would have been Goethe. Our conception of Gnosticism is coloured by scholarship that Solov'ev could not have known: Harnack's idea of Gnosticism as the acute Hellenization of Christianity, as he put it in his *History of Dogma*, Solov'ev could have known, but his theological works had been published earlier (*Dogmengeschichte* first began to appear in 1886; Solov'ev's relatively late *Russie et l'Église universelle* appeared in 1889); the influential view of Gnosticism that elaborates Harnack's, associated especially with Hans Jonas, belongs to the 1930s, and all this has come to seem rather old-fashioned since the discovery and publication of the Nag Hammadi library after the Second World War. But Solov'ev stands right at the beginning of modern scholarship, earlier even than Harnack. When he visited London in 1875, Gnosticism was nearly as exciting a subject as it was to become after the discovery of the Nag Hammadi library, and for a similar reason: Hippolytus' *Refutatio* had been recently published, giving a very philosophical view of Gnosticism, and in the British Museum, where Solov'ev worked, were to be found two Gnostic codices – *Askewianus* and *Brucianus* – which Solov'ev may have consulted. *Codex Askewianus* – also known as *Pistis Sophia* – had already been published in a Latin translation in 1851 (the same year in which Hippolytus' *Refutatio* was published as the *Philosophoumena*).

It is some sense of what was exciting about Gnosticism *circa* 1875 that we need to recover for understanding Solov'ev. The British Museum codices are quite late compilations, and assimilate their teaching to that of, say, the Hermetic Corpus, already well known. That means, however, that the Gnosticism Solov'ev encountered has less to do with the second century AD than with the traditions of esoteric wisdom that had flourished in Christian and Jewish circles since the Middle Ages, and were drawing traditions from further east into their ambit in the nineteenth century. This is confirmed by the fact that the only hint we have of what Solov'ev was reading beneath the dome of the British Museum Library comes from one of his friends of his London days, I. I. Ianzhul, who tells us that he spent his time engrossed 'in a strangely illustrated Cabalistic book', of which Solov'ev said that 'it is very interesting;

in every line of this book there is more life than in all of European scholarship. I am happy and content to have found this edition'.[7]

Another realm in which Solov'ev seems ahead of his time is ecumenism. A great deal has been made of the fact that Solov'ev received communion from a Uniate priest in Moscow in 1896. This did not mean that Solov'ev could be regarded as 'a Russian Newman';[8] though it points to the fact that Solov'ev abandoned the anti-Catholicism characteristic of the Slavophils, and in the last decade or so of his life began to envisage a universal Church that embraced the strengths of Catholicism, Orthodoxy and indeed Protestantism. It was his belief in such a universal Church that he affirmed by his receiving Catholic communion in 1896; when he died, four years later, in the last year of the nineteenth century (31 July or 1 August 1900), he made his confession to an Orthodox priest and received Holy Communion from him.

His return to Russia

Solov'ev is a protean figure: his importance for Russian culture is as great as his importance for Russian theology. Although our primary concern in this book is theology, we need to get some perspective on his more general cultural significance. We may perhaps approach this by continuing our account of his life from where we left it, after his third encounter with the lady Sophia in Egypt in 1875. In the following year Solov'ev returned to Moscow, and resumed his teaching post. However, in the years away he had changed, and after a year he resigned his post in Moscow and moved to St Petersburg, where he took up a minor post in the Department of Education. There he befriended Countess Sophia Andreevna Tolstaya, the widow of the poet Alexei Tolstoy, and her niece, a married woman, Sophia Petrovna Khitrovo, with whom he fell in love, and who has been described as 'the unique love of Solov'ev's entire life'.[9] She became one of his great supporters, and opened her estate to him, which provided him with the nearest thing to a permanent residence that he would ever know; she was with him when he died and was one of the women in whom Solov'ev found an incarnation of Sophia. He also came to know and was much influenced by Dostoevsky. From this emotional and family base, Solov'ev embarked on the major works of his life – *The Philosophical Foundation of Integral Knowledge, Treatise on Godmanhood*, and his monumental work, *The Criticism of Abstract Principles* – as well as becoming an immensely popular lecturer in the capital.

---

[7] D. Strémooukhof, *Vladimir Soloviev and His Messianic Work*, trans. Elizabeth Meyendorff (Belmont, MA: Nordland, 1980), 49. In a footnote Strémooukhof suggests that the book was Knorr's edition of Rosenroth's *Kabbala Denudata* (Frankfurt, 1677–84), 'a good source of Cabalistic knowledge for those who did not know Hebrew': Strémooukhof, *Vladimir Soloviev*, 343, n. 14.

[8] The title of a book by Michel d'Herbigny: *Un Newman russe: Vladimir Soloviev (1853–1900)* (Paris: Beauchesne, 1911).

[9] Quoted in Kornblatt, *Divine Sophia*, 17.

All this came to a dramatic end in 1881. On 1 March that year, the tsar Alexander II, the liberator of the serfs, was assassinated. On the 28th of that month, Solov'ev delivered the last of his series of lectures, and in it called on the new tsar to forgive his father's murderers and thus demonstrate to the world that Russia was a Christian country, capable of forgiveness.[10] There was an outcry, and Solov'ev was suspended from giving lectures, and lost all hope of a professorial chair.[11] The rest of his life – not quite 20 years – was spent, as he put it, in devoting himself to the reunion of the Church and the reconciliation of Christianity and Judaism. We have already seen that this led him to receive communion from the hands of a (Greek) Catholic priest, as a sign of the unity that already reposed in the universal Church, present in some way in the divided bodies of Christendom.

Major works of the 1880s include *The History and Future of Theocracy* and *Russia and the Universal Church.* To the last decade of the nineteenth century (and of his life) belong his major treatise, *The Justification of the Good*, and the *Three Dialogues on War, Progress and the End of History.* To these last two decades belong many of his most important works on literature and aesthetics: his three addresses on Dostoevsky, and works like *Beauty in Nature*, *The Universal Meaning of Art* and *The Meaning of Love.*

Addresses on Dostoevsky

Even a brief look at these apparently non-theological works reveals the seamlessness of Solov'ev's thought. In the first of his three addresses on Dostoevsky, he sees his importance as certainly that of an artist, but what it is that makes him a great artist is that 'all is in ferment here, nothing has been fixed, all is still only coming to be',[12] in contrast to his contemporaries (Solov'ev mentions Goncharov, Turgenev, Tolstoy), who analyse society as it is. This Solov'ev traces to his faith: 'he believed not only in a past, but also in an approaching Kingdom of God, and he understood the necessity of labour and action for its realization'.[13] The discourse has become theological; a little later on, Solov'ev says that the word that for Dostoevsky designates his social idea 'will not be the nation, but the *Church*'.[14] The other two addresses develop this in accordance with the Slavophil notion of *sobornost'*: the bringing about of a society in which the universal and the particular are reconciled without compromise, in the ideal of *vseedinstvo*, all-oneness. Russia transcends its national destiny and attains a universal destiny; what makes this

---

[10] A vision of Russia, not far removed from Elder Zossima's: 'God will save his people, for Russia is great in humility', Fyodor Dostoevsky, *The Brothers Karamazov* [published that very year], bk 6, ch. 3 (f), trans. Richard Pevear and Lara Volokhonsky (London: Everyman's Library, 1997), 316.

[11] For the significance of this for Solov'ev, see Oliver Smith, *Vladimir Soloviev and the Spiritualization of Matter* (Boston, MA: Academic Studies Press, 2011), 147–62.

[12] Quoted from Vladimir Wozniuk, ed. and trans., *The Heart of Reality: Essays on Beauty, Love, and Ethics by V. S. Soloviev* (Notre Dame, IN: University of Notre Dame Press, 2003), 6.

[13] Wozniuk, *Heart of Reality*, 7.

[14] Wozniuk, *Heart of Reality*, 11.

possible is the Russian nation's 'consciousness of its sinfulness, the incapability of elevating its imperfection to law and right and resting content upon it: from here comes the requirement of a better life, a thirst for purification and deed'.[15] In these addresses Solov'ev addresses the ugly stain of Dostoevsky's anti-Semitism by developing the role of the Jews in the progress towards all-humanity.

His understanding of aesthetics

Something similar can be observed in his works on aesthetics. What is perhaps particularly striking about *Beauty in Nature* is the way in which Solov'ev embraces Darwinian notions of evolution as a perspective that enables him to develop a theological vision, rather than finding it, as many of his contemporaries did, a problem for a Christian view of the world as created. Art, for Solov'ev, as he discusses it in *The Universal Meaning of Art*, is concerned with the embodiment of beauty. As he puts it, '[t]he highest task of art is the perfected incarnation of [God's] spiritual fullness in our reality, a realization in it of absolute beauty, or the creation of a universal spiritual organism'.[16] This requires something that draws one upwards towards the spiritual: Christ or, as he expresses it in the final pages of the work, the 'Eternal-Feminine', which, in Goethe's verse, 'draws us upwards'.

The longest of these aesthetic works is *The Meaning of Love*. At the heart of this work there is an engagement with Plato's understanding of *eros*, as expressed in the *Symposium* and *Phaedrus*. Essentially what Solov'ev seeks to do is extract Plato's ideas from their homoerotic context, and rethink them in terms of *eros* between man and woman. The essential reason for placing love between man and woman at the heart of his consideration of love – in contrast to Plato, who sees *eros* as essentially the ascent of the soul to the embrace of absolute beauty – is that the meaning of love is the creation of human individuality by overcoming egoism – the 'sacrifice of egoism' – and this involves an 'other', and for Solov'ev this other is encountered in the opposite sex: it is only sexual love that enables an encounter with the other that displaces the centre of the self, and overcomes egoism. Apart from sexual love, there is no real encounter with the other.

Plato's *eros* is aptly captured by perhaps the greatest reader of Plato, the third-century philosopher Plotinos, who speaks at the end of the last *Ennead* of 'the flight of the alone to the alone': here there is no encounter with the other, displacing the self, rather a pouring out of the self into the aloneness of the absolute. Other forms of love than sexual love between man and woman are part of the variety of ways in which human beings relate one to another, but cannot fulfil that role. Maternal love, for instance, sacrifices egoism, but at the expense, Solov'ev argues, of individuality – the mother's

---

[15] Wozniuk, *Heart of Reality*, 15.
[16] Wozniuk, *Heart of Reality*, 75.

sense of self (which is what I think Solov'ev means by 'individuality'). 'Still less', he argues,

> can the remaining forms of sympathetic feelings have a claim to take the place of sexual love. Friendship between persons of one and the same sex lacks an all-round formal distinction of qualities making up one another. But if, nevertheless, this friendship achieves a particular intensity, then it changes into an unnatural surrogate of sexual love. As for patriotism and love of humanity, these feelings, in all their importance, cannot in themselves concretely and vigorously abolish egoism, owing to the incommensurability of the lover and the loved one. Neither humanity nor even the nation can be for an individual man as concrete an object as he himself. It is certainly possible to sacrifice one's life for the nation or humanity, but to create out of oneself a new human being, to manifest and realize true human individuality on the basis of this extensive love is not possible. Here the real centre still remains one's old egoistic *I*, and the nation and humanity belong to the periphery of consciousness as ideal objects. The same could be said about love for science, art, etc.[17]

So, Solov'ev asserts:

> The meaning and value of love as feeling consists in the fact that love compels us effectively to acknowledge in *another*, with all our being, the unconditional, central significance that, on the strength of egoism, we sense only in ourselves.[18]

Solov'ev goes on to explore the nature of sexual love. He acknowledges the way in which lovers idealize each other, the way in which they see each other bathed in light, as it were. He does not, however, for all that he acknowledges its fleeting character, try to diminish it as an illusion; rather this experience of seeing the beloved suffused in light, finding her beautiful, is something genuine. The lover sees in the beloved something that is there, that is true, for he glimpses the image of God in which the human is created. Solov'ev alludes to the creation of the human in God's image, when he says: 'The mysterious divine image in which the human being is created originally refers to the true unity of its fundamental aspects, male and female, and not to any separate part of the human essence.'[19] For Solov'ev, Genesis 1.27, with its assertion that God created humankind as male and female, provides support for his analysis of the meaning of love. The 'archetypal cleft of sex'[20] is part of what it is to be human, because the achievement of true humanity entails the sacrifice of egoism through the encounter with the other as the beloved.

What we are finding in these primarily aesthetic and philosophical works is an attempt to think notions of all-humanity and all-oneness in a way that underlines a polarity in human experience and what it is to be human. It is

---

[17] Wozniuk, *Heart of Reality*, 99.

[18] Wozniuk, *Heart of Reality*, 100.

[19] Wozniuk, *Heart of Reality*, 116.

[20] Amy Clampitt's phrase from 'Dodona: Asked of the Oracle', in *The Collected Poems of Amy Clampitt* (New York: Knopf, 1997), 207.

a polarity that finds a dynamism in sexual distinction: man is drawn onwards and upwards by the woman (sexual distinction is invariably understood from the male side, which the female complements). In this context Solov'ev makes frequent reference to Goethe's notion of the eternal feminine, *das Ewig-Weibliche*, which, as Goethe puts it in the final line of Faust, Part II, 'Zieht uns hinan' – 'draws us upwards'. This is one of the ingredients in what becomes the central notion of his theology, and that aspect of his theology that was to exercise (and still exercises) a profound influence: his notion of Sophia, the Divine Wisdom, and its place in his understanding of reality as 'Godmanhood' (I prefer this older translation of *Bogochelovechestvo*, to the more recent translation, influenced by the French, 'divine humanity', for the Russian, as I read it, is an abstract noun based on [the] Godman, whereas 'divine humanity' rather suggests the abstract noun 'humanity', qualified as divine).

Sophia, the Wisdom of God

Let us now turn to exploring the ingredients of Solov'ev's notion of the Divine Wisdom, Sophia, and draw out the manifold facets of this idea for his thought, and for those who were influenced by him.[21]

We should start with the Scriptures of the Christian Church. The notion of wisdom begins to appear more consistently in the later strata of the Old Testament, both those books preserved in Hebrew – especially the book of Proverbs and also the book of Job – and those preserved in Greek – the book of Wisdom and the book called Ecclesiasticus or the Wisdom of Ben Sira. Wisdom also appears in the New Testament.

In Proverbs (and also in the Psalms) Wisdom appears in connection with creation. In Psalm 103 God is said to have made everything 'in Wisdom' (Ps. 103.24 LXX), and in Psalm 135 he is said to have made the heavens 'by understanding' (Ps. 135.5 LXX). In Proverbs 8, Wisdom herself declares that 'the Lord created me as the beginning of his ways, for the sake of his works' (8.22), and goes on to speak of her role in creation:

> When he prepared the heaven, I was present with him, and when he marked out his own throne on the winds ... when he made strong the foundations of the earth, I was beside him, fitting together; it is I who was the one in whom he took delight. And each day I was glad in his presence ...
>
> (Prov. 8.27, 29–30)

In the Hebrew text Wisdom, *Hokhmah*, describes herself as 'master workman' (Prov. 8.30 RSV): Solov'ev knew both the Hebrew and the Greek texts and it was important for him that the word for wisdom is feminine in both Hebrew, *hokhmah*, and in Greek, *sophia*. So Wisdom is God's companion in the work of creation: there is a male–female complementarity there at the

---

[21] For a more detailed account of the sources of Solov'ev's understanding of Wisdom see Kornblatt, *Divine Sophia*, 34–82, to which I am indebted.

bringing-into-being of the world. Closely allied with this function, Wisdom appears as one who knows God, one who can bring human beings to knowledge of God. In chapter 9, we are told:

> Wisdom has built her house, she has set up her seven pillars. She has slaughtered her beasts, she has mixed her wine, she has also set up her table. She has sent out her maids to call from the highest places in the town, 'Whoever is simple, let him turn in here!' To him who is without sense she says, 'Come, eat of my bread and drink of the wine I have mixed. Leave simpleness, and live, and walk in the way of insight.'   (Prov. 9.1–6 RSV)

Elsewhere, wisdom is presented as something to be sought out, more precious than anything in Creation. This is expressed very beautifully in the long hymn to wisdom in Job 28, which turns on the exclamation:

> But where shall wisdom be found? And where is the place of understanding? Man does not know the way to it, and it is not found in the land of the living ... It is hid from the eyes of all living, and concealed from the birds of the air ... God understands the way to it, and he knows its place.
>   (Job 28.12–13, 21, 23 RSV)

In Job wisdom is the secret that lies behind Creation, known to God alone, not – or not yet – personified, as in Proverbs.

These two aspects of Wisdom are found in the Greek books of Wisdom: the Wisdom of Solomon, and of Ben Sira. In Wisdom 7, we read that, on the one hand, 'And all such things as are either secret or manifest, them I know. For wisdom, which is the worker of all things, taught me' (Wisd. 7.21–22 AV), and then learn that,

> For in her is an understanding spirit, holy, one only, manifold, subtil, lively, clear, undefiled, plain, not subject to hurt, loving the thing that is good, quick, which cannot be letted, ready to do good, kind to man, stedfast, sure, free from care, having all power, overseeing all things, and going through all understanding, pure, and most subtil spirits ... For she is the breath of the power of God, and a pure influence flowing from the glory of the Almighty ... she is the brightness of the everlasting light, the unspotted mirror of the power of God, and the image of his goodness ... Wisdom reaches from one end to another mightily: and sweetly doth she order all things.   (Wisd. 7.22–23, 25, 26; 8.1 AV)

And then we switch to the other aspect of Wisdom: 'I loved her, and sought her out from my youth, I desired to make her my spouse, and I was a lover of her beauty' (8.2 AV). Something else happens to Wisdom in the book of Wisdom: she is not just involved in creation, but in all God's dealings with Israel – through salvation history, as we say. From chapter 10 onwards, the book of Wisdom tells the story from Paradise to the flight from Egypt as the story of Wisdom's engagement with humankind. This Wisdom of God is also called the Word, Logos, of God, notably at the high point of the story, when the author gives his account of the destruction of the firstborn of the Egyptians:

For while all things were in quiet silence, and that night was in the midst of her swift course, Thine Almighty word leaped down from heaven out of thy royal throne, as a fierce man of war into the midst of a land of destruction ... and it touched the heaven, but it stood upon the earth.

(Wisd. 18.14–15, 16c AV)[22]

In the New Testament, this tradition of Wisdom is associated with Christ, who is called 'the power of God and the wisdom of God' (1 Cor. 1.24 RSV), in whom 'are hid all the treasures of wisdom and knowledge' (Col. 2.3 RSV).

The 'in-between'

Solov'ev's understanding of Sophia draws together most of the areas of his wide learning; the scriptural understanding may be the main stream, but it has many tributaries. One of these is what he drew from Plato and Greek philosophy in general. There are several issues here, not so clearly related to Wisdom as the biblical material we have looked at. They are all concerned with what Plato occasionally, and his greatest follower, Plotinos, several times, refer to as *ta metaxu*, 'the in-between', as we might say in English. In the *Symposium*, when Plato considers Eros, he argues that Eros cannot be one of the gods, because he manifests need, and the gods are self-sufficient; Eros is one of the daemons, beings that exist between the gods and humans, and mediate between them. But *eros* itself – love that aspires after communion with the beautiful – typifies this state of 'betweenness': the beautiful is transcendent, beyond our reach; to experience *eros*, to pursue *eros*, is to advance into the realm of *ta metaxu*. Another candidate for the state of the between is the world soul, especially as this is treated in the *Timaeus*; the world soul exists between the realm of the Forms and the world as humans know it – it holds them together in some way.

Plato was of immense importance for Solov'ev. The poet Afanasii Fet laid on him the task of 'giving Plato to Russian literature', which Solov'ev fulfilled by translating seven of Plato's dialogues, published with an Introduction in 1899, intended as the first of several volumes, cut short, however, by his death in the following year. We have already seen something of Plato's significance for Solov'ev in his short treatise, *The Meaning of Love*. There he takes the central significance that love, *eros*, has for Plato, the inspiration behind the philosopher's search for ultimate truth and beauty, but, transposing it from the homoerotic context it had in Plato, introduces the polarity of the sexes, so that *eros* is no longer simply a yearning for the ultimate, but expresses itself in sexual love, in an engagement involving gendered difference. The world soul fits this context uneasily, which may explain the way in which the notion of the world soul seems fleeting in Solov'ev's thought, and was eventually abandoned.[23]

---

[22] For these quotations from the book of Wisdom, I have used the translation of the Authorized Version, which sounds so much better to my ear than other translations, even my own.

[23] See Kornblatt, *Divine Sophia*, 45–7.

The Christian tradition of Byzantium and Russia

Another tributary – or perhaps the confluence itself of other tributaries (though this metaphor is getting overworked) – is the Christian tradition as found in the Fathers of the Church and the Divine Liturgy. In the Fathers of the Church – notably the Cappadocian Fathers, Dionysios the Areopagite, Maximos the Confessor – there is much reflection on Sophia, which can probably be traced back to the second-century Christian scholar Origen, who uses Wisdom in relation to the Word, as complementing the outward movement of the Word with an inward movement of Wisdom: whereas the Word is made flesh, Wisdom is 'hidden in a mystery'.[24] But the sophiology of the Fathers is not very amenable to Solov'ev for one reason: invariably Wisdom is identified with Christ; wisdom ceases to be 'Lady Wisdom', she loses her feminine gender, and becomes an aspect of Christ the Word.

There is, however, evidence that in the Russian assumption of Byzantine Christianity, Wisdom once again assumes her identity as gendered (in doing this, it may be that Slav Christianity is articulating more clearly traditions that were muted in the Christianity of the Byzantine Empire, especially traditions about the Mother of God found in the apocryphal writings, such as the *Protevangelium of James*). 'To Holy Wisdom' was the dedication of the Great Cathedral Church in Constantinople, the capital of Constantine's Christian Empire. It is, however, very clear that that great church was dedicated to Christ, the Wisdom of God: this is evident in the mosaic in the narthex that greets one as one approaches the church; it is evident, too, in the feast of the dedication of the church, which is close to the feast of the Nativity of Christ. Churches dedicated to Holy Wisdom became very popular in Slav countries. However, and this is something to which Solov'ev himself draws attention,[25] the dedication of these churches – in Kiev, Vladimir, and several other cities, eventually too in Moscow – is clearly to the Mother of God, not Christ, as their feasts of dedication are either the feast of the Nativity of the Mother of God (8 September) or the feast of her Dormition (15 August). Holy Wisdom is, in some way, being associated with the Mother of God, rather than Christ, and this is eventually found in the Slav iconographic tradition. Solov'ev saw this as a discovery, or maybe a revelation, vouchsafed to the Slav soul: the restoration of femininity to the figure of Holy Wisdom.

Such a sense of the peculiar contribution of Slav Orthodoxy, in this case in contrast to the Byzantine and Greek traditions, clearly chimed in with Solov'ev's own Slavophil roots. It found further support in the use of readings from the Wisdom literature at feasts of the Mother of God in the Byzantine Rite (which found an echo in the use of Sirach 24.14–16 (Vulgate; 8–12 LXX) instead of the epistle in many masses in honour of the Blessed Virgin Mary in the old Roman Rite, abandoned at Vatican II). With this may

---

[24] Origen, *Hom. Exod.* 12. 4.
[25] See, e.g., *Russia and the Universal Church* (London: Geoffrey Bles, 1948), 177–8.

be related the place of Mother (Moist) Earth in Russian spirituality. Judith Kornblatt quotes a striking passage from George Fedotov's *The Russian Religious Mind*:

> In Mother Earth, who remains the core of Russian religion, converge the most secret and deep religious feelings of the folk. Beneath the beautiful veil of grass and flowers, the people venerate with awe the black moist depths, the source of all fertilizing powers, the nourishing breast of nature, and their own last resting place. The very epithet of the earth in the folk songs, 'Mother Earth, the Humid', known also in the Iranian mythology, alludes to the womb rather than to the face of the Earth. It means that not beauty but fertility is the supreme virtue of the earth, although the Russian is by no means insensible to the loveliness of its surface. Earth is the Russian 'eternal womanhood', not the celestial image of it: mother, not virgin; fertile, not pure; and black, for the best Russian soil is black.[26]

There is an evident echo of this in Dostoevsky's portrayal of the Elder Zossima, whose teaching includes:

> Love to throw yourself down on the earth and kiss it. Kiss the earth and love it, tirelessly, insatiably, love all men, love all things, seek this rapture and ecstasy. Water the earth with the tears of your joy, and love those tears.[27]

We have already seen something of the way in which Solov'ev drew on those writings that have been called Gnostic, since Solov'ev's day (though not much earlier), and the forms of early modern mysticism, notably associated with Jakob Boehme, where he found plenty about Sophia, and also an explicit acknowledgement of the place of sexual distinction and union in the attainment of enlightenment. Solov'ev was also familiar with the Jewish Kabbalistic tradition, where similar ideas flourished. I think that for our purposes, what I have sketched in earlier on is probably enough. Another source Kornblatt discusses is Goethe's notion of the eternal feminine and prefigurings of this she finds in Dante's Beatrice and Cervantes' Dulcinea.

This chapter may seem to have been all about the scaffolding of Solov'ev's theology, rather than about what he built up by means of this scaffolding. I think that is probably true, but perhaps as we explore his influence in what follows, we shall see something of the kind of theology that emerges from all this. Those who regarded themselves as, in some way at least, his disciples made use of his approach to theology, and as we look at Florensky, Bulgakov and Berdyaev, we shall see something of the way in which his theological intuitions could be developed. These intuitions were essentially rooted in experience, and it has been the terms in which Solov'ev rendered himself open to this experience that we have explored in this chapter.

---

[26] Quoted in Kornblatt, *Divine Sophia*, 53.
[27] Dostoevsky, *Brothers Karamazov*, bk 6, ch. 3 (h) (Pevear–Volokhonsky trans., 322).

3

Fr Pavel Florensky and the nature of reason

Fr Pavel Florensky was a phenomenon. Among the Christian intellectuals of the beginning of the twentieth century he stands out as exceptional, for multitudinous reasons. He was amazingly prolific; even very summary bibliographies run for pages and pages. His interests were exceptionally wide: if theology was at the centre, at least for some of the time, it overlapped into philosophy, history, art history, philology, the natural and biological sciences and mathematics; he was also in some ways a literary figure – in his early twenties he was familiar with most of the Symbolists through his friendship with Andrei Bely; furthermore, as we shall see, literary considerations impinge on his understanding of theology. In most of these areas, so far as I can judge, he was an expert, not a dilettante. For instance, the symbolic logic with which his most famous work, *The Pillar and Ground of the Truth*, is littered is that put forward in Russell and Whitehead's *Principia Mathematica*, the very latest thing when Florensky was writing. His knowledge of languages, both ancient and modern, was phenomenal; his footnotes refer to a huge range of works in all these languages with which he was familiar. He has been called 'Russia's unknown da Vinci',[1] and has been compared to Pascal, whose work he valued. His friend, Fr Sergii Bulgakov, said of him:

> For me Father Pavel was not only a phenomenon of genius, but also a work of art, so harmonious and beautiful was his image. We would need the words, the brush or the chisel of a great master to tell the world about him.[2]

This makes it exceptionally difficult to condense anything adequate into a single chapter. What I shall do, after sketching in his life, is concentrate on two issues – one taken from the earlier period of his life, and one from later on. The first issue is his analysis of the nature of reason, conducted in the earlier part of his great work, *The Pillar and Ground of the Truth*, and developed in the rest of it; the second issue I shall discuss is his theology of the icon, which belongs to the works he wrote in the 1920s, works not published then, because of the fiercely anti-Christian climate in early Bolshevik Russia, but only later, sometimes much later. The theology of the icon is related very closely, I shall suggest, to his analysis of reason. There is a further way in

---

[1] The (reluctant) subtitle of Avril Pyman's wonderful biography, *Pavel Florensky: A Quiet Genius: The Tragic and Extraordinary Life of Russia's Unknown da Vinci* (London: Continuum, 2010).
[2] Quoted in Nicoletta Misler's biographical sketch in *Beyond Vision: Essays on the Perception of Art*, comp. and ed. Nicoletta Misler, trans. Wendy Salmond (London: Reaktion Books, 2002), 13.

which Fr Pavel is exceptional among his contemporaries: unlike virtually all the non-communist intellectuals in Russia, he was not expelled from the Soviet Union in 1922/3, but remained there, because of his gifts as a scientist and the value that was placed on them.

Life

Pavel Florensky was born in 1882, the eldest of six children, in the village of Evlakh in Azerbaidjan. His father was a railway engineer, from whom he inherited his passion of science; to his mother, an intelligent and educated woman of ancient Armenian lineage, he owed his artistic talents. He attended the Second Classical Gymnasium in Tbilisi (Tiflis, as the Russians called it), Georgia, but regarded his real education as taking place outside school in his walks, or 'expeditions', in which he collected shells, stones and fossils, and drew and photographed the natural phenomena he observed – and also read. In 1899, on the threshold between adolescence and manhood, he went through a profound spiritual crisis, bound up with his sense of the inadequacy of what he called the 'knowledge of physics'. Later on he went through two other crises, one on the eve of his marriage in 1910, and the last in 1924, about which he was never very explicit. His first crisis opened to him the world of Orthodoxy, something that had no meaning for his educated, lay

Pavel Florensky: silhouette

family. This did not at all mean for Florensky that the world of science was abandoned – far from it – but it was no longer the only, or even the most important, way of understanding the nature of truth.

Having graduated from the gymnasium in Tbilisi, he enrolled in the Department of Physics and Mathematics at Moscow University, and studied under Nikolai Bugaev, whose son Andrei Bely, the novelist and poet, soon became a close friend, and through whom he came to know members of the Symbolist circle in Moscow: Briusov, Bal'mont, Dmitri Merezhkovsky and Zinaida Gippius. In 1904, he enrolled in the Moscow Spiritual Academy at Sergiev Posad, while still studying at the university in Moscow; he graduated from the academy in 1908 and was ordained priest in April 1911. Four years later he submitted his thesis for his master's degree in theology, and in May 1914 received the degree. It was a revised version of this thesis that was published later that year as *The Pillar and Ground of the Truth*. After his graduation, Florensky taught philosophy at the Moscow Spiritual Academy from 1908 until 1919, and also for a year (1908–9) at the Women's Gymnasium in Sergiev Posad; between 1912 and 1921 he served at the Church of St Mary Magdalene in Sergiev Posad, attached to the Shelter for Nurses of the Russian Red Cross. He also edited *Bogoslovsky Vestnik* ('Theological Messenger') for three years before the Revolution. In the two years after the Revolution, Florensky served on the Commission for the Preservation of Art and Antiquities of the Trinity-St Sergii Lavra, which provoked a series of important works on early Russian art and the nature of icons.

In the 1920s, Florensky devoted more and more time to his scientific activities, publishing prolifically. Though his activity was scientific, he continued to wear his priest's cassock and cross, even when lecturing. His evident Christian commitment led to periods of exile and harassment, and eventually in 1933 he was arrested, charged with criminal conspiracy, and condemned to ten years in a prison camp, ending up in the former monastery of Solovki in the far north of Russia, the origins of the Gulag. During his imprisonment, though he was deprived of his library and papers – something he felt deeply – he continued his scientific research. Finally, on 25 November 1937, the People's Commissariat for Internal Affairs (*Narodnyi Komissariat Vnutrennikh Del*, or NKVD) had him condemned to death. He was transferred to the Leningrad region, and executed by firing squad on 8 December 1937.

His writings

Florensky's theology was controversial. He inherited and developed Solov'ev's speculations about Sophia, which became a *cause célèbre* among the Russians of the emigration in the 1930s, leading to the condemnation of Fr Sergii Bulgakov's sophiology by the Moscow Patriarchate and the Russian Church in Exile – but not, however, by the Exarchate of Russian Parishes under the Œcumenical Patriarchate, to which Bulgakov belonged. That condemnation implicated Bulgakov's long-time friend and earlier mentor, Florensky, and it is likely for this reason that Florensky has not been included among the New

Martyrs canonized by the Moscow Patriarchate in 2000. That controversy continues, and has only been increased by the publication of his theological writings from the 1920s and 1930s, which were unpublished in his lifetime. The early pre-revolutionary works revolve around his great work, *The Pillar and Ground of the Truth*.[3]

In the twenties, Florensky was putting together materials for a massive work in many parts that was to be called *On the Watersheds of Thought*. It is not clear (certainly not to me) what this would have included. Works that have since been published and would doubtless have found a place in *Watersheds of Thought* include some of his art historical works, such as 'Reverse Perspective'[4] and *Iconostasis*,[5] a substantial volume, *Filosofia Kulta*, 'The Philosophy of Cult [or probably better, worship]', a work called *Names*, and a volume of auto-biographical reflections, *To My Children*. There is a good deal of discussion and disagreement as to the continuity between Florensky's earlier and later thought. What I propose to do is really to cut the Gordian knot, and take two subjects, one from his earlier thought as found in *The Pillar and Ground of the Truth*, and then his later reflections on the nature of the icon. This might look rather arbitrary, but I think similar, fundamental concerns manifest themselves in these two subjects.

The problem of reason

In this chapter we shall concentrate on the nature of reason, because it seems to me that this is the real heart of Florensky's concerns and significance. We have already seen that Russian thought in the late nineteenth century, not least in Solov'ev, often gives the impression of wanting desperately to catch up with all the developments of thought in the West that had passed the Russians by – Renaissance, Reformation, Enlightenment, Romanticism. Florensky, with his encyclopedic knowledge, not least his profound knowledge of mathematics and the sciences, was well placed to see what it was that had happened to Western thought since the late Middle Ages.

One might perhaps say that the Renaissance and Romanticism both led to a deepening of humanistic disciplines – a serious concern with philological issues, with language, with meaning – while the rise of the sciences that blossomed in the Enlightenment focused attention on how to understand the nature of reality by means of experiment and analytical reflection. This has led to a split between science and humanities, a split that became apparent in the eighteenth century and threatened to become a chasm in the nineteenth. The strides in the advance of knowledge in the natural sciences seemed to wrest the pursuit of truth from traditionally human approaches, locating it

---

[3] ET: Pavel Florensky, *The Pillar and Ground of the Truth*, trans. Boris Jakim (Princeton, NJ: Princeton University Press, 1997). References to this in brackets in the text: P + page number.

[4] ET: *Beyond Vision*, ed. Misler, trans. Wendy Salmond, 197–272.

[5] Pavel Florensky, *Iconostasis*, trans. Donald Sheehan and Olga Andrejev (Crestwood, NY: St Vladimir's Seminary Press, 1996).

in what can be discovered by the methods of the sciences. The popularity of the theory of evolution seemed to call in question still further the unique position of the human and threatened to evacuate human ways of understanding, including any religious understanding of the world of human experience, of any real meaning, despite the fact that the advance of the sciences was a fundamentally human story. Florensky, with his interests and learning, bridged that gulf, being equally at home in the most abstract mathematics and in a philological pursuit of meaning through etymology and poetry. As we have already noted in the brief sketch of his life, at the end of the century, while still in his teens, he had a spiritual crisis, as he realized that the 'knowledge of physics', as he called it, could not solve all the problems of human existence. Faith, prayer, worship could not be excluded; these, too, opened up dimensions of meaning of which 'physics' was unaware.

The Pillar and Ground of the Truth

Many of these issues are reflected in the early chapters of *The Pillar and Ground of the Truth*. However, before we look at what he has to say in detail, I think we need to reflect, at least briefly, on the way he says it. This is an issue we shall encounter throughout this book in different ways. Very few of the Russian theologians we shall be looking at had a formal training in theology, something we have already observed. Florensky is an exception (so, too, is Solov'ev): he had gained a master's degree at the Moscow Spiritual Academy. This was not the case with Bulgakov, or Florovsky, or Lossky. This lack of formal training meant that they approached the study of theology with fewer preconceptions; the same is true of Florensky, despite his exposure to the traditional methods of theological study. It was not obvious to him that the way to present theological truths and arguments was through a formal treatise, with a determined list of subjects. This is obvious as soon as one opens *The Pillar and Ground of the Truth*. It has chapters, but look! They are letters, addressed to someone, someone in particular. They do not have a form that can be traced back to the traditional structure of a lecture; they are letters, and make some attempt to sound like letters.

The first letter begins with an account of his return home. He writes to his friend, 'Our vaulted room greeted me with coldness, sadness, and loneliness when I opened its door for the first time after my trip'.[6] He goes on to talk about the sound of the wind in the trees, the trains that 'passed by with a deep-voiced roar'. It is autumn and he talks of the leaves that were falling to the ground: 'Like dying butterflies, they were describing slow circles in the air as they descended to earth'.[7] Another letter (the fourth) recalls 'a silent autumn night. Snow lies deep beneath the window. All is quiet; I do not even hear the night watchman's stick'.[8] The next begins: 'Do you remember, my

---

[6] Florensky, *Pillar*, 10.
[7] Florensky, *Pillar*, 11.
[8] Florensky, *Pillar*, 53.

gentle one, our long walks in the forest, the forest of dying August?"[9] There is no indication who the friend is to whom these letters are addressed. It seems to me clear that no one in particular is intended (it is certainly not Christ, as Richard Gustafson bizarrely suggests in his Introduction to the English translation[10]); it is rather a literary device to draw us into a conversation taking place in a particular place – in, or on the edge of, woods – at a particular time of year. Thought, for Florensky, is not a string of concepts, but a conversation taking place in the world, not in some abstract spiritual zone.

These descriptive touches seem to me not unlike the way in which Plato briefly sets the scene (outside the walls of Athens, in the *Phaedrus*, for example), and, as with Plato, it is rash to assume that this is mere scene-setting, of no real significance for what Plato, or Florensky, has to say. For in both cases, neither the dialogue nor the letter is superfluous to what is being said; it is not something that could be condensed into a few paragraphs – the 'meaning' of Plato or of Florensky. The engagement that the letter or the dialogue entails is part of what is being said, not some disposable packaging. This is not to say that the intellectual content is secondary – not at all; it is important and often demanding, just as a conversation can often require a lot of attention – but the intellectual argument is always that: an argument between people, not just between positions.

Antinomy

One way into what Florensky is saying in *The Pillar and Ground of the Truth* is found in the word he uses to capture something of the nature of theological assertion, and that word is *antinomy*.[11] Florensky is quite deliberate in his use of it: an Appendix (Chapter 26) surveys the history of the use of the term (for all the informality entailed by a series of letters, a work with 16 appendices and 1,057 endnotes has very serious academic pretensions!). The term goes back to classical times, with a primarily legal meaning – a conflict of laws, that is, a situation in which appeal to laws can be used to justify one solution, as well as its opposite. It was, as Florensky remarks, Kant who used the term with a philosophical meaning.

The term is very deliberately used by Florensky, for there are other terms he could have used, and indeed does use, that are much commoner in theological discourse. Paradox, for instance. It is everywhere in Christian theology. God is one and yet three; Christ is God and yet man; in the Eucharist there is what appears to be bread and wine, and yet after the calling on the Holy Spirit, we believe that it is the body and blood of Christ; we are ruled by providence and depend on grace, and yet we are free. These are all

---

[9] Florensky, *Pillar*, 80.

[10] Florensky, *Pillar*, xii.

[11] This discussion of antinomy is based on a paper I gave at a seminar in honour of Dr Avril Pyman at Pushkin House, celebrating the publication of her book on Florensky and her eightieth birthday, on 12 May 2010.

paradoxes. And in the Fathers of the Church we find what can only be described as a delight in paradox. St Ignatios of Antioch speaks of 'one physician, fleshly and spiritual, born and unborn, become God in the flesh, true life in death, from Mary and from God, first subject to suffering and then beyond suffering – Jesus Christ our Lord' (Ign. *Eph.* 7). Similarly St Gregory the Theologian says:

> He was begotten of a woman, yet he was already begotten. That he was from a woman makes him human, that she was a virgin makes him divine. On earth he has no father, in heaven he has no mother . . . He was wrapped in swaddling clothes, but at the Resurrection he unloosed the swaddling bands of the grave. He was laid in a manger, but was extolled by angels, disclosed by a star and adored by Magi.   (*Or. Bas.* 29. 19)

Some kinds of theology try to reconcile these contradictions; you could say this of the official theology of the ancient councils: God is three *Persons*, but one *substance* – there is no contradiction, as he is one and three in different ways; Christ is one person in two natures – again no contradiction. But the passages from St Ignatios and St Gregory the Theologian don't try to soften the contradictions; rather they seem to delight in them. So, too, does Florensky. He does more than just delight in them in a rhetorical way, however; he sees these contradictions as having a crucial role in theology, for they point to something fundamental about the nature of reason. This is why he chooses the word antinomy, rather than paradox, or contradiction, for the great German philosopher, the key figure in the development of modern philosophy, Immanuel Kant, also used the term antinomy to demonstrate something about the nature of reason. Kant, for Florensky, epitomizes the way in which the West has become blind to religion and to God, so it is Kant Florensky needs, and wants, to engage with, and he engages with him at the most fundamental point: over the nature of reason.

An alternative to Kant

Kant's antinomies occur in the treatise that was the turning point in his philosophical career, and ushered in the concerns that are characteristic of modern philosophy, his *Critique of Pure Reason*; they form part of his 'Transcendental Dialectic'. There are, he argues, four antinomies of pure reason: in each case the antinomy is a contradiction both terms of which can be demonstrated by reason alone, or pure reason. Because we can prove both sides of a contradiction, we have in effect demonstrated that reason here fails: we can go no further, there is no longer anything on the basis of which reason can proceed. His four antinomies are these:

1 Does the world, the cosmos, have a beginning in time and is it limited in space? Or does it have no limits with regard to time or space, as it is infinite? Kant shows how you can demonstrate both: that it can be shown to be both finite and infinite.

2 Is matter composed of atoms that cannot be divided further, or is matter infinitely divisible? Again it can be shown that either is true.
3 Is causality in accordance with the laws of nature the only causality there is? Or is it possible for humans freely to act as a cause of actions? Again, either can be demonstrated.
4 Is there within the cosmos an absolutely necessary being, either as a part of it or as its cause, or not? Again both positions can be argued for.[12]

For Kant this demonstrates that reason cannot establish anything sound about the nature of the cosmos, the nature of matter, the nature of causality, or the existence of God. All the so-called problems of metaphysics – about God, the soul and the cosmos – are beyond human reason. The antinomies constitute for Kant what one might call roadblocks to reason; they prevent reason from going any further in pursuing the central questions of metaphysics. For Kant, it follows that there is no speculative metaphysics; what speculative metaphysics is concerned with is relegated by Kant to the realm of the regulative, which is derived from moral presuppositions, but is not in any ordinary sense a matter of knowledge at all. We shall be better moral beings if we act as if God existed, as if the soul were immortal, if we believe that good will be rewarded beyond this life, and evil punished. But we have no reason to suppose that any of this is true.

Fr Pavel Florensky turns this on its head, and in so doing challenges Kant's notion of the nature of reason, and argues for something very different. In the Divine Liturgy, just before the creed is sung, when we confess our faith in what the Church teaches, the priest says: 'Let us love one another, that with one mind we may confess', and the people reply: 'Father, Son and Holy Spirit, Trinity consubstantial and undivided!' The third letter of *The Pillar and Ground of the Truth*, which is about Tri-unity, *Triëdinstvo*, picks up this response in its first words: '"Trinity consubstantial and undivided, unity trihypostatic and eternally co-existent" – that is the only scheme that promises to resolve *epoche*, if the doubt of scepticism is at all resolvable.'[13] It is the Trinity, the incomprehensible Three-in-Oneness, that can alone resolve the suspension of judgement, the *epoche*, of the ancient sceptics; only the apparently incomprehensible dogma of the Trinity can cut through the doubt that underlies, and undermines, all human thought.

How this is so is explored in Letter 6, concerned with contradiction, and it is here that Florensky introduces the term antinomy. For Florensky, antinomy is central to the recognition of truth, for without antinomies, without contradiction, we would simply be faced by rationally convincing proofs. This would mean that we would be *compelled* to accept the truth, for one cannot arbitrarily reject the conclusion of an argument, if one has accepted the premisses. This would have two consequences, both unacceptable to Florensky:

---

[12] See *Immanuel Kant's Critique of Pure Reason*, trans. Norman Kemp Smith (London: Macmillan, corrected impression, 1933), 393–421.
[13] Florensky, *Pillar*, 39 (trans. modified).

on the one hand freedom would be abolished – truth would be imposed, as it were, rather than accepted and embraced; but on the other hand truth would be transparent, obvious, 'clear and distinct', as Descartes put it; but such truth would bear no relation to the world we live in, which is fragmented by sin and finitude, and thus – far from being transparent – is utterly opaque. Truth without antinomy, Florensky maintains, is both tyrannical and also something that makes no sense in the world in which we live.

In fact, Florensky continues, reliance on rationality would lead to irreconcilable contradictions between different systems of belief, and therefore to conflict between those who are committed to them. We would be left with rationality's egoistical isolation *and* its egoistical opposition. Now this is indeed what we experience; this is the nature of fallen humanity. Argument based on reason sets humans one against another; it drives them more deeply into the fallen world that they constitute. Kant's deployment of antinomy is naive: the use of reason on which it is based is not going to stop at the roadblocks constituted by Kant's antinomies; it will lead back to where one started from – conflicting ways of understanding the world and humanity, a conflict that is not necessarily confined to learned argument, but can lead directly into conflict between different people and different societies. Kant's philosophical heritage seems to me to bear that out.

Florensky's solution is the *embrace of antinomy*, for such an embrace will lead us to question the claims of reason, its claims to coerce what it maintains is the truth. As he puts it in Letter 6:

> In other words, truth is an antinomy, and it cannot fail to be such. And truth cannot be anything else, for one can affirm in advance that knowledge of the truth demands spiritual life and therefore is an *ascesis*. But the ascesis of rationality is belief, i.e., self-renunciation. The act of the self-renunciation of rationality is an expression of antinomy. Indeed, only an antinomy can be believed. Every non-antinomic judgment is merely accepted or merely rejected by rationality, for such a judgment does not surpass the boundary of rationality's egoistical isolation. If truth were non-antinomic, then rationality, always revolving in its proper sphere, would not have a fulcrum, would not see extra-rational objects and therefore would not be induced to begin the ascesis of belief. That fulcrum is dogma. With dogma begins our salvation, for only dogma, being antinomic, does not constrain our freedom and allows voluntary belief or wicked unbelief. For it is impossible to compel one to believe, just as it is impossible to compel one not to believe. According to Augustine, 'no one believes except voluntarily' (*nemo credit nisi volens*).   (P 109)

Whereas for Kant the antinomies constitute roadblocks to reason, for Florensky they trip up reason, as it were, expose its deficiencies, and make us realize that truth can be attained by no method such as that of rationality, but only by the spiritual life, which demands self-renunciation, ascesis, which explores the world opened up by dogma, which is the realm of freedom, the freedom of the spirit that discovers truth through opening itself to God. This idea that the defeat of reason enables reason to transcend itself and attain what it is really searching for recalls the way in which Origen justifies allegory: the contradictions in the narrative of the Scriptures force us to look beyond the literal meaning and attain the true meaning of the Scriptures by a sensitivity to symbol and allegory – but this means moving into a realm where conventional certainties are abandoned, and the way forward proceeds through repentance, self-renunciation, progress in the spiritual life, which is not a matter of achievement, but of surrender to the love of God. More nearly it recalls Solov'ev who, as we saw last time, sees love as an encounter with the other that displaces the centre of the self, and overcomes egoism.

Another way of putting the point Florensky is making would be to say that rationality proceeds by *success*: arguments only convince if they are successful. But such success does not lead to the truth in any fundamental way, though it may help one to get some things right, especially in relation to the material world. The way to truth is through the spiritual life; it is a way that proceeds through repentance and self-renunciation. One could say that, in contrast to the way of rationality, it proceeds through failure, defeat, which dislodges the self, displaces it, and opens up the realm of freedom and dogma.

Antinomic truth

Several consequences follow from this understanding of the nature of truth and the way to embrace it. First, for Fr Pavel, the danger with rationality, or rationalism, is that it places the reasoning self at the centre; it entails an egoistic or egocentric view of the world, and that entails the illusion that here on earth it is possible to transcend the fragmentariness of the world, due to sin and finitude. In reality, this is impossible: lots of egos produce lots of clashing views of the world, which compete with each other, and prevail through power. In reality truth and its apprehension demand self-renunciation; there is an asceticism of the truth. As Florensky exclaims, 'Contradiction! It is always a mystery of the soul, a mystery of prayer and love. The closer one is to God, the more distinct are the contradictions'.[14]

Second, the ultimate overthrow of reason – by reason – is the realization that reason is not enough, that proof is not enough. What is needed is commitment to the spiritual life, to repentance and self-renunciation – to experience. As Florensky put it at the end of the prefatory letter to the reader in *The Pillar and Ground of the Truth*:

> The Orthodox taste, the Orthodox temper, is felt, but it is not subject to arithmetical calculation. Orthodoxy is shown, not proved [an anticipation of Wittgenstein!]. That is why there is only one way to understand Orthodoxy: through direct Orthodox experience ... To become Orthodox, it is necessary to immerse oneself all at once in the very element of Orthodoxy, to begin living in an Orthodox way. There is no other way.[15]

---

[14] Florensky, *Pillar*, 117.
[15] Florensky, *Pillar*, 9.

And third, for Florensky truth is dogma – not something we confect or make up, but something to which we surrender, and no brief moment of surrender, but a constant attempt to surrender to the truth that embraces us. Florensky would have been sympathetic to T. S. Eliot's conviction that sanctity involves a 'lifetime's death in love'.[16]

Dogma is hardly understood in our modern world; its overtones in use are almost always negative. But it is dogma, its apparent arbitrariness from a merely human perspective, that points us to truth enshrined in antinomy as offering the only possibility of meaning. So Florensky said, in the letter on Tri-unity, in a remark paraphrased by Vladimir Lossky, a theologian supposedly so far removed from the religious philosophy of Florensky:

> Either the Triune Christian God or dying in insanity. *Tertium non datur.* Pay attention: I do not exaggerate. That is precisely the way things are ... Between eternal life within the Trinity and eternal second death, there is no clearance, not even a hair's breadth. Either/or ...[17]

At moments like this, Florensky reminds one of Pascal, or of Anselm. Indeed Florensky mentions Pascal's wager in this letter (P 49) and quotes Anselm's *credo ut intelligam* (P 47). But Florensky takes a step further than Anselm: instead of an ontological argument for the existence of God, we might regard him as offering an epistemological argument for the existence of the Trinity.

Art and iconography

After the Communist Revolution, Fr Pavel served on the Commission for the Preservation of Art and Antiquities of the Trinity-St Sergii Lavra. This led to his reflecting on the nature of Russian iconography. At that time, Orthodox iconography had all but been buried beneath the traditions of Western painting. The treasures of the Trinity-St Sergii Lavra included some of the finest of Russian icons, from the period before the reforms of Patriarch Nikon in the seventeenth century, which opened the door to Western influence, a door that was pushed wide open with the reforms of State and Church under Tsar Peter the Great in the next century. Indeed, at the Trinity-St Sergii Lavra was the greatest of all Russian icons, Andrey Rublev's icon of the Holy Trinity, an icon that had been given quasi-canonical status at the Stoglav Council in 1551. Florensky stands right at the beginning of the rediscovery of the icon, a process that is now so advanced that it is difficult to imagine how ignored and even despised the traditional art of the icon had become at the end of the nineteenth century even among the Orthodox, for that rediscovery, associated with the name of Leonid Ouspensky of the Russian emigration in Paris, and in Greece with the name of Fotis Kontoglou, has transformed our perception of the icon.

---

[16] Cf. 'Dry Salvages, V', in T. S. Eliot, *Collected Poems 1909–1962* (London: Faber & Faber, 1963), 212.

[17] Florensky, *Pillar*, 48; paraphrased by Vladimir Lossky in his *The Mystical Theology of the Eastern Church* (London: James Clarke, 1957), 65–6.

Florensky's essays were among the first to explore the nature of the icon; I shall say something about two of these essays: 'Reverse Perspective' (1919) and *Iconostasis* (1922). The dates are the dates of their completion; since neither was published until long after Florensky's death – 'Reverse Perspective' in 1967; *Iconostasis* in 1977 in an incomplete form, finally in 1994 – it is not clear how much influence they could have had on the twentieth-century rediscovery of the icon. As the title of the first of these essays suggests, part of Florensky's intention was to overcome the prejudice against icons, derived from the fact that they do not use the linear perspective that has been characteristic of Western art since the Renaissance. The term 'reverse perspective' was coined by the German art historian Oskar Wulff, with whose work Florensky was clearly familiar.[18] Florensky's justification is not so much of 'reverse perspective' over against 'linear perspective', but rather an attack on the pretensions of 'linear perspective' to hegemony, as being the 'right way' of depicting objects in a painting or drawing, together with an appreciation of what icon painters who ignored the principles of linear perspective were trying to achieve.

This attack operates at two levels. On the one hand, there is an explanation of the unreality of linear perspective: unreal because it achieves an illusion, the illusion that the frame of the painting is a window through which one is looking on to the scene depicted, and unreal because what is achieved is something ultimately inhuman, unrelated to the way in which human beings see things. Florensky refers to the way in which the pursuit of linear perspective can lead to a mechanical way of seeing and painting, as if the world was being surveyed from one point.

Florensky's point can be illustrated by an example he doesn't use, from photography. Something one quickly learns, when one starts to take photographs, is that the camera is very limited in what it can focus on: you focus either on what is close up and the background is blurred, or on the distance and the foreground is blurred. The reason is simple: there is only one lens and it works mechanically. Human beings don't see like that: to start off with, we have two eyes and don't stay still; what we observe is a combination of what we see and what we know, while our eyes focus and refocus with amazing rapidity, and the brain lets us know what we know is there, not just what we see. (All that is reversed when you paint: if you want to depict in a realistic way, you have to forget what you know, and only paint what you see: a process which is quite unnatural, as is evident from children's pictures, who, untutored, depict what they know, not what they see.) Icon painters are not painting the way they do because they are ignorant of linear perspective (and, indeed, there are occasions when linear perspective is used in icons, as Florensky points out), but because they are not trying to achieve an illusion of reality, but something else.

---

[18] See Charles Lock, 'What Is Reverse Perspective and Who Was Oskar Wulff?', *Sobornost/ECR* 33:1 (2011), 60–89.

Furthermore, the desire to achieve an illusion of reality, characteristic of Western art since the Renaissance, is fairly limited; hardly any cultures have wanted to do it, not because they didn't know how to do it, but because they had no desire to. Florensky takes this cultural criticism into the heart of what he regards as the enemies' territory: the way in which the Renaissance world-view underlies Kant's understanding of reality – he speaks of the 'connection between the sweet Renaissance roots and their bitter Kantian fruits'.[19] According to Florensky, Kant worked with highly simplified notions of space and time; the space that he 'transcendentally deduces' is – lo and behold! – space as described by Euclid. Not many of Florensky's contemporaries were aware of the developments in geometry associated with the names of Riemann and Lobachevsky. Linear perspective is based on Euclidean space in which parallel lines never meet, but by the beginning of the twentieth century other geometries had been devised: Riemann's in which all 'straight' lines meet twice, and Lobachevsky's in which no 'straight' lines meet, whether parallel or not. Kantian–Euclidean space is not something 'transcendentally deduced' but a cultural convention, favouring a naive realism. As Avril Pyman remarks:

> But Florensky, of course, did know his geometry and was indeed a step ahead of all those who had not made a special study of non-Euclidean space, which give his arguments a persuasiveness that thrilled his first auditors in 1919 as it did his first readers in 1967. It was essentially liberating to be presented with reasoned proof that naturalistic representation of form (as imposed by socialist no less than nineteenth-century realism) is, in fact, a geometrical nonsense, and Florensky's debunking of a single viewpoint, in spite of its thorny technicalities, was welcomed as a riotously subversive *reductio ad absurdum*.[20]

In Florensky's assault on the hegemonic claims of Kantian–Euclidean space, we are finding something rather like what we have already encountered in his attack on rationality: an ego-centred view of a transparent world, bearing little relation to the world in which we really live, and promoting a view of the world and everything in it as objects that belong to my world. So Florensky says:

> It is hard not to recognize in such a perspectival artist the embodiment of a thought that is *passive* and doomed to every kind of passivity, that for an instant, as if by stealth, furtively spies on the world through a chink between subjective facets, that is lifeless and motionless, incapable of grasping movement and laying claim to a divine certainty, specifically about its <u>own</u> place and its <u>own</u> instant of peeking out. He is an observer who brings nothing of his own into the world, who cannot even synthesize his own fragmentary impressions; who, since he does not enter into a living interaction with the world and does not live in it, is not aware of his own reality either . . .[21]

---

[19] In 'Reverse Perspective': *Beyond Vision*, 216.
[20] Pyman, *Pavel Florensky*, 133.
[21] 'Reverse Perspective': *Beyond Vision*, 264.

Traditional forms of art, of which the icon is one, are not inadequate attempts to achieve what Western art has done since the Renaissance, but attempts to achieve something quite different. Their depictions of reality are not naive or unsophisticated. On the contrary, they are deeply considered and show an awareness of the complexity of reality that the Western artist has relinquished.

In *Iconostasis*, Florensky has more to say about what the icon is seeking to achieve. The work begins with a fascinating meditation on the world of dreams, on the strange disjunction between space and time in the dream and how it appears in our waking life. He notices the strange way in which dream time and waking time meet: often enough in the sound of the alarm clock, which certainly belongs to the normal time of waking life, but in the dream is the point towards which the dream seems to be progressing. It is as if time in the dream is measured backwards from when we wake up. Space, too, in dreams seems to belong to two worlds: we seem to be in familiar places, places familiar from our waking life, but unfamiliar too, often manifesting strange proximities. But space and time in the dream world are ruled by meaning:

> the dream is wholly teleological, saturated with the meanings of the invisible world, meanings that are invisible, immaterial, eternal yet nevertheless visibly manifest and (as it were) vividly material. A dream is therefore pure meaning wrapped in the thinnest membrane of materiality; it is almost wholly a phenomenon of the other world ... A dream then is a sign of a movement between two realms – and also a symbol: of what? From the heavenly point of view, the dream symbolizes earth; from the earthly perspective, it symbolizes heaven ...[22]

From this beginning Florensky develops the idea of the icon as similarly existing on the boundary between heaven and earth, belonging to one, disclosing the other. Central to the way this happens is the face, the central feature of the icon, which draws the beholder into a relationship with someone – Christ, the Mother of God, one of the saints – belonging to the heavenly realm. When the icon is beheld in the right spiritual state, its impact on the beholder is '*equally* physical and spiritual':

> Like light pouring from light, the icon stands revealed. And no matter where the icon is physically located in the space we encounter it, we can only describe our experience of seeing it as *a beholding that ascends*.[23]

As he develops his theme, Florensky adumbrates a whole understanding of worship as reaching out to the boundary between heaven and earth, a boundary that is traced in a way by the icon, and especially the icon screen. This is a small part of the vision that was to have been worked out in

---

[22] Florensky, *Iconostasis*, 43.
[23] Florensky, *Iconostasis*, 72.

On the Watersheds of Thought, to which his theological energies of the 1920s were directed.

This has been a possibly idiosyncratic introduction to one whom I am increasingly coming to regard as the greatest Orthodox thinker of recent times, one whose ideas have been preserved in an inevitably fragmented way, but who provides so many insights that we need to develop today.

4

Fr Sergii Bulgakov and the nature of theology[1]

Among the Russian émigrés who settled in Paris in the 1920s, Bulgakov was already an established theologian and, as dean of the newly established Institute of Orthodox Theology dedicated to St Sergii (the Institut St-Serge), he rapidly assumed theological leadership. He became one of the voices representing Russian Orthodoxy in the burgeoning ecumenical movement, and was particularly active in the newly founded Fellowship of St Alban and St Sergius, which though primarily concerned with Anglicans and Russian Orthodox had always a larger dimension. He spent the rest of his life in Paris, and during this period his theological interests predominated, issuing in two trilogies that represent a comprehensive attempt to set out the theological perspective of those Russian theologians who had sought to respond to the intellectual concerns of the nineteenth-century West, and who had been profoundly affected by German Idealism (and also by the Kierkegaardian reaction, something of which can be found, quite independently, in Dostoevsky). In these theological works, Bulgakov sought to engage with the theological world of the West, particularly as he encountered it among the Western intellectuals who welcomed him in Paris. Bulgakov's *œuvre*, then, represents a distinctive moment in an engagement between Russian Orthodoxy and the West, at the point at which the Russians of the emigration found themselves established there, and anxious to seize the opportunity to communicate to their Western contemporaries, in terms they could understand, the distinctive vision of Russian Orthodoxy.

Early years and life in Russia

Sergei Nikolaevich Bulgakov was born in 1871 in Livny, a small provincial town in the Orël province about 250 miles south of Moscow. His father was a priest serving the cemetery chapel and belonged to a priestly ('levitical') family, stretching back several generations. After schooling, Sergei was sent to the local theological seminary, where he was unhappy, and lost his faith.

---

[1] Most of the material in this chapter has already appeared in two of my articles: 'Sergei Bulgakov', in *Moderne teologi: Tradisjon og nytenkning hos det 20. århundrets teologer*, ed. Ståle Johannes Kristiansen and Svein Rise (Kristiansand: Høyskoleforlaget, 2008), 353–65, now available in English: *Key Theological Thinkers: From Modern to Postmodern* (Farnham: Ashgate, 2013), 341–51; 'Sergii Bulgakov and the Task of the Theologian', *ITQ* 74 (2009), 243–57.

As a young Marxist, he went to Moscow University, where he studied economics and law (1890–4). By the turn of the century, although still confessedly a Marxist, he was beginning to develop his own ideas, and in his thesis, submitted unsuccessfully for a doctorate in 1900, on agriculture and economics, he had broken with Marxism, though without developing any clear alternative. In the early years of the twentieth century, he began, like many of the intelligentsia, to turn back to his childhood faith. He was one of the contributors to the volume of essays, published in 1909, *Vekhi* ('Landmarks'), in which a group of intellectuals made clear their dissatisfaction with Marxism and its neglect of spiritual and metaphysical questions. By this time, Bulgakov occupied the chair of Political Economy at the Institute of Commerce in Moscow University, a position he held until 1911, when he resigned over government interference in university matters.

Writing of his return to Christianity, Bulgakov acknowledged the influence of Dostoevsky and the Russian philosopher and historian Vladimir Solov'ev; he also wrote about various experiences that unsettled his Marxist convictions, and drew him back to his childhood faith. As early as 1895, his first sight of the mountains of the Caucasus made him aware of the 'dull pain of seeing nature as a lifeless desert' to which a Marxist analysis of reality had committed him, and convinced him that he could not be 'reconciled to nature

Sergii Bulgakov
From a drawing by Sr Joanna Reitlinger

without God', with the realization that the 'pious feelings of his childhood' might be true.[2] A few years later, during his period of study in Germany, his encounter with Raphael's Sistine Madonna in the Zwinger Gallery in Dresden brought him to tears, and with them 'the ice melted from my soul';[3] thenceforth, his regular early morning visits to the gallery led him to an experience of prayer. His final conversion, ten years later in 1908, took place in a solitary hermitage deep in a forest. His *Autobiographical Sketches*, where these accounts are to be found, were only published in 1946 after his death; the three accounts of the steps towards his reconciliation with the Church were first published, however, in the first chapter of *Unfading Light* (1917), entitled 'Calls and Encounters'. These three encounters cannot but recall Solov'ev's three meetings with Sophia, related in his late set of poems, called 'Three Meetings' (1898). It can hardly be a coincidence.

His return to the Christian faith was an ecclesial awakening, too, leading him to participate in the movements seeking reform in the Church that were to culminate in the reform synod of Moscow in 1917–18, and also to his involvement in the controversy over the invocation of the divine name among the Russian monks on Mount Athos, which had led to their condemnation and the removal of most of them by Russian naval vessels in 1913. Bulgakov, like his friend Pavel Florensky, had great sympathy for the 'venerators of the Name' among the monks. For Bulgakov, the presence of Jesus was experienced by the invocation of his name, 'the temple for which is every human heart, and every member of the faithful, as having this Name imprinted in his heart, is a priest of this temple'.[4] The book Bulgakov wrote on the philosophy of the name remained, however, unpublished until after his death.

Bulgakov's commitment to church reform led to his being a delegate at the synod of 1917–18, which was cut short by the October Revolution and of which the only lasting result was the restoration of the patriarchate that had been abolished by Peter the Great. The very fact of the synod was decisive for Bulgakov: this act of independence gave the lie to the charge of caesaro-papism and freed Bulgakov to seek ordination to the priesthood. On the feast of Pentecost ('Trinity Sunday') 1918, Bulgakov was ordained deacon in the Danilov Monastery and the next day, the Day of the Holy Spirit, ordained to the priesthood (thereafter, as was the custom, adopting the more archaic spelling of his name: Sergii). The turmoil of the last years had not left him, however, and while a priest serving in Yalta in the Crimea, he wrote a dialogue called *Under the Ramparts of Cherson* ('Cherson' being the Byzantine – and ecclesiastical – name for Sevastopol in the Crimea), again not published in his lifetime, with the significant subtitle 'The "Catholic Temptation" of an Orthodox Theologian', in which he rehearsed the arguments

---

[2] Sergei Bulgakov, *Avtobiograficheskie Zametki* (Paris: YMCA Press, 1991; originally published 1946), 61–2; ET: *A Bulgakov Anthology: Sergius Bulgakov 1871–1944* (London: SPCK, 1976), 10.

[3] Bulgakov, *Avtobiograficheskie Zametki*, 64 (*Anthology*, 11).

[4] Sergius Bulgakov, *Icons and the Name of God* (Grand Rapids, MI: Eerdmans, 2012), 157.

of the various sides in the debate over the Russian Church, and finally exorcized the temptation to abandon Russian Orthodoxy for Roman Catholicism.[5]

Exile and controversy

In December 1922, Trotsky issued a decree exiling most non-Marxist intellectuals from Russia, and in January 1923, Bulgakov left the Crimea for Europe. After a brief period in Prague, he settled in Paris where he became the first dean of the Institut St-Serge and Professor of Dogmatic Theology. On his way to Prague, Bulgakov passed through Constantinople and visited the church of Hagia Sophia, then a mosque. There he had another remarkable experience, which he identified with the figure that had become, and was to remain, central to his theology: the figure of Sophia, the Divine Wisdom. The church of Hagia Sophia he experienced as

> the artistic and tangible proof and manifestation of holy Sophia – of the Sophianic nature of the world and the cosmic nature of Sophia ... neither heaven nor earth, but the vault of heaven above the earth ... neither God nor man, but divinity, the divine veil thrown over the world ...[6]

In Paris, Bulgakov sought, through his writings, his lectures, and perhaps above all through celebrating the Divine Liturgy and preaching and spiritual counsel, to make Russian Orthodoxy a living presence in the West.

The Russian Church in the West rapidly became divided. There were those who repudiated the Revolution and the patriarch's acquiescence with the communist authorities, most stridently those who formed the Russian Orthodox Church Abroad at a synod in Sremski-Karlovci in Yugoslavia in 1921 (the so-called 'Synodal Church'). Then in 1930, Metropolitan Evlogy, the Russian Orthodox exarch in Europe, broke off relations with the Russian Church and placed the parishes of the exarchate under the jurisdiction of the Œcumenical Patriarchate. Finally there were those – a minority – who remained faithful to Moscow, whatever the difficulties. The Institut St-Serge remained with Metropolitan Evlogy. In the 1930s, Bulgakov's theology, and especially the role of Sophia, the Divine Wisdom, in his theological reflections became controversial; both the Moscow Patriarchate and the Church in Exile condemned him, though Metropolitan Evlogy stood by him. This controversy clouded Bulgakov's last years, but he continued with his theological writing until his death from cancer in 1944.

The nature of theology

In the last decade or so of his life, Bulgakov composed his 'great' theological trilogy, *On Godmanhood*. In this trilogy he covers the ground of a traditional

---

[5] Published in Russian in 1997; French trans. with Introduction and notes by Bernard Marchadier: Serge Boulgakov, *Sous les remparts de Chersonèse* (Geneva: Ad Solem, 1999).

[6] Bulgakov, *Avtobiograficheskie Zametki*, 95 (*Anthology*, 14).

dogmatic theology, but he does this in a quite unusual way. This can hardly have been other than deliberate. It is striking, too, that round about the same time (the first volume, *The Lamb of God*, was published in 1933), another great theologian was also struggling with the problem of how to present a dogmatic theology: namely, Karl Barth, whose first attempt at dogmatic theology, *Die Christliche Dogmatik im Entwurf*,[7] the first volume of which appeared in 1927, was aborted, as Barth embarked on his monumental, and renamed, *Church* – not *Christian* – *Dogmatics* in 1932.

Dissatisfaction with the traditional shape of dogmatic treatises (though the traditional shape of Protestant dogmatics had already been altered by Schleiermacher, so that Barth's problems were not exactly the same as Bulgakov's, or indeed his Catholic contemporaries) was in the air, for in the Catholic world, the most vital movements in theology – those associated with the movement of *Ressourcement*, focused especially on the Jesuit house at Lyon-Fourviers, where de Lubac was teaching – pursued theology in a different vein, and also raised questions that affected the structural principles of a dogmatic theology (this seems true both of de Lubac's questioning of the traditional disjunction between the natural and the supernatural,[8] and Rahner's later reflections on the relationship between the traditional starting point of theology, 'On God', and 'On the Trinity'[9]). It is also a question raised by Hans Urs von Balthasar in what could be regarded as a methodological introduction to his own vast trilogy, published in English as *Love Alone: The Way of Revelation*.[10] Although we are primarily concerned with Bulgakov, it is worth setting our reflections against not dissimilar concerns expressed in Western theology, contemporary with him. What kind of historical links there might have been, I shall not explore, as it seems unlikely that any of these links are very secure.

The problem Bulgakov, Barth, Rahner and Balthasar all face is how and where to start. Traditionally, in East and West, dogmatic theologies had followed a basically credal order, an order already discernible in St John Damascene's *On the Orthodox Faith*, and even in some earlier patristic works, which seem to broach what we now would regard as a presentation of Christian dogmatic theology, such as Gregory of Nyssa's *Great Catechetical Oration* or Augustine's *Enchiridion*. As these earlier works are fundamentally catechetical, it is hardly surprising that they reflect, more or less, the order of the baptismal creed in their presentation of the faith. So they begin with God, and then progress through the Trinity, creation leading to the fall, Christology and redemption, the Church and the sacraments, eschatology. As the catechetical context of the earliest of these works suggests, the starting point is the believer coming to baptism and initiation in the faith epitomized

---

[7] Karl Barth, *Die Christliche Dogmatik im Entwurf*, vol. 1, *Prolegomena* (Munich: Chr. Kaiser Verlag, 1927).

[8] See Henri de Lubac, *Surnaturel*, Théologie 8 (Paris: Aubier, 1946), which grew into *Augustinisme et théologie moderne* and *Le Mystère du surnaturel*, Théologie 63 and 64 (Paris: Aubier, both 1965).

[9] Karl Rahner, *The Trinity*, trans. Joseph Donceel (London: Burns & Oates, 1970).

[10] Hans Urs von Balthasar, *Love Alone: The Way of Revelation* (London: Burns & Oates, 1968).

in the baptismal creeds, which from the beginning seem to have adopted a basically Trinitarian structure, itself probably reflecting the liturgical form of baptism in the threefold name. It is not exactly as a catechetical task that modern theologians understand their role. Their task is not just to expound, but to present coherently and critically the Christian faith. Principles of coherence are needed, and these are generally drawn from a broader understanding of the significance and meaning of the faith. It has long been observed, for instance, that Aquinas' *Summa Theologiae* adopts from Neoplatonism the idea of procession and return as a structural principle.[11]

Another issue in modern dogmatics concerns, more precisely, how to start: i.e. what are the prolegomena? What are the steps that take one into the realm of theology? A good deal of Western theology since scholasticism seems to see the prolegomena as philosophical considerations that establish a kind of rational basis – accessible to any honest thinker – on which the more detailed account that belongs to revelation can be based. Another version of this is to explore human experience and show how it is open to the transcendent, which is itself unfolded in the more particular experience of revelation. Barth, famously, is against all this, and the transition from the <u>Christian</u> to the <u>Church</u> *Dogmatics* took place, because he soon came to see that the *Christian Dogmatics* was not sufficiently radical.

One can get an initial impression of Barth's concerns by simply looking at the table of contents in each work. Both, after preliminaries (themselves significantly different in detail), see dogmatics as a response to the Word of God, but the *Christian Dogmatics* has chapters on 'The Word of God and Man as Preacher', and 'The Word of God and Man as Hearer', both of which Barth came to see compromised his insistence on the sovereignty of the Word of God; both inserted man, and man's innate capacity, into the consideration of the Word of God, so that the Word of God – its meaning and bearing – was qualified by man's capacity to understand and interpret. The point of contact (*Anknüpfungspunkt*) between God and man is not sovereignly created by God, but in some way conditioned by man. The consequences of Barth's radical understanding of the Word of God are a rejection of natural theology and any attempt to explore the human capacity to receive God's revelation. Another issue – explored in Section 7 of the first chapter of the *Church Dogmatics* – concerns the question of whether a Christian dogmatics can be a *systematic* theology, a term introduced by liberal theologians who disliked the associations of 'dogma' and 'dogmatic'.[12] Barth argues against 'systematic' theology, which he sees as introducing a humanly derived systematic principle and thus risks misrepresenting and distorting the Word of God.

For our part, the details of Barth's considerations here are less important than the kind of issues he is struggling with. Bulgakov came from a very

---

[11] See M.-D. Chenu OP, *Introduction à l'étude de saint Thomas d'Aquin* (Paris: Vrin/Montréal: Institut d'Études Médiévales, 1954), 266–76.

[12] Karl Barth, *Die Kirchliche Dogmatik*, I/1 (Zürich: Zollikon, 4th edn, 1944), 261–310.

different ecclesial experience, but there are analogies in the concerns of these theologians. There is something analogous, too, in Rahner's concerns in his essay on the Trinity, namely that the way into theology may compromise whatever it is one discovers, but the links between Bulgakov and Rahner, and indeed Balthasar, will become clearer after we have looked in more detail at Bulgakov's response to these issues.

The nature of dogma

One could simply go to the trilogy *On Godmanhood*, and ask why Bulgakov adopts what seems to be such an untraditional approach – Son, Spirit, and then Church and eschatology – but there is a short essay, 'Dogma and Dogmatic Theology', published in 1937, that is, just after he had published the first two volumes of his trilogy.[13] This is explicitly about the task of dogmatic theology, and thus demands our attention. The first part concerns the nature and remit of dogmatic theology, which he describes as 'the systematic setting out of dogmas which, taken together, express the fullness of Orthodox teaching'.[14] He initially makes two points: first, the limited scope of genuine dogmas – there is much that is not dogmatically defined – and second, the close link between *lex credendi* and *lex orandi* – dogma is rooted in the prayer of the Church; it is not a freestanding philosophical system. This link between dogma and prayer, both personal and liturgical, is one that he dwells on. He comments, 'That is why the altar and the theologian's cell – his workspace – must be conjoined. The deepest origins of the theologian's inspiration must be nourished from the altar'.[15]

It is in this context that we find Bulgakov echoing Barth's insistence on the sovereignty of the Word of God: 'The Word of God is the absolute criterion of theology . . . The Word of God has an unplumbable depth and an absolute character for us'.[16] But it is an insight that will be developed in different ways in the two theologians. Barth means the Word of God as preached, written and revealed. For Bulgakov, the Word of God is heard within the Church, in a liturgical context, so that he can affirm, 'The Holy Scriptures must be understood in the light of tradition'.[17] Bulgakov goes on to consider the role of the Fathers in theology. The Fathers are those who have passed on to us the apostolic faith. They are not to be identified with the Fathers of the first few centuries, important as these are; he mentions modern Fathers such as Fr John of Kronstadt and Bishop Theophan the Recluse (both now canonized). They constitute a chorus of reflection, a chorus of many voices, but not by any means a unison. There is much that

---

[13] ET: Peter Bouteneff in *Tradition Alive*, ed. Michael Plekon (Lanham, MD: Rowman & Littlefield, 2003), 67–80.
[14] *Tradition*, 67.
[15] *Tradition*, 69.
[16] *Tradition*, 69.
[17] *Tradition*, 70.

we can learn from listening to them, and we have to study them seriously, establishing the 'actual views of the Church writers', and understanding them 'in their historical context, their concrete circumstances and historical relativity'.[18]

The result of such an approach is that 'the Fathers' legacy of the past is a mosaic of different parts of history, produced by different historical circumstances. In no way is it comprehensive'.[19] He warns against what he calls a patristic 'rabbinism'.[20] He also remarks that much recent Orthodox theology has taken its categories from the West, and become 'more polemical, more reactive, than positive'.[21] The task of the modern theologian is daunting, for though the Fathers are a great resource, there are many questions they never considered, and which we cannot avoid. These questions 'one must treat in such a way that does not break with tradition, one should not cower from their "newness"'.[22] Bulgakov goes on to envisage modern Orthodox theology as ecumenical (though he does not use the word): ready to learn from contemporary Catholic and Protestant thinkers, while 'remain[ing] itself, nourished by the wellspring of truth entrusted to it'.[23]

Two further issues occupy Bulgakov in his essay: the question of the development of doctrine and that of the place of philosophy. Development is not something Orthodox have generally found acceptable,[24] and while Bulgakov is insistent that the 'fullness [of the divine life] is *given* in the incarnation of the Lord Jesus, in whom the whole fullness of God dwells bodily, and in the descent of the Holy Spirit at Pentecost, when the Spirit comes into the world hypostatically in the tongues of fire',[25] he is equally clear that

> in the divine-human conscience of the Church, insofar as it includes temporality and relativity, this fullness enters only successively and partially – which is why the history of dogma, as we observe it in reality, exists. New dogmas arise, and it is only in this sense that one can speak of the existence of dogmatic development.[26]

It is this sense of the Church as existing in culturally specific conditions that determines his attitude to philosophy. Dogmatic theology expresses the dogmatic consciousness of the Church in relation to current human problems, which means that it will utilize prevailing philosophical notions, even to the

---

[18] *Tradition*, 70.

[19] *Tradition*, 72.

[20] *Tradition*, 70–1.

[21] *Tradition*, 73.

[22] *Tradition*, 73.

[23] *Tradition*, 74.

[24] See my 'Is Development of Doctrine a Valid Category for Orthodox Theology?', in *Orthodoxy and Western Culture: A Collection of Essays Honoring Jaroslav Pelikan on His Eightieth Birthday*, ed. Valerie R. Hotchkiss and Patrick Henry (Crestwood, NY: St Vladimir's Seminary Press, 2005), 45–63.

[25] *Tradition*, 76.

[26] *Tradition*, 76.

extent of accepting principles of systematic coherence drawn from philosophy in its setting forth 'a system of dogmas'.[27]

Such an approach to dogmatics explains something of Bulgakov's approach to theology. Dogmatic theology is open-ended, exploring the implications and meaning of the dogmatic tradition of the Church. It is rooted in the life of the Church, and finds its confidence there in the daily encounter with Christ in the liturgical life of the Church and in personal prayer. This confidence drives out fear – fear of the new, fear of the unknown – so that Christian theologians can boldly avail themselves of the ways of thought of those they seek to communicate with. Above all, there is much to do. Theologians are not the keepers of a sacred tradition, but those who seek to engage with the issues of their day and of their culture. Of course, they do not do this uncritically – everything is to be tested against the word of God heard in the Church – but neither are they afraid of engagement with modern ideas and problems. Above all, theology, for Bulgakov, is not a collection of doctrines that you could list and run through; rather it is way of thinking, rooted in a way of praying: it is a vision, not a collection of truths, however accurate.

A liturgical theology

It is this last point that is most obviously carried over into Bulgakov's dogmatic theology. His readers are being encouraged to *look* at things in a certain way, or perhaps look at things from a certain position – and that position is standing in the Church before the face of the living God. We have already seen how closely Bulgakov associates the theologian's task with the prayer of the Church. I don't think this was merely a commonplace linking of *lex credendi* with *lex orandi*; rather it takes us to the heart of Bulgakov's understanding of the theologian, or at least, of his understanding of himself as a theologian. It is something we need to grasp fully, if we are to understand Bulgakov properly.

The achievement of Boris Jakim, Bulgakov's principal translator into English, in making him known – or at least accessible – in the English-speaking world, and the acclaim with which this has been received, risk obscuring how hard it seems to have been to hear Bulgakov at all in the past. It is only just over 40 years ago that Fr Alexander Schmemann could speak of the 'tragedy of Fr Sergii'. In an article published to commemorate the centenary of Bulgakov's birth (in 1871), Schmemann commented that,

> A hundred years after the birth, and more than twenty years after the death of someone who, whatever one thought of his work, must be recognized as one of the most remarkable men of this tragic half-century of Russian history, an almost total silence surrounds his name.[28]

---

[27] *Tradition*, 78.
[28] Alexandre Schmemann, 'Trois Images', *Le Messager orthodoxe* 57 (1972), 2–21, at 2–3 (my trans.).

Schmemann went on to say that, even if he is to be regarded as an irredeemable heretic, there was something about him that seemed to transcend that: the priest, the spiritual father. Schmemann proceeded to recount 'three images' of Bulgakov that remained with him. His first memory was of seeing him at some grand celebration, a priest, dressed simply, lost in thought, which led him to reflect on what he saw as the archetypal quality of Bulgakov as a priest, the descendant of a long 'levitical' family. His second memory was of Fr Sergii at the Vigil Service for Palm Sunday, and seeing his face, just for a moment:

> his eyes radiant with a calm enthusiasm, his tears, and the whole of his person turned towards 'the holy place' [the east end of the church], as if he were going to the next village where Christ was preparing the last passover for his disciples.[29]

The eschatology that breathes through the works of Bulgakov, an urgent waiting for the coming of Jesus, was something living and real for him. The third 'image' I would like to quote at greater length:

> My third memory of Fr Sergii, the third image, is not about a brief moment, a short encounter. It is the memory of Fr Sergii before the altar, celebrating the liturgy. In his last years, because of his illness and loss of voice, he celebrated only the morning liturgy. Because of the equipment he had about his throat, he celebrated in very light, white vestments.
>
> What memory have I kept of this? Not the 'beauty' of his celebration, if by beauty one means the rhythm and freedom of harmonious and solemn gestures, his 'savoir-faire'; in this sense Fr Sergii's way of celebrating was perhaps not beautiful. He never knew how to cense. And there was in his movements something awkward and jerky, something that had neither rhythm nor harmony . . .
>
> But there was in that very awkwardness and in those stiff gestures something that went back to the very source, which connected with the forces of nature, which recalled the sacrificing priest of the ancients or the princely priest of the Old Testament. He was not accomplishing a well-established rite, traditional in all its details. He delved down to the very depths, and one had the impression that the liturgy was being celebrated for the first time, that it had fallen down from heaven and been set up on the earth at the dawn of time. The Bread and the Chalice on the altar, the flame of the candles, the smoke of the incense, the hands raised to the heavens: all this was not simply an 'office'. There was accomplished here something involving the whole created world, something of the pre-eternal, the cosmic – the 'terrible and the glorious' [*strashnoe i slavnoe*], in the sense these liturgical words have in Slavonic. It seemed to me that it is not by chance that the writings of Fr Sergii are very often laden – so it seems – with liturgical Slavisms, that they themselves so often resonate with liturgical praise. It is not just a matter of style. For the theology of Fr Sergii, at its most profound, is precisely and above all liturgical – it is the revelation of an experience received in divine worship, the transmission of this mysterious 'glory', which penetrates the entire service, of this 'mystery', in

---

[29] Schmemann, 'Trois Images', 11.

which it is rooted and of which it is the 'epiphany'. The manifestation of God, and also of the world as God created it, of the divine roots of creation, destined to be filled with God, as that in which God is 'all in all'.[30]

And this from someone who thought of Bulgakov's works as a 'ponderous philosophical edifice'![31] Schmemann's sense of the centrality of the Divine Liturgy to Bulgakov's life and thought is something we encounter in many other reminiscences of him. It is there in Metropolitan Evlogy's address at his funeral, which recalls his ordination, and his last celebration of the liturgy, both on the Monday after Pentecost, the 'Day of the Spirit'.[32] It is there in Sister Joanna Reitlinger's recollections,[33] and it is significant that it is to Bulgakov that Fr Boris Bobrinskoy ascribes what is probably a priestly proverb – 'the whole of his theological vision he had drawn from the bottom of the eucharistic chalice'.[34]

What all this suggests, it seems to me, is that we need to catch something of the sense of Fr Sergii the priest, if we are to hear properly Bulgakov the theologian. In a profound sense Bulgakov is a *liturgical* theologian, not in the sense that he writes *about* the liturgy, but that he writes *out of* the liturgy. This can already be found in his earlier writings as a priest. There is an example in the very subjects of his so-called 'little trilogy' – *The Burning Bush*, *The Friend of the Bridegroom*, *Jacob's Ladder* – on the Mother of God, John the Baptist or the Forerunner, and the angels. The choice of the Mother of God and St John the Forerunner is certainly influenced by the iconographic tradition, and especially the icon called the *Deisis* – 'Intercession' – in which a seated Christ is flanked by the Mother of God and St John with their hands raised in an attitude of prayer. They are the two who are closest to Christ, and this closeness is manifest in prayer.

Such considerations are already liturgical, in that they are concerned with prayer, but the final volume on the angels focuses these considerations more precisely on the Divine Liturgy, for all these volumes are concerned with the conjunction of the two worlds – the earthly and the heavenly – a conjunction manifest in different ways in the Mother of God and St John the Forerunner, but realized most immediately for us in the celebration of the Divine Liturgy, when we join together with 'thousands of Archangels and ten thousands of Angels, the Cherubim and the Seraphim, six-winged and many-eyed'. But just considering together the Mother of God and the Forerunner has a more precisely eucharistic reference, which Bulgakov himself draws out

---

[30] Schmemann, 'Trois Images', 13–14 (my trans.).

[31] See also his remarks on Bulgakov as a thinker in his diary, entry for 31 March 1980: *The Journals of Father Alexander Schmemann 1973–83*, trans. Juliana Schmemann (Crestwood, NY: St Vladimir's Seminary Press, 2000), 261–2.

[32] Quoted in James Pain's Introduction to *A Bulgakov Anthology*, xvi–xvii.

[33] See Sister Joanna Reitlinger, 'The Final Days of Father Sergius Bulgakov: A Memoir', in *Sergius Bulgakov: Apocatastasis and Transfiguration*, trans. Boris Jakim, Variable Readings in Russian Philosophy 2 (New Haven, CT: Variable Press, 1995), 31–53.

[34] B. Bobrinskoy, *La Compassion du Père* (Paris: Cerf, 2000), 160, cf. 173; *La Mystère de la Trinité* (Paris: Cerf, 1986; 1996 imprint), 149 (presumably a reminiscence, as no reference is given).

when he recalls that in the preparation service, the *Proskomidi*, as the priest cuts fragments of bread to set beside the Lamb, the bread to be consecrated, the first two fragments are in honour of the Mother of God and then of the Forerunner. Similarly in the eucharistic prayer, after the epiclesis, the first to be commemorated is the Mother of God, followed immediately by St John the Forerunner.[35] The way in which such precise liturgical references feed Bulgakov's theological reflection is something very striking, and I don't really know anyone else of whom this is true to the same extent.

The structure of theology

If we think of Bulgakov as a liturgical theologian in this sense, then I think the structure of the great trilogy begins to make sense. But I want to lead into a discussion of the structure of the great trilogy by recalling Hans Urs von Balthasar's reflections on the history of theological reflection in the book already referred to, *Love Alone: The Way of Revelation*. Balthasar begins by outlining two historical approaches to theology: the first the cosmological approach, the second the anthropological approach. The cosmological approach presents the faith objectively, as a description of what is the case in the relationship of God to the world. Creation, the fall, the Incarnation, atonement, the Church, the sacraments, the last things: these are presented as a series of facts. It is the way the world is, as a result of God's activity; so we might well call it cosmological. This has characterized, and continues to characterize, traditional presentations of the faith, especially in the Catholic and Orthodox worlds. The anthropological approach, by contrast, starts from an understanding of what it is to be human, and in particular with the question, how do we humans come to know anything at all about all this? Historically, as Balthasar suggests, this approach takes its starting point from a central feature of the cosmological approach, the understanding of the human as in the image of God, as occupying a kind of frontier position (as a *methorion*) between God and the world, between the spiritual and material realms.[36] But this position has become isolated, and it is from the perspective of the human − its nature and potentialities, its needs and requirements − that any human understanding, of the world or God, is unfolded. This shift in approach constituted as radical a revolution as the more-or-less contemporary 'Copernican revolution'.

Festugière, long ago, suggested that we can see the contrast between the ancient approach (which Balthasar calls 'cosmological') and the modern approach (which Balthasar calls 'anthropological') by considering Descartes's *cogito ergo sum*, 'I think, therefore I am'. Descartes moves from thought to the one who thinks; the Greeks, Festugière suggests, would more naturally move

---

[35] Sergius Bulgakov, *The Friend of the Bridegroom*, trans. Boris Jakim (Grand Rapids, MI: Eerdmans, 2003), 136.

[36] Balthasar, *Love Alone*, 25.

from thought to those things of which one thinks, *ta noeta*.[37] Balthasar suggests that both these approaches are limited: the first, the cosmological, tends to become extrinsicist, presenting a list of objective 'facts'; the second, the anthropological, tends to an intrinsicism, an exploration of the conditions of being human, ending up in a kind of moralism, concerned above all with what humans ought to do. Balthasar seeks to combine the two approaches in what he calls the way of love, which is equally the way of aesthetics. God is approached neither simply as the Truth, the objectively real, underwriting the true state of affairs through his creative power; nor is he to be approached as the Good, underwriting a proper way of behaving; rather he is to be seen as Beauty, both someone to behold in objective forms that we can trace and describe, but also one who, through his beauty, inspires us with the longing of love, a love that shapes everything we do, so that the objectively true and the morally good are united in the pursuit of the beautiful.[38]

It is, it seems to me, precisely an attempt to hold together these two approaches that lies behind Bulgakov's approach to dogmatic theology, especially as we see it in the great trilogy. On the one hand, Bulgakov remains traditional in giving a systematic account of the objective truths of revelation – the way things are, seen in the light of revelation. On the other hand, he is concerned with the root question of the anthropological approach: how do we know any of this? and also: how does this make sense of my human experience? This leads him to be concerned for the place, as it were, from which we behold the revelation of the glory of God: standing before God in prayer, fundamentally in the Divine Liturgy. It is easy to see how this corresponds in a way to Balthasar's aesthetic approach, for the human being, according to Bulgakov, stands before God in prayer and beholds the revelation of God, participates in it, and is caught up with it – and, in particular, for Bulgakov, is drawn towards the fullness of the revelation of God at the end of time (remember the second of Schmemann's 'images', of Bulgakov looking for the coming of the kingdom with eagerness).

What fundamentally distinguishes Bulgakov from the anthropological approach is ultimately his conception of what it is to be human. The West, from Descartes onwards (and maybe earlier), has tended to reduce the human to the individual. Bulgakov inherits from nineteenth-century Russian thought, and especially the Slavophils, a sense of the person, as opposed to the individual:[39] the person coming into being shaped by and contributing towards

---

[37] See A.-J. Festugière, *Contemplation et vie contemplative selon Platon* (Paris: Vrin, 3rd edn, 1967), 210–49.

[38] There are some very striking parallels here with the approach of the Greek thinker Christos Yannaras. See, especially, his books recently translated by Norman Russell: *Person and Eros* and *Variations on the Song of Songs* (Brookline, MA: Holy Cross Orthodox Press, 2007, 2005). This cannot, however, be pursued here. On Yannaras, see below pp. 247–51, 254–9.

[39] This is such a commonplace of nineteenth-century Russian thought that it perhaps needs no reference, but see Tomáš Špidlík, *Die russische Idee: Eine andere Sicht des Menschen* (Würzburg: Der Christliche Osten, 2002), 21–99.

community, a togetherness to which the Russians give the term *sobornost'*.
So, for Bulgakov, the human being is not primarily an individual thinking,
nor an individual kneeling in prayer, separate from everyone else (though
that is an advance on an individual thinking), but a person standing before
God in prayer, side by side with others. Liturgical knowing comes about
through participation in a community standing before God in prayer; it is in
this way that we come to know anything about God at all, and as such our
knowledge is that of persons, not monads uttering individual *cogito*s, or even
individual *credo*s, but members of a community, formed by traditions that are
themselves bearers of wisdom. And who is this God before whom we stand
in prayer? Not the divine substance, not some indifferentiated divine monad
or God, but God the Father, revealing himself and his love for us through the
Son and the Holy Spirit, and drawing from us an answering love, that is
the Spirit poured out in our hearts, leading us back to the Father through
the Son.[40]

And so the structure of the great trilogy: two books on the Incarnate Son
and the Holy Spirit, passing by means of an Appendix on the Father to the
third volume, in which the Church is revealed as the Bride of the Lamb,
calling out with the Spirit to the coming Lord, so that the trilogy ends with
words from the final chapter of the New Testament: 'And the Spirit and the
bride say, Come. And let him that heareth say, Come ... Even so, come, Lord
Jesus' (Rev. 22.17, 20 AV).

It is striking how this approach to a 'systematic setting out of dogmas
which, taken together, express the fullness of Orthodox teaching', as Bulgakov
put it in the essay 'Dogma and Dogmatic Theology', anticipates some of
the concerns of both Balthasar and Rahner. Balthasar actually calls his
third way of love a 'personalist approach', though his understanding of
personalism is perhaps not as developed as Bulgakov's Slavophil-inspired
notion; Balthasar's personalism is more that of Buber's 'I–Thou' personalism,
though this parallels some aspects of Bulgakov's personalism, not least the
sense of the person as transcending nature. It also corresponds to the central
assertion of Rahner's essay on the Trinity, that we do not first engage with
an undifferentiated 'God', whom we later discern to be Trinitarian, but
rather encounter *ho Theos*, who is the Father, manifest through the Son and
the Spirit. Bulgakov solves Rahner's problem much more radically, starting
neither with the One God, nor the Trinity, but with the Son Incarnate and
the Spirit.

---

[40] Bulgakov's understanding of the person as shaped by love might suggest that Descartes's *cogito
ergo sum* be replaced by *amo ergo sum*, I love therefore I am. It is striking that this is the title of
Nikolai Sakharov's book on the spiritual teaching of Fr Sophrony, as one of the lessons of that
book is the debt Fr Sophrony owed to Fr Bulgakov, whose lectures he briefly attended at the
Institut St-Serge in the 1920s and whom he read throughout his life. See Nikolai Sakharov, *I
Love, Therefore I Am: The Theological Legacy of Archimandrite Sophrony* (Crestwood, NY: St Vladimir's
Seminary Press, 2002).

Theology drawn out of the liturgy

I have suggested that Bulgakov's theology can be seen to be liturgical in a general sense, in that it emerges from considering the human being who comes to know God by standing before him in prayer, first of all liturgical prayer. I think, however, the point can be made more precisely, by looking closely at the Divine Liturgy which Bulgakov celebrated daily.

At the heart of the Divine Liturgy is the anaphora, the eucharistic prayer, which, in the Byzantine Rite (and in the Roman *canon missae*) is addressed, not to God in general, or to the Trinity, but precisely to the Father. The anaphora most commonly used, that of St John Chrysostom, makes it clear, by the repeated addition of 'your only-begotten Son and your Holy Spirit', that the anaphora is offered to the Father – together with the Son and the Spirit. The anaphora of St John Chrysostom goes on to make clear that our engagement with the Father takes place through the Son and the Spirit – the Son, given as the love of God the Father for us, accomplishing the mystery of salvation through the Incarnation, of which the Eucharist is the representation, itself achieved through the invocation, the *epiklesis*, of the Holy Spirit. As Christ becomes present, heaven and earth are conjoined, and we find ourselves in the presence of the saints, pre-eminently the Mother of God, together with whom we offer intercessions for the Church and the world.

We can already see here the structure of Bulgakov's trilogy. In the anaphora the Father comes first, but is described in entirely apophatic terms – 'ineffable, incomprehensible, invisible, inconceivable, ever existing, eternally the same' – what we know of him, as Creator, and restorer of a fallen Creation, 'granting us [his] Kingdom that is to come', we know through the Son and the Spirit. So it is in a systematic theology that we start with the Son and the Spirit, who lead us back to the Father, who is God, *ho Theos*. (It is worth noting that the liturgical poetry of the Orthodox Church preserves this fundamental grammar of referring to God, while at the same time making clear the equality of the Persons of the Trinity, in the expressions *ho Theos kai Pater*, 'God and Father', i.e. the God who is Father, and *ho Logos kai Theos*, 'the Word and God', i.e. the Word who is God.)

The reference to the 'Kingdom that is to come' is also significant, for a sense of the coming kingdom is one of the striking features of Bulgakov's theology. The eschatology is not tagged on, or demythologized so that it only concerns the 'last things' in some quixotic way, as often seems to be the case in modern presentations of theology – it is integral, determining the movement of the work from the very beginning, right through to the final section, almost a third of the final volume, explicitly concerned with eschatology.[41] But this sense of the coming kingdom is itself a characteristic of the Byzantine

---

[41] This may underestimate the size of the final section, in that there are other sections that clearly belong in this final section that were, for some reason, not included, especially the section called 'On the Question of the Apocatastasis of the Fallen Spirits': see Bulgakov, *Apocatastasis and Transfiguration*, 7–30.

Liturgy from the opening proclamation, 'Blessed is the Kingdom of the Father and the Son and the Holy Spirit', through the Beatitudes, prefaced by 'In your Kingdom, remember us, O Lord', and the Great Entrance, with the commemoration of the faithful through their being remembered 'in your Kingdom', to the Communion, prefaced by the Lord's Prayer, with its petition for the coming of the kingdom, and the allusion of the prayer of the thief – 'Remember me, O Lord, in your kingdom' – in the prayers before communion. The repeated invocation of the kingdom lends to the Divine Liturgy a sense of standing on tiptoe on the threshold of the kingdom – something that Bulgakov incorporates into his dogmatic theology.

Sophiology

It would be possible to go through the great trilogy and illustrate the manifold ways in which Bulgakov appeals to liturgical facts and prayers to ground the teaching that he unfolds in the course of it. One particularly striking example is the way in which different aspects of the cult of the Virgin Mother of God undergird his understanding of her significance in the life of the Church. It is in these terms that I would want to present Bulgakov as essentially a liturgical theologian. But there is one matter of substance that I think makes more sense if we relate it to his fundamental sense of the liturgical origins of theology, and that is his sophiology.

Sophiology has experienced something of a revival, especially among the movement in modern theology known as 'radical orthodoxy'.[42] Nevertheless, it is still the case that in (authentically) Orthodox circles, sophiology is largely rejected, and even those willing to be sympathetic towards Bulgakov often take the line that everything that Bulgakov wants to say using the notion of Divine Sophia could be said just as adequately without invoking the notion of Wisdom or Sophia (Bulgakov's late work, *The Orthodox Church* (1935), in which he gives an account of Orthodox beliefs without using the notion of Sophia, can be cited in support of such an opinion). It may well be true that Sophia can be dispensed with, if one understands doctrine as a string of theological propositions. It is rather as one tries to understand the coherence and mutual entailments of these theological assertions that Sophia comes into its own for Bulgakov. However, that sense of coherence is also conveyed by the fundamentally liturgical inspiration of his theology.[43] This suggests that there is a link between Sophia and the liturgy, and it is this that I want to explore in these final paragraphs.

---

[42] My awareness of this has been greatly enhanced by the work of Brandon Gallaher, and conversation with him. See his 'Graced Creatureliness: Ontological Tension in the Uncreated/Created Distinction in the Sophiologies of Solov'ev, Bulgakov and Milbank', *Logos: A Journal of Eastern Christian Studies* 47 (2006), 163–90.

[43] It is also, of course, the case that all the Russian sophiologists appeal to liturgical evidence – especially the fact that the dedication festivals of several Slav churches of the Holy Wisdom are feasts of the Mother of God – in support of their ideas.

The fundamental intuition of sophiology is relatively easy to enunciate; it is that the gulf between the uncreated God and Creation, brought into being out of nothing, does not put Creation in opposition to God; rather Wisdom constitutes a kind of *metaxu*, 'between', between God and humans/Creation, for Wisdom is that through which God created the universe, and it is equally through wisdom that the human quest for God finds fulfilment.[44] Wisdom, one might say, is the face that God turns towards his Creation, and the face that Creation, in humankind, turns towards God. Creation is not abandoned by God, it is not godless, for apart from God it would not be at all; it is not deprived of grace, for it owes its existence to grace. Rather Creation is graced, it is holy; in Creation God may be encountered.

Bulgakov's account of the events that led to his own conversion, and his magnificent account of standing beneath the dome of the church of Hagia Sophia in Constantinople in January 1923, make clear how important this intuition was to him. It also lay at the heart of what he perceived to be wrong with the Roman Catholicism he encountered in the West as an exile: the idea of an ungraced 'pure nature' seemed to him fundamentally false. Moreover, the relationship between God and the world, constituted by Wisdom, cannot be an arbitrary relationship, nor can it be a necessary one. Uncreated wisdom and created wisdom differ only in their being uncreated or created. Why? Because if they differed in any other way, then God would be severed from Creation, and Creation from God. This line of thought indicates a further step involved in sophiology, which raises the issue: what must Creation be, if this is true? What is Creation like, if God indeed created it (through wisdom)?

As we ask these questions, we find ourselves asking questions that have exercised Christians for centuries, and perhaps most acutely at the beginning, when, in the second century, Christianity faced the manifold challenges of Greek philosophy and Gnosticism. Christianity was not consonant with just any view of the universe. Christians agreed with the Platonists over the existence of a transcendent divine, divine providence and human free will, and adopted Platonist arguments against other Greek philosophers – Aristotelians, Stoics and Epicureans – who rejected one or other of these positions.[45] They completely rejected the view, held by most of those scholars now call 'Gnostics', that the universe was the product of a God or gods who were either malevolent or negligent. At one point Irenaeus defends the Christian view of a universe, created out of nothing by a good God who rules it through his providence, by appealing to the Christian liturgy:

> How . . . can they say that flesh is destined for corruption, the flesh that has been nourished by the body and blood of the Lord? Either they must change

---

[44] For a longer account of my approach to Bulgakov's doctrine of Sophia, see 'Wisdom and the Russians: The Sophiology of Fr Sergei Bulgakov', in *Where Shall Wisdom Be Found?*, ed. Stephen C. Barton (Edinburgh: T&T Clark, 1999), 169–81.

[45] See my 'Pagans and Christians on Providence', in *Texts and Culture in Late Antiquity: Inheritance, Authority and Change*, ed. J. H. D. Scourfield (Swansea: The Classical Press of Wales, 2007), 279–97.

their opinion, or cease to offer him what they have said they do. Our opinion is consonant with the Eucharist, and the Eucharist confirms our faith. We offer him what belongs to him, harmoniously proclaiming the communion and union of flesh and spirit. For taking from the earth bread, after the invocation of the Lord it is no longer common bread, but Eucharist, joining together two realities, the earthly and the heavenly, so that our bodies, receiving the Eucharist, are no longer corruptible, but possess the hope of eternal resurrection. We make an offering to him, not because he needs anything, but to give thanks for his gifts and to sanctify the creation.[46]

For Irenaeus, to take bread and wine, to offer them to God and invoke the Holy Spirit to transform them into the Body and Blood of Christ, entails a certain view of Creation: that it is good, that the one to whom we offer the Eucharist is the Creator. In the same way, for Bulgakov, to celebrate the Eucharist entails that Creation belongs to God, that it is not alien to him, that to be a creature is already to be graced, something that Fr Schmemann's 'third image' seems to suggest: Bulgakov's celebration of the Divine Mysteries seemed to him something autochthonous, something rooted in the very being of Creation. It is this intuition that lay at the heart of his sophiology.

It is as we pursue such reflections as these that we find ourselves entering into the *arcanum* of Bulgakov's theology. It is a theology that invites the human spirit on a fascinating quest after the nature of things, but it is rooted in the simple turning of the creature towards God in joy and gratitude.

---

[46] Irenaeus, *Haer.* IV. 18.5–6.

5

Nikolai Berdyaev – creativity, freedom and the person

Fifty years ago, in any survey of Russian Orthodox theology in the diaspora there would have been something on Berdyaev. In Nicolas Zernov's book, *The Russian Religious Renaissance of the Twentieth Century*, published just over 50 years ago in 1963, a landmark in the study of Russian religious thought of the early twentieth century, there is a chapter on 'Four Notable Converts', one of whom is Nikolai Aleksandrovich Berdyaev (the others were Peter Struve, Fr Sergii Bulgakov and Sem'en Frank). At that time, and for several decades then, he was one of the best known among the Christian intellectuals of the Russian emigration: his works were readily available in French and English translations – I have on my shelves 16 volumes of his works in English translation, mostly by R. M. French, but also by Donald Attwater, Natalie Duddington and others, published mostly in the 1930s and 1940s. Nicolas Zernov said of Berdyaev:

> Among the four converts Berdyaev had the greatest reputation in the West. He was heard and studied in France, Germany, England and America. He knew how to sound a note that reverberated in non-Russian minds. He was the most European among the leaders of the renaissance, and here both his French ancestry and the direction of his thought were decisive. His defence of 'personalism', threatened by the rise of totalitarianism and the increasing pressure of impersonal forces brought into operation by scientific discoveries, found an eager response among the western intellectuals. In his person Russian religious thought spread beyond the limits of national boundaries and penetrated spheres which had previously dismissed Orthodox tradition as a decadent version of Christianity.[1]

That explains why Zernov thought him so important; it perhaps explains, too, why his star has somewhat declined in the last half-century. For it is less clear now how important his thought really was. Figures like Florensky, Bulgakov, Florovsky and Lossky attract more attention nowadays, at least among theologians, than Berdyaev. Fifty years ago, all except Lossky were ill-served by translations into English; that has now changed, and attention has shifted to these other Russians. Maybe Berdyaev was too much a figure of his times; it seems to me much easier to present Florensky as having something to say

---

[1] Nicolas Zernov, *The Russian Religious Renaissance of the Twentieth Century* (London: Darton, Longman & Todd, 1963), 158.

to our concerns today than Berdyaev. Nevertheless, historically he was a central figure among the émigrés in Paris, and historically, too, it was his voice that was, if not loudest, at least most easily heard in the intellectual world of Europe before and after the Second World War.

Furthermore, his voice is distinctive, in a number of ways. First of all, though Orthodox, and indeed one who had deliberately chosen Orthodoxy, he spoke rather as a Russian intellectual than an Orthodox thinker. This, I suspect, gave his voice greater reach at the time than, whatever their background, was the case with professors of theology such as Bulgakov and Florovsky. Also, as a layman, he is more easily associated with other figures of the Russian emigration who were not at all Orthodox: figures such as the thinker Lev Shestov, of Jewish origin, whose voice has perhaps gained in currency over the decades in contrast to Berdyaev's. His thought is also characterized by leading motifs that we encounter quite generally among other Russian émigrés: motifs such as freedom, creativity, the person (the subjects I have highlighted in my subtitle), the place of beauty, the role of ethics, as well as a philosophical stance perhaps more easily recognized in Berdyaev than in thinkers whose concern was more directly theological. There is something else about Berdyaev that makes him emblematic of his generation, and that is his sense of the importance of Dostoevsky as a profoundly Russian explorer of the human condition. It has been observed that in the 1930s, and even later, Orthodoxy was often presented as if Dostoevsky were its prophet: talks

Nikolai Berdyaev

on Orthodoxy were, in effect, talks on Dostoevsky, who seemed to have become almost a Father of the Russian Church.[2] There is something of this in Berdyaev (though with a critical distance, too); he wrote a book on Dostoevsky, which, as well as being a good book on the thought and concerns of the novelist, gives a lucid account of Berdyaev's own concerns.

Life

Nikolai Berdyaev was born in 1874 into Russia's military aristocracy. For all his emphasis on personal freedom and disdain for the *rod*, the family or the clan, he was very proud of his aristocratic roots, and indeed thought of himself as an aristocratic thinker. His paternal grandfather had the distinction of once defeating Napoleon. In 1814 Napoleon beat the Russian and German armies at the battle of Kulmsk. Berdyaev's grandfather, a young lieutenant at the time, was in a contingent of the Guards, all the officers of which had been killed. He rallied the brigade and mounted such a fierce attack that the French thought reinforcements had arrived and fled, leaving the field to Berdyaev's grandfather. This is a story Berdyaev tells himself, with understandable pride, in the biographical sketch with which he begins his intellectual autobiography, published in English as *Dream and Reality*.[3] Despite his pride in his descent, he had no inclination for the militaristic aspects of the Russian aristocracy; he was educated at a military academy in Kiev, but was miserable there and felt that he could not fit in with the masculine ethos of the military school. Although he went on to the Corps of Pages, he soon left, and studied in the university in Kiev. By this time he had become a Marxist and joined the Social Democratic Party; after two years at the university he was exiled for illegal activities to Vologda and expelled from the university.

His mother, born Princess Kudashev, was half-French (her mother was Countess Choiseul), and her Slav side was partly Polish. According to Berdyaev, his mother was more French than Russian; she had been educated in France and wrote letters in French (indeed was unable to write correct Russian); although Orthodox, she felt more at home in the Catholicism of her French ancestry, and always said her prayers using her mother's French Catholic prayer book. His paternal grandmother, as well as one of his mother's grandmothers, became Orthodox nuns. Nevertheless, Berdyaev says that he was not brought up in an Orthodox atmosphere, and his eventual embracing of Orthodoxy was not a homecoming, as it had been for Bulgakov, for example.

On his return from exile in Vologda, he went to St Petersburg and became editor, with Bulgakov, of a short-lived journal, called *Questions of Life* (*Voprosny Zhyzni*), which, for all its evanescence, became a focus for the intelligentsia –

---

[2] Again, Nicolas Zernov illustrates this: his book, *Three Russian Prophets* (London: SCM Press, 1944), treats of Khomiakov, Dostoevsky and Solov'ev.

[3] Nicolas Berdyaev, *Dream and Reality: An Essay in Autobiography*, trans. Katherine Lampert (London: Geoffrey Bles, 1950), 5.

poets, philosophers, writers – who were finding an interest in Orthodox Christianity: people such as Rozanov, Ivanov, Bely, Blok, Shestov. He also studied philosophy in Germany. In 1907, Berdyaev left Russia for Paris, but returned to Russia – to Moscow – the following year; there he lived as a freelance journalist and philosopher, radical in his views but moving closer and closer to Orthodoxy. An indication of this – and also of the problems he had with the Orthodox Church – is provided by his involvement in the Imiaslavtsy controversy, in which he defended the Athonite monks (the so-called 'worshippers of the Name') who had been forcibly removed from the Holy Mountain by Tsarist soldiers in 1913. Berdyaev, like others such as Florensky, Bulgakov and the young Losev, supported the monks, but his sharp criticism of the Holy Synod led to a proceeding against him that would have led to inner exile, again, had this not been cut short by the Communist Revolution.

With the Revolution, he stayed in Russia and was for a short time Professor of Philosophy at Moscow University, as well as teaching at a privately run 'Free Academy of Spiritual Culture'. He was among the intellectuals expelled from Russia by Trotsky's decree at the end of 1922, after twice being arrested and subject to interrogation in the hope of submitting him to a show trial. Initially he went to Berlin; in 1925 he moved to Paris, where he spent the rest of his life. In Paris he became editor of the review *The Way* (*Put'*), which became a forum for the Russian intelligentsia in Paris.[4] In this way, he occupied a role at the centre of the intellectual life of the Russian intelligentsia. In other ways, too, he was a central figure. In 1928 he founded what has been called the Berdyaev Colloquy, which became a meeting place for Catholic, Orthodox and (to begin with, before the Vatican put a stop to such dangerous ecumenism) Protestant thinkers: among the Catholics were Jacques Maritain (who appears to have become co-convenor with Berdyaev), Charles de Bos, Gabriel Marcel, Louis Massignon, Étienne Gilson; among the Orthodox, apart from Berdyaev himself, Bulgakov, Florovsky, and also Mother (now St) Maria Skobtsova and Myrrha Lot-Borodine; and among the Protestants, Boegner, Lesserer and Wilfred Monod. For a time, Maritain and Berdyaev became good, though always somewhat uneasy, friends.

Among his fellow émigrés, Berdyaev often cut an awkward figure. Although back in Russia he had become critical of Marxism to the point of rejecting it, among the émigrés he seemed too much a figure of the left, as indeed he was, for he rejected much that the Marxists rejected of the society that had been overthrown at the Revolution. He had no desire to put the clock back, and seemed to those who hankered for the restoration of Holy Russia something of a traitor. In religious terms, though he affirmed his Orthodoxy, what he said often sounded deeply unorthodox, and his support for Bulgakov

---

[4] On which see Antoine Arjakovsky, *La Génération des penseurs religieux de l'émigration russe: La revue La Voie (Put'), 1925–1940* (Kiev–Paris: L'Esprit et la Lettre, 2002); now in English translation: *The Way: Religious Thinkers of the Russian Emigration in Paris and Their Journal, 1925–1940*, trans. Jerry Ryan et al. (Notre Dame, IN: University of Notre Dame Press, 2013).

over the question of sophiology made him still more untrustworthy among Orthodox of a conservative stripe. Even more enlightened Orthodox thinkers, such as Bulgakov, often enough found his ideas uncongenial. In his thought, Berdyaev was something of a loner, even though his ideas belong to a cultural matrix that is obviously Russian and Orthodox.

Towards the end of the 1930s, with the help of a small legacy, Berdyaev was able to buy a house at Clamart for himself, his wife Lydia and her sister, Genia, who lived with them. There he lived throughout the war until his death in 1948.

Writings

Berdyaev was immensely prolific: the 16 volumes in English I referred to are only a part of his work, which included, too, articles in *Put'* and elsewhere. There is, however, a certain consistency, not to say sameness, about his works; sometimes the titles seem almost interchangeable – *Spirit and Reality*, *Freedom and the Spirit*, *Slavery and Freedom*, *Dream and Reality*. Despite that, it is really not easy to present his thought in any systematic way, or at least any attempt to present his thought as a system runs the risk of losing its aphoristic quality, which seems to me central, not just a matter of style. What I shall attempt to do is present his thought from two perspectives: first, by taking a number of issues and discussing the way he approaches them, and then, second, by looking at his short book on Dostoevsky, which provides a more rounded approach to his thought, without being too procrustean.

Towards the end of his life Berdyaev wrote an essay in an autobiography that we have already mentioned called *Dream and Reality*. In it he gives an account of his life, his books and the development of his ideas. It is a good introduction to the feel or flavour of his ideas, his approach to understanding. In the penultimate chapter he gives a sketch of his philosophical outlook. He begins a little forbiddingly by saying that in none of his books has he ever been able to express adequately what he thinks, and quotes a line from Tyutchev: 'a thought once spoken is a lie' (from the poem 'Silentium'). He insists, however, that his thought has 'as a whole revolved around a single axis', even though it seems to contain contradictions and inconsistencies; by this time the reader of the book has learnt that Berdyaev, like Florensky (to whom he rarely refers in a positive way), values antinomy, contradiction, as in some way intrinsic to our attempts to express the truth.[5]

Christian existentialism

The first notion he introduces is 'objectification'. It is something he is against: objectification, the attempt to see the world over against us, as a kind of reality we approach from the outside, seems to him a, or even the, fundamental error,

---

[5] Berdyaev, *Dream and Reality*, 285.

an error that he relates to the role the notion of being plays in Western philosophy from Plato (very much the criticism we find in Heidegger, though what they mean by this criticism is, I think, rather different). The notion of being, for Berdyaev, draws attention to some sense of objective reality, set over against us, whereas the truth is quite other. As he puts it:

> Reality in its primordial character and originality cannot in any sense be described as undifferentiated Being or essence or *ousia*. Original reality is creative act or freedom, and the bearer of original reality is the person, the subject, spirit, rather than Being, nature or object. Objectivity signifies the enslavement of the spirit to external things: it is the product of disruption, disunion, estrangement and enmity. Knowledge, which is an activity of the subject, depends on the victory over disunion and estrangement, on the extent and intensity of spiritual communion.[6]

We can get from this some sense of Berdyaev's starting point. One might describe it as 'existentialism', as he seems to privilege existence over essence, and he is often thought of, and rightly, as a famous representative of 'Christian existentialism', but this starting point seems to me to have more to do with his Idealist heritage, particularly in its Schelling-esque form, and perhaps even more to do with what Berdyaev thought to be the roots of Idealism, which he discerned in mystics such as Jakob Boehme. The key point in this quotation seems to be an identity of subject and object, to the extent that to speak of an 'object' is already to misrepresent reality. True knowing is not some kind of accurate surveying, from the outside as it were; it is an identity with what is known, a participation in the 'creative act and freedom' where we find the roots of reality, and where, too, we find the knower, the subject, ourselves. As Berdyaev goes on to put it, '[i]n true knowledge man transcends the object or, rather, possesses the object creatively and, indeed, creates it himself'.[7] 'Objective' knowledge is really a misnomer; it is not really knowledge at all, or at least only a lowly kind of knowledge that assesses something about how things appear to us. This kind of objective knowledge is concerned with a world that has already fallen into fragmentation, that is already 'fallen'. Another key theme for Berdyaev has already appeared and that is the notion of freedom. Objective knowledge is not 'free', it is enslaved to what it regards as external reality; it is not an expression of free, sovereign spirit, but cramped, servile.

Freedom and creativity

Berdyaev's association of Spirit, freedom and creativity seems on the face of it to be contrary to fundamental Christian beliefs. To ascribe freedom and creativity to the human in such a radical way seems to usurp the freedom and creativity – the creative freedom – that belong only to God. Freedom,

---

[6] Berdyaev, *Dream and Reality*, 286.
[7] Berdyaev, *Dream and Reality*, 287.

creativity and Spirit: these come together in another way for Berdyaev, as the characteristics of the *person*. The notion of the supreme value of the person, of the way in which the personal discloses the true nature of what it is to be human: this idea has been very popular in twentieth-century Christianity, and especially within Orthodoxy. Much has been made of the fact that the notion of the personal seems to have its origins in Christian reflection on the person of Christ and the three Persons of the Trinity. In all the Russians, both those who acknowledged their roots in the movements of thought in the late nineteenth century, and those who wanted to distance themselves from these roots, we find this sense of the value of the person over against the individual, an idea which, for the Russians, can be traced back to the Slavophils and – in the opposition of Western individualism to Russian personalism – is a commonplace of much late nineteenth-century Russian thought.

There are several notions here, all of which are picked up in Berdyaev's thought: person *v.* individual, person *v.* nature, true community (*sobornost'*) *v.* false community (some translators use commonality for true community, but it is hardly idiomatic). In each case there is a dichotomy between freedom and necessity or constraint: a person is free and *sobornost'* is a manifestation of freedom; in contrast, the individual is limited and constrained, nature is something already defined, and a false community is a product of rules and ideologies or institutional authority that are enemies to freedom. Modern urban society has reduced humans to individuals, defined by their job, their address, the number on their identity card: individuals represent the fragmented constituents of such a society, and the society itself nothing more than an aggregate of these fragments. The organic society of the past, especially in the village, allowed persons freedom to become themselves through the relationships they had with other persons. In contrast the individual in the modern city is lost in anonymity, and condemned to lack of freedom.

This sort of analysis is commonplace in the Slavophils and their successors. It is reflected in Berdyaev's thought, though with him we find a suspicion of the romanticism of the Slavophils and the analysis focuses more on the freedom of the person in contrast to the constraint of nature, as well as association of free persons found in *sobornost'* in contrast to the kind of society produced by institutions and hierarchies. In the background of Berdyaev's understanding of person and *sobornost'* lies a metaphysics that opposes the realm of the subject to that of objects, the one characterized by freedom and truth, the other by slavery and appearance. This metaphysics looks very much like that of the Christian thinker of the third century Origen, who similarly opposes an unfallen spiritual world to the material world of our experience; Origen, of course, was condemned as a heretic.

In several places, Berdyaev insists that he is often misunderstood, because his thought is pursued in too prosaic a fashion, whereas what he is interested in is the vision that he is trying, with inevitable lack of success (think of the Tyutchev line) to articulate. Something of this vision is expressed in a remark he makes in *Dream and Reality*:

In opposition to Schleiermacher and many others it must be stated that religion is not a 'sense of dependence' (*Abhaengigkeitsgefuehl*) but, on the contrary, a sense of independence. If God does not exist, man is a being wholly dependent on nature or society, on the world or the state. If God exists, man is a spiritually independent being; and his relation to God is to be defined as freedom.[8]

Similarly with his understanding of the person: Berdyaev's more interesting insights are less where he is typical of the tradition to which he belongs than in the striking observations that often accompany his thoughts. In his development of the notion of the personal he seeks to overcome the dualisms that, he maintains, have plagued our understanding of the personal. So the person is not the soul, inhabiting a body: the personal embraces both the soul and the body. It is not just that the soul is expressed through the body, in the sense that it can be inferred from the body that we perceive; rather the body itself is capable of spiritual expression. So he affirms: 'The vision of another person's countenance, the expression of his eyes, can often be a spiritual revelation. The eyes, the gestures, the words – all these are infinitely more eloquent of a man's soul than of his body.'[9]

Berdyaev and Martin Buber

Maybe one of the reasons for Berdyaev's popularity in his own time was his ability to sense the mood of the times. His development of the notion of the person differs from, say, Bulgakov's partly because of the way in which he picks up some of the ways of thinking that had become so popular from the later twenties onwards through Martin Buber's enormously influential book, *Ich und Du* (*I and Thou*).[10] There are some echoes of Buber's way of approaching personalism through the personal relationship expressed in and evoked by 'I' addressing the other as 'Thou' in some of the ways Berdyaev develops his own personalism. For example, just a couple of pages on from the quotation just given: 'The Ego remains isolated as long as it can only communicate with the object; its solitude can only be vanquished by the communion of personalities, of the Ego and the Thou, in the innermost depths of the We'[11] – in which sentence we can see Berdyaev developing Buberian themes in the direction of the Russian notion of *sobornost'*.

There are indeed broader parallels between Berdyaev and Buber: Buber's 'It-world' is much the same as Berdyaev's world of 'objectification', as is the personal world that possesses true reality for both of them. There are other ways in which there seem to be parallels between Buber and Berdyaev. The

---

[8] Berdyaev, *Dream and Reality*, 179–80.
[9] Nicolas Berdyaev, *Solitude and Society* (London: Geoffrey Bles, 1938; Russian original 1934), 109.
[10] Originally published in 1923; ETs: Ronald Gregor Smith (Edinburgh: T&T Clark, 1937; 2nd edn 1959); Walter Kaufmann (Edinburgh: T&T Clark, 1970).
[11] Berdyaev, *Solitude and Society*, 111.

communion that arises from the I finding the Thou in a relationship that is personal is not, for either of them, limited to human persons. There is a famous passage in *I and Thou* in which Buber considers what can be involved in our perception of a tree:

> I contemplate a tree.
>
> I can accept it as a picture: a rigid pillar in a flood of light, or splashes of green traversed by the gentleness of the blue silver ground.
>
> I can feel it as movement: the flowing veins around the sturdy, striving core, the sucking of the roots, the breathing of the leaves, the infinite commerce with earth and air – and the growing itself in its darkness ...
>
> But it can also happen, if will and grace are joined, that as I contemplate the tree I am drawn into a relation, and the tree ceases to be an It. The power of exclusiveness has seized me.[12]

So we find Berdyaev echoing Buber, when he says,

> The intimate communion of one Ego with another gives rise to an affective kind of knowledge. It is an error to think that communion can only be a human relationship, that it is the attribute solely of *human friendship*. It is common to the animal, vegetable and mineral worlds, which all enjoy an inner life of their own. Like Saint Francis one may commune with various manifestations of nature, such as ocean, the mountains, the forest, the fields, the rivers.[13]

Both Berdyaev and Buber move easily from such considerations into the human relationship with animals as pets. For Berdyaev it is the dog: 'A striking example of this type of affective communion is furnished by man's relationship to that true friend, the dog.'[14] Buber has a rather longer reflection on the glance we might exchange with a cat; this is a short extract:

> I sometimes look into the eyes of a house cat. The domesticated animal has not by any means received the gift of the truly 'eloquent' glance from *us*, as a human conceit suggests sometimes; what it has from us is only the ability ... to turn this glance upon us brutes ... Undeniably, this cat began its glance by asking me with a glance that was ignited by the breath of my glance: 'Can it be that you mean me? ...'[15]

My point is not that there is any influence from Buber to Berdyaev (though there may be), rather that there is a commonality of concern that may well have made Berdyaev's voice more immediately comprehensible in the intellectual world *entre deux guerres*.

Both Berdyaev and Buber relate this sense of the significance of the person to the idea of creativity. Speaking of the world opened up by the I uttering Thou, Buber asserts:

---

12 Buber, *I and Thou* (Kaufmann), 57–8.
13 Berdyaev, *Solitude and Society*, 112.
14 Berdyaev, *Solitude and Society*, 113.
15 Buber, *I and Thou* (Kaufmann), 145.

This is the eternal origin of art that a human being confronts a form that wants to become a work through him. Not a figment of his soul but something that appears to the soul and demands the soul's creative power. What is required is a deed that a man does with his whole being . . .[16]

The creative act

This is the central perception of Berdyaev's understanding of the creative act, expressed in his early book, *The Meaning of the Creative Act* (completed in 1914, though only published in English translation in 1954), and prominent in his account of his mature thought in *Dream and Reality*, where he summarizes his idea by saying that '[o]riginal reality is creative act and freedom, and the bearer of original reality is the person, the subject, spirit, rather than Being'.[17] In *The Meaning of the Creative Act*, Berdyaev pursues this insight throughout the whole realm of metaphysics and religion. Here I can only make a few observations.

Berdyaev himself affirms that *The Meaning of the Creative Act* was written in reaction against what he perceived to be taking place in Orthodox circles in Moscow. It is not difficult to guess what these might be, for it was round about this time that Orthodox, not just in Russia, but elsewhere (Romania, Greece), began to regain an appreciation of the traditional form of the icon, which had been overwhelmed by Western styles of art throughout the eighteenth and nineteenth centuries. The 'Recovery of the Icon', as it has been called,[18] was about to get under way; towards the end of the decade in which Berdyaev wrote his book Florensky's explorations of the origin and meaning of the icon were to be given as papers, if not actually published. As we have earlier seen, Florensky's defence of the icon involved a criticism and rejection of the Renaissance and all its works, not least the notion of artistic creativity, and of the artist as a near-divine creator, very much part of the Renaissance heritage. Berdyaev's making the notion of human creativity so central to his philosophical vision ran counter to much that was interesting Orthodox circles in Russia (and later in the diaspora, as well as elsewhere in the Orthodox world).

Furthermore, Berdyaev's understanding of creativity was inspired by Renaissance Italy; he tells us that the passages in *The Meaning of the Creative Act* about the Italian Renaissance were written in Italy, and says that 'Italy revealed to me the Renaissance as the dawn of a new age in which the Christian soul became conscious for the first time of a will to creation'.[19] If he goes on, as he does, to speak of the Renaissance as a failure, it is 'the most sublime, significant and tragic failure ever experienced by European man'.[20] Berdyaev's

---

[16] Buber, *I and Thou* (Kaufmann), 60.
[17] Berdyaev, *Dream and Reality*, 286 (already quoted above).
[18] The French title of a study of Leonid Ouspensky, published in English: Patrick Doolan, *Recovering the Icon: The Life and Work of Leonid Ouspensky* (Crestwood, NY: St Vladimir's Seminary Press, 2008).
[19] Berdyaev, *Dream and Reality*, 211.
[20] Berdyaev, *Dream and Reality*, 211.

thought was moving in a quite contrary direction to that of many of his Orthodox contemporaries; responses to his book were mostly hostile or uncomprehending.

There are, however, it seems to me, elements in his understanding of creativity as essential to what it is to be human that are profoundly Orthodox, even if expressed in an exaggerated way that was intended to provoke and was all too successful. Central to his understanding of creativity is an intuition that human activity, human knowledge, is in some way a reflection of divine activity; the human is created in the image of God, and as the image of God the Creator, the human is also creative. Berdyaev often suggests that one of the problems with much Christianity is that it confuses creatureliness with sinfulness: both are seen in negative terms. On one occasion, Berdyaev remarks, '[t]here can be no question of the work of a great artist being poor, low and insignificant simply because it is created';[21] seeing human creatureliness as almost some kind of defect would be an indictment of God the Creator. Human creation in the image of God is not primarily an index of frailty, but of potentiality for greatness. Even sin, Berdyaev sometimes seems to suggest, is not to be conceived in wholly negative terms, but rather in terms of the inevitable element of risk involved if finite human beings are to fulfil their creative destiny.

Beauty, death, tragedy

This leads to another dimension in Berdyaev's thought that is and was easily misunderstood. Often Berdyaev affirms that ethics is not really about right and wrong, good and evil. Part of what he means is that the question of moral conduct is not satisfactorily understood in terms of moral rules or commandments. And although it might seem that much biblical morality is concerned with obeying, or disobeying, divine commandments or rules, the dominant trend in traditional Orthodox reflection on moral behaviour focuses, not on adherence to rules, but on the fashioning of virtue: ethics is concerned, less with what one does, and more with who one is, what one wants to become. When Berdyaev suggests that a concern for moral rules is a shallow way of understanding human conduct, he is being much more traditional that many traditionalists think. What then is ethics about? Instead of good and evil, right and wrong, we find Berdyaev speaking about beauty, death and tragedy. It is about what is real and what is false. It is not about convention, behaviour, 'sanctification' (Berdyaev's – or his translator's – not perhaps entirely happy word); it is about 'love of truth, ontological veracity, absolutely unattainable for legalistic ethics; and it also means a striving to be truly human',[22] and this involves no mere sanctification, but transfiguration. He goes on to say:

---

[21] Nicolas Berdyaev, *The Destiny of Man* (London: Geoffrey Bles, 2nd edn, 1945), 27.
[22] Berdyaev, *Destiny of Man*, 247.

The real transfiguration and enlightenment of human nature means the attainment of beauty. The good realized actually, and not formally or symbolically, is beauty. The highest end is beauty and not goodness, which always bears a stamp of the law. Beauty will save the world, i.e. beauty *is* the salvation of the world. The transfiguration of the world is the attainment of beauty. The Kingdom of God is beauty. Art gives us merely symbols of beauty. Real beauty is given only in the religious transfiguration of the creature. Beauty is God's idea of the creature, of man and of the world.[23]

Ethics, then, is about the achievement of beauty in the world – beauty that, as Prince Myshkin says in Dostoevsky's *The Idiot*, will save the world: beauty that is what the world is meant to be, fashioned by the Creator. The world we know, however, is a world in which human plans are frustrated, confronted by death that reduces everything to nothing. Human life is, then, marked by tragedy, the defeat of human hopes, the twisting even of the good in ways that are frustrating and destructive. Tragedy, therefore, is a central category of Berdyaev's understanding of human life; he remarks at one point that it would be 'curious that the religion of the cross should deny tragedy',[24] as he claims, surely justly, that many forms of Christianity have, substituting for tragedy a stultifying moralism. For Christians, however, tragedy has to do with freedom, in contrast to pre-Christian, classical tragedy that is rather a tragedy of fate.

It is out of his understanding of human life in which freedom strives towards beauty, but is frustrated and experiences tragedy through the presence of death, that Berdyaev fashions his approach to ethics. Although he speaks little directly of the Resurrection of Christ, it seems to me that his ethics is an ethics of the Resurrection, an ethics founded on the affirmation of the Easter troparion: 'Christ has risen from the dead, by death trampling on death, and to those in the graves giving life'. So he says that '[o]ur attitude to all men would be Christian if we regarded them as though they were dying, and determine our relation to them in the light of death, both of their death and our own'.[25] Elsewhere he puts it like this: 'The fundamental principle of ethics may be formulated as follows: act so as to conquer death and affirm everywhere, in everything and in relation to all, eternal and immortal life.'[26] Affirmation of life is the acknowledgement and creation of beauty: beauty which lies beyond good and evil conceived in any moralistic sense.

> [P]aradise lies beyond good and evil and therefore is not exclusively the kingdom of 'the good' in our sense of the term. We come nearer to it when we think of it as beauty. The transfiguration and regeneration of the world is beauty and not goodness.[27]

---

[23] Berdyaev, *Destiny of Man*, 247.
[24] Berdyaev, *Destiny of Man*, 30–1.
[25] Berdyaev, *Destiny of Man*, 121.
[26] Berdyaev, *Destiny of Man*, 253.
[27] Berdyaev, *Destiny of Man*, 287.

This link between death and freedom is something borne out in Berdyaev's own experience. In *Gulag Archipelago*, Solzhenitsyn briefly mentions Berdyaev as one who retained his freedom, even in the face of interrogation by the Cheka, and did this by embracing death willingly. He has this to say:

> From the moment you go to prison you must put your cosy past firmly behind you. At the very threshold, you must say to yourself: 'My life is over, a little early to be sure, but there's nothing to be done about it. I shall never return to freedom. I am condemned to die – now or a little later. But later on, in truth, it will be even harder, and so the sooner the better. I no longer have any property whatsoever. For me those I love have died, and for them I have died. For today on, my body is useless and alien to me. Only my spirit and my conscience remain precious and important to me.'
> Confronted by such a prisoner, the interrogation will tremble.
> Only the man who has renounced everything can win that victory.
> But how can one turn one's body to stone?
> Well, they managed to turn some of the individuals from the Berdyaev circle into puppets for a trial, but they didn't succeed with Berdyaev. They wanted to drag him into an open trial; they arrested him twice; and (in 1922) he was subjected to a night interrogation by Dzerzhinsky himself... But Berdyaev did not humiliate himself. He did not beg or plead. He set forth firmly those religious and moral principles which had led him to refuse to accept the political authority established in Russia. And not only did they come to the conclusion that he would be useless for a trial, but they liberated him.[28]

And again, though personal, Berdyaev's vision of the beauty of the world encompasses more than human persons: '[m]y salvation is not only bound up with that of other men but also of animals, plants, minerals, of every blade of grass – all must be transfigured and brought into the Kingdom of God'.[29] This cosmic theme we have already encountered. One wonders if Berdyaev was aware of a parallel in a work he doesn't mention, but most likely knew – the work known in English as *The Way of the Pilgrim*. In that work, as the pilgrim begins to practise interior prayer, he remarks,

> And when with this in mind I prayed with my heart, everything around me seemed delightful and marvellous. The trees, the grass, the birds, the air, the light seemed to be telling me that they existed for man's sake, that they witnessed to the love of God for man, that everything proved the love of God for man, that all things prayed to God and sang His praise.[30]

Berdyaev and Dostoevsky

Berdyaev's book on Dostoevsky is as much a book on Berdyaev's own thought as it is a study of Dostoevsky: like many of the Russian émigrés, Berdyaev

---

[28] Alexander Solzhenitsyn, *The Gulag Archipelago: 1918–1956*, trans. Thomas P. Whitney (London: Collins/Fontana, 1974), 130.

[29] Berdyaev, *Destiny of Man*, 294.

[30] *The Way of the Pilgrim* and *The Pilgrim Continues His Way*, trans. R. M. French (London: SPCK, 1954), 31.

regarded Dostoevsky as a religious prophet as much as a novelist and man of letters. We have already encountered several themes of Dostoevskian provenance in our discussion of Berdyaev: the assertion that 'Beauty will save the world', the insistence on human freedom, a sense of human life as full of tragic possibilities, and allied to that an insistence that what is important for a human being is the choice, not so much between good and evil, as between truth and falsity. Berdyaev's book on Dostoevsky, like many other books on the writer, pursues two routes in conjunction, on the one hand, guided by the novels, from *A Raw Youth* to *The Brothers Karamazov*, and on the other, organized by general themes, from Spirit, Man, freedom, through evil and love, to a final discussion of the Legend of the Grand Inquisitor. There is something a bit old-fashioned about the work, in that it treats too readily Dostoevsky as a thinker, rather than a novelist. The difficulties in understanding Dostoevsky, discussed by Berdyaev in his final chapter,[31] where he outlines the problems faced by Tolstoyans and others, are not so much to do with the complexity of his thought, as Berdyaev seems to suggest, but more to do with what Mikhail Bakhtin identified as the 'polyphonic' dimension in his novels: Dostoevsky, from this point of view, is less concerned to promote his own ideas as to provide a space in which the fundamental issues of human existence — such as freedom, love, beauty and redemption — can be engaged with through the thoughts and actions of his characters, and their interaction one with another.

Early on in his book, Berdyaev makes the point — in connection with drawing a contrast between Tolstoy and Dostoevsky — that the problem of God, pursued by Tolstoy, is really a pagan quest, the Christian quest being rather occupied with the problem of the human, which stands at the centre of Dostoevsky's concern. What Dostoevsky does is to explore the nature of the human, illumined, certainly, by the fact that God has become man in Christ, that manhood finds its fulfilment in Godmanhood. Being human, then, opens out on to the infinity of the Godhead, for the human is not a being limited by its nature, as is the case with animals, for example. For this reason, human existence is characterized by an absolute freedom, which is the sign of the personal nature of the human. Freedom leads directly to the existence of evil and the possibility of redemption; implicated in it are the antinomies that mark human existence, caught between extremes that cannot be reconciled at some supposed middle point. In the chapter on evil, Berdyaev has this to say:

> Evil is essentially contradictory, and optimistically to conceive it as indispensable to the evolution of good and to try and remove its antinomy is to see only one aspect of it. The good that can be derived from evil is attained only by the way of suffering and the repudiation of evil. Dostoevsky believed firmly in the redemptive and regenerative power of suffering: life is the expiation of sin by suffering. Freedom has opened the path of evil to man, it is a

---

[31] Nicolas Berdyaev, *Dostoevsky* (London: Sheed & Ward, 1934), 216–20.

proof of freedom, and man must pay the price. The price is suffering, and by it the freedom that has been spoiled and turned into its contrary is reborn and given back to man. Therefore is Christ the Saviour freedom itself. In all Dostoevsky's novels man goes through this spiritual process, through freedom and evil to redemption.[32]

So, Berdyaev affirms, for Dostoevsky 'man is terribly free, liberty is a tragic and grievous burden to him'.[33] There is more to suffering, however, than the expiation of sin envisaged by this quotation; suffering is one of the ways – the most important way – in which a person attains the fullness of being human: 'suffering is the index of man's depth'.[34] Berdyaev explores briefly the way in which Dostoevsky came to learn this himself, drawing attention to his experience of debased and corrupt humanity during his imprisonment in Siberia, which he recounted in his *Memoirs from the House of the Dead*. There Dostoevsky came to know the peasant, the *muzhik*, not as foreign to himself, as an educated intellectual, but as part of himself. Berdyaev remarks, 'The "popular" element is not outside of myself, in the *muzhik*, but within myself, in that inmost part of my being where I am not like a closed monad'.[35]

The Legend of the Grand Inquisitor

Although Berdyaev pays tribute to the figure and teaching of Fr Zossima, who 'stands for the resurrection of Orthodoxy and the emergence in her of new life',[36] and sees Alesha as central to Dostoevsky's understanding of what the Christian life should mean, in truth the book is focused on the Legend of the Grand Inquisitor, 'the high point of Dostoevsky's work and the crown of his dialectic',[37] to which the last and longest chapter is devoted (it is, I think, odd that Berdyaev nowhere mentions one of the most striking elements of Fr Zossima's teaching: the conviction of his dying elder brother, Markel, after his conversion, that 'each of us is guilty before everyone, for everyone and everything').[38] I shall close by drawing out a couple of points that Berdyaev makes in his discussion.

For Berdyaev, the Legend of the Grand Inquisitor is about freedom, the essence of what Christ came to bring to human beings – genuine spiritual freedom. But this is, as we have just seen, 'a tragic and grievous burden' for humankind: a burden from which the Grand Inquisitor seeks to relieve human beings. For

[32] Berdyaev, *Dostoevsky*, 95.
[33] Berdyaev, *Dostoevsky*, 42.
[34] Berdyaev, *Dostoevsky*, 92.
[35] Berdyaev, *Dostoevsky*, 180.
[36] Berdyaev, *Dostoevsky*, 209.
[37] Berdyaev, *Dostoevsky*, 188.
[38] Fyodor Dostoevsky, *The Brothers Karamazov*, pt II, bk 6, ch. 2 (a), trans. Richard Pevear and Lara Volokhonsky (London: Everyman's Library, 1997), 289.

A man can bear neither his own sufferings nor those of other people, yet without suffering there can be no liberty of choice, so we are faced with a dilemma: on the one side, freedom; on the other, contentment, well-being, rationalized organization of life; either freedom with suffering or contentment without freedom.[39]

Berdyaev continues:

An overwhelming majority of people choose the last (*sic*). They give up the great ideas of God and immortality and freedom and come under the spell of a fallacious love of one's neighbour in which God has no part, a false compassion which promotes a godless systematization of the world.[40]

It is this overwhelming majority for whom the Grand Inquisitor provides, and it is a betrayal of Christ and his gospel of freedom. The Grand Inquisitor speaks of his 'secret', and reveals it to Christ: 'Listen then: we are not with you, but with *him*, that is our secret!'[41] – '*him*': the Antichrist, who has established himself in the Church. This is no difficult task, for '[t]he principle of authority that plays so large a part in the history of the Church can easily be transformed into a denial of the mystery of Christian freedom, the mystery of Christ crucified'.[42] And how does Christ, the one who was crucified, respond to the Grand Inquisitor? He says nothing; rather he 'suddenly approaches the old man in silence and gently kisses him on his bloodless, ninety-year-old lips'![43] Berdyaev comments on Dostoevsky's way of contrasting Christ and the Grand Inquisitor in the Legend:

[His] way of setting this out is admirable. His Christ is a shadowy figure who says nothing all the time: efficacious religion does not explain itself, the principle of freedom cannot be expressed in words; but the principle of compulsion puts its case very freely indeed.[44]

One of the Grand Inquisitor's taunts to Christ concerns his refusal to come down from the cross in response to the mocking passers-by. Berdyaev echoes the Grand Inquisitor's words of taunting:

Our Lord would not come down from the cross, as unbelievers called on him to do and still call on him to do, because he craved for 'the free gift of love, not the obsequious raptures of slaves before the might that has overawed them'.[45]

Berdyaev continues:

A divine Truth panoplied in power, triumphant over the world and conquering souls, would not be consonant with the freedom of man's spirit, and so the

[39] Berdyaev, *Dostoevsky*, 190.
[40] Berdyaev, *Dostoevsky*, 190.
[41] Dostoevsky, *Brothers Karamazov*, pt II, bk 5, ch. 5 (Pevear–Volokhonsky, 257); quoted by Berdyaev, *Dostoevsky*, 196.
[42] Berdyaev, *Dostoevsky*, 197.
[43] Dostoevsky, *Brothers Karamazov*, pt II, bk 5, ch. 5 (Pevear–Volokhonsky, 262).
[44] Berdyaev, *Dostoevsky*, 189.
[45] Berdyaev, *Dostoevsky*, 197 (passage from Dostoevsky, *Brothers Karamazov* (Pevear–Volokhonsky, 256)).

mystery of Golgotha is the mystery of liberty; the Son of God had to be crucified by the princes of this world in order that human freedom might be established and emphasized. The act of faith is an act of liberty, the world's unconstrained recognition of unseen things. Christ the Son of God, sitting at the right hand of the Father, can be seen only by a free act of faith, and he who so believes will witness the resurrection of the Crucified in glory. But the unbeliever, obsessed by the world of visible things, sees only the shameful punishment of a carpenter called Jesus, the downfall of one who had thought himself to be divine truth itself. There lies the whole secret of Christianity, and every time in history that man has tried to turn crucified Truth into coercive truth he has betrayed the fundamental principle of Christ.[46]

Berdyaev has sometimes been accused of being too much a philosopher and not clear enough about the place of Christ. His comments here perhaps explain why this is so: not a lack of faith, but an awareness of the indirectness of the witness of faith, an indirectness bound up with the way in which faith in Christ both confers and demands freedom, devoid of any compulsion – the free response of love.

---

[46] Berdyaev, *Dostoevsky*, 197–8.

6

Fr Georges Florovsky and the neo-patristic synthesis

When Fr Georges Florovsky died on 11 August 1979, he was probably the most famous Orthodox theologian in the world. In an obituary notice, Rowan Williams remarked that he had become the '"grand old man" of Orthodox theology', and went on to say,

> it is easy to forget that he was not a walking textbook but an original and radical mind. But of course his originality was always more than an eye-catching novelty. It was invariably a rediscovery of the perennial freshness of the heart of the gospel, in scripture and in liturgy, and in the great Fathers of the Church.[1]

Since then he has attracted intermittent attention. Already by the time of his death, the first four volumes of a projected *Collected Works of Georges Florovsky* had appeared: these volumes collected some of the articles he had written in English in the second part of his life. After his death, the series continued, mostly with works published in Russian, translated by various hands and edited by Richard S. Haugh, in another ten volumes, which appeared in the decade after Florovsky's death. The translations vary in quality, and it has to be said that they do not constitute a worthy memorial to Florovsky.

Various studies have appeared, notably a *Denkschrift*, edited by Andrew Blane, which includes a book-length biographical sketch by the editor, and notable contributions by Mark Raeff and George H. Williams, which make clear the very high regard in which Florovsky was held in Slavic and theological circles in the USA at the time of his death.[2] It has to be said, however, that the star of the 'grand old man' of Orthodox theology has declined over the decades, and far more attention has been paid recently to thinkers such as Fr Pavel Florensky and Fr Sergii Bulgakov, whose approach to theology Florovsky had deplored and had sought to replace with his own 'neo-patristic synthesis'. Nowadays one is much more likely to hear it said that Bulgakov was the greatest Orthodox theologian in the twentieth century, rather than Florovsky.[3]

---

[1] 'Georges Florovsky (1893–1979)', obituary by E. L. Mascall and Rowan Williams, *Sobornost/ECR* 2:1 (1980), 69–72, here 71–2.

[2] *Georges Florovsky: Russian Intellectual and Orthodox Churchman*, ed. Andrew Blane (Crestwood, NY: St Vladimir's Seminary Press, 1993).

[3] Since I gave the lectures on which this book is based, there has been published a brilliant monograph on Florovsky: Paul L. Gavrilyuk, *Georges Florovsky and the Russian Religious Renaissance* (Oxford: Oxford University Press, 2013). It provides a much more profound consideration of Florovsky than has been hitherto available. However, in revising this chapter for publication, I have not found anything that needed fundamental revision.

Life

Georges Florovsky was born in Odessa in 1893, the son of a priest. He did not, however, attend seminary, as priests' sons generally did, but studied at the University of Odessa, and graduated in arts in 1916. Later he lectured for the year 1919–20. He then left Russia, first going to Sofia and then to Prague, where he was lecturer in the Faculty of Law from 1922 to 1926. By this time there was no chance of his returning to Russia, as he had been included among the Russian intellectuals expelled from Russia by Trotsky's decree in 1922. In 1926, he became Professor of Patristics at the newly founded Institut St-Serge in Paris; later, he became Professor of Dogmatics there. In 1932 he was ordained priest. In Paris he was one of the intellectuals who attended the so-called Berdyaev Colloquy, convened by Berdyaev and Jacques Maritain. In the thirties, he was one of the Russian churchmen in Paris who became involved in the Fellowship of St Alban and St Sergius, an ecumenical society, founded by another Russian émigré, Nicolas Zernov, that sought to promote contacts between Eastern and Western Christians – to begin with, mainly Russians and Anglicans. Within that context he was something of a conservative, and did not warm to Bulgakov's proposal for limited sharing of the eucharistic sacrament ('intercommunion'), proposed by Bulgakov and

Georges Florovsky
With permission of St Vladimir's Orthodox Seminary

enthusiastically supported by Nicolas Zernov. He crossed Bulgakov, too, over another, much more important matter: in the controversy over sophiology.

In the 1930s, Bulgakov's ideas attracted criticism from many Orthodox, and he was condemned by the Synodal Church (now the Russian Orthodox Church Outside Russia) under Metropolitan Antony Khrapovitsky, as well as by the Patriarchate of Moscow. By this time Metropolitan Evlogy of Paris had led his exarchate (or most of it) under the jurisdiction of the Œcumenical Patriarchate to form the Exarchate of Parishes of the Russian Tradition in Europe, to which Bulgakov and the Institut St-Serge belonged. The condemnations of Bulgakov therefore came from Russian jurisdictions to which he did not belong. Metropolitan Evlogy, however, felt obliged to investigate Bulgakov's sophiology, and one of the theologians he asked to report on the question was Florovsky. Florovsky was deeply opposed to sophiology, and it was with reluctance that he accepted the task. For all his doubts about sophiology, in his report he judged that the doctrine was a *theologoumenon*, mistaken, but not, in itself, heretical (a much milder position than the shrill denunciation Vladimir Lossky had sent to the Moscow Patriarchate, to which he had continued to belong).

Bulgakov was not condemned by his own hierarchy, but Florovsky's lukewarm support led to some estrangement between the two men, and even more between Florovsky and Bulgakov's friends and supporters; Bulgakov himself soon forgave Florovsky and relations between the two men became once again cordial. Nonetheless, Florovsky now found the Institut St-Serge uncongenial. He spent most of the Second World War in Serbia and, after Bulgakov's death in 1944, sought actively to leave Paris. He had initially hoped to find an appointment in Oxford, but the post went to Nicolas Zernov, and in 1948 he moved to the USA, where he became Professor and Dean of St Vladimir's Orthodox Theological Seminary, then in Union Theological Seminary, New York City. In 1955 he left to become Professor of Eastern Church History at Harvard University (1956–64); while there he also taught at Holy Cross Greek Orthodox Seminary for a time. In 1964 he retired and took up a post as Visiting Professor at Princeton University, where he remained until his death in 1979.

Alongside this academic career, Florovsky played an important role in the ecumenical movement, from 1937 regularly serving as a delegate at assemblies of the Faith and Order movement, and being, too, one of the founding fathers of the World Council of Churches (WCC) at the assembly at Amsterdam in 1948. It is sometimes said that the credibility of the WCC as something more than a pan-Protestant organization was due to the efforts of Karl Barth, the Anglican Michael Ramsey, and Georges Florovsky.

Ways of Russian Theology

Florovsky's involvement in the ecumenical movement gave him an audience as an Orthodox theologian, especially in the English-speaking world, but it probably dissipated his energies in the latter period of his life, when he had settled in the USA. His only major work of theology is his vast history of Russian theology, *Puti Russkogo Bogosloviya* ('Ways of Russian Theology'), published in Paris in 1937 (the English translation appearing only after his death: in two volumes published in 1979 and 1987). For the rest there are articles and lectures, including several textbooks, based on lectures given at the Institut St-Serge in the 1920s and 1930s, put together by Mother (St) Maria Skobtsova, without – apparently – much attention from Florovsky himself.

Ways of Russian Theology is a protean work. On the one hand, it is a history of Russian theology from the beginnings until his contemporaries, the thinkers of what Nicolas Zernov has taught us to call the 'Russian Religious Renaissance'. Florovsky's training was as a historian and philosopher, and this work is full of illuminating information about the history of Russian theology from the fourteenth to the early twentieth century. It is not, however, a dispassionate history: Florovsky has a thesis to prove, and that thesis is radical, for it is in this work that Florovsky presents what he calls variously 'Christian Hellenism' or the 'neo-patristic synthesis' as the future that Russian Orthodox theology must pursue if it is to be faithful to the Christian revelation in Scripture and tradition.

This is manifest on the very title page of the book, though few have noticed it. The title of the work, *Ways of Russian Theology*, has generally been taken to be equivalent to something like 'Different Kinds of Russian Theology'. Berdyaev remarked on the inappropriateness of the title, saying it should have been called 'The Waywardness of Russian Theology'. But Florovsky meant something quite precise by talking about the 'ways' of Russian theology, and this he makes clear by his motto on the title page, taken from Psalm 1.6: 'For the Lord knows the way of the righteous, and the way of the ungodly shall perish' (omitted, alas, in the English translation). There are, for Florovsky, only two ways: his book is mostly about the 'way of the ungodly'; the way forward that he proposes is the 'way of the righteous'. Berdyaev was quite right; Florovsky casts the history of Russian theology as waywardness,[4] or worse, the pursuit of the 'way of the ungodly'. This way Florovsky analyses as the '"pseudomorphosis" of Russia's religious consciousness' or 'of Orthodox thought'[5] – borrowing the geological term from Oswald Spengler's analysis of the 'decline of the West' – or more dramatically (echoing this time Martin Luther) 'the "Babylonian captivity" of the Russian church',[6] which was held to be evident by the eighteenth century, and led, *via* the Slavophils and wayward genius of Vladimir Solov'ev, to what Florovsky regarded as the near-paganism

---

[4] Berdyaev in his review of *Ways of Russian Theology* in *Put'* 53 (1937), 53, which opens with the words: 'Fr Georges Florovsky's book bears the wrong title, it should have been called "The Waywardness of Russian Theology"' (quote by Gavrilyuk, *Florovsky*, 193).

[5] Georges Florovsky, *Ways of Russian Theology*, vol. I (Belmont, MA: Nordland, 1979), 85.

[6] Florovsky, *Ways* I, 121.

of sophiology.

Florovsky's *Ways of Russian Theology* recounts the errant wanderings of Russian theology to the point where it needed to be recalled to the 'patristic style and method', which had been 'lost'. This is the 'way of the righteous', what he came to call the 'neo-patristic synthesis'. It involves a return to the Fathers, whom Florovsky regarded as fundamentally Greek. However, this 'patristic theology must be grasped from within', he declared.[7] Florovsky spoke of 'intuition' as well as 'erudition', and argued that to regain this patristic way of thinking, or *phronema*, 'Russian theological thought must still pass through the strictest school of Christian Hellenism'.[8] 'Fully to follow the Fathers is possible only through creativity, not through imitation.'[9] The way forward he sketched on the last page of his book:

> A prayerful entry into the Church, a fidelity to Revelation, a return to the Fathers, a free encounter with the West, and other similar themes and elements make up the creative postulate of Russian theology in the contemporary circumstances ... The way of history has still not been fully travelled; the history of the Church is not yet finished; Russia's way has not yet been closed. The road is open, though difficult. A harsh historical verdict must be transformed into a creative call to complete what remains unfinished ... Russia's way has long been divided. It is a mysterious way of spiritual labour (*podvig*), a way of secret and silent labour in the acquisition of the Holy Spirit. There is also a separate way for those who have left this one ...[10]

In these closing words, Florovsky clearly recalls the words of Psalm 1.6, quoted on the title page: he is calling on Russian theology to repent and return to the 'way of the righteous' from which it has hitherto strayed.

Christian Hellenism? Neo-patristic synthesis?

Most recent reflection on Florovsky's programme for the future of theology has been very critical. On the one hand, he rarely seems to get beyond the programmatic: he sketches out the project of a return to the Fathers. He is quite clear that this does not mean simply repeating the theology of the Fathers; it involves something much deeper, more demanding. He talks, we have seen, of recovering the patristic *phronema*, that is, coming to *think* like the Fathers, rather than parrot their opinions. He sees this as above all a spiritual task, an ascetic *podvig*, leading to the acquisition of the Holy Spirit. All this is very inspiring, but in practice what does it mean? There is not that much in Florovsky's work that helps us to flesh out his meaning; it remains, at best, it would seem, inspiring rhetoric. Later on, I shall try and glean what

---

[7] Georges Florovsky, *Ways of Russian Theology*, vol. II (Vaduz: Büchervertriebsanstalt, 1987), 294.

[8] Florovsky, *Ways* II, 297.

[9] G. Florovsky, *Puti Russkogo Bogosloviya* (Paris: YMCA Press, 1981; reprint of 1937), 506 (my trans.); cf. *Ways* II, 294.

[10] Florovsky, *Ways* II, 308 (the translation there is lacunose and otherwise faulty, so I have modified it by reference to the Russian text: Florovsky, *Puti*, 520).

we can from some of his articles, many of which are compelling and give some insight into what he meant. He did not, however, produce anything comparable to Vladimir Lossky's *The Mystical Theology of the Eastern Church*, which has become, by default, the nearest thing there is to a compendium of the 'neo-patristic synthesis'.

On the other hand, there have recently been serious criticisms of what Florovsky actually proposed. 'Christian Hellenism' has been criticized as a limited aim. It was certainly polemical: as well as opposing Hellenism to Russianism, Florovsky had in his sights a whole raft of Protestant theologians from Harnack onwards, who regarded the Hellenic strand in patristic theology as a betrayal of, initially, the simplicity of the gospel (that is, more or less, Harnack's view), or (in the mid-twentieth century) of the essentially Hebraic nature of Judaeo-Christianity. Harnack called Gnosticism the 'acute Hellenization of Christianity' – the metaphor is medical – Catholicism, that is, the theology of the Church Fathers, being the chronic form of the disease of Hellenization; in the mid-twentieth century, there was much enthusiasm for an opposition between the Hebrew character of biblical thought, as opposed to Greek thought, which had corrupted the gospel. In that context, Florovsky is surely right. Once the Christian gospel became a missionary religion, appealing to the whole Mediterranean world, Christians used Greek, which is why the New Testament is in Greek: Christian Hellenism, it can be argued with Florovsky, is the original form of the worldwide Christian gospel.

What about, some say, other traditions: Christian Latin culture, Syriac culture, Armenian, Georgian, Coptic, Ethiopian? Christian Hellenism, it is claimed, represents a shrinking of the range and extent of the gospel. All languages, all cultures, contribute to the Pentecostal variety of the gospel. Florovsky never directly replied to these criticisms (indeed, I am not sure they were made very systematically during his lifetime), but he would, I think, have regarded these other traditions as stemming from Christian Hellenism (he regarded Augustine as a representative of Christian Hellenism – not such a weird idea as some people seem to think). Nevertheless, his ideal of Christian Hellenism is nowadays more likely to be regarded as a weakness than a strength.[11] (Incidentally, his preferred way of spelling his Christian name – Georges – was not so much because it is the French form of his name, as because it reminded him of the Greek form, Giorgios.)

Pseudomorphosis? Babylonian captivity?

It is perhaps worth spelling out a little more the argument of *Ways of Russian Theology*, before attempting to see what sense of the neo-patristic synthesis can be gleaned from his writings, occasional though most of them are.

---

[11] Criticisms of the sort outlined above are commonplace. The best attempt to think them through is found in an article by Paul Gavrilyuk: 'Harnack's Hellenized Christianity or Florovsky's "Sacred Hellenism": Questioning Two Metanarratives of Early Christian Engagement with Late Antique Culture', *SVTQ* 54 (2010), 323–44.

Both the terms – 'pseudomorphosis' and 'Babylonian captivity', the one borrowed from Spengler, the other from Luther – that Florovsky used to characterize the state of Russian theology refer to the influence of the West on Russian theology. He argues that Russian Christianity, because of the language barrier, drank only very meagrely from the wine of Christian Hellenism. Slavonic translation provided access to the Scriptures, the liturgy and the monastic office, and to some of the homiletic works of the Fathers, mostly Chrysostom, and mostly in a moralistic vein; this provided hardly any access to the theology of the Fathers, save for that provided by the (actually quite rich) theology of the liturgical texts. Icons were unaffected by this linguistic filter, and assumed a powerful role in Russian Christianity – something Florovsky recognized and related to his theme of Hellenism:

> The most powerful element in Russian ecclesiastical culture is the Russian icon, and this is so precisely because in iconography the Hellenic experience was spiritually assimilated and realized in a genuine creative intimacy by the Russian masters. Thus, in general, 'Hellenism' is more than merely a historical and transitional episode in the Church's life. When the 'Greek category' began to seem antiquated to the theologian, he only testified to his own departure from the rhythm of *sobornost'*. Theology can be catholic only in Hellenism.[12]

When the Russians encountered Latin theology, they had no resources of their own, so that, instead, Latin ideas took root in Russian soil, leading to 'pseudomorphosis' (a term originally botanical, which would fit well here, though Florovsky had in mind Spengler's mineralogical, or geological, use). Initially, what Florovsky has in mind is the period up to Peter Mogila, whose own theology was deeply indebted to Latin categories, and through whom such Latinized theology found institutional expression and influence through the Spiritual Academy he founded in Kiev. With the nineteenth century, things only got worse, with the Slavophils drinking deeply from the German Idealism of such as Hegel and Schelling, and Solov'ev and his circle drawing enthusiastically from the esoteric tradition in the West, with its roots in Boehme and Swedenborg, which was flourishing at the end of the century, with the likes of Madame Blavatsky. Sophiology is the misshapen child of this strange heritage.

This corrupt tradition, Florovsky believed, had to be uprooted and destroyed, and Russian theology had to return to its true Christian roots in the Christian Hellenism of the Fathers. It is curious how endemic anti-Westernism seems to be in Russian thought – as manifest in Florovsky, as in the Slavophils. 'Christian Hellenism' is very much a return to the pure source of Christianity in the East from the muddy waters of Western thought. It should perhaps be noted, too, that in recoiling against German Idealism, and its influence on

---

[12] Florovsky, *Ways* II, 297 (trans. slightly modified). At the very beginning of *Ways* Florovsky had described Russian iconography as 'speculation in colours' (*Puti*, 1; the English version mistranslates 'theology in colours': *Ways* I, 1) – a reference to Evgeny Trubetskoy's essay, 'Contemplation in Colours': see Eugène Troubetzkoï, *Trois études sur l'icône* (Paris: YMCA Press/OEIL, 1986).

Russian thought, Florovsky shows himself to be a man of his times, for it was in the period between the wars that philosophical movements, both on the continent and in the English-speaking world, began to turn their back on Idealism.

Florovsky and the neo-patristic synthesis

Although Florovsky never got round to writing any major work on the neo-patristic synthesis, it is, I shall argue, possible to discern the lineaments of his approach to theology by looking at the work that he published before and after the Second World War. Before the war, when he taught at the Institut St-Serge, he gave various courses of lectures on patristics. These were prepared for publication by the then Mrs Elizabeth Skobtsova (who later became a nun, Mother Maria, and died in Ravensbrück; she has since been glorified as St Maria) and published by Ilya Fondaminsky (who also died in a concentration camp and, too, has since been glorified). When they were republished, in 1972, Florovsky provided an Introduction in which he reflected on what he had been trying to achieve. There he says:

> When I began teaching at the Paris Institute, as Professor of Patrology, I had to face a preliminary methodological problem. The question of the scope and manner of Patristic studies had been vigorously debated by scholars for a long time. [He refers to J. de Ghellinck's discussion in *Patristique et Moyen Âge*, II, 1–180.] The prevailing tendency was to treat Patrology as a history of Ancient Christian Literature, and the best modern manuals of Patrology in the West were written precisely in this manner [he refers to the patrologies of Bardenhewer, Cayré, Tixeront and Quasten]. However, another cognate discipline came into existence during the last [i.e. the nineteenth] century, the *Dogmengeschichte*, or History of Doctrine school. Here scholars were concerned not so much with individual writers and thinkers, but rather with what can be defined as the 'internal dialectics' of the Christian Mind and with types and trends of Christian thought.
>
> In my opinion, these two approaches to the same material must be combined and correlated. Patrology must be more than a kind of literary history. It must be treated rather as a history of Christian Doctrine, although the Fathers were first of all *testes veritatis*, witnesses of faith. 'Theology' is wider and more comprehensive than 'Doctrine'. It is a kind of Christian Philosophy. Indeed, there is an obvious analogy between the study of Patristics and the study of the History of Philosophy. Historians of Philosophy are as primarily concerned with individual thinkers as they are interested ultimately in the dialectics of ideas. The 'essence' of Philosophy is exhibited in particular systems. Unity of the historical process is assured because of the identity of themes and problems to which both philosophers and theologians are committed. I would not claim originality for my method as it has been used occasionally by others. But I would underline the theological character of Patrology.[13]

---

[13] G. V. Florovsky, *Vostochnye Ottsy IV-go Veka* (reprint: Gregg International, 1972; original: Paris, 1931), Introduction to the reprint (unnumbered pages).

What is striking about what Florovsky says here is not its originality (which he rightly and modestly declines), but the clarity with which he expresses his understanding of the method of patristic studies as theology. J. N. D. Kelly's *Early Christian Doctrines* was first published in 1958, and follows something of the same method; the first volume of Jaroslav Pelikan's *The Christian Tradition: A History of the Development of Doctrine* was published in 1971, the year before Florovsky's words were published – Pelikan not only pursues much the same method, but is unusual in having made use of Florovsky's lectures, then still only available in Russian; even Bethune-Baker's *The Early History of Christian Doctrine* (published in 1903!) approaches the history of doctrine in much the spirit of Florovsky. Florovsky's training as a historian and philosopher is manifest in these methodological reflections. I think we can say that this was the method of the neo-patristic synthesis, as Florovsky conceived it. The fact that it is not purely Orthodox, but had been grasped by others, not least Anglicans, is no drawback.

Florovsky's presentation of patristic theology

These Paris lectures were published in four volumes; they are in many ways maddening, especially in that they have no references, despite the fact that Florovsky quotes the Fathers copiously.[14] The first concerns the Fathers of the fourth century, and is dominated by Athanasios and the Cappadocian Fathers, though there are brief discussions of several others, including Aphrahat and Ephrem the Syrian. The second is called *The Byzantine Fathers of the Fifth Century*, though the first 200 pages (of the English translation) provide background, covering the New Testament and the first three centuries; the rest of the volume is concerned with the Christological controversy and its culmination in the Council of Chalcedon. The third concerns the Byzantine Fathers from the sixth to the eighth century, with a long discussion of Monophysitism, before turning to Leontios of Byzantium, Maximos the Confessor and John Damascene. The fourth and final volume discusses the Byzantine ascetic and spiritual Fathers, with a long introductory section on asceticism in general, discussing the New Testament in connection with Anders Nygren's perceived rejection of asceticism (in his famous work, *Agape and Eros*), and further controversy over asceticism, in late antiquity and at the Reformation (Luther, Calvin), before turning to St Antony, St Pachomios, and the spread of monasticism in the fourth century, and then moving on to St Basil and St Gregory of Nyssa, the Macarian Homilies, Evagrios of Pontos, and various other ascetics treated more briefly, before closing with a discussion of the *Corpus Areopagiticum*.

---

[14] In the ET: *The Eastern Fathers of the Fourth Century, The Byzantine Fathers of the Fifth Century, The Byzantine Fathers of the Sixth to the Eighth Century, The Byzantine Ascetic and Spiritual Fathers*, translated by various hands, vols 7–10 of the Collected Works, ed. Richard S. Haugh (Vaduz: Büchervertriebsanstalt, 1987).

Simply to list the contents gives one some sense of Florovsky's understanding of patristics. It is Eastern, and for the most part Greek, though there is a nod towards the Syriac Fathers, and in his discussion of asceticism he makes reference to the Latin West. There is focus on individual thinkers. Florovsky has a clear sense of the main historical lines of Christian doctrine, but he is interested in the individual thinkers; for all his talk of the patristic *phronema*, he is well aware of differences between the Fathers, and seems to regard this diversity as richness, rather than a difficulty to be ironed out in the interests of a preconceived 'Orthodoxy'. Furthermore, his conception of patristics has a breadth that would have been unusual at the time he delivered the lectures: monasticism and asceticism are for him theological topics, not just phenomena belonging to church history. As we have seen above, the theologian is not simply concerned with an intellectual task of interpretation; his task involves asceticism and prayer.

Leading themes in his presentation of patristics

If we look more closely, we find some leading themes. There is, for instance, the theme of personhood. He asserts that '*[t]he classical world did not know the mystery of personal being*';[15] there is no word for person in the classical languages. One of the results of Christian theologians' reflecting on the mysteries of the Trinity and the Incarnation was a growing awareness of the mystery of personal being. This is a theme dear to the hearts of the thinkers of the Russian Religious Renaissance, whom Florovsky affected to despise: even he was not detached from his Russian roots in his return to the Fathers.

Another theme, to which we shall return, is the importance of the doctrine of creation out of nothing:

> Created from nothing, creation exists above the abyss of nothingness and is ready to fall back into it. The created world is generated and has an origin, and therefore its nature is 'fluctuating and subject to dissolution', since it has no support or foundation for existence within itself. True being belongs only to God, and God is first of all Being and Existence because he was not generated but is eternal. However, creation exists and at its origin it receives not only being but also stability and harmony. This is possible through participation in the Word, who is present in the world. Creation, illuminated by the dominion, works, and order of the Word, can attain stable being by 'participating in the Word, who truly exists from the Father'.[16]

Florovsky traces the way in which reflection on creation out of nothing underpins the emphasis on apophatic theology in Gregory the Theologian and Gregory of Nyssa.

Yet another theme, which runs through all the volumes, is the *nature* of the baptism of Hellenism that we find in the theology of the Church Fathers.

---

[15] Florovsky, *Eastern Fathers*, 32 (italics Florovsky's).
[16] Florovsky, *Eastern Fathers*, 43.

He pursues this especially in his treatment of the Cappadocian Fathers; associated with this theme is his distaste for Origen, in whose thought Hellenism remained largely unbaptized, he claimed, with the result that Origen's ideas are held responsible for heresy from Arianism to Iconoclasm.

Let us mention a final perception of Florovsky's in these lectures that seems to me of enduring significance. In his treatment of the Christological Definition upheld at the Council of Chalcedon, he makes much of its *asymmetry*: despite the rhetorical symmetry of the Definition – a rhetorical symmetry it shares with Leo's *Tome* – at the core of the Definition there lies an 'unspokenness' that discloses a fundamental asymmetry in the Incarnate Word, an asymmetry that Leo all but misses, for God and man are not equipollent in Christ; rather in Christ God has assumed human nature into his person, the sole person of Christ which is the person of God. Florovsky grasps this – something that has escaped many Western patristics scholars – because for him Chalcedon is not the end, but rather the centre of patristic reflection on Christ; he knows where the history of Christology is going, and does not cut short patristic meditation on Christ at Chalcedon.

The authority of the Fathers

Most of Fr Florovsky's writing took the form of articles, covering a wide range of topics.[17] I want to close by looking at a few topics covered in these articles. First, the question of authority, especially the authority of the Fathers, which is central to his understanding of the neo-patristic synthesis; second, his reflection on creation; third, his reflections on the task of the Christian historian; and finally, the centrality of Christ in his understanding of theology.

The question of authority in the Church was one to which Florovsky returned many times; the first volume of his collected works, *Bible, Church, Tradition: An Eastern Orthodox View*, gathers together several of his most significant articles on this subject. Because of the nature of what he hoped to promote in his neo-patristic synthesis, he has most to say about patristic authority. This was, however, secondary to the authority of the Scriptures and their reception in the tradition of the Church: it is as interpreters of the Scriptures that the Fathers possess what authority they have. He seeks to clarify what he means by the authority of the Fathers. First, appeal to the Fathers is not an appeal to antiquity, for, on the one hand, what is important is the vision of the Fathers, a vision we can share; patristic tradition cannot be reduced to a collection of abstract dogmas; while, on the other hand, the patristic period is not to be thought of as over and done with – it has not been succeeded, as in the Western conception of the history of theology, by scholasticism, for example. 'Our theological thinking has been dangerously affected by *the pattern of decay*,' Florovsky says, the result of an attempt to

---

[17] There is a list of Florovsky's publications (monographs, articles, compilations, book reviews, encyclopedia entries, forewords and introductions, sermons and homiletic writings) in *Georges Florovsky*, ed. Blane, 347–99.

restrict theology to a pristine period before the decay set in, whether the apostolic period, or that of the Seven Œcumenical Councils. He continues,

> it does not make much difference, whether we *restrict* the normative authority of the Church to one century, or to five, or to eight. *There should be no restriction at all.* Consequently, there is no room for any 'theology of repetition'. The Church is fully authoritative as she has been in the ages past, since the Spirit of Truth quickens her now no less effectively as in ancient times.[18]

Florovsky perhaps expressed his understanding of the authority of the Fathers most clearly in his Introduction to the original edition of his *Eastern Fathers of the Fourth Century* (not included in the English translation):

> This book was compiled from academic lectures. In the series of studies or chapters I strived to delineate and depict the images of the great teachers and Fathers of the Church. To us, they appear, first of all, as witnesses of the catholic faith, as custodians of universal tradition. But the patristic corpus of writings is not only an inviolable treasure-trove of tradition. For tradition is life; and the traditions are really being preserved only in their living reproduction and empathy [for them]. The Fathers give evidence concerning this in their own works. They show how the truths of the faith revive and transfigure the human spirit, how human thought is being renewed and revitalized in the experience of faith. They develop the truths of the faith into the integral and creative Christian worldview. In this respect, the patristic works are for us the source of creative inspiration, an example of Christian courage and wisdom. This is a school of Christian thought, of Christian philosophy. And first of all in my own lectures, I strived to enter into and to introduce [the reader/listener] into that creative world, into that eternal world of unaging experience and contemplation, in the world of unflickering light. I believe and I know that only in it and from it is revealed the straight and true way [*put'*] towards a new Christian synthesis, which the contemporary age longs for and thirsts after ...[19]

The Fathers of the fourth, fifth, seventh, fourteenth centuries have a special role in the witness of the Fathers, but that is because they have been received and reflected on in succeeding centuries; the age of the Fathers is not over. I am tempted to quote a remark of T. S. Eliot's, made in a rather different context: 'Someone said: "The dead writers are remote from us because we *know* so much more than they did". Precisely, and they are that which we know.'[20]

Doctrine of creation

A doctrine to which Florovsky returns repeatedly is the doctrine of creation out of nothing. He saw it as a perception fundamental to Christian Orthodoxy

---

[18] Georges Florovsky, *Bible, Church, Tradition: An Eastern Orthodox View* (Belmont, MA: Nordland, 1972), 111–12 (Florovsky's italics).

[19] Florovsky, *Vostochnye Ottsy*, 5; trans. Anastassy Brandon Gallaher, 'Georges Florovsky on Reading the Life of St Seraphim', *Sobornost* 27:1 (2005), 58–70, at 68, n. 34.

[20] T. S. Eliot, *Selected Essays* (London: Faber & Faber, 3rd edn, 1951), 16 (from the essay: 'Tradition and the Individual Talent').

as it took shape in the fourth and fifth centuries, and also as a perception that was threatened by muddle, as he saw it, that found expression in the preoccupation with Sophia, the Divine Wisdom, which seemed to straddle the clear distinction between the uncreated and the created. He often discusses the doctrine of creation out of nothing in connection with St Athanasios, for whom the doctrine was indeed fundamental in his opposition to Arianism, and in one of his later articles – a paper given at the Third International Patristics Conference in 1959, and published in 1962 – he professedly discusses the doctrine of creation out of nothing in relation to the Alexandrian saint. He finds the doctrine of creation *ex nihilo* in Athanasios at the beginning, even before the Arian controversy, in his work *On the Incarnation*. Here he finds Athanasios' vision of an 'ultimate and radical cleavage or *hiatus* between the absolute being of God and the contingent existence of the World':[21] the Being of God eternal and immutable, beyond death and corruption, while the created order is intrinsically mutable, marked by death, change and corruption. The whole Creation is only held in being at all by the Word of God, who binds it together and provides coherence. The Word of God, being truly God, is absolutely transcendent over the world, but it is present to and active in the world by its 'powers'. So Florovsky summarizes that,

> The world owes its very existence to God's sovereign will and goodness and stands, over the abyss of its own nothingness and impotence, solely by His quickening 'Grace' – as it were, *sola gratia*. But the Grace abides in the world.[22]

What is striking about this mature presentation by Florovsky of his thought on creation is his emphasis on the way in which it is through the Word that Creation comes into being and is sustained in being – the Word being present to and active in the created order by his powers: it is the Word, who became incarnate, who is at the centre of Athanasios' vision, as Florovsky expounds it.

Earlier on, Florovsky had discussed in much greater detail his understanding of creation in an article, 'Creation and Creaturehood', originally published in 1928, and included in English translation in volume 3 of his Collected Works: *Creation and Redemption*. Early on in the article, he notes that the notion of creation out of nothing was unknown, and indeed incomprehensible, to classical philosophy; it is a doctrine that grew out of reflection on the biblical witness to God and the world (even though the doctrine is hardly expressed explicitly in the Scriptures themselves). It means that the universe, the world, might not have existed: it is contingent, it is not self-sufficient. It is also radically new:

---

[21] G. Florovsky, 'St Athanasius' Concept of Creation', in *Aspects of Church History* (Belmont, MA: Norland, 1975), 39–62, 283–5 (notes); at 49.

[22] Florovsky, *Aspects*, 51.

In creation something *absolutely new*, an extra-divine *reality* is posited and built up. It is precisely in this that the supremely great and incomprehensible miracle of creation consists – that an 'other' springs up, that heterogeneous drops of creation exist side by side with 'the illimitable and infinite Ocean of being', as St Gregory of Nazianzus says of God.[23]

There is then an absolute contrast between the uncreated God and creation out of nothing. Florovsky illustrates this fundamental antinomy of creation in a vivid image from a sermon by St Philaret, the great Metropolitan of Moscow in the nineteenth century: 'the creative Word is like an adamantine bridge, upon which creatures stand balanced beneath the abyss of divine infinitude, and above that of their own nothingness'.[24]

This new thing, Creation, is manifested in creaturely freedom, which is more than simply the possibility of choice, but as it were enacts the fundamental choice faced by creatures, poised on Philaret's adamantine bridge, between the infinity of God and the infinity of nothingness. There is, as Florovsky puts it, the 'possibility of metaphysical suicide' – not self-annihilation, for Creation is God's gift and is indestructible. Creaturely freedom is but a reflection of the divine freedom with which the world was created, a divine freedom difficult to conceive, and easily compromised, as Florovsky maintains was the case with Origen, for whom God, as Pantokrator, needed the universe, *ta panta*, over which to rule. Not so, for the Fathers and Florovsky: God creates the world in radical freedom. In his later article, Florovsky quotes with approval a remark of Gilson's: 'it is quite true that a Creator is an eminently Christian God, but a God whose very existence it is to be a creator is not a Christian God at all'.[25] It is to God that the created order, through the human, who is a little cosmos, a microcosm, has to respond with its own freedom. It is through responding to God's presence in Creation in his energies that Creation moves towards its goal, which is deification, union with God. This is the meaning of creation, of history: 'The meaning of history consists in this – that the freedom of creation should respond by accepting the pre-temporal counsel of God, that it should respond both in word and deed'.[26]

Florovsky goes to great lengths in the article, drawing on his profound knowledge of the Greek patristic tradition, to grapple with how the temporal Creation is present to the mind of the eternal God. There is no time to explore this discussion here, but it seems to me that he is striving to express an understanding of that relationship that will compromise neither God's eternal freedom nor the temporal freedom of the creature nor their radical ontological distinctness. It is not difficult to see that Florovsky is trying to

---

[23] 'Creation and Creaturehood', in *Creation and Redemption* (Belmont, MA: Nordland, 1976), 43–78, 269–79 (notes); at 46.

[24] Cvyatitel' Filaret, Mitropolit Moskovsky, *Slova i Rechi* [Homilies and Speeches], ed. I.Yu. Smirnova et al., vol. 2, 1825–36 (Sergiev Posad: Cvyato-Troitskaya Sergieva Lavra, 2009), 277 (my trans.). Florovsky quotes it: *Creation and Redemption*, 45.

[25] Florovsky, *Aspects*, 41.

[26] Florovsky, *Creation and Redemption*, 77.

put forward an understanding of the engagement of God and the created order that responds to the concerns expressed by sophiology, without positing some realm, or being, in-between God and the world, which, for Florovsky, would compromise the radical ontological gulf that exists between the creature and the Creator. It is perhaps also worth remarking – though it should not appear, as it does here, as an aside – that the patristic sources that Florovsky uses are wide-ranging, and focused on Athanasios and the Cappadocians; it is this, I think, that anchors his theology in the mystery of Christ, rather than some philosophical concept – a topic we shall return to later.

The Christian historian

Florovsky was by training and inclination a historian (he was also trained in philosophy, but I do not have the impression that he was by inclination a philosopher). In his contribution to the Festschrift for the great liberal Protestant theologian Paul Tillich, published in 1959, he addressed the question of '[t]he Predicament of the Christian Historian'.[27] He argues that Christianity has indeed made a difference to the study of history since, before the rise of Christianity, classical culture considered history either subject to fate or utterly random; either human freedom was denied, or history rendered null – either way any sense of a meaning in history to which human beings contributed was rendered nugatory. Having affirmed that, he is very cautious about how the profession of Christianity affects the pursuit of history by the historian. The idea of a 'Christian interpretation' he shies away from; rather he sees the role of Christian faith in the historian's profession as more to do with the sense the Christian is bound to have that history is about the free activity of human beings. So, as he asserts in his concluding paragraph,

> The Christian historian pursues his professional task of interpreting human life in the light of his Christian vision of that life, sorely distorted by sin, yet redeemed by Divine mercy, and healed by Divine grace ... The Christian historian will, first of all, vindicate 'the dignity of man', even of fallen man ...

As to the meaning of history, Florovsky is wary of too readily detecting any providential structure:

> Even in the history of the Church 'the hand of Providence' is emphatically hidden, though it would be blasphemous to deny that this Hand does exist or that God is truly the Lord of History. Actually, the purpose of a historical understanding is not so much to detect the Divine action in history as to understand the human action, that is, human activities, in the bewildering variety and confusion in which they appear to a human observer. Above all, *the Christian historian will regard history at once as a mystery and as a tragedy – a mystery of salvation and a tragedy of sin.*[28]

---

[27] Reprinted in Georges Florovsky, *Christianity and Culture* (Belmont, MA: Nordland, 1974), 31–65, 233–6 (notes).

[28] Florovsky, *Christianity and Culture*, 64–5 (Florovsky's italics).

This seems to me to bear the marks of his approach to the neo-patristic synthesis, at once scholarly, and marked by a respect for personhood, and awe before the mystery of God.

The centrality of Christ

Florovsky's theology in general, and his pursuit of the neo-patristic synthesis in particular, is deeply Christocentric. In a letter to his friend Dobbie Bateman, apropos Bateman's study of St Seraphim of Sarov, Florovsky remarked:

> The Spirit is the Spirit of Christ, and is sent by Christ from the Father in order to remind the Disciples, those of Christ, or Christians, of Him. *Pneumatic* should not be played against *Christological*. I am coming to see it with increasing clarity. The Spirit, and His gifts, the *charismata*, can be 'acquired' only in the name of Christ. And, in the order of Salvation, there is no higher Name. One addresses the Father in the Name of Christ, the Incarnate Son. The Pentecost is the mystery of the Crucified Lord, who rose again to send the Paraclete. Thus, Cross, Resurrection, Pentecost belong together as aspects of one mystery, distinct in the dimension of time, but integrated in the one Divine deed of Redemption.[29]

He goes on to refer to the Foreword he wrote for the first English edition of Fr Sophrony's work on St Silouan, *The Undistorted Image*. There he had said:

> Grace is given only to the humble and meek. Moreover, humility itself is never a human achievement. It is always the gift of God, granted freely, *gratia gratis data*. The whole structure of spiritual life is indeed paradoxical. The riches of the Kingdom are given only to the poor. And with the riches authority is also given. The humble do not say anything of their own. Yet, they speak with authority, whenever they are moved to speak at all . . .[30]

Christ stands at the centre of Florovsky's understanding of theology, and theological authority; the human exercise of that authority is only possible owing to the presence of the Spirit of Christ, whether exercised by synods, bishops, or the radical authority of those who have emptied themselves in humility and become vessels of the Spirit. Once one sees this, then I think we can detect a thread running through Florovsky's understanding of the neo-patristic synthesis. So far as we humans are concerned, it is first of all an ascetic path, a way in which we enter more and more deeply into the mystery of Christ. It seems to me particularly striking that Florovsky's use of the distinction between essence and energies, characteristic of most modern Orthodox theology, is fundamentally Christological, rather than philosophical, as it is often presented. It is the Word, made flesh as Christ, who is the one

---

[29] Florovsky, 'Georges Florovsky on Reading the Life of St Seraphim', 61.
[30] Archimandrite Sofrony [Sophrony], *The Undistorted Image: Staretz Silouan 1866–1938* (London: Faith Press, 1958), 5.

who created the world and is present to it by his activities or powers. I think it could be argued that it was the danger of edging Christ to one side and finding some other figure or – worse – notion to be the centre of our theological endeavour that was what Florovsky was always most afraid of. His fears may have been unjustified in particular cases, but the neo-patristic synthesis was intended to refocus theology on the mystery of Christ, crucified and risen.

7

Apophatic theology and deification:
Myrrha Lot–Borodine and Vladimir Lossky

After thinking about Fr Georges Florovsky and the neo-patristic synthesis, it seems natural to turn to Myrrha Lot-Borodine and Vladimir Lossky,[1] for in both these thinkers we can find some sense of what might be meant by the 'neo-patristic synthesis' that Florovsky was convinced must be the true way of Orthodox theology. This may seem obvious in the case of Lossky, since, for many of us in the West, myself included, it was his little book, published in 1944 with the title *Essai sur la théologie mystique de l'Église d'Orient*,[2] known in English as *The Mystical Theology of the Eastern Church*,[3] that opened up the theological tradition of the Orthodox Church, a tradition based on the Fathers of the Church. It is manifestly an exercise in the 'neo-patristic synthesis', whether Lossky himself thought in these terms or not. However, by that date, Myrrha Lot-Borodine had published several series of influential articles that, as we know from the testimony of the great Jesuit patristic scholar, Jean (later Cardinal) Daniélou, had had a decisive role in opening up to that astonishing young generation of Catholic scholars the world of the Fathers as more than a branch of learned study, but a vital source of spiritual and theological insight. Daniélou wrote (in his Introduction to the posthumous publication of a book of her articles on deification in the Greek patristic tradition):

> What was exceptional in the work of Myrrha Lot-Borodine was not simply her learned research, but the way she gave vivid expression to the mystical heart of the Byzantine tradition. Her work was nourished by her reading of the great Greek and Byzantine spiritual writers and theologians. One found here the echo of the Gregories and of Evagrios, of Maximos the Confessor and Pseudo-Denys, of Symeon the New Theologian and Nicholas Cabasilas. She mentioned these authors frequently, but not by means of citation. Her articles have a minimum of the apparatus of erudition. That makes them difficult to use. The boundaries between the experience of the author and that of her sources are difficult to trace.

---

[1] Published after I had written this is an important study of Lot-Borodine and Lossky by Michel Stavrou: Michel Stavrou, 'La Démarche néopatristique de Myrrha Lot-Borodine et de Vladimir Lossky', in *Les Pères de l'Église aux sources de l'Europe*, ed. Dominique Gonnet and Michel Stavrou (Paris: Cerf, 2014), 200–25.

[2] Paris: Aubier, 1944; republished with an Introduction by Saulias Rumšas OP (Paris: Cerf, 2005) (with the same pagination as the original).

[3] London: James Clarke, 1957.

But what she gave us is more precious than a work of erudition ... It is a certain experience that is discerned and described.[4]

Who were these two Russians: Myrrha Lot-Borodine and Vladimir Lossky? As we shall see, there were many parallels in their lives and interests. Let us start with Myrrha Lot-Borodine, who was the elder of the two.

Myrrha Lot-Borodine: Life

Myrrha Lot-Borodine was born in St Petersburg in 1882.[5] She attended there the Prince Obolensky University for Women, and in 1906 went to Paris for further study. There she attended the courses in medieval literature given by Joseph Bédier at the Collège de France, and in 1909 was awarded the degree of 'Docteur de l'Université' for a thesis on 'Woman in the Work of Chrétien de Troyes'. In the same year she married the by then distinguished medieval historian and professor at the École des Hautes-Études, Ferdinand Lot. She continued her research on the courtly literature of the Middle Ages, publishing several works in the course of the next few decades on Chrétien and the Grail legend, not least the lay Cistercian adaptation of it in *La Queste del saint-Graal* (some of these works are still in print; her doctoral thesis, *La Femme dans l'œuvre de Chrétien de Troyes* (1909) was reprinted as recently as 2011).

Alongside this life of professional academic scholarship, she became part of the Russian émigré community in Paris, which had expanded dramatically after the expulsion of the intellectuals from Soviet Russia with Trotsky's decree of 1922. She became an active member of the Berdyaev Colloquy, which we have met already. It was in these circles that her interest in the theology of the East was inspired, when she heard a paper by Fr Florovsky on deification.[6] In the thirties she wrote several series of articles, the most

---

[4] From Daniélou's Introduction to Myrrha Lot-Borodine, *La Déification de l'homme selon la doctrine des Pères grecs* (Paris: Cerf, 1970), 11.

[5] I have been much stimulated by Heleen Zorgdrager's article, 'A Practice of Love: Myrrha Lot-Borodine (1882–1954) and the Modern Revival of the Doctrine of Deification', *JECS* 64 (2012), 285–305. Zorgdrager has an account of her life based on the article by Lot-Borodine's daughter, Marianne Mahn-Lot, 'Ma mère, Myrrha Lot-Borodine (1882–1954): Esquisse d'itinéraire spirituel', *RSPT* (2004), 745–54. The obituary in *Irén.* 30 (1957), 340–5, is reprinted in Myrrha Lot-Borodine, *Un maître de la spiritualité byzantine au XIVe siècle: Nicolas Cabasilas* (Paris: Éditions de l'Orante, 1958), ix–xiii.

[6] During her early years in France, her interest in, and practice of, religion had ceased. According to her daughter (Mahn-Lot, 'Ma mère, Myrrha Lot-Borodine', 748), her interest in religion revived from about 1920, and her route back to Orthodoxy involved some kind of encounter with Catholics. Her interest in the theology of the East was, by Lot-Borodine's own account (quoted by her daughter), inspired by the paper by Florovsky. Arjakovsky (repeated by Gavrilyuk, *Florovsky*, 197, 232, n. 2) states that she 'était devenu (*sic*) orthodoxe en 1934' under the influence of Florovsky (*La Génération*, 483). This seems to be a misunderstanding; by the time she participated in the Berdyaev Colloquy she had rediscovered her native faith, or was well on the way to doing so; what Florovsky did was inspire an interest in the *theology* of the East in a learned medievalist. By 1934, this interest had already borne fruit in the articles on deification (published 1932–3).

notable being a series of articles on the Greek patristic doctrine of deification, published after her death in the volume I have already referred to.[7] There were, however, two other series of articles that should be mentioned: a translation of St Maximos the Confessor's *Mystagogia* with an Introduction,[8] and a series of studies of Nicolas Cabasilas, which she gathered together and prepared as a book, published just after her death, as *Un maître de la spiritualité byzantine au XIVe siècle: Nicolas Cabasilas* (Paris, 1958).[9] There were other articles, too, notably a long article on the gift of tears in the Christian Orient (as Heleen Zorgdrager notes, Lot-Borodine never seems to refer to Orthodoxy, but speaks of Greece and the Orient).[10] Initially Lot-Borodine was wary of the ecumenical movement, afraid of dilution or distortion of the Orthodoxy of the Greek or Slav East. However, through the Fellowship of St Alban and St Sergius, she encountered friendly Anglicans and her ecumenical leanings became warmer, as her participation in journals such as *Irénikon* and *Dieu Vivant* makes clear. She died in 1957.[11] Although in the last years of her life, to judge from her publications, she seemed to be preoccupied mostly with Nicolas Cabasilas, there was published posthumously in 1961 her study of courtly love, *De l'Amour profane à l'amour sacré: Études de psychologie sentimentale au Moyen Âge*, with a Preface by Étienne Gilson. The final monument to her scholarship was, then, her first love.[12]

Vladimir Lossky: Life

Vladimir Lossky was brought up in St Petersburg, though he was born in 1903 in Göttingen, where his father, the philosopher Nicolas Lossky, was staying with his family for academic reasons.[13] He studied in St Petersburg from 1920 to 1922, by then called Petrograd. Vladimir's interest in the Western Middle Ages had already been awakened. Despite the Revolution, like his father he refused to emigrate, but at the end of 1922 the family was exiled from Russia, early victims of Trotsky's decree, and went to Prague, where

---

[7] The articles were published in 1932 and 1933 in *RHR*. In the published volume, further articles were added: 'La Doctrine de la grâce et de la liberté dans l'orthodoxie gréco-orientale', from *Œcumenica* 9 (1939), and 'La Béatitude dans l'Orient chrétien' from *Dieu Vivant* 15 (1950).

[8] *Irén.* 13–15 (1936–8).

[9] Paris: Éditions de l'Orante, 1958. Various articles on Cabasilas appeared in *RSPT* (1935–7), *Irén.* 13 (1936), 26 (1953), *Dieu Vivant* 24 (1953); the relationship between these and the book is not clear.

[10] *La Vie spirituelle*, suppl. (1936), 65–110; reprinted in O. Clément et al., *La Douloureuse Joie*, Spiritualité Orientale 14 (Bégrolles-en-Mauge: Abbaye de Bellefontaine, 1981), 133–95.

[11] Although the article by her daughter gives the date of her death as 1954, this must be a printer's error; there is ample confirmation that she died in 1957.

[12] Myrrha Lot-Borodine, *De l'Amour profane à l'amour sacré: Études de psychologie sentimentale au Moyen Âge* (Paris: Nizet, 1961). Although half of the chapters (four out of eight) are reprints of articles published in the 1920s, the publication of the whole testifies to her continued interest in medieval courtly love.

[13] This biographical account is drawn from the 'notice biographique' in Olivier Clément, *Orient–Occident: Deux passeurs: Vladimir Lossky et Paul Evdokimov* (Geneva: Labor et Fides, 1985), 94–9.

he studied for two years with the expert on archaeology and Byzantine art N. P. Kondakov. In 1924 he arrived in Paris and enrolled at the Sorbonne, where he studied with Ferdinand Lot, Myrrha's husband, and Étienne Gilson, the great historian of medieval philosophy and neo-Thomist, whose courses he was to follow for many years. Very soon, together with Evgraf Kovalevsky, he founded the 'Confrérie de saint Photius', which was to witness in the West, and more precisely in France, to a resolutely universal Orthodoxy, capable of reviving in France the authentic traditions of French Christianity. Round about the same time, he began his long work on Meister Eckhart. In 1928, on the Day of the Holy Spirit (the day of his birth in the church calendar), he married Madeleine Schapiro; they were to have four children. In the following years, Lossky's studies on Meister Eckhart led him to further studies of Aquinas and Dionysios the Areopagite.

In 1931, when Metropolitan Evlogy left the Moscow Patriarchate and led his exarchate under the jurisdiction of the Œcumenical Patriarchate, Lossky refused to follow and became part of the small group of Russian Christians in Paris faithful to Moscow. In 1935–6, Lossky became involved in the sophiological controversy over the works and thought of Fr Sergii Bulgakov. It was his assessment of Bulgakov's sophiology that led to the condemnation

Vladimir Lossky
Copyright © revue *Contacts*

of Bulgakov by the Moscow Patriarchate.[14] His opposition to Bulgakov was theological, not personal. When Bulgakov died in 1944, he walked many miles to be present at his funeral. In 1939, Lossky became a French citizen, and on the outbreak of war he tried to join the French army, but was rejected on account of a heart condition. When the Germans invaded France, he followed on foot the French army in retreat as far as Orléans in an attempt to play his part in the defence of France. The diary he kept during those days was published 40 years after his death as *Sept Jours sur les routes de France*;[15] it bears eloquent testimony to his sense of French belonging. During the war Lossky was engaged in the French Resistance; owing to his wife Madeleine's Jewish origins, the family had to hide. It was also during the war that Lossky gave a course of lectures that was published as *Essai sur la théologie mystique de l'Église d'Orient*.

In 1945, there was founded the Institut Saint-Denis, where Orthodox theology was taught in French (unlike the Institut St-Serge, where the language of instruction was Russian); Lossky was the dean of the institute, teaching dogmatic theology and church history. In the same year he was involved in the establishment of the ecumenical journal *Dieu Vivant*, to which he contributed several articles. Also in the same year, Lossky became attached to the Centre National de la Recherche Scientifique (CNRS), under the auspices of which he continued his research on Eckhart. In the next year, he gave a course at the École des Hautes-Études, which was published after his death as *Vision de Dieu*.[16] For the next decade, Lossky was involved in academic and ecumenical matters, attending the first Oxford Patristics Conference in 1951, and participating in the conferences of the Fellowship of St Alban and St Sergius. In 1952, together with Leonid Ouspensky, he published the influential book *Der Sinn der Ikonen* ('The Meaning of Icons').[17] In 1956, at the invitation of the Moscow Patriarchate, he visited Russia. He died, quickly and simply, of a heart attack on 7 February 1958. Two years later, the great work that he had been preparing for the *doctorat d'état* was published as *Théologie négative et connaissance de Dieu chez Maître Eckhart*, edited by the great medieval scholar and friend of Lossky's, Maurice de Gandillac, assisted by Olivier Clément, with a Preface by Étienne Gilson, who had supervised the progress of the work over many years.[18]

Lot-Borodine and Lossky: parallels and contrasts

There are striking parallels between these two Russians, Myrrha Lot-Borodine and Vladimir Lossky. Both from St Petersburg, both in love with France and

---

[14] Vladimir Lossky, *Spor o Sofii: Statii Raznyx Let* [Controversy over Sophia: Articles from Various Years] (Moscow: Izdatel'stvo Svyato-Vladimirskogo Bratstva, 1996), 7–79.

[15] Paris: Cerf, 1998; ET, Crestwood, NY: St Vladimir's Seminary Press, 2012.

[16] Neuchâtel: Delachaux et Niestlé, 1962; ET, London: Faith Press, 1963.

[17] Bern–Olten: Urs Graf-Verlag, 1952; ET: *The Meaning of Icons* (Boston, MA: Boston Book and Art Shop, 1969).

[18] Vladimir Lossky, *Théologie negative et connaissance de Dieu chez Maître Eckhart* (Paris: Vrin, 1960).

French culture, especially medieval French culture, both with what one might think of as a secular academic career – as medievalists, working on courtly love and the Grail legend in Lot-Borodine's case, on Meister Eckhart in Lossky's case – but both of them distinguished exponents of Greek patristic thought, scholars of great erudition, certainly, but possessing something more valuable – a sense of speaking from within the Orthodox tradition to which they belonged. They were also active participants in the ecumenical Fellowship of St Alban and St Sergius, both standing for an uncompromising Orthodoxy, yet keen to communicate Orthodoxy in a Western context. How far Lot-Borodine shared Lossky's conviction that the Russian emigration was providential, helping Orthodoxy to realize its universal dimension and find a presence in the West, I do not know. They died within a year of each other; both had an *opus postumum* published, again within a year of each other, and both with a Preface by Étienne Gilson.

It also seems – it is certainly commonly said in the case of Lossky, and Lot-Borodine herself talks of the 'deux domaines' of her work[19] – that their two academic tracks were indeed parallel lines that never meet. In fact, I am not sure that is true, though it is certainly the case that there is not much marked engagement. There are a few links between Lossky's book on Eckhart and his theological work, for instance when he notes how the Western interpretation of Plato's 'region of unlikeness' puts this unlikeness down to the fundamental gulf that exists between Creator and creature, whereas the East would relate the unlikeness to the way in which the affinity between human beings and God, implicit in being created in the image of God, has been compromised by unlikeness as a result of the fall.[20] In the case of Lot-Borodine, there is at least one issue where she speaks both as theologian and as medievalist: in an article published in 1951 she criticized Gilson's attempt to identify the Grail in *La Queste del saint-Graal* with the scholastic notion of created grace.[21] She argued that the background of the Grail legend was to be sought in the common monastic heritage of both East and West, rather than in scholasticism, where Gilson sought to locate it, and that the Grail designates the presence of Christ, not some created effect. Furthermore, as Heleen Zorgdrager has argued, there is a very evident thread running through both Lot-Borodine's academic interests, summed up in the title of her posthumous work: 'from profane love to sacred love'.

There are, however, contrasts between Lossky and Lot-Borodine. They took different sides over the ecclesiastical divide in the Russian diaspora, Lossky remaining faithful to Moscow, whereas Lot-Borodine attached herself to Metropolitan Evlogy and his exarchate. Furthermore, although as theologians

---

[19] From papers quoted by her daughter in Mahn-Lot, 'Ma mère, Myrrha Lot-Borodine', 747.

[20] See Lossky, *Théologie négative*, 175–6, though Lossky does not make it explicit that 'la plume du théologien chrétien' is that of one belonging to the Greek patristic tradition.

[21] Myrrha Lot-Borodine, 'Les Grands Secrets du Saint-Graal dans la Queste du pseudo-Map', in *Lumière du Graal*, ed. R. Nelli (Paris: Cahiers de Sud, 1951), 151–74, criticizing an article by Étienne Gilson, 'La Mystique de la grâce dans «la Queste del saint-Graal»', originally published in *Romania* 51 (1925), 321–47, and reprinted in Étienne Gilson, *Les Idées et les lettres* (Paris: Vrin, 1932).

they are both indebted to the Greek Fathers, the Fathers they appeal to are rather different. Lossky turns to the Fathers most celebrated in the Orthodox tradition – Athanasios and Cyril of Alexandria, and the Cappadocian Fathers (Basil the Great, Gregory the Theologian, Gregory of Nyssa), Maximos the Confessor and Gregory Palamas; Lot-Borodine, although attached to Palamas and his distinction between the uncreated divine essence and energies, presents rather a different patristic palette: Clement and Origen of Alexandria, Gregory of Nyssa, and the ascetical and mystical Fathers of the fourth and later centuries, including Maximos the Confessor. They both share an enthusiasm for Dionysios the Areopagite and Symeon the New Theologian. Lossky, indeed, fits much more easily into the 'neo-patristic synthesis', as Florovsky conceived it. In contrast, Lot-Borodine seems to be a much more independent spirit, though heresy held no attractions for her, and her attitude to the figures of the Russian Religious Renaissance seems to have been guarded.[22]

Lossky: 'mystical theology'

The very title of Lossky's most famous work, *The Mystical Theology of the Eastern Church*, makes one wonder about engagement between his two academic interests, for notions of the 'mystical' are clearly central to any study of Eckhart. Indeed the first pages of both books have clearly overlapping concerns. This might be a place to start considering Lossky's ideas and achievement. Lossky begins his enormous work on Eckhart by considering what meaning the 'apophatic' has for 'the Dominican from Thuringia', 'le dominicain thuringien' (as he frequently calls him). This depends, he says, on the different ways in which God can be understood to be ineffable, beyond thought or language. The discussion invokes Augustine, Plotinos, Dionysios the Areopagite, Thomas Aquinas, and reaches a point where he compares Aquinas, many of whose metaphysical principles Eckhart shares, with Eckhart himself. For Thomas, God is unknowable, unnameable, because

> a created intellect, whether angelic or human, can only know by its natural powers the *esse* determined by an essence . . . But the pure act of existing, 'whose very essence is to exist', the *puritas essendi*, the *ipsum esse subsistens*, not being distinct from but identical with its essence, remains indeterminable and cannot be named from what He is. That is why the name which is best fitted to designate God is *Qui est* [He who is]: it names, without determining, That which is its own existence . . . Separated from all beings whose act of existing is determined by an essence which distinguishes it, God then remains ineffable so far as his own existence is concerned. That is the reason why saint Thomas . . . has transformed the 'unnameable' of Denys into *Esse innominabile* [unnameable Being].[23]

---

22 In contrast to what Zorgdrager asserts (Zorgdrager, 'A Practice of Love', 289, basing herself on what I fear is a misunderstanding of something quoted by Mahn-Lot, 'Ma mère, Myrrha Lot-Borodine', 748). Lot-Borodine says that all heresy inspired in her an 'instinctive mistrust', and the whiff of Gnosticism she detects in Solov'ev and Bulgakov does not seem to be something she shares.

23 Lossky, *Théologie negative*, 25.

But for Eckhart God is *Deus absconditus*, the God who hides himself (Isa. 45.15), *Esse absconditum*, Being that hides itself: hiding itself in the inner recesses of the mind or heart, for as Augustine affirmed, addressing God in his *Confessions*: *tu autem eras interior intimo meo et superior summo meo* [you were more inward than my innermost self and higher than my highest] (*Conf.* III. 6.11). With a movement of thought characteristic of the Western Middle Ages, Dionysios is read with Augustinian eyes, so that Eckhart 'enters into himself to search for the *Esse absconditum* in the innermost depths of the soul': 'Is not this [Lossky asks] to try to transform into the mystical [transformer en mystique] the natural theology of Saint Thomas?'[24] Lossky concludes:

> When he searches for the God-*Esse* of Saint Thomas in the *abditum mentis* [hidden place of the mind] of Saint Augustine, Eckhart draws on the two theologians, uniting them on a mystical level [sur le plan d'une mystique] which he is able to express in terms of a speculative theology.[25]

We are not concerned here with Eckhart, but this brief exposition shows that Lossky has a clear sense of what is meant by *la mystique*, the mystical (which is usually translated into English as 'mysticism', a term that has I think the wrong overtones here). The mystical Lossky takes to be the inward, something beyond conceptualization, grasped by experience. Eckhart's speculative theology is presented by Lossky as a kind of conceptual transcript of this inward experience, *la mystique*. This is important, for the title of the only book he published in his lifetime is *The Mystical Theology of the Eastern Church*: what did he mean by that? In his Introduction he has a few pages in which he discusses 'the mystical':

> The eastern tradition has never made a sharp distinction between the mystical and theology; between personal experience of the divine mysteries and the dogma affirmed by the Church ... To put it another way, we must live the dogma expressing a revealed truth, which appears to us as an unfathomable mystery, in such a fashion that instead of assimilating the mystery to our mode of understanding, we should, on the contrary, look for a profound change, an inner transformation of the spirit, enabling us to experience it mystically ... For the Christian, therefore, the mystical cannot exist without theology, but, above all, there is no theology without the mystical ... The mystical is accordingly treated in the present work as the perfecting and crown of all theology: as theology *par excellence*.[26]

The mystical and theology relate as experience and theory, but experience of what? Ultimately of God, but that is not where Lossky begins: he begins by speaking of 'personal experience of the divine mysteries', the term 'mysteries' being, not exactly ambiguous, but with at least two connotations – meaning

---

[24] Lossky, *Théologie negative*, 30–1.
[25] Lossky, *Théologie negative*, 32.
[26] Vladimir Lossky, *The Mystical Theology of the Eastern Church* (London: James Clarke, 1957), 8–9. I have modified the translation since 'la mystique' in the original French is rendered in English as 'mysticism', not perhaps quite the same thing.

both the sacraments of the Church, and also mysterious truths about the Godhead. That double meaning is no chance homonymity; the two meanings seem to me to be closely related for Lossky and the Orthodox Church, because the mysterious truths about God – his existence as a Trinity of love, his creation of the world, his care for the world and his redemption of it, pre-eminently in the Incarnation – are truths that we experience and celebrate in the Divine Mysteries, or the sacraments, of the Church. The sacramental aspect remains largely implicit in Lossky's book, and we can see why, I think, from the understanding of the mystical we find in his treatise on Eckhart: for there the mystical is a matter of union with God in the depths of the soul. It is an experience, not necessarily experience*s* of a strange and unusual kind, but an experience involving, as he puts it in the quotation just given, 'a profound change, an inner transformation of the spirit'. It is, too, an experience that is apophatic, ineffable, in ways that we have yet to explore. Lossky goes on to show how this experience lies at the heart of the dogmas expounded and defended by the Church:

> The main preoccupation, the issue at stake, in the questions which succes-sively arise respecting the Holy Spirit, grace and the Church herself . . . is always the possibility, the manner, or the means of our union with God. All the history of Christian dogma unfolds itself about this mystical centre, guarded by different weapons against its many and diverse assailants in the course of successive ages.[27]

This relates the mystical to the emergence of dogmas in the history of the Church: dogmas are concerned to safeguard 'the possibility, the manner, or the means of our union with God'. Later on, Lossky will say that,

> [i]n the Church and through the sacraments our nature enters into union with the divine nature in the hypostasis of the Son, the Head of the mystical body. Our humanity becomes consubstantial with the deified humanity, united with the Person of Christ . . .[28]

The mysteries, in both senses of the term, are concerned with an experienced union with God in Christ, mediated by the sacraments, or mysteries, and felt in the heart. Note, however, that this experienced union is founded on '[o]ur humanity becom[ing] consubstantial with the deified humanity . . . of Christ': it is not experience that gives a conviction of reality, but experience of a – dogmatically defined – union, in this case expressed by the assertion found in the Chalcedonian Definition that Christ is *homoousios hēmin*, con-substantial with us, just as he is *homoousios toi patri*, consubstantial with the Father. It is this that gives Lossky's presentation such a different orientation from what is normally associated with mysticism in the West: it is not detached from dogma, but founded on the dogmatic truths of the Christian tradition; it is not indifferent to Church organization, hierarchy and sacraments, but

---

27 Lossky, *Mystical Theology*, 10.
28 Lossky, *Mystical Theology*, 181.

rooted in the structured life of the Church; it is not individualistic, but grows out of the experience of the eucharistic community.

... and the 'apophatic'

The mystical, for Lossky, is bound up with the apophatic. The second chapter of his *Mystical Theology* is entitled 'The Divine Darkness': the darkness Moses entered as he climbed Mount Sinai to receive God's revelation – a darkness, the meaning of which was explored by the Fathers of the Church: Clement of Alexandria, the two Gregories, and epitomized by Dionysios the Areopagite in his short treatise, *The Mystical Theology*. In the darkness, we can no longer see; what is revealed is beyond conceptual understanding – it can only be felt, it is a presence. Lossky introduces Dionysios' distinction between kataphatic and apophatic theology: the theology of affirmation and the theology of denial. He is insistent (both in *The Mystical Theology* and in his book on Eckhart) that these theologies are not to be understood as equal (as he argues they are understood in the West), as if affirmative theology is simply to be corrected by negative theology – a kind of tacking, as in sailing, to keep one's thought about God on course; rather, apophatic theology is more fundamental: it does not so much correct affirmative theology as actually undergird it, for the deepest truth is that God is ineffable, beyond name and concept. Lossky comments:

> Indeed, not only does he [the theologian, the one who seeks God] go forth from his own self ... but he belongs wholly to the Unknowable, being deified in this union with the uncreated. Here union means deification. At the same time, while intimately united with God he knows Him only as Unknowable, in other words as infinitely set apart by His nature, remaining even in union, inaccessible in that which He is in His essential being.[29]

Lossky raises the question as to whether in speaking of union thus we are envisaging an ecstatic experience, and responds:

> Apophaticism is not necessarily a theology of ecstasy. It is, above all, an attitude of mind which refuses to form concepts about God. Such an attitude utterly excludes all abstract and purely intellectual theology which would adapt the mysteries of the wisdom of God to human ways of thought. It is an existential attitude which involves the whole man: there is no theology apart from experience; it is necessary to change, to become a new man. To know God one must draw near to Him. No one who does not follow the path of union with God can be a theologian ... Apophaticism is, therefore, a criterion: the sure sign of an attitude of mind conformed to truth. In this sense all true theology is fundamentally apophatic.[30]

This apophatic approach has manifold implications for the pursuit of theology. An apophatic theology is tentative:

---

[29] Lossky, *Mystical Theology*, 38.
[30] Lossky, *Mystical Theology*, 38–9.

Any theological doctrine which pretends to be a perfect explanation of the revealed mystery will inevitably appear to be false: by the very fact of pretending to the fulness of knowledge it will set itself in opposition to the fulness in which the Truth is known in part.[31]

This does not at all mean that Lossky sits light to dogma: dogmas are important, but not as the building blocks of some comprehensive account of the Divine Mysteries, but rather as a series of decisions, arrived at by the Church, that are there to prevent ways of thinking that might obscure or bypass the mystery of God before which we stand in awe. One might say that it is impossible to understand God and his ways; nevertheless it is very easy to misunderstand God and his ways, and the dogmas are there to help prevent such misunderstanding. As Olivier Clément put it, summarizing the lectures he heard Lossky give in the 1950s:

> The whole purpose of the Church, in defining [dogma], is to preserve the possibility, for each Christian, of participating with all his being in the whole of revelation, that is to say, of sharing in the very life of Him who reveals himself. That is why, said Vladimir Lossky, Orthodoxy refuses to multiply dogmatic definitions. The definition, when it can no longer be avoided, is there to correspond to a precise, practical necessity, is there as evidence to bar the route to erroneous interpretations.[32]

In interpreting and exploring the meaning of dogma this sense of reserve remains. Lossky cites a remark of St Ignatios of Antioch: 'He who possesses the word of Jesus can even hear his silence'.[33] Lossky comments: 'The words of Revelation have then a margin of silence which cannot be picked up by the ears of those who are outside'.[34] There is a margin of silence that surrounds any manifestation of mystery. One is reminded of a remark of Mallarmé's: 'Toute chose sacrée et qui veut demeurer sacrée s'enveloppe de mystère.'[35] If we are to understand what is revealed, we need to be attuned to the margin of silence that surrounds it. That margin of silence is only discerned in prayer. The kind of dogmatic attitude, if we can call it that, which is necessary if we are to engage with the mysteries of the Church, the mystery of God, is, in many ways, a quite 'undogmatic' attitude, using the word in its commonly accepted sense. It reminds me very much of what the English poet Keats called 'negative capability': 'that is, when a man is capable of being in uncertainties, mysteries, doubts, without any irritable reaching after fact and reason'.[36]

---

[31] Vladimir Lossky, 'Tradition and Traditions', in *In the Image and Likeness of God*, ed. John H. Erickson and Thomas E. Bird (Crestwood, NY: St Vladimir's Seminary Press, 1974), 161–2.

[32] Clément, *Orient–Occident*, 25.

[33] Ign. *Eph.* 15. 2.

[34] Lossky, 'Tradition and Traditions', 150–1.

[35] [Everything sacred that wants to remain sacred wraps itself in mystery] Quoted by Anthony Hartley in his Introduction to *Mallarmé* (Harmondsworth: The Penguin Poets, 1965), xi.

[36] Letter to George and Thomas Keats, Sunday 21 December 1817, in *The Letters of John Keats*, ed. M. B. Forman (London: Oxford University Press, 2nd edn, 1935), 72.

... and personhood

The notion of the apophatic permeates the whole of Lossky's theology. In particular, it is central to his analysis of the personal. The very notion of the personal, he suggests, arises only from reflection on the mystery of the Trinity: apart from the Trinity the mystery of personal being is closed to us. A personal apophaticism is only revealed to us by the doctrine of the Trinity. For personhood itself is beyond conceptualization:

> Personality can only be grasped in this life by a direct intuition; it can only be expressed in a work of art. When we say 'this is by Mozart', or 'this is by Rembrandt', we are in both cases dealing with a personal world which has no equivalent anywhere.[37]

The apophatic and the personal reflect each other, as it were, but not in a merely conceptual way: it is only the person that can make the apophatic approach to the divine mystery, for the apophatic is concerned with a personal, or existential, attitude. We have no time to pursue this further now, but before we leave Lossky, we must underline this point by quoting from the last chapter of his book, *The Mystical Theology of the Eastern Church*. There we read, in his recapitulation:

> We have had again and again, in the course of our study of the mystical theology of the Eastern Church, to refer to the apophatic attitude which is characteristic of its religious thought. As we have seen, the negations which draw attention to the divine incomprehensibility are not prohibitions upon knowledge: apophaticism, so far from being a limitation, enables us to transcend all concepts, every sphere of philosophical speculation. It is a tendency towards an ever-greater plenitude, in which knowledge is transformed into ignorance, the theology of concepts into contemplation, dogmas into experience of ineffable mysteries. It is, moreover, an existential theology involving man's entire being, which sets him upon the way of union, which obliges him to be changed, to transform his nature that he may attain the true *gnosis* which is the contemplation of the Holy Trinity. Now, this 'change of heart', this *metanoia*, means repentance. The apophatic way of Eastern theology is the repentance of the human person before the face of the living God.[38]

Lot-Borodine and deification

If now we turn to Myrrha Lot-Borodine, it is evident that we are turning to a presentation of Orthodox theology (both Lot-Borodine and Lossky speak rather of 'Eastern theology') of much the same complexion. The apophatic is a guiding theme for Lossky, a thread that runs through his whole theology, but it is a theme closely bound up with the theme of deification, *theosis*. As Heleen Zorgdrager comments in her article, Lot-Borodine's articles on

---

[37] Lossky, *Mystical Theology*, 53.
[38] Lossky, *Mystical Theology*, 238–9.

deification can be regarded as having introduced the doctrine to the Western world: Jules Gross' book appeared a few years later.[39] I want to pick up two other points that Heleen Zorgdrager made in her article on Lot-Borodine. The first point is the link she draws between Lot-Borodine's understanding of courtly love in medieval Romance literature and her approach to deification. For Lot-Borodine, the profane love, celebrated by the troubadours and their followers, shocking and transgressive as it is, trembles on the brink of sacred devotion. Giving the example of Lancelot, Lot-Borodine comments:

> Overcome by vertigo, love can no longer be sustained at this altitude without a complete transformation. In this respect, the edifying end of Lancelot du Lac, who, returning from so far away, dies a hermit in the last part of the tetralogy, is profoundly symptomatic. What remains of the carnal in the adoration of the lady must be burnt up, so much impure dross, in the brazier of asceticism, must melt, like wax, in the fire of the mystic sun. Souls were ready and awaited only the call.[40]

As we shall see, for Lot-Borodine deification is the end of such purification of love. Another significant point made by Zorgdrager concerns Lot-Borodine's understanding of *nous*, usually translated 'intellect'. Zorgdrager suggests that it is more properly understood as 'intuition'. It is interesting to reflect that in another seminal work, published in the 1930s (in 1936, to be exact), it is very much this point that is made about the meaning of the Greek word *nous*. In his book, *Contemplation et vie contemplative selon Platon*, the great Dominican classical scholar André-Jean Festugière had discussed the meaning of *nous* and unfolded its meaning in terms of likeness and contact.[41] Later, in his vast collection of reflections on the Hermetic literature he had summarized this earlier discussion by saying that, by means of *nous* – referred to as an 'intuitive faculty' – the soul 'aspires to a knowledge that is a direct contact, a "feeling", a touching, something seen [un «sentiment», un toucher, une vue]. It aspires to a union where there is total fusion, the interpenetration of two living beings.'[42] Lot-Borodine develops this in a typically rhapsodic manner:

> The Logos manifests itself in man under the form of sovereign intelligence, uniting reason and being. The *nous*, 'eye of the understanding', is the depository in the soul of the *eikon* (icon, image) of God, the secret repository of his triune image: the effigy of the Son imprinted by the seal of the Holy Spirit, the unction of the Father ... It is intellection *modo divino*. One can then say that the *nous* is the organ of apprehension of a charismatic knowledge-intuition; not simply a prolongation of the discursive reason ... It is a doctrine concerning what is innate, which, restructuring all the psychological categories, places

---

[39] Jules Gross, *La Divinisation du chrétien d'après les pères grecs: Contribution historique à la doctrine de la grâce* (Paris: J. Gabalda, 1938); ET, Anaheim, CA: A. & C. Press, 2002.

[40] Lot-Borodine, *De l'Amour profane à l'amour sacré*, 27.

[41] A.-J. Festugière, *Contemplation et vie contemplative selon Platon* (Paris: Vrin, 3rd edn, 1967), 220–49.

[42] A.-J. Festugière, *La Révélation d'Hermès Trismégiste*, I (Paris, 2nd edn, 1950), 65.

God at the very centre of ontogeny, as unique reality: the triune God who at once is decomposed and unified in the very depths of the soul.[43]

The implications of this are profound: not only does this understanding of *nous* take us beyond the rational; it takes us to a point where soul and body are found in union in the deep centre of human being. Deification, mediated through the reforming of the image of God in the *nous*, does not simply concern the human rational faculties, but pervades the whole psycho-somatic unity of the human. Lot-Borodine goes on to remark that,

> As the all-powerful means of arriving at this goal, supernaturally natural – [that is, 'the final metamorphosis, entirely submissive to the charismatic action of the Spirit'] – man, whose perfect life is the glory of God [an echo of Irenaeus' famous dictum], possessed this innate gift, *love*: fruit of will and intelligence, immanent desire for perfection, infused knowledge of the Light.[44]

All through this, Lot-Borodine is weighing her words so as to oppose the dichotomies she found in the Catholic theology of the West: natural–supernatural, knowledge–love, body–soul, grace–free will. If anything, Lot-Borodine's anti-Westernism is even more pronounced than what we find in her contemporaries such as Bulgakov and Lossky; she sought out striking images of this contrast (which, I think we must admit, are overdrawn), a contrast between the *sensibilité pathétique* of the West and the *frisson sacré* of the East.[45] Her own understanding of the deification of the human through a working together of God and the human, synergism, was intended to point beyond the dichotomies characteristic of Western theology and spirituality.

... and asceticism

The second, and longer part, of her articles on deification explores the ways in which deification is attained in the Eastern tradition. It constitutes a brilliant introduction to the asceticism of Byzantine monasticism, rooted in the experience of the Fathers (and Mothers) of the Egyptian desert. She expounds the central notion of *apatheia*, freedom from the passions, a concept that quickly dropped out of the ascetic vocabulary of the West, after attacks on it by Jerome and Augustine. She takes these notions back to her beloved Clement of Alexandria (an intuition that has been confirmed by more recent research). Long footnotes bristle with her irritation at the misunderstanding of the Greek tradition by Western scholars. A central bone of contention concerns the Western inability to understand the meaning of synergism between God and humankind, which leads to the opposition of grace and free will and ends in the 'anguishing problem of predestination'.[46]

---

[43] Lot-Borodine, *Déification de l'homme*, 44.
[44] Lot-Borodine, *Déification de l'homme*, 46.
[45] See Lot-Borodine, *Déification de l'homme*, 61–6.
[46] Lot-Borodine, *Déification de l'homme*, 97.

Read patiently, however, Lot-Borodine provides a wonderful account of the heart of the Eastern tradition, with a view of humanity that, fully conscious of the distortions introduced into the human condition by sin, is nevertheless constantly aware that the image of God in which the human has been created cannot be destroyed by a mere creature, and that there is a proportion between God's grace and the human search for God. She also brings out the way in which asceticism, far from denigrating the body, is a way in which the body participates in the transfiguration that deification entails – this a consequence of her seeing *nous* as the core of the human. Her account is detailed, full of striking insights, impossible to summarize at all adequately. She draws on a wide range of Eastern sources, from her favourite Alexandrines, whom she defends from Western misunderstanding, through the Desert Fathers, not least the *Life of St Antony*, the Cappadocian Fathers, mainly Gregory of Nyssa, Evagrios, the Macarian Homilies, Maximos (whom she discusses at some length) and finally Symeon the New Theologian. It is worth noting that not only was the subject of deification one that had been little discussed when she wrote, but many of her sources were little known, too (though maybe better known in Russia than in the West: Symeon, for instance, and even Maximos).

... and the liturgical

If we confine our attention to this remarkable series of articles (something very easy to do, as the book *La Déification de l'homme* is her only theological work in print), we might come away with a false impression, for virtually all we find in this volume concerns the individual search for union with God; deification might appear the goal of an individual ascetic exercise, undertaken, of course, only with the grace of God.

However, later on in the 1930s various other articles appeared that suggest a broader perspective. These were articles (mentioned above) that contained a translation of Maximos the Confessor's *Mystagogia*, the first into any Western language, and the beginning of what was to be a long engagement with the works of Nicolas Cabasilas. What is striking in both cases is that Lot-Borodine shifts her attention from what we might call the ascetical and mystical to the liturgical, or maybe not 'shifts', but extends her attention to embrace the liturgical. For in both Maximos and Nicolas we are engaging with texts that seek to integrate the ascetical/mystical and the liturgical. This is explicitly the case in Chapter 5 of Maximos' *Mystagogia*, which sets out an elaborate parallel between the structure of the church in which the liturgy takes place and the soul, with contemplative and practical aspects, the one pursued through the *nous*, the other through *logos*, with *nous* advancing from wisdom, to contemplation, to knowledge, to enduring knowledge, to truth; while *logos* passes from moral wisdom, to practice, to virtue, to faith, and finally comes to goodness. For Maximos, this is mirrored in and nourished by the celebration of the Divine Liturgy, which is the principal subject of the treatise.

Lot-Borodine's interest in this aspect of Maximos' *Mystagogia* is evident in the early pages of her book on Cabasilas, where she comments directly (if a little puzzlingly) on precisely this chapter from the *Mystagogia*,[47] and in the Introduction to her translation of the *Mystagogia*, she says that in this work, 'a bridge is thrown, like a rainbow, linking the two banks of Eastern spirituality: the mystic ritual, called hierurgy, and the inward, individual experience of the soul in quest of the Best-Beloved'.[48]

We are on firmer ground with Nicolas Cabasilas as, in addition to the articles she wrote from 1935 onwards, there is also the book on Cabasilas already referred to. Here again Lot-Borodine was breaking new ground: when she wrote there was one obscure monograph and only a few articles on Cabasilas (Salaville's important article came in the year after Lot-Borodine had begun to publish on Cabasilas[49]).

Cabasilas was a distinguished fourteenth-century Byzantine layman, with strong theological interests; he was a supporter of Palamas in the hesychast controversy. His works are very varied, but he is most famous for two works: *The Life in Christ* and a commentary *On the Divine Liturgy*; it is these that interested Lot-Borodine, along with some of his sermons (written in the dense and elaborate style popular in the Byzantine court).[50] Both these works are characterized by a kind of osmosis between the Christian life and the liturgy: this is obvious in *On the Divine Liturgy*, while *The Life in Christ* is constructed around the three sacraments of baptism, chrismation and the Divine Liturgy (this list of three, though not the order, being reminiscent of Dionysios the Areopagite). The sacraments and the ascetical–mystical aspect of the Christian life converge in the doctrine of deification, exactly as we have seen that they do with Lossky. There is no time to explore this more deeply here. Let us just look briefly at the third part of her book on Cabasilas. Part One explored the treatise *On the Divine Liturgy*, focusing on the symbolism of the liturgy and the nature of the eucharistic sacrifice; Part Two turned to *The Life in Christ* and discussed the nature of the sacraments of baptism,

---

[47] Lot-Borodine, *Un maître*, 17–18.

[48] Myrrha Lot-Borodine, 'Lecture patristique: *Mystagogie de saint Maxime*', *Irén.* 13 (1936), 467. She concludes her Introduction with the following observation: 'What is most important, in our opinion, in this essay of symbolist ecclesiology, is not the strict parallelism, but the permanent *contact* of these elements habitually separated, the sacral and the mystical proper. For Saint Maximos they are rooted in the supreme unity of the idea-energy which is *theosis kata charin* [deification by grace] – veritable symbiosis-synergy of grace and freedom, these "two wings", as the illustrious Confessor calls them, which lift the human, without ever alienating it, up to the divine': Lot-Borodine, 'Lecture patristique', 468.

[49] S. Salaville, 'Le Christocentrisme de Nicolas Cabasilas', *Échos d'Orient* 35 (1936), 129–67. Salaville also produced a translation of *On the Divine Liturgy*, SC 4 (Paris: Cerf, 1943), which Lot-Borodine used in her book.

[50] For an up-to-date and detailed survey of Cabasilas, and scholarship on him, see Yannis Spiteris and Carmelo Giuseppe Conticello, 'Nicola Cabasilas Chamaetos', in *La Théologie byzantine et sa tradition*, II, ed. Carmelo Giuseppe Conticello and Vassa Conticello (Turnhout: Brepols, 2002), 315–410.

chrismation and the Eucharist, and Christian participation in them. Part Three is on 'The Experimental Doctrine of *amor Dei*'.

We return to the theme that had occupied Lot-Borodine (and continued to occupy her) in her researches on courtly literature: love. The heart of Cabasilas' teaching is, for Lot-Borodine, the practice of love, a love inspired in us by God's creation of the world and his redemption of the world through the Incarnation: a love that leads us to participate in God's own love, and thus attain deification. It seems to me characteristic of Lot-Borodine that she first singles out a kind of serenity in Cabasilas' teaching.

> This moralist – for he was one, and of stature – remains far removed, by nature and by argument, from a *dolourism*, cultivated as such. Also Cabasilas will oppose, on principle this time, the excesses even of contrition, considered as a conditional good. On this delicate point, he produces a detailed analysis, separating two aspects of contrition: the indispensable and sane repentance for a fault committed, and the morbid remorse that leads to despair, a mortal sin ...With a great deal of finesse and tact, the author signals the individual reactions of different subjects to the effects of mortification; in some cases an excellent stimulant, but more often leading directly to a 'sort of numbness', a danger in itself to the mental equilibrium of the subject. He will counsel, too, with prudence, 'avoiding as much the presumption *before* sin as the *perfectly vain* shame and fear (our italics) *after* the sin'. The conclusion is then: 'Fear, shame, contrition, mortification are good only when they carry us towards God'.[51]

And there we must leave our two Russian émigré theologians, who strove to bring to a Western audience, first of all French, the riches of the theological tradition of the Greek East.

---

[51] Lot-Borodine, *Un maître*, 123–4.

8

St Maria of Paris
(Mother Maria Skobtsova) and
Orthodoxy in the modern world

St Maria of Paris might seem in strange company in a book on Orthodox thinkers. She is not known primarily, if at all, as a thinker – though, as we shall see, this is a misconception; she had a powerful mind and thought very deeply about the problems facing Christianity in the twentieth century – rather she is known as someone who worked tirelessly for the Russian émigrés in France, and especially in Paris, many of whom were utterly disorientated by exile and poverty. Among them were Jews, and after the fall of France to Nazi Germany in 1940, St Maria did everything she could to protect and shield the Jews from extermination, and herself ended up a martyr in Ravensbrück camp in Germany. Before being glorified as a saint of the Orthodox Church in 2004, she was inscribed as one of the 'Righteous among the Nations' at Yad Vashem in Jerusalem and a tree was planted in her memory in 1985.

St Maria (Skobtsova) of Paris

Yet she fits into this book very well. She might well have been included alongside Vladimir Lossky and Myrrha Lot-Borodine in the last chapter. Like them she spent formative years of her life in St Petersburg, and like them belongs to the blossoming of Russian theology in émigré Paris. Whereas Lossky and Lot-Borodine fit among those seeking a renewal of theology through some version of a neo-patristic synthesis, St Maria belongs much more clearly to the Russian Religious Renaissance; in some ways her links with movements in Russian culture – the so-called Silver Age – are closer than many of the other Paris émigrés: she knew Aleksandr Blok from her time in St Petersburg, and also Anna Akhmatova, to whom she was related by marriage through her first husband. St Maria was herself a poet. Unlike Lossky, who remained faithful to the Moscow Patriarchate, and Lot-Borodine, who seems to have attached herself both to the exarchate under Metropolitan Evlogy and the Moscow Patriarchate, St Maria was a passionate supporter of the exarchate, and had hard things to say about both the Synodal Church – the Russian Orthodox Church Abroad (as it then was) – and the supporters of the Moscow Patriarchate. As we shall see, she was nothing if not passionate – about everything. Even in strictly theological terms, St Maria played an important role in making available the theology being taught at the Institut St-Serge, and took an unambiguous role in the sophiological controversy in the 1930s. Furthermore, as we have seen, the Orthodox theology we have been looking at has rarely been the theology of the academy: there have been few trained theologians among our cast, though that hasn't stopped them from being profound thinkers. In many ways, the Orthodox thinkers who have had most impact have broken the mould of the traditional Orthodox theology of the universities and spiritual academies. Nor is she alone in this volume in being a glorified saint: later on we shall discuss the Serbian theologian St Justin Popović, and also St Silouan the Athonite.

Life

St Maria's life is more difficult to recount in a short span than most of the people we have been concerned with. The life of a thinker is generally uneventful, and most of them, after the turmoil of the Revolution and exile, settled down to their intellectual pursuits. Not so with St Maria, whose life never settled down, but was characterized by ceaseless activity on behalf of the poor and wretched.[1]

---

[1] On St Maria, see the pioneering biography by Sergei Hackel, *One, of Great Price* (London: Darton Longman & Todd, 1965); published in a revised version as *Pearl of Great Price* (Crestwood, NY: St Vladimir's Seminary Press, 1982). Also: Sainte Marie de Paris (Mère Marie Skobtsova, 1891–1945), *Le Jour du Saint-Esprit* (Paris: Cerf, 2011), a collection of various materials in translation. *Contacts* 224 (2008) is devoted to her; see also Tatiana Victoroff, 'Mère Marie, poète', *Le Messager orthodoxe* 140 (2004): *Les Nouveaux Saints orthodoxes de France*, 29–34; Sainte Marie Skobtsov, 'Poèmes'; 'Le Présent et l'avenir de l'Église', *Le Messager orthodoxe* 140 (2004): *Les Nouveaux Saints orthodoxes de France*: 35–7; 38–46; Elisabeth Skobtsov, '«Terre Sainte»', *Le Messager orthodoxe* 146 (2008), 4–21.

She was born Elisabeth Pilenko in 1891, in Riga in what is now Latvia, then the Baltic Province of the Russian Empire. When she was four, the family moved to Anapa, in the very south of Russia (Caucasia) on the north-eastern coast of the Black Sea. Elisabeth lived there with her family until, after the death of her father in 1906, she moved with her mother, Sophia, to St Petersburg. Her schooling, which had begun in the girls' lycée at Yalta, continued at St Petersburg. She already knew St Petersburg, as her godmother, Elisabeth Yamikovich, lived there and they visited regularly. When only five, she came to know the friend of the family, the Oberprokuror of the Russian Synod, Konstantin Petrovich Pobedonostsev. Later, she asked him Pilate's question: What is truth? He replied: 'the truth lies in love, of course. But there are many people who think that the truth lies in love for distant people. Love for distant people is no love. If only everyone loved his neighbour, his immediate neighbour . . .'[2] That answer remained with her.

While still at school, Elisabeth (as we'll call her for the time being) met Aleksandr Blok, the Silver Age poet, and around the same time, took part in a Marxist study group with other students from her lycée. In 1910, aged 18, she married D. V. Kuzmin-Karavaev, son of the estranged father of the poet Nikolai Gumilev. Her husband was a member of the Social-Democratic (Bolshevik) party. She became part of the well-to-do, radical and artistic circles of St Petersburg that revolved round Anna Akhmatova and Nikolai Gumilev, she herself both painting and writing poems and at least one novel; she seems to have met everybody – as well as Blok and Akhmatova, Marina Tsvetaeva, Ivanov, Alexei Tolstoy, Berdyaev, and many others. She continued her education, as well, both attending the women's courses associated with St Petersburg University and embarking on a course of studies at the Spiritual Academy, reading the text of lectures she was not, as a woman, allowed to attend.

In 1913, Elisabeth left her husband and St Petersburg, and returned to Anapa; later in the year she gave birth to her first child, Gaiana, in Moscow, where she was to spend a few years, again very much part of the artistic and radical circles she had frequented in St Petersburg. In 1917, Elisabeth joined the Socialist-Revolutionary party. As Russia descended into chaos, she found herself both in Moscow and Anapa, where first the Bolsheviks and then the White Russians took control. As mayor of Anapa, Elisabeth was directly involved in the conflict, and found herself arrested and condemned by both sides. In 1919, she married again, to Daniel Skobtsov, with whom she was to have two children: Yuri and Nastya (Anastasia). In 1920, the Skobtsov family, together with Elisabeth's mother Sophia, left Russia. At the end of the year they found themselves together in Constantinople, and by 1924 they had arrived, via Serbia, in Paris. In 1926, her daughter, Nastya, died. This was a turning point in St Maria's life. Later, she spoke about how death can affect one as a 'sudden opening of doors into eternity: one's whole natural life

---

[2] Quoted in Hackel, *One, of Great Price*, 70.

has been shaken, has disintegrated, desires have faded, meaning has lost its meaning and another incomprehensible Meaning has caused wings to grow at one's back'.[3] And so with St Maria: she felt that the death of her child obliged her

> to become a mother for all. This is God's will: that that, which was so precious in a blood relationship, should be passed on, out of love, to those who are not related; and that we should care for them as we would care for our own children.[4]

This precipitated St Maria's decision to become a nun. In 1927, she and her husband separated. In 1932, an ecclesiastical divorce was issued (they did not seek a civil divorce, so in the eyes of the state they remained married), and ten days later, Elisabeth Skobtsova received the monastic tonsure from Metropolitan Evlogy, and took the name Maria, after St Mary of Egypt. Metropolitan Evlogy had great hopes for Mother Maria; he wanted her to become the founder of convent life in the emigration: he later remarked,

> Ascetic, contemplative ... monasticism, that is to say, monasticism in its pure state, did not succeed in the Emigration. I say this with great sorrow, for ascetic monasticism is the flower and decoration of the Church, a sign of her vitality.[5]

Mother Maria visited monasticism 'in its pure state', in Latvia and Estonia, and also at Valaam in Finland, but was not impressed. She was to pursue another ideal of monasticism, far from the traditional form of contemplative monasticism found in the Orthodox Churches.

Already by this time, Elisabeth, as she still was, had been involved in theological discussions and lectures at the Institut St-Serge. In autumn 1928, she had attended weekly discussions on the question of the Divine Wisdom, Sophia, led by Fr Sergii Bulgakov, who was to become her spiritual father; present at these discussions was another remarkable woman of the Russian diaspora, Yulia Reitlinger, later Sister Joanna, the icon painter, and much later one of the supporters of Fr Aleksandr Men' in Moscow. She also attended the lectures on the Church Fathers given by Fr Georges Florovsky: it was she who typed up the lectures and prepared them for publication, which took place in the 1930s.

In 1931 Metropolitan Evlogy placed the churches of the Exarchate of Western Europe of which he had pastoral charge under the jurisdiction of the Œcumenical Patriarchate – a decision which Mother Maria supported wholeheartedly. In a paper given in 1936, Mother Maria characterized the Russian Orthodox Church Abroad as hankering after the State–Church union of the pre-revolutionary period, while the 'Church called patriarchal' had a 'tendency to transpose to the free countries ... the psychology of the

---

[3] Hackel, *One, of Great Price*, 4.
[4] Hackel, *One, of Great Price*, 17.
[5] Hackel, *One, of Great Price*, 22.

persecuted, their clandestinity, an ecstasy sometimes a little bit hysterical'; it was left to the Church of the Exarchate to attempt to create new values: 'spiritual freedom, an attention directed to the world, to the spiritual problems that tear it apart, to culture, to the sciences, to art, to forms of a new life'.[6] In the controversy over Fr Bulgakov's sophiology that took place in the 1930s, Mother Maria supported Bulgakov passionately. When Vladimir Lossky sent Mother Maria his then-unpublished critique of Bulgakov, she returned it, unopened, with the indignant message: 'I don't read texts signed by writers of denunciations!'[7]

Elisabeth was involved from the beginnings in 1925 in the affairs of the French branch of *Action chrétienne des étudiants russes* (ACER: Russian Student Christian Movement), which had been founded in Czechoslovakia in 1923. She was elected to the council and remained very active. For it was action that she sought: active ways of supporting the Russian emigration in France, both through study days and summer camps and through providing food and shelter and other help for those who were suffering. Once a nun, she fashioned a form of monasticism that made such practical support possible. The centre of her activities, though there were others, was the house she rented at 77, rue de Lourmel. Here the destitute could find shelter, food was provided, cheap or free, the door was never closed to anyone. It became a cultural centre, too; a church was built there; an organization, 'Orthodox Action', was founded there – a cultural and charitable association, independent of the church hierarchy, though with the blessing of Metropolitan Evlogy.

As the days darkened, Orthodox Action sought to address the problems facing Christians; in the autumn of 1938 there was a public conference on 'The Christian World and Racism'. A little later Mother Maria visited psychiatric hospitals throughout France and discovered many Russians consigned to these places through dire misfortune and inability to communicate rather than any malady. Mother Maria never had any doubts about the direction her work should take; not everyone could cope with the constant risk-taking and the resultant chaos that seemed to threaten – a Russian nun, Evdokia, found her impossible, and eventually left for a more normal monastic environment, after the war, founding the monastery at Bussy-en-Othe; Fr Kiprian Kern was chaplain at rue Lourmel for a time, and again found Mother Maria impossible to work with. Eventually a priest was found with whom Mother Maria could work: Fr Dimitri Klepinine, who arrived in autumn 1939. By this time the Second World War had begun, and Paris soon began to suffer bombardment, and then defeat. Using her establishments, especially 77, rue de Lourmel, Mother Maria sought to meet the needs of the population: as well as the canteen, she opened a cheap market for necessities.

---

[6] Skobtsov, 'Le Présent et l'avenir de l'Église', 41–2.
[7] Quoted in Alexis Klimoff, 'Georges Florovsky and the Sophiological Controversy', *SVTQ* 49 (2005), 67–100, at 85.

After the defeat and German occupation, Jews began to suffer, and again Mother Maria sought to respond. When, in July 1942, the Jews were herded into the Vélodrome d'Hiver, Mother Maria managed to enter and enabled four children to escape in the refuse bins – a story beautifully told in Jim Forest's children's book, *Silent as a Stone*.[8] The next year arrests began. In February 1943 Mother Maria and Fr Dimitri were arrested. The day before, her son, Yuri, had been arrested, and Ilya Fondaminsky, a Russian Jew who had been a great support to Mother Maria, had died at Auschwitz, two months after being baptized. Mother Maria and Fr Dimitri were incarcerated at Romainville, and then moved to Compiègne, the site of the Carmel whose nuns were guillotined during the French Revolution, and whose fate is celebrated in Georges Bernanos' *Dialogues des Carmélites* and in Poulenc's opera based on it. Soon Mother Maria was transferred to Ravensbrück; in December, Fr Dimitri was transferred with Yuri to Buchenwald, where they perished in February 1944. Finally, on 31 March 1945, Mother Maria died in a gas chamber at Ravensbrück, having taken the place of one of the prisoners.

Some characteristics of her theology

The enormity of her death, her courage, the encouragement she gave to others, her optimism – right at the beginning of the war, she was convinced Germany would be defeated; in the last days at Ravensbrück, she remained cheerful, smiling, and said to a fellow prisoner, 'I am deeply convinced that we may not walk out, but we shall be carried out and we shall stay alive. There is no doubt about that'[9] – all this focuses our attention on her person, her faith, her hope, her love. I want to suggest, however, that the faith she lived by and died for is seamless with her understanding of the nature of the Church, the demands of the gospel, and what is involved in trying to follow Christ.

Her theology is, it seems to me, very simple, but pursued in a dramatically radical way. In an article published in 1939 – the first item in the volume *Essential Writings*[10] – she makes clear where she stands, and also how she sees herself as belonging to a tradition of Orthodox theology. It is called 'The Second Gospel Commandment' – to love one's neighbour as oneself – and her main gravamen is how easily this commandment has been sidelined or relativized. Because it is 'second', it is often treated as secondary, an appendix to the first commandment. She starts out by pointing out how we are never encouraged to pray alone: the prayers that we say morning and night as Orthodox are all prayers in which we pray, not as 'I', but as 'we' – culminating, of course, in the Lord's Prayer, the 'Our Father'. Her first conclusion takes this form:

---

[8] Jim Forest, *Silent as a Stone* (Crestwood, NY: St Vladimir's Seminary Press, 2007).
[9] Hackel, *One, of Great Price*, 126.
[10] Mother Maria Skobtsova, *Essential Writings*, trans. Richard Pevear and Larissa Volokhonsky, with an Introduction by Jim Forest (Maryknoll, NY: Orbis Books, 2003), 45–60.

> Thus what is most personal, what is most intimate in an Orthodox person's life, is thoroughly pervaded by this sense of being united with everyone, the sense of the principle of *sobornost'*, characteristic of the Orthodox Church. This is a fact of great significance; this forces us to reflect.[11]

She relates it immediately to Khomiakov, Dostoevsky, Solov'ev: the great nineteenth-century figures who are the pillars of the Russian Religious Renaissance. She then faces two ways that seem to her to turn away the force of this sense of the fundamental place of *sobornost'*. First, what she calls a 'holy egoism', which accepts the value of the second commandment, the need to feed the hungry, shelter beggars and so on, but treats this as an ascetic exercise, undertaken for the salvation of the soul of each one of us. The neighbour, the one in need, provides an opportunity to further our salvation: to love like that is not to love the other at all, but use him or her as a way of loving oneself. 'One cannot love sacrificially in one's own name, but only in the name of Christ, in the name of the image of God that is revealed to us in man'.[12]

The next problem is: the *Philokalia*, the pre-eminent work of Orthodox spirituality. She remarks that 'in the first volume of the *Philokalia*, material about the attitude towards one's neighbour takes up only two pages out of six hundred, and in the second volume, only three out of seven hundred and fifty' – quite a different proportion from the Gospels and the Epistles of the New Testament.[13] Nevertheless, from these few pages she quotes from St Makarios the Great, from St John Cassian, from St Neilos of Sinai (actually from Evagrios), from St Ephrem the Syrian, and St Isaac the Syrian. Here she finds enough to establish an Orthodox tradition that leads to genuine attention to our neighbour, the other, and his or her needs, and she goes on to sketch out what this entails. She talks of work and abstinence – work that is not merely 'an unavoidable evil, the curse of Adam', but also 'participation in the divine economy', in which work is 'transfigured and sanctified'; abstinence that frees one to attend, an abstinence of which one is virtually unconscious, for it is the attention enabled that is important. Attention, to the other, to his or her needs, is paramount for Mother Maria. This requires the cultivation of inwardness, an inwardness that enables us to discern and respond to the inwardness of the other – something very different from an ascetic impersonality – but this respect for and attention to the other is to be neither judgemental nor indulgent. As she puts it:

> On the one hand, it is dangerous to approach a man with the yardstick of all-measuring doctrine and begin to dissect his living and sick soul; on the other hand, it is no less dangerous to accept sentimentally the whole of a man as he is, his soul along with all its sores and growths.

We are to discern the image of God in the other, and fall before him in veneration, yet at the same time, not to ignore the way the image has been

---

[11] Skobtsova, *Essential Writings*, 47.
[12] Skobtsova, *Essential Writings*, 49.
[13] Skobtsova, *Essential Writings*, 50.

ravaged by sin, and to long 'to become an instrument of God in this terrible and scorching work'.[14]

I am summarizing an essay that is brief anyway, and I am sure that some of the power of what St Maria says is being lost, but the central point is clear: that love of God and love of one's neighbour coinhere in one another, and they are both authentically love. Therefore we need to explore what is meant by this loving encounter with one's neighbour, and be aware of the ways in which the demands of this love can be turned aside and evaded – even in the name of the love of God. Before she closes her essay, she remarks that for the Russian Orthodox this ought to be easier to understand, 'because it was precisely this commandment that captivated and interested Russian religious thought'. She mentions Khomiakov and the notion of *sobornost'*, 'which rests entirely on love, on lofty human communion', and goes on to say that it is this that makes sense of Solov'ev's notion of Godmanhood, 'because it becomes one and organic, the genuine Body of Christ, only when united and brought to life by the flow of fraternal love that unites everyone at one Cup and brings everyone to partake of one Divine Love'. Finally, she asserts, 'Only this commandment makes clear Dostoevsky's words about each of us being guilty for all, and each of us being answerable for each other's sins.'[15]

It is this commandment, she affirms, that contains the answer to the problems facing the modern world:

> [W]e are called to oppose the mystery of authentic human communion to all false relations among people. This is the only path on which Christ's love can live; moreover, this is the only path of life – outside it is death. Death in the fire and ashes of various hatreds that corrode modern mankind, class, national, and race hatreds, the godless and giftless death of cool, uncreative, imitative, essentially secular democracy. To all forms of mystical totalitarianism we oppose only one thing: the person, the image of God in man. And to all forms of passively collectivist mentality in democracy we oppose *sobornost'*.
>
> But we do not even oppose. We simply want to live as we are taught by the second commandment of Christ ... in such a way that all those who are outside it can see and feel the unique, saving, unsurpassable beauty, the indisputable truth of precisely this Christian path.[16]

It is not hard to see here the values that Khomiakov sought to express through the notion of *sobornost'* given a precision, as St Maria contemplates the problems facing Orthodoxy in the modern world. It is no harking back to a bygone age of 'Holy Russia': the challenge of socialism has been acknowledged and embraced. Neither is it some easy acquiescence in the new circumstances of modernity. It is simply an acceptance of the radical demands of the gospel. This, it seems to me, characterizes all of St Maria's reflection on human living, and the demands of the other on us.

---

[14] Skobtsova, *Essential Writings*, 55–7.
[15] Skobtsova, *Essential Writings*, 58–9.
[16] Skobtsova, *Essential Writings*, 60.

Let me briefly mention two other dimensions of St Maria's teaching, both of which seem to me to show how close her vision was to that of her spiritual father, Sergii Bulgakov. In several places, but particularly in her meditation 'On the Imitation of the Mother of God',[17] St Maria develops a complementarity between Christ and his Mother, in a way very reminiscent of passages especially in his last work, *The Bride of the Lamb*. At the foot of the cross which bore her suffering Son, the Mother of God knew the truth of Symeon's prophecy, that a sword would pierce her own soul also. As Christ accepted the voluntary passion, voluntary suffering, so the Mother of God co-suffered with him:

> the cross of the Son, in all its scope, in all its pain, becomes a two-edged sword that pierces the maternal heart. These two torments are equally measureless. The only difference is that the Son's active, voluntary, and willing acceptance becomes the Mother's passive, unavoidable *co*-acceptance.[18]

And as we follow the way of the cross, we follow the way of the Mother, too: 'in this sense she always walks with us on our own way of the cross, she is always there beside us, each of our crosses is a sword for her'.[19] And so we are not only an image of God, but also an image of the Mother of God, 'who bears Christ in herself through the Holy Spirit';[20] we do not only discern the image of God in our neighbour, but in loving him or her adopt them as a son or daughter, and so fulfil the image of the Mother of God that we bear – 'The Christian soul should be filial, that is, cross-bearing, but also maternal, that is, receptive of the sword in the heart'.[21] And we all fall short of this demand: 'All we see is falling away, betrayal, coldness, and indifference'.[22] We need to learn to pray with the Son, 'your will be done', and with his Mother, 'Behold, the handmaid of the Lord': then we shall approach 'the innermost depths of our human hearts, God-like and maternal in their spiritual essence'.[23]

All the way through this, there is a constant message against any tendency to limit Christianity to a concern for 'God and the soul' – what she calls, maybe a little unfairly, 'mystical Protestantism'. The commandment to love embraces the brother or sister, draws people into a co-humanity that is an entailment of the Godmanhood we see in Christ.

Sometimes St Maria's vision can seem relentless, even joyless, but that would be profoundly to misunderstand her. For there is no effort, no strain: the vision is of being caught up in God's love, becoming a vehicle of his love, resting in his providence and love. There is a rather beautiful illustration

---

[17] Skobtsova, *Essential Writings*, 61–74.
[18] Skobtsova, *Essential Writings*, 68.
[19] Skobtsova, *Essential Writings*, 69.
[20] Skobtsova, *Essential Writings*, 69.
[21] Skobtsova, *Essential Writings*, 73.
[22] Skobtsova, *Essential Writings*, 73–4.
[23] Skobtsova, *Essential Writings*, 74.

of this in some words she spoke to Konstantin Mochul′sky, one of her closest friends, as the German armies entered France in early summer, 1940: 'I am not afraid to suffer,' she said, 'I love death.' He asked her what it would be like after death, to which she replied, 'I don't know. Spacious. And then we shall learn a small secret, that hell has already been.'[24]

One should add to this that her establishment at 77, rue de Lourmel was not just a centre for the needy and abandoned, though that was at the heart of her life there. She wrote, not just the kind of theological works we are going to look at, but poetry, too; they held musical evenings there, and engaged in heated discussions. As well as poetry, St Maria was a gifted artist. Along with Sister Joanna Reitlinger, she tried to reconceive the icon in modern terms, and though her efforts – their efforts – met with a mixed reception, their attempts to reconceive the icon should be considered alongside the better known 'rediscovery of the icon', associated with Leonid Ouspensky and Gregory Krug.[25]

Types of religious life

Long after St Maria's death, there was discovered in her mother's archive a somewhat longer reflection on the various ways in which Christians have negotiated their relationship with the world, which has become known as 'Types of Religious Life'. It was written in 1937, first published in the Paris-based *Vestnik* in 1997;[26] an English translation soon followed in *Sourozh*,[27] the journal of the Russian Orthodox Diocese in Britain, which has been reprinted in *Essential Writings*.[28]

Writing in 1937, St Maria had in mind the ways in which Russian Orthodox Christians in the diaspora had responded to their situation, but it is of much wider relevance. In it she distinguishes five types of religious life, what she calls: the synodal, the ritualist, the aesthetic, the ascetic, and finally, the option she presents as the true one, the evangelical. If the ritualist, the aesthetic and the ascetic seem plain enough, a comment is needed on the terms 'synodal' and 'evangelical'. The 'synodal' refers primarily to the period in Russian church history from the introduction of the reforms under Tsar Peter the Great at the beginning of the eighteenth century to the aborted Russian *sobor* (council) of 1917–18. During this period the Russian Church was governed by a 'Holy Synod', Peter the Great having abolished the patriarchate (which was re-established by the 1917–18 *sobor*, virtually the

---

[24] Quoted in Hackel, *One, of Great Price*, 88.
[25] On St Maria's art, see Xenia Krivochéine, *La Beauté salvatrice: Mère Marie (Skobtsov): Peintures – Dessins – Broderies* (Paris: Cerf, 2012); also Paul Ladouceur, 'The Saint as Artist: The Art of Saint Maria of Paris (Mother Maria Skobtsova). The Making of a Poet-Artist', *Sobornost* 36:1 (2014), 48–72.
[26] *Vestnik* 176 (II–III 1997), 5–50 (actually appearing in 1998).
[27] *Sourozh* 74 (November 1998), 4–10; 75 (February 1999), 13–27; 76 (May 1999), 21–35.
[28] Skobtsova, *Essential Writings*, 144–86.

only thing it achieved), so it is often called the 'synodal period'. The 'synodal' Church could also refer to the branch of the Russian Orthodox Church that rejected the alleged compromises of the Church in Russia after the Revolution, and established itself as the Church in exile, at a synod held in Sremski-Karlovci in 1921 (and which, for Mother Maria, preserved many of the faults of the pre-revolutionary Church). Mother Maria makes it clear that she means 'synodal' in the first sense, and given that Peter the Great's inspiration for his 'Spiritual Regulation' of 1721 was not just Lutheran models, but also the Church of England, which he had visited while deliberating about his reform, in English one might think of this as the 'Establishment' model. 'Evangelical', in English, has connotations of 'Protestant'; the Russian word has no such suggestion, being simply the adjective from gospel, *evangelie*. By 'evangelical', Mother Maria means 'gospel Christianity' (though she is aware of the narrower use).

Mother Maria starts with the 'synodal' religious type. For Russians it means the identity of being Russian and being Orthodox: Orthodoxy is the outward expression of national identity. As a result of the Petrine reforms, the Church was subordinated to the state; it became a religious branch of the state: higher clergy were appointed by the state, the 'Holy Synod' that governed the Church was organized by the Oberprokuror, a layman, appointed by the tsar (he had no vote, but he had what was more important: influence). Religious observance was part of what was expected of one as a citizen (or rather, subject of the tsar); moderate, sober devotion was encouraged. Those whose devotion was more fervent either turned to the monasteries (such as were left: under both Peter the Great and Catherine the Great, monasteries suffered and many were closed) or simply rebelled, and sought refuge in un-Russian forms of religion – Catholicism, or some forms of Protestantism. What was expected was sober conformity; creativity was frowned on and any form of innovation stamped out. This was not, of course, the whole story, but it was the predominant one.

If the details of the picture, as Mother Maria presents it, are Russian, the general picture is much more widespread: established national churches came to characterize Europe in the modern period; denominations expressed aspects of national character – even Catholicism, with its universal aspirations, hardly escaped such subordination of the Church to the state and society. It is often traced back, as it is by Mother Maria, to the conversion of the emperor Constantine and the eventual emergence of established Christianity: the fire of the gospel was tamed and became a gentle heat promoting decency. It seems to me that all Christians in Western Europe face the problems of what Mother Maria calls the 'synodal' type of religious life. The fact that these problems are being solved by rising secularism which has caused the link between State and Church to wither away often seems only to make the problems worse, as Christians seek to hang on to the tatters of a fabric that should really have been abandoned willingly, rather than snatched piece by piece from the churches' anxious grasp.

Mother Maria's next type is the 'ritualist'. For a Russian, there is a very specific archetype here, for what we in English call an 'Old Believer' is, in Russian, called 'Old Ritualist', *staroobryadets*, if one is being polite: they are usually called just schismatics, *raskolniki*. They go back to the schism that occurred in Russia in the sixteenth century, when Patriarch Nikon removed what he thought were corruptions that had crept into the liturgical books, and brought Russian liturgical customs into line with current Greek practice. The Old Ritualists rejected the reforms and separated from the Russian Church. The schism intensified their attachment to the customs that had been changed – making the sign of the cross with three fingers instead of two being the most obvious – and as a result they preserved practices – traditions of icon-painting and church singing, for instance – that, though not part of Nikon's reform, ensued on it. In the nineteenth century, Old Believers, as a persecuted minority, attracted a lot of sympathy from the intellectuals, including Tolstoy. In schism, they found themselves more and more distant from the life of the Church. One group ended up with no priests, and there-fore no sacraments: the cost of liturgical purity was sacramental sterility – as Mother Maria comments, speaking of an Old Believer meeting house:

> It lacks only one thing: its magnificent iconostasis, completely covered with icons in massive metalwork covers, shelters nothing, it preserves nothing. For behind the iconostasis is a blank wall, to which the iconostasis is fixed. There is no sanctuary, no altar table, no table of oblation, since there is no Mystery, no Sacrament.[29]

What is left, Mother Maria suggests, is a concern with ritual detail, of which there is plenty in Orthodoxy. This is not, in itself, worthless; much is achieved: 'a very high degree of self-discipline, a large measure of control over oneself and over all the chaos of the human soul, even control over others, a complete structuring of one's inner and outer life', as she puts it,[30] but there is nothing particularly Christian about it. It relies on 'a passionate belief in the magic of the word and of combinations of words, of gestures and sequences of gestures', all of which has 'very real roots'.[31] What is lacking is any real engage-ment with the mystery of Christ, any real inspiration of love. Loving acts can spring from the ritualist type, but as a by-product; it is not the heart of the matter. This ritualist type is not by any means confined to the Old Believers; it is very common among the Orthodox who do have the mysteries, the sacraments. Indeed, I would guess that to many Western Christians the ritualist mentality seems endemic in Orthodoxy, and they are not completely wrong. What causes recourse to such ritualism? Surely it is fear, fear of change, fear of new circumstances – new circumstances that, in the modern world, we cannot avoid. Such dependence on ritual creates a cocoon, a place where

---

[29] Skobtsova, *Essential Writings*, 150.
[30] Skobtsova, *Essential Writings*, 152.
[31] Skobtsova, *Essential Writings*, 152.

there is certainty and safety – not something to be despised. The danger is, however, that the cocoon will deafen us to the demands of love, will stifle any creativity.

And then the 'aesthetic type': perhaps the besetting temptation of Russian Orthodoxy. The conversion of Rus' is presented in the *Russian Primary Chronicle* as a response to the experience of the ambassadors to Constantinople:

> we knew not whether we were in heaven or on earth. For on earth there is no splendour or such beauty, and we are at a loss how to describe it. We only know that God dwells there among men, and their service is fairer than the ceremonies of other nations. For we cannot forget that beauty.[32]

And Russians are fond of quoting the words ascribed to Prince Myshkin in Dostoevsky's *Idiot*: 'Beauty will save the world'. In itself the aesthetic sensitivity for beauty is good, at least as a starting point, but it can become limiting. The aesthete thinks of himself as belonging to a privileged minority, who can alone appreciate the aesthetic delights of the Orthodox Liturgy; a condescending attitude is adopted to those who do not have this appreciation. The aesthetic type will find little room for love, or even for hatred: '[t]here is only that cold, exacting contempt for the profane crowd and an ecstatic admiration for beauty'.[33] In the end, this aesthetic attitude misses what is most central to Christianity: Christ himself. As Mother Maria puts it:

> The eyes of love will perhaps be able to see how Christ Himself departs, quietly and invisibly, from the sanctuary that is protected by a splendid iconostasis. The singing will continue to resound, clouds of incense will still rise, the faithful will be overcome by the ecstatic beauty of the services. But Christ will go out on to the church steps and mingle with the crowd: the poor, the lepers, the desperate, the embittered, the holy fools. Christ will go out into the streets, the prisons, the hospitals, the low haunts and dives. Again and again Christ lays down his soul for his friends.[34]

Mother Maria is acutely aware of the way in which the aesthetic attitude can turn aside the demands of love, turn them into something to admire:

> Even the suffering and death of the Lord Himself, His human exhaustion, acquires an aura of beauty, inviting admiration and delight. Love is a very dangerous thing. At times it must reach down into the fathomless lower levels of the human spirit, it must expose itself to ugliness, to the violation of harmony. There is no room for it where beauty, when once discovered and sanctioned, reigns forever.[35]

Mother Maria's fourth religious type is the 'ascetic'. It is very widespread: not particularly Christian, it is found in a pure form in Eastern religions, for

---

[32] *Russian Primary Chronicle*, 108 (ed. and trans. S. H. Cross and O. P Sherbowitz-Wetzor (Cambridge, MA: Mediaeval Academy of America, 1953), 111).

[33] Skobtsova, *Essential Writings*, 158.

[34] Skobtsova, *Essential Writings*, 161.

[35] Skobtsova, *Essential Writings*, 162.

instance in the practice of yoga in Hinduism; it is also found in quite non-religious contexts, revolutionary movements, for instance, with which Mother Maria herself was well acquainted. In some ways it is an essential ingredient in any serious, strenuous religious commitment, which only makes its dangers more insidious. She begins by talking about what she calls a 'natural' form of asceticism, which is concerned with acquiring control over oneself, by pursuing various fundamentally psychological techniques whose 'aim is the acquisition of spiritual power'.[36] In response to this, Mother Maria says,

> The only thing in this world more powerful than this is the Church's teaching about spiritual poverty, about the spending, the squandering of one's spiritual powers, about the utmost impoverishment of the spirit. The only definition of self that is more powerful than it are the words: 'Behold the handmaid of the Lord.'[37]

In Christianity, however, the true danger of the ascetic approach is revealed if one thinks about the question of salvation. There is no doubt at all that the salvation of the soul is, as Mother Maria puts it, the 'mature fruit of a true and authentic Christian life', but there are two fundamentally different ways of pursuing this: the ascetic approach is one of them. For the ascetic approach, salvation of the soul is paramount: it is attained by ascetic mortification of the flesh, by prayer and fasting, by obedience. Yes, the individual lives in the world and has duties to fulfil, but, in truth, '[t]he whole world, its woes, its sufferings, its labours on all levels – this is a kind of a huge laboratory, a kind of experimental arena, where I can practise my obedience and humble my will'.[38] This leads to what Mother Maria calls 'an extraordinary spiritual stinginess, a kind of miserliness', for '[t]he other person, the other person's soul – a stranger's, of course – becomes not the object of love, but a means of benefiting one's own soul'.[39] Such asceticism is a barely veiled egoism, and a 'unique process of self-poisoning by spiritual means takes place',[40] all the more dangerous because it looks so authentically religious.

The last type in Mother Maria's analysis is the 'evangelical' type. She begins by distinguishing this from the way 'evangelical' is often used – which she sees as marked by sectarianism, moralism and a 'distorted and impoverished view of salvation' – and also from attempts to 'Christianize' or 'enchurch' society, which are only milder versions of the same thing. The word she wants to use here is 'Christify', based on the apostle Paul's words, 'I live, and yet no longer I, but Christ lives within me' (Gal. 2.20). 'The image of God, the icon of Christ, which truly is my real and authentic essence or being, is the only measure of all things, the only path or way which is given to me.'[41] Mother Maria's

---

[36] Skobtsova, *Essential Writings*, 164.
[37] Skobtsova, *Essential Writings*, 165.
[38] Skobtsova, *Essential Writings*, 167.
[39] Skobtsova, *Essential Writings*, 168.
[40] Skobtsova, *Essential Writings*, 173.
[41] Skobtsova, *Essential Writings*, 174.

discussion of what this entails is dense and urgent, not easy to summarize. I shall just pick out a few points and comment on them in my own words.

First of all, this is the way of love, and as we have seen from all that follows, it is all too easy to side-step the demands of love, to seem to be loving, when really love itself has been set aside, or turned into a means to an end. This is avoided by realizing the complementarity of the two commands to love. There are two ways of loving to be avoided: one which subordinates love of our fellow humans to love of God, so that humans become means whereby we ascend to God, and the other of which forgets love of God, and so loves our fellow humans in a merely human way, not discerning in them the image of God, or the ways in which it has been damaged or distorted.

St Maria then points to the source of this love, in the 'path of Godmanhood, Christ's path on earth', where we behold 'limitless, sacrificial, self-abnegating, and self-humbling love'. It seems to me that she alludes here to a central point in Bulgakov's theology, when she says that there are not 'two Gods ... one who abides in blessedness within the bosom of the Holy Trinity and another who took on the form of a servant'.[42] Although she is not explicit, I find here an allusion to Bulgakov's understanding of *kenosis*, self-emptying, which we see in Christ, who humbled himself, taking the form of a servant, but also in the relationships within the Blessed Trinity, where the Persons of the Trinity yield to each other in constituting one God. The entailment of this is that the love we behold in the Son's *kenosis* in his Incarnation and death is the very same as the love that, through mutual *kenosis*, we find in the bosom of the Trinity. This leads St Maria to speak of love as the way of non-possession (a conscious allusion to the controversy in fifteenth-century Russian monasticism between the 'Possessors', led by Iosif Volotsky, and the 'Non-possessors', led by Nil Sorsky, over whether monasteries should possess land or not). Opposed to non-possession are the vices of stinginess and greed:

> Nonpossession teaches us not only that we should not greedily seek advantage for our soul, but that we must not be stingy with our soul, that we should squander our soul in love, that we should achieve spiritual nakedness, that spiritually we should be stripped bare. There should be nothing so sacred or valuable that we would not be ready to give it up in the name of Christ's love to those who have need of it.[43]

The way of non-possession, St Maria suggests, is completely foreign to the way of the world, characterized as it is by a quantitative approach and sense of contract: if I give something away, I lose something, and at the same time make a claim on the one to whom I give it. The way of non-possession enables love to be completely free. It is enshrined at the heart of the Eucharist, in the offering in which we all participate in union with Christ: 'Offering you your own of your own, in all and for all'.

---

[42] Skobtsova, *Essential Writings*, 179.
[43] Skobtsova, *Essential Writings*, 181.

St Maria's vision was radical, uncompromising, demanding; it led directly to her death in Ravensbrück. It was not just some personal charism of utterly generous, self-giving love, however, for we see from her writings how it was rooted in a vision of God and the world. That vision is something that we are by now familiar with: the lineaments of St Maria's vision we have already found in the great thinkers of the Russian Religious Renaissance, from Solov'ev to Berdyaev and Bulgakov. Her vision is expressed in terms of *Bogochelovechestvo*, Godmanhood, the central theme in Solov'ev's philosophy, and *sobornost'*, a theme Solov'ev inherited from Khomiakov. She directly appeals to Dostoevsky to underscore the paradoxical nature of love. Although she does not make much use, that I can see, of Bulgakov's notion of Sophia, there are plenty of other striking parallels with his theology, not least the complementarity she finds between Christ and his Virgin Mother – in Bulgakov himself bound up with his ideas of Sophia. In her discussion of 'Types of Religious Life', one of her criteria constantly called on is the essential place of creativity and freedom in any authentically Christian life, something we have explored in little in thinking about Berdyaev. It seems to me that in St Maria we find the themes of Russian religious philosophy fused into the burning light of her life, and raised to the heights of true holiness.

9

Modern Orthodox dogmatic theology: 1 Fr Dumitru Stăniloae

So far we have followed the development from the influence of the *Philokalia* in nineteenth-century Russia through to the Russian émigrés who found themselves in Paris between the two world wars; we shall now take something of a detour and look at two Orthodox theologians who represent the renewal of theology in their native lands, both of which fell to communism after the Second World War. Both these theologians – Fr Dumitru Stăniloae in Romania and Fr (now St) Justin Popović in Serbia – produced extensive dogmatic theologies of the traditional kind, unlike any of the thinkers we are considering in this volume. They were more or less contemporaries: St Justin was older by nearly a decade and died on his eighty-fifth birthday, just over a decade before Fr Dumitru. They bear other similarities: both were devoted to their homeland, and thus wrote in languages not widely understood elsewhere, so that their influence has been limited by these factors; both were

Dumitru Stăniloae

127

deeply influenced by the Fathers, and their dogmatic theologies can be seen as attempts to articulate a patristic vision in today's world – they are both, then, exemplars of the 'neo-patristic synthesis'; they also studied abroad, both of them in Athens, Fr Dumitru in Berlin and Paris, St Justin in Petrograd (as it then was) and Oxford; both were in touch with the currents of Russian Orthodoxy we have been exploring so far, and both were dissatisfied with the way in which Orthodox dogmatic theology was taught in the seminaries of their youth (and more recently).

Life

We shall start with the Romanian, although he was the younger of the two. He was born on 16 November 1903, the youngest child of his parents, inVlădeni, in what is now the district of Braşov, on the southern edge of Transylvania, close to the South Carpathian mountains. His village was Orthodox, but it is an area of Romania where there were also Protestants and Eastern Rite Catholics. He was a bright child, and in 1917 went to Braşov to attend high school. After finishing high school, the young Dumitru went to Sibiu, where he was recommended to the bishop, Nicolae Bălan, who proved to be an important influence on his theological education. First, he went to Cernăuţi, where he studied theology. It was, however, a disappointing experience, and he moved to Bucharest, where he studied Romanian literature. A meeting in Bucharest with Bishop Bălan led to his returning to Transylvania and studying theology at Sibiu. After completing his degree, Dumitru went to Athens to study for a doctorate in theology, which he completed on the seventeenth-century patriarch Dositheos of Jerusalem and his relations with Romania. Dumitru's studies continued in Munich, Berlin, Paris and Belgrade; during this time he studied the theology of St Gregory Palamas, working from manuscripts, not content with the (meagre) published editions.

In 1929 he returned to Sibiu and began teaching at the Department of Dogmatics in the Andrei Şaguna Theological Academy, remaining there until 1947. At the beginning of his time there, Bishop Nicolae Bălan asked him to translate the *Dogmatics* of the Greek theologian Christos Androutsos, which he did, only to find himself dissatisfied with Androutsos' 'scholastic' approach to theology. In 1930 he married. In the same year he was ordained deacon, and in 1932 ordained priest. In 1931, again at the request of his bishop, he began a long association with the cultural and religious journal *Telegraful Român*, lasting until 1945 (becoming manager in 1934). Dumitru's journalistic work was extensive; he also wrote for the journal *Gândirea* ('Thought'). This work was clearly important to him; in the bibliography that forms part of the Festschrift prepared for his ninetieth birthday (in the event a *Denkschrift*), there are listed 420 items of journalism, just twice the number of theological articles listed – such journalism was considered by Fr Dumitru part of the task of a theologian, who is to interpret the times for the benefit of his fellow Christians. In 1934 he met Nichifor Crainic at his bishop's house, and became good friends with this remarkable man. Crainic had discovered the mystical dimension of his native Orthodoxy in Vienna, and deeply influenced the no less remarkable Hugo Ball, in whose person Byzantine mysticism and Dadaism were united.[1]

The 1930s were a difficult period for Romania. In a country that had achieved its dream of a united nation only at the end of the First World War, nationalist sentiments were powerful and widespread; these were often tinged with anti-Semitism and right-wing sympathies. Fr Dumitru was not free of these influences, in this at one with other intellectuals such as Mircea Eliade, E. M. Cioran and Petru Ţuţea. From his youth, Fr Dumitru had been dogged by bad health, and the decade of the thirties was no exception to what became a continuing feature of his life.

At the end of the war, Fr Dumitru was relieved of his position at the Andrei Şaguna Theological Academy, and only in 1947 was he appointed to the Department of Asceticism and Mysticism (which had been established at the insistence of Crainic, when he was appointed there) in the Faculty of Theology at Bucharest; the following year he was appointed Professor of Dogmatic and Symbolic Theology, and there he taught until his retirement in 1973, mostly concerned with doctoral students. During his time in Bucharest he became a fervent supporter of the group called *Rugul aprins* ('The Burning Bush'), which fostered Christian reflection among the Christian intelligentsia in the capital, and quickly found itself at odds with the communist régime, imposed on Romania at the end of the Second World War as a result of the Yalta conference. Nevertheless, the Church continued to celebrate its heritage, and in 1955 Fr Dumitru was involved in the glorification of St Callinicus of Cernica, a monastery just outside Bucharest.[2]

The Hungarian uprising in 1956 alarmed the communist régime in Romania, and very soon, Fr Dumitru found himself in deepening trouble with the communists. His articles were censored and then banned. In 1958, he was arrested, along with other members of the 'Burning Bush', subjected to a show trial and sentenced to five years' imprisonment, most of which was spent in the notorious prison at Aiud. He never made much of his period of imprisonment, other than to say that he was not physically maltreated, and that there he simply carried his cross, which was the normal condition of any Christian and that one needed not to speak of it.[3] He also said that his

---

[1] On Crainic, see Christine Hall, *'Pancosmic' Church – Specific Românesc: Ecclesiological Themes in Nichifor Crainic's Writings between 1922 and 1944*, Uppsala Universitet, 2008. On Ball and Dadaism, see Leonard Aldea, 'The Implicit Apophaticism of Dada Zurich: A Spiritual Quest by Means of Nihilist Procedures', *Modern Theology* 29 (2013), 157–75.

[2] See *The Tradition of Life: Romanian Essays in Spirituality and Theology*, ed. A. M. Allchin, SSTS 2 (Oxford: Fellowship of St Alban and St Sergius, 1971), which contains articles on St Callinicus by Patriarch Justinian (Marina) and Fr Stăniloae.

[3] Olivier Clément, 'Le Père Dumitru Stăniloae et le génie de l'Orthodoxie roumaine', in *Persoană şi Comuniune: Prinos de Cinstire. Preotului Profesor Academician Dumitru Stăniloae 1903–1993*, ed. Mircea Păcurariu and Ioan I. Ică Jr (Sibiu: Editura şi tiparul Arhiepiscopiei ortodoxe Sibiu, 1993), 82–9, at 82–3.

time in prison was the one time in his life when he was able continually to pray the Jesus Prayer.[4]

In 1963 he returned to Bucharest. It was only with difficulty, and after some delay, that he was restored to his chair in the Theological Institute in Bucharest. Soon he was permitted to travel abroad – as a living symbol of the religious freedom that the communist authorities wanted the West to believe existed in Romania – and accepted invitations to lecture in many universities, visiting Pope Paul VI in 1971, and in the same year the Monastery of Chevetogne and also the University of Uppsala. In 1973, he retired as professor, but continued to work with doctoral students; he also began to write more and more. In 1990 he was elected to the Romanian Academy; in these latter years, he received many honorary doctorates. In March 1993, his wife, Maria, died, and on 5 October, Fr Dumitru followed her.

Simply through his life, his friendships, his teaching and direction of doctoral students, Fr Dumitru made a signal contribution to the life of the Romanian Church during one of the worst periods of its history, under the communist régime imposed on the country as part of the settlement after the Second World War. He involved himself in the challenges facing his country, and was not afraid to reflect on its fate and future. He also wrote and published, and left a lasting legacy for Romania and for the world.

Writings

The list of his publications is colossal; the Festschrift has 50 pages of bibliography (though it includes translations of his works as well), and when it was published there were still items yet to appear. There are very many articles, over 600, more than two-thirds of them, as we have seen, of a popular nature, appearing in cultural journals. There are several major works: a volume on Orthodox spirituality, based on lectures given in Bucharest, that go back to 1946 even before he was appointed to the Department of Asceticism and Mysticism there. These were first published in 1981 as volume 3 of *Orthodox Moral Theology* (volumes 1 and 2 never existed), and reissued in 1992 as *Orthodox, Ascetical and Mystical Spirituality*;[5] also his best-known work, *Orthodox Dogmatic Theology*, published in 1978.[6] These works belong to the period of his retirement, though they represent the substance of lectures he had given

[4] See Charles Miller, *The Gift of the World: An Introduction to the Theology of Dumitru Stăniloae* (Edinburgh: T&T Clark, 2000), 20.

[5] Dumitru Stăniloae, *Spiritualitatea Ortodoxă: Ascetica şi Mistica* (Bucharest: Editura Institutului Biblic şi de Misiune al Bisericii Ortodoxe Române, 1992); ET: *Orthodox Spirituality*, trans. Archimandrite Jerome (Newville) and Otilia Kloos (South Canaan, PA: St Tikhon's Seminary Press, 2002).

[6] Dumitru Stăniloae, *Teologia Dogmatică Ortodoxă*, 3 vols (Bucharest: Editura Institutului Biblic şi de Misiune al Bisericii Ortodoxe Române, 1978, 2nd edn, 1996–7). First translated into German by Hermann Pitters of the Lutheran Hochschule in Sibiu (Hermannstatt): *Orthodoxe Dogmatik*, 3 vols (Zürich: Benziger Verlag/Gütersloh: Gerd Mohn, 1994–5). ET: *The Experience of God: Orthodox Dogmatic Theology*, trans. Ioan Ioniţă and, for some volumes, Robert Barringer (Brookline, MA: Holy Cross Orthodox Press, 1989–2013).

throughout the course of his long academic career. The circumstances of their publication need to be noticed: published during the communist period, they were intended as an up-to-date substitute for older textbooks, and so they had to look like textbooks to pass the censors. This is why a work on spirituality appears initially as part of a set of works on moral theology (the reissue in 1992 taking place soon after the fall of Ceauşescu), and it explains the curious mismatch that the reader of the *Orthodox Dogmatic Theology* feels between the very traditional order of the chapters and what these chapters actually contain, which sometimes undermines traditional expectations.

The Romanian *Philokalia*

Dwarfing the theological articles and the published volumes, however, is Fr Dumitru's vast work of translation, at the heart of which is his Romanian *Philokalia*. I have already maintained that the publication of the original *Philokalia* in 1782 heralds (sometimes in a distant way) the course that Orthodox theology (or the most significant Orthodox theology) was to take in the modern period. With Fr Dumitru this is explicit, and it is worth pausing for a moment to consider what is meant by the central position the Romanian *Philokalia* represents in Fr Dumitru's conception of theology.

Between 1946 and 1991, there appeared 12 substantial volumes (typically of about 400 pages each) of the Romanian translation of the *Philokalia*. It is based on the Greek *Philokalia*, published in 1782 and compiled by St Nikodimos of the Holy Mountain and St Makarios of Corinth. In fact, few of the different versions, in different languages, of the *Philokalia* are simply translations of the original selection – perhaps the English version, very slowly nearing completion, is the closest to the original[7] – but the Romanian version departs from the original most dramatically: the original texts are supplemented, or sometimes replaced by others, and as well as providing his own introductions to the works involved, Fr Dumitru also provided commentary. The Romanian *Philokalia* is also, as is evident, much larger than the original: a veritable library rather than the 'anthology' implied by the title *Philokalia*. Every element in Fr Dumitru's conception of the Romanian *Philokalia* – the choice of the *Philokalia* itself, its supplementation and his commentary – is significant for Fr Dumitru's understanding of the role Orthodox theology is to play in the modern world.

The *Philokalia* itself suggests a particular approach to theology. In the Introduction to the English translation of the *Philokalia*, the editors draw attention to the subtitle of the work, according to which 'the intellect is purified, illumined and made perfect', and remark:

---

[7] For an account of the different versions of the *Philokalia*, see my article, 'The Influence of the *Philokalia* in the Orthodox World', in *The* Philokalia: *A Classic Text of Orthodox Spirituality*, ed. Brock Bingaman and Bradley Nassif (New York: Oxford University Press, 2012), 50–60, 286–7 (notes).

The *Philokalia* is an itinerary through the labyrinth of time, a silent way of love and gnosis through the deserts and emptinesses of life, especially of modern life, a vivifying and fadeless presence. It is an active force revealing a spiritual path and inducing man to follow it. It is a summons to him to overcome his ignorance, to uncover the knowledge that lies within, to rid himself of illusion, and to be receptive to the grace of the Holy Spirit who teaches all things and brings all things to remembrance.[8]

Such an approach to theology is not just a 'return to the sources', but to embark on a spiritual journey.

The *Philokalia* is an anthology of texts, spreading over about a millennium, initiating readers into a tradition of prayer that developed on the Holy Mountain of Athos and led to the so-called hesychast controversy of the fourteenth century over the use of the Jesus Prayer and the claims of the Athonite monks to experience the uncreated light of the Godhead. They were defended by St Gregory Palamas, who is one of the theologians most extensively anthologized, along with St Maximos the Confessor. The focus of the Greek *Philokalia* is predominantly devotional; the more speculative works of St Gregory and St Maximos, for example, are either omitted or present in a truncated form. Fr Dumitru had greater confidence in his readers' ability to scale the heights of Byzantine theology, and perhaps a greater sense of the significance of, in particular, the cosmic dimension of Byzantine theology, not least for his century, than did the saints Nikodimos and Makarios. So, as well as the more devotional works of Maximos, Fr Dumitru included the whole of one of his great theological works, *Questions to Thalassios*, which had been present in the original *Philokalia* as a series of 'centuries' of excerpts. St Symeon the New Theologian is expanded from a few pages (including one dubiously ascribed to him) to virtually the whole of his prose works. Authors not present at all are added: notably the *Ladder* of St John of Sinai, Dorotheos of Gaza, the 'Questions and Answers' of the 'Great Old Man' and the 'Other Old Man' of Gaza, the hermits Varsanouphios and John, as well as St Isaac the Syrian, seventh-century Nestorian bishop of Nineveh.

Alongside the Romanian *Philokalia*, Fr Dumitru also published translations (with introductions and notes) of other Fathers: St Athanasios, the Cappadocian Fathers, St Gregory the Theologian and St Gregory of Nyssa, St Cyril of Alexandria and Dionysios the Areopagite. He also published translations of two other works of St Maximos: his *Mystagogia*, a commentary on the eucharistic liturgy, and his massive *Ambigua*.

If one looks at the Greek Fathers who are central to Fr Dumitru, a familiar pattern emerges, for these are the Fathers usually invoked in connection with the neo-patristic synthesis of Fr Georges Florovsky and Vladimir Lossky. Fr Dumitru then emerges not as a marginal figure, not even simply a bridge

---

[8] *The Philokalia: The Complete Text Compiled by St Nikodimos of the Holy Mountain and St Makarios of Corinth*, trans. from the Greek and ed. G. E. H. Palmer, Philip Sherrard, Kallistos Ware, I (London: Faber & Faber, 1979), 13–14.

between East and West, or between Russian and Greek Orthodoxy (roles Romanians have often adopted), but rather at the very centre of what can claim to have been the liveliest and most significant movement in modern Orthodox theology. Fr Dumitru's endeavours, however, dwarf those of his contemporaries.

And the commentaries (or notes). The lack of commentary in the original *Philokalia* was not oversight; the volumes were not intended for private reading, but for reading under the guidance of a spiritual father. But as the West learnt at the end of the Middle Ages, the printed word cannot be bound to institutions in the way manuscripts can. St Nikodimos envisaged that the *Philokalia* would be read outside a monastic context, but was prepared to take the risk. The experience of the Russian pilgrim of *The Way of the Pilgrim* suggests that reading the *Philokalia* on one's own could occasion as much puzzlement as enlightenment. However, from the beginning, Fr Dumitru envisaged readers who would need commentary, not simply because of the straitened circumstance of the Church under the communists, but also because, with his inclusion of intellectually demanding texts, there was need to make clear the coinherence of the mind and the heart, of theology and prayer, that the *Philokalia* presupposes.

The importance of commentary on the Fathers, however, goes further than that for Fr Dumitru: it is his preferred way of interpreting the Fathers for the modern world. Much of his theological insight finds its clearest expression as he seeks to draw out the meaning of the Fathers. The case of St Maximos provides a good example: Fr Dumitru's comments on the major works of St Maximos draw out theological themes the importance of which is enduring. In his published books, reflection achieved in commentary finds its way into the lineaments of Fr Dumitru's own theological vision. There is a symbiosis between scholarly commentary and creative theological reflection, but above all there is the desire to communicate. One of the few things that Fr Dumitru said about his prison experiences is relevant here: once in reply to a question about it he said, 'I realized that our theology had been too abstract and theoretical. We needed to be closer to the people in our teaching, nearer to where they really are. I decided that I would always try to be nearer to people and their present predicaments in my writing.'[9] Later he was said to have remarked that, when writing, he would ask himself, 'What would the people of my old village have made of this?'

The created order

Perhaps a good place to start in considering his theology is a remark reported by several who knew him: 'We have made the distinction between heaven and earth far too absolute and far too neat. There is constant overlap'.[10] This

---

[9] Reported in A. M. Allchin's obituary for Fr Dumitru: *Sobornost* 16:1 (1994), 38–44, at 40.

[10] Allchin, obituary, 42.

echoes a concern we have already met in some of the theologians we have considered so far, for instance Fr Sergii Bulgakov, for whom the sense that nothing is bereft of God is one of the informing insights of his sophiology, though in the case of Fr Dumitru it is an Orthodox self-criticism, rather than being directed against the West. We find this awareness, too, in the frequent evocation in the Russian tradition of the words of Prince Vladimir's envoys to Constantinople of the Divine Liturgy they experienced in the church of Hagia Sophia: 'we knew not whether we were in heaven or on earth ... We only know that God dwells there among men ... For we cannot forget that beauty.'[11] The place of beauty in Orthodox theology belongs here, too, for beauty in this sense is to be seen as a sense of the radiance of heaven experienced here on earth. The tendency that Fr Dumitru is warning against is something that very easily affects theology: a desire to define, to keep our notions clear and distinct, to protect the reality and transcendence of God, as if he needed our efforts! The alternative is a lack of clarity, a tolerance of a certain confusion, a certain muddle: which is characteristic of something experienced, rather than simply conceived. For Fr Stăniloae's theology is a theology of experience – not of experiences, but of engagement.

The remark of Fr Dumitru's just quoted is about the created order, traditionally understood as consisting of heaven and earth, as is affirmed in the creed, for example, when we confess God the Father as 'creator of heaven and earth'. It is easy to set heaven and earth in opposition: the one spiritual and invisible, the other material and visible. For Fr Dumitru, however, there is 'constant overlap': we find heaven in earth, that earth discloses heaven. Partly this means that we find meaning in Creation, that the created order is full of symbols – a theme that we find in the Fathers. Meaning and symbols, however, need a mind to discern them. I remarked earlier that, while Fr Dumitru was obliged to stick to the structure of a traditional textbook of dogmatic theology, what he has to say constantly disrupts the structure, and so here.

Creation is the explicit subject of the second part of the *Orthodox Dogmatic Theology* (that is, the second part of the first volume of the Romanian original and the German translation, the second volume of the English translation), but the theme of creation is introduced in the first pages, for the knowledge of God, traditionally the initial topic of a dogmatic theology, cannot, for Stăniloae, be discussed without raising the question of creation, for it is through created beings that God manifests himself, whether we are thinking of natural revelation or supernatural revelation (a distinction that Stăniloae finds fault with, too). So, right at the beginning of his *Orthodox Dogmatic Theology*, he introduces the idea that the human and the cosmic mutually reflect each other. As he puts it:

---

[11] *Russian Primary Chronicle*, 108 (ed. and trans. S. H. Cross and O. P. Sherbowitz-Wetzor (Cambridge, MA: Mediaeval Academy of America, 1953), 111).

Some of the Fathers of the Church have said that man is a microcosm, a world which sums up in itself the larger world. Saint Maximos the Confessor remarked that the more correct way would be to consider man as a macrocosm, because he is called to comprehend the whole world within himself as one capable of comprehending it without losing himself, for he is distinct from the world. Therefore, man effects a unity greater than the world exterior to himself, whereas, on the contrary, the world, as cosmos, as nature, cannot contain man fully within itself without losing him, that is, without losing in this way the most important part of reality, that part which, more than all others, gives reality its meaning.

The idea that man is called to become a world writ large has a more precise expression, however, in the term 'macro-anthropos'. The term conveys the fact that, in the strictest sense, the world is called to be humanized entirely, that is, to bear the entire stamp of the human, to become pan-human, making real through that stamp a need which is implicit in the world's own meaning: to become, in its entirety, a humanized cosmos, in a way that the human being is not called to become, nor can ever fully become, even at the farthest limit of his attachment to the world where he is completely identified with it, a 'cosmicized' man. The destiny of the cosmos is found in man, not man's destiny in the cosmos.[12]

Note, first of all, how Stăniloae develops his theme from a remark of St Maximos', his favourite Father. Furthermore, note how this insight is directed to a new problem, that of understanding the significance of the human in the world as revealed by modern science, and doing this in a way that preserves the insights of the patristic vision. Too often the Christian story has been understood as fundamentally about the human, the rest of the Creation acting as a kind of backdrop. This is emphatically not the case with the Fathers, nor the liturgy of the Church (as a glance at the traditional eucharistic anaphoras will reveal, or even more so the prayer of the blessing of the water in the baptismal service): nor is it so with Stăniloae's theology. The refusal to isolate the human from nature is repeated when Stăniloae comes to consider Creation explicitly, in Part 2. There he affirms: 'For nature depends on man or makes him whole, and man cannot reach perfection if he does not reflect nature and is not at work upon it. Thus by the "world" both nature and humanity are understood'.[13]

Another feature of Stăniloae's doctrine of creation needs to be noted: Part 2 is subtitled, 'The World: Creation and Deification'. To speak about creation is to speak about the cosmos that God created to be deified: we have noted earlier how Orthodox theologians think of the great arc of the divine economy as stretching from creation to deification, and reaching over the lesser arc of the fall and redemption. Fr Dumitru simply reflects a fundamental Orthodox intuition by considering creation in relation to deification, as an expression of God's love and goodness the purpose of which is to be raised to union with him.

---

[12] Stăniloae, *Experience* I, 4–5.

[13] Stăniloae, *Experience* II, 1.

'The Cross on the Gift of the World'

Stăniloae has another theme, characteristic of his doctrine of creation, what he calls 'The Cross on the Gift of the World'. Again, this takes its inspiration from a remark of St Maximos', found in his *Centuries on Theology and the Incarnate Dispensation*:

> All visible things need a cross, that is, the state in which what is active in them through the senses is cut off; all intelligible realities need a tomb, the complete quiescence of what is active in them according to the intellect.[14]

The cross is the cross of blessing, in which we acknowledge everything created as a gift from God the Creator. A gift, however, is not just a transaction: it establishes, and is a sign of, a relationship between the giver and the one who receives. The 'cutting off' that the cross symbolizes is a cutting off so that the gift does not become an end in itself, but rather a sign of the relationship it establishes or furthers, a relationship of generosity and thankfulness. The whole world is a gift from God, a gift on which he has set his cross. It is a gift that establishes a condition of gift-giving: we take the gifts we have been given, and give them to others, as well as giving them back to God, pre-eminently in the Eucharist, the Divine Liturgy. If we fail in this, we experience the cross in another way:

> Over the world and over our lives, the cross is raised in this way. When, of our own will, we no longer see God through the cross, leaving the world and our own lives behind in the love for God, then he makes himself transparent to us through the cross against our will.[15]

This chapter, which speaks of the cross on the gift of the world, goes on to develop more themes, again largely drawing on St Maximos: his doctrine of the presence of God in his Creation through his *logoi*, deep structures of meaning. This leads into reflection on human responsibility for the cosmos, a timely theme, even more timely now than when it was written (in the mid-1970s).

I have started to look at Fr Dumitru's theology by homing in on his doctrine of creation. I have only touched on it, however – there is much more, even in the section on creation – but as I have suggested, and as will emerge later on, the implications of his doctrine of creation permeate his theology. Before going any further, it might be worth outlining the structure of his *Dogmatic Theology*, and also saying something about his book on *Orthodox Spirituality*.

Orthodox Dogmatic Theology (The Experience of God)

The *Orthodox Dogmatic Theology* is in six sections (two sections a volume in the Romanian original and German translation): the first section is concerned

---

[14] Maximos the Confessor, *Capitum theologicorum and œonomicorum Centuria* I. 67 (PG 90:1108B).
[15] Stăniloae, *Experience* I, 24.

with revelation and knowledge of God; the second with the world as the work of God's love, which is to be deified; the third with Christology; the fourth with Christ's redemptive activity; the fifth with the sacraments; the sixth with eschatology. Put like that it sounds very traditional, as of course it had to be, if it was to pass the censors. If one looks more closely, these neat divisions begin to seem porous. For example, the first section begins with revelation and ends with the doctrine of the Trinity. Despite this, the doctrine of the Trinity is integral to the discussion of revelation, which is seen as the revelation of the Father through the Son and the Holy Spirit. The danger of the traditional model – a danger famously raised in Roman Catholic theology by Karl Rahner – is that an abstract knowledge of God is presented without reference to the Trinity, which is then seen as a further fact about God. Stăniloae avoids this danger very deftly.

Furthermore, although to speak of natural and supernatural revelation runs the risk of an artificial separation between what we can discover about God and what God reveals of himself, this risk is again avoided by Stăniloae who sees both natural and supernatural revelation as God's revelation, and moreover refuses to countenance any neat separation between nature and supernature. Again, the third and fourth sections seem to separate very clearly Christ's person and his work, Christology and redemption, but closer attention to what Stăniloae has to say reveals that any such separation is quite breached, mostly by his use of the notion of Christ as prophet, priest and king, which is treated both as three ways of seeing the person of Christ – who is he? – and as three ways of understanding Christ's office and work – what does he do? How does he achieve it?

In passing, it is worth noting that this notion of Christ's threefold office as prophet, priest and king first seems to be found in Calvin, at least as an explicitly 'threefold' office; individually, the ideas can be found in the Fathers and in the West in many later theologians, but the idea of thinking in terms of a threefold office seems to have been Calvin's. I doubt if Stăniloae would have been aware of this – the notion had probably entered traditional dogmatic treatises long before he started on his dogmatics – so I do not think we can regard this as evidence of any kind of openness on his part towards Western theology. Indeed, even though it is claimed that Stăniloae is unusual in his knowledge of and engagement with Western theology, my impression is that, especially in the *Orthodox Dogmatic Theology*, he is usually critical of Western theology, to the point of unfairness.[16] Whatever the source of the doctrine of Christ's threefold office, Stăniloae's use of it as a way of bridging a traditional separation between Christ's person and work is remarkable.

We shall pursue this way in which Stăniloae relates rather than separates with some other examples in a moment, but it should be noticed that behind

---

[16] I discuss this very briefly in a review article on the *Orthodox Dogmatic Theology* in *Dumitru Stăniloae: Tradition and Modernity in Theology*, ed. Lucian Turcescu (Iaşi: Center of Romanian Studies, 2002), 53–70, at 63–4 (originally published in *Modern Theology* 13 (1997), 253–67).

this lies a more fundamental intuition: theology is not concerned with concepts, though it makes use of them, but concerned with engagement with God (to call the English translation *The Experience of God* was an inspiration). *Orthodox Spirituality* is a companion to Stăniloae's *Dogmatic Theology*. It is an immensely rich work, a distillation of all that he had learnt in his translation of the *Philokalia*. His principal guiding light is once again St Maximos, and ideas that are explored as part of a Christian metaphysic of reality in the dogmatics are here explored as part of the ascent of the Christian to union with God. A good example of this would be the complementary treatment of the doctrine of the *logoi*, the deep structures of Creation. In *Orthodox Dogmatic Theology*, they serve to expound a sense of the integrity of Creation and the presence of God within it; in *Orthodox Spirituality* they help us to understand the place of nature and its contemplation in the development of our spiritual life.

It follows from this that it is dangerous to discuss Stăniloae's theology too much in terms of generalities. So I want to conclude by taking two specific examples.

The apophatic dimension of theology

Fr Stăniloae, like most (though not all) modern Orthodox theologians, gives an important place to apophatic theology in our knowledge of God, that is, to the knowledge of God that approaches him through denial of human concepts. In his *Orthodox Spirituality* he pays tribute to Vladimir Lossky's role in seeing the importance of apophatic theology for Orthodox thinking about God.[17] He goes further, and credits Lossky with seeing that apophatic theology lies beyond what might be called negative theology, simply as counterbalance to a theology of affirmation, and is really concerned with union with God, who is utterly incomprehensible:

> Unknowability does not mean agnosticism or refusal to know God. Nevertheless, this knowledge will only be attained in the way which leads not to knowledge but to union – to deification. Thus theology will never be abstract, working through concepts, but contemplative: raising the mind to those realities which pass all understanding.[18]

Fr Stăniloae's treatment of apophatic theology has its own distinctiveness. First of all, he opposes it not so much to kataphatic theology as to rational theology, and begins by emphasizing that apophatic theology does not dispose of rational theology, but transposes it:

> To rise above the things of the world does not mean that these disappear; it means, through them, to rise beyond them. And since they remain, the apophatic

---

17 Stăniloae, *Orthodox Spirituality*, 230–5.
18 Stăniloae, *Orthodox Spirituality*, 235, quoting Vladimir Lossky, *The Mystical Theology of the Eastern Church* (London: James Clarke, 1957), 43.

knowledge of God does not exclude affirmative rational knowledge ... In apophatic knowledge the world remains, but it has become transparent of God. This knowledge is apophatic because God who now is perceived cannot be defined; he is experienced as a reality which transcends all possibility of definition.[19]

This complementarity of apophatic and rational theology is true of our natural knowledge of God, but it is fleeting. It is true of revealed theology in a deeper way, for revelation reveals a God who is unknown, by which Fr Dumitru means that through faith in revelation there is disclosed to us both conceptions of God but, much more important, a sense of God as transcending anything we can grasp of him. The apophatic is the experiential: it is a sense of God's overwhelming reality that grows within faith. Fr Dumitru then takes a further step: this sense of God is something that will grow as we become more open to it, and that openness is a function of a growing purity and limpidity of our spiritual nature (something that is expressed through our bodily nature, not in contrast to it). Fr Stăniloae sees this sense of God as developing from a kind of 'pressure', as he puts it, to a sense of the personal presence of God. Its inexpressibility means that capturing it in terms of knowledge is abandoned in favour of experiencing it in terms of union: as it grows in intensity and purity, it escapes any kind of definition and becomes totally apophatic. 'The apophatic experience is equivalent to a sense of mystery that excludes neither reason nor sentiment, but it is more profound than these.'[20]

This might sound, especially to Western ears, as all rather mystical. Fr Stăniloae does not exclude such an interpretation, but it is not his primary meaning, for that last remark follows on from the assertion that 'the apophatic experience of God is a characteristic that gives definition to Orthodoxy in its liturgy, its sacraments, and sacramentals',[21] and the next section begins with this affirmation: 'If intellectual knowledge, both affirmative and negative, is more the product of theoretical reflection while it is in apophatic knowledge that people grow spiritually, then this latter knowledge is essential for all Christians in their practical life.'[22] This apophatic knowledge of God is found in the daily circumstances of our life, as we experience God's care and guidance in joyful circumstances, in the demands others make on us, in the qualms of conscience when we do wrong, and in the way God leads us through all circumstances to himself, if only we will let him. 'It is a thrilling, burdensome, painful, and joyful knowledge; it awakens with us our ability to respond; it gives fervour to prayer, and it causes our being to draw closer to God'.[23] This sense of the mystery of God

---

[19] Stăniloae, *Experience* I, 99.
[20] Stăniloae, *Experience* I, 117.
[21] Stăniloae, *Experience* I, 117.
[22] Stăniloae, *Experience* I, 117.
[23] Stăniloae, *Experience* I, 118.

is experienced especially in those states of responsibility, consciousness of
sinfulness, need of repentance, and in the insurmountable difficulties of life ...
The difficult circumstances which pierce our being like nails urge us towards
more deeply felt prayer. And during this kind of prayer the presence of God
is more evident to us.[24]

Such experience of God is apophatic because, although we can reflect on it,
we cannot figure it out; it is something to endure in silence, in the silence
of prayer.

Doctrine of the sacraments

My final example is Fr Stăniloae's treatment of the sacraments, 'The Sanctifying
Mysteries', as the English translation has it, rather over-translating, it seems
to me, the original 'Despre Sfintile Taine'. It is a rather traditional treatment
of the seven sacraments; Stăniloae does not reflect on the invasion of the
Western notion of seven sacraments into Orthodox theology. The first
chapter is on sacraments in general.

It is marred – I have to say this – by Fr Stăniloae's apparent need to position the Orthodox understanding of the sacraments in relation to what seem
to me caricatures of Protestant and Roman Catholic teaching, repeated later
on in the chapter.[25] What he has to say positively is pure gold.

I want to take three of what seem to me structural points in his development of the understanding of the sacrament. First, his sense of the way
sacramental activity flows from the very nature of the Creation, created by
God, who is the 'creator of all things, visible and invisible', or, we might
say, material and spiritual. So he begins by saying: 'The general basis of the
mysteries of the Church is the faith that God can operate upon the creature
in his visible reality'.[26] From this Stăniloae develops a sense of how visible
and invisible, material and spiritual, are interwoven in Creation: an interweav-
ing manifest pre-eminently in the human, who stands on the borders between
the material and the spiritual, as the 'macrocosm' and bond of the cosmos
(*syndesmos tou kosmou*). He makes special mention of the place of touch in
the sacraments: '[s]piritual powers flow out through the touch of the human
hand'.[27]

The second point I want to draw attention to is the way in which the
mystery of the union of God and Creation – the metaphysical basis of
the possibility of sacramental reality – is related to two other mysteries: the
mystery of Christ, which establishes a still deeper union between Creator
and creature, and the 'third mystery', the mystery of the Church, 'in which
God the Word restores and raises to an even higher degree His union

---

[24] Stăniloae, *Experience* I, 118–19.
[25] Stăniloae, *Experience* V, 1, cf. 15.
[26] Stăniloae, *Experience* V, 3.
[27] Stăniloae, *Experience* V, 2.

with the world, a world brought into being through the act of creation but weakened through human sin'.[28] As the third mystery, the Church extends the mystery of Creation and the mystery of Christ:

> The universe, become once again Church, has become the all-encompassing mystery, for mystery is the presence and action of God in the whole of creation. Moreover, inasmuch as each element within this all-encompassing mystery is also a mystery, it can also be said that each of its components is a church.[29]

The third point is entailed by these: a profound sense of the coinherence of material and spiritual, body and soul, and more precisely a sense of the profoundly personal nature of the sacraments. Although the achievement of union with God means transformation, transfiguration, by the Spirit of God,

> this reality is not achieved in a way that is purely invisible, or spiritual. There are two reasons for this: on one hand His body, even filled with the Spirit, has remained a real body, and on the other hand our body has to start from the visible, earthly image that the body of Christ possessed in order to advance through the various stages through which His body also passed, so that our bodies may attain to resurrection and spiritualization in the life eternal.[30]

He goes on to speak of 'the great importance and eternal worth of the human body as the medium through which the divine riches and depths become transparent', remarking that '[e]very gesture of the body has repercussions on the life of the soul, and every thought or sentiment of the soul has repercussions in the body'. These gestures, however, are personal: they involve personal communication, personal communion. At one level, this means personal communion between the human persons engaged in the sacrament. That is why, in all the sacraments, the person receiving them is called by name: 'The servant of God N. is baptized', 'The servant of God N. is granted communion in the precious and all-holy Body and Blood'. The person administering the sacraments, the priest or bishop is a person,

> a human being among the rest, yet is himself sent with a mission from above. He has the palpable warmth of a human being but also the responsibility of bringing Christ into intimacy and union with his brothers and sisters.[31]

Still more, the sacraments are personal, since, through the persons engaged in the sacrament, Christ himself is personally present, and engages personally with his people, one by one. For this reason, Fr Stăniloae is reluctant to see the sacraments as acts of the Church; rather they are actions of Christ through his Church.

> The light of that same ocean of grace, of brilliance and power that shines forth from Christ, penetrates into all those who receive the sacraments, and within

---

[28] Stăniloae, *Experience* V, 6.
[29] Stăniloae, *Experience* V, 7.
[30] Stăniloae, *Experience* V, 9.
[31] Stăniloae, *Experience* V, 23.

this light and its penetrating energy, the same Sun of Righteousness is present and active. Just as the look of a father, filled with an identical affection and penetrating love, will concurrently light upon all his children, so Christ enters through the energy of His own love within all those who receive the sacraments, bringing them into union with Himself and with one another and in this way expanding the Church and strengthening her unity.[32]

This emphasis on the personal has been characteristic of Fr Dumitru's theology from the beginning: the 'cross on the gift of the world' makes personal the relationship with the Creator we have through seeing the whole of Creation as a gift from the hand of the Creator. In the sacraments, this exchange of gifts between persons finds its fulfilment. Mysteries, or sacraments, are then not simply religious ceremonies, more or less necessary, but absolutely essential ways of expressing the nature of God's involvement, his personal engagement, with the created order through creation and Incarnation.

Fr Dumitru's dogmatic reflection is immensely rich, and I have only touched on a few points, but enough, I hope, to show something of his immense power of synthesis, and his sense that the deepest theology is close to the experience of the ordinary Christian, though for Fr Dumitru, to be a Christian, genuinely to yield to the transfiguring power of grace, is to be far from ordinary!

---

[32] Stăniloae, *Experience* V, 17.

10

Modern Orthodox dogmatic theology: 2 St Justin Popović

In this chapter, we shall find ourselves entering different, yet not unfamiliar, territory. Hitherto, through the thinkers we have been discussing, we have found ourselves looking at the so-called 'Paris School' of Orthodox theology, and its sources in nineteenth- and twentieth-century Russia. We shall soon take up this approach again by looking at other thinkers associated with the Paris School – Evdokimov, Meyendorff and Schmemann – and with the last two, at the continuation of this school in North America, in the theological circles associated with St Vladimir's Orthodox Theological Seminary in New York, where Fr Georges Florovsky, Fr John Meyendorff and Fr Alexander Schmemann taught. Because of the renown of these theologians in the English-speaking world, and partly, too, because of the dominance of the Press of the Seminary as a provider of Orthodox theological literature (most of the major works of twentieth-century Orthodox theology, originally published in the UK, are now issued by St Vladimir's Seminary Press), it is difficult in the English-speaking diaspora, and I expect further afield in the diaspora, to avoid a perception of Orthodox theology that operates on what one might call the Paris–New York, or St Serge–St Vladimir's, axis. This is, however, only part of the story of the reception of Russian theological and philosophical ideas in the West, just as the history of the so-called Rue Daru jurisdiction and the Orthodox Church in America is only part of the story of the Russian Orthodox diaspora.

The other Russian diaspora: Metropolitan Antony Khrapovitsky and the Church in Exile

As we look at St Justin Popović, or St Justin the New, as he has been called since his glorification in 2010, we shall find ourselves at least catching a glimpse of another story. For St Justin the New was a Serb, and it was Serbia that provided hospitality for another part of the Russian Orthodox Church outside the Russian homeland: that part of the Russian Church that has been called the Church in Exile, the Russian Orthodox Church Abroad (ROCA) or, more recently, the Russian Orthodox Church Outside Russia (ROCOR). This branch of the Russian Church consisted of those who had fought against the Revolution – the White Russians – and lost, those who refused to acquiesce in the Revolution and the accommodation that the recently established Patriarchate of Moscow had been forced to accept from the time of the first patriarch, Tikhon, onwards. This Church, which thought of itself as the true successor of the Russian Orthodox Church, was led by Metropolitan Antony Khrapovitsky. He was a highly respected bishop, Metropolitan of Kiev, and had in fact received the largest number of the votes in the final ballot for the new patriarch at the 1917/18 synod, though in the end the bishops' choice went to Metropolitan Tikhon of Moscow.[1]

It was in Serbia, in Sremski Karlovci, that Khrapovitsky gathered together his synod which defied Moscow and the patriarchate. Khrapovitsky was immensely respected, and Patriarch Dimitrije of Serbia – the Patriarchate of Serbia was also newly established – allowed Metropolitan Antony to rule his church from Karlovci. The reputation of the Russian Orthodox Church Abroad, the so-called Synodal Church, has on the whole been very negative: a Church clinging fiercely to the old traditions, the old language, and deeply opposed to ecumenism. This is true, but it is a partial truth. Khrapovitsky himself, though in many ways conservative, had some original, even surprising, theological views. He was opposed to substitutionary views of the atonement, and though this might be put down to his deep anti-Westernism, the truth is probably more complex. For him, it was in Gethsemane, in the Agony in the Garden, not at Golgotha, on the cross, that Christ achieved the redemption of humankind, for it was not Christ's death that wrought salvation, but his solidarity with the sinful condition of the whole of humanity: it was this that was the cause of his agony, and his prayer to the Father, 'Let this cup pass from me', expressed his overwhelming grief for the sinful human race that he so deeply loved.[2]

Certainly, it was Metropolitan Antony Khrapovitsky who led the heresy hunt against Fr Sergii Bulgakov's sophiology, but he was not himself a man without theological imagination. Even his anti-ecumenism is not unrelieved: he shared in the common positive attitude towards Anglicans on the part of the Orthodox that we find in the 1920s, and in some way recognized Anglican orders, proposing that Anglican clergy should be received into Orthodoxy by simple penance.[3] I mention all this because in the twenties Khrapovitsky had immense influence within the Serbian Church, and it is in this world that St Justin seems to me to make sense. It is a different world from the Paris of Bulgakov, Florovsky and Lossky, but it is a world just as indebted to Russia,

---

[1] See *My Life's Journey: The Memoirs of Metropolitan Evlogy*, trans. Alexander Lisenko, 2 vols (Yonkers, NY: St Vladimir's Seminary Press, 2014), I, 350–2. On Metropolitan Antony Khrapovitsky, see *Metropolitan Antonii (Khrapovitskii): Archpastor of the Russian Diaspora*, ed. Vladimir Tsurikov, Readings in Russian Religious Culture 5 (Jordanville, NY: Foundation of Russian History, 2014).

[2] On Khrapovitsky's soteriology, see Archpriest Nikolai Artemov, 'O soterilogii mitropolita Antoniya (Khrapovitsogo)', in *Metropolitan Antonii*, 19–68.

[3] On Metropolitan Khrapovitsky's relations with the Anglican Church, see Andrei V. Psarev, '"The soul and heart of a faithful Englishman is not limited by utilitarian goals and plans": The Relations of Metropolitan Anthony Khrapovitskii with the Anglican Church', *Sobornost* 33:2 (2011), 28–55; reprinted in *Metropolitan Antonii*, 92–113.

and a world we need to make something of, especially as ROCOR and the Moscow Patriarchate are now moving closer together.

Life

St Justin was born in Vranje, Serbia, in 1894 on the feast of the Annunciation, *Blagovest*, and therefore called Blagoje.[4] He was born into a devout family, which had had seven generations of priests. The healing of his mother from a severe illness in response to prayers to the wonderworker St Prohor, at the monastery of Pčinsk, gave him a profound and lasting sense of the reality of the spiritual world. He attended the St Sava seminary in Belgrade, where one of his teachers was Nikolaj Velimirović, later the famous bishop of Ohrid, now also glorified. At the outbreak of the First World War, Blagoje joined a student brigade of medical orderlies and went through the horrors of that war and the sufferings of those he tended; this reinforced his longing to become a monk.

In 1916 he was professed a monk by the Serbian metropolitan Dimitrije, and given the name Justin, after Justin the Philosopher, or the Martyr, and was sent by Metropolitan Dimitrije to the Spiritual Academy in Petrograd (as it then was). There he read the Russian thinkers: the Slavophils, Leont'ev, Solov'ev and Dostoevsky. Seven months later, however, the beginnings of

St Justin Popović
With permission of Boris Lubardić

---

[4] For my account of St Justin's life, I am largely reliant on Dame Elizabeth Hill's obituary in *Sobornost/ECR*, 2:1 (1980), 73–9.

the Communist Revolution cut short his stay in Russia and he went to Oxford instead. There he embarked on a thesis for the BLitt, the only research degree then available there, on the religion of Dostoevsky. The examiners took exception to his sweeping criticism of Catholicism, Protestantism and Western Europe, and advised him to revise his thesis. He refused, and left Oxford without a degree (the thesis was later published in Serbian).

Justin returned to Serbia, now Yugoslavia, the Kingdom of the Serbs, Croats and Slovenes, and taught theology at the St Sava Orthodox Seminary in Sremski Karlovci. He was soon sent to Athens where he completed a doctoral thesis on person and knowledge in St Makarios of Egypt. Returning to Karlovci, he combined his teaching with editing the monthly journal *Christian Life*; he soon became the main editor. In Karlovci, he came to know and revere Metropolitan Antony Khrapovitsky. His editorials in *Christian Life* became, as Dame Elizabeth Hill put it in her obituary, increasingly trenchant in their criticism of Western European civilization, which he felt was being imposed on Serbia. He lamented that 'never was there less God in man than today, never less God on earth than today'. He lamented the secularization of the schools, arguing for religious education and prayer. He deplored the neglect of St Sava, the patron saint of Serbia: 'The Turks burned St Sava's relics – whereas we, his undeserving descendants, burn him today: just as on Vračar his ashes were scattered, so we scatter his ashes by throwing him out of our education and culture.' In the last issue of *Christian Life* in 1927, he defended the periodical for having been alone in voicing opposition to what he saw as dangerous non-Orthodox innovations proposed at the Pan-Orthodox Congress held in Constantinople in 1923, not least the replacement of the Julian Calendar with the New Revised Julian Calendar (coincident for many centuries with the Gregorian Calendar, used elsewhere in Europe).

After a brief period teaching at Prizren, Fr Justin was reappointed to Karlovci. In 1931 he accompanied Metropolitan Josip Cvijic to Subcarpathian Rus' in Czechoslovakia. There he worked with such success among Uniates, bringing them back to Orthodoxy, that he was offered a bishopric. He refused and would rather have become the rector of St Sava's Seminary in Karlovci, but was not offered that post. Instead he went to the seminary in Bitolj. There he taught, translated the *Lausiac History* into Serbian and began to publish one of his major works, *The Dogmatics of the Orthodox Church: The Orthodox Philosophy of Truth*, the first volume of which was published in 1933. This led to his appointment to the Theological Faculty in Belgrade in 1934. He remained there teaching throughout the Second World War, during the occupation of Belgrade by the Nazis, though he was clear in his condemnation of Nazism. He had enormous influence among his students, encouraging several of them to embrace the monastic state.

After the war and the advent of the communist régime under Tito, he left Belgrade, and after spending time at various Serbian monasteries, settled in

1948 in Ćelije, up in the mountains near Valjevo, at a small monastery founded by King Dragutin (1276–1316) and dedicated to the archangel Michael. He remained there almost without interruption for the rest of his life. For years the monastery at Ćelije had been guarded, empty, by a lone monk; in 1946 the local bishop had sent a few nuns there to rekindle the religious life. Fr Justin became their spiritual father and shared with them an incredibly austere life of poverty, prayer and work. Much of the monastery had been destroyed. Slowly over the years – decades, really – with the help of local devout peasants, the monastic buildings were restored or rebuilt. Other convents grew from the convent at Ćelije.

Writings and influence within Serbia

St Justin's principal literary work during his years at Ćelije was the composition, in 12 volumes, of the *Lives of the Saints* (published between 1972 and 1977), a complement to St Nikolai Velimirović's *Ohrid Prologue*, in the preparation of which Justin had helped St Nikolai. Its importance for St Justin is manifest in the fact that in icons of the saint he is usually depicted holding a volume of the *Lives of the Saints*, although this is an unusual iconographical convention. He also published, while at Ćelije, *Svetosavlje as a Philosophy of Life* (that is, St Sava-ism, or Serbian Orthodoxy, as a Philosophy of Life; 1950), *The Life of St Sava and St Symeon* (1962), *Man and Godman: A Study in Orthodox Theology* (1969), and *The Orthodox Church and Ecumenism* (1974). His attitude to ecumenism was uncompromising: the Orthodox Church was the one true Church of Christ; ecumenism was a matter of politics, and unacceptable: Greek and Russian theologians engaged in the ecumenical movement were naively unaware of the dogmatic differences between Christians in the modern world. Various other tasks of publication occupied Fr Justin – translations of the Divine Liturgy, of the small and great *Euchologia*, the Akathist to the Mother of God and other saints, as well as commentaries on the Pauline Epistles, and the Gospels of Matthew and John (the latter unfinished) – so that only in 1976, with the help of his spiritual son, Bishop Atanasije Jevtić, and Mother Glikerija, the abbess of Ćelije, was Fr Justin able to bring his *Dogmatics* to completion with the third volume on the Church and eschatology, published in 1978, the year before he died.

St Justin's influence in Serbia has been, and still is, profound, though in his lifetime he had problems with the church hierarchy, largely owing to his outspokenness. Theology in Serbia today is dominated – so it seems to me, looking from outside, through a language barrier, as my Serbian is very rudimentary – by St Justin and his disciples, especially Amfilokije Radović, Atanasije Jevtić, Artemije Radosavljević, and Irinej Bulović, all bishops (or in the case of Artemije a former bishop). He was also highly regarded by those of the tradition of the Paris School, such as Fr John Meyendorff, who, in an obituary, listed these characteristics of his theology:

not only his love for the Fathers, not only the severe but enlightened monastic tradition of which he was the spokesman, but also his concern for Orthodoxy as a whole, his openness to and appreciation of both Greek and Russian theological thought and, above all, his ability to see theology as a living philosophy of Truth.[5]

St Justin and Serbian Orthodoxy

Because we are moving into a somewhat different world in considering St Justin the New, I think it might be useful to reflect on Serbia's history and its place in the Orthodox world, by way of placing St Justin in relation to the history of Orthodox thinking we have pursued so far.

The presence of Slav tribes in the territory of what is now Serbia goes back to the sixth century. Literary evidence for this is found in the work *De Administrando Imperio*, compiled from Byzantine archival material under the supervision of Constantine VII Porphyrogennetos in the tenth century, and can be supplemented by archaeological evidence. By that time the Serbs, or at least the nobility, had embraced Christianity, probably as a result of the mission of Cyril and Methodius to Moravia and the subsequent conversion of the Bulgarians in the ninth century. The creation of Serb Christian identity is, however, firmly bound up with St Sava, the youngest son of Stefan Nemanjić, who in the twelfth century managed to unite most of the Serbian lands into a single state. Stefan and his son, Stefan the 'First-Crowned', built the monastery of Studenica, the 'mother of all Serbian churches', where Stefan Nemanjić took monastic vows on his abdication in 1196, and where his earthly remains were eventually laid to rest (after returning from Hilandar, on Mount Athos, founded by Stefan and Sava, where he died); there they still lie. St Sava became the first Archbishop of Serbia, with his see in Žiča. The importance of St Sava for Serbia's Orthodox identity is difficult to exaggerate. The distinctive nature of Serbian Orthodoxy is referred to as 'Svetosavlje', 'St Sava-ism'. The great Serbian poet of the twentieth century, Vasco Popa, celebrated St Sava in a sequence of poems:

> Hungry and thirsty for holiness
> He left the world
> His own people and himself ...

> He lives without years without death
> Surrounded by his wolves ...

> He journeys over the dark land

> With his staff he cuts
> The dark beyond him into four ...

> He journeys without a path
> And the path is born behind him.[6]

---

[5] John Meyendorff, '*In Memoriam*: Archimandrite Justin Popovich', *SVTQ* 23 (1979), 118–19, at 118.
[6] Vasco Popa, *Earth Erect*, trans. Anne Pennington (London: Anvil Press Poetry, 1973), 24, 29. With permission of Lady Margaret Hall, Oxford.

We have already seen something of St Justin's devotion to St Sava, the neglect of whom he deplored in his journal, *Christian Life*; he also wrote a book, as we have seen, with *Svetosavlje* in the title. The nation, fashioned by the royal line to which St Sava belonged, and the Church inspired by St Sava's austere monastic spirituality, came to form an indissoluble unity. Very soon its sense of Orthodox identity was to undergo a long period of testing. As the Ottoman Turks advanced triumphantly across Europe, Serbia fragmented and the Serbian forces underwent inevitable defeat in the battle of Kosovo Polje – the blackbirds' field – in which Prince Lazar died. This defeat became another defining factor in Serbian identity, and Prince Lazar is celebrated as a martyr. With the final victory of the Turks over the Byzantine Empire and the fall of Constantinople in 1453, most of Serbia (its heartlands) was incorporated into the Ottoman Empire. The Serbs, as Orthodox, found themselves part of the *Rum Millet*, under the immediate jurisdiction of the Patriarchate of Constantinople; they lost their patriarchate (initially within a decade of the fall of Constantinople, and then, after a period of restoration, finally in 1766). The position of the Serbs within the Ottoman Empire was wretched.

In the nineteenth century, caught between the Ottoman Empire, the Austro-Hungarian Empire and the Russian Empire, Serbia embarked on a bloody path to freedom, achieved finally in 1920, with the re-establishment of the Serbian Church and its patriarchate, as part of the new state of Yugoslavia, the Kingdom of the Serbs, Croats and Slovenes, uniting different religious traditions of Orthodoxy, Catholicism and Islam. After the Second World War, Yugoslavia became a communist state under Tito, and with the collapse of communism, Yugoslavia succumbed to civil war between its constituent parts. This recent conflict means that the tensions implicit in standing between, and oppressed by, Catholic Europe and the Muslim Empire of the Ottomans are not simply historical memories, but bitter experiences.

Given such a history, it is hardly surprising that Orthodoxy for the Serbs is a fragile and wonderful thing, something that links them with Russia to the north and Greece to the south, but which is experienced as something quite special to the Serbs, 'Svetosavlje', while at the same time they are acutely conscious of the distinctiveness of Orthodoxy in relation both to the Catholicism (and Protestantism) of Europe and to Islam, under the yoke of which they suffered for so many centuries. Also woven into their consciousness is the sense of their Orthodoxy as something to fight for, even to the point of death. The hopeless defeat of the Serbian forces by the Ottomans on the Field of the Blackbirds, and the death of Prince Martyr Lazar, lends the Orthodoxy of the Serbs a profound sense of life or death.

> Singing we ride over the field
> To encounter the armoured dragons
>
> Our most lovely wolf-shepherd
> His flowering staff in his hand
> Flies through the air on his white steed

> The crazed thirsty weapons
> Savage each other alone in the field . . .[7]

This sense of standing between enemies who will destroy the precious heritage of the Serbs, if they are failing in diligence, powerfully informs St Justin's concern to preserve Orthodoxy without compromise.

St Justin and the Western threat to Orthodoxy

What is it, however, that threatens to compromise Orthodoxy? St Justin's answer is both simple and complex: simple in its analysis, complex in its ramifications. It is, however, fair to say that St Justin's understanding of what threatens Orthodoxy, and his ways of defending this, fall into a, by now, familiar pattern. His analysis of the threat to Orthodoxy is fundamentally one that can be traced back to the Slavophils, whom St Justin read eagerly during his few months in Petrograd before the Revolution: it is modern Western society. His own theological contribution is to draw the remedy from the well of the Fathers. Right from the beginning, with his thesis written in Athens in the early twenties, we can see Justin reaching back to the Fathers to enable him to deepen his analysis of the threat and develop his remedy, but we can see, too, even in the title of the thesis the Slavophil roots of his analysis; his thesis (in Greek) was entitled, 'The Problem of Person and Knowledge [gnosis] According to St Makarios the Egyptian'. The idea of person and personhood as possessing the key to what Orthodoxy has preserved and the West lost is one we have encountered several times already; it is, indeed, a commonplace.

St Justin charges Western culture with humanism, rationalism and individualism – precisely the kind of analysis we have found in the Slavophils and their followers – to which he opposes Godmanhood, integral knowledge and *sobornost'*.

Slavophil inheritance

As we have already seen, the Slavophils, Russian thinkers such as Khomiakov and Kireevsky, were concerned to discern what it was that characterized Russian experience over against the influence of Western ideas that had been promoted in Russia from the time of Peter the Great. Tsar Peter the Great, and his successors, notably Catherine the Great, had sought to bring Russia from what they saw as a backward Asianism into the new Europe of the Renaissance and the Enlightenment; the transfer of the capital of Russia from Moscow to the newly built city of St Petersburg was a symbol of this change. Peter the Great wanted a modern Russia, commercially successful, politically powerful. Symbols of Russian difference were banned – beards, for instance – and the Church itself subordinated to the state on a Lutheran

---

[7] Popa, *Earth Erect*, 36.

model, the patriarchate abolished, and the Church governed by a misleadingly called 'Holy Synod', a committee supervised by a lay Oberprokuror, appointed by the tsar. The Slavophils sought to rediscover the true nature of Russian experience of reality, in contradistinction to the Europeanization or Westernization introduced by the Petrine reforms. Though opposed to the West, they drew on the West, and especially Western Idealist philosophy, as they developed their ideas. This was not difficult, as there were movements in nineteenth-century thought in the West, already distressed by the way in which traditional values were being weakened by industrialization and urbanization: thinkers whom one of the most perceptive writers on the Slavophils, Andrzej Walicki, has, as we have seen, dubbed 'conservative romantics'.

What was it, then, that was distinctive about Russian culture and experience? Early on, Khomiakov had argued that no other people, other than the Scots, has 'such legends and songs as ours': this, in a century, when, following the Grimm brothers, all the European nations were busily gathering the tales of traditional wisdom! (In making the Scots an exception, Khomiakov simply reveals the popularity of the novels of Sir Walter Scott!) The village, the traditional community, with its organs of self-government: this was idealized by Khomiakov, who developed from it the ideal of *sobornost'*, the sense that it is together, in a traditional community, or in the Church, that we discover the truth about reality, not on our own, as isolated individual thinkers (Descartes, thinking on the warmth of his stove in Sweden!).

With Kireevsky, we find other ways of characterizing what it is that makes Russian experience different from that found in Western Europe. From the twelfth century, Europe had developed a system of education culminating in the university, something that Peter the Great was concerned to emulate with his reforms. Kireevsky, in contrast, looked to where the Russians had preserved and developed their learning: in the monasteries, where learning was not pursued for its own sake, but as part of a way of life. From this Kireevsky developed the notion of 'integral knowledge': in contrast to the rationalist analysis that came to characterize the learning of the university, Kireevsky set an ideal of learning that involved the whole person, not just the mind, but the imagination, the senses, the heart – a knowledge that demanded initiation into a way of life, an ascetic struggle, the attempt to discover the heart, where all these human faculties are concentrated, where one becomes conscious of God, and discerns a light that illuminates all the powers that make up being human.

All of this remained largely implicit in the Slavophils themselves who, apparently, never used the abstract expressions that designate these ideas, *sobornost'* and integral knowledge. These were provided by Vladimir Solov'ev, who added a further element implicit in the Slavophils. For the Slavophils saw Russia and its experience as fundamentally Christian: made explicit, this means that human experience exists in response to God, more precisely, in response to God's manifestation of himself among humankind as the Godman, *Bogochelovek*. The pursuit of human knowledge, the achievement of *sobornost'* and integral knowledge, is something that takes place as the human moves towards experience of Godmanhood, that union with God and man implicit in, and expressed by, the Incarnation, conceived of as much more than a historical event, but a union between God and man implicit in the creation of the human, and manifest in the historical Incarnation of the Son of God. Among the Slavophils, including Solov'ev, all of this is expressed in the rather forbidding concepts of German Idealism, which was also attracted to ways of transcending rationalism and achieving an experience of wholeness, all-in-oneness, *Alleinheit*, in Russian *vseedinstvo*.

St Justin's appropriation of Slavophilism

All this was clearly very attractive to St Justin: the terms Godman, integral knowledge and *sobornost'* (in Serbian, *sabornost*) are encountered frequently in his works. The philosophical background is there, too, but in a very simplified way; for the most part, it seems to me that St Justin uses a rather schematic history of Western European philosophy mostly as a way of developing and justifying his anti-Westernism. For it is indeed very difficult to escape a sharply anti-Western note in his works. In an as yet unpublished paper, the Serbian thinker Vladimir Cvetković (to whom I owe a great debt in my attempts to understand St Justin) compares St Justin's anti-Westernism with that of the Greek thinker Christos Yannaras, who recently maintained that the West is not for him an 'other', but something that is part of himself, so that his 'critical stance towards the West is self-criticism'.[8] I would like to believe that, but I have not encountered much self-criticism in St Justin. Even if it can be claimed that in his concern for Europe, he is convinced, like Yannaras, that Orthodoxy and the West are not incompatible, I cannot imagine him referring to his 'own wholly Western mode of life'.[9]

Frequently St Justin traces a history of the West from the Middle Ages onwards, finding a gradual progress – or rather decline – in humanism, a concentration on the human that ignores or denies God. (St Justin supports his pessimistic view of Europe by reference to Maurice Maeterlinck and Oswald Spengler.[10]) The beginnings are found in the papacy and scholasticism which 'drained the creative, vital powers of European man',[11] and continue with Rousseau, Locke and Hume, who abstract the human from nature and

---

[8] Christos Yannaras, *Orthodoxy and the West*, trans. Peter Chamberas and Norman Russell (Brookline, MA: Holy Cross Orthodox Press, 2006), ix.

[9] Yannaras, *Orthodoxy*, ix.

[10] For Maeterlinck, see 'Meterlink: "Pred veliko ćutanje"' [Maeterlinck: 'Before the great silence'], *Hrišćanska misao* 4 (1935), reprinted in Popović, *Filozofske urvine* [Philosophical crevasses] (Munich, 1957), 141–51; for Spengler, 'Na vododelnici kultur' [At the watershed of culture], first published in *Filozofske urvine*, 178–89. I owe these references to Dr Cvetković.

[11] Father Justin Popovich [Popović], *Orthodox Faith and Life in Christ*, trans. etc. by Asterios Gerostergios et al. (Belmont, MA: Institute for Byzantine and Modern Greek Studies, 1994), 57 (from the essay, 'Humanistic and Theanthropic Education').

reduce his or her own nature to the senses; Descartes and Kant suggest another notion of human beings as no more than intellect; Schopenhauer and others reduce them to their will. With Nietzsche and Darwin, 'Europe was directed towards a search for the new man among inferior creatures in order to, based on the animal kingdom, create man without God'.[12] Having dispensed with God, Nietzsche proposes man as superman, devoid of pity for one's neighbour, and pursuing an 'irresponsible and merciless desire for power' – 'beyond good and evil, beyond truth and error, beyond conscience and responsibility'.[13]

In other essays, this culmination of the dehumanization of man, consequent on the rejection of God, St Justin brings into conjunction with Nietzsche's proclamation of the superman and the pope's proclamation of infallibility: 'infallibility of the pope is the Nietzschean assertion – *Ja-sagung* – extended to the entire conception of European humanism'.[14] A little later on he affirms that '[i]n the history of the human race there have been three principal falls: that of Adam, that of Judas, and that of the pope'.[15] In reading this, one needs to remember how St Justin experienced the beginnings of a dilution, or sidelining, of *Svetosavlje*, in the new united Kingdom of Yugoslavia, with the forced conjunction of Catholic Croats and Slovenes with Orthodox Serbs, accompanied by memories, before that and since, of murderous hostility. His attitude to the papacy underlies his attitude to ecumenism, for, as with Khomiakov – for whom 'all the West knows but one datum, *a*; whether it be preceded by the positive sign +, as with the Romanists, or with the negative –, as with the Protestants, the *a* remains the same'[16] – Protestantism and Catholicism are but different sides of the same coin, so he speaks of 'Papist–Protestant Ecumenism'.[17]

Nevertheless, the points that St Justin makes – that the Orthodox Church is the Church of Christ; that unity is given, not negotiated; that papal claims seem to envisage an understanding of the Church at odds with Orthodox conviction – are shared by virtually all Orthodox, even if not asserted so aggressively. Furthermore, one should not miss his insistence that the attitude of all of us – Orthodox and non-Orthodox – in the presence of Christ, the Godman, can only be one of repentance, and for this reason the councils of the Church made Christology the centre of their declarations: '[f]or them Christ the Godman is the unique value of the Church of Christ in all the worlds. Their unending and eternal message is: Give up everything for Christ; do not give Christ up for anything'.[18]

---

[12] Popović, *Orthodox Faith*, 58.

[13] Popović, *Orthodox Faith*, 59.

[14] Popović, *Orthodox Faith*, 103 (from an essay, 'Reflections on the Infallibility of European Man').

[15] Popović, *Orthodox Faith*, 105.

[16] *Russia and the English Church*, vol. 1, ed. W. J. Birkbeck (London: Rivington, Percival & Co., 1895), 67.

[17] Popović, *Orthodox Faith*, 170 (from an essay called 'Humanistic Ecumenism').

[18] Popović, *Orthodox Faith*, 113.

The neo-patristic synthesis according to St Justin

However, it seems to me more profitable to pursue, not the way in which the anti-Westernism of the Slavophils manifests itself in St Justin's thought, but rather the way he treats the Slavophils' fundamental affirmations in quite a different way from the Slavophils themselves. As I have already remarked, Khomiakov and Kireevsky – and also Solov'ev – develop the fundamental notions of Godmanhood, integral knowledge and *sobornost'* by drawing on contemporary German Idealist philosophy, and in particular Schelling. What we find in St Justin is something quite different, which links him with the other approach we find in the Paris School: the attempt to create a neo-patristic synthesis. For St Justin develops his understanding of these key Slavophil notions by a return to the Fathers. Of course, the Slavophils themselves were interested in the Fathers, and promoted, in conjunction with the monks of Optina Pustyn', translations of the works of the Fathers. There is, however, little use of the Fathers in their works, as opposed to enthusiastic utterances about the Fathers as witnesses to a country, which is their homeland, as Kireevsky put it.

With St Justin, we find several attempts to develop what seem to be ideas of fundamentally Slavophil origin by drawing on the works of the Fathers. And it is interesting whom he chooses among the Fathers: not the Cappadocian Fathers, or Athanasios or Cyril, but ascetic Fathers (in the *Orthodox Philosophy of Truth*, there is plenty of use of such Fathers, but in a more directly doctrinal context). His thesis, already mentioned, on 'Personhood and Knowledge in St Makarios the Egyptian' is a study based on the Macarian Homilies. Later on, he wrote a long essay on 'The Theory of Knowledge of St Isaac the Syrian'.[19] It is this latter that I want to discuss in more detail.

St Justin begins by exploring a little his idea that, in European philosophy, the human being always appears as a fragmented being: all attempts at self-understanding start either from the intellect, or from the senses, and fail to achieve a sense of the person as a whole. In trying to overcome this sense of fragmentation Western philosophy makes conjectures that seek to transcend both humankind and matter, in Idealist philosophy by a leap into the super-natural, which, frustrated, leads back to scepticism. So humans come to see a great gulf between themselves and the truth. The only solution is for the truth itself to cross the gulf and become immanent in humankind. This can only take place if Truth is a person, the person of the Godman, in whom the gulf is bridged. In Christ, the Godman,

> transcendent Truth becomes immanent in man. The Godman reveals the truth in and through Himself. He reveals it, not through thought or reason, but by

---

[19] The Greek originals are published in Archim. Ioustinos Popovits, *Odos Theognosias* (Athens: Ekdoseis Grigori, 1992). 'The Theory of Knowledge of St Isaac the Syrian', trans. (from Serbian) by Mother Maria Rule, is reprinted in Popović, *Orthodox Faith*, 117–68 (originally published in *Sourozh* 15, 16, 17 (1984)).

the life that is His. He not only has the truth, He is Himself the Truth. In Him Being and Truth are one. Therefore, He, in his person, not only defines truth but shows the way to it.[20]

Encountering Christ, '[m]an's understanding is not overthrown, but is renewed, purified, sanctified'. The truth that Christ embodies, St Justin calls 'integral knowledge':

> In the Godman, absolute Truth has in its entirety been given in a real and personal way. This is why He alone, among those born on earth, both has integral knowledge of the truth and can pass it on. The man who desires to know the truth has only to be made one with the Godman, to become one flesh with Him, to become a member of his divine and human Body, the Church.

In experiencing the truth, human beings encounter contradictions, antinomies (a key notion, we have seen, in Florensky and Bulgakov). These, for St Justin, are 'not irreconcilable opposites; they are simply ruptures caused by the upheaval of original sin in man'.[21] As man unites himself to Christ, he 'feels in himself a coming-together of fragmented parts, a healing of the intellect, a wholeness and integration that makes him capable of integrated understanding'.[22] So, truth is given, objectively, in the person of Christ: 'the way in which this becomes subjective – that is, the practical side of the Christian theory of knowledge (the Greek is *gnosiologia*) – was fully developed by the Fathers'. Not surprisingly, it is the ascetic Fathers to whom St Justin turns at this point – in his doctoral thesis to the Macarian Homilies, in the essay we are summarizing to St Isaac the Syrian – for it is from these ascetic Fathers that we learn how the human is made whole and the intellect freed to contemplate God.

First, we need to grasp that the human organs of understanding have been damaged by sin – original and actual; they have been weakened and diseased. So St Justin quotes St Isaac: 'Evil is a sickness of soul', 'passions are illnesses of the soul' – they are not natural to the soul, but 'accidents, adventitious, and intrusive, an unnatural addition to the soul'.[23] Nevertheless, their effects on the soul are profound, filling it with confusion and distraction: '[a] feeble soul, a diseased intellect, a weakened heart and will – in brief, sick organs of understanding – can only engender, fashion, and produce sick thoughts, sick feelings, sick desires, and sick knowledge'.[24]

St Isaac does not, however, leave us with a graphic analysis of our fallen, weakened state; he details the remedy, a remedy which amounts to bringing to life our incorporation in Christ the Godman, and this is achieved through the virtues. 'The acquisition of the virtues is a progressive and organic process . . .

---

[20] Popović, *Orthodox Faith*, 119.
[21] Popović, *Orthodox Faith*, 119–20.
[22] Popović, *Orthodox Faith*, 120.
[23] Popović, *Orthodox Faith*, 121.
[24] Popović, *Orthodox Faith*, 122.

"Every virtue is the mother of the next." Among the virtues there is not only an ontological order, but also a chronological one.'[25]

The sequence of virtues is faith – prayer – love – humility; this leads to a consideration of grace and freedom, for in the practice of the virtues a person is not achieving something of his or her own, but responding to the grace of God; nonetheless, the acquiring of the virtues is no easy task, but one of unremitting toil. St Justin then follows St Isaac to consider the purification of the intellect:

> Perseverance in prayer cleanses the intellect, illumines it, and fills it with the light of truth. The virtues, led by compassion, give the intellect peace and light. The cleansing of the intellect is not a dialectical, discursive and theoretical activity, but an act of grace through experience and is ethical in every respect. The intellect is purified by fasting, vigils, silence, prayer, and other ascetic practices.[26]

This leads to a consideration of the mystery of knowledge; the purified intellect passes beyond natural knowledge, which is achieved by 'examination and experimentation' and is itself, as St Isaac puts it, 'a sign of uncertainty about the truth', and achieves spiritual knowledge, the fruit of 'simplicity of heart and simplicity of thought'. In the realm of spiritual knowledge, we pass beyond nature and natural knowledge – it is a realm of miracles, such as the miracle of healing St Justin witnessed in his mother, when a child.

Ascetic epistemology

St Justin discerns in St Isaac three degrees of knowledge: the first concerned with the senses, the second a product of the union of body and soul through the virtues, and the third that of perfection. St Justin comments that in the first degree of knowledge 'is included virtually the whole of European philosophy, from naïve realism to idealism – and all science from the atomism of Democritus to Einstein's relativity'.[27]

Of the third and highest degree of knowledge, that of perfection, St Justin quotes this passage from St Isaac, about how then the intellect can

> take wing and fly to the realm of incorporeal spirits and plumb the depths of the fathomless ocean, pondering on the divine and wondrous things that govern the nature of spiritual and physical beings and penetrating the spiritual mysteries that can only be grasped by a simple and supple mind. Then the inner senses awaken to the work of the spirit in those things that belong to that other realm, immortal and incorruptible. The knowledge has, in a hidden way, here in this world, received already spiritual resurrection so as to bear true witness to the renewal of all things.[28]

---

[25] Popović, *Orthodox Faith*, 123.
[26] Popović, *Orthodox Faith*, 136.
[27] Popović, *Orthodox Faith*, 145.
[28] Quoted in Popović, *Orthodox Faith*, 145–6.

This third degree of knowledge turns into contemplation, which,

> in the philosophy of the holy fathers ... has an ontological, ethical and gnoseological significance. It means prayerful concentration of the soul, through the action of grace, on the mysteries that surpass our understanding and are abundantly present not only in the Holy Trinity but in the person of man himself and in the whole of God's creation.[29]

The soul that has acquired contemplation, when it turns towards the created order, is filled with love and compassion. 'What is a merciful heart?' asks St Isaac, and he replies in the much-quoted words:

> It is a heart burning with love towards the whole of creation: towards men, birds, animals, demons, and every creature. His eyes overflow with tears at the thought and sight of them. For the great and powerful sorrow that constrains his heart and form his great patience, his heart contracts and he cannot bear to hear or see the least harm done to or misfortune suffered by creation. Therefore, he prays with tears incessantly for irrational beasts, for opponents of the truth, and for those who do him harm, that they may be preserved and receive mercy. He also prays for the reptiles with great sorrow, a sorrow that is without measure in his heart and which likens him to God.[30]

In his conclusion, St Justin remarks that, for St Isaac, 'the problem of knowledge is fundamentally a religious and an ethical one'.[31] Knowledge is bound up with man's moral state. St Justin suggests that it goes further than the virtues being simply a condition of true knowledge:

> There is no doubt that knowledge progresses through man's virtues and regresses through the passions. Knowledge is like a fabric woven by the virtues on the loom of the human soul. The loom of the soul extends through all the visible and invisible worlds. The virtues are not only powers creating knowledge; they are the principles and sources of knowledge. By transforming the virtues into constituent elements of his being through ascetic endeavour, a man advances from knowledge to knowledge. It could even be possible to say that the virtues are the sense organs of knowledge. Advancing from one virtue to another, a man moves from one form of comprehension to another.[32]

In this essay, we can see how St Justin fleshes out the themes of Godmanhood and integral knowledge, drawn from the Slavophils. The theme of *sobornost'* is less clearly developed, though it seems to me implicit in the bonds of compassion that are developed as the soul grows in union with God. What St Justin has found in St Isaac (and he found much the same in the Macarian Homilies, as a glance at the chapter heading of his doctoral thesis reveals) is an understanding of human nature and personality, the fruit of ascetic experience, that enables him to work out in some degree of detail how the human

---

[29] Popović, *Orthodox Faith*, 153.
[30] Quoted in Popović, *Orthodox Faith*, 161–2.
[31] Popović, *Orthodox Faith*, 163.
[32] Popović, *Orthodox Faith*, 163–4.

being is transformed and transfigured in responding to the Godman through grace and ascetic endeavour. What St Justin has done can be seen as another way of pursuing the neo-patristic synthesis. Whereas Lossky and Florovsky looked to the Fathers for notions of personhood, in relation to both Trinitarian theology and anthropology, and also for a sense of the cosmic, St Justin supplements this approach by drawing more directly on the ascetic tradition in the Fathers, both for his understanding of personhood and for his analysis of the fallen human condition and how this is remedied in practice. The approaches of Lossky and Florovsky are by no means absent from St Justin; a glance at his *Orthodox Philosophy of Truth* reveals how much he draws on Fathers such as St Athanasios, the Cappadocian Fathers and St Maximos the Confessor.

I have attempted in this chapter to explore a less-well-known region of modern Orthodox theology, less well known partly because of the barriers of language, and because of the way St Justin's theology is rooted in the experience of Serbian Orthodoxy, and partly because its closest affinities are with the Russians who formed the Synodal Church after the Revolution. There is much that I have not attempted to cover, notably his vast dogmatics, *The Orthodox Philosophy of Truth*. Nevertheless, I think it has become clear that this rootedness in the experience of a particular people does not at all entail any parochialness in his theology. If St Justin is unusual in drawing to the extent that he does on the ascetic wisdom of Orthodox monasticism (though in this there are remarkable parallels with Fr Dumitru Stăniloae), he is simply opening up to all Orthodox, and indeed all Christians, treasures that belong to us all.

11

Paul Evdokimov and the love and beauty of God

Paul Evdokimov was a man of contrasts, even contradictions. Born and brought up in Russia, he was deeply embued with Russian literary and theological culture; yet, after he came to France, unlike many of the other émigrés, he wrote little, and certainly published virtually nothing, in Russian: all his books and articles appeared in French. His father was a soldier, and he himself studied in a cadet school, and during the civil war that followed on the Bolshevik Revolution he fought in the White Army; yet, a decade or so later, married with a young family, he stayed at home looking after his children, while his wife went out to work – not altogether usual even today, but very unusual in the 1930s. He was married, and indeed, after his first wife died of cancer, he later married again a much younger woman; yet, one of the

Paul Evdokimov

central themes of his writing is the notion of 'interior monasticism'. There are other contrasts that we shall encounter as we explore his theological *œuvre*.

Life

First, however, his life.[1] Paul Evdokimov was born on 2 August 1901; he was therefore a couple of years older than Vladimir Lossky. In 1907, his father was assassinated by a soldier belonging to a revolutionary group. Paul and his elder brother left for central Asia to join their mother and their dead father; scarcely was he able to catch a last glimpse of his father's face. Olivier Clément, who later became a close friend of Evdokimov, suggests that perhaps this experience introduced him to two of the themes of his theology: that of the sacrificial love of the Father, and that of the smile of the Father, which we shall have all eternity to contemplate.

Paul's mother, of the old aristocracy, was a fervent Christian, and it was from her that Paul learnt his faith, a faith he never called in question. As his second wife said of him, after his death, 'he believed as one breathes'. Following the normal pattern, Evdokimov went to a cadet school for the Imperial Army. During the vacations, however, his mother took him to visit monasteries; from that period dates his acquaintance with, and deep sympathy for, Orthodox monasticism. At the time of the October Revolution, his family found themselves in Kiev, where, despite his military education, the young Paul enrolled in the Spiritual Academy (a quite exceptional thing for someone to do from the *noblesse d'épée*; most of his peers there would have been sons of priests) and began his theological studies. After a few months, he joined the White Army and fought in the cavalry, on several occasions narrowly missing death. A little later, he was back with his family, and in 1922, along with hundreds of thousands of Russians, his family embarked on the paths of exile. Like several of his fellow Russians, the experience of exile impressed on him the sense of the Christian life as essentially one of exile, 'for here we have no abiding city, but we seek one to come', as the author of the Epistle to the Hebrews put it (Heb. 13.14).

After spending time in Constantinople, Berlin, Prague and Belgrade, he ended up in Paris in September 1923. He continued his studies at the Sorbonne, and the next year became one of the first students at the newly founded Institut St-Serge. To support himself while studying, he worked at night for Citroën, or at railway stations cleaning carriages. He spent four years

---

[1] For material on Evdokimov's life, see Olivier Clément, *Orient–Occident: Deux passeurs: Vladimir Lossky et Paul Evdokimov* (Geneva: Labor et Fides, 1985), 105–210 (for his life, especially 105–16); Michel Stavrou, 'Note bio-bibliographique sur l'œuvre de Paul Evdokimov', *Contacts* 235–6 (July–December 2011), 267–75; the double issue is devoted to Evdokimov. And in English: Michael Plekon, in Paul Evdokimov, *Ages of the Spiritual Life* (Crestwood, NY: St Vladimir's Seminary Press, 1998), 1–10; and *In the World, Of the Church: A Paul Evdokimov Reader*, ed. Michael Plekon and Alexis Vinogradoff (Crestwood, NY: St Vladimir's Seminary Press, 2001), 1–9. See also Evdokimov's own autobiographical notes, 'Some Landmarks on Life's Journey', in Evdokimov, *In the World*, 37–47.

studying at St-Serge; the two teachers to whom he owed most were Fr Sergii Bulgakov and Nicolas Berdyaev. Evdokimov spoke of what he owed to them, 'one a free-thinking philosopher, the other a priest and professor of dogmatic theology', each speaking of the freedom of Orthodoxy and its prophetic mission, 'deepening the "institution" by the "event", each placing great emphasis on the Holy Spirit'. From Fr Sergii, he learnt to

> cultivate the 'instinct of Orthodoxy' which placed you in the path of Tradition ... where you rediscovered the immediacy of the Bible ... it was also necessary to plunge oneself into the thinking of the Fathers, to live the Liturgy, to 'consume the eucharistic fire', to discover the icon, eschatology, all of the faith that lay beyond history, the meta-historical.[2]

In 1927, Paul married Natasha Brunel, Provençale from Nîmes on her father's side, Russian and Caucasian by her mother, a Protestant. They set up home in Menton, where Natasha taught Italian. Two children were born, Nina in 1928, Michel in 1930. While Natasha earned a living as a teacher, Paul remained at home and looked after the children, while at the same time preparing a doctoral thesis, not in theology, but in philosophy, which he later defended in 1942 at the University of Aix-en-Provence; it was published as *Dostoïevski et le problème du mal*.[3] In his thesis, he presented Dostoevsky as the prophet of a Christianity renewed by atheism. Two years later, he published his book, *Le Mariage, sacrement de l'amour*.[4] By this time Paul and his family had left Menton, occupied by Italian troops in 1940, and eventually settled in Valence.

At the end of the war, in 1945, Natasha died from cancer, and Paul returned with his children to the region of Paris. In 1942, the year when he submitted his thesis, his mother died, and the Germans occupied the 'free zone'. Paul became involved with his Protestant friends in the Resistance through the *Comité inter-Mouvements pour l'accueil des évacués* (CIMADE), which aimed to save lives, especially those of Jews; he was arrested and detained for several weeks, but eventually released at the intercession of a friend, a judge from Orange. After the war, his involvement with CIMADE continued, now concerned especially with the fate of refugees. In 1946 he directed a house of refuge for displaced persons, and then from 1947 to 1968 a house for foreign students from central and Eastern Europe, after 1956 from Hungary, and then from the Third World.

From 1948 until 1961, he was a member of the committee of direction of the Ecumenical Institute of Bossey, in Switzerland. In 1953, he became professor at the Institut St-Serge in Paris, teaching Western Christianity and moral theology. In 1954, he married again, to Tomoko Sakaï, an interpreter, 25 years old, the daughter of a Japanese diplomat and an English woman. His

---

[2] Evdokimov, 'Some Landmarks', 38–9.

[3] *Dostoïevski et le problème du mal* (Lyon: Éditions du Livre Français, 1942; reissued Paris: Desclée de Brouwer, 1978).

[4] *Le Mariage, sacrement de l'amour* (Lyon: Éditions du Livre Français, 1944).

marriage to Tomoko seemed to unlock his creative energies, as well as, according to Olivier Clément, widening his cultural sympathies, hitherto determined by Russia.

In 1958, there appeared his book, *La Femme et le salut de monde*,[5] the next year the longest of his books, *L'Orthodoxie*,[6] for which he was awarded a doctorate in theology at the Institut St-Serge; two years later in 1961, an exploration of the Russian roots of his thought, *Gogol et Dostoïevski ou la descente aux enfers*;[7] in 1962 another book on marriage, *Le Sacrement de l'amour: Le mystère conjugal à la lumière de la tradition orthodoxe*;[8] in 1964, one of his major works, *Les Âges de la vie spirituelle: Des pères du desert à nos jours*;[9] in 1968, *La Connaissance de Dieu selon la tradition orientale*;[10] in 1969, *L'Esprit-Saint dans la tradition orthodoxe*;[11] and then in 1970, the year of his death, two further works, *Le Christ dans la pensée russe*[12] and *L'Art de l'icône: Théologie de la beauté*.[13]

In this last decade of his life, his ecumenical endeavours continued: in 1964, he was invited to attend Vatican II as one of the Orthodox observers from St-Serge; in 1967, he became professor at the Ecumenical Institute at Bossey, and at the Institut Supérieur d'Études Œcuméniques, newly established in Paris. In 1968 he was made doctor *honoris causa* of the University of Thessaloniki. He died suddenly in his sleep on 16 September 1970.

Evdokimov's place in the émigré tradition in Paris

You might be wondering why I have left Paul Evdokimov until now, given that he was older than some of the thinkers already considered – Lossky and Fr Stăniloae, for example. I have been wondering myself, and I think the reason is that, whatever his age, his impact on Orthodox theology comes after that of Lossky and, in a more complicated way, even of Stăniloae. For the bulk of his work belongs to the last decade of his life, the 1960s; he died at the height of his recognition. In contrast, the younger man, Vladimir Lossky, died young, in 1958; he was already well known, not least in the English-speaking world, through his involvement in the English ecumenical Fellowship of St Alban and St Sergius, and his most important work, *The Mystical Theology of the Eastern Church*, was already translated in English at the time of his death.

[5] *La Femme et la salut de monde* (Paris–Tournai: Desclée de Brouwer, 1958; reissued 1978).
[6] *L'Orthodoxie* (Neuchâtel: Delachaux et Niestlé, 1959).
[7] *Gogol et Dostoïevski ou la descente aux enfers* (Paris: Desclée de Brouwer, 1961; reissued Paris: Éditions de Corlevour, 2011).
[8] *Le Sacrement de l'amour: Le mystère conjugal à la lumière de la tradition orthodoxe* (Paris: Éditions de l'Épi, 1962; reissued 1980).
[9] *Les Âges de la vie spirituelle: Des pères du desert à nos jours* (Paris: Desclée de Brouwer, 1964; reissued 1980).
[10] *La Connaissance de Dieu selon la tradition orientale* (Lyon: Xavier Mappus, 1968).
[11] *L'Esprit-Saint dans la tradition orthodoxe* (Paris: Cerf, 1969; reissued 2011).
[12] *Le Christ dans la pensée russe* (Paris: Cerf, 1970).
[13] *L'Art de l'icône: Théologie de la beauté* (Paris: Desclée de Brouwer, 1970).

For the West, the 1960s were a watershed, with the 'Death of God' movement and the cultural shifts of that decade. Lossky's apophatic theology already provided something of a response, which was picked by Orthodox thinkers in the sixties; although Evdokimov knew Nietzsche and Heidegger, his reading of these seems removed from the turmoil of the sixties. As we shall see, although the 1960s affected the Orthodox theological world very differently from the West, most of the thinkers that we have yet to encounter were aware of the challenges of this decade. Paul Evdokimov seems to me to stand on the cusp, and so we shall consider him first.

Just from the subjects that he writes about, we can form an impression of where he is coming from. We have already noted the effect on him of the horrifying death of his father when he was a young child. It is hardly surprising that his first book is on Dostoevsky and the problem of evil. Hardly surprising personally, but not surprising, either, if we think of his roots in the Russian tradition, strengthened as they will have been by his mentors at St-Serge, Bulgakov and Berdyaev. Both Florensky and Bulgakov began their theological careers by writing on the problem of evil: Florensky's *The Pillar and Ground of the Truth* is an essay in theodicy; Bulgakov's *Unfading Light* is similarly concerned with the problem of evil. Berdyaev himself wrote a book on Dostoevsky, which could easily have been called 'Dostoevsky and the Problem of Evil': Ivan's questions and the Legend of the Grand Inquisitor form the backbone of the book. The extent to which Dostoevsky's questions, especially in *The Brothers Karamazov*, but not only there, fired the imagination of the thinkers of the Russian Religious Renaissance can hardly be exaggerated; the notion of Dostoevsky as a prophet of a renewed and cleansed Christianity – cleansed by atheism, even – is widespread.[14]

Evdokimov starts, then, with the preoccupations of the tradition of the Russian Religious Renaissance. His next book, *Marriage, the Sacrament of Love*, fits too within this tradition and takes up the preoccupations of Solov'ev's *The Meaning of Love*, with its sense of the role of the polarity between male and female in any true understanding of love (and maybe marriage, though Solov'ev is perhaps not the best guide here). Both these two books perhaps suggest another thinker with whom Evdokimov was to engage, for the problem of evil preoccupied the psychologist Carl Gustav Jung, especially in his *Answer to Job* (but also very profoundly in his autobiographical *Memories, Dreams, Reflections*), while Evdokimov's sense of the complementarity of male and female was something he would follow up by drawing on Jung in his later works (an aspect of his work to which some of his Orthodox readers were not sympathetic). The notion of Sophia, especially in Solov'ev, but also in Bulgakov, involves an appropriation of male–female complementarity; Evdokimov is one of the few who will continue to think through the sophianic ideas of Bulgakov (again drawing on Jung, to whose sophiological

---

[14] The chapter on Dostoevsky in Nicolas Zernov, *Three Russian Prophets* (London: SCM Press, 1944), 82–115, is representative.

notions his attention had been drawn by the authority on Sufism, Henry Corbin, who contributed ideas from his own research into Sufism[15]).

'Forward to the Fathers of the Church!'

It is difficult to trace the development of Evdokimov's thought. After the first two books there is a long gap – the gap in his life from the death of his first wife, Natasha, to his remarriage to Tomoko – which is followed by a helter-skelter of books, one of the earliest of which is *L'Orthodoxie*. In this book we find ourselves in territory that appears, at first sight at least, to be very different. His historical sweep goes back to Hellenism and sees the Slav contribution as something of an appendix. His theological method involves the Fathers. One might be inclined to enlist him as a supporter of Florovsky's 'neo-patristic synthesis', save that Evdokimov himself warns us that 'the discovery of the Fathers must not lapse in a "neo-patristic" theology which would simply come to replace a neo-scholastic theology';[16] nevertheless he affirms that

> always, the deeper study of the thought of the Fathers, a certain identification with their experience, with their catholicity, is a condition *sine qua non* for any real theologian: a *ressourcement en arrière* but also and above all *en avant* in eschatology, as St Gregory of Nyssa said: 'one remembers what is to come'.[17]

Not surprisingly, one priest from Moscow said that Evdokimov's motto could be: '*En avant* vers les Pères de l'Église' – 'Forward to the Fathers of the Church'.[18]

What is it to be human?

The structure of the book that follows these introductory ideas is significant. The first part is called 'Anthropology', introducing notions such as the heart, the human person, freedom and the image of God. Evdokimov then moves on to creation and fall, and beyond that to deification, which he introduces by way of the liturgy, as a cosmic event, drawing the whole of God's Creation together in worship, celebrated by human beings whose very essence is liturgical:

> A saint is not a superman, but one who finds and lives the truth of being human as a liturgical being. The definition of the human finds its most exact and fullest expression in liturgical adoration: the human being is the person of the *Trisagion* and the *Sanctus*: 'I shall sing to my God as long as I live'.[19]

The section on anthropology ends with chapters on asceticism and mysticism: deification involves a working together, a *synergeia*, with God. The few pages on asceticism introduce the idea of attaining a state of simplicity:

---

[15] So Clément, *Orient–Occident*, 124–5.
[16] Evdokimov, *Orthodoxie*, 194.
[17] Evdokimov, *Orthodoxie*, 194.
[18] Clément, *Orient–Occident*, 121.
[19] Evdokimov, *Orthodoxie*, 96.

God is simple, and the bosom of the Father is unity. Evil is complicated and by that dispersed. Asceticism reunites and integrates 'according to the image' of the divine simplicity. An ascetic, in the unity of his interior world, contemplates 'the truth of things', the thoughts of God, and by the power of his own unity, inclines the material level towards its ultimate destiny, which is to be the praise of God: liturgy.[20]

Evdokimov goes on to point to an apparent contradiction at the heart of Orthodoxy (he does not use, though he might well have, the term 'antinomy'):

Orthodoxy, mystically, is most refractory to all imagination, to any figurative representation, visual or auditory, and at the same time has created the cult of the icon, surrounds itself with images, and from them has constructed the visible reality of the Church. 'As the eyes of those who see are sanctified by the sacred icons, so the mind is led to the knowledge of God' [*Synodikon of Orthodoxy*]. By means of the theology of symbols, [Orthodoxy] raises us up to a presence without form and without image. The icon comes from the Incarnation and ascends again to the immaterial God. Nature is manifest – and this is the point of all iconosophical teaching – as dematerialized, 'de-thingified', but not at all made unreal.[21]

Evdokimov broaches here two subjects – asceticism and the icon – that would occupy him in the sixties and issue in two of his most important books, *Les Âges de la vie spirituelle*, and *L'Art de l'icône: Théologie de beauté*.

In his section on mysticism, Evdokimov leads us through prayer as a form of love – not just *agape* but also *eros*, using the terms then very popular (though usually opposed) – expressed in the Jesus Prayer, where the repetition of the name of the Beloved as a kind of babbling love discloses something deeper:

In this tradition, the name is considered as a place of theophany; the invocation of the name of Jesus prolongs the Incarnation, the heart receives the Lord, the force of the divine presence is a greatness in itself... Hermas said: 'The name of the Son of God ... sustains the whole world', for he is present there and we worship him in his name.[22]

Our ascent of love is a response to the *amour fou* of God, as Evdokimov often put it, a love that breaks all limits: our love for God defines who we are. As Evdokimov puts it elsewhere, 'To the God who *is love* there corresponds the human *amo ergo sum* [I love, therefore I am]'.[23]

Doctrine of the Church

The second part of *L'Orthodoxie* is entitled 'Ecclesiology'. Although Evdokimov, like many Orthodox of the last century, adheres to a form of 'eucharistic ecclesiology', he places his ecclesiology in a broader context:

---

[20] Evdokimov, *Orthodoxie*, 106.
[21] Evdokimov, *Orthodoxie*, 106–7.
[22] Evdokimov, *Orthodoxie*, 115.
[23] Evdokimov, *La Femme*, 63; quoted by Clément, *Orient–Occident*, 155.

The world is created with a view to the Incarnation; in its very foundation, the world is the Church potentially, virtually. Saint Clement of Rome (2 Clem. 14.2) says: 'God created man and woman, the man is Christ and the woman is the Church'. Similarly, Hermas, in the second vision of his *Shepherd*, describes the Church in the features of an aged woman and says: 'she is aged because she has been created first, before everything else, and it is for her sake that the world was created'... Indeed, God 'came in the cool of the evening' (Gen. 3:8), to converse with human kind: the *essence of the Church* is thus expressed in the *communion between God and human kind*; prefigured in the Edenic state, anticipated prophetically in the society of the Old Covenant, she is fulfilled in the Incarnation and revealed completely in the heavenly City (Apoc. 21:22): the living temple of the wedding feast of the Lamb.[24]

There follow a series of short chapters expounding aspects of the Church: the longest of these deals with the 'Mariological aspect'; a little shorter is the chapter on the 'pneumatological aspect'. The latter chapter develops the notion of the Church as essentially 'epicletic', constantly invoking God to send the Spirit, the Giver of Life, to his Church. The Church is certainly an institution, a historical community, and in that reality fulfils the role of being a 'theandric [God–human] link', uniting the vertical axis, the descent of the Holy Spirit on the Church, with the horizontal axis, the reality of the Church in the world.

Theandrism constitutes the Church, places it at the centre of the world, fills the human content with its reality, transforms it into theandric substance, and by that, establishes the horizontal continuity: the apostolic succession, the sacraments (which continue Christ's visibility), the incorporation of the faithful into an historical body.[25]

The Church is also an event,[26] constantly called into being by the descent of the Holy Spirit, in response to the Church's *epiklesis* or invocation.

The Mother of God

The chapter on the Mariological aspect, for all its brevity, is very rich, and I want to draw attention to just two points. The first takes its cue from the *dogmatikon* in the third tone, where the Mother of God is addressed: 'without a Father, you bore in the flesh the Son, who, before the ages, was begotten from the Father without a mother'. Evdokimov comments:

To the paternity of the Father in the divine corresponds the maternity of the *Theotokos* in the human, figure of the *maternal virginity* of the Church. This led Cyprian to say: 'You cannot have God for your Father if you no longer have the Church for your mother'.[27]

---

[24] Evdokimov, *Orthodoxie*, 124.
[25] Evdokimov, *Orthodoxie*, 126.
[26] Cf. Evdokimov, *Orthodoxie*, 126–7.
[27] Evdokimov, *Orthodoxie*, 149.

This theme of seeing God's paternity reflected in Mary's maternity is one Evdokimov develops elsewhere. Here he develops the traditional idea of the Mother of God as the Mother of all Christians:

> In giving birth to Christ, in so far as she is universal Eve, she gives birth to him for *all*, and thus gives birth to him also in every soul, which is why the whole Church 'rejoices in the blessed Virgin' (St Ephrem). The Church, then, is represented in her function as the mystical matrix, of the continual childbirth, of the perpetual *Theotokos*.[28]

The other point to be noticed is the parallelism, this time, between Mary and the Spirit: Evdokimov refers to the reading of Philippians 2.5–11 on the feast of the Mother of God, remarking that it 'underlines the *kenosis* that the Mother shares with the Son and above all with the Holy Spirit, whose divinity is proclaimed simultaneously with the proclamation of the dignity of the *Theotokos*'.[29] What, too, links the Virgin and the Holy Spirit is prayer: '"Purification of the world" and "Burning Bush" – "*Orans*", the Virgin represents the ministry of prayer, the charism of intercession. As bride, with the Spirit, she says, "Come, Lord"'.[30]

The third part of *L'Orthodoxie* is concerned with the faith of the Church, not an exposition of Christian belief, rather a brief account of what kind of faith the Church professes and on what grounds: apophatic, the place of councils and creeds, canon law, the Scriptures and tradition.

The fourth part concerns the prayer of the Church, beginning with an exploration of sacred space and church building, and then discussing, again quite briefly, the icon, the Divine Liturgy and the sacraments. Part Five concerns the 'Eschaton, or the Last Things', and closes with a discussion of the relationship of Orthodoxy to other Christians, in fact, the place of ecumenism. His last paragraph reads:

> Each and all are thus invited to enter more deeply into the dazzling presence of Christ, his birth-parousia by the breath of the Spirit, and it is at the level of the miracle of this Spirit-bearing Nativity – already the Kingdom – that separation can be changed into a bond, into unity. Orthodox, Catholics, Protestants passing along the road of holiness to the end, which is Christ, are able to rediscover themselves as living icons reunited in the iconostasis of the Temple of God, the Royal Gate opening on to the abyss of the Father.[31]

The nature of his theology

If we look back over this presentation of Orthodoxy, there are several points worth observing. First of all, Evdokimov does not argue; only very occasionally does he argue *against* anyone – there are a few references to Karl Barth,

---

[28] Evdokimov, *Orthodoxie*, 151.
[29] Evdokimov, *Orthodoxie*, 153.
[30] Evdokimov, *Orthodoxie*, 153.
[31] Evdokimov, *Orthodoxie*, 346.

discussions of questions like the *Filioque* in the creed address Latin objections, and Evdokimov is clear in his rejection of the papacy (or indeed any Orthodox equivalent): in his caption to the icon of Pentecost (the version without the Mother of God, so with an empty seat between the apostles Peter and Paul), he remarks that 'the empty place represents the invisible, but most real, presence of the Lord in the Church ... No one could ever sit there. Neither pope nor patriarch'.[32] In fact he makes clear this aspect of his approach in the book:

> We have consciously chosen a descriptive method, strictly objective. Our faith teaches us that the truth has no need of demonstration, still less of proofs – its evidence suffices for itself. In the face of misunderstandings or an attitude violently polemical, one sees the criticism turning itself fatally against simplistic apologists like the friends of Job. And was it not Job, that being who disturbed and confused any representation too well designed, that God, in the murmurs of his Wisdom, made his messenger?[33]

A serene presentation of Orthodoxy by one who 'believed, as one breathes' – a presentation of Orthodoxy that finds its heart in the acknowledgement of God as the one we worship, to whom we pray.

Let us now look in a little more detail, though still briefly, at four particular themes in Evdokimov's theology. They are, in no particular order, woman, the inner life, the icon, and what he loved to call *amour fou de Dieu*.

Woman

Three books and several articles discuss the role of woman and the nature of marriage. I shall concentrate on what Evdokimov has to say about woman. He warns us straight away in an article on 'The Charisms of Woman'[34] that to speak of the 'problem of woman' is to succumb to a male-orientated approach, something all too easy to do in a society marked by patriarchy, a society which the Church, with its male priesthood and forms of government dominated by men, is all too likely to exemplify. He comments:

> In a male-dominated world where everything is marked by the patriarchal system, man, armed with his reason, his being, and existence, loses his cosmic connection with heaven and nature, also with the feminine as a mystery complementary to his own being. Eliminating the metaphysical and the mystical which generated him, sliding toward cerebral abstraction, man sees the deeper dimension closing before him, that of the Holy Spirit.[35]

Rather, Evdokimov is keen to see man and woman as complementary, with different gifts or charisms, different ways of being and feeling. It is only as a

---

32 Evdokimov, *Orthodoxie*, opposite page 160.
33 Evdokimov, *Orthodoxie*, 41.
34 In Evdokimov, *In the World*, 231–42.
35 Evdokimov, *In the World*, 231–2.

result of the fall that man and woman find themselves opposed to each other. Evdokimov goes on to say:

> Man overflows his own being, more external to himself, his charism of expansion directs his vision constantly outside of himself. He constantly fills the world with his creative energies, imposing his mastery upon it and conquering it as engineer and constructor. Man receives at his side woman, who is to be his companion and helper. She is at one and the same time beloved, spouse, and mother. Far more interiorized than man, woman is completely at ease within the limits of her being by which she fills the world with her radiant presence. 'The glory of man' (1 Cor. 11:7) in her luminous purity, woman is like a mirror in which the face of man is reflected and revealed to himself and by which he is corrected. Thus she assists man in understanding himself and in realizing the meaning of his own being. Woman accomplishes this by discerning her destiny, for it is only through woman that man becomes what and who he really is.[36]

One might object to this that, though it is more positive towards woman, it still sees the man–woman relationship from a male perspective: it is through woman that man gains self-understanding; woman still seems to remain functional for man. There is clearly, too, a danger of stereotypes here (even if, using Jungian language, they are dubbed 'archetypes': the third part of *La Femme et le salut de monde* is called 'Les Archétypes'). Although sex seems rooted in biology, gender, it is increasingly argued, is socially constructed, and has varied in different human societies. Nevertheless, gender roles are in some way based on sexual distinction, and biological motherhood is the exclusive preserve of woman. So Evdokimov declares:

> The ontological relationship of mother and child makes woman like Eve, 'the source of life'. She watches over every being, protects life and the world. Her interiorized and universalized charism of 'motherhood' bears every woman toward the famished and needy and makes admirably precise her feminine essence: married or not, every woman is *mother in aeternum*.[37]

In contrast, fatherhood is much less fundamental to being man than motherhood is to being woman – 'Conqueror, adventurer, builder, man is not fatherly in his being'.[38] This leads Evdokimov to the bold suggestion, inspired by the *dogmatikon* quoted above, in which it is said of the Virgin that 'she gave birth without a Father to the Son, who was begotten before the ages by the Father without a mother', that '[t]he virgin Mary's motherhood is thus a human figure or image of the fatherhood of God'.[39] This is supported by the way in which the human is presented as feminine in relation to God, in the Bible and indeed in other religious traditions, and by the fact that, though the Incarnation could, and did, take place without a man, it could not have

---

[36] Evdokimov, *In the World*, 232.
[37] Evdokimov, *In the World*, 233.
[38] Evdokimov, *In the World*, 233.
[39] Evdokimov, *In the World*, 234.

taken place without a woman, as well as by the place of women in the accounts of the Resurrection, in which they became apostles to the Apostles, and finally by the way in which the eschatological vision of the Apocalypse focuses on a woman 'clothed in the sun'. Evdokimov goes on to draw this out, remarking that '[m]an establishes himself in the world by his tools. Woman however does this by the gift of herself. In her very being she is intimately connected to the rhythms of nature'.[40]

Very similar themes are developed in another article, 'Panagion and Panagia: The Holy Spirit and the Mother of God'.[41] Here Evdokimov works more closely with a parallelism between the 'all-holy' (neuter = the Holy Spirit) and the 'all-holy' (feminine = the Mother of God). He draws attention to the tradition of the role of the Holy Spirit in the birth of Christ in the soul, and remarks, '[t]he breath of giving birth, in the expression of Fr Sergii Bulgakov, is the Spirit's "hypostatic maternity". This is why the virginal maternity of the Theotokos, according to Tradition, is a figure of the Holy Spirit, the Advocate'.[42] He draws on an image from Heraclitus:

> In Heraclitus one finds an image of astonishing depth, that of the bow and the lyre. The Greek word *bios* means both life and the bow, whose arrows signify death. The bow is a cord under tension. The bow of many strings, sublimated one might say, becomes a lyre. Thus in place of death-bearing arrows, the bow become a lyre brings forth music, harmony, beauty. The masculine instinct for destruction, the 'father of war', can be brought into concord, harmony, transformed by the feminine, the 'mother of life', given the instinct for life, for a constructive and positive cultural existence.[43]

Evdokimov goes on to illustrate this from an icon of St George and the Dragon, found in a church in the north of Russia, in which the dragon is not slain by the (unarmed) saint, but held on a lead by a queen, representing both the Mother of God and the Church (actually not an uncommon depiction in Western art). 'How relevant this vision is to us!' Evdokimov exclaims. 'Evil is not destroyed by a man but is converted by a woman.'[44]

Interior monasticism

One of the most important of Evdokimov's later works is his *Les Âges de la vie spirituelle*, first published in 1964. We can trace in this themes developed elsewhere in his works, not least his concern for the problem of evil and his notion of 'interiorized monasticism', both themes that were inspired by his reading of Dostoevsky. Concern with the problem of evil leads to an impatience with conventional piety. Even though Evdokimov was himself deeply,

---

[40] Evdokimov, *In the World*, 236.
[41] In Evdokimov, *In the World*, 155–73.
[42] Evdokimov, *In the World*, 161.
[43] Evdokimov, *In the World*, 164.
[44] Evdokimov, *In the World*, 165.

unconsciously, pious, he was aware of the dangers of a kind of spiritually blind pietism that could prevent one from being aware of the difficulties of believing in the modern world. *Ages of the Spiritual Life* begins with a chapter on atheism. Evdokimov considers the challenges to theism provided by the society in which we live in the West, a society that acts on the basis of atheism, looking at the world through the eyes of modern science and technology, for which God is irrelevant as a hypothesis, as Laplace put it. Instead of seeking to overcome atheism through argument, he sees atheism as a movement of the human spirit that can purify faith. Too easy a rebuttal of the problem provided by the existence of evil in the world leaves us with too naive a notion of God. Apologetic pragmatism, Evdokimov declares,

> does not treat the problem of evil in itself, but as a necessary component of the world. Now evil has an astonishing power. It has drawn God forth from his silence and has made him pass through death and Resurrection. And it is still the existence of evil that is the most striking proof of God's existence.[45]

What is really dangerous is what he calls 'the *latent atheism of ordinary believers,* drowsy in their own inspired good conscience, which out of thrift, avoids conversion of the heart'.[46] He remarks that Simone Weil noted that there are two kinds of atheism, 'one of which is a purification of the idea of God'.[47] A little later on, Evdokimov speaks of a 'purifying atheism', which, according to Jules Lagneau, is 'that salt which hinders belief in God from corrupting itself'. He comments: 'In this role of protection and safeguard, this unbelief cooperates with grace. That is why the Christ of Dostoevsky's *Legend* is silent, and kisses the suffering face of the Grand Inquisitor'.[48] This is where the spiritual life begins. Such a notion of a faith purified by atheism he had already found in Dostoevsky in his first book, *Dostoïevski et le problème du mal.* There he had linked it to the figure of Alesha in *The Brothers Karamazov*: the Alesha who wants to become a monk, but is persuaded by his elder, Zossima, that his vocation is not in the monastery, withdrawn from the cares and concerns of the world, but in the world itself. This was to be the subject of the last volume of the novel, never written.

Alesha becomes, though only mentioned occasionally, the central character in Evdokimov's *Ages of the Spiritual Life*. The central notion is that of 'interiorized monasticism', which he traces back to the great eighteenth-century spiritual teacher St Tikhon of Zadonsk (though very much the same idea is found in the spiritual letters of the nineteenth-century spiritual writer St Theophan the Recluse). His chapter opens by drawing attention to what he calls a 'universal crisis' in monasticism, which 'suggests that an historic

---

[45] Paul Evdokimov, *Ages of the Spiritual Life*, trans. Sister Gertrude SP, rev. Michael Plekon and Alexis Vinogradoff (Crestwood, NY: St Vladimir's Seminary Press, 1998), 44.

[46] Evdokimov, *Ages*, 45.

[47] Evdokimov, *Ages*, 46.

[48] Evdokimov, *Ages*, 88.

cycle is coming to a close'.[49] Although that might seem to have been borne out in Western Christendom, it could be regarded as an unduly pessimistic prognosis for Orthodox monasticism. Evdokimov, however, was writing in the 1960s, when indeed Athonite monasticism seemed on the point of expiring – most books on Athos written in the sixties held out little hope for the continuation of the monastic communities there. However, the decades since the sixties have seen a revival of monasticism on the Holy Mountain, and indeed elsewhere in the Orthodox world. Evdokimov's solution is, however, still worth heeding: what he calls the universal vocation of *interiorized monasticism*, that is, a monastic form of life, lived in the world by Christians both single and married. He quotes Fr Florovsky as saying that

> too often one forgets the provisory character of monasticism. St John Chrysostom declared that monasteries are necessary because the world is not Christian. Let it be converted, and the need for a monastic separation will disappear.[50]

Evdokimov also points out that the Orthodox Church, for all its veneration for the monastic state, has never accepted the idea that grew up in the West, that there are two forms of the Christian life, one for ordinary Christians bound by the commandments, the other for monks and nuns, 'religious', heeding the evangelical precepts of poverty, chastity and obedience. Evdokimov develops his understanding of interior monasticism with reference to the Legend of the Grand Inquisitor, recounted by Ivan in *The Brothers Karamazov* (Part II, Book 5, Chapter 5). The Grand Inquisitor has developed his parody of Christianity by turning the three temptations of Christ on their head. Whereas Christ refused to turn stones into bread by miracle, refused the mystery of leaping from the pinnacle of the Temple and landing safely in the Temple court, refused to acknowledge Satan's authority in return for power over the nations of the earth, the religion of the Grand Inquisitor is precisely based on 'miracle, mystery, and authority', in doing so depriving ordinary humans of freedom, a freedom he claims they are all too ready to relinquish. The three monastic vows of poverty, chastity and obedience are based on Christ's response to the three temptations, Evdokimov claims, and goes on to argue that they can be taken out of the cloister, as it were, and become the basis of an interior monasticism, lived in the world (or indeed in the cloister: think back to St Maria Skobtsova's criticisms of traditional Orthodox monasticism).

So the vow of poverty becomes a way of renouncing the *need to have*, which

> becomes a *need not to have*. The disinterested freedom of the spirit in regard to things restores its capacity for loving them as gifts from God. To live in what is 'given in abundance' is to live between destitution and the superfluous. The monastic ideal does not preach formal poverty but a wise frugality of needs.[51]

---

[49] Evdokimov, *Ages*, 133.
[50] Quoted in Evdokimov, *Ages*, 135.
[51] Evdokimov, *Ages*, 146.

Similarly the vow of chastity, understood as renunciation of mystery, is concerned with accepting one's own human integrity. Evdokimov quotes Christ's words to his disciples, 'Do not rejoice in this, that the spirits are subject to you [the submission of which Satan speaks]; rejoice rather in this, that your names are written in heaven'. He comments: 'The *name* designates the person. The text speaks of the joy of seeing oneself admitted to the spiritual heaven of the divine presence'.[52] Chastity is about renouncing the magic power of the 'guru', about refusing to confuse spiritual power with magical power over the material, gained maybe by a redirection of one's sexual drive.

> We must remember the close relationship between woman and the cosmos. The whole gamut of pagan mysteries prefigured this even up to the cult of the Virgin Mary – 'Blessed Land, Promised Land, Abundant Harvest'. These liturgical names are the cosmic symbols of the new Eve – *Virgin and Mother*. This mysterious linkage explains the command not to tempt God, not to sully and profane *chastity*.[53]

'Chastity – *sophrosyne* –' Evdokimov remarks, 'integrates all the elements of the human being into a whole that is virginal and interior to the spirit.' He speaks of chastity as purifying the way we regard things, and mentions how familiarity with icons purifies the imagination, teaching 'the fasting of the eyes'.[54]

His treatment of obedience begins like this:

> 'You shall love the Lord your God and him only shall you worship.' The liturgical definition of man, the being who sings 'Holy, holy, holy,' the *Trisagion* and the *Sanctus*, excludes all passivity. True obedience to God implies the supreme freedom that is always creative.[55]

This leads Evdokimov to consider the role of the elder, the spiritual father. He is never a 'director of conscience', but above all else a charismatic. 'He does not engender his spiritual son, he engenders a son of God. Both *mutually* place themselves in the school of truth.'[56] And goes on to remark that 'the very counsel of a *staretz* leads one to a state of freedom before the face of God'.[57]

With this rethinking of the traditional vows of poverty, chastity and obedience, we see delineated the fundamental features of Evdokimov's 'interior monasticism', no less demanding than conventional monasticism, for it envisages a state of freedom before the face of God that can only take place in prayer, both personal and liturgical.

---

[52] Evdokimov, *Ages*, 147–8.
[53] Evdokimov, *Ages*, 148.
[54] Evdokimov, *Ages*, 149.
[55] Evdokimov, *Ages*, 151.
[56] Evdokimov, *Ages*, 152.
[57] Evdokimov, *Ages*, 153.

Theology of beauty

L'Art de l'icône: Théologie de la beauté was published in the last year of Evdokimov's life. From what people say about him, one easily gets the impression that here we find the heart of the man and his thought: both issues of *Contacts* devoted to his thought have the title 'Paul Evdokimov ... témoin de la beauté de Dieu' ('Paul Evdokimov ... witness to the beauty of God').[58] Again it is easy to see how he fits into the development of the Russian Religious tradition, for one of the themes of early twentieth-century Russian theology is the rediscovery of the icon. We have already seen something of the beginnings of this in discussing Florensky, and glimpsed more of it in St Maria of Paris and (very fleetingly) in her friend, Sister Joanna Reitlinger; we shall pick up the thread later on when we come to Fr Sophrony, who came to Paris in the early 1920s as a budding professional painter and then, later in his life, became himself an icon painter and inspired others. The main part of the story in Paris we have, alas, passed over: the reflections of Evgeny Trubetskoy before the Revolution,[59] and the endeavours of Leonid Ouspensky and the monk Fr Gregory Krug, who between them drew the practice of icon-painting among the Russians in Paris back to its roots after the period in the eighteenth and nineteenth centuries when the style of icon-painting – throughout the whole Orthodox world – succumbed to Western artistic styles. Parallel with Ouspensky and Krug, the Greek Orthodox world rediscovered the icon through the advocacy of Fotis Kontoglou. The story is fascinating, but cannot be told here.[60]

Evdokimov undoubtedly draws on and develops the approach of Ouspensky. Together with Vladimir Lossky, Ouspensky had published his seminal work, *The Meaning of Icons*,[61] and then followed it up with *Essai sur la théologie de l'icône de l'Église Orthodoxe*, which was later supplemented and expanded as *Theology of the Icon*.[62] In a recent article, Alexandre Musin wonders why Evdokimov's book was not more of a response to Ouspensky, who belonged to the other Russian jurisdiction in Paris;[63] I am not sure why one should raise this – by the sixties the two jurisdictions were much less antagonistic.

Nevertheless, Evdokimov's work is in no sense a critical response to Ouspensky; he adopts much the same approach (though with no reference at all, so far as I can recall, to the older man's work, save in the brief Bibliography):

---

[58] *Contacts* 73–4 (2001); 235–6 (2011).

[59] See Eugène Troubetzkoï, *Trois études sur l'icône* (Paris: YMCA Press/OEIL, 1986).

[60] For an account that gathers together an immense amount of evidence, see Kari Kotkavaara, *Progeny of the Icon: Émigré Russian Revivalism and the Vicissitudes of the Eastern Orthodox Sacred Image* (Turku: Åbo Akademi University Press, 1999). See also my 2015 Zernov Lecture, 'The Recovery of the Icon', *Sobornost/ECR* (forthcoming, 2015).

[61] *Der Sinn der Ikonen* (Bern–Olten: Urs Graf-Verlag, 1952); ET: *The Meaning of Icons* (Boston, MA: Boston Book and Art Shop, 1969).

[62] 2 vols (Crestwood, NY: St Vladimir's Seminary Press, 1992); for the French translation of both parts of the Russian original, see the edition in Patrimoines: Orthodoxie (Paris: Cerf, 2003).

[63] Alexandre Musin, 'La Théologie de l'icône chez Paul Evdokimov: Une approche ecclésiale de l'art chrétien', *Contacts* 235–6 (2011), 388–400, at 391.

the same attitude to the history of iconoclasm and the post-medieval Wester-nization of the icon, the same response to modern art as betraying the bankruptcy of the Western artistic tradition. Indeed, this seems to have been virtually universal among the Russian émigrés we have looked at, despite the fact that other Russian émigrés, such as Kandinsky (in fact, Sergii Bulga-kov's brother-in-law), in their advocacy of modernism were maybe reflecting an artistic sensitivity born of their familiarity with the icon tradition. Evdokimov's attitude to modern art is, however, well informed; he knows of Matisse's interest in the colour of the icons, and his visit to Russia to study them, commenting, however, 'but their sense remained totally closed to him'.[64]

There are three aspects of the icon that are important to Evdokimov which, while not unique, together make up something distinctive. First, there is the emphasis on the Face: the icon is about encounter with Christ, the Mother of God, or the saint depicted, revealed through the *face*. The icon is not a work of art to be admired, but the means to an encounter with God's revela-tion in the face of Jesus Christ, or with those who have been transfigured in their following of Christ. The purpose of the icon is the transfiguration of those who behold them: we are to be caught up into the beauty of the transfigured cosmos; the end of the Christian life is transfiguration in the glory of God. Second, the encounter with the icon is an ecclesial experience: the icon belongs to the liturgy of the Church; even the icon in a private home creates a sacred space, analogous to that of the church. The experience of beholding, encountering, the icon is ecclesial. Evdokimov quotes the first line of the Cherubic hymn, 'We who in a mystery represent the Cherubim' [or better: are images/icons of the Cherubim: *eikonizontes*].[65] Third, there is what Evdokimov calls the *apophasis* of the icon. He draws attention to the idea that in prayer we pass beyond images, an idea emphasized by the hesychasts. This is in *antinomy* to the icon; and it is a true antinomy – we must embrace both poles of this antinomy: the inexpressibility of God, and his manifestation in the *face*. Without the witness of the icon, the apophatic runs the risk of becoming an intellectual abstraction, a privileging of the spiritual over the material.

> It is on the lintel of his existence that man is struck by the divine effigy. The image searches for the divine Original, aspires to its Archetype, orients man, breaks his solitude: 'There where man is alone, I am with him'. The content of thought about God, his Name traced, the icon, is not a content simply thought or imagined, but an encounter, presence immediate, bringing about unity. If man can no longer say anything *about* God, he can still say *God*, you, Father . . .[66]

---

[64] Evdokimov, *L'Art de l'icône*, 145. For a more nuanced account of the link between the rediscovery of the icon and modernism in the arts, see Charles Lock, 'The Space of Hospitality: On the Icon of the Trinity Ascribed to Andrei Rublev', *Sobornost/ECR* 31:1 (2008), 21–53, esp. 23–36.

[65] Evdokimov, *L'Art de l'icône*, 152.

[66] Evdokimov, *L'Art de l'icône*, 200, and see the whole chapter: 195–201.

Amour fou de Dieu

In our discussion, a little while back, of Evdokimov's *Ages of the Spiritual Life*, we began, as the book does, with his discussion of atheism and the problem of evil, in which he says of evil that 'it has drawn God forth from his silence and has made him pass through death and Resurrection. And it is still the existence of evil that is the most striking proof of God's existence.'[67] Instead of turning his back on the evil humans have brought into the world, a world which nowadays in the West, through widespread atheism, has come itself to turn its back on God, God continues to love the world. As we read in St John's Gospel, 'For God loved the world in such a way that he gave his only-begotten Son' (John 3.16).

St Paul picks up the same theme, speaking of the way in which God loved human beings who had turned their backs on him (cf. Rom. 5.8). A love that disregards lack of response, that just goes on loving *quand même*, is called, in French, *amour fou*. This idea of God's *amour fou* runs throughout Evdokimov's theology; the first collection of his articles published after his death was thus called *L'Amour fou de Dieu*.[68] It begins with an article called 'L'Amour fou de Dieu et le mystère de son silence'.[69] This, too, starts from the fact of modern atheism, and leads quickly to the idea of God who loves the world with an *amour fou*, a seemingly blind and crazy love. Instead of making his presence clear and undeniable, which would constrain human beings to respond, God simply goes on loving, with the love we see on the cross, the love of One who emptied himself. He quotes a striking remark of Joseph Malègue – 'The form under which God takes us by the hand is the very same that renders this hand invisible' – and goes on to comment:

> The hand of Christ crucified covers our eyes, but it is pierced and our eyes look through. Faith is the response to this kenotic attitude of God. It is because man can say *no* that his *yes* takes on its full resonance and is placed on the same register as God's *yes*.[70]

One must, therefore, speak, not of God's omnipotence, but of his frailty (*faiblesse*), or better: speak of God's omnipotence in terms of his frailty:

> The omnipotence of the *manikos eros* [the expression of Nicolas Cabasilas, which Evdokimov translates *amour fou*], of the *amour fou* of God, does not simply destroy evil and death, but assumes them: 'by death he has trampled on death'. His light shines forth as that of the Truth, crucified and risen.
>
> It is in this light that, faced with the suffering of the innocent, of abnormal children, of absurd accidents, there is space to apply to God the most paradoxical notion of invincible frailty. The only adequate response is to say that 'God is frail' and that he can only suffer with us, that suffering is 'the bread

---

[67] Evdokimov, *Ages*, 44.
[68] Paul Evdokimov, *L'Amour fou de Dieu* (Paris: Seuil, 1973).
[69] Evdokimov, *L'Amour fou*, 11–39.
[70] Evdokimov, *L'Amour fou*, 30–1.

that God shares with man'. Frail, certainly, not in its formal omnipotence, but in his Love which renounces freely its power and it is under this aspect of frailty that it appears to Nicolas Cabasilas as 'God's *amour fou* for mankind'.[71]

God's *amour fou* is a kenotic love, and our response to that partakes of God's self-emptying. To the atheist who demands proofs of God's existence, all we can say is:

> when one enters into oneself, and finds again the true silence, one will experience it as a waiting which comes to us from the 'Father who is present in secret' (Matt. 6:6).[72]

> It is in a like silence and in the royal freedom of his spirit that everyone is invited to respond to the very simple question: what is God? Someone like St Gregory of Nyssa lets it escape quite simply: 'You, whom my soul loves . . .'[73]

---

[71] Evdokimov, *L'Amour fou*, 35–6.
[72] Evdokimov, *L'Amour fou*, 37.
[73] Evdokimov, *L'Amour fou*, 39.

12

Neo-Palamism: Fr John Meyendorff and some Greek neo-Palamites

Neo-Palamism and the neo-patristic synthesis

Neo-Palamism: the term is often used almost interchangeably with Florovsky's term 'neo-patristic synthesis', and like that term is rarely given any clear meaning. Several factors suggest this near equivalence. First of all, the notion of a 'neo-patristic synthesis' was evoked in the context of defining the future of Orthodox theology in the years *entre deux guerres* in Paris. It served two purposes: first, it sought a redirection of Orthodoxy from the tradition represented by Vladimir Solov'ev, Pavel Florensky and Sergii Bulgakov, which in the eyes of Florovsky was far too much in hock to the philosophy of the West, especially German Idealism; second, however, it sought to define the nature of Orthodox theology against the Catholic theology of the West, which the Russian émigrés had encountered in Paris.

The liveliest form of Catholic theology in Paris at that time was (maybe, though one should not forget Maurice Blondel's 'philosophie de l'action') the neo-Thomism associated with Jacques Maritain and Étienne Gilson, both of whom we have already encountered as members of the so-called Berdyaev Colloquy, convoked by Berdyaev and Maritain: neo-Thomism, a theology (or rather philosophy) drawing on the thought of the Angelic Doctor, but responding to the problems of the twentieth century. Not surprisingly, Florovsky's appeal to the Fathers included the same desire to speak to the contemporary world, and not be content with repeating the formulae of the past: so, neo-patristic synthesis. However, the last great theological controversy of the Byzantine period, the hesychast controversy, was often understood as resistance to ideas from the West, infiltrating the world of Orthodoxy, as the Byzantine emperors sought the support of the West against the inexorable advance of the Ottoman Turks, which had its final triumph with the fall of Constantinople in 1453. The hero of that controversy was St Gregory Palamas, an Athonite monk, who for the last decade of his life had been Archbishop of Thessaloniki. To define the neo-patristic synthesis further, by focusing on Palamas, must have seemed natural: hence, neo-Palamism.

There was, however, immediately a problem: Palamas was well known as the champion of the hesychasts, and in the great hesychast anthology, the *Philokalia*, compiled by St Makarios of Corinth and St Nikodimos of the Holy Mountain, several works of the saint are included, as a kind of final peak in the mountain range of treatises, but apart from these treatises Palamas' works were little known. Nikodimos had prepared an edition of the saint from manuscripts on the Holy Mountain, but the manuscript of his edition was destroyed by the Austrian authorities in Vienna in 1798 when, at the prompting of the Ottoman authorities, they arrested Rhigas Velestinlis, protomartyr of the Greek revolution, and confiscated the manuscripts found in the office of the printer, George Makridis-Poulios, with whom Rhigas had found refuge.[1]

In the 1920s and 1930s, some work had been done on the manuscripts of Palamas held in Paris – by Fr Dumitru Stăniloae and Fr Basil Krivocheine – but the task of copying and editing the manuscripts was colossal and little progress had been made when Meyendorff began his research in the 1950s. What was known of Palamas' teaching was the distinction he had drawn within God between his essence and energies, a distinction that enabled him to reconcile the affirmation of God's unknowability with a genuine experience of God himself through his energies, which are identical with God and therefore uncreated. The Palamite contrast between essence and energies was well known in Russian circles: Bulgakov was well aware of it, using it to support his sophiological notions, and in a paper significant for the enterprise of the neo-patristic synthesis, 'St Gregory Palamas and the Tradition of the Fathers', Florovsky's summary of Palamas focuses on the essence–energies distinction and its importance for articulating the doctrine of *theosis*, deification, though Palamas was not otherwise particularly important to Florovsky in his own elaboration of the neo-patristic synthesis.[2] It is perhaps not a matter of chance that neo-Palamism, understood in such terms, propounds a philosophical doctrine that can be compared, and contrasted, with the identity in God of his essence and existence, a central principle of neo-Thomism. The contrast between East and West could be encapsulated in a neat pair of incompatible philosophical tenets, and could be characterized as Thomas Aquinas *versus* Gregory Palamas!

Perhaps Fr John Meyendorff's most important achievement for scholarship and Orthodox theology was his work on St Gregory Palamas, which culminated in his major study, *Introduction à l'étude de Grégoire Palamas*,[3] and his edition of perhaps the most important of the saint's works, his *Triads in Defence of the Holy Hesychasts*,[4] both published in 1959. There is, however, very much more to Meyendorff than this, and I shall begin by a brief account of his life and achievements.

---

[1] See Kallistos Ware, 'St Nikodimos and the *Philokalia*', in *The* Philokalia: *A Classic Text of Orthodox Spirituality*, ed. Brock Bingaman and Bradley Nassif (New York: Oxford University Press, 2012), 9–35, at 16.

[2] Georges Florovsky, 'St Gregory Palamas and the Tradition of the Fathers', in *Bible, Church, Tradition: An Eastern Orthodox View* (Belmont, MA: Nordland, 1972), 105–20, 127 (notes).

[3] Jean Meyendorff, *Introduction à l'étude de Grégoire Palamas*, Patristica Sorbonensia 3 (Paris: Seuil, 1959); ET (with abridged footnotes and lacking the Appendices and Bibliography, but with minor updating): *A Study of Gregory Palamas*, trans. George Lawrence (London: Faith Press, 1964; now published by St Vladimir's Seminary Press).

[4] Grégoire Palamas, *Défense des saints hésychastes* (Leuven-Louvain: Spicilegium Sacrum Lovaniense: Études et documents, fascicule 30–1, 1959; rev. edn, 1973); very partial ET: Gregory Palamas, *The Triads*, trans. Nicholas Gendle (London: SPCK, 1983).

Meyendorff's life

John Meyendorff was born of Russian émigré parents on 17 February 1926, in Neuilly-sur-Seine, a residential suburb of Paris (where Kandinsky lived for the last decade of his life – 1933–44).[5] After schooling, he studied at the Institut St-Serge in Paris, graduating in 1949; in 1958 he was awarded the *Doctorat ès lettres* by the Sorbonne. In the same year, he was ordained to the priesthood. In 1959, the fruits of his doctoral work were published. In the same year he migrated to the USA, and became Professor of Patristics and Church History at St Vladimir's Orthodox Seminary, then housed in Union Theological Seminary, soon to move to Crestwood, New York (in 1962). He became the third in a line of Russian teachers who made their home in the USA: after Fr Georges Florovsky and Fr Alexander Schmemann. At St-Serge he had encountered many distinguished theologians and historians of the Russian emigration, among whom he later singled out as of special importance for him Fr Kiprian Kern and Fr Nicholas Afanasiev. While at St Vladimir's

John Meyendorff
With permission of St Vladimir's Orthodox Seminary

---

[5] For Meyendorff's life, I have relied on Dimitri Obolensky's obituary in *Sobornost/ECR* 15:2 (1993), 44–51.

he was also closely involved in Dumbarton Oaks, the centre for Byzantine Studies (among other matters) in Washington, DC, and was Adjunct Professor of Byzantine Studies at nearby Fordham University. He became Dean of St Vladimir's Seminary in 1984, succeeding Fr Alexander Schmemann after his death in 1983.

As well as his scholarly work, he became deeply involved in the life of the Russian Orthodox in the USA and, together with Fr Alexander, was instrumental in the creation of the Orthodox Church in America, which received its status as autocephalous from the Patriarchate of Moscow in 1970.[6] He was deeply involved in the pastoral and liturgical life of the seminary, and had a profound influence on those who studied with him. Meyendorff was also involved in matters outside his adopted country. He was a founder and first general secretary of *Syndesmos*, an international organization of Orthodox youth movements. He also represented the Orthodox Church in America (before 1970, the Russian Orthodox Church in North America) on the World Council of Churches, and served for eight years as moderator of the Faith and Order commission. He was openly critical of the tendency of the WCC to move from theological discussion to political involvement, a tendency that has increased and led to still deeper reservations about the WCC on the part of the Orthodox. He retired as dean of the seminary on 1 July 1992, and died later that month (22 July).

His scholarly work falls into three categories: his work on Palamas, which combined theological, historical and philological expertise; his work as a church historian; and his work as a theologian. Let us treat them in reverse order.

His work as a theologian

His most important works of theology are his early *L'Église orthodoxe: Hier et aujourd'hui*, published in English as *The Orthodox Church: Its Past and Its Role in the World Today*,[7] which presents the Orthodox Church, as is often done, through its history; *Le Christ dans la théologie byzantine* (1969, published in English in the same year as *Christ in Eastern Christian Thought*),[8] presented, maybe a little unwisely, as a successor to Aloys Grillmeier's *Christ in Christian Tradition* (1965), then apparently a work on its own – only in 1975 did a revised version appear with the subheading 'volume 1', presaging a volume 2 in eventually five parts, which rather dwarfed Meyendorff's account of post-Chalcedonian Christology; *Byzantine Theology*;[9] and his *Marriage – An Orthodox Perspective*.[10] All these books are fine introductions to their several

---

[6] On what was involved in this venture, see Alexander Bogolepov, *Towards an American Orthodox Church: The Establishment of an Autocephalous Orthodox Church* (Crestwood, NY: St Vladimir's Seminary Press, 1963; rev. edn, 2001).

[7] Paris: Seuil, 1960; London: Darton, Longman & Todd, 1962.

[8] Paris: Cerf/Crestwood, NY: St Vladimir's Seminary Press, 1969.

[9] Bronx, NY: Fordham University Press/London: Mowbrays, 1974.

[10] Crestwood, NY: St Vladimir's Seminary Press, 1970; rev. edn, 1975.

subjects, well grounded in the Fathers, the Holy Canons and history; indeed, apart from *The Orthodox Church*, they go beyond mere introductions and provide substantial discussions, in English, of a number of important issues. There are also several collections of essays, or articles, mostly on theological or historical themes.

...as a historian

Meyendorff, the scholar, was probably happiest, or most at home, as a historian. As a historian, he covered a wide range: the early centuries of the Christian Church, the Byzantine Middle Ages and early Russian history. His most important, original work of history was his *Byzantium and the Rise of Russia*.[11] In this book, he discussed the recovery of the lands of Rus' from subjection to the Mongols, and the shift of the Metropolitanate of all Russia from Kiev to Moscow (where it was eventually to become the patriarchate). It is a very tangled story, and Meyendorff's account is enviably clear. Among the important aspects of his account is the role he ascribes to what Sir Dimitri Obolensky had called the 'Byzantine Commonwealth', formed by the ties based on common faith and common political theory that linked the, then rapidly diminishing, Byzantine Empire to the countries to which it had bequeathed its Christian faith, in which the Patriarch of Constantinople played a part alongside the emperor, as well as the way in which fourteenth-century hesychasm inspired a revival of monasticism through the Byzantine Commonwealth, with the monks and their communities deepening and inspiring the faith of the Orthodox in the regions recovering from the depredations of the Golden Horde, and providing a sense of identity in which Orthodoxy and nationhood went hand in hand. The figure of St Sergii of Radonezh played a large role in his account.

Meyendorff's other venture as a historian was his conceiving of a church history to be published by St Vladimir's Seminary Press, entitled *The Church in History*, of which he was the first general editor. His conception was a history of the whole Church from the perspective of Orthodoxy, and so to provide a counterbalance to virtually all church histories available in the West, where the story of the Church is conceived from a Western point of view, with the Eastern Church more or less fading from the scene after the fifth century, to appear again briefly as the 'other side' of the Great Schism in the eleventh century. Meyendorff's aim in his history of the Church was to see things from the point of view of the Eastern Church (as far as possible not only the Orthodox Churches, but also the Oriental Orthodox Churches that separated from the Church of the Byzantine Empire after the councils of Ephesos and Chalcedon in the fifth century), and to tell the story even-handedly with the gradual separation of, but continuing engagement between, the Churches of the East and the West at the centre of the account. Meyendorff's

---

[11] New York: Cambridge University Press, 1981.

own volume, the second planned, *Imperial Unity and Christian Divisions: The Church 450–680 AD* (1989), admirably fulfilled these aims, presenting the Byzantine Empire as a multicultural state, embracing a great diversity, cultural and linguistic, which became the seedbed for Christian divisions. The next volume to appear, the fourth, *The Christian East and the Rise of the Papacy: The Church 1071–1453 AD*, was by Aristeides Papadakis, with Meyendorff contributing the chapters concerned with Russia and the Balkans; it was published in 1994, the year after Meyendorff's death.

...and on Palamas

Meyendorff's most original and enduring contribution to church history was, unquestionably, his work on St Gregory Palamas. It is hard to imagine how difficult was the task he had set himself in deciding to work on Gregory Palamas. As he remarked in the first sentence of the Preface of his book on the saint, 'Mediaeval Byzantine thought is still virgin land which has only just begun to be cleared'.[12] In the articles Meyendorff wrote during the 1950s, and indeed in his book, many of the citations from the works of Palamas and his contemporaries are taken from manuscripts. As well as the huge work of preparing an edition of the *Triads*, Meyendorff had made himself familiar with many of the works of the saint's contemporaries, themselves only to be found in manuscripts. Lack of published editions meant lack of general surveys (at least, surveys based on any serious evidence): Meyendorff's work opened up a new era of scholarship – and not only of scholarship, for the hesychast controversy and its repercussions have had a profound impact both on the subsequent life of the Orthodox Church itself and on the relationship between the Churches of the East and the West. Meyendorff followed up his great treatise on Palamas with a short and very attractive little book, *St Grégoire Palamas et la mystique orthodoxe*, published in the same year in the series Maîtres spirituels, which was soon translated into English.[13]

Let us look in a little more detail at Meyendorff's work on Palamas. As I have already suggested, the way Palamas had defended a radical doctrine of deification by recourse to the distinction within God between his essence and his energies was already well known in Orthodox circles – and attacked in Western Catholic circles, notably by Martin Jugie in his vast and learned work, *Theologia dogmatica Christianorum Orientalium ab Ecclesia Catholica dissendentium* (5 vols, 1926–35).[14] For although most of Palamas' works were unavailable before Meyendorff's endeavours, the essence of the controversy was contained in the *Hagioretic Tome* (1340), easily accessible, as it was included in the *Philokalia*. There is nothing wrong with identifying this with Palamism:

[12] Meyendorff, *Study*, 5.

[13] Jean Meyendorff, *St Grégoire Palamas et la mystique orthodoxe*, Maîtres spirituels 20 (Paris: Seuil, 1959; ET, Crestwood, NY: St Vladimir's Seminary Press, 1980).

[14] See Martin Jugie, *Theologia dogmatica Christianorum Orientalium ab Ecclesia Catholica dissendentium*, 5 vols (Paris: Letouzey et Ané, 1926–35), De Theologia Palamitica, II, 47–183.

it is certainly the core of the matter so far as the controversy was concerned, but it represents a narrowing of the theological vision of Palamas. The principal achievement of Meyendorff's book was the way he set the hesychast controversy in its historical context and provided a much fuller picture of the theology of St Gregory.

The hesychast controversy and Palamas

We perhaps need to begin by reminding ourselves in outline of the events of the controversy.[15] The first figure whom Palamas opposed was Barlaam the Calabrian, from the then Greek-speaking toe of Italy. Initially the subject was the burning issue between East and West in the discussions over reunion – discussions that sought success after the failure of the reunion council of 1274, the Second Council of Lyon – the question of the double procession of the Holy Spirit, the *Filioque*. Barlaam had argued that the question was beyond the reach of human reason, and that therefore the *Filioque* should be dropped by the Latins, and all agree on the tenet that the Holy Spirit proceeded from the Father. As Gregory learnt more about Barlaam's arguments, he became alarmed, and argued in his *Apodeictic Treatises on the Procession of the Holy Spirit* that the error of the *Filioque* can be demonstrated; it is not something we are to be simply agnostic about. (Incidentally, although without attribution, it is Barlaam's arguments that figure in the treatise on the Holy Spirit by Nilos Cabasilas, a successor of Palamas' in the see of Thessaloniki, which was the principal source of the arguments on the Orthodox side at the Council of Florence in 1439.)[16]

From 1337, Barlaam turned his attention to the hesychast monks of the Holy Mountain, and their claims to behold in their prayer the uncreated light of the Godhead, which they identified with the light of Tabor, the Mount of the Transfiguration: he denounced them as Messalians, and drew down upon himself the wrath of Palamas, who defended the monks in his set of treatises called the *Triads*. The first *Triad*, written in spring 1338, consisted of three parts (hence the title), the first against profane philosophy and its dangers; the second a defence of the hesychast way of prayer, the prayer of the heart (this treatise was included in the *Philokalia*); the third, a demonstration that the true way to knowledge of God is through the divine charism of spiritual perception (*noera aisthesis*). Late in 1338, Barlaam wrote his own treatises against the hesychasts, to which Palamas replied in the first half of 1339 with his second *Triad*, with the same structure as the first. In the winter of 1339/40, Barlaam replied with a set of treatises called *Against the Messalians*, to which Palamas responded in early 1340 with his third *Triad*, in which he deals

---

[15] For a good up-to-date account of Palamas, the controversy and his theology, see R. E. Sinkewicz, 'Gregory Palamas', in *La Théologie byzantine et sa tradition*, II, ed. Carmelo Giuseppe Conticello and Vassa Conticello (Turnhout: Brepols, 2002), 31–188.

[16] See Nil Cabasilas, *Sur le Saint-Esprit*, ed., trans., with Introduction and notes by Théophile Kislas (Paris: Cerf, 2002), esp. 145.

at length with the Orthodox doctrine of deification, his theology of the Light of Tabor as an uncreated activity (or energy) of God, and the distinction between the divine essence and the divine energies. At the same time, Palamas enlisted the support of the monastic authorities on Mt Athos, who endorsed the *Hagioretic Tome* (or *Tome of the Holy Mountain*), composed by Palamas and directed against Barlaam, though Barlaam is not mentioned by name.

The controversy continued from 1341 to 1347, with Gregory Akindynos now as the opponent of Palamas, Barlaam having left the scene. Akindynos had been on good terms with both Barlaam and Palamas and had, initially, sought to mediate between them, but the Palamite doctrine of the distinction between the essence and energies of God seemed to him to compromise the unity of God. The controversy with Akindynos produced several treatises on both sides. Akindynos was himself a monk and spiritual father, almost certainly counting among his spiritual children Irene-Eulogia Choumnaina-Palaeologina, the widow of John Palaiologos, the Despot, the son of Emperor Andronikos II: he was well connected in court circles.[17] We must pass over the details, but during this stage of the controversy, which coincided with a period of civil war in the Byzantine Empire, Palamas found himself condemned, and for a time imprisoned, and it was only with the ascendancy of Emperor John VI Kantakouzenos from 1346 (emperor 1347–54) that Palamas was vindicated by synods in Constantinople in 1347 and 1351. Nevertheless, Palamas still faced opponents, this time the learned scholar Nikephoros Gregoras, who mounted the most significant intellectual challenge to Palamism.

Meyendorff's understanding of the controversy

The controversy between Palamas and his opponents has traditionally been considered as a controversy between Western-inclined Eastern theologians – Latin-minded, *latinophrones* – and truly Orthodox Eastern theologians, or between humanists and monks or mystical theologians. This way of looking at the controversy seemed quite inadequate to Meyendorff; to him the controversy appeared more complex . . . and more Byzantine. In particular, he tried to suggest that the difference between Barlaam and Palamas was a difference that could be traced back to their diverging interpretations of the theologian who called himself Dionysios the Areopagite, and whose works had been so influential in subsequent Christian thought, in both East and West. He interpreted Barlaam as giving a purely intellectual interpretation of Dionysios' apophatic theology: an interpretation that led to agnosticism. Whereas Gregory Palamas, he argued, interpreted Dionysios' apophatic theology quite differently, not leading to agnosticism, but rather preparing the way for an encounter with God in which there was genuine knowledge of God

---

[17] See Juan Nadal Cañellas, *La Résistance d'Akindynos à Grégoire Palamas: Enquête historique, avec traduction et commentaire de quatre traits édités récemment,* vol. 2 (Leuven: Peeters, 2006), 83–9; also in Nadal Cañellas' article on Akindynos in *La Théologie byzantine,* II, 189–314.

transcending the human intellect, a knowledge found in union with God, a union made possible through grace, grace flowing from God's union with humankind in the Incarnation.

Another aspect of Meyendorff's interpretation of Palamas' conflict with Barlaam concerned the way in which he saw Barlaam as representing a kind of intellectual Platonism or Neoplatonism, in which it was the intellect that came to know God, by detaching itself from matter and the body, contrasted with a holistic understanding of human nature, which he argued Palamas endorsed. For Barlaam it was simply ridiculous for the hesychast monks to claim that they had seen the uncreated light of the Godhead – and therefore God himself – with their very eyes, whereas for Gregory the monks' prayer of the heart, in response to God's grace that healed fallen, fractured human nature, was a prayer that involved the whole of the human being, body as well as soul, so that the idea of seeing God with our very eyes seemed not in the least ridiculous. Behind these contrasts, Meyendorff saw a very different understanding of asceticism: Barlaam's asceticism was concerned to subdue the body, to detach the intellect from the body and its emotions and passions by mortifying it, whereas for Gregory asceticism was concerned with the transfiguration of the body and the redirection of human emotions and passions. Towards the end of the third *Triad*, Gregory had argued against Barlaam's understanding of *apatheia* as killing the passionate part of the soul, asserting that 'lovers of good things work a transformation [*metathesis*] of this faculty, not its killing [or mortification: *nekrosis*]' (*Triads* III. 3.15).

Meyendorff's interpretation of Palamas was not received without criticism; within a few years of the publication of his book, two articles by Fr John Romanides appeared in the *Greek Orthodox Theological Review*.[18] Romanides had a number of criticisms, some of them very telling. In particular, he criticized Meyendorff's presentation of Barlaam as a Platonist or Neoplatonist nominalist, which he argued was very nearly a contradiction in terms, as one could hardly be a Platonist without a belief in the theory of forms or ideas, and it is precisely the contention of nominalists that such forms or ideas are no more than names (*nomina*), corresponding to no reality. This seems a fair point, and Romanides indeed refers to Barlaam's notion of the *logoi* of creatures, an idea incompatible with nominalism. It seems odd that Palamas rejected this notion of the *logoi*, so central to the thought of St Maximos, whom he revered (though what Palamas was objecting to was the idea that merely by learning, and not grace, the intellect could come to know the *logoi*, something Maximos would have rejected, too).

---

[18] John S. Romanides, 'Notes on the Palamite Controversy and Related Topics', *GOTR*, I: 6 (1960–1), 186–205; II: 9 (1963–4), 225–70. The second article concludes with: 'To be concluded', but I do not think it ever was. In the English version, *A Study of Gregory Palamas*, Meyendorff refers to the first of these articles, noting Romanides' criticism of his '*tentative* interpretation of Barlaam's thinking', and summarizing his critic's position as seeing Barlaam 'in the line of classical Western Augustinism', which, he argues, would reduce the controversy to a 'simple episode in the debate between East and West' (*Study*, 116, n. 1ª).

Recently it has been argued by Fr Maximos of Simonopetra that we can discern here a missed opportunity in the controversy, for had he not dismissed the doctrine of the *logoi*, Palamas might have developed an Orthodox version of *analogia entis*, more satisfactory than what we find in St Thomas Aquinas.[19] Romanides' criticism could have been pushed further by pointing out that Meyendorff's understanding of nominalism seems muddled, mixing up the philosophical doctrine (discussed in the West at least from the time of Abelard) with the theological doctrine known as the 'two powers' doctrine, which distinguishes between God's *potentia absoluta* and his *potentia ordinata* – what God can do absolutely, and what he has chosen to do – the doctrine applied by Scotus and Ockham and others, which certainly undermined the theological vision of St Thomas Aquinas. It could be argued, and has recently by Marcus Plested,[20] that the Byzantines preserved an interest in and respect for Thomas throughout the rest of the Byzantine period, a period (mid-fourteenth to mid-fifteenth centuries) when Thomas' star was distinctly in decline in the West.

Meyendorff's Palamas

Meyendorff's attempt to escape from the traditional ways of approaching the hesychast controversy is to be welcomed, and for many his view of the controversy has seemed convincing. Nevertheless, Meyendorff does not seem to escape the broad tendency we noticed at the beginning of this chapter, namely, to read out of the controversy a sense of the fundamental divide between East and West as encapsulated in a contrast between Thomist scholasticism and Palamite mystical theology, which still remains powerful at a popular level as well as among theologians. Although Meyendorff gives no countenance to seeing the hesychast controversy as a conflict between Thomism and Palamism, there are aspects of his book that encourage a way of opposing Orthodox theology with Catholic theology in terms of an opposition between Palamas and Aquinas. The chapter on the distinction between essence and energies in Part II of his book on Palamas is entitled 'Une théologie existentielle: essence et énergie', and this opposition is manifest in the way he interprets the distinction in personalist terms: God, unknown in himself, makes himself known personally through his energies in which we can participate. He quotes words Palamas addressed to Barlaam:

> God, when he conversed with Moses, did not say: I am essence, but: I am He who is (Exod. 3:14). It is not then He who is who comes from the essence, but the essence that comes from Him who is, for He who is embraces in Himself the whole of Being.[21]

---

[19] Fr Maximos Simonopetrites (Nicholas Constas), 'St Maximus the Confessor: The Reception of His Thought in East and West', in *Knowing the Purpose of Creation through the Resurrection*, ed. Bishop Maxim (Vasiljević) (Alhambra, CA: Sebastian Press, 2013), 25–53, at 44–6.

[20] Marcus Plested, *Orthodox Readings of Aquinas* (Oxford: Oxford University Press, 2012).

[21] *Étude*, 292 (cf. *Study*, 213).

It is striking that Meyendorff refers to Palamas' interpretation of Exodus 3.14, for this was a key text in Étienne Gilson's interpretation of Aquinas, and indeed of the best of medieval Latin theology in general, of which Aquinas was the supreme example. God, as 'He Who is', declares himself to Moses as a person, not a principle. Gilson spoke of Christian personalism in terms of 'une métaphysique de l'Exode'.[22] He interprets Aquinas' use of *ipsum esse* of God in what he called existentialist, not essentialist, terms.[23] In his great work, *Le Thomisme*, Thomas' philosophy is presented as existential: in Part I, called 'Dieu', the burden of the first chapter, called 'Existence et réalité', is to demonstrate Thomas' existentialism.[24] It is not fanciful to see Meyendorff as matching Palamas against Thomas as another great existential theologian. The familiar opposition appears again: in contemporary dress!

The great merit of Meyendorff's work on Palamas is to turn him from the representative of a principle to a theologian of power and originality. Hesychasm becomes a way of characterizing the whole Christian life, rooted in baptism, deepened through prayer and participation in the sacraments, and finding its fulfilment in deification. Much of Palamas' pastoral and spiritual theology was already accessible through his sermons, in which Palamas never raises such recondite matters as the distinction between God's essence and energy. Meyendorff's exploration of the fundamental structure of his thought in the *Triads* enabled him (and others) to place the pastoral and sacramental theology of the sermons in a sharper theological context. The goal of human creation, according to Palamas, was to unite the human with God. In our fallen condition, deification entailed the restoration to wholeness of fallen fractured humanity: in this process, personal prayer and asceticism, participation in the sacraments, and acts of love and care for one's fellow men and women were united. Meyendorff's work restored to the whole Christian world, East and West, all the lineaments of St Gregory Palamas' theological vision.

Meyendorff's influence

Fr Meyendorff's work on St Gregory Palamas – his edition of the *Triads*, his *Study of Gregory Palamas*, and the articles, mostly from the 1950s, collected in *Byzantine Hesychasm: Historical, Theological, and Social Problems*[25] – changed the landscape of studies of hesychasm in general and St Gregory Palamas in particular. There were, as we have seen, a lot of loose ends – in particular, it is a pity that Meyendorff never engaged with Romanides' criticisms – and in the years since 1959 there has been a great deal of scholarship devoted to

---

[22] Étienne Gilson, *L'Esprit de la philosophie médiévale* (Paris: Vrin, 2nd edn, 1948), 210 (in a chapter called 'Le Personnalisme chrétien').

[23] Étienne Gilson, *Le Thomisme* (Paris: Vrin, 5th edn, 1945), 51.

[24] Gilson, *Thomisme*, 44–68; cf. 83, 505 ('on ajoutait que «la philosophe thomiste est une philosophie existentielle»').

[25] John Meyendorff, *Byzantine Hesychasm: Historical, Theological, and Social Problems* (Aldershot: Variorum, 1974).

the 'long last century' of Byzantium: editions of the writings and treatises, and many studies, of Palamas and his contemporaries and successors. On the question of the engagement between the thought of the Latin West and the Byzantine East, there is now a major research project devoted to editing and reflecting on the host of Byzantine texts that translated and commented on St Thomas Aquinas: *Thomas de Aquino Byzantinus*, based in Royal Holloway under the supervision of Charalambos Dendrinos and John Demetracopoulos.

Meyendorff's achievement stimulated a revival of interest in Palamas, especially, maybe rather surprisingly, in Greece. There was no comparable devotion to hesychast theology in France (except for a few professors at the Institut St-Serge, notably Fr Boris Bobrinskoy), which Meyendorff left in his *annus mirabilis* of 1959, nor in the USA, where Meyendorff was to spend the rest of his life; indeed, once in the USA, Meyendorff's energies were increasingly taken up with St Vladimir's Seminary, the Orthodox Church of America and ecumenism – his work on Palamas seems to have ceased. There were a few Catholic scholars who interested themselves in Palamas: the indefatigable Gerhard Podskalsky,[26] for example, and the Canadian Dominican Jacques Lison, whose work on Gregory's doctrine of the Holy Spirit was dedicated to John Meyendorff.[27]

Immediately in the wake of Meyendorff's work on Palamas, there was, however, an explosion of interest in the saint in Greece. The central symbol of this awakened interest in St Gregory Palamas was the projected critical edition with Panayiotis Christou, Professor at the Aristotle University in Thessaloniki, as general editor. He provided introductions to the individual works, which were edited by a team of scholars, including Fr Boris Bobrinskoy, for many years Dean of the Institut St-Serge in Paris, and some of Christou's colleagues at the Aristotle University, such as George Mantzaridis and Nikos Matsoukas: the first volume was published in 1962 and volume 5, the last to appear before Christou's death, in 1992.[28] As it stands, it included most of Palamas' works, apart from the homilies.

Neo-Palamism in Greece

As the edition progressed, Palamas became a central inspiration for what one might almost call a hesychast school of Orthodox theology in Greece. This school, loosely conceived, included scholars such as George Mantzaridis and Panayiotis Nellas, whom we shall discuss in the rest of this chapter, and later scholars who wrote dissertations on Palamas and related hesychast subjects in Greece, including Serbians such as (later, Metropolitan) Amfilokije

---

[26] Gerhard Podskalsky, *Theologie und Philosophie in Byzanz*, Byzantinisches Archiv 15 (Munich: C. H. Beck, 1977): this is one of his shorter books on the history of Orthodox theology, all marked by immense learning.

[27] Jacques Lison, *L'Esprit répandu: La pneumatologie de Grégoire Palamas* (Paris: Cerf, 1994).

[28] Gregoriou tou Palama, *Suggrammata*, ed. Panayiotis Christou, 5 vols (Thessaloniki: Kyromanos (for the last volume), 1962–92).

Radović,[29] and other Greeks such as Stavros Yagkazoglou,[30] or even Chrysostomos Stamoulis, a systematic theologian clearly inspired by Palamas.[31]

Both George Mantzaridis and Panayiotis Nellas were scholars with strong links with Orthodox monasticism, especially with the monasteries of the Holy Mountain, not always a feature of Greek Orthodox theology. George Mantzaridis is a native of Thessaloniki, who studied there and, until his recent retirement, was Professor of Moral Theology and the Sociology of Christendom at the Aristotle University. His book, translated into English as *The Deification of Man*,[32] 'supplements Fr John [Meyendorff]'s general survey in a most illuminating fashion', as Metropolitan Kallistos remarks in his Foreword to the English translation.[33] It is an exposition of Palamas' doctrine of deification, and its ramifications. Metropolitan Kallistos' remark is abundantly borne out by the book, which approaches St Gregory from very much the standpoint of Meyendorff, though there are few direct references to Meyendorff's work; indeed, the scholar on whom he seems most to rely is Fr Kiprian Kern, one of Meyendorff's mentors, who wrote a book on Palamas' anthropology, relying, inevitably, on the relatively few works of Palamas then available.[34]

George Mantzaridis

According to Mantzaridis, Palamas' doctrine of the deification of man is based on three premisses: the doctrine of the creation of humankind in the image and likeness of God; the Incarnation of the Word of God; the strength of human communion with God in the Holy Spirit. In creating humankind in his image, God intended human beings to live in communion with him. Alas, because of the fall, humans turned away from God, and in the Incarnation, God restored that lost communion. However, the final perfection of communion with God, deification, can only take place as humans respond to the grace of the Holy Spirit, and enable the divine image and likeness to be reformed in themselves, a process that requires effort, indeed struggle, on the part of man. Mantzaridis' book explores the way in which the process of deification takes place according to the teaching of the saint. He starts by exploring the way in which the Church and the sacraments are involved in this process. Deification is founded on baptism and nurtured by the Eucharist: this sacramental dimension makes clear that deification is not a matter for the individual, however much the picture of an isolated ascetic, praying the Jesus Prayer alone, might suggest this – rather deification is ecclesial. As Palamas puts it in one of his sermons:

---

[29] Amphilochios Radović, *To Mysterion tes Agias Triados kata ton Agion Gregorion Palaman* (Thessaloniki: Analekta Vlatadon, 16, 1991; now in French trans., Paris: Cerf, 2012).

[30] Stavros Yagkazoglou, *Koinonia Theoseos* (Athens: Ekdoseis Domos), 2001.

[31] See Chrysostomos A. Stamoulis, *Peri Photos* (Thessaloniki: Ekdoseis «To Palimpseston», 1999).

[32] Georgios I. Mantzaridis, *The Deification of Man*, trans. Liadain Sherrard (Crestwood, NY: St Vladimir's Seminary Press, 1984).

[33] Mantzaridis, *Deification of Man*, 7.

[34] Kiprian Kern, *Antropologija sv. Grigorija Palamy* (Paris: YMCA Press, 1950).

Through his grace we are all one in our faith in Him, and we constitute the one body of His Church, having Him as sole head, and we have been given to drink from one spirit through the grace of the Holy Spirit, and we have received one baptism, and one hope is in all, and we have one God, above all things and with all things and in us all.[35]

Mantzaridis then turns to the moral and ascetic dimension of deification, to prayer and the vision of the Uncreated Light of the Godhead and participation in God. Finally he comes to the fulfilment of deification, and the vision of God 'face to face'. One of the most important features of Mantzaridis' presentation is the way in which he links what could appear to be two separate sides of Palamas' thought. For in the polemical treatises, his discussion is mostly philosophical and ascetic, the pastoral and sacramental side of his thought being mostly developed in the homilies. By deft use of the polemical treatises, Mantzaridis shows how the two sides of Palamas' thought fit together. By focusing on deification, not only is the theological underpinning of the doctrine explored, but also its pastoral and sacramental – and indeed ecclesiological – implications.

Panayiotis Nellas

The other Greek theologian we shall explore a little in this context is Panayiotis Nellas. He died young, at the age of 50 in 1986, having already achieved much, and promising more. Like Christos Yannaras, whom we shall discuss later, his contemporary and friend from student days, he studied theology at Athens, and then went abroad, in his case to France and Rome. Like Yannaras, he was connected with the revival movement called Zoë, and like Yannaras again, he came under the influence of an extraordinary man, Dimitrios Koutroubis (1921–83), who inspired a whole generation of Greek theologians in the 1960s, ending his life in Norfolk, England.

Unmarried, never ordained, Nellas was a lay theologian; neither was he a monk, though he had a deep love of monasticism, and wrote his book translated as *Deification in Christ*[36] at the Athonite monastery of Stavronikita, whose abbot, Fr Vasileios, was a close friend. His commitment to the promotion of theology and patristics is manifest in two ventures. In 1968, he launched a series called *Epi tas pigas*, 'to the sources', a kind of Greek equivalent of the French Sources Chrétiennes, which produced editions of the Fathers – the Marian homilies of Nicolas Cabasilas, edited by himself, the Marian Homilies of St John Damascene, edited by the Serbian theologian Fr Atanasije Jevtić, and two volumes of Maximos, his *Mystagogia* and the first (and only) volume of the *Ambigua*, edited by Fr Dumitru Stăniloae – with the original Greek

---

[35] *Homily* 15, quoted in Mantzaridis, *Deification of Man*, 57.

[36] Panayiotis Nellas, *Deification in Christ: The Nature of the Human Person*, trans. Norman Russell (Crestwood, NY: St Vladimir's Seminary Press, 1987). The Foreword by Metropolitan Kallistos contains a warm account of Nellas' life, on which I have drawn.

text, a modern Greek translation, and Introduction and notes. This series did not survive his death. His other venture was a journal, *Synaxi*, started in 1982, a lively theological journal, still the most worthwhile in Greece.

His book, *Deification in Christ*, is not on Palamas, but on Nicolas Cabasilas, a younger contemporary of Palamas and his supporter during the hesychast controversy. Cabasilas is mostly known for two works, his *Commentary on the Divine Liturgy*, and his *The Life in Christ*, an account of the Christian life focused on the three sacraments of baptism, chrismation and the Eucharist. The Greek title of Nellas' book, *Zōon theoumenon*, suggests a contrast with other definitions of the human as *zōon logikon*, 'rational animal', or Aristotle's *zōon politikon*, 'animal of the city': in contrast to these the nature of the human is to be found in its capacity to be deified, to share the divine life. Nellas begins his book with this observation:

> There are times when one feels oneself literally 'cast down and abandoned in a corner of the universe yet obliged to go on living'. But there are other times when a strange inspiration, which nevertheless comes from deep within oneself, seems to raise one up above necessity and grant one a taste of true freedom and joy. The Church Fathers speak at length about this inspiration.[37]

These two sides of the human condition – Pascal's *misère et grandeur de l'homme* – Nellas relates to the image of God, in which we were created, and the 'garments of skin' that God provided for the human couple after their fall and turning away from him. Nellas points out that for most of the Fathers (especially the Greek Fathers) the 'image of God' is Christ, and we are created after, or according to (Greek: *kata*), the image of God, which is Christ. It is then in Christ that we see both what it is to be God and what it is to be human; we are not dealing with abstract qualities – mortal–immortal, created–uncreated – but with the Lord of the Gospels, the Lord of the Church, the one we encounter in the sacraments. Human life is about assimilation to Christ, through the Church, through the sacraments, through our stumbling attempts to follow him. Already we are talking about the image, not abstractly, but about the presence of the image to us in our fallen condition. And it is to that fallen condition that the 'garments of skin' belong: both a sign of what we have lost – in the garden before the fall Adam and Eve were naked and not ashamed – but also a comfort to us in our fallen condition, and more than that, something to enable us to turn to God and begin the process of the restoration of the image. As Nellas puts it:

> On the one hand, then, the garments of skin are the physiological result of sin, constituting an obscuring of the image, a fall from what is according to nature, and introducing 'hubris', 'penalty' and 'trauma'; on the other they constitute a 'remedy' and blessing, introducing a new potentiality which God gives to man, enabling him, since he has forfeited life, to survive in death

---

[37] Nellas, *Deification in Christ*, 15.

and even to survive in the right way so as to reach the point of finding again the fullness of life and the beauty of form that belongs to his nature in Christ.[38]

In the rest of the book, which we can do no more than summarize very briefly, Nellas develops, drawing mostly on Nicolas Cabasilas, the spiritual life in Christ, in which he introduces notions such as 'theocentric humanism' – an affirmation of the human, through seeing it as opening up towards communion with God – and the transformation of Creation into ecclesial communion, which presages the eschatological transfiguration of the universe as the cosmic body of Christ.

* * *

In considering the legacy of Fr John Meyendorff, as we encounter it in what might be called the hesychast revival of theology among Greek theologians of the second half of the twentieth century, we find, I think, a holding together of two themes that seem to me characteristic of Orthodox theology: first, an emphasis on deification as the human destiny – the idea that the human is open to the infinite, that the human is destined to be like God in everything save identity of being, as St Maximos put it; and second, combined with this, or an aspect of this, the discovery of the true nature of personhood, as *zōon theoumenon*, an animal, a living being, in the process of being transformed into God, a person not 'cribb'd, cabin'd, confined', but open to the infinite, self-transcending.

---

[38] Nellas, *Deification in Christ*, 63.

13

Liturgical theology: Fr Alexander Schmemann and the Greeks Ioannis Foundoulis and Fr Vasileios

The notion of liturgical theology

'Liturgical theology' is a relatively new concept and it is, I think, pretty well universally agreed that the very notion of 'liturgical theology' is closely associated with the name of Fr Alexander Schmemann: liturgical theology, that is, as opposed to liturgiology – the study of liturgical rites (usually actually liturgical texts) over the ages – or the theology of liturgy, or of worship. Liturgical theology is theology that springs from the liturgy, that is implicit in the liturgical worship of the Church, above all the celebration of the Eucharist, but stretching beyond that to encompass the daily offices of the Church, the sacramental rites, and also the structure of the liturgical day, week, year. Its watchword is: *lex orandi lex credendi* (properly, in Prosper of Aquitaine: *legem credendi lex statuat supplicandi* – the law of praying supports the law of believing). It is difficult for us (especially for anyone younger than me) to grasp how new an approach this is. In the Roman Catholic Church, liturgy was not a specific area of theology until after the reforms of the Second Vatican Council; before that liturgical studies were assigned to moral theology, canon law – and for the history of the liturgical rites themselves, church history. The case was not that much different in the Orthodox Churches: here, too, liturgical study was largely a question of the study of the liturgical rubrics. As I have already argued, I think we can see the beginnings of liturgical theology in one of Fr Alexander's teachers, Fr Sergii Bulgakov, who made a habit of using liturgical texts and liturgical practice as a springboard for his theology. This was not, however, much noticed at the time (nor indeed since), as Bulgakov's theological writings mostly attracted attention for their sophiological speculation.

The turn to liturgical theology was not, however, something that Fr Alexander achieved on his own; it is part of a movement in theology in the last century, a movement associated with the return to the Fathers in Western, and especially Roman Catholic, theology, that we have already noticed in connection with the neo-patristic synthesis. Just as the theologians of the neo-patristic synthesis – Florovsky, Lossky, Lot-Borodine – were friendly with

Alexander Schmemann
With permission of St Vladimir's Orthodox Seminary

and owed much to the theologians of what Catholic theologians nowadays call the movement of *Ressourcement* – Henri de Lubac, Jean Daniélou, Hans Urs von Balthasar, Louis Bouyer, Aloys Grillmeier, and others – so Schmemann's liturgical theology owed a good deal to the liturgical movement in the Western Church, which culminated in the reforms of the Second Vatican Council. In his Introduction to the book published in the UK as *The World as Sacrament* – now known by the title of the US edition as *For the Life of the World: Sacraments and Orthodoxy* – Schmemann mentioned by name scholars associated with the liturgical movement – Odo Casel, Lambert Beauduin, J. A. Jungmann, Louis Bouyer, Romano Guardini, H. A. Reinhold (to whom one could add Anton Baumstark and the Anglican Benedictine liturgical scholar Dom Gregory Dix) – whose work

> did more than merely initiate a liturgical revival within Roman Catholicism. It helped to establish a common theological and spiritual perspective, to restore a truly catholic language without which no fruitful encounter, no ecumenical conversation is possible. Their writings were and still are as significant for us Orthodox as they are for our Western brothers. For not only did they help us better to understand the liturgical and spiritual heritage

of the West, they also helped us – paradoxically as it sounds – to understand better our own *lex orandi*.[1]

It is not surprising that some of these names are associated, too, with the ecumenical movement, and especially with deepening relations between Orthodox and Catholics. It is also significant that some of these scholars attended the Second Vatican Council as *periti*, 'experts': indeed Schmemann himself attended the council as one of the Orthodox observers. Schmemann, then, can be seen as belonging to a movement of thought and scholarship that transformed perceptions of the liturgy in the twentieth century, and bore fruit in the reforms of Vatican II. If nowadays there are many who find these fruits to have a bitter taste, it can hardly be claimed that the liturgical reforms of Vatican II were all bad, though the reforms took on a life of their own that went beyond anything the fathers of the council envisaged – something that some of the theologians we have mentioned were to come to protest against: Balthasar and Bouyer, for example.

Schmemann acknowledged, as we have seen, what he owed to the scholarship and reflection of Western scholars. It seems also to be the case that, however great his influence has been in the Orthodox world, his influence in Roman Catholicism, especially in the USA, has been nearly as significant: one not infrequently hears mention of a 'Schmemann–Kavanaugh–Fagerberg–Galadza' school of liturgical theology.

Liturgical theology in East and West

A slight digression might be useful here (you may think I am proceeding by digression!). There is, it seems to me, a very significant difference between the application of liturgical theology in East and West. In the West – notably in the Roman Catholic Church with the Vatican II reforms, but in fact generally (and synchronically) among the Western Churches – liturgical theology has been put into practice: the ideas scholars have thought up in their studies and libraries, and proclaimed in lecture halls, have had a direct influence on the worship of the Western Churches. Old liturgies have been abandoned and new 'revised' liturgies have been introduced. Rarely have scholars found themselves in possession of such power. What has happened in the East has been very different: the *way* the Divine Liturgy, for example, is celebrated has changed – the music is often simpler and less intrusive, the 'secret' prayers are often said audibly (this was Fr Alexander's practice), frequent communion is much more common than it used to be – but the prayers and the ceremonial have remained the same. Liturgy is still thought of as received from

---

[1] Alexander Schmemann, *The World as Sacrament* (London: Darton, Longman & Todd, 1966), 8. This book was originally published as *Sacraments and Orthodoxy* (Crestwood, NY: St Vladimir's Seminary Press, 1963); references henceforth are given to the second, revised and expanded edition, 1973, which is called *For the Life of the World*, with 'Sacraments and Orthodoxy' as a subtitle. The Preface of *For the Life of the World*, at least in the second edition, differs from that in the UK edition, and no longer includes the passage cited.

tradition – a good defence of this way of understanding the liturgy can be found in *The Spirit of the Liturgy* by Joseph Ratzinger, cardinal, when he wrote it, now Pope Emeritus[2] – rather than thought up by scholars in their studies and decided upon by liturgical committees. Of course, the Orthodox Liturgy has changed, and is changing, but not by a process (one might think of as brutal) of abandonment and replacement.

Schmemann needs to be understood in the context of developments in Western liturgical scholarship. He needs, too, to be understood in the wider context of the decade of the 1960s: this is something we shall come across in many of the thinkers we shall be considering in this book. The Second Vatican Council is one of the events of the sixties, and ushered in (or was the catalyst for) changes that the fathers of the council can hardly have expected. The 1960s was also the decade of the theology of the 'Death of God', a slogan to be traced back in German thought via Nietzsche to Heine and 'Jean Paul' (Richter), ultimately to Martin Luther himself (though his understanding of the death of God was perfectly orthodox); there was talk of 'religionless Christianity' and the acceptance of a post-Christian society. The 1960s was also an important decade, something of a turning point, for Greek theology, partly as the concerns of the West reached Greece, and partly for more local reasons, as Greece emerged from a long period of war, occupation and civil war.[3] There are echoes of the situation in Western theology in Schmemann's writings, especially *For the Life of the World*, which can be seen as his bid to reach beyond the liberals who proclaimed the death of religion and the conservatives who clung to religion to an encounter with God himself, the Creator who calls us to the transfiguration of his Creation. For one of the most important facts about Schmemann was that, as a theologian, he spoke not just to his fellow Orthodox, or his fellow Russians, but had a voice that was heard throughout the world, and first of all in the USA.

Alexander Schmemann

Alexander Schmemann was born in Reval, a district of Tallinn in Estonia, the son of aristocratic White Russian émigrés (his father had been an office in the Imperial Life-Guards), on 13 September 1921.[4] When he was seven, the family moved to Paris. There he attended the Russian cadet school, and later transferred to the Lycée. He attended the Russian Cathedral of

---

[2] Joseph Cardinal Ratzinger, *The Spirit of the Liturgy*, trans. John Saward (San Francisco: Ignatius Press, 2000).

[3] On this see *Anataraxeis sti Metapolemiki Theologia* [Unrest in Post-War Theology], ed. P. Kalaïtzidis et al. (Athens: Indiktos, 2009).

[4] For an account of his life, see the obituary by Peter Scorer in *Sobornost/ECR* 6:2 (1984), 64–8, and also the Afterword by John Meyendorff to *The Journals of Father Alexander Schmemann, 1973–1983* (Crestwood, NY: St Vladimir's Seminary Press, 2000), 343–51 (originally published as 'A Life Worth Living', *SVTQ* 28 (1984), 3–10). See also William C. Mills, *Church, World, Kingdom: The Eucharistic Foundations of Alexander Schmemann's Pastoral Theology* (Chicago–Mundelein, IL: Hillenbrand, 2012), 23–36.

St Alexander Nevsky in the rue Daru, where he served as an altar boy under Metropolitan Evlogy. In 1939, he enrolled in the Institut St-Serge, where he was to remain for 12 years, from 1946 teaching church history. There he was taught by Fr Sergii Bulgakov, whom he revered, unimpressed though he was by his sophiological speculations, Fr Nikolai Afanasiev, whose eucharistic ecclesiology greatly influenced him, Professor A. V. Kartashev, who inspired in him a love for church history and under whom he prepared a 'candidate's thesis' on Byzantine theocracy, and Fr Kiprian Kern, who was to have a profound influence on his future work in liturgical theology. In 1943 he married Juliana Osorguine; in 1946 he was ordained to the priesthood, and served in the church in Clamart with Fr Kiprian, who became his spiritual father.

In 1951, he followed Fr Georges Florovsky to the USA, and joined him in the newly founded St Vladimir's Orthodox Theological Seminary, where Fr Georges was dean. There he continued to teach church history. At that time the seminary was housed in cramped quarters in New York City, near Columbia University. In 1955, Florovsky retired as dean, and when the seminary moved to a new site in Crestwood, New York, in 1962, Fr Alexander became dean, a position he would hold for 21 years, until his death in 1983 (on 13 December).

Fr Alexander spent just over half his life in the USA, and had a profound influence not only over the seminarians at St Vladimir's, but also as a distinctive and audible voice of Orthodoxy in his adopted country, and beyond, as well as over the organization of the Orthodox Church in the USA. Although he did not found St Vladimir's Seminary, the institution as it now is owes much to his energy and his vision. Under him the language of teaching and worship became English, and by the time he died he had seen the building of a remarkable chapel there, built in native American wood, with fine icons in the style developed by Leonid Ouspensky in émigré Paris: it feels both Russian and American. Though Fr Alexander became immersed in his adopted country, he remained deeply Russian, steeped in Russian literature, with an especial love of Aleksandr Blok, Anna Akhmatova and Osip Mandel'shtam; each summer he read *Anna Karenina*; all his books were written in Russian, though he lectured in English.

For many years he preached a weekly Russian sermon that was broadcast in the Soviet Union by Radio Liberty, which made his name known to many oppressed Christians in Russia, and indeed others, among whom was Aleksandr Solzhenitsyn, whom he came to know after his expulsion from Russia in 1974.

At the institutional level, probably his greatest achievement was securing autocephaly for what came to be called the OCA (Orthodox Church in America), which was granted in 1970 by the Patriarch of Moscow. Also involved in the negotiations was his slightly younger colleague, Fr John Meyendorff.

His writings

At the seminary Schmemann taught church history, liturgical theology and pastoral theology. His first book to be published appeared in English translation as *The Historical Road of Eastern Orthodoxy* (1963);[5] the reviews were lukewarm, as the book was largely derivative, and his view of the Byzantine period much influenced by a hostility towards Tsar Peter the Great projected on to the Byzantine emperors.[6] Most of his books, beginning with his *Introduction to Liturgical Theology*,[7] are concerned with what he called liturgical theology: as well as the *Introduction*, there are his books, *For the Life of the World, Great Lent: The Journey to Pascha*,[8] *Of Water and the Spirit*,[9] and his last book, *The Eucharist*,[10] as well as a collection of papers, published posthumously, *Liturgy and Tradition*.[11] There is another collection of papers, *Church, World, Mission: Reflections on Orthodoxy in the West*,[12] as well as three volumes of sermons, translated into English as *Celebration of Faith*,[13] from the more than 3,000 sermons that survive in Russian. From what we have said about the links between Schmemann's liturgical theology and the Western liturgical movement, which grew out of the movement of patristic *Ressourcement* among Western theologians, one might suppose that Schmemann himself could be regarded as aligned with the neo-patristic synthesis. However, this does not look very likely. It has to be said, however, that, because of the publication of his diary covering the last decade of his life, we are perhaps too well informed about Schmemann's opinions.[14] Nevertheless, in his entry for Thursday, 2 October 1980, he remarks,

> Once, Father John [Meyendorff] told me in a moment of candour that he could not understand why people are obsessed with the Fathers. So many people propagate this fashion, which prevents them from understanding anything in the real world, and at the same time are convinced that they serve the Church and Orthodoxy. I'm afraid that people are attracted not by the thoughts of the Fathers, not by the content of their writings, but by their style. It is quite close to the Orthodox understanding of liturgical services: love them without understanding; and inasmuch as they are not understood, come to no conclusion. We sit in our shell, charmed by a melody, and do not notice that the Church is suffering, and for a long time already has left the battlefield.[15]

His attachment to the Russian religious tradition might seem to be evidenced in his book, *Ultimate Questions: An Anthology of Modern Russian Religious Thought*,[16]

---

[5] *The Historical Road of Eastern Orthodoxy* (London: Harvill Press, 1963).

[6] See the review by George Every in *Sobornost* 5:2 (1966), 144.

[7] *Introduction to Liturgical Theology* (London: Faith Press, 1966).

[8] *Great Lent: The Journey to Pascha* (Crestwood, NY: St Vladimir's Seminary Press, 1969).

[9] *Of Water and the Spirit* (Crestwood, NY: St Vladimir's Seminary Press, 1974).

[10] *The Eucharist: Sacrament of the Kingdom* (Crestwood, NY: St Vladimir's Seminary Press, 1988).

[11] *Liturgy and Tradition*, ed. Thomas Fitch (Crestwood, NY: St Vladimir's Seminary Press, 1990).

[12] *Church, World, Mission: Reflections on Orthodoxy in the West* (Crestwood, NY: St Vladimir's Seminary Press, 1979).

[13] *Celebration of Faith*, 3 vols (Crestwood, NY: St Vladimir's Seminary Press, 1990–5).

[14] Original text: Archpriest Aleksandr Schmemann, *Dnevniki 1973–1983* (Moscow: Russkii Put', 2007); abridged ET: *The Journals of Father Alexander Schmemann, 1973–1983* (Crestwood, NY: St Vladimir's Seminary Press, 2000).

[15] Schmemann, *Journals*, 269.

[16] *Ultimate Questions: An Anthology of Modern Russian Religious Thought* (Crestwood, NY: St Vladimir's Seminary Press, 1977; originally published in 1965).

an invaluable introduction to a wide range of Russian thinkers, in which Bulgakov is represented by one of his sermons. Nevertheless, in his entry for Holy Monday, 31 March 1980, he has this to say of Father Sergii Bulgakov:

> After all, his is a 'capricious' theology, very personal and, in a sense, emotional so that it probably won't 'survive'. It seems to me that it can also be said about 'the Russian religious thought' – about Berdyaev, Florensky, Rosanov.[17] Bulgakov uses a thoroughly Orthodox terminology, everything is a sort of 'brocade' – at the same time, romantic, almost subjective. 'My' theology! – 'There! I will impose on Orthodoxy my "Sophia". I will show everybody what they really believe in.'... In Bulgakov's theology, there is no humility. Whatever he touches, he must immediately change it into his own, explain it in his own way. He never blends with the Church; he always feels *himself* in the Church.[18]

Harsh words, but these two comments tell us something about what he felt were the real exigencies of theology. To discover more, we must turn to his presentation of what he called liturgical theology.

Liturgical theology

Fr Alexander's conviction of the central place of the liturgy grew out of his own experience, an experience he shared with many in the Russian émigré community in Paris, where he grew up. In one of the early entries in his diary, however, he gives another picture from his life in Paris:

> During my school years in Paris, on my way to the Lycée Carnot, I would stop by the Church of St Charles of Monceau for two or three minutes. And always, in this huge, dark church, at one of the altars, a silent Mass was being said. The Christian West: it is part of my childhood and youth, when I lived a double life. On the one hand it was a worldly and very Russian émigré life; on the other, a secret, religious life. Sometimes I think of the contrast: a noisy, proletarian rue Legendre (a small street in the 19th *arrondissement*, in Paris) and this never-changing Mass (...a spot of light on the dark wall ...) – one step, and one is in a totally different world. This contrast somehow determined in my religious experience the intuition that has never left me: the coexistence of two heterogeneous worlds, the presence in this world of something absolutely and totally 'other'. This 'other' illumines everything, in one way or another. Everything is related to it – the Church as the Kingdom of God among and inside us. For me, rue Legendre never became unnecessary, or hostile, or nonexistent – hence my aversion to pure 'spiritualism'.[19]

And Schmemann goes on to relate this experience to his vocation as a liturgical theologian:

---

[17] All included in Schmemann, *Ultimate Questions*.

[18] Schmemann, *Journals*, 261–2.

[19] Schmemann, *Journals*, 19 (10 December 1973); quoted by David Fagerberg in his article, 'The Cost of Understanding Schmemann in the West', *SVTQ* 53 (2009), 179–207, here 204.

This experience remains with me forever: a very strong sense of 'life' in its physical, bodily reality, in the uniqueness of every minute and of its correlation with life's reality. At the same time, this interest has always been rooted solely in the correlation of all of this with what the silent Mass was a witness to and reminder of, the presence and the joy. What is that correlation? It seems to me that I am quite unable to explain and determine it, although it is actually the only thing that I talk and write about ('liturgical theology'). It is not an 'idea': I feel repulsed by 'ideas'; I have an ever-growing conviction that Christianity cannot be expressed by 'ideas'…This correlation is a tie, not an idea; an experience. It is the experience of the world and life literally in the light of the Kingdom of God revealed through everything that makes up the world: colours, sounds, movements, time, space – concrete, not abstract.[20]

This experience, we may be sure, Schmemann would have had elsewhere as a Russian émigré in Paris. Although he habitually worshipped in the cathedral in rue Daru, many Orthodox places of worship were tucked away in rooms and other very unecclesiastical spaces (as today the church of Notre-Dame, Joie des Affligés et Ste Geneviève, in what looks from outside like a launderette, in rue St-Victor): in such liturgical spaces it is the liturgy that makes the church. Just as this experience was the inspiration for Fr Nikolai Afanasiev's eucharistic ecclesiology, so it was for Fr Schmemann's liturgical theology. Elsewhere in his diary, he talks about the way church services 'create a different dimension': 'to reveal this dimension the Church exists. Without this different dimension, the whole teaching, structure, and order of the Church mean nothing'.[21]

The purpose of liturgical theology is to reveal this 'different dimension': the dimension revealed by the perception of the world as belonging to the kingdom of God. In his book, *Introduction to Liturgical Theology*, Schmemann tries to draw out from the history of the liturgical experience of the Church the fundamental structure – what he calls the *ordo* – that underlies and expresses this perception of the dimension of the kingdom. He discerns four *strata* in its evolution.[22]

First, there is the pre-Constantinian *stratum*, where we find the origin of the daily cycle, the weekly cycle with the Eucharist celebrated on Sunday, and the yearly cycle, based on Easter (and Pentecost), the practice of fasting (on Wednesdays and Fridays, and in preparation for Easter), and the predominance of psalmody. Second, there is the *stratum* of the secular (or cathedral) *ordo*, with the development of liturgical practice in the post-Constantinian Church, with the growing importance of the Constantinopolitan liturgy, with the development of singing, liturgical music, dramatic elements in the ceremonial,

---

[20] Schmemann, *Journals*, 20; cf. Fagerberg, 'The Cost of Understanding Schmemann', 205.

[21] Schmemann, *Journals*, 9 (3 April 1973).

[22] See (now Archbishop) Job Getcha's article in the issue of *SVTQ* already mentioned: 'From Master to Disciple: The Notion of "Liturgical Theology" in Fr Kiprian Kern and Fr Alexander Schmemann', 53 (2009), 251–72, esp. 266; the whole article, as well as exploring Schmemann's relation to Fr Kiprian Kern, also relates him to the earlier Russian liturgiological tradition.

and the multiplication of liturgical feast days, together with the growth of the cult of saints, and the veneration of relics. Third, there is the monastic *stratum*, with the inclusion of many more prayers, the recitation of the psalter in sequence and the development of longer periods of fasting. Finally, there is the *stratum* in which the cathedral and monastic *ordines* are combined in the Byzantine *ordo*, in which there is eventually a predominance of the monastic *ordo*.

The purpose of this analysis is manifold: there is a genuinely scholarly element, concerned to clarify the development of liturgical structure in the life of the Church. Like his Western colleagues, there is a concern to show how the later *strata* overlay and obscure the earlier experience: Schmemann is concerned to recover, or rediscover, aspects of liturgical experience that have become obscured by later developments. For Schmemann this is not so much to guide liturgical reform, as happened in the West, as to inform liturgical practice by recovering important themes that have become obscured, though still present (the Orthodox Liturgy is a bit like a house where nothing is ever thrown away). This difference has something to do with the different liturgical histories of the Church in the East and the West: the reforms of Vatican II were not unprecedented; the Council of Trent had sought, too, to reform the liturgy, replacing older forms with what was then deemed to be more acceptable. There was also an authority capable of effecting such reforms, namely the papacy. (Orthodoxy's principal experience of such liturgical reforms was the reforms introduced into the Russian Church by Patriarch Nikon: a muddled and dispiriting episode.)

Many of the aims of the Western liturgical movement are shared by Schmemann: the desire for greater participation in the liturgy by the laity, for greater understanding of the liturgical texts, not least the scriptural readings, more frequent communion, and an attempt to promote a liturgical piety, rather than one that had become too individualistic. And it does mean, as liturgical reform did in the West, privileging the ancient, and regretting what came later – both the outward splendour of the Constantinian and post-Constantinian Church and the influence of monasticism.

There is sometimes an uneasy tension between the *ordo* he discerns in the past, which is where he finds his liturgical meaning, and the *ordo* that he actually follows in his own liturgical experience. To anticipate: in his account of the Eucharist in *For the Life of the World*, he says that the liturgy begins with our leaving our homes and proceeding to church: 'the liturgy of the Eucharist is best understood as a journey, a procession'.[23] In this, Schmemann is harking back to the earlier practice of the Church, where the bishop, with the people and some of the clergy, made a procession to the church, and entered at what is now called the Little Entrance. There are still elements of this in the current Byzantine Liturgy, but it has really been replaced by a different symbolism, based on a series of circuits of the church with incense

---

[23] Schmemann, *For the Life of the World* (2nd edn, 1973), 26.

(found as early as Dionysios the Areopagite, that is, early sixth century). On what ground Schmemann prefers the one symbolism to the other is not made explicit.

For the Life of the World

The underlying pastoral purpose of liturgical theology for Schmemann becomes clearer in his next work, the one already mentioned, *For the Life of the World*. Here it becomes apparent that, for Schmemann, there is a liturgical crisis in the Orthodox world, though the remedy involves less liturgical reform than attention to the deeper themes of the liturgy that have become obscured (an example of which we have given). For Schmemann, the Eucharist is about the realization of the presence of the kingdom of God, in which we are invited to participate at the heavenly banquet. This heavenly banquet reveals the purpose of creation: communion with God, sharing his life. This is the goal to which our life is to be directed. Early on in *For the Life of the World*, Schmemann affirms:

> Man is a hungry being. But he is hungry for God. Behind all the hunger of our life is God. All desire is finally a desire for him. To be sure, man is not the only hungry being. All that exists lives by 'eating'. The whole creation depends on food. But the unique position of man in the universe is that he alone is to *bless* God for the food and the life he receives from Him. He alone is to respond to God's blessing with his blessing.[24]

Schmemann goes on to talk about Adam's naming the animals, pointing out that in the Bible the name is not a label that distinguishes one thing from another: '[i]t reveals the very essence of a thing, or rather its essence as God's gift'.[25] In naming each animal, Adam was blessing God for it and in it. Furthermore, blessing God is 'not a "religious" or a "cultic" act, but the very *way of life*'.[26]

> God blessed the world, blessed the man, blessed the seventh day (that is, time), and this means that he filled all that exists with His love and goodness, made all this 'very good'. So the only *natural* (and not 'supernatural') reaction of man, to whom God gave this blessed and sanctified world, is to bless God in return, to thank him, to *see* the world as God sees it – and in that act of gratitude and adoration – to know, name, and possess the world.[27]

So the human being is to be seen as standing at the centre of this world, receiving it from God and offering it back to him in thanksgiving, *eucharistia*. 'The world was created as the "matter", the material of one all-embracing eucharist, and man was created as the priest of his cosmic sacrament.'[28]

---

[24] Schmemann, *For the Life of the World*, 14–15.
[25] Schmemann, *For the Life of the World*, 15.
[26] Schmemann, *For the Life of the World*, 15.
[27] Schmemann, *For the Life of the World*, 15.
[28] Schmemann, *For the Life of the World*, 15.

All this was spoilt by the fall – symbolized in the eating of a fruit that had *not* been given humans to eat, a fruit consumed in secret, not received with thanksgiving. In doing so, men and women have failed to return God's love, and come to regard the world as apart from God, not as what God created as 'very good'. Human beings have lost the power to bless the world, to accept it as God's gift. For them, the world has become opaque, no longer transparent to God's love: it has become worldly, 'secular', separate from God. Fallen man's attempt to make contact with God becomes 'religion', which accepts a division between the sacred (= God) and the profane (= the world) and tries to bring them into harmony – without success, as it is beyond human power. Religion and secularism alike accept the fallenness of the world. The only solution to the human plight is not religion, but God: accepting that God has not abandoned fallen human beings, but entered their darkness and brought light. Moreover, this is on God's part no

> rescue operation, to recover lost man: it was rather for the completing of what he had undertaken from the beginning. God acted so that man might understand who he really was and where his hunger had been driving him.[29]

> The light God sent was his Son: the same light that had been shining unextinguished in the world's darkness all along, seen now in full brightness.[30]

There are a number of themes here that run through the book: the rejection of the opposition of natural and supernatural (very much on the lines of his misunderstood teacher, Bulgakov), or sacred and profane, and the rejection of both 'religion' and 'secularism'. This latter point echoes some of the discussion of the 1960s in the West. Karl Barth had long before rejected religion, and the notion of 'religionless Christianity' had become popular with the publication in English of Dietrich Bonhoeffer's *Letters and Papers from Prison*. Moreover, it was popular among the theologians of the 1960s to embrace secularism, to speak of 'Christianity come of age'.

Schmemann's rejection of religion meant something rather different from what either Barth or Bonhoeffer had envisaged: the idea of man, 'hungry for God', would have seemed to Barth precisely to open the door to religion. Nor was Schmemann's 'religionless Christianity' Christianity without liturgy (neither indeed was Bonhoeffer's, unless he is held to have changed his ideas dramatically once in prison): as we have noticed, Schmemann's liturgical theology did not lead in the direction of liturgical reform of the kind beginning in the 1960s to be practised in the West. Liturgy, one could say, was not for Schmemann 'religious', an attempt to make contact with a remote God; rather liturgy was the celebration of the kingdom present in Christ. For Schmemann, 'sacramental theology' is not primarily about the details and rubrics of sacramental rites; rather sacramental theology re-establishes the conviction of the world as sacrament, that is, as revealing God's presence, and

---

[29] Schmemann, *For the Life of the World*, 19.
[30] Schmemann, *For the Life of the World*, 19.

the conviction of Christ as the primordial sacrament, of which the Church's seven sacraments are different aspects, revealing different dimensions of the life in Christ, the life of the kingdom, proclaimed in the opening exclamation of the Divine Liturgy: 'Blessed is the Kingdom of the Father, and the Son, and the Holy Spirit, now and for ever and to the ages of ages. Amen'.

Such an approach to the sacraments was not peculiar to Schmemann: very similar ideas are to be found in work of the Dominican theologian Edward Schillebeeckx, published in English as *Christ the Sacrament of the Encounter with God*.[31] Religion, for Schmemann, manifests itself as an attempt to withdraw from the world into some sacred preserve. Secularism, based on the same premises, seeks to improve man's lot in this world, and may indeed be very successful, save that we live in a fallen world, bounded by death.

Eschatology and the liturgy

The heart of what Schmemann thought liturgical theology to be can be put in another way: in terms of *eschatology* – eschatology, not as concerned with what lies beyond death, but rather with the presence of the ultimate, the end, communion with God, in this life: what is sometimes called 'realized eschatology', again very much one of the themes of Western theology from the interwar period onwards (beginning with C. H. Dodd and Joachim Jeremias on the parables and reaching beyond that into most post-war systematic theology). There is an interesting passage on eschatology in his *Journals*:

> *This* is the essence of Christianity as Eschatology. The Kingdom of God is the goal of history, and the Kingdom of God is already now *among us, within us*. Christianity is a unique historical event, and Christianity is the presence of that event as the completion of all events and of history itself. And only in order that it be so, only for that, only in that, is the Church, its essence, its meaning.
>
> This all seems like elementary truths. But then why are they not effective? Is it not because Christianity started being, on the one hand, 'perceived' (piety), and on the other hand, 'interpreted', 'explained' (theology) – according to the views of this world and not *in Christ*.
>
> Here is, for me, *the whole meaning of liturgical theology*. The Liturgy: the joining, revelation, actualization of the historicity of Christianity (remembrance) and of its transcendence over that historicity ('*Today*, the Son of God . . .'). The joining of the end with the beginning, but the joining today, here . . .
>
> Hence, the link of the Church and the world, the Church *for the world*, but as its beginning and its end, as the affirmation that the world is *for the Church*, since the Church is the presence of the Kingdom of God.
>
> Here is the eternal antinomy of Christianity and the essence of all contemporary discussion about Christianity. The task of theology is to be faithful to the antinomy, which disappears in the experience of the Church as *Pascha*:

---

[31] Edward Schillebeeckx, *Christ the Sacrament of the Encounter with God* (London: Sheed & Ward, 1963; original Dutch, 1959).

a *continuous* (not only historical) passage of the world to the Kingdom. All the time one must leave the world and all the time one must remain in it.

The temptation of piety is to reduce Christianity to piety; the temptation of theology – to reduce it totally to history.[32]

Reflections and influence

There is much that is attractive and powerful about Schmemann's vision (his own word, one he repeated) of the liturgy: the dangers of pietism and secularism are evident, and what Schmemann has to say about the dangers of the Church giving in to secularism by presenting itself as a kind of spiritual psychotherapy that will make humans happier and more contented is compelling, as true now as when he uttered it in the 1960s.[33] It is, in many respects, Schmemann's vision that has guided the changes in the way the Divine Liturgy has been celebrated over the last half-century or so: introduction of the vernacular, greater simplicity in ceremonial and music, a way of celebrating that follows the structure of the liturgical action, greater participation by the laity, not least in terms of frequency of communion, and so on, though these are all a matter of degree, not fundamental changes of the kind the West has seen over the same period, at least in the Catholic and Anglican Churches (the only ones I have much knowledge of).

There are, however, criticisms that must be mentioned. It is evident from the papers given at symposia at St Vladimir's and St-Serge honouring the twenty-fifth anniversary of Fr Alexander Schmemann's death, and published in *St Vladimir's Theological Quarterly*, that his influence among Western liturgical scholars has been great, though at the same time, it is felt that concentration on the Byzantine Rite is constricting in a way that is unnecessary and unhelpful. It is not just that Schmemann spoke of what he knew – the Byzantine Rite of the Orthodox Church – but that, looking from this perspective, he ignored elements of liturgical history that are not irrelevant, but not obvious: an example would be the stational liturgies, which get no consideration. Another way of putting this would be to say that Schmemann makes little of the *variety* of liturgical traditions that seems to have characterized Christian liturgical practice from the beginning. This is not something I want to pursue here, for there are other criticisms more relevant to the reception of Schmemann among the Orthodox. The criticisms that strike me as most important are related: his rejection of what he calls mysteriological piety, which, on investigation, disposes of a good deal of Orthodox liturgical reflection over the centuries, and what I think we could call his distaste for monasticism. These are bound up with each other, as it is in monastic circles that what Schmemann called mysteriological piety flourished. They are also fundamental, for, as I shall argue, they are closely related to Schmemann's central vision of the liturgy.

---

[32] Schmemann, *Journals*, 234 (14 October 1979).
[33] See Schmemann, *For the Life of the World*, 98–100, indeed the whole chapter (on the sacrament of healing) called 'Trampling Down Death by Death' (95–106).

Mysteriological piety?

Both these issues are raised in the third chapter of *Introduction to Liturgical Theology*, entitled 'The Problem of the Development of the *Ordo*' (the fact that Schmemann speaks of *ordo*, rather than *typikon*, suggests that, in this book, at least, he has in mind a Western audience). There are a couple of ways of looking at what Schmemann is talking about. Like most Western liturgical scholars, he tends to see the history of liturgy on the lines of decline and fall: all the developments since the time of Constantine are regretted, and in particular the influence on Christian worship of the imperial liturgy, which brought in pagan ideas by the back door, as it were. The chapter is difficult to read (or, at any rate, I find it so), for it lurches between an attempt to survey the evidence and expression of fairly sharply defined values – prejudices, one might call them. His use of evidence is sometimes disingenuous: for example, a wonderful quotation from St John Chrysostom about how 'when Christ came ... He purified the whole earth, and made every place suitable for prayer' is used as evidence against the growing sense of the sacred, manifest in consecrated buildings and the cult of saints, which was in its beginnings very localized in sacred places, regardless of the fact that Chrysostom himself is one of the most eloquent witnesses to the growing cult of the saints.[34] Chrysostom presumably found no contradiction in the notion that God can be prayed to everywhere, and yet there are sacred places.

The real villain, however, is the thinker who wrote under the name of Dionysios the Areopagite: 'We find the first pure expression of this theory of the cult and initiation in the writings of Dionysius the Areopagite'.[35] 'Mysteriological piety' arises from this, and amounts to reducing the liturgy to a drama which is to be interpreted by the individual: instead of liturgical participation, we have sacred actions to be observed and interpreted.

There is some truth in what Schmemann says, but he takes it to extremes, as when he discounts any kind of mysteriological piety, and dismisses altogether the work of Dom Odo Casel, who saw the notion of mystery as central to liturgical worship; indeed, his treatment of mystery, *mysterion*, is very one-sided and makes no mention of the important work by Louis Bouyer, published more than a decade before Schmemann's book.[36] In dismissing 'mysteriological piety', Schmemann dismisses not just the Dionysian *corpus*, but the writings on the liturgy by St Maximos the Confessor, St Germanos of Constantinople, and others, right up to Nicolas Cabasilas' works, his *Commentary on the Divine Liturgy* and his *Life in Christ*, and indeed beyond – St Symeon of Thessaloniki, and indeed Gogol. Schmemann's attitude to the

---

[34] See Schmemann, *Introduction*, 90.
[35] Schmemann, *Introduction*, 101.
[36] I have in mind two of Bouyer's articles – ' "Mystique": Essai sur l'histoire d'un mot', and 'Mysterion' – published in *Supplément de la Vie spirituelle* 9 (1949), 3–23; 23 (1952), 397–412 (ET in *Mystery and Mysticism: A Symposium* (London: Blackfriars, 1956), 119–37, 18–32); later worked up into a book: *Mysterion: Du mystère à la mystique* (Paris: OEIL, 1986).

Areopagite, never argued, just expressed as a distaste, is curious; it is something he shared with his younger colleague, John Meyendorff, and something that separates these two from other theologians of the Russian emigration, Vladimir Lossky, Myrrha Lot-Borodine, and even Fr Georges Florovsky. It seems to me almost a kind of blind spot, which shuts him off from a whole dimension of the Byzantine liturgical tradition. It is also something that echoes a very common attitude in Western scholarship on Dionysios, an attitude that was beginning to be challenged during Schmemann's lifetime.[37]

Schmemann's distaste for monasticism also echoes scholarly prejudices in the West, at least among Protestants, and is bound up closely with his rejection of mysteriological piety: Chapter 3 of his *Introduction to Liturgical Theology* discusses both of them, and sometimes runs them together, as when he says, 'The "mysteriological" terminology became a kind of common language for describing the rise of monasticism and for speaking of the sanctifying quality of worship'.[38] Sister Vassa Larin has a good discussion of this aspect of Schmemann in the issue of *St Vladimir's Theological Quarterly* already referred to.[39] Sister Vassa draws together material from different parts of Schmemann's *œuvre* and presents a full picture of the different ways in which he expressed his distaste for monasticism. It was, for instance, very much bound up with his distaste for 'spirituality', which he interpreted as withdrawal from the real world into one's own world. As Sister Vassa asserts, Schmemann had little place for what she called *repentance* and the *inner mission*, and she suggests that this might be because he was '*simply not the monastic type*'.[40] She is doubtless right. There are, however, a number of ways in which this distaste for monasticism might be put. First of all, more generally, as we have had occasion to notice already, the Russian emigration, at least those belonging to the exarchate under Metropolitan Evlogy, seems to have had problems about monasticism, problems it seems to have bequeathed to the Orthodox Church in America. We noted earlier Metropolitan Evlogy's lament that,

> Ascetic, contemplative ... monasticism, that is to say, monasticism in its pure state, did not succeed in the Emigration. I say this with great sorrow, for ascetic monasticism is the flower and decoration of the Church, a sign of her vitality.[41]

Schmemann's attitude to, his distaste for, monasticism was something that seems to have characterized at least part of the Russian diaspora. But there is something more. Schmemann is important for the way in which liturgical

---

[37] See, for example, the discussion of more recent scholarship on Dionysios by Adolf Martin Ritter ('Das Werk und seine Deutung: Neuere Forschungsansätze (von Roques zu Louth)') in his Introduction to his German translation of *Mystical Theology* and *Letters*: Pseudo-Areopagita, *Über die Mystische Theologie und Briefe*, Bibliothek der Griechischen Literatur 40 (Stuttgart: Anton Hiersemann, 1994), 19–31.

[38] Schmemann, *Introduction*, 113.

[39] Vassa Larin, 'Fr Alexander Schmemann and Monasticism', *SVTQ* 53 (2009), 301–18.

[40] Larin, 'Fr Alexander Schmemann', 311 (and elsewhere), 310.

[41] Sergei Hackel, *One, of Great Price* (London: Darton, Longman & Todd, 1965), 22.

piety came to be understood in the Orthodox world in the twentieth century (I have put that carefully; I am not convinced that liturgical piety was something discovered, or even invented, by the Russian émigrés; it was, however, something they emphasized). And this manifestation of liturgical piety saw the encounter between God and man in Christ as taking place *par excellence* in the Eucharist, the Divine Liturgy. Such an emphasis almost inevitably carries with it a mistrust of individual piety, understood as *individualistic* piety. This seems to me a great mistake, but there is plenty of evidence that it has become widespread among Orthodox Christians who see eucharistic participation as the pre-eminent way in which we engage with the truth: other examples we shall encounter include Metropolitan John of Pergamon (John Zizioulas) and Christos Yannaras. It seems to me important to hold together the ascetic piety of the *Philokalia* and the liturgical piety focused on eucharistic participation.[42] There is no necessary opposition, though sometimes we speak as if there were (for example, Jean-Claude Larchet cites a bishop who is said to have told a group of nuns: 'The prayer that you make with your *komvoskini* when you are alone in your cells has no value; what has value is your being together in the church'[43]).

Finally, there is some kind of conflict between Schmemann's emphasis on eschatology and the way in which monasticism, at its best, sees itself as preserving an eschatological dimension in relation to a Church that has reached some sort of compromise with the world; it is almost as if Schmemann feared that the very existence of monasticism might let the Church in the world off the hook, rather than being a constant, and often awkward, reminder of the Church's true vocation.

Schmemann's influence . . . in Greece

Schmemann's influence has been profound, though uneven. Clearly he had an enormous influence on the seminarians at St Vladimir's during his time there, and more generally, as an Orthodox voice along with those of Florovsky and Meyendorff on the US scene. The influence of his liturgical theology in the USA has been mostly among younger Catholic scholars, as we have seen, rather than with the (in comparison fewer) Orthodox scholars.

In Greece, however, his influence has been widespread. He first appeared in Greek translation in 1959 with an article in a diocesan periodical of the Metropolis of Mytilene, translated by the young Ioannis Foundoulis (1927–2007), later for many years Professor of Liturgy at the University of Thessaloniki, well known for his liturgical scholarship, notably his five-volume collection, *Answers to Liturgical Problems*.[44] A few years later two other articles were

---

[42] See David W. Fagerberg, *On Liturgical Asceticism* (Washington, DC: CUA Press, 2013).

[43] Jean-Claude Larchet, *Personne et nature: La Trinité – Le Christ – L'homme* (Paris: Cerf, 2011), 387–8, n. 710.

[44] Ioannou M. Foundouli, *Apantiseis eis Leitourgikas Aporias*, 5 vols (Athens: Apostoliki Diakonia, 1967–2003).

published under the aegis of the Zoë Brotherhood, in one case, at least, translated by the remarkable Greek theologian Dimitris Koutroubis, who was a profound influence in the awakening of theology in Greece in the 1960s. So we find Schmemann brought to the attention of the Greeks by precisely those who were leading the renaissance of theology among the Greeks. Other theologians of the Russian emigration in Paris, such as Florovsky, Lossky and Meyendorff, had a role in this renewal (we have already seen something of Meyendorff's influence). In 1970, Schmemann's book, *For the Life of the World*, was translated by the great Greek man of letters, Zissimos Lorenzatos. All his works are now available in Greek translation.[45]

One element of Schmemann's approach to liturgy that has not found much of an echo in Greece is his wholesale rejection of the Byzantine liturgical commentaries, a tradition inaugurated by Schmemann's *bête-noire*, Dionysios the Areopagite.[46] The first major work on Schmemann, appreciative, though critical, has also appeared in Greece.[47]

Let us turn to two exponents of liturgical theology in Greece: Ioannis Foundoulis and Fr Vasileios (Gondidakis).

Ioannis Foundoulis

As already mentioned, Foundoulis is most famous for his five-volume collection called *Answers to Liturgical Problems*, which consists of relatively short answers to a host of liturgical problems, all of which originally appeared in a periodical called *O Efimerios* ('The Parish Priest'), an official publication of the Church of Greece, sent to all the clergy. The focus is very much practical, dealing with a host of specific problems; the answers deal with the sacraments (the largest group of questions in each volume deals with 'the Divine Liturgy, in general'), other services, the liturgical year, and 'various'; in all there are 600 questions gathered together in five volumes. As one can imagine, the liturgical problems vary enormously, from the colour of vestments, their form and when they are worn, through details of particular prayers, whether white wine can be used in the liturgy, whether the homily should come after the Gospel or at the time of the priests' communion (the former, very firmly), and so on. All this detail might seem to run the risk of losing the meaning of the liturgy in a host of details of ceremonial. Foundoulis' genius lies in never letting this happen; he always points beyond the detail to the theological meaning of the elaborate ceremonial of the Byzantine Liturgy.[48]

---

[45] For details, see Stefanos Alexopoulos, 'Did the Work of Fr Alexander Schmemann Influence Modern Greek Theological Thought? A Preliminary Assessment', *SVTQ* 53 (2009), 273–99.

[46] Alexopoulos, 'Work of Fr Alexander', 281.

[47] George Basioudis, *I dynami tis latreias: I symboli tou p. Alexandrou Schmemann sti Leitourgiki Theologia* [The power of worship: The contribution of Fr Alexander Schmemann to liturgical theology] (Athens: En Plo, 2008), discussed by Alexopoulos, 'Work of Fr Alexander', 283–4.

[48] For another example of theology drawn, in this case, from a liturgical gesture, by a young Greek theologian, see Andreas Andreopoulos, *The Sign of the Cross: The Gesture, the Mystery, the History* (Brewster, MA: Paraclete Press, 2006).

Let us take as an example what might seem a minor detail of ceremonial, dealt with (together) as questions' 51 and 52: when and why the veil of the Holy Doors is drawn across, and whether the priest should receive the Holy Gifts with the veil drawn or open.[49] Foundoulis' first point is that it is quite wrong to associate the question of the opening or closing of the veil with the communion of the priest, as if its closing was to do with hiding the priest when performing a sacred, or intimate, action. The reasons behind the opening and closing of the veil are symbolic: the drawn veil recalls the veil of the Hebrew Temple, which separated the Holy of Holies, entered only once a year by the high priest, from the sanctuary; it also symbolizes the distinction between heaven and earth. The drawn veil speaks of the holiness of God, and reminds us of both our unworthiness and the privilege of entering into the presence of God. Foundoulis quotes from the Prayer of the Veil in the Liturgy of St James, which asks that we may be counted worthy 'to enter into the place of God's Tabernacle of Glory, to be within the Veil and behold the Holy of Holies'.[50] The drawing aside of the veil when the priest (or deacon) brings the Holy Gifts to the people for communion with the cry, 'With fear of God, in faith and love draw near', declares the breaking down of any barrier between God and his people at the Holy Communion.

> The closing of the veil emphasizes more the mysterious character of the Divine Liturgy; the performing of the rite with the veil drawn open makes much easier the participation of the people and emphasizes more the communal character of the Divine Liturgy ... So there can be joined together two related traditions, that, as we have seen, are equally ancient and equally reverent.[51]

Many other answers illustrate in the same way Foundoulis' ability to look beyond the detail and discern the theological meaning of the liturgy.

Fr Vasileios (Gondidakis)

My other example of liturgical theology in Greece is to be found in the short work, known in English as *Hymn of Entry*,[52] by Fr Vasileios, then (1974) igumen of the Stavronikita monastery on the Holy Mountain (now at Iveron). Fr Vasileios was linked by bonds of friendship with Panayiotis Nellas and others of that group of Greek theologians, influenced by Dimitris Koutroubis, who brought about a renewal of Greek theology in the 1960s and 1970s. *Hymn of Entry* was originally written, as Metropolitan Kallistos makes clear in his Foreword (and indeed as is clearer from the subtitle in Greek: 'Elements of liturgical life of the mystery of unity in the Orthodox Church'),[53] to

---

[49] Foundouli, *Apantiseis* I, 103–7.
[50] Foundouli, *Apantiseis* I, 104.
[51] Foundouli, *Apantiseis* I, 107.
[52] Archimandrite Vasileios, *Hymn of Entry* (Crestwood, NY: St Vladimir's Seminary Press, 1997).
[53] Vasileios, *Hymn of Entry*, 8 (the original Greek edition was called *Eisodikon*, Holy Mountain: Iera Moni Stavronikita, 1974; reprinted several times).

explain the deep reserve of the monks of the Holy Mountain to ecumenism, and especially to dialogue between Orthodox and Roman Catholics. Fr Vasileios wrote something of much wider significance: an introduction of theology as rooted in the Christian experience of prayer, both personal and liturgical, and specifically rooted in the witness of the Fathers. Rooted in prayer, theology is also rooted in silence: 'Patristic theology is an area of silence ... The Fathers are liturgical persons who gather round the altar with the blessed spirits'.[54] It follows from this that '[o]utside the framework of the Divine Liturgy, where God manifests his glory ... it is impossible to understand Orthodox faith and theology, "for faith and love are everything, and there is nothing higher than them"'.[55] For Fr Vasileios, there is no separation between the prayer of the Divine Liturgy and personal prayer: 'The material offered to each person to struggle with, to write theology with, and to speak about to the Church, is none other than his own self, his very being, hidden and unknown'.[56] This statement reminds one that the root meaning of the verb *askein*, from which the word 'asceticism' is derived, is 'to work with raw materials' – in ascetic struggle, the raw materials of one's own being. Our approach to the Fathers is not as to dead figures of the past, but living voices that speak to us now:

> living patristic word is not conveyed mechanically, nor preserved archaeologically, nor approached through excursions into history. It is conveyed whole as it passes from generation to generation through living organisms, altering them, creating 'fathers' who make it their personal word, a new possession, a miracle, a wealth which increases as it is given away.[57]

The Church is then revealed as more than a human institution, but created by the Lord himself, an image of the Holy Trinity, in which the cosmos itself finds its fulfilment:

> The Church is the kosmos, the order and beauty of the world. In it the whole world finds meaning and harmony. Outside it, it falls into chaos and ruin ... The unity of the Church is not an administrative system ... It is a theanthropic mystery made known in the Spirit who 'unites the whole institution of the Church'.[58]

Fr Vasileios continues:

> Every believer is called to live theologically, and the whole body of the Church is creating theology in its life and its struggle. Thus the *ex cathedra* of Orthodoxy, the way in which it experiences itself infallibly, is from the Cross. The responsibility that is spread over the whole body of the people is a cross. Apophatic theology is an ascent to Golgotha.[59]

---

54 Vasileios, *Hymn of Entry*, 22.
55 Vasileios, *Hymn of Entry*, 30; quoting Ignatios of Antioch, *To the Smyrnaeans* 6.1 (not *To the Ephesians* 20.2, as the footnote gives it).
56 Vasileios, *Hymn of Entry*, 33.
57 Vasileios, *Hymn of Entry*, 35.
58 Vasileios, *Hymn of Entry*, 46.
59 Vasileios, *Hymn of Entry*, 51.

Fr Vasileios develops his theme by what often amounts to a commentary on the Divine Liturgy itself, understood, however, as consisting 'not of sacred words, but of sacred actions'.[60] Apophatic theology, the theology of the denial of concepts, is found asserted early on in the anaphora of St John Chrysostom:

> The statement 'for you are God, ineffable, incomprehensible, invisible, inconceivable ...' rises before us 'truly like a mountain, steep and hard to approach', from which the uncreated breeze descends and swells the lungs of man, bringing life to his innermost parts with the joy of freedom, of something unqualified, dangerous and wholly alive.[61]

Fr Vasileios' words are lyrical, full of allusions to the Fathers and quotations from the liturgical texts, presenting a theology that inspires rather than instructs. He sums up his meaning in these words:

> All things liturgically transfigured in Orthodoxy show the same apophatic character of freedom:
>
> > The *inexpressible* is manifested in its *theology*,
> > the *invisible* in the *icon*,
> > and the *incomprehensible* in *holiness*.[62]

Fr Vasileios' theology is a liturgical theology, rooted in the Divine Liturgy, finding there its touchstone. Unlike some other liturgical theologies, it does not pass over, or ignore, the personal prayer of the believer, but demands it, requires such prayer, and the struggle to pray, to enable the life of the believer to be taken up in the incarnate life and love of God manifest, made present, in the Divine Liturgy. For 'man's vocation in love is one. It is love: an exodus, a departure from the narrow prison of self-love for the promised land, the land of the Other, of "my brother, my God"'.[63]

---

[60] Vasileios, *Hymn of Entry*, 61–2.
[61] Vasileios, *Hymn of Entry*, 64.
[62] Vasileios, *Hymn of Entry*, 64.
[63] Vasileios, *Hymn of Entry*, 109.

14

Theology of patristic renewal: Metropolitan John of Pergamon (Zizioulas) and Fr John Romanides

So far we have focused for the most part on the Russians who settled in Paris, their immediate predecessors and their successors; hitherto, only St Justin Popović represents a distinctly different tradition. Though we are by no means saying goodbye to the so-called 'Paris School', the focus of our attention will now turn to the revival of Greek theology in the twentieth century, though, as we shall see (and indeed have seen), the influence of the Paris School will still be felt, transferred, however, to the different soil and concerns of Greece.

This chapter is devoted to two theologians considered under the umbrella term 'Theology of patristic renewal', though some might be surprised to find them classified together, and indeed reach for other terminology. Yannis Spiteris, the Italian Roman Catholic writer on modern Greek theology, in his book that then marked out new territory, *La teologia ortodossa neo-greca*, placed together Romanides and Yannaras under the title 'The currents of the "neo-Orthodox"' and devoted a separate chapter to Zizioulas called 'The theologian of Christian personalism'.[1] As we shall see, Yannaras himself might well have been included under the title of 'Christian personalism', but there are good reasons for putting Romanides and Zizioulas together under the title 'Theology of patristic renewal', for both of them sought to renew theology by recourse to the Fathers, though in somewhat different ways. It is, perhaps, useful to have umbrella terms that shelter rather different theologians, for it reminds us that thinkers often pursue what could be called the same course in very different ways.

In several other ways, Romanides and Zizioulas can be linked together. They were both born in Greece; both studied in the USA and came under the influence of Fr Georges Florovsky. Both can be seen as inheriting from Fr Georges the pursuit of some kind of 'neo-patristic synthesis', though in rather different ways. Each of them has taught both in the West and in Greece; both published much of their significant work in Greek, and have had a major influence on modern Greek theology, in both cases, too, breaking the mould

---

[1] Yannis Spiteris, *La teologia ortodossa neo-greca* (Bologna: Edizioni Dehoniane, 1992), 281–95 (Romanides), 363–416 (Zizioulas).

John Romanides

With permission of Fr Adrian Agachi

John Zizioulas

215

of traditional Greek Orthodox theology in a controversial way. Both have been engaged in the ecumenical movement in ways that overlap, even though one would probably characterize their contribution to ecumenism in rather different terms. Both have a sense of Orthodox theology as being in some fundamental ways opposed to the West – a theme that, it has to be said, is hardly absent anywhere in twentieth-century Orthodox theology – though in markedly different ways. It follows that, considering them together, we shall form some sense of the different ways in which common traits in Orthodox theology express themselves. Again, I am tempted to discuss them in what might seem a back-to-front way, taking Metropolitan John first, though he was born four years after Romanides and is still alive, whereas Romanides died in 2001. That has something to do with the way in which they came to my theological consciousness, though in this case I can see that it is very subjective.

Metropolitan John Zizioulas

Let us start then with John Zizioulas. He was born in 1931 in Greece, and studied at the universities of Thessaloniki and Athens.[2] His first encounter with the West came through a semester spent at the Ecumenical Institute at Bossey, near Geneva, in 1954–5, and it is from this time that his engagement with ecumenism dates. He then went to the USA, where he studied for a master's degree at Harvard with Fr Georges Florovsky as his professor in theology and Paul Tillich in philosophy. Florovsky's influence on him was profound, and like him he sees the task of modern Orthodox theology in terms of the 'neo-patristic synthesis'. A little later he returned to Harvard for three years and prepared two doctoral theses, one on the Christology of St Maximos the Confessor with Florovsky, which was submitted to Harvard, but never published (and is now, apparently, lost), and the other on patristic ecclesiology under Professor A. G. Williams, which was submitted at the University of Athens, and published in Greek in 1965 (English translation: *Eucharist, Bishop, Church: The Unity of the Church in the Divine Eucharist and the Bishop during the First Three Centuries*).[3] While in the USA, he taught at St Vladimir's Orthodox Seminary, where he came to know John Meyendorff and Alexander Schmemann.

In 1964 Zizioulas returned to Athens, where in 1965 he was appointed Professor of Church History. In the late sixties, he was involved in various ways with the Faith and Order commission of the World Council of Churches, and spent two and a half years in Geneva as a permanent member. In 1970, he left Geneva to teach patristics at the University of Edinburgh, where

---

[2] Biographical information is not easy to find; I have followed that given in Lars Erik Rikheim's chapter on Johannes Zizioulas in *Key Theological Thinkers: From Modern to Postmodern*, ed. Staale Johannes Kristiansen and Svein Rise (Farnham: Ashgate, 2013), 435–47.

[3] *Eucharist, Bishop, Church: The Unity of the Church in the Divine Eucharist and the Bishop during the First Three Centuries*, trans. Elizabeth Theokritoff (Brookline, MA: Holy Cross Orthodox Press, 2001).

he came to know T. F. Torrance. Three years later, he became Professor of Systematic Theology at Glasgow, where he remained until 1986, when he was ordained bishop and appointed Metropolitan of Pergamon, a titular see belonging to the Œcumenical Patriarchate; as a result he became a member of the Holy Synod in Constantinople. He has held chairs (or visiting chairs) at the universities of Thessaloniki, Geneva, King's College London and the Gregorian University in Rome. He was a founding member of the International Commission for Theological Dialogue between the Orthodox and Roman Catholic Churches in 1979, and is presently the Orthodox chairman; he has also been a member of the International Anglican–Orthodox Dialogue.

Zizioulas has written only one monograph, his thesis *Eucharist, Bishop, Church*, and much of his work has appeared in the form of articles, often in ecumenical journals. There are, however, several volumes of collected articles, the most important being *Being as Communion: Studies in Personhood and the Church*,[4] *Communion and Otherness: Further Studies in Personhood and the Church*,[5] and most recently *The One and the Many: Studies on God, Man, the Church, and the World Today*.[6] Many articles, however, remain scattered throughout journals, which, as one scholar has complained, 'makes them extremely difficult to access, with the result that most of us have only a partial knowledge of the corpus of his work'.[7]

There are, it seems to me, a couple of other problems with Metropolitan John's *œuvre*, owing to its existing in the form of articles. First of all, many of these articles had their origin in the Metropolitan's ecumenical work, both formal (in connection with the WCC) and informal (participation as an Orthodox theologian in Western theological *fora*): that is, in talks and lectures. This means that in many of his articles Metropolitan John is seeking to explain Orthodox ideas to an interested audience, though not one necessarily very familiar with Orthodox approaches. This makes for a certain clarity, but also a certain repetitiveness, which leads on to the other problem. The form of the article does not make it very easy to develop and explore ideas. As with his mentor, Fr Georges Florovsky, it is often clear enough what the agenda is, but detailed exploration of the items on the agenda has not always been possible.

Koinonia

In the last few decades of the ecumenical movement, especially as it manifests itself officially through the World Council of Churches, a central theme has

---

[4] *Being as Communion: Studies in Personhood and the Church* (London: Darton, Longman & Todd, 1985; 2nd edn, 2004; Crestwood, NY: St Vladimir's Seminary Press).

[5] *Communion and Otherness: Further Studies in Personhood and the Church* (London: T&T Clark, 2006; Crestwood, NY: St Vladimir's Seminary Press).

[6] *The One and the Many: Studies on God, Man, the Church, and the World Today* (Alhambra, CA: Sebastian Press, 2010).

[7] Dimitrios Bathrellos in his contribution to the Festschrift for Zizioulas, *The Theology of John Zizioulas: Personhood and the Church*, ed. Douglas H. Knight (Farnham: Ashgate, 2007), 138, n. 8.

been that of *koinonia*, meaning communion (the Greek word literally means 'holding in common', and has a wide variety of meanings, including 'participation'). I think it cannot be a matter of chance that this notion is central to Zizioulas' thought in all its dimensions. The word 'communion' occurs in the titles of the first two volumes of collected articles – *Being and Communion* and *Communion and Otherness*. It is a central term in his understanding of what is meant by being truly human, something that he sums up in the notion of personhood. Zizoulas' fundamental contention – one that we have encountered frequently already – is that the West has lost any sense of what it means to be a person, and instead conceives human beings as essentially individuals. An individual is simply an instance of what it is to be human, distinct from other individuals. It is in contrast with this that Zizioulas thinks in terms of personhood. The notion of the person, he maintains, is essentially relational; it is out of relationships that persons emerge, in which persons are formed. I am not, as a person, separated from others, as I am if I think of myself as an individual; rather as a person I am united to others in communion: it is through relationships with others that I discover who I really am; it is through relationships with others, through communion, that I become who I really am.

Zizioulas develops this notion in two directions, which are in fact closely related: on the one hand, it is related to the Christian notion of God as a Trinity of Persons; on the other hand, it is related to the Eucharist, in which communion, *koinonia*, is manifested and created. In relation to the Trinity, Zizioulas maintains that the notion of personhood is something unknown outside the Christian revelation of the Trinity, for it is through reflection on the Trinity that the notion of personhood has been discovered. In particular, Zizioulas sees in the term *hypostasis*, used by the Cappadocian Fathers to refer to Father, Son and Holy Spirit, in contrast to *ousia*, used to refer to the one Godhead, the crystallization of the notion of personhood. Indeed, Zizioulas sees the term *hypostasis* as much the best term to use for what, for lack of a better word, we call person, though he does use the term *prosopon* as an equivalent of *hypostasis*, following the example of the Cappadocian Fathers. What was discovered was not just a term for person, but the perception that personhood is prior to essence; persons are not instances of an essence. Persons find union or unity, not in possession of a common essence, but through *koinonia*, communion. This applies to the Trinity, too: the Persons of the Trinity manifest their union, not through possession of a common essence, through being *homoousios*, but in the *koinonia* they share. The Trinity of Persons in the Godhead gives us a picture of true *koinonia*, of which human *koinonia* is, at best, a partial reflection.

Personhood

In very concise terms, these are the main points that Zizioulas makes when he is considering personhood in the light of the Trinity. These ideas were expressed in an article, published in Greek in 1977, 'From Mask to Person: The Contribution of Patristic Theology to the Concept of the Person', which forms the first chapter of *Being as Communion*.[8] There is a mixture of elements in this picture. The contrast between individual and person we have already encountered. It was particularly popular among Russians in the nineteenth century who used the contrast to characterize the difference between Russian and Western understandings of what it is to be human. The parallel with the Trinity begins to be made about the turn of the century, and the use of *hypostasis* (Russian: *ipostas*) to designate true personhood is something we find in Bulgakov, who may have invented the usage (earlier Russians, and early Bulgakov, make a distinction between two senses of *lichnost'*, personality or personhood, one in which the person sets himself against other humans, which comes to be described as 'individualistic' (*individualny*), and the other in which personhood unites persons in communion and the person grows out of true community, or communion, for which *ipostas* is used). The Russian use of the term *ipostas* suggests that the parallel with the Trinity had already been made; the famous Trinity icon of Andrey Rublev has come to be seen as disclosing a picture of persons existing in true *koinonia*.[9]

Zizioulas' notion of personhood is, then, something already familiar in the Russian Orthodox tradition, at least, and it must be something that Zizioulas picked up as a disciple of Florovsky. Zizioulas, however, develops the notion of personhood in distinctive ways. First of all, he sees the notion of a person as something that distinguishes Christianity from the Hellenic environment in which it developed and which formed it, to some extent. This observation is nothing new; we have heard Florovsky remarking that *'[t]he classical world did not know the mystery of personal being'*;[10] Zizioulas develops the conviction of his mentor. For Zizioulas, the classical world-view was governed by necessity; only the doctrine of creation out of nothing made possible a sense of freedom that enabled the notion of the person. Second, it was the need to develop an understanding of God as Trinity, itself a challenge to the tendency to monism in the classical tradition, that enabled the emergence of the sense of personhood.

Third, however, Zizioulas runs up against problems in his interpretation of the theology of the fourth century that are caused by his sense of the primacy of the person, for a central element of the doctrine of the Trinity in the fourth century, and especially in the Cappadocian Fathers, is the doctrine of the *homoousion*, the central conviction of the Nicene Creed – also the central element in the defence of that Council by Athanasios and the Cappadocians and the emergence of what we call 'Nicene Orthodoxy' – that

---

[8] Zizioulas, *Being as Communion*, 27–65.

[9] See Paul Evdokimov, *L'Art de l'icône* (Paris: Desclée de Brouwer, 1970), 205–16. For a fine study of the Rublev Trinity, see Gabriel Bunge, *The Rublev Trinity* (Crestwood, NY: St Vladimir's Seminary Press, 2007).

[10] Georges Florovsky, *The Eastern Fathers of the Fourth Century* (Vaduz: Büchervertriebsanstalt, 1987), 32 (italics Florovsky's).

the Son is *homoousios* with the Father, and indeed, as it is later put, that the Trinity is *homoousios*: *Triada homoousion kai achoriston*, 'Trinity consubstantial and undivided', as we exclaim in the liturgy, just before singing the creed.

For Zizioulas this is a problem, for *homoousios* tells us something about the being of God, or his essence, whereas for him it is the Persons that come first. He tries to maintain that *homoousios* is only of secondary importance for the Cappadocian Fathers, arguing that *koinonia* is more fundamental. He even argues that the 'omission' of 'from the substance of the Father', used in the Creed of Nicaea in explanation of the term *homoousios*, from the Creed of Constantinople, the one used liturgically, indicates a withdrawal from an essentialist understanding of the *homoousion*, and therefore of the unity of God.[11]

None of these arguments has carried much weight with patristic scholars,[12] and Zizioulas' notion that 'from the substance of the Father' was deliberately omitted from the creed suggests an odd understanding of the relationship of the Creed of Nicaea to the creed promulgated as 'Nicene' at the First Council of Constantinople.[13]

On a more general level, the contrast drawn by Zizioulas (and Florovsky) between classical philosophy in hock to notions of necessity and the emergence of freedom as a purely Christian concept is not, I think, something it would be easy to defend. We encounter here one of the problems in dealing with Zizioulas as a theologian: as a *historical* theologian, he accepts too easily ideas that correspond to the argument that he wants to develop as a *systematic* theologian. It must be the case that we can find a notion of personhood in the use of *hypostasis* by the Cappadocian Fathers, and furthermore it must follow that the use of *hypostasis*, or *way of existing*, was envisaged by the Fathers themselves as illuminating the nature of human personhood, even though there is virtually no evidence that this transition was ever made by the Fathers themselves. Zizioulas tends to respond to annoying historical criticism by repeating his position at greater length, which does not make for very easy dialogue.[14]

Eucharistic ecclesiology

There is, however, another line of development of the notion of personhood and *koinonia* in Zizioulas' thought, and that is its connection with the Eucharist.

---

[11] Zizioulas, *Communion and Otherness*, 120.
[12] See the three articles by André de Halleux: '«Hypostase» et «personne» dans la formation du dogme trinitaire', 'Personnalisme ou essentialisme trinitaire chez les Pères cappadociens?', 'Le IIe concile œcuménique: Une evaluation dogmatique et ecclésiologique', most conveniently found in de Halleux, *Patrologie et œcuménisme: Recueil d'études* (Leuven: Leuven University Press, 1990), 113–299.
[13] Zizioulas' argument only makes sense if it is thought that the creed agreed at Constantinople I was a revision of the Creed of Nicaea. It is perfectly evident that this is not the case; the basis of the creed of Constantinople I is a baptismal creed (maybe of Constantinople itself), to which Nicene phraseology had been introduced. See J. N. D. Kelly, *Early Christian Creeds* (London: Longman, 3rd edn, 1972), 296–331.
[14] See, for example, Zizioulas, *Communion and Otherness*, 171–7.

Indeed, reflection on the implications of the eucharistic celebration was occupying Zizioulas before he developed the more philosophical approach I have just tried to sketch. It is notable that the article, 'From Mask to Person', was published in 1977, whereas there is a host of articles on various aspects of the Eucharist in the 15 or so years before this – articles contributing to, or developing from, his Athens dissertation of 1965.[15]

Zizioulas stands in the tradition, mostly associated with the Paris émigré theologian Fr Nikolai Afanasiev, of 'eucharistic ecclesiology'. Afanasiev's principal exposition of eucharistic ecclesiology, *The Church of the Holy Spirit*, written between 1950 and 1955, was only published in 1971, after his death;[16] his approach to eucharistic ecclesiology was known well before this, principally from an article, 'The Church Which Presides in Love', published in French in 1960 (and in an English translation in 1963) in a volume of essays, *La Primauté de Pierre dans l'Église orthodoxe*.[17] The key idea of such eucharistic ecclesiology is very simple: it is the Eucharist that makes the Church, for the Church is, in essence, the eucharistic assembly, gathered together, under the bishop, to proclaim Christ's death and rejoice in his risen presence with his people. In each eucharistic assembly the whole church is present, is instantiated in the celebration of the Eucharist under the bishop. The origins of such an ecclesiology can be found in the conditions of the Russian diaspora. Hitherto, really from the time of the emperor Constantine, or at least the end of the fourth century with the emperor Theodosios, the Church had accepted the structures of the Roman Empire. This sense of the mutual entailment of Church and empire was so strong that, barely half a century before Constantinople fell to the Ottoman Turks, we find the Œcumenical Patriarch Antony of Constantinople writing to Grand Prince Vasily I of Moscow, saying,

> Therefore, my son, you are wrong to affirm that we have the church without an emperor, for it is impossible for Christians to have a church and no empire. The Empire (*basileia*) and the Church have a great unity and community – indeed they cannot be separated.[18]

This idea of the unity of Church and State was inherited by the Rus', after the fall of Constantinople, leading to the idea of Moscow as the 'Third Rome'. All this was swept away by the Russian Revolution, and one finds in the

---

[15] See the Bibliography of published writings by Zizioulas (up to 1991) in Paul McPartland, *The Eucharist Makes the Church: Henri de Lubac and John Zizioulas in Dialogue* (Edinburgh: T&T Clark, 1993), 316–21.

[16] ET: *The Church of the Holy Spirit*, trans. Vitaly Permiakov (Notre Dame, IN: University of Notre Dame Press, 2007).

[17] Nicolas Afanassieff, 'L'Église qui preside dans l'Amour', in *La Primauté de Pierre dans l'Église orthodoxe* (Neuchâtel: Delachaux et Niestlé, 1960), 7–62; ET in *The Primacy of Peter in the Orthodox Church* (Leighton Buzzard: Faith Press, 1963), 57–110.

[18] Letter from Patriarch Antony to Grand Prince Vasily I (1395), in Deno John Geanakoplos, *Byzantium: Church, Society, and Civilization Seen through Contemporary Eyes* (Chicago–London: University of Chicago Press, 1984), 143 (§105).

diaspora attempts to reconceive what it might mean to be the Church, now that there was no empire. Among the Russians, Nikolai Afanasiev (1893–1966) was the most articulate in developing an alternative ecclesiology. Reaching back behind the conversion of Constantine, and the vision of *symphonia* between Church and State first adumbrated by Eusebius of Caesarea in his encomia on the emperor Constantine, Fr Afanasiev looked back to St Ignatios of Antioch, with his notion of the Church as found in the eucharistic community assembled together with its bishop: 'wherever the bishop appears, there let the people be; just as wherever is Christ Jesus, there is the catholic Church' (Ign. *Smyrn.* 8.2). St Ignatios' remark is condensed into the slogan: 'Where the Eucharist is, there is the Church.'[19] Afanasiev's article had already attracted attention in the Greek Orthodox world, as can be seen from an article by Fr John Romanides, 'The Ecclesiology of St Ignatius of Antioch', published in 1961/2.[20] Afanasiev himself, on the basis of his article and a couple of others, is discussed and criticized by Zizioulas in the last chapter of his book *Eucharist, Bishop, Church*, though Afanasiev had anticipated many of the criticisms (e.g. the apparent danger of congregationalism) or otherwise had outflanked them (disregard for the canonical unity of the Church).[21]

It was such a model of eucharistic ecclesiology that Zizioulas explored in his Athens doctoral thesis, published as *Eucharist, Bishop, Church*. The eucharistic assembly provides, not just a model for, but the very reality of *koinonia*: the Eucharist makes the Church, indeed the Eucharist makes Christians – it is pre-eminently in the Eucharist (continued in the 'liturgy after the liturgy') that Christians learn what it means to be persons, formed in a communion of love. Zizioulas' book is best read as containing the reflection that led to his developing the idea of eucharistic communion as the foundation for ecclesiology: the prolegomena to his reflection as a systematic theologian on the nature of *koinonia* and the Church. It is important, because Zizioulas' reflection on this has had a profound impact on the theology of the ecumenical movement.

. . . and episcopacy

In his great high-priestly prayer, the Lord prayed for his disciples and 'those who believe in me through their word', 'that they all may be one, as you, Father, are in me, and I in you, that they all may be in us, that the world may believe that you have sent me' (John 17.20–21). These words have been repeatedly invoked in connection with the ecumenical movement, and added urgency to the call for union, but the idea they primarily express is that the unity of the Church is in some way modelled on the union of the Father and the Son, or – expressed in later language – that the unity of the Church

---

[19] See my article, 'Ignatios or Eusebios: Two Models of Patristic Ecclesiology', *IJSCC* 10 (2010), 46–56.
[20] John Romanides, 'The Ecclesiology of St Ignatius of Antioch', *GOTR* 7 (1961–2), 53–77.
[21] Zizioulas, *Eucharist, Bishop, Church*, 247–64.

is, in some way, derived from and modelled after the unity of the Trinity. It is this idea that Zizioulas develops, seeing a parallel between the unity of Father, Son and Holy Spirit in the communion that binds them together and the unity of the Church, manifest in the local church gathered together as a eucharistic community under its bishop. The parallelism is taken to entail that just as the principle of union in the Godhead is the Father, so in the eucharistic community the principle of unity is the bishop. Just as the Son and the Spirit receive their being, *homoousios* with the Father, from the Father, so in the Church, the members of the church receive their union with God and one another through the bishop.

This notion has had a mixed reception, on two grounds, which are not directly linked. First, the notion of the Trinity as receiving its union from the Father needs to be qualified by the realization that the Son and the Spirit are in no way inferior to the Father: subordinationism is ruled out in the Orthodox doctrine of the Trinity. Second, the notion of episcopal authority implicit in this way of thinking seems to run counter to the notion of synodality (or conciliarity, or *sobornost'*), equally important as constituting the union experienced in the Church. Zizioulas is well aware of this latter criticism, and meets it by insisting that primacy does not exclude synodality, but rather safeguards it.

In terms of actual church politics, however, there are fears that Zizioulas will be invoked to justify a kind of monepiscopism: something not a remote danger in the Orthodox Church, but rather a very real one. What might seem matters of simply theological import are in fact questions of real significance for the life of the Church. Zizioulas' ideas here can seem to justify injustice and to ignore real problems that need to be faced.

There is also an air of unreality about such an ecclesiology, in that the actual local parish community is not one led by a bishop, but by a priest, acting on his behalf, and commemorating him in the liturgy, and that actual living community should not be overlooked in the interests of an ideal that is rarely, if ever, actualized.[22] It is also not irrelevant that Zizioulas' own personal exercise of episcopacy seems anomalous: a titular bishop of a see that is, in present-day reality (whatever its fame in the past), a Turkish village with an important archaeological site.

The fragility of the theological model of the Trinity needs to be heeded, too: it makes no historical sense to sideline the doctrine of the *homoousios* or to subordinate it to a doctrine of the *koinonia* of the Persons, yet this seems to be the presupposition of Zizioulas' ecclesiology.

Another dimension of his ecclesiology concerns the way it is used to justify primacy at all levels of the Church's life: not just the primacy of the bishop over (but also within) the local eucharistic community, but also the metropolitan principle (the primacy of metropolitan bishop over the other bishops

---

[22] See Demetrios Bathrellos, 'Church, Eucharist, Bishop: The Early Church in the Ecclesiology of John Zizioulas', in *The Theology of John Zizioulas*, 133–45.

in his province), the patriarchal principle (the pentarchy of ancient patriar-
chates, which has been extended, whatever the justification, to the notion of
ethnic patriarchs, as developed in the nineteenth century), and beyond that
some form of universal primacy, such as that envisaged in the recent Ravenna
Statement of the Joint International Commission for the Theological Dialogue
between the Roman Catholic Church and the Orthodox Church, with
which Metropolitan John was closely associated.[23] The acceptance in the early
centuries of some modelling of the administrative structures of the Church
on those of the Roman or Byzantine Empire is not necessarily anything
more than an acceptance of the transient structures of the state by a Church
that has no abiding city here: that such was what was envisaged is suggested
by the reason given in the canons of Constantinople I and Chalcedon for
raising the see of Constantinople to parity with that of Rome – 'because
it is new Rome' (Constantinople 3; recalled in Chalcedon 28). The refusal
by the Church of Rome to accept these canons was because it justified its
primacy in terms of apostolicity, rather than reflecting the structures of the
empire, however apparently enduring.

Other problems

There are other problems with Zizioulas' doctrine of *koinonia* and personhood.[24] Although he has defended himself eloquently (most recently in 2012
at a conference in Belgrade[25]), there are still ambiguities in his ontology
of person and communion. It is important to recognize, however, that, in
insisting on personhood as an ontological question, he is making a valid point.
There has been a historical tendency to see ontology in terms of the
general and the universal – and therefore the impersonal. Metropolitan
John's iterated insistence that personhood is also concerned with being, with
ontology – that ontology is primarily personal – is important. In this he
would seem to acknowledge, and implicitly welcome, a broad movement in
Western metaphysics over the last century (mostly on the European continent)
that places the person (*Dasein* in Heidegger's terms) at the centre of metaphysical reflection about the nature of being. It is not just *what* we are that
raises ontological concerns, but also the question of *who* we are.

Metropolitan John's adoption of St Maximos the Confessor's distinction
between *logos* of being and *tropos* (mode) of existence, as expressing an

---

[23] For a helpful analysis of the Ravenna Statement from an Anglican perspective, see Colin Davey,
'Orthodox–Roman Catholic Dialogue: The Ravenna Agreed Statement', *Sobornost* 30:2 (2008),
7–36. For Zizioulas on primacy, see *The One and the Many*, 262–87.

[24] See, most recently, Chrysostomos Koutloumousianos, *The One and the Three: Triadic Monarchy in
the Byzantine and Irish Patristic Tradition and Its Anthropological Repercussions* (London: Lutterworth,
due in 2015), though there is more in this book than criticism of Zizioulas.

[25] Metropolitan John (Zizioulas) of Pergamon, 'Person and Nature in the Theology of St Maximus
the Confessor', in *Knowing the Purpose of Creation through the Resurrection: Proceedings of the Symposium
of St Maximus the Confessor, Belgrade, October 18–21, 2012*, ed. Bishop Maxim (Vasiljević) (Alhambra,
CA: Sebastian Press, 2013), 85–113.

ontological distinction between what we are – *logos* of being – and who we are – mode of existence – is something that promises to be fruitful. We face the same problem here, however, as in his deriving the notion of personhood from the Cappadocian use of the term *hypostasis* for Father, Son and Holy Spirit. Just as we cannot maintain that *hypostasis*, as used by the Cappadocian Fathers, simply unfolds into everything that Zizioulas (and others in the twentieth and twenty-first centuries) understand by the notion of person, neither can we maintain that Maximos' distinction between *logos* and *tropos* envisaged everything that we might derive from it.

It is surely enough, however, to claim that reflection on what could be meant by three Persons existing as one Godhead, and how one Person (that is, Christ) could embrace two natures (that is, the divine and the human), and indeed the difference between what we are and what we have made of ourselves – the Cappadocian and Maximian contributions, respectively – led to ways of thinking about personhood that blossomed later in the intellectual history of humankind: such a claim would not only be enough, but really quite a lot. And to that reflection on what it is to be human Augustine contributed, just as much as Maximos. It does no favours to the Orthodox to misread Augustine, and cast him as some kind of intellectual villain.

Zizioulas' understanding of nature and the individual, and the way in which he draws a link between the necessity imposed by nature and its manifestation in the unfreedom of the individual, is often expressed in an unfortunate way. He protests that by nature he always means *fallen* nature, not *created* nature,[26] but too often that distinction is barely visible, and his notion of 'nature' reads too much like Pascal's notion of 'une seconde nature, qui détruit la première' – an idea redolent of Pascal's Jansenism.[27] Zizioulas' opposition of 'biological *hypostasis*' and 'ecclesial *hypostasis*' seems to me to go even beyond the Jansenist notion of a second nature, constituted by custom.

John Romanides

There we must leave Metropolitan John for the moment, and turn to our other John: Fr John Romanides. Fr John was born in Athens in 1927, of parents who originated from Cappadocia and had come to Athens as a result of the exchange of populations after the war with the Turks at the beginning of the 1920s. Along with many others, they left Greece for the USA while John was still a baby. Romanides was educated in the USA, and received degrees from Holy Cross Orthodox School of Theology (1949) and Yale University (1954). He spent a year at the Institut St-Serge in 1954/5, before returning to Greece in 1955 to pursue doctoral studies at the University of Athens.

In 1957, he submitted his doctoral dissertation, which was published as *To Propatorikon Amartima* ('Ancestral Sin'). This book provoked a major theological

---

[26] For example, in his contribution to *Knowing the Purpose of Creation*, 106–8.
[27] Blaise Pascal, *Pensées* 117 in *Œuvres complètes*, ed. Michel Le Guern (Paris: Gallimard, 2000), II. 578.

row, and was attacked by one of the most distinguished professors of the Athens Theological Faculty, Panagiotis Trembelas. Trembelas was one of the last theologians of the old school in Greece. The theological faculty in Athens had been founded in the nineteenth century on the German model; theology was taught in the Western way, leaning towards either Protestantism or Catholicism. Since independence, Greece had emerged slowly as an Orthodox country, and one of the organizations that sought to promote spiritual renewal was the Zoë Brotherhood. This was a fairly strictly organized group of men (with a parallel women's organization). It was modelled on similar movements in the West, and had a very strong Protestant ethos (though there were parallels in Catholicism, such as Opus Dei). Zoë did much to contribute to the recovery of church life after the Second World War, during which Greece had been occupied by the Germans, and in the civil war that ensued, and there were many academics, like Trembelas, who were closely associated with it.

Romanides had arrived in Greece after being brought up in the USA; Zoë's Protestant ethos was very apparent to him.[28] Romanides' own theological formation had included, as we have seen, a year at the Institut St-Serge in Paris, which had given him an initiation into the tradition of the Russian émigrés there. Certainly Romanides arrived in Athens with an idea of theology based on the Greek Fathers, very much at odds with what he encountered in Greece. Trembelas' sustained attack on Romanides' doctoral thesis led to a lengthy correspondence between them, only recently published as *Encheiridion* (in 2009;[29] though earlier than that there had been access to it in unpublished form: Sopko makes use of it in his study of Romanides[30]).

Ancestral sin

His Athens thesis, despite the title 'Ancestral Sin', is not just about original or ancestral sin. One of the book's reviewers noted, with some surprise, that 'Father Romanides devotes most of his study to such related doctrines as creation, cosmology, divine energies, grace and the *imago Dei*'.[31] It is rather a book that seeks to present a sustained account of Orthodox theology, based on the Greek Fathers, and eschewing the Western categories and sources so marked in much Greek Orthodox theology of the time, not least in Trembelas' own work. It is a measure of its influence that much of it seems all rather obvious nowadays. After lengthy methodological introductions, successive chapters deal with the relationship between God and the world, discussing creation out of nothing, divine freedom, and divine activity (*energeia*) in the universe. The next chapter discusses Satan. This is followed by a chapter on

---

[28] For more on the Zoë Brotherhood, and some bibliography, see below in Chapter 16.

[29] *Encheiridion: Allilographia p. I. S. Romanidou kai kath. P. N. Trembela*, ed. Fr George D. Metallinos (Athens: Ekdoseis Armos, 2009).

[30] Andrew J. Sopko, *Prophet of Roman Orthodoxy: The Theology of John Romanides* (Dewdney, BC: Synaxis Press, 1998).

[31] E. A. Stephanou, in *GOTR* 4:2 (1958–9), 174.

the definition of the human – ethical perfection, the fall, immortality. There is a chapter on the human in the image of God. And finally there is a chapter on original, or ancestral, sin. What is striking about it is that its categories are drawn from the Greek theological tradition; Romanides abandons the approach found in the theological manuals used hitherto in Greece (and, indeed, still), which is much more redolent of scholasticism (at least in its modern textbook form).

There is a fairly strident anti-Westernism about the book: his methodological section attacks the notion of *analogia entis*, then still (just) thought of as characterizing Thomism (barely 20 years earlier, Karl Barth had singled out the doctrine of *analogia entis* as *the* reason why one could not become Catholic[32]), argues for the essence–energies distinction against the West, and attacks the Western doctrine of the *Filioque* and Augustine's notion of original sin; he is also opposed to an Anselmian doctrine of the atonement, as well as Anselm's understanding of theology as *fides quaerens intellectum* ('faith seeking understanding'). Fr Romanides' book, *To Propatorikon Amartima*, seems to me the most significant of his works, but let us continue with his life.

Back in the USA

Shortly after the controversy with Trembelas, Romanides returned to the USA and taught at Holy Cross until 1965. It was there that he came to know Fr Georges Florovsky, who was teaching both at Holy Cross and at Harvard at that time. Growing acquaintance with Florovsky can only have strengthened him in the position he had taken in his doctoral dissertation and in the controversy with Trembelas: a position which can be seen pre-eminently as an example of the kind of neo-patristic synthesis that Florovsky regarded as the only future for Orthodox theology. While teaching at Holy Cross in the 1960s, Romanides was one of the Orthodox observers to the Second Vatican Council. During this decade, too, he began to participate – along with Florovsky – in the consultations between the Eastern Orthodox Churches and the Oriental Orthodox Churches, and played a significant role in the wide measure of agreement that these consultations arrived at. In 1970, Romanides returned to Greece again and became Professor of Dogmatic Theology at the University of Thessaloniki. In 1973, he published his *Dogmatic and Symbolic Theology of the Orthodox Catholic Church*, in two volumes: text and documents (not unlike Trembelas' own work).[33] Another work of Romanides that has gained some fame (or notoriety) is his lectures, given in English at

---

[32] 'Ich halte die *analogia entis* für die Entfindung des Antichrist und denke, daß man ihretwegen nicht katholisch werden kann' [I hold the *analogia entis* to be the invention of Antichrist and think that, for this reason, one cannot become a Catholic]: Foreword to *Kirchliche Dogmatik*, I/1 (Zürich: A. G. Zollikon, 4th edn, 1944; original edn, 1932), VIII.

[33] *Dogmatiki kai Symboliki Theologia tis Orthodoxou Katholikis Ekklesias*, 2 vols (Thessaloniki: Pournaras, 1973; 2nd edn, 1999–2000).

Holy Cross, *Franks, Romans, Feudalism, and Doctrine: An Interplay between Theology and Society*.[34]

A theology of experience

Though no mean debater with words and concepts, for Fr Romanides theology is not about concepts, but about experience. This is why he is opposed to Anselm's programme of *fides quaerens intellectum*, which must seem puzzling to a Westerner, for whom this phrase expresses precisely the notion of theology as a form of prayer, as found, for example, in the treatise to which the phrase forms a subtitle: Anselm's *Proslogion*. What is wrong with Anselm's idea of faith seeking understanding is that this seems to Romanides a complete digression. Faith seeks God, and finds fulfilment in an experience of God, of union with him. Romanides is fully behind St Gregory Palamas and his defence of the hesychasts, for in that defence Palamas was defending the *experience* of the hesychast monks. Theology is about unfolding something of that experience, and its importance lies in helping others to come to that experience of God and union with him. More starkly, perhaps, than any other Orthodox academic theologian, he lays emphasis on the importance of experience of God, an experience to which the dogmas of the faith direct us.

One might put it in this way: Romanides has a very *Dionysian* understanding of the Church – not, perhaps, in the way most people conceive of Dionysios' approach to ecclesiology, as being very hierarchical, though Romanides is not insensitive to that side of ecclesiology – but more deeply. For he sees the Church as the place, context, society, in which we come to be united with God through purification, illumination, and what he usually calls, not perfection or deification, as Dionysios does, but glorification. This experience of glorification, or deification, is the purpose of the Church as an institution or community. Other ways of understanding the Church – as an institution, or even as a community gathered under a bishop – are secondary to his sense of the Church as the place for the deification of the human, and the reconciliation of the whole created order with the Uncreated God.

East and West

This experience is something that he found was shared with the Oriental Orthodox Churches – which is why he found the consultations with them so fruitful – but it was not an experience he could discern in the theology of the West. It is this perception that gives his theology such a negative attitude towards the West. He tends to trace the divide between Orthodox and Western theology back to Augustine, which must seem very strange to Western theologians, for whom Augustine is very much a theologian of experience.

---

[34] *Franks, Romans, Feudalism, and Doctrine: An Interplay between Theology and Society* (Brookline, MA: Holy Cross Orthodox Press, 1982).

Augustine is also held responsible for two of the doctrines that divide East and West: the doctrine of original sin and the doctrine of the double procession of the Holy Spirit, the doctrine that lies behind the addition of the *Filioque* to the Nicene (or strictly, the Niceno-Constantinopolitan) Creed. The addition of the *Filioque* to the creed is, however, as a matter of history, bound up with the history of the West in a different way. For it is well known that the Roman Church and the pope showed great reluctance in adding the *Filioque* to the creed; as late as the early ninth century Pope Leo III provided two silver shields to be placed each side of the entrance to the *confessio* in St Peter's, inscribed with the creed in Greek and Latin, in neither case including the *Filioque*.[35] Already Pope Leo was under pressure from the Carolingians, indeed from Charlemagne himself, whom he had crowned as Emperor of the Romans, on Christmas Day, 800, to include the *Filioque* in the creed used by the Church of Rome, but he refused. This story provides a kind of introduction to one of Romanides' books and one of his themes. The book is *Franks, Romans, Feudalism, and Doctrine: An Interplay between Theology and Society*, and the theme the reason for the divide between Eastern and Western Christendom. For Romanides the fundamental reason for the historic divide in Christendom has to do with the way in which Western Christendom (including, eventually, the papacy) came under the sway of the Franks, people of a very different culture from the people of the Mediterranean.

It seems to me that there is something in this, that the underlying reasons for lack of understanding between East and West have to do with the way in which the ascendancy of the barbarian kingdoms, and finally the Carolingians and the Holy Roman Empire, drew the Church into a culture very different from the Mediterranean culture of its origins. This gave rise to a host of problems concerned with translating the faith into everyday life, and underlay the issues that were articulated theologically. Having said this, I would add that I would find this perception something that enables us to understand why the Churches drifted apart, but I would not follow Romanides in interpreting these differences as theological.[36]

* * *

There we must leave Romanides. I would end, however, by emphasizing the importance of the insights that he expressed most clearly in his first book, *To Propatorikon Amartima*: insights based on his desire to develop the theology of the Orthodox Church from categories to be found in the Greek Fathers. That was an important contribution to the emergence of Orthodox theology in the twentieth century, one of enduring significance.

---

[35] See *Liber Pontificalis*, Leo. 84, in *The Lives of the Eighth-Century Popes* (Liber Pontificalis), trans. with commentary by Raymond Davis, Translated Texts for Historians 13 (Liverpool; Liverpool University Press, 1992), 219, and n. 171.

[36] For my take on this, see my *Greek East and Latin West: The Church AD 681–1071* (Crestwood, NY: St Vladimir's Seminary Press, 2007), especially, perhaps, 305–18.

15

Lay theologians: 1 Philip Sherrard

In the course of his life, Philip Sherrard became well known in at least three contexts: as a translator and interpreter of modern Greek poetry; as an Orthodox lay theologian, both for his numerous books and articles, and for his role in the English translation of the *Philokalia*; as a founding member, with the English poet Kathleen Raine, of the journal *Temenos*, and the Temenos Academy, concerned with rediscovering a sense of the sacred, and preserving the 'revered traditions of mankind', found in the sacred traditions of the great religions. Linked to all these was a concern for the damage that modern Western society is inflicting on the natural world, and a conviction that only the rediscovery of a sense of the sacred, as understood in the great religions

Philip Sherrard
With permission of Denise Harvey

of the world, could save humankind from the catastrophe towards which it seems to be inexorably moving. For Philip Sherrard, all of these concerns overlapped and interpenetrated one another, and most of those who know his work in one area or another are in some way aware of his renown in some at least of the other areas.

Early life and encounter with George Seferis

He was born in Oxford on 23 September 1922, of Anglo-Irish stock, with some Spanish ancestry.[1] His family background was not at all religious; his mother had links with the Bloomsbury Group (she knew Rupert Brooke and Virginia Woolf, when she was Virginia Stephen), among whom religious ideas were regarded as simply outdated. Educated at Dauntsey's School, in 1940 he went up to Peterhouse, Cambridge, to read history. Two years later he joined up in the army, eventually becoming a lieutenant in the Royal Artillery. His war ended in Italy (where he spent two years); he was finally concerned with mopping up the mess left by liaisons that had been formed between British soldiers in Italy and the local women.

Shortly after the end of the war, he travelled, still a soldier, from Naples to Greece. As soon as he got to Athens, moved, no doubt, as he says, by the literary affinities of his Bloomsbury background, he went to a leading book-shop there, and asked if they had any contemporary Greek verse in translation. He was offered, and bought, a volume of verse by George Seferis, with the Greek text and a facing French translation (by Levesque). He began to read these poems, and described their impact thus:

> And that was the real starting-point of my experience of Greece, or of my contact with what I have called the other mind of Europe, for when I began to read these poems I was at once aware that here was a voice, a resonance, a response to life – call it what you will – which, for all its links with what other European and American poetry I knew, possessed some quality I had never encountered before. It defeated, quite literally, my framework of references, challenged, as it were, the whole ground on which I stood, demanded of me that I should step through a door which I didn't even know existed.[2]

---

[1] For some details of Sherrard's life, I have used Metropolitan Kallistos' obituary: *Sobornost/ECR* 17:2 (1995), 45–52, supplemented by what I have learnt from conversations with Denise Harvey and Liadain Sherrard. See also Kathleen Raine, *Philip Sherrard (1922–1995): A Tribute* (Birmingham: The Delos Press/Clun: The Redlake Press, 1996). I am further indebted to Denise Harvey for access to the correspondence between Philip Sherrard and George Seferis. This correspondence was annotated by Philip Sherrard with a view to publication. It has been edited by Denise Harvey, and is to be published with introductions by Peter Mackridge and Vincent Rossi in the near future. Along with the correspondence, Denise Harvey has included a few other relevant essays by Sherrard, including an essay called 'The Other Mind of Europe' and an early essay on Seferis, called 'An Approach to the Poetry of Seferis' (1948). References to this book, provisional at the moment, are to the numbered pages of the PDFs of individual chapters. The letters for 1950 are divided into 'Letters 1950' and 'Letters 1950 cont.' I am very grateful to Denise Harvey for permission to quote from this material.

[2] Sherrard, 'The Other Mind', 4.

Philip soon wrote to the poet and began a correspondence that was to span many years, but there in 1946 began a process that led to his being baptized into the Orthodox Church in 1956. Immediately after his baptism, in June, he received Holy Communion for the first time in a church on the edge of the Pedion Areos park in Athens. The Divine Liturgy was being celebrated by Fr John Romanides; also present were Dimitrios Koutroubis, receiving Holy Communion for the first time since his return from abroad to Greece and to the Orthodox Church from Roman Catholicism, as well as Fotis Kontoglou, the writer and icon painter, who did more than anyone else in the Greek Church to restore the traditional style of iconography, parallel with Leonid Ouspensky in the Russian diaspora in Paris. We have already met Fr Romanides: at the time of celebrating this liturgy he had already embarked on his thesis, published as the book *The Ancestral Sin*, which awakened Greek theology to its true patristic inheritance. Dimitrios Koutroubis has been mentioned, but we shall encounter him again later when we look at the decisive turn Greek theology took in the 1960s. Kontoglou represents an aspect of modern Orthodox theology – the rediscovery of traditional iconography – which is only touched on in this book. In that church in Athens in June, we find a remarkable microcosm of the renewal of Greek theology in the post-war years.

Life continued, and writings

We are getting ahead of ourselves. On his return to England from Greece, Sherrard enrolled in King's College London, and began work on a thesis on modern Greek poetry, studying the poets Solomos, Palamas and Seferis; the thesis was later expanded into a book, *The Marble Threshing Floor* (1956),[3] in which he discussed as well the poets Cavafy and Sikelianos. In the course of his life, Sherrard held various academic positions in Athens and England, and from 1970 to 1977, he was University Lecturer in the History of the Orthodox Church, a position attached jointly to King's College and the School of Slavonic and Eastern European Studies, but he never settled to a conventional academic career, supporting himself, meagrely, as a writer and translator. Greece, however, drew him as a magnet; he returned as often as he could, and was never able to settle outside Greece. In the late 1950s, on an exploratory trip to Evia to find somewhere to rent for the summer, he came across a group of houses that had been built for a by-then-disused magnesite mine at Katounia near Limni: a remote and little-frequented site between the sea and the steep pine forest. No one wanted to live in remote locations in Greece so soon after the violence and insecurity of the civil war, and Sherrard found, in combination with some friends, that he could afford to buy them. He began to live there with his first wife Anna Mirodia and their young

---

[3] *The Marble Threshing Floor* (London: Vallentine, Mitchell & Co., 1956; reprinted in the Romiosyni Series, Limni, Evia, Greece: Denise Harvey & Co., 1981).

daughters, Selga and Liadain, in conditions of extreme simplicity – no telephone, no electricity, heating provided by wood stoves. This remained his home until his death in 1995, though there were periods when he was living and working in England.

Philip Sherrard was an amazingly prolific writer. Together with the American scholar Edmund Keeley, he produced translations of the major poets of modern Greece, which have become the standard translations. In 1961, they published *Six Poets of Modern Greece*, with selections (in translation) from Cavafy, Sikelianos, Seferis, Antoniou, Elytis and Gatsos.[4] This was followed in 1966 with a volume in the series Penguin Modern European Poets, *Four Greek Poets*, with selections from Cavafy, Elytis, Gatsos and Seferis.[5] This was followed by translations of the collected poems of George Seferis (with the Greek text, 1967)[6] and Constantine Cavafy,[7] and selected poems by Angelos Sikelianos (with the Greek text, 1979)[8] and Odysseus Elytis[9]. He wrote two books of criticism: *The Marble Threshing Floor*, his doctoral thesis, already mentioned, and *The Wound of Greece: Studies in Neo-Hellenism*.[10]

He was himself a poet; a volume of selected poems, *In the Sign of the Rainbow*, was published in 1994, the year before his death.[11] He wrote various other books on Greece (understood in a broad sense): *Athos: The Holy Mountain*,[12] *Constantinople: The Iconography of a Sacred City*;[13] he edited an anthology – which has wonderful pictures by Dimitri – *The Pursuit of Greece* (1964),[14] and also *Edward Lear: The Corfu Years*, a selection from Lear's letters and journals, accompanied by pictures, especially his watercolours.[15]

Other works were concerned with Orthodox theology, beginning with *The Greek East and the Latin West*,[16] and continuing with *Christianity and Eros*,[17] and *Church, Papacy and Schism* (1978),[18] though perhaps his greatest contribution to Orthodox theology was his involvement in the English translation of the *Philokalia*.[19] Philip's works on ecology grow out of his theological concerns

---

[4] *Six Poets of Modern Greece* (New York: Alfred A. Knopf, 1961).

[5] *Four Greek Poets* (Harmondsworth: Penguin, 1966).

[6] *George Seferis: Collected Poems* (London: Anvil Press, 1967).

[7] *C. P. Cavafy: Collected Poems* (London: Chatto & Windus, 1975).

[8] *Angelos Sikelianos: Selected Poems* (Princeton, NJ; Princeton University Press, 1979; reprinted in the Romiosyni Series, 1996).

[9] *Odysseus Elytis: Selected Poems* (London: Anvil Press, 1981).

[10] *The Wound of Greece: Studies in Neo-Hellenism* (London: Rex Collings, 1978).

[11] *In the Sign of the Rainbow: Selected Poems 1940–89* (London: Anvil Press, 1994).

[12] *Athos: The Holy Mountain* (London: Sidgwick & Jackson, 1982; originally published in German in 1959, and then as *Athos: The Mountain of Silence* the following year).

[13] *Constantinople: The Iconography of a Sacred City* (London: Oxford University Press, 1965).

[14] *The Pursuit of Greece* (London: John Murray, 1964).

[15] *Edward Lear: The Corfu Years* (Limni: Denise Harvey & Co., 1988).

[16] *The Greek East and the Latin West* (London: Oxford University Press, 1959; reprinted in the Romiosyni Series, 1992).

[17] *Christianity and Eros* (London: SPCK, 1976; reprinted in the Romiosyni Series, 1995).

[18] *Church, Papacy and Schism* (London: SPCK, 1978; reprinted in the Romiosyni Series, 1996).

[19] *The Philokalia: The Complete Text Compiled by St Nikodimos of the Holy Mountain and St Makarios of Corinth*, trans. G. E. H. Palmer, Philip Sherrard, Kallistos Ware, 5 vols (so far only 1–4) (London: Faber & Faber, 1979–95). Philip Sherrard completed his draft translation of vol. 5 before his death in 1995.

(and also out of what Greece came to mean for him): *The Rape of Man and Nature*,[20] *Human Image: World Image. The Death and Resurrection of Sacred Cosmology*;[21] they were also closely related to his involvement with *Temenos* and the Temenos Academy.

Two other works must be mentioned: *The Sacred in Life and Art*,[22] which expresses with urgent lucidity Philip's understanding of the nature and place of the sacred, and a volume of collected essays and lectures published posthumously, edited by his widow, his second wife, Denise Harvey: *Christianity: Lineaments of a Sacred Tradition*.[23] In my view, in these two works Philip expressed his fundamental theological and philosophical intuitions with the greatest lucidity and tranquillity, though with no diminishment of his sense of urgency.

Greek: Hellenic or Romaic?

If one looks over his published works, there emerges immediately what might seem to be a paradox: Philip's engagement with Greek literature is almost entirely concerned with what may be called the Hellenic strand in modern Greek literature, and yet his interest in Greek literature is an interest that led him to embrace Orthodoxy. It has often been observed, in various contexts, that modern Greece has two rather different ways of articulating its identity: one looks back to the ancient pagan past, which one might call Hellenic; the other looks back to its Byzantine past (as we still in the West perversely call it), which is best called 'Romaic' (for the Byzantines thought of themselves as Romans, their empire the Roman Empire, and their capital, Constantinople, they more usually referred to as 'New Rome'). Some unforgettable pages in Patrick Leigh Fermor's *Roumeli* catalogue the differences between the 'Romios' and the 'Hellene', beginning with 'Practice : Theory', continuing through 'Love of the recent past : Love of the remote past', 'Fatalism : Philosophic doubt', with the odd coincidence – 'A passion for newspapers, especially the political sections : A passion for newspapers, especially the political sections' – and concluding with 'Demotic : *Katharévousa*', 'The Dome of St Sophia : The columns of the Parthenon'! It runs to six pages.[24]

Philip was profoundly Orthodox, a characteristic of the Romios, and yet his energies as literary translator and critic were devoted almost exclusively to the Hellenic heritage (the translation of the *Philokalia* is an exception, admittedly a large exception). He wrote nothing about the great writer of the Romaic tradition, Alexandros Papadiamandis, though the English translation of Papadiamandis' short stories, *The Boundless Garden*, pays tribute to the

---

[20] *The Rape of Man and Nature* (Ipswich: Golgonooza Press, 1987).
[21] *Human Image: World Image. The Death and Resurrection of Sacred Cosmology* (Ipswich: Golgonooza Press, 1992).
[22] *The Sacred in Life and Art* (Ipswich: Golgonooza Press, 1990).
[23] *Christianity: Lineaments of a Sacred Tradition* (Brookline, MA: Holy Cross Orthodox Press, 1998).
[24] Patrick Leigh Fermor, *Roumeli: Travels in Northern Greece* (London: John Murray, 1966), 107–13.

'late Zissimos Lorenzatos and Philip Sherrard' for 'guiding, inspiring and sustaining this work from its inception'.[25]

Seferis and Orthodoxy

A good way of understanding Philip Sherrard's vision is to tackle this problem directly, and there is no better way of doing this than going back to the correspondence with George Seferis that began with Philip's writing a letter to the poet in 1947, after reading Seferis' poems in Athens in 1946.[26] As we have seen, reading these poems called in question all the assumptions of his background and education: as he put it, they 'demanded of me that I should step through a door which I didn't even know existed'. That door was eventually to lead into the Orthodox Church. Why?

George Seferis himself was hardly a devout Orthodox Christian. Indeed, he found somewhat puzzling what the young Sherrard had found in his poems, and though initially moved to go along with him and explore it, encouraged in this by his friendship with one who was to become a great man of letters, Zissimos Lorenzatos, by the mid-1950s, when Philip embraced Orthodoxy, Seferis found himself backing off from what Sherrard had discerned in his writings, and breaking off for a time with Lorenzatos, who analysed what he found to be a failure to grasp the wholeness of the Greek experience on Seferis' part (not his alone, however) in an important essay, 'The Lost Centre'.[27] This aspect of the story is, however, beyond our remit here.

Nevertheless, one facet of Lorenzatos' analysis of Seferis (which, in fact, he owed to Philip)[28] is worth commenting on. Seferis published a translation of T. S. Eliot's *The Waste Land* and some other poems (not, perhaps significantly, *Four Quartets*). In a kind of second Introduction, 'Letter to a Foreign Friend', he remarked, 'There's no way of getting away from it – we are a people who have great Fathers of the Church, but no mystics'.[29] Lorenzatos comments:

> This passage seems to me not so much the confession of a man who has acquired firsthand knowledge of the living spiritual tradition of Greece (the only one we have), but the involuntary repetition ... of the familiar self-projection of

[25] Alexandros Papadiamandis, *The Boundless Garden*, vol. 1 (Limni: Denise Harvey & Co., 2007), v.

[26] See note 1.

[27] This essay can be found, in English translation by Kay Cicellis, in *The Lost Center and Other Essays in Greek Poetry* (Princeton, NJ: Princeton University Press, 1980), 85–146 (the title of the essay is an echo of a line in Yeats' poem, 'The Second Coming': 'Things fall apart; the centre cannot hold').

[28] See Philip's letter to Seferis, 2 March 1950 (Letters 50 cont., 5); see also letter of 8 January 1959 (Letters 1950, 6, n. 2, and 77–8 with n. 153).

[29] Quoted by Lorenzatos, *Lost Center*, 140. The letter can be found (in a different English translation by Edmund Keeley and Nanos Valaoritis) in George Seferis, *On the Greek Style*, trans. with an Introduction by Rex Warner (Athens: Denise Harvey & Co., 1982; originally London: The Bodley Head, 1967), 163–81.

European *rationalismus* on ancient Greece, thanks to which our spiritual tradition has been consistently deformed and ignored by the still flourishing humanism of the Renaissance.[30]

Lorenzatos goes on to illustrate, with many names cited, the 'mystical tradition' of the Eastern Church, the origin of the mystics of the West, the only ones Seferis seemed aware of, and comments on the 'neglected, or misinterpreted, fact that our Eastern Orthodox tradition gave the West all that is deepest and most substantial in its own spiritual tradition'. He continues:

> When I say 'our' tradition, I do not mean that we Greeks gave others some precious possession of which we were the sole depositories, or that the Orthodox tradition was our own exclusive privilege, a kind of national or racial heritage, but simply that we belong to that tradition, insofar as we allow ourselves to become 'the holy people of Christ', as Photius wrote from his place of exile [*ep.* 126]; in other words, only as long as we cherish it and follow it are we entitled to call this tradition 'ours'; never in the national or racial sense.[31]

It was, it seems to me, this sense of Greek tradition that Philip Sherrard sensed in Seferis' poems, something that the poet himself was perhaps only partly aware of, and maybe was finally unable to hold on to. In the same 'Letter to a Foreign Friend', Seferis also remarked, following on from the passage on which Lorenzatos commented:

> we are devoted to emotions and ideas, but we like to have even the most abstract notions presented in a familiar form, something which a Christian of the West would call idolatry. Also we are – in the original sense of the word – very conservative. None of our traditions, Christian or pre-Christian, have really died out. Often when I attend the ritual procession on Good Friday, it is difficult for me to decide whether the god that is being buried is Christ or Adonis. Is it the climate? Is it the race? I can't tell. I believe it's really the light. There must surely be something about the light that makes us what we are. In Greece one is more friendly, more at one with the universe. I find this difficult to express.[32]

This interpenetration of the Pagan/Hellenic and the Christian Seferis experienced from the Hellenic side, as a Greek; the same interpenetration Sherrard, coming from outside Greece, experienced as a complete coinherence, *perichoresis*, drawing him to the wholeness of the Greek experience in which the Hellenic blends with the Christian (as in the thought and experience of the fourth-century Cappadocian Fathers, especially, perhaps, St Gregory the Theologian), which demanded his embrace of Greek Orthodoxy. That it is this aspect of Seferis that struck Philip is confirmed by something Philip himself says in the Introduction that he wrote to his edition of the correspondence he had with Seferis:

---

[30] Lorenzatos, *Lost Center*, 140.
[31] Lorenzatos, *Lost Center*, 142.
[32] Seferis, *Greek Style*, 170–1.

I still remember my bewilderment when Seferis sent me a letter in which occur such phrases as: 'I have a very organic feeling which identifies my human life with the life of nature', and went on to speak of the Greek world – the world of Greek nature – as 'lines which occur and recur; bodies and features, the tragic silence of a *face* ... There is a process of humanization in the Greek light ... Just think of those cords that bind man and the elements of nature together, this tragedy which is at once natural and human, this intimacy. Just think how the light of day and man's blood are one and the same thing.'[33]

Philip retained this sense of a fundamental unity of experience, transcending any distinction between the human and the natural, and, for him, the created and the uncreated. It can be found in his discussions of Greek literature – mostly, as I have remarked, concerned with the Hellenic strand – in which he feels the coinherence of the Hellenic and the Christian in a way that has become less fashionable in more recent writing on Greek literature.[34]

The sense of wholeness, connectedness, that he discovered in Greece is expressed in an early essay he wrote on Seferis. In this essay, written in 1948 – eight years before he became Orthodox – many of the themes that were to characterize Philip's own vision are already apparent. The essay is, in some ways, a comparison between T. S. Eliot and Seferis. In both he finds an analysis of the meaninglessness that faces modern Western society, but he finds, too, perhaps more clearly developed in Seferis, an alternative:

> There is, however, quite another way in which history may be understood and this, far from enslaving and crushing man, opens the way to freedom. From this point of view history is an inner act of comprehension. Man is not simply his exterior self, bound to a set of impersonal forces; he possesses within himself a sort of microcosm in which the whole world of objective reality and all the past historical periods – in fact everything that has happened, and possibly everything that will happen – exist and assert themselves. Man is not what he seems – a fragment of a meaningless world – but is rather a world in his own right. He possesses as it were a fourth dimension in which he is no longer a being conditioned from outside, but is able to condition himself from within; he is able to be free. But to enter into that dimension requires a prodigious feat of creative memory. 'This is the use of memory: for liberation'.[35]

Already there are adumbrations of themes that will be important for Sherrard's later theology, especially the notion of man as a microcosm. The use of memory in the rediscovery of freedom and meaning is related to Plato's doctrine of knowledge as *anamnesis*. He goes on to remark,

> Memory, then, in the sense used here, is simply the interior bond that connects the history of one's own spiritual development to the story of the world; and the history of the world, properly viewed, is nothing more than the reflection

---

[33] Sherrard, 'The Other Mind', 9 (the letter from which he quotes is Seferis' letter to George Katsimbalis on his poem, 'Thrush').

[34] See, e.g., Anthony Hirst, *God and the Poetic Ego: The Appropriation of Biblical and Liturgical Language in the Poetry of Palamas, Sikelianos and Elytis* (Oxford: Peter Lang, 2004).

[35] Sherrard, 'An Approach', 9.

of the history of one's own spirit in the past. That is why the search to unite man to his spiritual depths becomes a descent into the abyss of history.[36]

This use of memory is more immediately available in Greece than anywhere else, Sherrard suggests; 'no country is more haunted by history than Greece ... no country in which the divine has dwelt so close to man, or in which its absence is more poignant'.[37]

> The Greek land and seascape is perhaps more immediately symbolic than that of any other country; never has more been conceived in the realm of ideas than became actual there; no where else does the actual demand so immediately to be imaginatively recreated.[38]

Plato and Aristotle: East and West

The language Philip uses is redolent of Plato, and he goes on to contrast the genius of Platonism, which he finds in the Greek East, with the spirit of Aristotle, an organizing, controlling spirit, which he finds characteristic of the Latin West. He continues:

> In the Orthodox East, on the other hand, Platonic thought plays a larger part. The natural world is rooted in the supernatural ... This world is rooted in the world of ideas, and the world of ideas rests upon God. Thus this world and everything in it is capable of reflecting and in its turn is capable of being lit up by the highest processes of life. The imperfection of man is not the same thing as his powerlessness in the face of his destiny, nor is it a consequence of his imperfection that he must submit to an external authority in order to achieve anything of value. In fact, anything of value can only be achieved where institutions leave off, and man's obedience to them is something which he accepts and suffers negatively, because other people need them ... Imperfection is not the same thing as badness, and the one does not imply the other. The excessive monotheism of Puritanism always reduces the world to poverty, since one ideal dominates, and the forces which have no positive relation to this ideal are denied, or ignored, or suppressed. The world is organized and moralized; the characters of monotheists are strong, they have firm principles, their forms of life are good. On the other hand, their souls lack colour, they become rigid and sterile; they talk about transfiguration and illumination but they cannot experience it: non-sensuous natures are incapable of profundity in religious experience; their world is full of striving and bitterness, it is a tortured world, internally and externally, without joy, without liberation. Man is debased, he almost ceases to exist. The East gives man a more positive role. Man is imperfect, but his imperfection is a blessing which contains within it the possibilities of immense development, and is in fact the starting point of the creative impulse without which even the gods would cease to exist. Hence there is less concern with morality and with original sin as such, and more with redemption and the coming of the millennium.[39]

---

[36] Sherrard, 'An Approach', 10.
[37] Sherrard, 'An Approach', 11–12.
[38] Sherrard, 'An Approach', 12.
[39] Sherrard, 'An Approach', 16–17.

I have quoted at length – though, alas, omitted the quotations from Seferis' poems – because there is expressed here, succinctly, the polarities that are characteristic of Philip's thought. Accepting the analysis of modern Western society implicit in such works as Eliot's *The Waste Land,* or Yeats' 'The Second Coming', he finds hope for escaping the meaninglessness and lack of connection with oneself, the world and God, in what he has discovered in Greece, as mirrored in the poems of Seferis. The sense of the connectedness of this world with the divine world, expressed in Plato's doctrine of the Ideas, and realized through the memory of man, aware of himself, not as an isolated individual, but as a microcosm, capable of containing the whole of history in himself. The redemption of the senses, the sense of human imperfection as containing within itself 'possibilities of immense development', opening out a horizon of hope. All this seen as a huge contrast to the state in which the West and the Western Church finds itself, a contrast maybe overdrawn, but not fundamentally false. These were to be the guiding lines of Sherrard's theological and philosophical vision.

The division of Christendom: the Great Schism between East and West

His expressly theological works explore the implications of such a realization. Two works are explicitly concerned with the schism between Orthodoxy and the West: *The Greek East and the Latin West* and *Church, Papacy and Schism.* The first, in particular, has been much criticized. In what is no more than a single chapter on Sherrard, it is impossible to enter into detailed discussion of points of interpretation. Instead, I think it more useful to recall the contrast Philip drew between the Latin and the Greek, included in a letter to Seferis, sent on 20 March 1950. Trying to express the different ways in which an artist may experience the contrast between the longing for liberation and the sense of being determined by external cultural forces, Sherrard suggested that there are two ways of trying to resolve the tension:

1   Feeling that both his emotions and the outside world threaten his existence, he may try, through a labour which is largely intellectual, to reduce the irrational forces which surround him to a rational harmony; and his beatitude, his liberation, will consist in the contemplation of an ordered world from which all the accidents of personal emotion and illogical behaviour are purged.
2   Still with the sense that he is immersed in an alien world, he may feel not that liberation consists in reducing this world and its forces to a single rational unity, an intellectual order; but that it consists rather in communication with and participation in another life beyond both the physical and the intellectual frontiers of this life.

The artist whose 'way' corresponds to 1. will possess what I call a Latin temperament; he whose 'way' corresponds to 2. will possess a Greek temperament.[40]

---

[40] Letters 1950 cont., 11.

And he goes on to distinguish between these two temperaments thus:

1 The Latin temperament is rooted in the intellectual order of life. An artist of this temperament, suspicious of if not hostile towards his emotions, will give his feeling rein only up to that point at which it does not interfere with the clarity of his intellectual vision. If what his feeling tells him to be true is contradicted by what his intellect can prove to him is not true, he will discipline the truth of his feeling until it is subordinate to the truth of his Reason.

2 The Greek temperament is rooted in the emotional order of life. An artist of this temperament, possessed of strong human emotion and relying on that strength, instinctively distrusts anything which is not human; at the same time – this may sound like but is not a paradox – all that he feels for he endows with a vital human personality. If what his feeling tells him to be true is contradicted by what his intellect can prove to him is not true, he will discipline the truth of his Reason until it is obedient to the truth of his feeling.[41]

It is not too much to say that it is this analysis that undergirds the historical analysis undertaken in *The Greek East and the Latin West*. Although talk of 'two temperaments' suggests a polarity between equals, closer attention reveals something rather different. The Greek temperament manages to reconcile reason with emotion in the wholeness of a mature person; the Latin temperament, on the other hand, suppresses the emotions and manifests itself, all too easily, in a tendency to exclude what it cannot understand and to dominate. This latter attitude led the Latin West to sever its link with the original Christian Church of the Greek world (it is not a matter of chance that the New Testament is written in Greek); it is the same attitude, Philip will argue, that underlies the malaise of the West and the ecological crisis it has brought on the world

Church, Papacy and Schism is a much easier book to read, and its analysis clearer to grasp. It also fits well with the contrast just outlined. In this little book, Philip develops his understanding of the nature of the Church, 'in the first place . . . a spiritual reality, rooted in the divine life'. Such an approach accords entirely with the understanding of the Church of the Fathers, none of whom wrote a treatise devoted simply to the Church, for the Church is bound up with the whole mystery of the divine *oikonomia*, and cannot be detached from it. The Church then is the place of our participation through Christ in the divine life of the Trinity; it is a real community, gathered together with its bishop. Philip rarely quotes the Fathers, but here he might have cited St Maximos, who in his *Mystagogia* remarks of the Church:

For many and of nearly boundless number are the men, women and children who are distinct from one another and vastly different by birth and appearance, by race and language, by way of life and age, by opinions and skills, by manners and customs, by pursuits and studies, and still again by reputation, fortune,

---

[41] Letters 1950 cont., 12.

characteristics and habits: all are born into the Church and through it are reborn and recreated in the Spirit. To all in equal measures it gives and bestows one divine form and designation: to be Christ's and to bear his name.[42]

The universality, or catholicity, of the Church is manifest in the local community, but also in another way in the assemblies known as councils. However, the authentic Christian, that is, Orthodox, understanding of the Church never allows the institution to predominate, and as the book develops, Philip shows how this indeed happened in the history of the Church, and became formally defined in the emergence of the papacy, with the pope as the supreme ruler of the Church, itself more and more conceived as a worldwide political organization. I cannot think that Philip would have been at all happy about the notion of primacy put forward by the Orthodox (and endorsed by many Orthodox jursidictions) in the recent *Ravenna Statement*. Institutions, as we have seen in the quotations from his 1948 essay on Seferis, were for Philip no more than a necessary evil.

The *Philokalia*

Philip's principal contribution to Orthodox theology was his part (a major part) in the English translation of the *Philokalia*. I want to try and draw out what I think this meant for Philip. This is not easy, for he wrote virtually nothing on the *Philokalia*, but the immense investment represented by his work of translation deeply affected the way he thought. He was, as is evident from Metropolitan Kallistos' accounts of their working together on the translation, a meticulous translator, who had in his lifetime acquired enormous skill in translating (and more than that, a feel for the language) through his rendering of Greek poetry into English poetry (certainly the greatest challenge to a translator). Perhaps what was most important for him in the *Philokalia* was the understanding of human nature he found enshrined in it: a fundamentally Platonic anthropology (to use the word in its older sense), based on the accounts of the soul in dialogues such as the *Symposium* and the *Phaedrus*, which sees the soul as a complex of desire and energy, to be ruled by reason, where reason itself includes both a lower level, concerned with planning and devising, and a higher level, concerned with contemplation. The whole purpose of the *Philokalia*, as stated on the title page, is to purify and illumine the soul, so that the higher reason, the *nous*, can turn in contemplation towards God; such a purified *nous* is also capable of understanding the created order and discerning its inner reality, as expressed in the *logoi*, or inner principles, of being.

Beside that fundamental intuition, found in the writings collected in the *Philokalia*, there are other aspects that seem to me to have been valuable for Philip. I shall discuss these in two stages: first, by reflecting on a couple of passages from the Introduction by the translators to the English version

---

[42] Maximos the Confessor, *Mystagogia* 1.

of the *Philokalia*; second, by drawing out one theme found there, the central theme of love, to which Philip did indeed devote much reflection.

First, the Introduction to the *Philokalia*. As well as explaining the nature of the *Philokalia*, a collection of ascetic texts compiled by St Makarios of Corinth and St Nikodimos of the Holy Mountain and published in Venice in 1792, arranged in what was thought to be their chronological order from the fourth to the fifteenth century and culminating in texts associated with the fourteenth-century hesychast controversy, the translators have a few passages that try to capture something of the spirit of the *Philokalia*:

> The *Philokalia* is an itinerary through the labyrinth of time, a silent way of love and gnosis through the deserts and emptinesses of life, especially of modern life, a vivifying and fadeless presence. It is an active force revealing a spiritual path and inducing man to follow it. It is a summons to him to overcome his ignorance, to uncover the knowledge that lies within, to rid himself of illusion, and to be receptive to the grace of the Holy Spirit who teaches all things and brings all things to remembrance.[43]

And, in relation to the question how far this collection of largely monastic texts envisages a solely monastic audience:

> Indeed, in this respect the distinction between the monastic life and life 'in the world' is but relative: every human being, by virtue of the fact that he or she is created in the image of God, is summoned to be perfect, is summoned to love God with all his or her heart, soul and mind. In this sense all have the same vocation and all must follow the same spiritual path. Some no doubt will follow it further than others; and again for some the intensity of the desire with which they pursue it may well lead them to embrace a pattern of life more in harmony with its demands, and this pattern may well be provided by the monastic life. But the path with its goal is one and the same whether followed within or outside a monastic environment.[44]

The first quotation, to which it is difficult to think that Philip did not contribute some of the imagery used, at least, sees the *Philokalia* very much in terms of seeking to enable the transition from the meaninglessness of modern life to a world transfigured by the divine presence, a transition Philip found already on the way to being accomplished in the Greek world he had discovered. The second sees this as the development and purification of love – a love for God in which heart, soul and mind find union: something that must take place not only within the monastic life, but in married life in the world. Philip thought much about the place of love, of *eros*, within the Christian life, of, precisely, the place of sexual love. He devoted a book to the subject – *Christianity and Eros: Essays on the Theme of Sexual Love* – and also discussed it in one of the chapters of *The Sacred in Life and Art*, called 'The Nuptial Mystagogy'. It is this latter chapter that I want to dwell on briefly.

---

[43] *Philokalia*, 13–14.
[44] *Philokalia*, 16.

Man and woman: *eros*

Philip begins by reflecting on the story of the creation of man, 'in the image and likeness of God', in the book of Genesis. His interpretation is, so far as I am aware, quite original, though it is developed from the wording of the text, especially in the Greek Septuagint. At the end of the first account, God surveys his Creation and finds it *kala lian*, 'very good', even better: 'exceedingly good', and better still: 'exceedingly beautiful' (Gen. 1.31), for the Greek *kalos* conveys the sense of beautiful as well as good. And then we read that God sees that for man to be on his own is *ou kalon*, 'not beautiful', 'not good' (Gen. 2.18). The woman, Eve, is therefore created 'as the finishing touch to the divine work of art', which is the created order.[45] Eve is therefore not to be regarded as 'adventitious or second best', as traditional interpretations of the Genesis story often suggest, but as completing the beauty of Creation. Philip goes on to comment:

> It is as if the two complementary principles that we describe as the masculine and feminine principles, united and reconciled in God Himself, require this polarization on the human plane if the full potentiality of their creative energies is to be actualized. Each of the two beings stands in a particular relationship to one of these principles, which is its own source of identity, its own *logos* and *sophia*, and which determines its destiny. The differentiation into male and female, far from being a compromise or a concession to human weakness, is intrinsic to human nature as such: it is a condition of the very existence of human nature itself.[46]

From this it follows that the image of God is found in its fullness in the *relationship* between a man and a woman, a relationship which is a relationship of love, but more than this a relationship in which the love that holds them together is recognized as a divine 'quality and gift'.

> Nor is it simply in God that they love each other ... Everything is an unveiling of God, a theophany in which God discloses Himself in His own image. Hence in loving each other what they love is God as He has revealed Himself in each of them to the other. Each becomes an icon to the other; and because God has revealed Himself as an icon in the form of the living being who is the beloved, so in loving that being the lover will be loving God. In the icon it is God who manifests Himself; and what the man loves in the woman is the mystery she discloses as such an icon, just as what the woman loves in the man is the mystery that he discloses in a similar way. Each thus discloses for the other that unknown Being who is the sacred core of their existence and Who Himself aspires to find a birthplace in the hearts of both of them.[47]

The distinction between man and woman is, in each case, a matter of the predominance, not exclusive possession, of the two principles, masculine and

---

[45] Sherrard, *The Sacred in Life and Art*, 112.
[46] Sherrard, *The Sacred in Life and Art*, 112–13.
[47] Sherrard, *The Sacred in Life and Art*, 117.

feminine, and these principles are distinguished by qualities, for the man, of majesty and impartial judgement and, for the woman, of beauty and a sense of infinite tenderness and compassion – a distinction reflected in a verse of the prophet Isaias (which Philip does not quote): 'he has set a crown on me as a bridegroom, and as a bride is adorned with jewels, so has he adorned me' (Isa. 61.10 LXX).

This ideal is, perhaps, rarely realized, but we can see these principles manifest in a distorted way, when sexual love fails to be a way of loving God, and is simply directed to worldly concerns, and manifests itself as concupiscence and sensual covetousness, which 'turns the love between man and woman into little more than a blind search to assuage ego-centred desires'.[48] Nevertheless,

> Man has not forfeited the divine image in which he is created ... He can recover what he has lost ... But to do this he has to recognize that in essence he is a spiritual being whose deepest needs and aspirations can be fulfilled only through self-realization in God. Yet since God is love, this realization can be achieved only through the rebirth of divine love in his soul. Hence the crucial role in the whole process of regeneration or redemption that can and should be played by the nuptial relationship between man and woman.[49]

There remain two topics to be discussed if I am to do anything like justice to the breadth of Philip's concerns: the role and nature of sacred tradition, and how everything that we have discussed bears on the ecological crisis we are facing.

Sacred tradition

The question of sacred tradition was of paramount importance to Philip; it is the loss of sacred tradition, through neglect and also through a sense that we have passed, as a civilization, beyond the need for such things, that lies at the root of the problems of Western culture. It is, indeed, this notion of sacred tradition that Philip encountered through his reading of the poems of Seferis, back in 1946, for there he encountered the Greek tradition as just such a tradition, a tradition, as Lorenzatos was to say, that was specifically Greek, but only possessed by the Greeks as 'ours', if 'we cherish and follow it' – 'never in the national or racial sense'.[50] For Philip, sacred tradition was something preserved in the great religions of the world, not confined to Christianity; indeed, the problems with Western Christianity could be traced back to its abandonment of sacred tradition. This explains what might otherwise seem a paradox in Philip's thought: a strident rejection of the kind of Christian ecumenism associated with the World Council of Churches, combined with a willingness, even eagerness, to learn from the spiritual traditions of the great religions.

---

[48] Sherrard, *The Sacred in Life and Art*, 125.
[49] Sherrard, *The Sacred in Life and Art*, 127.
[50] Lorenzatos, *Lost Center*, 142.

It was in this spirit that Philip participated with Kathleen Raine and others in the setting up of the *Temenos Journal*; later, after Philip's death, the Temenos Academy was established, with its journal, *Temenos Academy Review*. Indeed, Kathleen Raine has said that '[i]t was Philip who introduced me to the definition of Tradition as a timeless reality embracing mental and spiritual worlds'.[51] Unlike Kathleen Raine, however, for whom the different spiritual traditions were a resource from which one could develop one's own spirituality, Philip saw participation in sacred tradition as something that could only be achieved by wholehearted adherence to one such tradition, in his case that of (Greek) Orthodoxy. In this, he was at one with the perennialist philosopher René Guénon, though he differed sharply from him over how this was to be worked out.[52] Perhaps the most obvious way of seeing how Philip understood the nature of sacred tradition is to explore how he interpreted this in relation to Christianity.[53]

Sacred tradition, Philip asserts, 'in the highest sense consists in the preservation and handing-down of a method of contemplation':[54] contemplation, by which we realize our affinity with the divine and spiritual world of which the world of everyday reality is, at best, some kind of reflection. This is not something we can achieve on our own, which is why there is sacred tradition: something handed down to us, not something we confect. The tradition is manifest in sacred writings, sacred rites and sacred initiation. For Christianity, the sacred writings are primarily the Holy Scriptures, but these are not understood in any exclusive sense, and certainly not understood as some kind of infallible revelation; rather they provide access to the world of God's revelation, not least to the world of symbols that disclose to us the nature of the divine and spiritual world, an access provided by other sacred writings, including the works of the Fathers, and an anthology such as the *Philokalia*. The sacred rites are the sacraments, especially the Divine Liturgy, in which we find ourselves caught up in the creative and redemptive movement of God in Christ, formed into the body of Christ, and through ourselves extending that movement into the world in which we live.

Sacred initiation is the meaning of all this, found through participation in the sacraments, and in the rhythms of personal prayer and asceticism; here, too, is the role of the spiritual master, father or mother, who passes on the living tradition. All the great religions revolve round sacred writings, sacred rites, sacred initiation, which constitute sacred tradition. It is the fragile grasp of the notion of the sacred, the deconstruction of sacred writings through the secular methods of biblical criticism, the dissolution of sacred rites into confected ways of fostering human community, and the way in which sacred

---

[51] Raine, *Sherrard*, 13.

[52] See the chapter, 'Christianity and the Metaphysics of Logic', in Sherrard, *Christianity: Lineaments*, 76–113.

[53] What follows is based on Sherrard, *Christianity: Lineaments*, in particular, Chapter 1, 'The Meaning and Necessity of Sacred Tradition', 1–26.

[54] Sherrard, *Christianity: Lineaments*, 11.

initiation has been surrendered to the pursuit of the scientific method, that has weakened the hold of Western forms of Christianity on sacred tradition.

The ecological crisis

There is little space left to say much about what could be regarded as the most urgent of Philip Sherrard's concerns: the ecological crisis. Philip's indictment is fundamental: it is not a matter simply of excessive and selfish use of the power that has been put in human hands by the methods of modern technology; it is more fundamentally the loss of a sense of who we are as human beings created in God's image. As a result, as Philip put it in his Introduction to *Human Image: World Image*, we have come to

> look upon ourselves as little more than two-legged animals whose destiny and needs can best be fulfilled through the pursuit of social, political, and personal and economic self-interest. And to correspond with this self-image we have invented a world-view in which nature is seen as an impersonal commodity, a soulless source of food, raw materials, wealth, power and so on, which we think we are quite entitled to experiment with, exploit, remodel and generally abuse ... in order to satisfy and deploy this self-interest.[55]

All this has its origin 'in a loss of memory, in a forgetfulness of who we are, and in our fall to a level of ignorance and stupidity that threatens the survival of our race'.[56]

Philip's analysis of the crisis Western society and science has brought on the world is withering, but his attitude was not one of despair. However much damage we do to the world and ourselves, it remains the truth that the world is created by God – there is nothing in the universe opposed to God, as such – and we human beings are created in God's image. The bedrock of the reality of things cannot be destroyed by human contriving. The solution, however, is radical: not simply a tempering of our raid on, or rape of, nature, not fixing a supposedly moderate limit for carbon emissions, but rather a radical change of heart, *metanoia*, and the recovery of a sense of who we are, and what the world is.

> Once we repossess a sense of our own holiness, we will recover the sense of the holiness of the world about us as well, and we will then act towards the world about us with the awe and humility that we should possess when we enter a sacred shrine, a temple of love and beauty in which we worship and adore. Only in this way will we once again become aware that our destiny and the destiny of nature are one and the same. Only in this way can we restore cosmic harmony.[57]

Philip's question is an urgent question, and there is no real evidence that it is being heeded now, 20 years after his death.

---

[55] Sherrard, *Human Image: World Image*, 3.
[56] Sherrard, *Human Image: World Image*, 3.
[57] Sherrard, *Human Image: World Image*, 9.

16

Lay theologians: 2 Dimitris Koutroubis, Christos Yannaras, Stelios Ramfos

Lay theology?

As we begin the second of three chapters on lay theologians, it is perhaps worth reflecting on the role of lay theologians in modern Orthodox theology. The word 'lay' has various connotations. Originally, of course, it derives from the Greek *laos*, people, and referred to the Church as the 'people of God', *laos tou Theou*, but, too soon, it came to mean the 'laypeople' in contrast with the clergy, and so acquired a negative sense of 'not-the-clergy', not-the-experts, and lost its original sense of the people of God, among whom the clergy are numbered, not in opposition to the clergy. So lay came to mean 'non-ordained', and then in an extended metaphorical sense, non-expert, someone interested in something but not trained. The term 'lay theologian' can therefore mean either a theologian who is not ordained, or a theologian who has not been trained as a theologian, by, for example, pursuing a university course in theology. In both these senses, we have come across many 'lay theologians': Khomiakov, Solov'ev, Berdyaev, Lot-Borodine, Lossky, Evdokimov, Philip Sherrard, and Greeks such as Christou, Nellas and Mantzaridis, were not ordained, and even priests such as Bulgakov and Florovsky had no training as academic theologians – at university they had studied economics, philosophy or history.

One might say that Orthodox theology, in the last two centuries, has been predominantly a *lay* phenomenon. This could be regarded as a strength or a weakness, though in my view, as one both a priest and a trained theologian (though not a trained *Orthodox* theologian), it seems to me more of a strength. For it seems to me that lay theology is less likely to become inward-looking, less likely to address a narrow circle of professionals; and indeed this seems to me to have been so with the thinkers we have been exploring.

Whatever the case generally, in the case of Greek theology over the last half-century, we find ourselves dealing with a pronounced lay theology. Those we shall be discussing here are both lay, in the sense of not ordained, and lay in pursuing their careers outside the groves of theological academe, or indeed often outside academe altogether. Nor is this some kind of exceptional condition: it is still the case that the liveliest *fora* of Greek theology lie outside the formal confines of Church or university: the Greek theological journal most worth reading nowadays is *Synaxi*, founded by Panayiotis Nellas in 1982, and now edited by Thanasis Papathanasiou, both laymen.[1] Furthermore, neither Nellas nor Papathanasiou belongs to the academic establishment: Nellas taught in a high school in Athens, and Papathanasiou is a tutor at the Open University in Greece.

Yannaras and Ramfos

There are doubtless historical reasons for this situation; here, however, is not the place to pursue them, save in so far as they are directly relevant to our subject, modern Greek lay theological reflection, especially as exemplified in Christos Yannaras and Stelios Ramfos (and more briefly in Dimitris Koutroubis). Both Yannaras and Ramfos are well-known public intellectuals in Greece. For many years now, Yannaras has had a weekly political column in the newspaper *Kathimerini*, and periodically has appeared regularly on television debates and interviews; Ramfos is popular and well known as a public lecturer. For decades now they have addressed the political, cultural and economic problems Greece faces, and both of them have drawn on the riches of the Byzantine theological and ascetical tradition. It is a phenomenon it is difficult to imagine in the UK, where there are certainly public intellectuals who can be found discussing the issues of the day, though more commonly in the rarefied quarters of Radio 3 rather than on the public screen of popular television channels; as a rule, none of these intellectuals displays any sympathy towards Christianity, indeed, rather the reverse.

Our two Greek thinkers were both born in Athens: Yannaras in 1935, Ramfos in 1939. Both studied at the University of Athens – Yannaras theology, Ramfos law. Both then pursued their university studies abroad: Yannaras studied philosophy at the universities of Bonn and Paris, Ramfos studied philosophy in Paris. Thereafter, Ramfos lectured in philosophy at the University of Paris-VII from 1969 to 1974. That date marked the end of the dictatorship of the colonels in Greece (1967–74), and in the same year Ramfos returned to Athens, where he has devoted himself to writing and lecturing. He has produced a prodigious number of books, few of which have been translated into English. Other than that, I have been unable to find out much about his life, maybe because of lack of diligence. We shall come back to Ramfos later.

About Yannaras' life we are much better informed, not least because Yannaras himself has published two autobiographical volumes, *Katafygio ideon: Martyria* ('Refuge of ideas: Testimony') and *Ta kath' eauton* ('About himself').[2] These are illuminating about the course of Yannaras' life, both inner and outer, as

---

[1] For an illuminating selection in English translation from *Synaxi*, see *Synaxis: An Anthology of the Most Significant Orthodox Theology in Greece Appearing in the Journal SYNAXI from 1982 to 2002*, 3 vols (Montreal: Alexander Press, 2006).

[2] Christos Yannaras, *Katafygio ideon: Martyria* (Athens: Ikaros, 5th rev. edn, 2000, originally published by Domos in 1987); *Ta kath' eauton* (Athens: Ikaros, 1995).

well as about the state of theology and church life in Greece from the 1950s to the 1970s.[3]

In the 1950s, Greece emerged from the civil war that had followed on the Second World War, in which Greece, after providing decisive support for the UK in the early stages, was occupied by the Germans. Greece, however, could be regarded as emerging from a much longer struggle, beginning with its liberation from the Ottoman yoke in the nineteenth century, followed by a fumbling attempt to become a European nation, with an initially foreign (German) king and the introduction of the accoutrements of such a nation, such as universities (initially one, in Athens).

It is against this background that Yannaras' account of his own development needs to be seen (as well as his account of the state of theology, and culture generally, in Greece in works such as his *Orthodoxy and the West*[4]). Greece had

Stelios Ramfos

Copyright © *Kathimerini* – Yiannis Bardopoulos

---

[3] For a less personal account, see *Anataraxeis sti Metapolemiki Theologia: I «Theologia tou '60»*, ed. P. Kalaïtzidis, Th. N. Papathanasiou, Th. Ampatzidis (Athens: Indiktos, 2009). For my understanding of Yannaras, especially the early years, I am indebted to the Durham University PhD thesis of my former research student, Evaggelia Grigoropoulou, 'The Early Development of the Thought of Christos Yannaras' (2008), though I have not been able to consult it in preparing this chapter.

[4] Christos Yannaras, *Orthodoxy and the West*, trans. Peter Chamberas and Norman Russell (Brookline, MA: Holy Cross Orthodox Press, 2006); trans. of *Orthodoxia kai Dysi sti Neoteri Ellada* (Athens: Domos, 1992).

emerged from the Ottoman yoke as the result of a series of bloody wars (ending with the disastrous Greek invasion of what was becoming Turkey, the homeland for many Orthodox Greeks, in the early 1920s); the German occupation and the subsequent civil war only added to the condition of devastation and despair.

Many of the attempts to restore the fortunes of Greece involved the adoption of Western models. In the religious sphere, this included the establishment of theological faculties on the German model in Athens and eventually Thessaloniki, and in the sphere of religious life, movements of revival and missionary endeavour, the principal of which was the movement Zoë ('Life'). Christos Yannaras himself was a member of Zoë for several years, a period of which he gives a scathing account in the first volume of his autobiography, *Katafygio ideon*. Zoë grew from the missionary activity of Apostolos Makrakes and Fr Eusebios Matthopoulos in the latter half of the nineteenth century; it was a brotherhood of men, by the 1950s about 90 men, all graduates, mostly from the Faculty of Theology in Athens, both priests and laymen, devoted to religious revival in Greece. A positive account of this movement, written in the 1950s, can be found in Peter Hammond's book, *The Waters of Marah: The Present State of the Greek Church*.[5]

Christos Yannaras
With permission of Christos Yannaras

---

[5] Peter Hammond, *The Waters of Marah: The Present State of the Greek Church* (London: Rockliff, 1956).

Yannaras' account is much less sanguine, drawing attention to the regimented and moralistic pattern of life it inculcated, its almost Manichaean attitude to sexual relations, its detachment from, or independence of, the authentic life of the Orthodox Church, and bound up with that its reliance on Western pietistic models, both Protestant and Catholic (for instance, Opus Dei). When Yannaras arrived in Bonn, he found himself in an environment all too familiar, and repellent – that of a kind of extra-ecclesial sect. He began to feel deeply the polarities that he was to wrestle with for the rest of his life: Orthodoxy–the West, Greece–Europe, tradition–ideology, Church–religion.[6]

He then moved to Paris, and encountered the Russian Orthodoxy of the diaspora; he seems not to have made much of the Greeks in Paris: he speaks more warmly of the Russians he met – Nicolas Lossky, Boris Bobrinskoy, Pierre Struve, Michel Evdokimov, and the French Orthodox thinker Olivier Clément, who belonged with the Russians – of the Russian cathedral in rue Daru, and the French-speaking Russian Orthodox parish of Notre-Dame des Affligés et Ste Geneviève, which belongs to the Moscow Patriarchate, founded by Vladimir Lossky and Leonid Ouspensky, among others, by then, as it still is, in rue St-Victor. He was also conscious of the heritage of the so-called Paris School of Russian Orthodox theology.[7] It was this experience that gave him some of the fixed points for the way his theology was to begin to develop.

Dimitris Koutroubis

There were, however, other influences that led Yannaras from the confines of Zoë to his distinctive style of theology and philosophy. Notable among these was the Greek lay theologian Dimitris Koutroubis. We have already met him, receiving the Holy Gifts together with Philip Sherrard in Athens in 1956: Philip's first communion as Orthodox, and Koutroubis' first communion after his return to Orthodoxy from spending some time in the West and becoming a member of the Roman Catholic Church.

Dimitris Koutroubis was born in Athens in 1921.[8] Initially he sought to become a doctor, but his studies were cut short by an accident, from which he nearly died. In the prolonged period of convalescence, he began to reflect more deeply on spiritual questions, and came in touch with the Jesuits in Athens. Impressed by their theological learning, and the services of the Latin Rite, he decided to join the Society of Jesus, and in 1946 became a Jesuit novice at Manresa House, in Roehampton, south London. He began his philosophical studies at Heythrop College, then in Oxfordshire near Chipping Norton, and continued them at the Scholastic House of Studies at Fourvière,

---

[6] See Yannaras, *Ta kath' eauton*, 41–3. On Zoë, see also Ampatzidis' paper in *Anataraxeis*, 17–51.

[7] See Yannaras, *Ta kath' eauton*, 87–94.

[8] All the biographical material is drawn from '*In Memoriam Demetrios Koutroubis*', collection of tributes to him by (then) Bishop Kallistos of Diokleia, Elias Mastroiannopoulos, Christos Yannaras and A. M. Allchin, *Sobornost/ECR* 6:1 (1984), 67–77.

Dimitris Koutroubis
Copyright © David Paskett PPRWS

Lyon, where Henri de Lubac was still teaching, and there was keen interest in the Greek Fathers. In 1950 he was transferred to Beirut, where he taught at the Université St Joseph. While there Dimitris became less happy among the Jesuits, and he began to feel the attraction of his Orthodox roots. As Metropolitan Kallistos puts it, drawing on his own memories of Koutroubis, 'Childhood memories of his mother's piety, the influence of de Lubac's writing on the Greek Fathers, and meetings with Fr Lev Gillet, all drew him towards Orthodoxy'.[9]

In May 1952, at his own request, he was released from the Society of Jesus. He travelled widely, and in 1954 settled in Athens with his widowed mother. In 1956, as we have seen, he became once more a member of the Orthodox Church. After a brief period working for the refugee service of the United Nations in Greece, he lived, for many years with his mother, in conditions of hardship and poverty in Greece. He exercised what was to be a considerable influence entirely through personal contact. Again to quote Metropolitan Kallistos:

---

[9] Bishop Kallistos et al., '*In Memoriam*', 68.

With rare sensitivity, in a hidden self-effacing way, he succeeded in creating an environment – a 'little oasis', as he termed it – in which he and his friends could together explore the meaning of God, the world and their own selves.[10]

He was involved, with others, such as Yannaras and Panayiotis Nellas, in the journal *Synoro* ('Frontier'), which appeared from 1964 until April 1967, when the military junta seized power. He spent the last few years of his life in England, near the Shrine of Our Lady at Walsingham, and died in Downham Market in March 1983. After his death, a volume of his essays and reviews was published, *I Charis tis Theologias* ('The Grace of Theology'),[11] which gives some impression of his approach to theology. Several of the pieces collected here were published after his death in *Synaxi* (which could be regarded as a successor to the journal *Synoro*, closed down by the colonels); otherwise they seem to have been published between 1959 and the mid-1960s, and could be regarded as introducing the works of the Paris School to the Greeks. There are reviews of Meyendorff's books on Palamas, of Myrrha Lot-Borodine's book on Nicolas Cabasilas (as much on her as him), works by Evdokimov (*L'Orthodoxie* and *La Femme et le salut du monde*), a brief review called 'The Throne of Wisdom', which takes its title from the book by Louis Bouyer, the French Oratorian priest, a convert from Protestantism who was deeply interested in the Russian tradition, and includes remarks on Evdokimov's book on woman, and a book, 'known already to readers of *Zoë*',[12] by the Protestant monk from Taizé, Max Thurian.

Even that brief, and incomplete, survey of only one section of the book gives some impression of the range of Koutroubis' interests: the patristic theology of the Russians in Paris, understood in no narrow sense, but aware of, and appreciative of, its echoes among Catholics and Protestants. There are also a couple of articles on the Vatican Council that was to dominate the 1960s, at least in the West. Koutroubis, one might say, was alive to the signs of new life in the Orthodox theology of the diaspora, of its ecumenical implications, as well as the way in which it could become a source of new life for Orthodox theology in Greece.

Christos Yannaras, in his tribute to Koutroubis in *Sobornost*, sees the theology of modern Greece as 'divided into the period before Demetrios Koutroubis and the period after him'.[13] He summarized the changes in these terms:

> For we have seen the wonderful rebirth of monastic spirituality on the Holy Mountain; the reuniting of theology with the eucharistic foundations of religious truth and liturgical experience; the re-examination of the criteria of Orthodoxy in the apophatic language of the Fathers, as well as through

---

[10] Bishop Kallistos et al., '*In Memoriam*', 68–70.
[11] D. K. Koutroubis, *I Charis tis Theologias* (Athens: Domos, 1995).
[12] Koutroubis, *Charis*, 227.
[13] Bishop Kallistos et al., '*In Memoriam*', 72.

ascetic discipline and inner prayer; the awakening of the consciousness of the parish as a community; the search for answers to the problems of modern man by means of Orthodox tradition.[14]

He goes on to speak of Koutroubis as 'the first to speak the "new" language':

> It was he who wrote the earliest articles in Greek about the theology of St Gregory Palamas and St Nicolas Cabasilas, he who translated for the first time the texts of the great theologians of the Russian diaspora, and – above all – he who gathered around himself a new generation of theologians and trained them by means of the discreet humility of his Socratic method.[15]

Koutroubis' disciples made their own way: he enabled his disciples to think for themselves, he helped them to find the freedom to embrace the new, while drawing strength and inspiration from the tradition of the Orthodox Church, a tradition both dogmatic and ascetic, concerned both with what we believe and how we pray.

Yannaras and Heidegger

Yannaras' own words bear testimony to what he owed Koutroubis, but he found his own way, as he encountered philosophical and theological traditions in the West. In the Paris School (among whom one must include Vladimir Lossky, though he did not belong to the circles of the Institut St-Serge), he discovered Jean-Paul Sartre: one of the chapters of *Ta kath' eauton* begins with the words, *Agápisa ton Sartre* – 'I loved Sartre'.[16] What he found in Heidegger (and in a way in Sartre) was an analysis of the history of Western philosophy and culture that made sense of the polarities, such as Orthodoxy–the West, that he had found himself struggling with from his arrival in the West in Bonn.

Put simply, too simply, I expect, Heidegger's indictment of the Western metaphysical tradition from Plato onwards (like many modern thinkers, he makes much more of the pre-Socratic philosophers such as Herakleitos and Parmenides) is that it treats the ultimate – God or the Absolute – as a being alongside other beings, even though it is thought of as transcendent, and thus in some way removed from ordinary finite beings. Heidegger called such a metaphysics 'ontotheology', a study of, or account of, God (*theos*) thought of in terms of being (the root *ont-* is a form of the verb 'to be'). Such a theology is ultimately incoherent: it makes no sense to think of a being as the source of being. This is no new problem: the metaphysics of the great scholastic theologian, Thomas Aquinas, tries to solve it by the doctrine of analogy, according to which we are indeed not using the verb 'to be' in precisely the same way when we say that God is, and that human beings are, or a tree is: we are using the verb 'to be' analogically, not in the same way,

---

[14] Bishop Kallistos et al., '*In Memoriam*', 72.
[15] Bishop Kallistos et al., '*In Memoriam*', 72.
[16] Yannaras, *Ta kath' eauton*, 104.

but not in utterly unrelated ways either. Whether the doctrine of analogy, in this context usually called *analogia entis*, solves the problem is a matter of discussion. For Heidegger it makes little difference: what we have is simply a more sophisticated version of ontotheology, which only disguises, but does not remove, the incoherence of thinking of the Ultimate in terms of being. For Heidegger, the incoherence of ontotheology leads inexorably to atheism, or more dramatically to the doctrine of the 'death of God', of which Nietzsche spoke so eloquently in, for example, *Die fröhliche Wissenschaft* (traditionally translated as *The Gay Science*).

It was shortly after discovering Heidegger that Yannaras discovered the Russian theologians of the diaspora, not least Vladimir Lossky, whose influence was strong in Paris, as it still is, though he had died in 1958, before Yannaras arrived there. Lossky is known, and not mistakenly, as a proponent of the apophatic nature of theology, and in his development of apophatic theology makes much of the writings attributed to Dionysios the Areopagite. Yannaras saw the more strictly philosophical implications of the apophatic, in particular, how the notion of the apophatic provides something of an answer to the bankruptcy of the Western philosophical tradition, as Heidegger had expounded it. It was in the 1960s when Yannaras arrived in the West: the decade of the 'Death of God' theology, which was itself a manifestation of the end of the road for Western theistic metaphysics. Of course, it was not as simple as that, for the Western theistic metaphysical tradition had rather more resources than those who proclaimed the death of God bargained for. Nevertheless for many in the West – my contemporaries, reading theology in the sixties – much Western theology seemed to have run into the sand. Yannaras' take on this was rather different from that of many of the students and teachers of the 1960s in the West; he accepted the critique of Nietzsche and Heidegger of the Western metaphysical tradition, their conviction of the cultural death of God and the utter inadequacy of what Heidegger dubbed ontotheology, but saw this not as a judgement on the Christian gospel, but rather a judgement on a way of thinking about God as a being, or a concept, that formed part of the mental world of Western philosophy.

It was in the mysterious author of the *Corpus Areopagiticum*, who called himself after the apostle Paul's convert, Dionysios the Areopagite of Acts 17, that Yannaras found the true tradition of Christian thought that had been misunderstood and distorted in the West, and even in much of the East. Central to Dionysios' theology was the conviction that God is utterly unknowable, we can say nothing about him, we cannot capture him in our concepts, nor can we construct an ontology that applies to him. What Yannaras took from his reading of Dionysios in the light of Heidegger went beyond this; indeed, the host of books that he wrote after *Heidegger and the Areopagite*,[17]

---

[17] Christos Yannaras, *Heidegger kai Areopagitis* (first published as a thesis, Athens, 1967; Athens: Ekdoseis Dodoni, 1972; 2nd rev. edn, Athens: Domos, 1988); ET: *On the Absence and Unknowability of God: Heidegger and the Areopagite* (London: T&T Clark, 2005).

and continues to write, can be regarded as exploring all the avenues that this commanding insight opened up.

The apophatic and personhood

If Yannaras took the notion of the apophatic from Lossky, and through him from Dionysios the Areopagite, he took something else from Lossky: his conviction that the unknowability of God, acknowledged by the fundamentally apophatic nature of theology, makes the knowledge of God something quite different from our knowledge of other beings: it is not a matter of putting together information drawn from various sources and building up an understanding of God, which we call theology. It is really an opening of ourselves to the mystery of the Trinity, an opening of ourselves in which we come to understand ourselves as personal, as related to one another, as sharing in experience. For Lossky, the personal is only revealed through the mystery of the Trinity, through the perception of relatedness in the Ultimate. And yet the personal is not something beyond our experience: it comes through openness to experience of the Other. For personhood itself is beyond conceptualization:

> Personality can only be grasped in this life by a direct intuition; it can only be expressed in a work of art. When we say 'this is by Mozart', or 'this is by Rembrandt', we are in both cases dealing with a personal world which has no equivalent anywhere.[18]

The apophatic and the personal reflect each other, as it were, but not in a merely conceptual way: it is only the person that can make the apophatic approach to the divine mystery, for the apophatic is concerned with a personal, or existential, attitude. Lossky spoke of the 'apophatic way of Eastern theology [as] the repentance of the human person before the face of the living God'.[19]

All of this resonated deeply with Yannaras. Where he differs from Lossky is in his seeing the *philosophical* implications of the apophatic and the personal: philosophical implications concerned with a whole range of questions to do with being human, not just how we know and how we love, but political and economic questions, and again more recently fundamental philosophical questions.[20]

The most fundamental of Yannaras' books is perhaps his *Person and Eros*,[21] originally a doctoral thesis submitted at the University of Thessaloniki in

---

[18] Vladimir Lossky, *The Mystical Theology of the Eastern Church* (London: James Clarke, 1957), 53. Yannaras uses virtually the same example in his *Heidegger and the Areopagite*, 85.

[19] Lossky, *Mystical Theology*, 239.

[20] For a brief, but valuable, account of Yannaras as a philosopher, see Sotiris Mitralexis, 'Person, Eros, Critical Ontology: An Attempt to Recapitulate Christos Yannaras' Philosophy', *Sobornost/ECR* 34:1 (2012), 33–40.

[21] Christos Yannaras, *To prosopo kai o eros* (Athens: Ekdoseis Domos, 4th edn, 1987); ET: *Person and Eros*, trans. Norman Russell (Brookline, MA: Holy Cross Orthodox Press, 2007).

1970, called 'The ontological content of the theological notion of the person'.[22] It is a quite extraordinary book – at one level rigorously philosophical, but at another level, grounded in a living experience. The West tends to keep these in separate compartments, to the detriment of both. To engage with this book at any depth would go beyond the limits of this chapter. All I can do here is point to his discussions of the nature of personhood in its ecstatic character, its universality (or 'catholicity') and its unity; the way the notion of the person penetrates an understanding of the cosmos, of space and time; the idea of *logos*, in its authentic sense, as rooted in the disclosure of the person, and closely related to the notion of image; and the long analysis of nothingness, inspired by, but quite different from, Heidegger's discussion in *Sein und Zeit*. Central to Yannaras' understanding of personhood – an idea already adumbrated in *Heidegger and the Areopagite* – is the term 'mode of existence', *tropos hyparxeos*, one of the characterizations of *hypostasis* or person suggested by the Cappadocian Fathers in the fourth century and developed in the seventh by St Maximos, in contrast to (though not, I think, in opposition to) nature as characterized by the principle of being, *logos ousias*. The way of existence, which is personhood, is not predetermined, like our human nature, as a collection of properties, but is the way our human nature is lived out, or expressed, in a personal way of existence experienced as self-transcendence – an ecstatic moving beyond oneself in loving freedom. This perception is the starting point of Yannaras' thought, a notion that is explored at length in the first part of *Person and Eros*, the longest of the four parts of the book. What, in my view, makes Yannaras' thought distinctive among adherents of what could seem a fashionable 'personalist existentialism' is the care and thoroughness with which he explores this notion from a philosophical perspective.

Anti-Westernism?

There is another feature of Yannaras' thought that runs through his work, and which some find rather disconcerting; it is possibly one of the reasons for his lack of influence in the West. This is what appears to be a consistent anti-Westernism. Yannaras, as we have seen, accepts Heidegger's analysis, according to which the West is tied to ontotheology, and embarked on a course leading to atheism and the cultural death of God. Yannaras develops this analysis, drawing frequently on Heidegger himself, and comes up with a view of the West that has abandoned the original understanding of the gospel and the Church, and settled into a rationalist and legalistic understanding of human existence, subject to law and custom; this course was bound, sooner or later, to turn to the ashes of nihilism, while at the same time reducing value to

---

[22] *To ontologikon periechomenon tis theologikis ennoias tou prosopou*, Athens, 1970. I am grateful to the former Archbishop of Canterbury, Rowan Williams, now Lord Williams of Oystermouth, for the loan of this rare book.

price and ushering in the consumerism that is so marked in modern Western society (and one of its most successful, and baleful, exports).

These ideas, expressed here all too briefly and crudely, lie at the heart of Yannaras' analysis of the problems facing modern theology, and indeed modern society as a whole. A Western reader is likely to feel that this analysis is too simplistic, and he or she may be right. One needs, however, to acknowledge that Yannaras sees this not as simply a matter of blaming the West for the ills of the modern world, for in his Introduction to the English edition of *Orthodoxy and the West*, he remarks,

> Let me therefore make one thing absolutely clear. The critique of Western theology and tradition which I offer in this book does not contrast 'Western' with something 'right' which as an Orthodox I use to oppose something 'wrong' outside myself. I am not attacking an external Western adversary. As a modern Greek, I myself embody both the thirst for what is 'right' and the reality of what is 'wrong': a contradictory and alienated survival of ecclesiastical Orthodoxy in a society radically and unhappily Westernized. My critical stance towards the West is self-criticism; it refers to my own wholly Western mode of life.
>
> I am a Western person searching for answers to the problems tormenting Western people today . . .[23]

But even if the analysis is too simplistic, *what* it is seeking to analyse is a set of problems that are undeniable: as Yannaras puts it a few lines later, 'the threat to the environment, the assimilation of politics to business models, the yawning gulf between society and the state, the pursuit of ever-greater consumption, the loneliness and weakness of social relations, the prevailing loveless sexuality'. There is no question that we need answers to these issues, nor that, for whatever reason, it is this that Western civilization has created for itself and spawns throughout the world.

There is a great deal more that I could say about Yannaras, and before moving on, I must say something about the rest of his life. We have advanced to the end of the 1960s, and the publication of his books, *Heidegger and the Areopagite*, *Hunger and Thirst*,[24] *The Metaphysics of the Body* (on St John Climacus),[25] the original version of *Person and Eros*, and *The Freedom of Morality*.[26] In the dark, tense days of the rule of the colonels, Yannaras quickly became a highly controversial figure: when *The Freedom of Morality* 'was first published in Greece, it caused an explosion', as an English reviewer put it.[27] Yannaras has remained a controversial figure, and something of an outsider. When Yannaras was eventually appointed to a university chair, as Professor of Philosophy at

---

[23] Yannaras, *Orthodoxy and the West*, viii–ix.

[24] *Peina kai Dipsa* (Athens: Ekdoseis Grigori, 1969; though there was an earlier version as a pamphlet in 1961).

[25] *I metafysiki tou somatos: Spoudi ston Ioanni tis Klimakos* (Athens: Ekdoseis Dodoni, 1971).

[26] *I elefteria tou ithous* (Athens: Ekdoseis Domos, 2nd expanded edn, 1979; original edn, 1970); ET: *The Freedom of Morality*, trans. Elizabeth Brière (Crestwood, NY: St Vladimir's Seminary Press, 1984).

[27] Yannaras, *Ta kath' eauton*, 96. The reference is to *ECR* 5 (1973), 205.

the Panteion University of Social and Political Sciences in Athens, there was an outcry: theologians felt he should have no such public position; secular thinkers felt that such a committed Orthodox thinker should not hold a chair in the new secular university in Athens.[28]

Stelios Ramfos

Ramfos, we have seen, has, since the expulsion of the colonels in 1974, lived and worked in Athens. He has written a very great deal, little of which has been translated into English. In his earlier works, he, like Yannaras, looked to the Orthodox theological tradition for sources of wisdom: *Like a Pelican in the Wilderness*[29] is a series of reflections on the sayings of the Desert Fathers. I shall concentrate on a more recent work, *Yearning for the One: Chapters in the Inner Life of the Greeks* (2000, ET 2011),[30] which is concerned with a notion central to Yannaras, as also to much modern Orthodox theology, the notion of the person.

The notion of personhood

What is striking about Ramfos' approach to the notion of the person is that, unlike most Orthodox thinkers, such as Yannaras and Metropolitan John (Zizioulas), he does not see the notion of the personal as in any way something that is the special preserve of the Orthodox. It often seems to be taken for granted by Orthodox thinkers that the notion of the personal is something that the West has lost, or never knew. To characterize the West as individualistic, and to oppose to that a sense of community and the personal, is to stand in a long tradition: it is commonplace in writing on Russian nineteenth-century literature, and we have seen that all the Russians of the diaspora found themselves at home in making a distinction between the personal and the individual: the person being defined by relations, the individual an isolated monad, cut off from everything and everyone else. Ramfos calls such an analysis in question; indeed he turns it on its head. Through developing a notion of the individual, the West has been able to discover a sense of the personal, while in the East the failure to achieve any adequate sense of individuation has prevented the awareness of any sense of inwardness, necessary, he argues, for an adequate notion of the personal.

Ramfos' *Yearning for the One* begins by surveying the controversy over the personalism of Yannaras and Zizioulas in the Greek world, especially as it emerged in the pages of *Synaxi* with responses to Yannaras' *Person and Eros*

---

[28] See Yannaras' own account: *Ta kath' eauton*, 158–73.

[29] *Pelikanoi erimikoi* (Athens: Ekdoseis Armos, 1994); abridged ET: *Like a Pelican in the Wilderness*, trans. Norman Russell (Brookline, MA: Holy Cross Orthodox Press, 2000).

[30] *I kaimos tou enos* (Athens: Ekdoseis Armos, 2000); abridged ET: *Yearning for the One: Chapters in the Inner Life of the Greeks*, trans. Norman Russell (Brookline, MA: Holy Cross Orthodox Press, 2011).

and Zizioulas' *From Mask to Person* by John Panagopoulos (in *Synaxi* 13–14, 1985) and Savvas Agouridis (in *Synaxi* 33, 1990), to which there were responses by Yannaras and Zizioulas in *Synaxi* 37, 1991. The criticisms of Panagopoulos and Agouridis are pertinent: both find the identification of the gospel with a personalist ontology gravely inadequate. As Panagopoulos puts it (in Ramfos' summary):

> Christ . . . accomplishes a work that is much more important than the historical manifestation of the ontological principle. In his person the created is identified by grace with the uncreated; human nature is assumed in an unconfused union by the divine nature. The personal character of human nature lies in the fact that it receives and manifests by grace the fullness of the Triadic Godhead: human nature is personal because it is theanthropic. The believer manifests the theanthropic hypostasis of Christ in an individual manner and in this sense can become a true person, a real image of him. He can now 'recognize' as an incomprehensible mystery the personal life of the Trinity and thus see reflected in a mirror the mystery of his own truth.[31]

Panagopoulos and Agouridis also object to the finding of the modern notion of the person in the Cappadocian Trinitarian language: a not uncommon criticism.

Ramfos' survey of the controversy takes the discussion on to another level. He sets the whole question of personal existentialism/ontology in a broader context, both theologically (going back to Lossky) and intellectually (scrutinizing Zizioulas' presentation of the way the personal is a distinctive Christian contribution, of which the classical world knew nothing). Ramfos draws on an impressive range of classical scholarship, in contrast to the rather thinly supported case we find in Zizioulas, with whom he sometimes deals quite sharply. Zizioulas, for example, had made play with the 'blind, colourless, cold marble' of Greek statues and drew from it the notion of a cold, impersonal beauty he attributes to the Greeks. As Ramfos points out, such an understanding of Greek statuary is simply mistaken: Greek statues were coloured, and would have seemed anything but 'blind, colourless, cold'. Furthermore, Greek statuary has a history: it cannot be characterized as all the same, as Zizioulas seems to do. All this makes the historical account Zizioulas gives quite unreliable.

Ramfos goes well beyond this, however. Not only does he call in question Zizioulas' narrative of the emergence of the notion of the person in Cappadocian Trinitarian theology (interestingly, his discussion is mostly concerned with Zizioulas; as with Larchet's criticism of their personalism,[32] Yannaras seems entangled with Zizioulas' coat-tails, or should I say mandyas?), he calls in question whether the Greeks ever developed a notion of the personal at all. He sketches out his case in three stages. The first suggests a contrast between the search of the personal in the Latin West and the Greek

---

[31] Ramfos, *Yearning*, 29.
[32] Jean-Claude Larchet, *Personne et nature* (Paris: Cerf, 2011), 207–396.

East. The basis of this is a contrast he explores between St Augustine's search for inwardness, pre-eminently in the *Confessions*, and the, in many ways parallel, search for inwardness in St Gregory the Theologian's poems *peri eautou*, about himself (the parallels are largely due to their common Neoplatonic background). Ramfos sketches out the way in which Augustine's notion of inwardness is developed by Boethius into a notion of the *persona*. He finds a similar exploration of inwardness in Gregory, but finds the notion of inwardness less well developed. As he puts it:

> Although Gregory anticipates Augustine on many points, he differs from him in the following way: he believes that the ancient world soul is humanized through becoming like the divine original on the model of imitation in art. In Augustine this is achieved through the will, which corresponds to humanity's psychological individuality even though the latter is potential rather than actual. In other words, what predominates in Gregory's thinking is optical theory, not the principle and practice of touch.[33]

I find this fascinating, though not altogether pellucid! He goes on to develop the idea that Gregory's thinking remains optical by suggesting that the Byzantine East remains fundamentally symbolic, rather than through inwardness finding contact with ultimate reality, as he finds in Augustine. The contrast Ramfos is delineating seems to me real, and conforms to the perception of others about Augustine's contribution to the history of thought. Another way of putting it would be that Augustine's inwardness absorbs all ontological categories, whereas Gregory's comparative toying with inwardness leaves intact a sense of the cosmic. Ramfos, however, is quite clear that it is the Augustinian route that we need to emulate, and in this he is quite unusual among Orthodox thinkers. I wonder, however, how much is lost by the cosmic being swallowed up by the inward.

The second stage of Ramfos' endeavour is to document the way in which the Byzantine and later Greek East failed to achieve individuation: the discussion is learned and fascinating, but we cannot pause over it here. The final stage is concerned to show how the lack of individuation has prevented the development of the notion of the personal, so vaunted as the achievement of the Orthodox tradition by Yannaras and Zizioulas. What he has argued, it seems to me, is that, whatever might be meant by an opposition between the individual and the person, without some notion of individuation relations, on their own, are insufficient to generate a notion of the personal. (Ramfos does have an idea of how the Byzantine tradition might have developed a sense of the personal, through making more of the notion of *enhypostasia*, which he finds in Leontios of Byzantium and St Maximos the Confessor. We cannot pursue this now, not least because in my view the notion of *enhypostasia*, far from being 'deposited in the Orthodox Christian tradition',[34] is in reality a not-very-bright idea, thought up by the nineteenth-century

---

[33] Ramfos, *Yearning*, 117.

[34] Ramfos, *Yearning*, 286.

German scholar Friedrich Loofs, that has had an extraordinarily long run for its money!)

The third stage develops this notion of *enhypostasia*, and gathers together some reflections on person, community, history and tradition. There is much that is interesting in this final section, and many wise observations, but it reads too much like a tract for the times, and especially the present times in Greece, to express anything very clearly. There are problems with a society facing modernity; some solutions are suggested by the collective wisdom of the Greeks, but these solutions do not go deep enough.

What, perhaps, is most important about Ramfos is his willingness to embrace the challenges of modernity, and learn from them, not simply flee before them. In doing this he strikes notes that will seem discordant to many Orthodox. His attitude to Philokalic spirituality is mostly rather negative (though that is true of some of Yannaras' more recent utterances, in contrast to the way he characterized the new way of Greek theology in his tribute to Koutroubis[35]). His emphasis on the need for the person to have inwardness, as well as related-ness, seems to me well made, but there seem to me problems, for the Western way of inwardness has eclipsed the ancient notion of the cosmic, with poten-tially dire consequences, both for who we are as human beings, and for our relationship to the world in which we live.

Another, related, aspect of Ramfos' thought that we should heed is his willingness to learn from the West. Augustine is not demonized, but represents a positive step in the intellectual history of the West, to which the Orthodox East belongs, through our common debt to the classical tradition and the Christian Scriptures.

Orthodoxy and the West – again

I want to end with a more general point. It is a fairly constant contention in the Orthodox thinkers we have been looking at that the Orthodox have preserved a deeper sense of the personal, and not allowed it to be reduced to the notion of the individual. But reflection on the nature of the personal often remains at the level of the rhetorical: there is not much analysis, rather that adoption of a certain, generally anti-Western, stance. Part of the reason for the emphasis we find among the Russian thinkers of the diaspora on the personal is the way it chimed in with the kind of personal existen-tialism that was popular in Western intellectual circles in the middle of the twentieth century. Much has been thought and written in the West on the notion of the personal; it is by no means something neglected or overlooked. Yannaras is from time to time aware of this; he speaks appreciatively of the Protestant psychiatrist and psychotherapist Paul Tournier, whose book,

---

[35] See Yannaras' ultimately negative account of the *Philokalia* and St Nikodimos in *Orthodoxy and the West*, 126–37, though he begins quite positively, noting the role of the *Philokalia* in 'initiating the "theological spring" of the sixties' (128).

The Meaning of Persons (in the original, *Le Personnage et la personne*), was popular in the 1950s and 1960s.[36] The Gifford Lectures, given by the Scottish philosopher John Macmurray, in 1953–4, were entitled *The Form of the Personal*.[37] More recently, the German philosopher Robert Spaemann has seen his book on persons published in English translation as *Persons: The Difference between 'Someone' and 'Something'*.[38] Orthodox reading this book will find some things said that are often claimed as distinctively Orthodox:

> For Aristotle the *noēsis noēseōs*, the divine consciousness, must, as the solitary 'One', lie beyond being, like the Platonic good. To think of God as Absolute Being, by contrast, means to think that in himself he has what it is to be another – *another*, not *other*. That is to think of him as Trinity, an always-open sphere of mutual Letting-be.[39]

> The idea of a single person existing in the world cannot be thought, for although the identity of any one person is unique, personhood as such arises only in plurality. That is why philosophical monotheism is invariably ambiguous: either it advances to become trinitarianism, or it slips back into pantheism. The thought of a single unipersonal divinity depends upon a concept of the person that has lost touch with its historical roots. We began to speak of God as a person only when we began to speak of three persons in one God.[40]

> But to think of a personal God, which is to say, a three-personal God, is to think of an inwardness that does not incessantly slip away to become objective, but has inward being precisely in self-utterance, looking on himself, and looked on, through 'another of himself'. This thought is what transforms the idea of timelessness from indifference into eternity, what Augustine called a 'permanent now'.[41]

Persons is a short, but densely written, book, and discusses questions such as transcendence, fiction, religion, time, death and the future perfect tense, souls, conscience, recognition, freedom, promise and forgiveness: all topics we need to consider if we are to develop an adequate notion of the personal. The anti-Westernism of much Orthodox theology is self-mutilating, if it prevents us from attending to such traditions of thought in the West.

---

[36] Paul Tournier, *The Meaning of Persons* (London: SCM Press, 1957). See Yannaras, *Katafygio ideon*, 295–6.

[37] Published as *The Self as Agent; Persons in Relation* (London: Faber & Faber, 1957–61).

[38] Robert Spaemann, *Persons: The Difference between 'Someone' and 'Something'*, trans. Oliver O'Donovan (Oxford: Oxford University Press, 2006).

[39] Spaemann, *Persons*, 68.

[40] Spaemann, *Persons*, 40.

[41] Spaemann, *Persons*, 111.

17

Lay theologians: 3 Elisabeth Behr-Sigel, Olivier Clément

It occurs to me that these three chapters on 'Lay theologians' might well have been called 'Orthodoxy and the modern world': the thinkers we have discussed in the last two chapters – Philip Sherrard, Dimitris Koutroubis, Christos Yannaras and Stelios Ramfos – have all been concerned to relate the insights of Orthodoxy to the modern world, conceived of in different ways: culture, literature, politics, and also the way in which modernity has come to be characterized by what is called globalization, a sense of the presence to one another of different cultures, once separated geographically, now living side by side, an experience found in microcosm with Orthodoxy in the West.

Deux passeurs

We shall discuss two French thinkers and theologians, who have a great deal in common: they were near contemporaries, Behr-Sigel being nearly 15 years older than Clément; both were converts to Orthodoxy, the one from a family in Alsace, non-practising but not hostile to religion, the other from the secularism that marked the teaching profession in France, though in his parents' case without actual hostility to religion, as was often the case among French teachers. Both came to Orthodoxy through their encounter with the Orthodox in Paris (one before the Second World War, one after). Both embraced Orthodoxy without rejecting their past, and both were deeply committed to ecumenism, having wide contacts throughout the world of Western Christendom. Both were deeply concerned to relate the insights they had come to through being Orthodox to the world in which they lived, and were conscious of the danger of Orthodoxy settling for an isolated position in the modern world, exotic, maybe, but irrelevant. They were also close friends and collaborators: both were for many years on the editorial board of the journal *Contacts*, perhaps the finest journal of modern Orthodox theology and thinking.

Clément wrote a book on Lossky and Evdokimov, called *Deux passeurs* – 'Two people who pass between one culture and another', as one has to say long-windedly in English (the dictionary equivalents of *passeur* are ferryman, smuggler!). We might call our two thinkers *deux passeurs*, two who made the transition from the secularized, or semi-secularized, condition of the West to the experience of Orthodoxy, while still remaining in the West.

Elisabeth Behr-Sigel

Olivier Clément

Behr–Sigel: Life

Elisabeth Behr-Sigel was born in 1907 in Schiltigheim, near Strasbourg, in Alsace, then part of the German Empire.[1] Her father was a Protestant from Alsace, her mother Jewish of Middle European ancestry; neither of them was particularly religious, or anti-religious. She studied philosophy at the University of Strasbourg, and then, having become an active Christian, became one of the first women to study theology at the Protestant Faculty in Strasbourg. Already she was being drawn to Orthodoxy, primarily by the liturgy and worship, and especially through participation in the Easter Vigil, and the experience of the joy of the Resurrection. Her thesis at Strasbourg was on the nineteenth-century Russian theologian Aleksandr Bukharev, to which she returned many years later, submitting a doctoral thesis on him to the University of Nancy-II in 1976, which was published a year later.

Having graduated in theology, she became for a time a pastoral assistant in the Reformed Church, desperately short of clergy after the carnage of the First World War. By this time she was already Orthodox – she was received into the Orthodox Church by Fr Lev Gillet in December 1929, in Strasbourg – but she held this position until her marriage to André Behr in 1933, when she moved with her husband to Nancy. During her studies on Bukharev, she came into contact with various Orthodox thinkers in Paris, especially Fr Sergii Bulgakov, as well as others more of her generation such as Paul Evdokimov, Vladimir Lossky and Evgraf Kovalevsky, who were also committed to giving Orthodoxy liturgical expression in French. With them she found an understanding of Orthodoxy 'open at once to Western thought and to dialogue with other Christian Churches'.[2] In Paris, too, she met Fr Lev Gillet, a former Benedictine monk of Amay (later Chevetogne), who had himself just passed from Eastern-rite Catholicism to Orthodoxy.

From 1939 until 1975, Elisabeth (Liselotte, as she was known to her friends) taught literature and philosophy at lycées, mostly in Nancy. Increasingly after the war she became involved in the ecumenical movement, working for the journal *Dieu Vivant*, and from 1947 participating in the meetings of the Anglican–Orthodox Fellowship of St Alban and St Sergius, to which Fr Lev became the Orthodox chaplain, living in London at St Basil's House in Ladbroke Grove. She had strong links with the Abbey of Chevetogne, the monks of which followed the Benedictine and Eastern Rites in parallel, as part of their commitment to deepening links between Catholicism and Orthodoxy, as well as with the Carmelite sisters of Montbard (Côte-d'Or).

---

[1] For Behr-Sigel's life, see primarily Olga Lossky, *Vers le jour sans déclin: Une vie d'Élisabeth Behr-Sigel (1907–2005)* (Paris: Cerf, 2007); there is an abridged ET published by the Fellowship of St Alban and St Sergius. See also the tributes gathered in *Contacts* 220 (October–December 2007), and the obituary by Marcus Plested in *Sobornost/ECR* 27:2 (2005), 62–4. For her theology, see Sarah Hinlicky Wilson, *Woman, Women, and the Priesthood in the Trinitarian Theology of Elisabeth Behr-Sigel* (London: Bloomsbury T&T Clark, 2013).

[2] Quoted by Fr Boris Bobrinskoy in *Contacts* 220, 398.

As already mentioned, she served on the editorial committee of *Contacts* for 45 years.

After the death of her husband in 1969, Elisabeth moved to the Paris region, soon settling at Épinay-sur-Seine, where she spent the last 35 years of her life. She became a member of the French-speaking parish in the crypt of the cathedral of St Alexander Nevsky in rue Daru in the centre of Paris. Père Bobrinskoy remarks how she was very attentive to any depreciation of the place of women in the sacramental life of the Church; under her influence, Fr Bobrinskoy learnt to take baby girls, as well as baby boys, into the altar of the church during the ceremony of Entry into the Church of newly baptized children.

...themes and writings

A central theme of Elisabeth's theology was the place of women in the Church, and in particular the ordination of women. She had a great influence on attitudes to the ordination of women: an example being Metropolitan Kallistos Ware's change in attitude to the question in the last decades of the twentieth century.[3] The question of the place of women was, however, really part of a much wider issue, the place of Orthodoxy in the modern world. The place of women was just one of the more obvious ways in which the Orthodox Church found itself ill at ease in the modern Western world – with the result that its message was compromised, if heard at all.

In the period 1970–90, Elisabeth was much involved in teaching as a theologian: at the Institut St-Serge and the Institut Supérieur d'Études Œcuméniques in Paris, at the Ecumenical Institute in Bossey, associated with the World Council of Churches, the Ecumenical Institute of Tantur, in Jerusalem, and at the Dominican College of Theology and Philosophy in Ottawa, as well as at the fledgling Institute for Orthodox Christian Studies in Cambridge, UK. It was in these years that most of her books were published: *Prière et sainteté dans l'Église russe*,[4] her thesis on Bukharev (1977),[5] *Le Lieu du cœur*,[6] two works on the ministry of women, *Le Ministère de la femme dans l'Église*[7] and *L'Ordination de femmes dans l'Église orthodoxe* (1998),[8] her biography of Lev Gillet, *Lev Gillet,*

---

[3] Compare his contributions to the two editions of *Women and the Priesthood*, ed. Thomas Hopko (Crestwood, NY: St Vladimir's Seminary Press, 1983; 2nd edn, 1999), and Fr Hopko's remarks in the Preface to the second edition (p. 1). From being firmly opposed to the ordination of women, Metropolitan Kallistos is now unconvinced by the arguments adduced by opponents (including his own) and regards the question as open, in need of further reflection.

[4] *Prière et sainteté dans l'Église russe* (Paris: Cerf, 1950; reissued: Spiritualité Orientale 33; Bégrolles-en-Mauge: Abbaye de la Bellefontaine, 1982).

[5] *Alexandre Boukharev: Un théologien de l'Église orthodoxe russe en dialogue avec le monde moderne* (Paris: Éditions Beauchesne, 1977).

[6] *Le Lieu du cœur: Initiation à la spiritualité de l'Église orthodoxe* (Paris: Cerf, 1989); ET: *The Place of the Heart: Introduction to Orthodox Spirituality*, trans. Stephen Bigham (Torrance, CA: Oakwood, 1992).

[7] *Le Ministère de la femme dans l'Église* (Paris: Cerf, 1987); ET: *The Ministry of Women in the Church*, trans. Stephen Bigham (Redondo Beach, CA: Oakwood, 1991).

[8] *L'Ordination de femmes dans l'Église orthodoxe* with Kallistos Ware (Paris: Cerf, 1998); ET: *The Ordination of Women in the Orthodox Church* (Geneva: WCC Publications, 2000).

«*un moine de l'Église d'Orient*» (1993),[9] and her final collection of articles, *Discerner les signes du temps* (2002).[10] To two of these books – *Le Lieu du cœur* and *L'Ordination de femmes* – Metropolitan Kallistos contributed or collaborated.[11] Elisabeth died, on the night of 25/26 November 2005, in her flat in Épinay, at the age of 98.

Clément: Life

Olivier Clément's life was in one way fairly straightforward.[12] He was born in 1921 at Aniane (Hérault) in the south of France, near the Mediterranean, to which he remained deeply attached all his life. His parents were school-teachers, atheists, like many at that time (and since), though not aggressively so. In his childhood Olivier became obsessed by death and what there might be afterwards. Intellectually very gifted, he finished his secondary education in 1939, and entered the University of Montpellier to read history, for which he had a passion. There in Vichy France, he benefited from having outstand-ing professors who had left German-occupied France in Paris and the north. Among them were distinguished historians such as Marc Bloch, one of the founders of the *Annales* school, and the great Christian historian (and much else), Henri-Irénée Marrou. He was also impressed by Alphonse Dupront, a great historian of religion, with whom he joined the Resistance. In 1943, he passed the *agrégation* in history at an exceptionally early age.

In the following years, Clément read widely, trying to quench his spir-itual thirst, turning to the Indian religions, Judaism, especially the Kabbalah, and esoteric traditions, such as alchemy. He read Nicolas Berdyaev, and was deeply attracted by his sense of the person and the significance of the human face (which he was later to find in the Jewish-Lithuanian philosopher, Emmanuel Levinas). He also discovered Dostoevsky. Finally he read Vladimir Lossky's *Essai sur la théologie mystique de l'Église d'Orient*, published in 1944, which converted him to Christianity, and led him to search out the author and ask for baptism; he was baptized in the Orthodox Church in November 1952 at the age of 30. By this time Clément was teaching at the famous Lycée Louis le Grand in Paris, where he remained until he retired. After his baptism, he became a faithful disciple of Vladimir Lossky, attending his courses

---

[9] *Lev Gillet, «un moine de l'Église d'Orient»* (Paris: Cerf, 1993); ET: *Lev Gillet, 'A Monk of the Eastern Church'*, trans. Helen Wright (Oxford: Fellowship of St Alban and St Sergius, 1999).

[10] *Discerning the Signs of the Times: The Vision of Elisabeth Behr-Sigel*, ed. Michael Plekon and Sarah E. Hinlicky (Crestwood, NY: St Vladimir's Seminary Press, 2001); in French, *Discerner les signes du temps* (Paris: Cerf, 2002).

[11] For an extensive (surely complete) bibliography of Elisabeth's works, see Hinlicky Wilson, *Woman, Women, and the Priesthood*, 167–82.

[12] Information on his life is more difficult of access. See Nicholas Lossky's obituary in *Sobornost/ECR* 31:1 (2009), 61–3. *Contacts* 228 (October–December 2009) was a tribute to him; apart from the tributes at his funeral and messages *in memoriam* (383–406), it contains Clément's own 'Notes autobiographiques', and what is described as a 'bibliographie succincte' (not at all complete); the rest of it consists of pieces by Clément himself; see also *Contacts* 247 (July–September 2014).

at the Institut St-Denis. After Lossky's untimely death in 1958, Clément was instrumental in preserving his legacy, helping to complete the thesis that Lossky had been engaged on for many years for the *doctorat d'état*, which was published posthumously, writing a long essay on the theology of Lossky, published in the *Messager* of the Exarchate of the Russian Patriarchate, and later in his book, *Deux passeurs*, which used the notes he had taken of Lossky's lectures, later published separately. Later Clément taught at the Institut St-Serge, belonging to the Russian jurisdiction under the Œcumenical Patriarchate.

By his own confession – and it is evident from his works – he owes a great deal to the thought of the Orthodox Russians, without ignoring the Byzantine or Syrian traditions. Furthermore, although conscious of the apparent polarity between 'Russian religious thought' and the 'neo-patristic synthesis', he is keen to transcend it, while learning from both traditions. He speaks of the role Paul Evdokimov and Père Vladimir Zelinsky played in helping him to overcome this tension.[13] His urge to reconcile contradictions without losing anything from either side seems to me to run deep. Clément presents his journey as one of finding doors to open, not shutting doors behind him. Even the atheism of his parents is presented as a stage in his life, not something abandoned. His urge to reconcile lies behind his engagement with ecumenism, not so much at the level of official discussions as at the level of personal engagement.

He met Pope John Paul II in Rome in 1996, at the request of the pope, who had been impressed by his book, *Corps de mort et de gloire*.[14] He has something of the dragoman about him, helping people communicate with each other and with the world: his two volumes of conversations with Patriarch Athenagoras and Patriarch Bartholomew are intended to make their concerns evident to a wider world.[15] Clément ends his autobiographical notes by quoting a remark of Patriarch Athenagoras: 'My business is not to give human beings laws, but to remind them of the meaning of life . . . Christianity is not made up of prohibitions: it is fire, creation, illumination'.[16]

Olivier Clément was very prolific; the 'succinct Bibliography' lists 41 books and over a hundred articles published in *Contacts*; he published in many other journals, not least the well-known weekly *Le Nouvel Observateur*. As we shall see, it is difficult to summarize his essential message, difficult to find over-riding themes, as we have been able to do for Elisabeth Behr-Sigel. Nicholas Lossky spoke of him as 'probably the greatest French Orthodox theologian of our century', that is, the 'long' twentieth century. Part of the problem is revealed by Clément in his autobiographical notes. Much, most even, of what

---

[13] *Contacts* 228, 409.

[14] *Corps de mort et de gloire: Petite introduction à une théopoétique de corps* (Paris: Desclée de Brouwer, 1995).

[15] *Dialogues avec le patriarche Athénagoras* (Paris: Fayard, 1969; 2nd augmented edn, 1976); *La vérité vous rendra libre: Entretiens avec le patriarche œcuménique Bartholomée Ier* (Paris: Desclée de Brouwer, 1996). Both available in English (Crestwood, NY: St Vladimir's Seminary Press).

[16] *Contacts* 228, 412.

he has published has been occasional: written because he was requested to. There are no major tomes; most of his books are under 100 pages long; some of his bigger books are collections of articles. As he says himself, he has two interests: to underline the universality of Orthodoxy (but with a love for all its particular ways of expression), and to place it at the frontier between the faith and the secularized world. And he admits the drawbacks: no overall plan, everything scattered according to the chances of history.[17]

Olivier Clément died in January 2009, after a long illness that confined him to his bed.[18] Nicholas Lossky records an event from his deathbed. As he was about to die, he said, 'I want to go.' His son said something to the effect that he should not worry, that things would come in their time. But Olivier said, 'No! I want to go to Marsillargues' – back in his native territory, where he had a house. Clément was of the soil of his native France.[19] Lossky has also said that

> it is extremely difficult to translate him into any language.[20] The reason is that his French is not only very French, but profoundly marked by his Mediterranean origin and his attachment to those southern roots of his.[21]

Elisabeth Behr-Sigel's theology

Whether one looks at the works she wrote during the course of her life, or her last book, *Discerning the Signs of the Times*, which collected together what she regarded as significant articles, there emerges a consistent pattern. The Orthodoxy she embraced, as a young woman in her early twenties, had deep Russian roots: she read Russian, and for her dissertation at the Protestant Faculty of Strasbourg she worked on Aleksandr Bukharev, pursuing much of her research in Paris, where she encountered, as we have seen, the Russians of the emigration, at the cathedral of St Alexander Nevsky in rue Daru and at the newly established Institut St-Serge: Fr Sergii Bulgakov and others at St-Serge, as well as, most importantly for her, Fr Lev Gillet, le 'moine de l'Église d'Orient', to give him his pen-name. She was attracted, as she herself says, by the Divine Liturgy, and the joy of the Resurrection that permeates it. She was attracted, too, by the saints of the Russian Church, by its spirituality, not least the Jesus Prayer, on which she wrote a standard book, *Le Lieu du cœur*, and also by those strands in nineteenth-century Russian thought that sought to engage with the challenges of modernity: strands summed up in the figure of Aleksandr Bukharev.

From this we can, I think, disentangle a number of overriding themes: the notion of sanctity, especially in its peculiarly Russian manifestation; the

---

[17] *Contacts* 228, 408.
[18] See Andrea Riccardi's Preface to Olivier Clément, *Petite boussole spirituelle pour notre temps* (Paris: Desclée de Brouwer, 2008), 7–23.
[19] *Sobornost* 31:1, 63.
[20] As one who has tried, I would concur!
[21] *Sobornost* 31:1, 62.

centrality of the prayer of the heart; the way in which both of these lay bare a way in which the central mysteries of the faith, especially the Resurrection, permeate the world in which we live. This presence of the power of Christ in the world took various particular forms with Elisabeth: her commitment to peace, and especially to the eradication of torture through her involvement in ACAT (*Action des chrétiens pour l'abolition de la torture*), and her commitment to deepening and expanding the place of women in the Church, which she pursued at an ecumenical level and within the Orthodox Church.

...and Aleksandr Bukharev

Given all this, it is not surprising that Elisabeth found herself drawn to the figure of Aleksandr Bukharev.[22] Bukharev was born in 1824[23] into a village deacon's family in Tver province. An intellectually precocious child, he made such progress at school that in 1842 he proceeded to the Moscow Spiritual Academy. On graduation in 1846, he took monastic vows with the name Feodor, remaining a teacher at the Academy. In 1852, he became professor and the following year archimandrite. At the Academy, he benefited from a stimulating theological atmosphere provided by professors such as the great church historian A.V. Gorsky and the philosophical theologian F. A. Golubinsky, who inspired the young Bukharev in his openness to modern European thought; he also benefited from the influence of the great Metropolitan of Moscow, Philaret.

Very soon, however, Bukharev was involved in controversy. In 1848, he wrote *Three Letters to N. V. Gogol*, defending Gogol against attacks on letters he had published addressing the problems of Russia as an Orthodox Christian. Gogol believed that these problems could be engaged with by drawing on the resources of the Orthodox tradition, bringing down on his head attacks from liberals, who could not understand what Christian teaching had to do with it, and conservatives, who could not see that there were any problems to be faced. Bukharev's letters were not published; monks were not expected to be involved in controversy, even in defence of the Orthodox tradition. In 1854, Bukharev left Moscow for the Kazan Spiritual Academy, where he was Dean of Students, modelling his dealings with the students on Christ, who emptied himself and came alongside humankind. This followed up some ideas from the *Three Letters*, where Bukharev had affirmed 'that "God's saving love in Christ" is not an abstract ideal or external rule, but an indwelling presence, a "heavenly guest" and "inner teacher" imparting divine things to the one in whom it resides'.[24]

---

[22] Apart from Elisabeth's book, see Paul Evdokimov, *Le Christ dans la pensée russe* (Paris: Cerf, 1970), 85–9; Paul Valliere, *Modern Russian Theology: Bukharev, Soloviev, Bulgakov. Orthodox Theology in a New Key* (Edinburgh: T&T Clark, 2000), 19–106; also Nadejda Gorodetzky, *The Humiliated Christ in Modern Russian Thought* (London: SPCK, 1938), esp. 116–26.

[23] There is dispute about the date: see Valliere, *Modern Russian Theology*, 19.

[24] Valliere, *Modern Russian Theology*, 27.

From Kazan, Bukharev moved in 1858 to St Petersburg to take up the post of an ecclesiastical censor. This enabled him to get some of his own works published, including his best-known work, *On Orthodoxy in Relation to the Modern World* (1860), in which he proposed that the Orthodox Church should embark on a dialogue with 'modernity'. This stirred up controversy, one of his conservative opponents being V. I. Askochensky, a journalist and one-time professor at the Kiev Spiritual Academy. One of Bukharev's views Askochensky objected to was his conviction that all human beings are created in the image of God, which provoked the response: 'What! So gypsy girls, prostitutes, Jews, and can-can dancers are all icons of God Himself and worthy of honour! Lord, have mercy! This is blatant iconoclasm, which has now spoken its final word'.[25]

So began the vituperative Bukharev Affair, which ended in Bukharev's being removed from his post and confined to a monastery, from where in 1863 he petitioned to be laicized and to return to life in the world. So Archimandrite Feodor became Aleksandr Matveevich Bukharev once more. A fortnight later he married Anna Sergeeva Rodyshevskaya. The marriage was happy, despite the death in infancy of their only child, Aleksandra, in 1869, and initially he was able to continue with his writing. In 1871, however, at the age of only 47, he died in poverty. Eventually, Bukharev came to be seen as foreshadowing the ideas of Solov'ev and other thinkers of the Russian Religious Renaissance. At the beginning of the twentieth century, Rozanov and Fr Florensky drew attention to his ideas. Paul Evdokimov has a few pages on him in his *Le Christ dans la pensée russe*, and it was likely he who suggested to Elisabeth that she should study Bukharev. It seems to me there are three things that inspired Elisabeth about Bukharev: first, his conviction that Orthodoxy needed to engage with the world, not just to teach it, but to learn from it; second, his idea of 'interiorized monasticism', to be pursued in both the monastic and the married state; and third, his emphasis on the self-emptying, the *kenosis*, of Christ.

Prayer and sanctity

Elisabeth's first book to be published was *Prière et sainteté dans l'Église russe*. In this book, she distinguishes three distinctive types of Russian sanctity: the 'passion-bearers' (*strastoterpsy*), the 'fools for Christ' (*yurodivi*), the 'spiritual elders' (*startsy*). The 'passion-bearers' are generally princes, such as Boris and Gleb, who gave up their lives rather than defend themselves, thus leading to further fratricidal wars: rulers who suffered what amounted to political murder for the sake of the ordinary people, who are the real sufferers in war. Tsar Nicolas and the rest of the imperial family who were murdered in Ekaterinburg by the Bolsheviks are also numbered by the Russian Church among the passion-bearers.

---

[25] Quoted by Valliere, *Modern Russian Theology*, 36–7.

'Fools for Christ' were characterized by outrageous behaviour, breaking conventions by eating meat in Lent, or social conventions disguising hypocrisy, walking about naked, behaving as if mad (it is a moot point whether they were mad or simply feigning madness). As Elisabeth puts it, 'humiliation is the point of it, whether it is a matter of madness simulated for ascetic reasons, or simply the consequence, in the case of those genuinely "simple" in mind'.[26] Following the humiliated Christ, they shared in the wisdom of Christ, with uncanny gifts of prophecy. In Russia, they were fearless in the face of the mighty, and respected for it. St Basil the Fool, of Moscow, was revered by Tsar Ivan the Terrible, even as he criticized him.

Spiritual elders, *startsy*, have been a feature of Christianity, especially in the East, for centuries; the nineteenth century saw a striking revival of the institution of *starchestvo*, or elderhood, as we can see from the early chapters of Dostoevsky's *The Brothers Karamazov*. The wisdom of the *startsy* is a fruit of their closeness to Christ, pursued by prayer and often dramatic asceticism: it is a wisdom that frequently enabled them to see into the souls of those who sought their counsel. Elisabeth draws attention to the paradox of the *startsy*: withdrawn from the world by prayer and asceticism, and yet given back to the world in their care for those who seek them out. She quotes from the Diveevo Chronicle: 'Everyone who came to Father Serafim was touched by the flame of the divine fire that burnt in him, and the human heart began to be set ablaze'.[27]

In all these forms of holiness, we find a following of the Christ of the *kenosis*, the Christ who hides himself among humans, who tastes what it is to be human to the utmost. Sanctity is not a model of respectability, nor for the respectable. One finds oneself recalling the idea of sanctity we found in St Maria Skobtsova, who was a close friend of Elisabeth's and with whom she worked in protecting Jews, and especially children, from the murderous activity of the Nazis. The *kenosis* of Christ was central to Elisabeth's theology. It was, as we have seen, one of the themes Elisabeth found central in the theology of Bukharev. As Michel Evdokimov put it, in his article in *Contacts*:

> It is the theme, developed above all in *Prière et Sainteté*, of a compassionate God, of the suffering servant come on earth to take responsibility for the mortal condition of his creature, to raise him up and restore to him his dignity in the kingdom. The similar vision of the kenotic Christ is, for Elisabeth Behr-Sigel, at the centre of the intellectual, theological, and spiritual preoccupations of the former archimandrite, who saw, too, in Christ, dead on the cross, the strong God, 'the vigorous athlete who bears the weight of the world'. One could then inverse the image of the authoritarian God, whose main concern is to punish the rebellious creature – an image that bears a heavy responsibility for a certain modern atheism –, into a God, crucified by love, who descends into hell 'to transform despair into hope' (Olivier Clément), to raise up mankind and restore to him the dignity of a friend of God.[28]

---

[26] Behr-Sigel, *Prière et sainteté*, 165.
[27] Behr-Sigel, *Prière et sainteté*, 178.
[28] *Contacts* 220, 409.

This idea of Christ, hidden among human beings, is one that was popular in Russian piety, as witnessed in the famous poem of Tyutchev, quoted by Elisabeth:[29]

> Those poor villages,
> That featureless nature …
> Land of patient fortitude,
> Land of the Russian folk.
>
> The proud glance of a stranger
> Will not notice or understand
> The radiance which shines dimly through
> Thy naked poverty,
>
> Laden with the burden of the cross,
> All through thee, my native land,
> In the form of a servant, the King of Heaven
> Went about bestowing his blessing.[30]

This was the soil from which the concerns of Elisabeth Behr-Sigel grew and were nourished. There are two other points I want to touch on before turning to Olivier Clément. First, the place of prayer and her friendship with Fr Lev Gillet. Fr Lev Gillet is well known as 'Un moine de l'Église d'Orient', the author of many books, of what, for want of a better word, we call 'spirituality'. Those works are matched in Elisabeth's *œuvre* by *Prière et sainteté* and *Le Lieu du cœur*, not to mention her article on 'Le Prière à Jésus' in *La Douloureuse Joie* along with articles by Clément, Bobrinskoy, Koppel, and Lot-Borodine.[31] For all the activism of Elisabeth, at the heart of her teaching, as of her life, was prayer, both participation in the liturgy and, flowing out from that, private prayer, the prayer of the heart, practised through the Jesus Prayer. This matches the notion of 'interiorized monasticism', which she found in Bukharev and was, as we have seen, a significant theme in the thought of her friend, Paul Evdokimov. The practice of the Jesus Prayer, and the pursuit of 'interiorized monasticism', establishes the mystery of Christ in the world, enabling Christ to reach out from the sanctuary, where he is celebrated, to the world that needs him.

The place of women in the Church

Finally, though it could well have been the main topic: the place of women in the Church and their ministry. There is, it seems to me, a danger in Elisabeth Behr-Sigel being thought of as a woman of one issue, the ministry of women. I have already suggested that her concern for the ministry of women is to

---

[29] Behr-Sigel, *Discerner*, 41.
[30] Trans. Nadejda Gorodetzky (with a minor modification), in Gorodetzky, *Humiliated Christ*, 7; quoted by Behr-Sigel, *Discerner*, 41.
[31] O. Clément et al., *La Douloureuse Joie*, Spiritualité Orientale 14 (Bégrolles-en-Mauges: Abbaye de Bellefontaine, 1981); Behr-Sigel's article: 83–129.

be seen as part of a wider concern for dialogue of the Orthodox Church with the modern world. Her final book illustrates that, and a couple of other things. First, she begins by talking about Jesus and women, Mary and women; and explains that she wants to talk about 'women', not 'woman' – persons, not a concept. Elisabeth's theology is not a theology of concepts, but a theology that grows out of lives, lives transfigured by the presence of Christ through the Spirit. That volume also shows how her central concerns are always ecumenical. Ecumenism was not an issue, for Elisabeth: it was a dimension of any theology in dialogue with the world.

It is perhaps true to say that Elisabeth Behr-Sigel herself was more important than any of her books, that her impact was the impact of her presence, her actual engagement in dialogue, which cannot be reduced to any positions she held or causes she espoused. One of the causes she embraced, as we have seen, was opposition to the use of torture, including recourse to the death penalty. On one occasion in 1986, she was part of a delegation of ACAT at an audience with Pope John Paul II about the ambiguous position of the Catholic Church over the death penalty. The pope explained that these ambiguities were difficult to dispel because of the theological and philosophical traditions that had justified the death penalty for many centuries. At the end of the discussion, Elisabeth addressed the pope directly: 'Mais très Saint Père – But, most holy Father, it seems to me that two thousand years ago there was someone who did not hesitate to call in question certain traditions.'[32] I rather suspect that if someone had tried to curtail a discussion of the ordination of women by appealing to the centuries-old tradition of the Church, she would have replied in like terms.

Olivier Clément's thought

I have already quoted Fr Nicholas Lossky's opinion of his friend, Olivier Clément – 'probably the greatest French Orthodox theologian of our century' – and also given some account of his life and concerns. He was enormously prolific – 41 books and hundreds of articles, over a hundred in *Contacts* alone. But his writing was, as he admitted, mostly occasional, nearly always responses to requests to contribute an article, give a lecture, answer some question. His work is therefore very diffuse; it is very difficult to set out his thought in a number of themes or concerns. Indeed, it is precisely that which makes him worth reading.

Clément had the training of a scholar, and benefited from studying under some of the great minds of the mid-twentieth century, but he did not become a scholar himself; his approach was quite different. He was immensely widely read; in the decade or so before his baptism in 1952, he was searching, searching for an understanding of the mystery of death, the mystery of life. He read widely: in the different religious traditions, especially those we

---

[32] Quoted by Guy Aurenche in *Contacts* 220, 468.

call 'mystical' – Eckhart, Boehme among the Christians, but also Jewish Kabbalah, the ancient traditions of India, the Vedas, Buddhism, as well as esoteric traditions such as alchemy; but also among the philosophers, not least those who were popular in France after the Second World War – Sartre, Levinas, novelists, poets – Rilke is often cited, and writers of all kinds. As he approached Christianity, he was particularly drawn to the Russians, not just the theologians, but the poets and novelists – predictably, Dostoevsky was important; he wrote a book on Solzhenitsyn, published in 1974, the year Solzhenitsyn was expelled from the Soviet Union.[33]

He was a man of dialogue: as well as the well-known volumes based on conversations with two œcumenical patriarchs, Athenagoras and Bartholomew, there is also a volume of dialogue on Islam with Mohamed Talbi, *Un respect têtu* ('An obstinate respect').[34] All his works, however, are dialogues, as Clément draws on a wide range of traditions, bringing them into fruitful engagement, whatever he is writing on.

There is an autobiography, *L'Autre Soleil* (1975),[35] and, though not autobiographical, a work, *Rome, autrement* (1997),[36] which can be read against his rejection of what might have seemed his natural home, Catholicism, as he turned to Christianity in 1952. His most systematic work – in French, *Sources*, translated as *The Roots of Christian Mysticism* – is revealing, for the text – an exposition of Christianity seen as a pathway to the contemplation of God – is accompanied by extensive extracts from the Fathers, among whom the Syrian Fathers, the fourth-century Ephrem and the seventh-century Isaac of Nineveh, feature prominently.[37]

Theological alchemy

The host of sources that Clément draws on, whatever he writes about, must be evidence of a capacious memory, and indeed one most often comes away from reading Clément with some arresting image or remark in one's head. He makes connections, but more than that, what is connected is fused into something new and fresh. I am tempted to suggest that we should see Clément under the rubric of 'The theologian as alchemist', for alchemy was concerned with the transmutation of elements, and there is always something of this in Clément's writing. This is not an entirely idle suggestion, for in 1953, the year after he became Orthodox, there appeared in a volume called *Yoga – Science de l'homme intégral*, an essay of his called 'L'alchimie occidentale, science et art de la transmutation cosmique'. Forty-one years later it was republished

---

[33] Olivier Clément, *The Spirit of Solzhenitsyn* (London: Search Press, 1976; French original, Paris: Stock, 1974. The English version has an additional chapter).

[34] Mohamed Talbi–Olivier Clément, *Un respect têtu* (Paris: Nouvelle Cité, 1989).

[35] *L'Autre Soleil* (Paris: Stock, 1975).

[36] *Rome, autrement* (Paris: Desclée de Brouwer, 1997).

[37] *Sources: Les mystiques chrétiens des origines. Textes et commentaire* (Paris: Stock, 1982); ET: *The Roots of Christian Mysticism*, trans. Theodore Berkeley, rev. Jeremy Hummerstone (London: New City, 1993).

with the title *L'Œil de feu*, this time, at Clément's insistence, topped and tailed by more recent essays by Clément: 'Éros et cosmos: Révolte ou assomption', and 'Transfigurer l'univers (Le cosmos dans la mystique de l'orient chrétien)'.[38]

The later essays wrap a discussion of alchemical ways of transmutation with expositions of transfiguration (and it is worth mentioning that the first of Clément's books was *Transfigurer le temps*, 1959[39]). The essay on alchemy clearly grows out of Clément's years of searching, a search that led him finally to Orthodoxy. Clément's essay is long (longer than most of his articles) and rich; all I can do is pick out some observations. He suggests we see alchemy and Christianity as complementary:

> Thus alchemy could not have survived in the West without the prodigious initiating effusion of Christianity: just as the archaic house only exists because of the chimney which makes it communicate with the 'sky', just as a cosmology is only possible around the 'central' condition by which one can go out from the cosmos.
>
> But without alchemy Christianity could not have been 'incarnated' in an all-embracing order: it would have been monks and saints, it would not have had a sacred conception of nature capable of giving to the arts, the crafts, to heraldry, their character of 'little mysteries'.
>
> In a time when the weight of gravity [pesanteur] crushes us, it is perhaps urgent to remind Christianity that, for centuries, it had not only accepted, but even given life to, its most noble incarnation, a veritable illumination of gravity.[40]

He introduces his discussion of alchemy in these words:

> Alchemy, contrary to what is repeated in histories of science, has never been, save in its dimmer aspects, a kind of infant, stammering chemistry. It was a 'sacramental' science for which material appearances had no autonomy, but represented solely the 'condensation' of mental and spiritual realities. Nature, when one penetrates its spontaneity and its mystery, becomes transparent: it is transfigured on the one hand under the radiance of divine energies, on the other it incorporates and symbolizes the 'angelic' states that fallen man can only endure for brief moments, hearing a music and contemplating a face.[41]

I am not interested, for now, in exploring Clément's understanding of alchemy, relating it to ideas in the Kabbalah, both Jewish and 'Christian', as well as Tantric Buddhism, fascinating though this would be, but simply with drawing attention to how the alchemical notion of transmutation, seen as discerning gold in dull elements such as lead, gives an insight into Clément's method. Striking ideas are brought into conjunction and spark off each other; one finds oneself looking at ideas from a different perspective, seeing things for the first time, as it were, finding familiar ideas exciting.

---

[38] This has been reprinted since his death: *L'Œil de feu* (Clichy (Hauts-de-Seine): Éditions de Corlevour, 2012).

[39] *Transfigurer le temps* (Paris–Neuchâtel: Delachaux et Niestlé, 1959).

[40] Clément, *L'Œil*, 33.

[41] Clément, *L'Œil*, 33–4.

The Archangel of Death

It would be best to give an example. In a journal called *Planète St Serge*, the students' journal of the Institut St-Serge in Paris, a short article appeared called 'L'Ange de la Résurrection' by Olivier Clément, which was translated and published in the English Orthodox journal *The Forerunner*.[42] Clément begins by relating a story about the angel of death, who is sent to those who are about to die. The angels' wings are covered with eyes, as were the cherubim in Ezekiel's vision. But it may happen – because of a prayer or a tear – that God decides to spare the one to whom he has sent his angel: he or she must go on living, is still needed on earth. So the angel is told to return, but before departing, he leaves behind, discreetly, without showing himself, a pair of eyes from his wings. The one restored to life now sees, not just with his or her natural eyes, but with the eyes left by the angel. Now much that seemed important appears ridiculous, and vice versa.[43]

Clément then goes on to tell the story of a Russian priest, who spent many years in the camps, who one day felt that he was at the end of his strength, going to die. He felt himself suddenly transported to the church where he used to serve, hundreds of miles away, and there he found himself celebrating the liturgy with priests long dead. Then a voice was heard, telling him to go back to the camp, he was still needed there. His friends, already reciting the prayers for the dead beside his mortal remains, were astonished as he came back to life. But thereafter in whomever he met, he could see a flame burning, steadily or just flickering, in their soul; in the souls of some taken for ruffians the flame burned strongly, but was practically extinct in some who were well-wishers.

Clément goes on to reflect on this mystery, the contrast between the inner reality, only seen with the eyes of the angel of death, and the outward appearance. He refers to Solzhenitsyn, who spoke of the eyes of some who had gone through the frozen hell of the camps as having the purity of mountain lakes: their eyes were, in reality, the eyes left by the angel. He speaks of Cézanne, and the way he sees all that he painted as ordinary things – fruits, the wind, rocks – as revealing of deeper reality: the 'rock, taciturn density, lightning turned to stone', for example. And then he mentions Levinas, a philosopher, he said, who wanted a philosophy, not of concepts, but of faces: not of concepts that we can grasp and use, but faces, which we can only contemplate, if they are to remain faces.

---

[42] *The Forerunner* 32 (Winter 1998–9), 17–19.

[43] This story is curiously reminiscent of an experience of Bulgakov's: in 1926, he suffered a heart attack and nearly died. In the Introduction to *Jacob's Ladder*, he tells that he dreamt that he was walking quickly and freely towards the lights of heaven; he then had a sense of his guardian angel with him, who told him that 'we had gone too far ahead and it was necessary to return ... to life' (Sergius Bulgakov, *Jacob's Ladder: On Angels*, trans. Thomas Allan Smith (Grand Rapids, MI–Cambridge: Eerdmans, 2010), 19).

The story of the priest comes from the early pages of a wonderful book called in English, *Father Arseny 1893–1973: Priest, Prisoner, Spiritual Father*.[44] The story of the angel of death is a traditional legend. The references to Solzhenitsyn, Cézanne, Levinas, we can follow up for ourselves. It is interesting that what he says about Cézanne suggests that his painting was a kind of alchemy, and the idea of seeing the true, underlying reality is very much how he interpreted alchemy in the essay I've referred to.

Transfiguration

But he turned from alchemical transmutation to Christian transfiguration, from human attempts to penetrate the secret reality of things, to the revelation of the glory of God in the face of Jesus Christ, a revelation not of the power that the alchemists were all too prone to crave, but of the glory of a face full of love. The editor of the recent edition of *L'Œil de feu*, Franck Damour, remarks in his introductory note that, 'the passage from "alchemical transmutation" to "Christian transfiguration" is that of the discovery of the "figure", that God is a face'.[45] The discovery of the face of God seems to me at the very heart of Clément's understanding of Orthodoxy. It was a discovery helped by one of his early Russian mentors, Nicolas Berdyaev, who had, as we have seen, a profound sense of the particularity of the material face as revelatory of spiritual reality. Later on it was developed by his reading of the philosopher Emmanuel Levinas. Levinas was a philosopher of the phenomenological school, instrumental in the introduction of Husserl into French philosophical culture.

One of his most important books has the title, *Totalité et infini*,[46] central to which is the contrast between the ideas of what he called totality and the infinite. Most philosophers in the West had pursued totality, seeking some way of understanding reality that would give a complete, total account; inevitably, such an approach leans towards generalities, universals. The 'minute particular' is a problem. But a human account of totality can only be a large, even huge, marshalling together of finite quantities. To the total, and totalizing, Levinas opposes the infinite, which we can never reach by piling up finite quantities. It belongs to another order of reality altogether. Levinas finds this order of reality in ethical demands that emerge from our engagement with persons, for these demands are not calculable, and so do not partake of the finite; they are infinite, boundless, qualitatively different from what can be measured and calculated. The symbol of the personal is the face, which reveals this infinite demand: a face which is not universal or generalized,

---

[44] Olivier Clément, *Father Arseny 1893–1973: Priest, Prisoner, Spiritual Father* (Crestwood, NY: St Vladimir's Seminary Press, 1999), 44–8.

[45] Clément, *L'Œil*, 8.

[46] Emmanuel Levinas, *Totalité et infini: Essai sur l'extériorité* (The Hague: Martinus Nijhoff, 4th edn, 1980).

but quite particular, unique in every case. And this unique particular face is also fragile: it can easily be liquidated (I use the word deliberately). I can ignore the face by smashing it, by killing it – for it is very fragile. I can also ignore the face by not beholding it, not giving it time, treating it instead as little more than the particular aspect of the universal called humanity. For Levinas the command, Thou shalt not kill, arises from the infinite demand of the unique and particular face. Levinas wrote against the background of the Holocaust; his other major work, *Autrement qu'être ou au-delà de l'essence*, is dedicated (in French and Hebrew):

> To the memory of the close to six million beings assassinated by the national socialists, alongside the millions and millions of humans of all confessions and all nations, victims of the same hatred of the other man, the same anti-semitism.[47]

...of the Face in Glory

As Clément's reflection on the face developed, he drew more and more on Levinas, or perhaps more accurately returned time and again to Levinas' fundamental intuition. The theme of the face is found everywhere in his writings (even in the 1953 article: see the second of the passages quoted above), but there is one volume devoted to the face, *Le Visage intérieur* (1978).[48] Levinas' own development of the theme of the face is not very easy reading; he was schooled too much in the German of his mentor, Husserl. Clément's version is lyrical, poetic:

> Any face, however worn or almost destroyed, the moment we regard it with the heart's gaze, reveals itself as unique, inimitable, free from any repetition. One can analyse its components, take apart coldly, or cruelly, the way they are assembled, and thus consign it to the world of objects that one can explain, that is to say, possess. Regarded against the background of the night, of the nothing, the face is an inhabited archipelago, a disqualifying caricature. Regarded from the side of the sun, the face reveals an other, someone, a reality that one cannot decompose, classify, 'understand', for it is always beyond, strangely absent when one wants to seize it, but which radiates from its beyond whenever one agrees to open oneself to it, to 'put one's faith' in it, as the old language admirably puts it.[49]

One can see how Clément is going to develop this, how it links up with so many aspects of the Orthodox faith, not least the icon. In this way, Clément's theology transforms 'concepts into contemplation', which his mentor, Vladimir Lossky, claimed to be the way of the mystical theology of the Eastern Church.[50]

---

[47] Emmanuel Levinas, *Autrement qu'être ou au-delà de l'essence* (The Hague: Martinus Nijhoff, 2nd edn, 1978), V.

[48] *Le Visage intérieur* (Paris: Stock, 1978).

[49] Clément, *Le Visage*, 13.

[50] Cf. Vladimir Lossky, *The Mystical Theology of the Eastern Church* (London: James Clarke, 1957), 238.

18

Spiritual elders: 1 Mother Thekla (Sharf) and the English acculturation of Orthodoxy

Spiritual elders

The contribution of the spiritual elders to Orthodox theology, not least in the modern period, cannot be passed over. In Greece the influence of elders such as Fr Vasileios of Stavronikita/Iviron (already discussed briefly in connection with Fr Schmemann and liturgical theology), Fr Joseph, Fr Paisios, Fr Aimilianos and Fr Porphyrios is widespread and well known. In the two chapters devoted to spiritual elders I shall take spiritual elders whom I myself knew: Mother Thekla and Fr Sophrony. Mother Thekla I knew much better (though Fr Sophrony had been a (largely hidden) presence in my life since I first met him in 1964), for shortly after becoming Orthodox, I found myself in the north of England, where in those days there were few opportunities to attend the Divine Liturgy, and thus went to the Monastery of the Assumption near Whitby regularly for a period of about six years. Very soon I came to know Mother Thekla, and I owe her a great deal. One reason for limiting myself to spiritual elders I have personally known is that, however much spiritual elders might have written, the primary way in which they convey their understanding of the Christian life is through personal encounter. What a spiritual elder says is personal to you, not a generalized message; inevitably something written down – even collections of letters – takes on the character of a general message, and so loses something of its original power.

Spiritual eldership – called in Russian *starchestvo*, an elder being a *starets* – has long been an important feature of Orthodoxy, to be traced back to the Fathers of the Egyptian Desert in the fourth century, whose sayings and example were gathered together in the *Apophthegmata Patrum*, the 'Sayings of the Desert Fathers', or the *Gerontikon* ('Book of the Elders'). The tradition continued from then, sometimes with periods of decline and at other times periods of renewal. The publication of the *Philokalia* in the eighteenth century was both evidence of a renewal of spiritual eldership on the Holy Mountain, and itself contributed to further renewal, especially in Russia, evidence of which is found in the early chapters of Dostoevsky's novel *The Brothers Karamazov*. *Starchestvo* continued to be important, though often

Mother Thekla
With permission of Ann Hamblen

hidden, during the Soviet period.[1] As well as in Greece, as already mentioned, spiritual eldership has been important in the last century in Serbia (mentioned in passing in the chapter on St Justin Popović) and in Romania, where among others Fr Cleopa and Fr Teofil were outstanding.[2] The relevance of spiritual eldership to theology in Orthodoxy is not far to seek, for, as we have seen, Orthodox theology is rarely limited to purely speculative questions, but concerns the implications of living the Christian life.

Acculturation of Orthodoxy in the West

Our discussion of Mother Thekla has a more precise focus, one that seems to me of great importance. The picture of Orthodox theology that I have presented in this book is largely focused on the presence of Orthodoxy in the West, and especially the influence of the Russians who found themselves in Paris after their expulsion from Russia in 1922. The experience of exile,

---

[1] On *starchestvo* in Russia, see Irina Paert, *Spiritual Elders: Charisma and Tradition in Russian Orthodoxy* (Dekalb, IL: Northern Illinois University Press, 2010).
[2] On spiritual elders in Romania, see Nicolas Stebbing CR, *Bearers of the Spirit: Spiritual Fatherhood in Romanian Orthodoxy*, Cistercian Studies Series 201 (Kalamazoo, MI: Cistercian Publications, 2003).

of being a diaspora, was in many ways a liberating experience: the engagement of these thinkers with the Western thinkers who welcomed them led to a rediscovery of elements of Orthodox theology that had been forgotten or overlaid in the immediate past. Often enough there were times when it became difficult to distinguish between the presentation of Orthodox insights and an unfolding of a specifically *Russian* experience, and the encounter of Western thinkers with Orthodoxy has often been bound up with an encounter with another national or linguistic culture, not simply with Orthodoxy itself, as we saw in the case of Philip Sherrard. Often enough in the West in the middle decades of the last century, Russian Orthodoxy, for example, was presented through the medium of Russian culture, or more specifically, Dostoevsky and the vision found in his novels.

It is a serious question how Orthodoxy can find itself at home in the culture of a Western nation, and this question is raised acutely in the thinking of Mother Thekla. Born in Russia, and educated in England, she was equally at home in Russian literature and English literature (which she taught for many years). She did not sound at all Russian, and was somewhat dismissive of Russians who retained a distinctly Russian accent; she sounded like what she was – a well-educated and highly cultured English lady. In a few works she sought to expound Orthodoxy in terms of English literature; a short book on Shakespeare's Hamlet (she completed a more substantial work on Shakespeare, which she sent to a London publisher; since then nothing has been heard of it), and larger works on John Keats and George Herbert. She thought of what she was doing as growing Orthodoxy on English soil. One might think of her work in these books as parallel with the rediscovery of the saints of the first millennium – Aidan and Cuthbert of Lindisfarne, Bede of Jarrow, Wilfrid of Hexham and Ripon, and many others – and their veneration by modern English Orthodox (and not them alone: the Celtic and Anglo-Saxon saints are popular in Russia and Greece, for instance), and with similar attempts to recover the saints we have in common with the Churches of Western Europe in the Low Countries and France, for example.[3]

As veneration of the saints of the lands where Orthodox in the West find themselves is something of an attempt to find a sense of being at home as Orthodox in the West, so Mother Thekla's attempt to find the spiritual values of Orthodoxy in English poets such as Shakespeare, Herbert and Keats (rather than Pushkin, Gogol and Dostoevsky) is an attempt to find a sense of belonging as Orthodox in the culture of the West (there is a parallel to Mother Thekla's attempts in Olivier Clément's more essayistic references to, and discussions of, modern poets such as Rilke and Pierre Emmanuel). Why poets, one might wonder? I recall reading somewhere (the reference I have not been able to recover) that poets deal in essences; if so, then it would seem natural to turn to them for insight into spiritual matters.

---

[3] This theme is present in Vladimir Lossky's *Sept jours sur les routes de France: Juin 1940* (Paris: Cerf, 1998).

Life

First, however, something about Mother Thekla's life.[4] She was born Marina Sharf on 18 July 1918 at Kislovodsk in the Caucasus (where, barely five months later, Aleksandr Solzhenitsyn was born). Her family was of Jewish descent, her mother having converted to Christianity. (After the Second World War her brother, Andrew, returned to his Jewish roots; an expert on Byzantine Jewry, he became a professor at the Bar-Ilan University in Israel.) The turmoil caused by the Russian Revolution led her father, a barrister, to bring his young family to England, where they lived in Richmond, Surrey, and later in Chelsea. Crossfire in the streets of Kislovodsk had prevented her parents taking the baby Marina to church, so she was baptized in a flower vase, an episode she loved to relate. She was educated at the City of London Girls' School, and went from there to Girton College, Cambridge, where she read Part I of the English Tripos and then Russian for Part II of the Modern Languages Tripos, graduating in 1940. During the Second World War, she served in RAF Intelligence (1941–6), partly in India, and then worked in the Ministry of Education, before taking up a teaching post at Kettering High School in 1952, where she soon became Head of English.

Marina's life changed in 1965: on her way to a retreat at the Anglican Abbey of West Malling, she attended the Divine Liturgy at the Russian Cathedral in Ennismore Gardens, and there saw Mother Maria, 'a *real* nun'. Mother Maria (born Lydia Gysi) was living at West Malling, and Marina met her again there, and knew that she must herself become a nun with Mother Maria. Mother Maria had been professed by Father (later Metropolitan) Anthony Bloom, and had for 14 years lived in the Anglican enclosure at West Malling. Two Orthodox nuns was felt to be too much, and soon after her profession Sister Marina and Mother Maria found themselves setting up the Monastery of the Assumption at Filgrave in Buckinghamshire. The Anglican nuns, and Michael Ramsey, the Archbishop of Canterbury, their visitor, had feared that two Orthodox nuns might attract recruits from their own ranks – and with reason, for a few years later, the novice mistress at West Malling, Dame Mary Thomas, became convinced that her vocation lay with the nuns in Filgrave.

In 1970, Patriarch Aleksii of Moscow died, and the nuns felt that their link with Russia had died with him; they therefore sought admission to the Œcumenical Patriarchate. In 1971 their monastery changed its canonical allegiance and Sister Marina became Sister Thekla; in the same year Dame Mary Thomas joined them as Sister Katherine. Two years later, Mother Maria was diagnosed with cancer; she eventually died in 1977. With Mother Maria's

---

[4] For her life, see Mother Thekla, *The Monastery of the Assumption: A History*, Pamphlet 8 (Normanby, Whitby: Library of Orthodox Thinking, 1984). See also her Introduction to *Mother Maria: Her Life in Letters*, ed. Sister Thekla (London: Darton, Longman & Todd, 1979), xiii–xlviii. The text here is based partly on the obituary I wrote for *The Times* (27 August 2011).

death imminent, Sisters Thekla and Katherine sought to preserve her heritage by setting up a publishing venture, the Library of Orthodox Thinking. The title was deliberate: the sisters wanted to present Orthodoxy, not as a system of thought opposed to the West, but as a way of thinking, rooted in their way of life and prayer. Mother Thekla spoke of 'the one innermost battle-cry of the monastery, the austere demand of refusing to discuss what is not lived, and the impossibility of living up to this ourselves: back into the revolving wheel of repentance. Face God, not man'.[5] Mother Maria's doctoral thesis had been on the Cambridge Platonist Ralph Cudworth, and a brief monograph of hers on Cudworth was an early pamphlet in the Library.[6] Other works of Mother Maria's followed, and then works by Sister Thekla on Shakespeare,[7] on Keats[8] and on George Herbert,[9] as well as translations of liturgical texts, the work of Sisters Thekla and Katherine together,[10] and the Psalms, translated from the Hebrew by Mother Maria, the version of the psalms used by the nuns in their worship.[11] The sisters were seeking what one might call an English acculturation of Orthodoxy. Sister Thekla also edited *Mother Maria: Her Life in Letters*.[12]

Mother Maria's imminent death also led the sisters to seek a more remote and inaccessible situation for their monastery, which they found in some old farm buildings at Normanby, just south of Whitby, several hundred yards down a track off the road to Scarborough, on the edge of the North York Moors. There, under the shadow of St Hilda, the Monastery of the Assumption was re-established in 1975 – three nuns and Nimrod, the cat. Mother Maria soon died. In 1988, Sister Katherine also died, a victim of cancer. In that year, Archimandrite Ephrem (Lash) returned from Mount Athos, and became chaplain to the community, which soon comprised a single nun, Mother Thekla.

At Normanby, Mother Thekla kept sheep, and then goats, of whom she was very fond. It was while she was there that Mother Thekla became an inspiration for (Sir) John Tavener; she suggested the words for what became the *Song for Athene* (1993), and wrote the texts for his opera, *Mary of Egypt* (1989), and many of his choral works. She was the inspiration for one of his most popular works, *The Protecting Veil* (1987), referring to the *pokrov* (the Russian word meaning either veil or protection), with which the Mother of

---

[5] Mother Thekla, *Monastery of the Assumption*, 16.

[6] *Ralph Cudworth: Mystical Thinker* (Newport Pagnell: Library of Orthodox Thinking, 1973).

[7] *Hamlet: The Noble Mind* (Newport Pagnell: Library of Orthodox Thinking, 1972).

[8] *John Keats: The Disinterested Heart* (Newport Pagnell: Library of Orthodox Thinking, 1973).

[9] *George Herbert: Idea and Image* (Newport Pagnell: Library of Orthodox Thinking, 1974).

[10] For example, St Andrew of Crete, *The Great Canon: The Life of St Mary of Egypt*, ed. and trans. Sister Katherine and Sister Thekla (Newport Pagnell: Library of Orthodox Thinking, 1974); *The Service of Vespers*, trans. with Introduction, Sister Thekla (Normanby, Whitby: Library of Orthodox Thinking, 1976).

[11] Mother Maria, *The Psalms: An Exploratory Translation* (Newport Pagnell: Library of Orthodox Thinking, 1973).

[12] See note 4.

God protects the world. They were joint authors of a volume, *Ikons: Meditations in Words and Music*.[13] The fame she acquired from her association with Tavener led to two works of hers being published with established presses: *The Dark Glass*[14] and *Eternity Now*.[15]

Mother Thekla remained the only professed nun at the Monastery of the Assumption; various people sought their vocation there, but none of them persevered. In 1994 she was joined by an American nun, Sister Hilda, whom Mother Thekla hoped might succeed her. In the event, Sister Hilda alienated virtually all Mother Thekla's friends, securing Fr Ephrem's departure in 1996. Soon Mother Thekla found herself expelled from her own monastery on the alleged grounds of senility, but was rescued by the sisters of the Anglican Order of the Holy Paraclete, who welcomed her to the infirmary at the Abbey of St Hilda in Whitby. There she spent the declining years of her long life, being quickly reconciled to her many friends. In her last years she was cared for pastorally by Fr Stephen Robson, an Orthodox priest in nearby York. Mother Thekla died in the early hours of Sunday 7 August 2011, and was buried at Whitby on 16 August. At her funeral several pieces by Tavener were performed, including a newly written piece, 'They are all gone into the World of Light', a setting of Henry Vaughan's poem.

Relationship with Mother Maria (Gysi)

There is a great deal that could be discussed in a thorough study of Mother Thekla. Her relationship to Mother Maria would need to be explored, for providentially they had a great deal in common. Mother Maria, Lydia Gysi before her profession, was Swiss, born in Basle in 1912, and had studied, first theology (especially Old Testament), then philosophy, at the university there, eventually submitting a doctoral thesis on the Cambridge Platonist Ralph Cudworth, later published in English with the title, *Platonism and Cartesianism in the Philosophy of Ralph Cudworth*; she also wrote a shorter piece on Ralph Cudworth for the Library of Orthodox Thinking.[16] Mother Thekla herself read English at Cambridge, and then taught English literature in a grammar school (or high school) for 13 years. Neither English by birth, they both knew and loved English literature from Shakespeare onwards, Mother Maria interested in the Platonist tradition in England, then, as now, largely neglected, Mother Thekla more interested in poetry, much of which she knew by heart (though she had a love for the novel, too, especially the novels of Charlotte M. Yonge).

---

[13] John Tavener and Mother Thekla, *Ikons: Meditations in Words and Music* (London: Fount, 1994).

[14] Mother Thekla, *The Dark Glass: Meditations in Orthodox Spirituality* (London: Fount, 1996).

[15] Mother Thekla, *Eternity Now: An Introduction to Orthodox Spirituality* (Norwich: Canterbury Press, 1997).

[16] Lydia Gysi, *Platonism and Cartesianism in the Philosophy of Ralph Cudworth* (Bern: Herbert Lang, 1962); Mother Maria, *Ralph Cudworth: Mystical Thinker* (Newport Pagnell: Library of Orthodox Thinking, 1973).

Most of the works published in the Library of Orthodox Thinking were by Mother Maria; Mother (then Sister) Thekla published the three studies of English literature already referred to, as well as a commentary on two of the psalms – 136 (137) and 125 (126) – *A Story of Babylon*.[17] These works of Mother Thekla's clearly owe much to her relationship with Mother Maria; much, too, can be learnt about what Mother Thekla owed to Mother Maria from the *Life in Letters*.

… and John Tavener

There is also her relationship with John Tavener: this again is part of a story of the English acculturation of Orthodoxy, for though Tavener did write music for the Orthodox Liturgy, most of his works belong to the tradition of Western music, introducing to that tradition elements of Russian and Greek chant (and later, from other religious traditions). They are, often, works that present Orthodox theology and Orthodox sensibility within a clearly Western setting (Orthodox liturgical music makes no use of instruments, save the human voice; Tavener makes extraordinary use of instruments, especially stringed instruments, particularly the cello): it is Western music that is Orthodox, rather than Orthodox music. The texts that Mother Thekla provided express Orthodox theological intuitions uncompromisingly, but they find their way into compositions recognizably Western (opera, oratorio, for instance).

… as spiritual mother

Beyond this there is Mother Thekla's role as a spiritual mother to many who turned to her – the 'cloud of witnesses', as one of her spiritual daughters calls us (for I was one of them). Helping people, mostly converts to Orthodoxy, to live an authentically Orthodox life in modern England is perhaps her deepest contribution to the English acculturation of Orthodoxy, but it is one that, by its nature, is difficult to talk about at all adequately.

Orthodoxy in English dress

So I shall confine myself to one aspect of Mother Thekla's engagement with the English world she made her own, while remaining deeply, authentically Orthodox: her explicit attempt to express Orthodox insight and intuition through works of English literature. The three works I shall discuss came out rapidly one after another: *Hamlet: The Noble Mind* in 1972; *John Keats: The Disinterested Heart* in 1973; and *George Herbert: Idea and Image* in 1974. I shall discuss them in their order of publication, though I am not claiming that there is any development to be discerned; indeed it seems to me most unlikely.

---

[17] Sister Thekla, *A Story of Babylon* (Newport Pagnell: Library of Orthodox Thinking, 1973).

Shakespeare's Hamlet

Hamlet: The Noble Mind is a study of Hamlet's seven soliloquies. For Mother Thekla, the problem of Hamlet can be expressed thus:

> Scholar, soldier, courtier, Hamlet fell headlong into the trap of the infinite potentiality of human capability. He refuted the limitation of the human mind, he rejected the liberating compromise of the partial, and he subjected his will to the assault of the consequence, the numbing guilt and the paralysis which would follow inevitably this unrealisable demand upon himself for sovereign decision and boundless discrimination.
>
> Hamlet denied the presence of the last step into an acknowledgment of the limitation of the human mind, of human reason, and of human judgment. For him, failure, as he saw it, to find the absolute answer to the apparent choice between absolute right and absolute wrong, demonstrated only his own personal failure, his wonted inexplicable weakness.[18]

Or, as she puts it a little later on in the Introduction: 'He rejected the validity of failure, and, thereby, he excluded himself from the grace of error.'[19]

Hamlet's first soliloquy ('O! that this too, too solid [sullied] flesh would melt ...' Act I, Sc. 2, 129ff.) is in response to his mother's marriage to Claudius. In this soliloquy, Mother Thekla draws attention to the way in which Hamlet's response devalues personal experience, deflecting it into generalized, impersonal reflection on the human condition. In this way the possibility of action is abandoned, and Hamlet is left to paralysis of the will, inertia.

> The personal experience of revulsion, of pity, and of love, which he violently rejected as weakness, would have been the strength which might have helped him to escape out of the trap into victory. But, what he substituted for strength was not his greatness but his sickness, and what he saw as sickness, and others after him, would have been his health.[20]

Hamlet's second soliloquy (Act I, Sc. 5, 91ff.) takes place after his encounter with the ghost of his father, who reveals his murderer to be Claudius, his brother, and departs with the words: 'Adieu, adieu! Hamlet, remember me.' Mother Thekla remarks that the ghost implores Hamlet not to remember 'the crime of murder, nor the sin of adultery, but the loved person of his father'.[21] In doing so, the ghost challenges the premiss of Hamlet's attitude, as revealed in the first soliloquy: 'he demands the acknowledgment of human limitation in the personal re-action, he rejects the assumed superiority of the extra-personal, and he pleads the love of the person as the sole balanced driving force'.[22] The ghost had revealed the brutal reality of the details of his murder, which might have precipitated Hamlet into an impassioned act of

---

[18] Mother Thekla, *Hamlet*, 2.
[19] Mother Thekla, *Hamlet*, 3.
[20] Mother Thekla, *Hamlet*, 7.
[21] Mother Thekla, *Hamlet*, 8.
[22] Mother Thekla, *Hamlet*, 8.

revenge. Mother Thekla comments: 'One act of such rash un-reason, deriving from personal emotion, yet might have eased his way into the awareness of limitation, thence to true reason, and to the possibility of living'.[23]

After the third soliloquy (Act II, Sc. 2, 543ff.), occasioned by Hamlet's meeting with the troupe of players visiting Elsinore, the next, fourth soliloquy is the most famous of them all: 'To be, or not to be; that is the question:' (Act III, Sc. 1, 58ff.), which begins by Hamlet's considering his action in terms of nobility of mind:

> To be, or not to be; that is the question:
> Whether 'tis nobler in the mind to suffer
> The slings and arrows of outrageous fortune,
> Or to take arms against a sea of troubles,
> And by opposing end them?

What, however, did Hamlet mean by mind? Mother Thekla remarks:

> He certainly did not include any quality of awareness for human failing, or common fears, or obligations, or of love. He meant nothing of the acknowledgment of ignorance, of the going forward in faith, of the victory in defeat, the wisdom in foolishness. The mind would seem for him the sacred vessel which holds the preconceived criterion of the unlimited potentiality of human reason, of nobility which must be satisfied before he can move one step in any direction. Failure, however slight, would be the betrayal of the nobility imposed on the top-most rung of the ladder. Hamlet stood alone, the prey to vultures. He was torn asunder, he must know precisely, exactly, with no shade of relieving doubt, where lay the absolute right, and where the absolute wrong.[24]

The next three soliloquies (Act III, Sc. 2, 381ff.; Act III, Sc. 3, 73ff.; Act IV, Sc. 4 [from the second Quarto], 23ff.) provide further material for Mother Thekla's analysis of Hamlet's paralysis of will rooted in his conviction of the nobility of his mind. She concludes,

> Such was the isolation of Hamlet's sublime position that it is not surprising that the soliloquies are the medium for his tragedy. He denied himself communication, advice, consolation, or even the stimulation of hatred. Where Othello could still hear the voice of Iago, and Lear could bend down into the love of the Fool, Hamlet condemned himself to total sterile solitude. It was his destiny to remain aloof.[25]

And she goes on to quote from one of Hamlet's earlier speeches (delivered just after the second soliloquy, in conversation with Rosencrantz and Guildenstern):

> What a piece of work is man! How noble in reason, how infinite in faculty, in form, in moving how express and admirable, in acting how like an angel, in apprehension how like a God – the beauty of the world, the paragon of animals!
> (Act II, Sc. 2, 305–9)

---

[23] Mother Thekla, *Hamlet*, 9.
[24] Mother Thekla, *Hamlet*, 18–19.
[25] Mother Thekla, *Hamlet*, 34.

Hamlet says this derisively ('And yet to me what is this quintessence of dust?'); it is, however, often quoted as epitomizing the high understanding of human-kind recovered – from classical antiquity and the Church Fathers – by the Renaissance. Mother Thekla's analysis suggests that in his heart Hamlet was wedded to this estimate of the human: an estimate that sets the human on a pinnacle, unable to admit failure, contradiction, doubt, uncertainty, any limitation – and therefore condemned to sterility and paralysis. To be able to act at all, one needs to acknowledge one's limitations, one's dependence on others, to see failure as a way of learning, and love as engaging with real persons: yet all of this Hamlet sees as a betrayal of the nobility of the mind, a mind solitary in its eminence. Mother Thekla closes her study (save for the Appendix on Brutus) by saying: 'The despairing self-praise wafts down from the height from which no road can lead into the valley of tears, where, alone, true reason may rise from within the depths'.[26]

John Keats

Mother Thekla's book on Keats – *John Keats: The Disinterested Heart* – is much longer than the study of Hamlet's soliloquies, though still a fairly short book. It is, however, very condensed, so I shall pick out the themes that seem to me essential. The book has a clear structure: Mother Thekla starts with words, the essential toolkit of the poet, as it were, paying attention not just to their meaning, but to their resonances, and also to their sound. The book then moves from the world of the senses, through the world of the imagination, to the world of reason, which finally opens up to the world of truth (these are the headings of the successive chapters). As is inevitable in a book on Keats, Mother Thekla draws not just on her deep familiarity with Keats' poems (for which she makes no extravagant claims – 'not . . . consistently great poetry, much of what he wrote on the level of poetry was poor verse'),[27] but also on his remarkable letters. I shall pass over the early chapters, save to remark that Mother Thekla draws attention to Keats' amazingly rich use of words, to his positive attitude to the world of the senses, seeing the snares of the world thus revealed as not at all intrinsic to that world (there is no world-denying asceticism in Keats), but more to do with the way in which human beings prize that world. Keats' understanding of the imagination fits easily with the ideas found among the Romantic poets: the imagination relying on the senses, but moving beyond them. Mother Thekla summarizes the role of the imagination in these terms:

> The World of Imagination has striven towards the divine but, it seems, that it may not achieve the way. Its very striving away from the world of the senses has inevitably fixed it relatively to the material world which it would avoid. Direct exclusion, efforts at placation, at conscious transcending, may not suffice.

---

[26] Mother Thekla, *Hamlet*, 34.
[27] Mother Thekla, *Heart*, 191.

> The emphasis needs shifting. Only a re-orientation, and a final one, can help: Action into stillness, observation into contemplation, speculation into reason.[28]

We might pick up a more detailed account of the 'philosophy' of the poet, as Mother Thekla calls it, with Chapter Four, 'The World of Reason'. We begin, now, where we were with Hamlet. In a discussion of Keats' long poem *Endymion*, Mother Thekla remarks at one point that 'Endymion has sought to stray outside and beyond his natural sphere of action. He has forgotten and ignored the proper limits set to man'.[29] The acknowledgement of limits, which Hamlet's conception of the nobility of mind prevented, leads one not up, by way of some kind of idealism, but to a 'sober going down'.[30] 'True spirituality will always come from within, not from the false stimulation of seeming mystery.'[31] This leads to an acceptance of the world in which we live as the world where we shall discover our place, our home. Keats disliked the idea of this world as 'a vale of tears': 'Call the world if you Please "The vale of Soul-making". Then you will find the use of the world', he remarks in one of his letters.[32]

There is, however, some truth in the phrase 'a vale of tears', which Mother Thekla had used in the last sentence of her book on Hamlet, for the way in which the soul is made in this world is through suffering, though it is not any kind of morbid suffering. In another letter, Keats ends a passage, in which he has made a distinction between 'imaginary woes ... conjured up by our passions' and 'real grievances' which 'come of themselves', with what Mother Thekla calls 'an image, which strangely startles': 'The imaginary nail a man down for a sufferer, as on a cross; the real spur him up into an agent'.[33] She comments:

> The echoes here sound and re-sound. The cross was meant to be the end. It would have been the end, if not for the love which had always been. Thus, the end never was. The End always is. The wings of the Imagination fly. Suffering (love) out-distances flight. Suffering spurs up into work. The *up* and the *down* are simultaneous. The cross and the resurrection are outside time and inside time eternally, and in strict sequence. They are cause and effect. They are effect and the cause. The cross and the resurrection are the final blessing upon suffering, which remove it for ever from the sphere of the senses, of the imagination, of human ratiocination and dispute. Suffering is not the scourge, but the gift. Imperceptibly Keats has moved into the radiance of redemptive suffering, into the heart of the problem of evil.[34]

---

[28] Mother Thekla, *Heart*, 103.

[29] Mother Thekla, *Heart*, 110.

[30] Mother Thekla, *Heart*, 110.

[31] Mother Thekla, *Heart*, 110.

[32] See Mother Thekla, *Heart*, 111, quoting Letter 123, to George and Georgiana Keats, 14 February– 3 May 1819, in *The Letters of John Keats*, ed. Maurice Buxton Forman (London: Oxford University Press, 2nd edn, 1942), 335–6.

[33] See Mother Thekla, *Heart*, 120, quoting Letter 155, to Charles Brown, 23 September 1819, *Letters of John Keats*, 397.

[34] Mother Thekla, *Heart*, 121.

Suffering leads to humility. Humility is not at all a matter of self-abasement. It is a matter of realism, seeing things as they are: 'A life, in which evil is accepted, means a way of life in which self-limitation predominates. Reason dictates, not passion. And, reason, first and foremost, sees and approves its own frontiers'.[35] This leads to what Mother Thekla calls 'active humility': 'no subservience but a lack of interest in the faults of other people ... [it] leads to an eager acceptance of help, however seemingly inadequate ... to a startling disregard of being "right" or "wrong" ... humility is an undreamed of freedom'.[36] She quotes from a letter in which Keats says, 'I care not to be in the right'.[37] In the same letter, Keats speaks of a 'proper philosophical temper', on which Mother Thekla comments:

> The *proper philosophical temper* has no achievement ... From the very outset into genuine philosophy, fear is shown impotent for *I care not to be in the right*. This dangerous way without shelter is yet the safest. No abyss will open.[38]

The acceptance of self-limitation that is bound up with humility points to the need for thought:

> Thought, for Keats, is carefully distinguished from speculation at the one extreme, and from planning for some kind of immanent profit at the other. Thought is closely akin to meditation; hence to prayer. The negative capability of the poet-genius merges unassumingly into the contemplation of the mystic.[39]

'Negative capability' is here a key concept for Keats. Mother Thekla had already introduced the notion,[40] but now she treats it at greater length. Keats mentioned it in a letter to his brothers, where he spoke of the 'quality [that] went to form a Man of Achievement, especially in literature, and which Shakespeare possessed so enormously':

> I mean *Negative Capability*, that is, when a man is capable of being in uncertainties, mysteries, doubts, without any irritable reaching after fact and reason – Coleridge, for instance, would let go by a fine isolated verisimilitude caught from the Penetralium of mystery, from being incapable of remaining content with half-knowledge.[41]

Mother Thekla comments that,

> To follow the way of thought is ..., for Keats, the practical application at its highest of the principle of negative capability, the resignation, with the gladdest participation, to a vocation which has no end, no fulfilment, no reward, in this life ... The demand is defencelessness ... But the contrary demand follows:

---

[35] Mother Thekla, *Heart*, 125.
[36] Mother Thekla, *Heart*, 125.
[37] Mother Thekla, *Heart*, 126.
[38] Mother Thekla, *Heart*, 126.
[39] Mother Thekla, *Heart*, 134.
[40] Cf. Mother Thekla, *Heart*, 100.
[41] Letter 32, to George and Thomas Keats, 21 December 1817, *Letters of John Keats*, 72. I am not sure that the comment on Coleridge is altogether fair, or not always.

to be open to all; to all good and to all evil; to suffer all; and to work with this sacrifice of prejudice, to work through it. There must be no secret hiding-places of self-will ...[42]

A little later on, Mother Thekla remarks:

Again and again, the same plea comes from the one provision to thinking: the total abnegation from self-opinion, the vigilant listening, in stillness. But, this brings with it the further implication of the vital step of faith – the including of doubt into the life and the overcoming of the fear of mistakes, the fear of lack of proof, the fear of lack of palpable answers. Resignation of will means the readiness to work always in darkness towards the light which may never be seen.[43]

And Mother Thekla goes on to quote the passage from Keats' letters about negative capability, and remarks:

In this flash of intuition, Keats caught the torment of the sensitive soul who dared not be in doubt, torn in the conflict of *half knowledge*, unable to turn the key into the safety of love which includes doubt and denies any possibility of finding the absolute answer within the partial world inside the realm of human thought.[44]

There follows a chapter on sleep, for thought, as Keats conceives it – thought characterized by negative capability – has something dreamlike about it; it craves no longer the certainty after which reason strives, but finds itself in the half-light of uncertainties, doubts, resignation. No longer seeking knowledge 'out of logic', it becomes a search in the transcendent, searching for a knowledge 'out of vision'. In this context, Mother Thekla comments, 'the weight that Keats puts on sleep is surely of significance', and continues:

In his poetry, Keats repeatedly presents sleep as the image of the mystical condition of contemplation. It is, at times, even difficult to be to any degree sure as to whether sleep is the image or whether it is, in fact, the condition itself. There may be the alternative, that sleep is both symbol and content.[45]

She gives various examples from Keats' poems, including this, from *Endymion*:

> O magic sleep! O comfortable bird,
> That broodest o'er the troubled sea of the mind
> Till it is hush'd and smooth! O unconfined
> Restraint! imprison'd liberty! great key
> To golden palaces, strange minstrelsy,
> Fountains grotesque, new trees, bespangled caves,
> Echoing grottos, full of tumbling waves
> And moonlight; ay, to all the mazy world

---

[42] Mother Thekla, *Heart*, 135.
[43] Mother Thekla, *Heart*, 138.
[44] Mother Thekla, *Heart*, 138–9.
[45] Mother Thekla, *Heart*, 143.

Of silvery enchantment! – who, upfurl'd
Beneath thy drowsy wing a triple hour,
But renovates and lives?[46]

Mother Thekla comments, '*Comfortable bird*: – Comforter and Dove': that is, the Holy Spirit; she continues:

> The presence of the bird, the symbol of sleep, confers upon the human spirit both death and life in a new and hitherto unknown freedom. Sleep, the bird, are one in bestowing this *imprison'd liberty*. Sleep, the bird, take on the third symbol of the *great key*.[47]

Sleep, whether actual or symbolic, renews the soul, and prepares it for the 'ordinary work of waking life'. Keats goes further, and sees sleep 'as a spiritual condition to be sought': '[i]t is not always available. It may come unawares, as a gift. Here [that is, in the poem *Endymion*], the pre-condition for its descent was solitude and silence'.[48]

The soul now moves towards the goal of its journey – its encounter with reality: '[w]ith Keats, from out of sleep, we awaken to Beauty'.[49] Mother Thekla quotes the opening words of *Endymion*, in which we see sleep opening on to beauty:

> A thing of beauty is a joy for ever:
> Its loveliness increases; it will never
> Pass into nothingness; but still will keep
> A bower quiet for us, and a sleep
> Full of sweet dreams, and health, and quiet breathing.[50]

Beauty, however, by its very nature leads us beyond: '[t]he beautiful things penetrate into our darkness with the light of eternity. The creature is mortal. The beautiful thing is mortal, the very thing which stirs us with the radiance of the immortality that works through it'.[51] Beauty leads to the final reality, which is truth. Mother Thekla explores the meaning of this for Keats in a series of profound meditations on Keats' great odes: the 'Ode on a Grecian Urn', the 'Ode to a Nightingale', and 'To Autumn'. We cannot now follow her development in any detail, but just pick up the way she introduces the title of her book: 'The Disinterested Heart'. The heart, Mother Thekla tells us,

> lives only towards the transcendent with no worldly concern, no demand of success or reward. The disinterested heart is man's highest aim on earth, and, it is not an ideal aim, it is a possibility in practice, as has been shown in history.[52]

---

[46] *Endymion*, bk I, 453–63, in *The Poems of John Keats*, ed. H. Buxton Forman (London: Reeves & Turner, 5th edn, 1896), 92.
[47] Mother Thekla, *Heart*, 145.
[48] Mother Thekla, *Heart*, 145.
[49] Mother Thekla, *Heart*, 147.
[50] *Endymion*, bk I, 1–5, *Poems of John Keats*, 79.
[51] Mother Thekla, *Heart*, 150.
[52] Mother Thekla, *Heart*, 174.

Later on, she asserts:

> To die into life is finally the only way to live towards the now coveted end. There must be no question of escape from life, by rejection, by flight into the Imagination, by self-willed seeking of physical death. That is not dying into life. To die into life is to live every moment of it, every problem of it, every suffering of it. But, to live it ever directed to the End. It is to live with the love of the disinterested heart. It is to this vision of death that Keats came.[53]

George Herbert

The third book in which Mother Thekla tried to unfold a spiritual vision by discussing an English poet was her book, *George Herbert: Idea and Image*. We could begin by making a bridge from the kind of considerations we have been following in her book on Keats to her discussion of Herbert, for, in her comment on his poem, 'To all Angels and Saints', she remarks that 'the poem suggests how untenable a spiritual position, founded on balance, may come to be if it once seeks for proof in rationalization, and forsakes active and mute carrying of the contradiction'.[54] In the poem, George Herbert, an early seventeenth-century Anglican priest, evokes the angels and saints, and especially the Virgin Mother of God, and speaks of his desire to seek their aid. Of the Virgin Mary he says,

> Thou art the holy mine, whence came the gold,
> The great restorative for all decay
> > In young and old;
> Thou art the cabinet where the jewell lay:
> Chiefly to thee would I my soul unfold:

And yet, he dare not,

> > ...for our King...
> > Bids no such thing:
> And where his pleasure no injunction layes,
> ('Tis your own case) ye never move a wing.[55]

And so, for all his sense of the succour that can be found with the angels and saints, especially with the Mother of God, he cannot turn to them. And why? According to Mother Thekla, because he cannot endure the 'active and mute carrying of the contradiction': the movement of his heart is held back by his rationalizing intellect.

Mother Thekla's book on Herbert is rather different from the other books we have looked at. One might suggest that Shakespeare and Keats were more amenable to Mother Thekla's approach, because the theological intuitions

---

[53] Mother Thekla, *Heart*, 186.
[54] Mother Thekla, *Herbert*, 73.
[55] 'To all Angels and Saints', 11–15, 18–20; in *The Works of George Herbert*, ed. F. E. Hutchinson (Oxford: Clarendon Press, 1941), 78.

she finds in them are largely implicit and inchoate. George Herbert was, however, a priest of the Church of England, bound by the *39 Articles of Religion*, to which all Anglican priests have to subscribe, so that his theology was not in the least implicit; frequently it was all too explicit.

Earlier on, Mother Maria had written a short essay on Herbert, 'George Herbert: Aspects of His Theology', published in the Library of Orthodox Thinking, which is included in Mother Thekla's book as an Appendix.[56] In this essay, Mother Maria traced what she believed to be a fundamental shortcoming in his poetry to an unresolved contradiction in his thought, a contradiction caused by the way in which Anglicans of Herbert's ilk saw the Church of England as treading a middle way between Catholicism and Protestantism. This left him, Mother Maria maintained, with an unresolved contradiction between the Protestant conviction of the imputation of the righteousness of Christ as the outward or forensic justification of the soul and the Catholic conviction about inner grace which guides and leads the soul in the daily work of progressive sanctification. Indeed, a better way of putting this might be to say that, for all the sense of Anglicanism as a *via media*, in practice, fear of Catholicism pushes the Anglican into a Protestant understanding of salvation as external, simply a change in the human being's standing before God, with a reluctance to consider how this works inwardly in the Christian soul. This frustrates, she maintained, many of Herbert's insights, making it impossible for him to see the Christian life as an ascent towards God, or the sacraments as an objective encounter with, and feeding on, Christ; at best, there is a juxtaposition that prescinds any union. (Incidentally, in the final page of the essay, Mother Maria seems to suggest that, whatever may be the case with George Herbert, Anglicans who found their way back to the Greek Fathers discovered with them that 'the proportion is preserved of redemption without us, with us, and in us', making it possible for the Anglican *via media* to be seen as no compromise, but at least a first step towards a healing of the breach of the Reformation.)[57]

Mother Thekla largely accepts and explores at greater length this failing in Herbert, a failing she traces back to his inability to accept 'the active and mute carrying of contradiction'. Nevertheless, she does find some poems in which she suggests we can see the rational contradictions of George Herbert's theology pointing beyond themselves to a deeper mystery: 'mystery' is the word Mother Thekla uses. She says that,

> The positive recognition of the love of God, of Christ's redeeming action as that of Incarnate Love, inevitably leads out of any dark apprehension of passive redemption into the light of released and free reciprocal activity. Incomprehensible passivity to an arbitrary dispensation of Grace can now be interpreted as participation in love.[58]

---

[56] Mother Thekla, *Herbert*, 279–305.
[57] Mother Thekla, *Herbert*, 305.
[58] Mother Thekla, *Herbert*, 152.

It is in the moments when Herbert passes beyond the stultifying fear of Catholicism to participation in the mystery of love that Mother Thekla finds spiritual theology of great depth in the Anglican poet. As she puts it:

> This Mystery of Love is inalienable and inexorable in its powerful demand of our activity. The Mystery of Love claims our practical life of spirituality not on a foundation of fear, nor of mute hope, nor of dependence on the Church, but on the explicit promise of the Mystery of human love going forward, in total trust, into the Mystery of the Divine Love. Disciplinary fear is replaced by the far more potent, and inescapable, experience of facing Love. Sin becomes, already in this world, the agony of hell, for it can not bear the confrontation with Love. Repentance takes on another meaning, and, so too, daily morality is drawn into its transcendent rather than social dimension. Death too is seen with different eyes. And, as long as we live, life is re-orientated. In fact, theology faced with the Love of the Person of Christ, becomes a practical spirituality.[59]

Mother Thekla finds at least intimations of this in various of the poems which she discusses. Part III discusses what she calls the key poems, in which, as she puts it,

> all the possible flatness of theology falls away and there stands out strongly and simply the fabric of Herbert's spirit, a fabric woven with the single thread of his unceasing prayer, his life, within the Mystery. Herein lies his greatness.[60]

In the end, however, the book on George Herbert fails to enunciate an understanding of the spiritual path, and problems on the way, in the way we find in her other books on Shakespeare and John Keats. Perhaps the most fascinating aspect of the book, alongside the close reading of the key poems, is the way she analyses Herbert's language, setting out the intricate network of imagery that he developed.

* * *

In these books, Mother Thekla was seeking to express the insights of Orthodox spirituality through the intuitions of the English poets she discussed. It was something very deliberate, and very important for her. Orthodoxy need not, she was convinced, be expressed with the use of lots of Greek and Russian words; it need not sound foreign. She tried to show how in some of the English poets – and indeed the greatest of them – there can be found the perceptions and language, the images and feelings, in which to express a genuinely Orthodox spirituality. This would express a genuinely English – or, if you like, British – Orthodoxy, which did not sound foreign, or apologetic, even less, anti-Western. The example of George Herbert points to some of

---

[59] Mother Thekla, *Herbert*, 152.
[60] Mother Thekla, *Herbert*, 209. The key poems are: 'Divinitie', 'The Flower', 'The Answer', 'The Collar', 'Miserie', 'Jordan (II)', 'Josephs Coat', 'Love unknown', 'The Pulley', 'Mans medley', 'Home', 'The Pilgrimage', 'Hope'.

the problems with such an endeavour: it can be argued that the religious dimension of English culture *is* inexorably Protestant. Nevertheless, her discussion of Herbert shows how it may be possible to go deeper, to reach beyond the limitations of Western Christian controversy, and recover the reality of facing the Love of the Incarnate Christ, which is truly Orthodox, truly Christian.

19

Spiritual elders: 2 St Silouan and Fr Sophrony: seeing God as he is

The first UK edition of Fr Sophrony's book on St Silouan, *The Undistorted Image* (but not, so far as I can tell, any other editions, not even the later UK editions) carried a Foreword by Fr Georges Florovsky. This is what Fr Georges had to say:

> Father Silouan was a humble man. But his teaching was daring. It was not a daring of the inquisitive mind, engaged in speculative scrutiny and argument. It was a daring of spiritual assurance. For, in the words of the Father himself, 'the perfect never say anything of themselves, they only say what the Spirit gives them to say'. Father Silouan, surely, must be counted among the perfect. Now, this 'perfection' is the fruit of humility. It can be acquired – and, what is no less important, kept and preserved – only by a constant and continuous effort of self-humbling and self-denial. This process of self-abnegation however, is not just a negative endeavour. It is not just a denial, a subtraction, or a reduction of the self. On the contrary, it is a recovery of the true self. The process is guided by a positive purpose. The objective is always constructive. It is 'the acquiring of the Holy Spirit', as St Seraphim of Sarov used to say. There is here, indeed, a paradoxical tension, The purpose of the spiritual quest is high and ambitious: *consortium divinae naturae*, 'a participation in the Divine nature' (2 Peter 1:4). In whatever manner this startling phrase of the Scripture may be interpreted, it points, clearly and distinctly, to the ultimate goal of all Christian existence: 'life everlasting', life 'in Christ', 'fellowship of the Holy Ghost'. The Greek Fathers used even the daring expression: *theosis*, 'divinization'. Yet, the method, i.e., precisely 'the way', by which this goal can be attained, is the method of radical self-renunciation. Grace is given only to the humble and the meek. Moreover, humility itself is never a human achievement. It is always the gift of God, granted freely, *gratia gratis data*. The whole structure of spiritual life is indeed paradoxical. The riches of the Kingdom are given only to the poor. And with the riches authority is also given. The humble do not say anything of their own. Yet, they speak with authority, whenever they are moved to speak at all. They do not claim any authority for themselves. But they claim authority for that which has been disclosed, through their mediation, from above. Otherwise they would keep silence. 'But you have an anointing from the Holy One and you know all things' (1 John 2:20).
>
> The sayings of Father Silouan are simple. There is nothing spectacular in them, except indeed their simplicity itself. He had no special 'revelations' to disclose. He spoke usually about common things. Yet even about the common things he spoke in a very uncommon manner. He spoke out of his intimate

experience. Love is both the starting point and the core of Christian endeavour. But the 'novelty' of Christian Love is so often overlooked and disregarded. According to Christ Himself, the only true love is 'love for enemies'. It is in no case just a supererogatory advice, and not just a free option. It is rather the first criterion, and the distinctive mark, of genuine Love. St Paul was also quite emphatic at this point. God loved us while we were His enemies. The Cross itself is the perennial symbol and sign of that Love. Now, Christians must share in that redemptive Love of their Lord. Otherwise they cannot 'abide in His Love'. Father Silouan not only spoke of Love. He practised it. In a humble, and yet daring, manner he devoted his life to prayer for enemies, for the perishing and alienated world. This prayer is a dangerous and ambiguous endeavour, unless it is offered in utter humility. One can easily become conscious of one's love, and then it is corroded and infected by vanity and pride. One cannot love purely, except with the love of Christ Himself, infused and operating in the humble heart. One cannot be a 'saint', except when one knows that one is one's self but a 'miserable sinner', in utter need of help and forgiveness. And yet the Grace of God washes away all stain and heals all infirmity. The glory of the Saints is manifested in their humility, just as the glory of the Only Begotten has been manifested in the utter humiliation of His earthly life. Love itself has been crucified in the world.

In his spiritual ascent Father Silouan went through the saddening experience of the 'dark night', of utter loneliness and abandonment. And yet there was nothing grim or morbid in him. He was always calm and quiet, always radiant with joy. It was a joy in Christ, very different indeed from any worldly joy. As we learn from the story of his life, this joy has been acquired by a long and exacting contest, by an unceasing 'invisible warfare'. Left alone, man is left to despair and desolation. Salvation is only in the Lord. The soul must cling to Him. Man is never left alone, except when he chooses himself to leave God. Father Silouan knew by experience the dread and dangers of the outer darkness. But he also learned by experience the immensity of the Divine Love. It shines even over the abyss of trials, torments, and tribulation. Precisely because God *is* Love.

Father Silouan stands in a long and venerable tradition. Nor was he alone even in his own time. There was in every generation a cloud of witnesses of the Mysteries of the Kingdom. Our predicament is in that we do not know them, nor do we care for them and for their witness. We are overtaken by worldly cares. The story of Father Silouan is a timely reminder for our generation of that only 'good thing', which is never taken away. It is also an invitation to the pilgrimage of faith and hope.[1]

I have quoted this at length, because it seems to me to sum up exactly what there is to learn from Fr (now St) Silouan. He was an Athonite monk, and if exceptional, only because he was exceptionally what an Athonite monk is meant to be; he is one of a 'cloud of witnesses', most of whom remain unknown. Fr Georges put his finger on what, nonetheless, is distinctive about St Silouan: his teaching on love, especially love of our enemies, and alongside

---

[1] Archimandrite Sofrony [Sophrony], *The Undistorted Image: Staretz Silouan 1866–1938*, trans. Rosemary Edmonds (London: Faith Press, 1958), 5–6; I have somewhat modified the translation.

St Silouan
With permission of the Stavropegic Monastery of St John the Baptist, Essex

that, his experience of darkness, of the 'dark night' – a point of comparison with the great Western mystic, St John of the Cross, who likewise emphasized the role of love: A la tarde te examinarán en el amor – In the evening [of life] you will be examined in love.[2] St Silouan's experience reminds one, too, of another Western saint, this time a contemporary of his, St Thérèse de Lisieux.[3] A further reason for quoting Fr Georges' words is that, while on the one hand Fr Sophrony had sought and received from the monks of Mount Athos the acknowledgement of his account of St Silouan as an authentic presentation of Athonite spirituality,[4] Fr Georges, speaking from the academy, as it were, acknowledges St Silouan as representing the wisdom of the saints.

Life of St Silouan

Who was he, this monk who became St Silouan? The monastery register records of him:

---

[2] *Dichos de luz y amor*, I, 59: in San Juan de la Cruz, *Obras Completas*, ed. Lucinio Ruano de la Iglesia (Madrid: Biblioteca de Autores Cristianos, 11th edn, 1982), 48.

[3] Ysabel de Andia notes this parallel, but does not develop it: de Andia, *Mystiques d'Orient et d'Occident*, Spiritualité Orientale 62 (Bégrolles-en-Mauges: Abbaye de Bellefontaine, 1994), 36–7.

[4] Archimandrite Sophrony, *His Life Is Mine* (London and Oxford: Mowbrays, 1977), 11.

Schema-monk Father Silouan. Name 'in the world' – Simeon Ivanovich Antonov. Peasant from the province of Tambov, district of Lebedyan, village of Shovsk. Born 1866. Came to Athos 1892. Professed 1896. *Schema* 1911. Performed his duties of obedience at the mill, at Kalomar at Old Rossikon, and as steward. Died 11/24 September 1938.[5]

If we press a little, we can fill out the details a bit. He was brought up as a devout peasant, and remembered an early interest in religion. He worked as a member of an *artel*, a group of artisans, as a carpenter. The old country-woman who cooked for them once went on pilgrimage and visited the tomb of a hermit, John Sezenov. On her return, she spoke of his holy life and the miracles that took place at his tomb. This convinced the young Simeon of the reality of God, and he began to pray and felt drawn to the monastic life. First, however, he had to do his military service, and found himself drawn into a more worldly way of life. On one occasion, he was involved in a brawl and nearly killed a man, the memory of which remained with him all his life. A little later on, he felt himself called again, through a dream in which he saw a snake crawling down his throat; he awoke, sick with revulsion, to

Fr Sophrony

With permission of the Stavropegic Monastery of St John the Baptist, Essex

---

[5] Sophrony, *Undistorted Image*, 15.

hear a voice saying: 'just as you found it loathsome to swallow a snake in your dream, so I find your ways ugly to look upon'. He was convinced this voice, 'unusually sweet and beautiful', was that of the Mother of God, calling him. At the end of his military service he set off to see Father (now Saint) John of Kronstadt. He failed to meet him, but left a letter, written by the company scribe who had accompanied him, to which he added a few words asking for the priest's prayers for him, as he wanted to become a monk. Soon he was on his way to Athos.

Fr Sophrony records what he learnt from St Silouan about his time on Athos, the temptations, initially to return to the world and marriage, and soon, as he discovered his aptitude for prayer, the danger of vanity and self-satisfaction. He continues this account through to the experience in which he heard in his prayer the words, 'Keep your mind in hell, and despair not', and then closes with an account of the death of the *starets*. All of this Fr Sophrony discussed in his book, *St Silouan*, and we shall follow some of this later. First, we need to pause, for one problem we face is that we have no account of St Silouan other than that given us by Fr Sophrony. It is, indeed, not easy to distinguish between the teaching of the one and of the other, simply because Fr Sophrony acknowledges how much he owed to the *starets*, and how much he saw his own vocation as one of making known what he had learnt from St Silouan.

In the book, called in its first English version, *The Undistorted Image*, Fr Sophrony presents his account in two parts: the first called 'Life and Commentary', the second 'From the Staretz' Writings' – which encourages the idea that we first have Fr Sophrony's account, and then the writings on which it is based. Closer inspection reveals that it is not so simple. The first part is full of lengthy quotations from St Silouan, and it is not clear how the second part has been put together: some parts seem to be compiled, other parts to have an integrity of their own. In short, it is difficult to separate the master and the disciple. And yet, they were very different. The saint is presented to us as a peasant with little formal education; Fr Sophrony was highly educated, and continued to read and think deeply throughout his life. What he made of what he learnt from St Silouan cannot all be traced back to the saint himself.

Life of Fr Sophrony

Who then was Fr Sophrony? The best account of his life so far, both in terms of events and in terms of intellectual influence, is that by his great-nephew, who himself became a monk of the monastery Fr Sophrony founded in England, Fr Nikolai, in his book, based on a doctoral thesis, *I Love, Therefore I Am: The Theological Legacy of Archimandrite Sophrony*.[6] There is also a briefer

---

[6] Nicholas V. Sakharov, *I Love, Therefore I Am: The Theological Legacy of Archimandrite Sophrony* (Crestwood, NY: St Vladimir's Seminary Press, 2002).

account, by the English translator of his works, Rosemary Edmonds, which she wrote as an Introduction to his work, *His Life Is Mine*.[7]

Fr Sophrony was born Sergei Symeonovich Sakharov in Moscow on 22 September 1896, into a devoutly Orthodox family. He soon demonstrated an aptitude for prayer. He read widely from a young age in Russian literature, and absorbed the kenotic perception of Christianity characteristic of Russian culture. From his early years he was interested in painting and also in Oriental mysticism. He proved to be a talented painter and studied in Moscow at the Academy of Arts and the Moscow School of Painting, Sculpture and Architecture; he was deeply involved in the mystical trends that characterized the theory and practice of art among the Russians at that time. While still in Russia, he read deeply in the works of such as Berdyaev and Rozanov.

In 1921 he came west to Paris, a little before the 'ship of the philosophers', expelled from Russia by Trotsky's decree, and pursued his artistic career there, exhibiting at the Salon d'Automne, and the more exclusive Salon des Tuileries. After a few years, he tired of his artistic quest, and, through an experience of the uncreated light over Easter in 1924, embraced Christianity in a wholehearted way.[8] He quickly became one of the first students at the newly founded Institut St-Serge in Paris, where Bulgakov was the dean. In his theological development, he owed a great deal to Fr Bulgakov. After a year, however, he felt that a purely intellectual approach to Orthodox Christianity did not fulfil his real desire, which was to pray and experience God in prayer. He left Paris and went to Mount Athos, where he joined the Russian Monastery of St Panteleimon. After a few years, he discovered St Silouan, and became his spiritual disciple. After the saint's death in 1938, Fr Sophrony lived for several years as a hermit. In 1941 he was ordained priest, and continuing to live an eremitical life, became confessor and spiritual father for many ascetics on the Holy Mountain. These were the years of the Second World War, in which he felt called to such intense prayer for the sufferings of the world that his health was affected.

After the war, he left Athos and came to Western Europe with a sense of his vocation to make known the teaching of his *starets* in the West. He returned initially to Paris, where he spent 12 years. There he came to know the persons and writings of the so-called Paris School, and came to know Vladimir Lossky: they shared a great deal, but also differed over many issues.

In 1959, he came to England and established the monastery of St John the Baptist at a former rectory in the Essex village of Tolleshunt Knights. Gradually a community of both monks and nuns grew around him. He began, too, to publish books setting out the spiritual vision of St Silouan, and his own

---

[7] Sophrony, *His Life Is Mine*, 7–13.

[8] Later, as a monk, Fr Sophrony turned to icon-painting, and should be considered, too, as part of the revival of iconography in the twentieth century, a story only touched on in this book. On the place of art in his spiritual journey, see Sister Gabriela, *Seeking Perfection in the World of Art: The Artistic Path of Father Sophrony* (Essex: Stavropegic Monastery of St John the Baptist, 2013).

understanding of it. The first book, published in 1958 before he arrived in England, was *The Undistorted Image*.[9] In his next major work, *His Life Is Mine*, he began to develop his own theological ideas, based on what he had learnt from St Silouan. The final work published in his lifetime, published initially in French in 1984, *We Shall See Him as He Is*, proved very controversial.[10] In it, Fr Sophrony developed further his theological ideas, and expressed them quite boldly. Well received among Western Christians sympathetic to Orthodoxy, it was received very negatively among the Orthodox, especially among the Russians. Since his death in 1993, many more works have been published: the talks that he gave to his community, letters to various recipients, and articles that he published through his life, mostly in the 1950s.

The teaching of St Silouan

What was it that Fr Sophrony learnt from his Athonite elder? In *The Undistorted Image*, there are two chapters on 'The Staretz' Doctrinal Teaching',[11] though the chapters that follow in Part I continue to give the spiritual teaching of the saint. We shall first look at these chapters, and then go on to discuss the two issues mentioned by Fr Georges – love for one's enemies, and the words the saint heard, 'Keep your mind in hell, and despair not!'

Fr Sophrony notes, as does Fr Georges, that St Silouan knew from experience; his knowledge was not the result of argument or thought. Fr Sophrony gives an example from his writings:

> We know that the greater the love, the greater the sufferings of the soul. The fuller the love, the fuller the knowledge [of God]. The more ardent the love, the more fervent the prayer. The more perfect the love, the holier the life.[12]

He comments, 'Each of these four propositions might have been the precious culmination of complex philosophical, psychological and theological arguments, but the Staretz had no need of such arguments and did not descend

---

[9] *The Undistorted Image* was republished in two volumes with some additional material – *The Monk from Mount Athos*, with a brief Foreword by Metropolitan Anthony of Sourozh, and *Wisdom from Mount Athos*, with a Foreword by Archimandrite Sophrony (London: Mowbrays, 1973–4); fullest version: *Saint Silouan the Athonite* (Essex: Stavropegic Monastery of St John the Baptist, 1991; Crestwood, NY: St Vladimir's Seminary Press, 1998); French trans.: *Starets Silouane, moine du Mont-Athos: Vie – Doctrine – Écrits* (Sisteron: Éditions Présence, 1973). Original version: *Prepodobny Siluan Afonsky* (Paris, 1952; facsimile published with additional texts by the monastery, 1990).

[10] *Voir Dieu tel qu'il est* (Geneva: Labor et Fides, 1984); *La Félicité de connaître la voie* (Geneva: Labor et Fides, 1988). *We Shall See Him as He Is* (Essex: Stavropegic Monastery of St John the Baptist, 1988). Original Russian: *Videt' Bog kak On est'* (published jointly by the Trinity-St Sergii Lavra, Moscow, and the Essex Monastery, 2006). It should be noted that the different versions of Fr Sophrony's books in different languages are often different books: different bits are included or excluded, frequently at Fr Sophrony's direction. The three versions of *We Shall See Him as He Is* mentioned have rather different contents, though the contents of the French version (the shortest) appear in the other two.

[11] Sophrony, *Undistorted Image*, 54–74; which appears as one, much extended, chapter in *Saint Silouan the Athonite*, 75–130.

[12] Sophrony, *Undistorted Image*, 54.

to them'.[13] At the end of the previous chapter, Fr Sophrony had told a story about a 'certain Orthodox foreigner' who had visited the monastery over a long period and been deeply impressed by the saint. When asked by one of the monks what a 'scholar' like him found in 'Father Silouan, an illiterate peasant', he replied, 'It needs a "scholar" to understand Father Silouan'. The monk later expressed his amazement to Father Methodios, who ran the monastic bookshop, at this interest in St Silouan, for '[a]fter all, he reads nothing'. Father Methodios replied, 'He reads nothing but fulfils everything, while others read a lot and perform nothing.'[14]

Fr Sophrony presents the saint's teaching by beginning with 'Discovering the Will of God'. To know God's will is the most important thing in a person's life, but very hard, because of the 'endless complexity of situations' in the tangled state of the fallen world. To have the love of God in our heart will mean that our actions approximate to the will of God, but only approximate: perfection is beyond our reach. The way is to reject our own knowledge, our preconceived ideas, and turn to God in prayer and attention. Since we are all created in God's image and likeness, we are all called to the fullness of direct communing with God, but this seems not to be the path for everyone. There is an alternative: to search out a spiritual father. The relation with the spiritual father is very delicate: if he meets with resistance on the part of the questioner, he does not insist, or demand, but, as man, withdraws. Fr Sophrony goes on to speak of the nature of obedience, and recalls the ancient teaching of the Church that the spiritual father is to be trusted implicitly, even when he is clearly not without faults himself (St John Climacus is emphatic on this, for example), not because the spiritual father is infallible, but because the Holy Spirit uses this relationship (which includes the delicacy already mentioned) to help the one who has sought out the spiritual father to find what God's will is for him. Fr Sophrony remarks,

> In the vast sea which is the life of the Church the true tradition of the Spirit flows like a thin pure stream, and he who would be in this stream must renounce argument. When anything of self is introduced the waters no longer flow clear, for God's supreme wisdom and truth are the opposite of human wisdom and truth. Such renunciation appears intolerable, insane even, to the self-willed, but the man who is not afraid to 'become a fool' has found true life and true wisdom.[15]

The ultimate source of the will of God is to be found in tradition and the Scriptures. 'For the Staretz the life of the Church meant life in the Holy Spirit, and Sacred Tradition the unceasing action of the Holy Spirit in her.'[16] The saint was convinced that this living tradition, the life of the Holy Spirit, was the real source of authority. Even if the Church lost all her books – the Scriptures, the writings of the Fathers, the whole body of liturgical texts –

---

[13] Sophrony, *Undistorted Image*, 54.
[14] Sophrony, *Undistorted Image*, 53.
[15] Sophrony, *Undistorted Image*, 58.
[16] Sophrony, *Undistorted Image*, 58.

'Sacred Tradition would restore the Scriptures, not word for word perhaps –
the verbal form might be different – but in essence the new Scriptures would
be the expression of that same "faith which was once delivered unto the
saints".'[17] The saint had, Fr Sophrony tells us, the greatest respect for the work
of scholars, but their work only related to the historical aspect of the Church,
'not to the real, eternal life of the Spirit'.[18] The whole of Scripture is summed
up in *love*, the meaning of which 'will remain a mystery for the philologist
to all eternity. The word *love* is the very name of God, and its true sense only
revealed by the action of God Himself'.[19]

Following the will of God, keeping the commandments, leads to our being
in the likeness of Christ – 'we shall be like him, for we shall see him as he is'
(1 John 3.2 RSV). Within that likeness, we find ourselves one with our fellow
human beings: our relationship with them is the test of our love. Various
consequences follow from this. First of all, it opens up the idea of the unity
of the spiritual world: through this love the unity of spiritual beings is made
real. There is an 'intangible communion in the existence of all things', which
is 'peculiar to the Saints'. This awareness, 'which exceeds the bounds of human
knowledge, [the saint] ascribed to the action of the Holy Spirit in whom the
soul "sees" and embraces the whole world in her love'.[20] In this spiritual
vision, '[t]he spiritual man soars like an eagle in the heights, and with his soul
feels God, and beholds the whole world, though his prayer be in the darkness
of the night'.[21] In this state, 'the soul, detached from everything and seeing
nothing, in God beholds the entire world and knows that she is one with
this world, as she prays for it'.[22] If there seems to be a paradox here, in that
the soul seems both detached from the world, and yet united to it, it is
a paradox well known in the Byzantine ascetic tradition: Evagrios spoke of
the monk as 'one who is separated from all and united to all'.[23]

Another topic about which the saint spoke was the nature of human
freedom. Human beings seek freedom, but in the wrong way.

> 'Men seek their own freedom,' that is to say, freedom outside God, outside true
> life, in 'outer darkness', where there is and can be no freedom, for freedom can
> only exist where there is no death, where there is authentic eternal existence –
> that is, in God.[24]

St Silouan recognized 'with his whole soul that there is only one real servitude –
the servitude of sin – and one real freedom, which is resurrection in God'.[25]
And this leads again into further insights into the nature of love, the love

[17] Sophrony, *Undistorted Image*, 59.
[18] Sophrony, *Undistorted Image*, 60.
[19] Sophrony, *Undistorted Image*, 60.
[20] Sophrony, *Undistorted Image*, 62.
[21] Sophrony, *Undistorted Image*, 62.
[22] Sophrony, *Undistorted Image*, 63.
[23] Evagrios, *On Prayer*, 124.
[24] Sophrony, *Undistorted Image*, 65.
[25] Sophrony, *Undistorted Image*, 66.

that seeks the salvation of fallen humankind. St Silouan believed that 'Christ-like love cannot suffer any man to perish, and in its care for the salvation of all men walks the way of Calvary'.[26] Such love works 'by attracting people. There is no place for any kind of compulsion'.[27] Nor is there any sense of this love being limited: it embraces all, the 'whole race of Adam'.[28] For the saint, this seemed perfectly simple: 'there is no need to cudgel our brains: we all have one and the same nature, and so it should be natural for us to love all men; but it is the Holy Spirit who gives the power to love'.[29] This might seem to be leading in the direction of universal salvation – and there is no doubt that for the saint the salvation of all was something to be hoped for – but human freedom makes it possible to resist even perfect love: that remained a possibility, however difficult to conceive.

Further themes Fr Sophrony explored in his chapters on the doctrinal teaching of St Silouan include love for enemies, which we shall touch on separately, the nature of good and evil, where the saint was convinced of the reality of the good and the essentially parasitic nature of evil, and the nature of justice, where he drew a sharp distinction between the notion of legal responsibility and the love of Christ, which sees 'nothing strange, but rather something entirely natural, in sharing the guilt of those we love, and even in assuming full responsibility for their wrong-doing':[30] something that does away with any notion of self-justification. All this was the result of the saint's experience of prayer, on which Fr Sophrony commented: 'Intense prayer, like Father Silouan's, for the world leads to an awareness of the ontological community between one's personal existence and the existence of all mankind'.[31]

Love of one's enemies

The test of this way of love was, for the saint, love of one's enemies. The command of Christ – 'Love your enemies; bless those who curse you, do good to those who hate you, and pray for those who persecute you' (Matt. 5.44) – and the example of Christ – 'when we were enemies, we were reconciled to God through the death of his Son' (Rom. 5.10) – teach us to love our enemies. In speaking of 'enemies', the saint was adopting current language. In reality, in Christ there are no enemies, no one rejected by God's love. The 'enemies' are those who reject the Creator's love, but they are not outside that love. Nor are they outside the prayer of those who pray in that love. 'God is love and in the Saints the Holy Spirit is love. Dwelling in the Holy Spirit, the Saints behold hell and embrace it, too, in their love.'[32]

---

26 Sophrony, *Undistorted Image*, 66.
27 Sophrony, *Undistorted Image*, 67.
28 Sophrony, *Undistorted Image*, 67.
29 Sophrony, *Undistorted Image*, 67.
30 Sophrony, *Undistorted Image*, 72.
31 Sophrony, *Undistorted Image*, 74.
32 Sophrony, *Undistorted Image*, 70.

To love the enemy, the true enemy of God, is to embrace the hell that they have brought on themselves. St Silouan lived through the horrors of the First World War, when enmity between nations became for many a rule of life; Fr Sophrony spoke of himself as 'condemned to live in this appalling century'.[33] To pray for such a world was to embrace the hell human beings had brought on themselves, to enter into that hell.

'Keep your mind in hell, and despair not'

Keep your mind in hell, and despair not. Those were the words the saint heard at the end of a time of prayer. What could they mean? They seem, indeed, paradoxical, even contradictory: after all, Dante saw written on the lintel of Hell the words, *Lasciate ogni speranza voi ch'entrate* – 'Leave behind all hope, you who enter'[34] – for Hell is a place devoid of hope, a place of despair. To be in hell and *not* to despair: how could that be? Fr Sophrony suggested various ways of understanding these words.[35] One way was ascetic: to keep the mind in hell, to despair of one's own salvation, is a way of dealing with the assaults of the passions, especially the passion of pride, the conviction that one has achieved perfection. Fr Sophrony speaks of Silouan's 'beloved song':

> Soon shall I die, and my accursed soul will descend into hell. There I shall suffer alone in the darkness of the prison-house, and weep with bitter tears: My soul is weary for the Lord and seeks Him in tears. How should I not seek Him? He first sought me and showed Himself to the sinner.[36]

The real experience of hell, of abandonment, sears away the passions and casts the saint on the love of Christ; it was the experience of that love from which the words 'and despair not' arose.

Fr Sophrony suggested another meaning, which flowed from the sense of abandonment embraced in praying for the whole Adam:

> Man's consciousness that he is unworthy of God, and his condemnation of himself to hell for every sin, in strange fashion makes him kin with the Spirit of Truth, and sets his heart free for Divine love. And with the increase of love and the light of truth comes revelation of the mystery of the redeeming descent into hell of the Son of God. Man himself becomes more fully like Christ; and through this likeness to Christ in the 'impoverishment' (*kenosis* [self-emptying]) of His earthly being he becomes like to Him also in the fullness of Eternal Being. God embraces all things, even the bottomless abysses of hell, for there is no domain outside His reach, and the Saints behold and abide in hell, but it has no power over them, and the manner of their abiding differs from the abiding of those who constitute hell.[37]

---

[33] Sophrony, *We Shall See Him*, 81.

[34] *Inferno* III. 7.

[35] See Sophrony, *Undistorted Image*, 103–6; *Saint Silouan the Athonite*, 208–13 (the chapters are not at all the same, though they overlap to some extent).

[36] Sophrony, *Undistorted Image*, 104–5.

[37] Sophrony, *Undistorted Image*, 105–6.

The teaching of Fr Sophrony

Such is a brief and inevitably inadequate sketch of the teaching of St Silouan, as Fr Sophrony presented it. But the teaching of Fr Sophrony himself? In most respects it is, as we would expect, a development of what he had learnt from the saint. However, Fr Sophrony's experience of the love of God went back in his life before his meeting with his spiritual father. In *We Shall See Him as He Is*, he recounts his experiences of the Divine Light. The first account he gives is from his time in Paris, just after leaving Russia.

> And suddenly one Great Saturday – it must have been in 1924 – the Light visited me after I had received Communion; I felt it like the touch of divine eternity on my soul. Soft, full of peace and love, the Light remained with me for three days. It dispersed the shadows of nothingness that were rising up before me. I was risen; and in me and with me, the whole world was risen. The words of John Chrysostom read at the end of Easter Matins resounded with striking force: 'Christ is risen and no longer is there anyone dead in the tombs'. Until then I had been weighed down by the spectre of universal death, but at that moment I came back to life: yes, my soul was raised up, and from then on I saw no one in death . . . If our God is such, then we must abandon everything as quickly as possible and seek union with him alone.[38]

The theme of the Divine Light is important to Fr Sophrony, as we shall see; it goes back in his life before his arrival on Athos.

Although Fr Sophrony's teaching can be located in the traditions of Russian thought in a way that is not really possible with the teaching of St Silouan (Fr Nikolai is very illuminating over all this), his thought is not really very systematic, though there are leading themes. Indeed, one might say that any intellectual ideas are strictly subordinated to his ascetic programme. I shall attempt in what follows to take some of these leading themes, and pursue them a little, as an introduction to the thought of Fr Sophrony.

The unity of the Church in the image of the Trinity

An important early text by Fr Sophrony is his long article, 'The Unity of the Church in the Image of the Holy Trinity', which is contained in the volume, *La Félicité de connaître la voie*, where it is collected together with other chapters from the Russian original of *We Shall See Him as He Is*, which were not included in the French *Voir Dieu tel qu'il est*.[39] In this article, Fr Sophrony explores the nature of the unity of the Church as a reflection of the unity of the Trinity, in accordance with the prayer of Christ: 'that they may be one, as we are one, I in them and you in me, that they may be made perfect in

---

[38] Sophrony, *Voir Dieu tel qu'il est*, 125 (my trans.).

[39] Sophrony, *La Félicité*, 9–55. My realization of the importance of this text I owe to my former research student, Fr Serafim (Aldea).

one' (John 17.22–23). The unity of the Church is based on the fact that the Church consists of human beings, created in the image of God. It is, however, not so much man, as an individual, who is in the image of God, but man, as summing up the unity of mankind, as Adam. This is unity created and manifest through love: a reflection of the unity of love that we find in the Holy Trinity:

> Love transfers the existence of the person who loves into the being loved and thus it is assimilated to the life of the beloved. Person is then permeable to love. The absolute perfection of love in the bosom of the Trinity reveals to us the perfect reciprocity of the compenetration of the Three Persons, to the point that there are in Them only a single will, a single energy, a single power.
>
> In the image of that Love, the observing of the second commandment – 'You shall love your neighbour as yourself' – re-establishes the consubstantiality of the human race, rent asunder by sin. Realized in its ultimate perfection, this commandment demonstrates that *man is one*, in the image of the Holy Trinity: unique in his essence, multiple in his *hypostases*. When each human *hypostasis*, by virtue of the fact that he dwells in the plenitude of the consubstantial unity, becomes bearer of human existence in its entirety, it is dynamically equal to the whole of humanity, in the image of Christ, of the perfect Man who contains in Himself all human beings.[40]

Out of this Fr Sophrony develops an ascetic strategy: that of taking human beings from their fallen state as disparate, indeed warring, individuals to their perfect state in the image of God as persons, *hypostases*. This contrast between fragmented individuals and persons bound together in a communion of love is something we have frequently encountered among the thinkers of the Russian emigration. It was, however, Fr Bulgakov who made use of the Russian word *ipostas* to designate human beings as they are meant to be, persons bound together in a united human nature by love, in the image of God the Trinity, in contrast to the human fallen state, in which human nature is fragmented and humans are manifest as individuals, at odds with one another, unable to love, constrained by necessity. It is in the Church that this renewed human nature is to be found, and so in the Church we find human-kind restored (at least potentially) to a unity in which persons exist in love, and therefore in freedom. Fr Sophrony says that,

> It is equally in this way that we must understand the image of God in man, that is to say, that humanity, while being one in its essence, comprises a plural-ity of *hypostases*, each of which must finally contain the fullness of divine-human being and be presented, not as just a part of human nature, but as the whole fullness of human being, or in other words, to become *universal man*. And that is realized fully only in the Church and by the Church.
>
> Existing in the image of the Holy Trinity, the Church equally presents in its being the antinomic character of identity and diversity simultaneously. On the example of the divine Being where one distinguishes three moments:

---

[40] Sophrony, *La Félicité*, 21.

Person, Essence, and Energy, we see in the Church persons, nature and acts, which, in the ultimate accomplishment of human being, must be identical. Just as in the Trinity each *hypostasis* is bearer of the absolute fullness of divine Being, so, in our human existence, each *hypostasis* must, in its supreme realization, become bearer of the divine-human fullness, the condition *sine qua non* of unity in the image of the Holy Trinity. For if the identity is not complete, the unity, too, will remain incomplete.[41]

There flow from this vision of humanity restored in the image of the Trinity – a restoration found in its fullest in the Church – two corollaries on which I want to dwell just a little.

Spirituality as ontology

First, there is the use of *ontological* language, the language of *being*, to describe the nature of the change that has to take place as we respond to the gospel and seek to follow Christ. This is quite deliberate on Fr Sophrony's part; it lends to his words a distinctive character. It seems to me to have several purposes. One is ascetic: this use of ontological language underlines the nature of ascetical effort. It is not just a matter of some change in behaviour, or even moral practice; it goes deeper than that – it involves an ontological change, a change at the level of being. Ultimately, it leads into the idea of transformation in Christ as coming to partake of the divine nature, deification. We shall come back to that. There is another level, manifest in the early chapters of *His Life Is Mine*. The first chapter begins:

> O Thou Who art:
> O God the Father, Almighty Master:
> Who hast created us and brought us into this life:
> Vouchsafe that we may know Thee,
> The one true God.[42]

The first words of this prayer are the first words of the Anaphora of St Basil, themselves a quotation from the Septuagint text of Jeremias 1.6 (cf. 14.13). God is addressed by the name he gives to Moses at the Burning Bush: *Ho Ōn*, 'the One who is', 'I am that I am' in English Bibles (and in the English translation of Fr Sophrony's works). The first few chapters of *His Life Is Mine* revolve round the revelation of God as 'He who is': one who simply exists in an unqualified way, one who declares himself as the One who is, as a person addressing persons – as calling persons into being – as a, or rather the, *Hypostasis*. This has the effect of moving the horizon of theology to the level of being, to the doctrines of creation out of nothing, the Incarnation, the Resurrection: all of which focus on creation and re-creation.

---

[41] Sophrony, *La Félicité*, 49–50.
[42] Sophrony, *His Life Is Mine*, 17.

Becoming persons

The second corollary, as I see it, of this vision of humanity restored in the image of the Trinity is the close relationship thus effected between human persons and divine Persons, human society and the divine coinherence or *perichoresis*. The divine Person is the goal to which the human person, or *hypostasis*, is heading: that is what is meant by deification. It is not a metaphor; it is a reality, a reality in which human persons become permeable to each other through love and permeable, as it were, to the love of the divine Persons. Fr Nikolai speaks of this as a theological 'maximalism'. In *We Shall See Him as He Is*, Fr Sophrony speaks of an 'identity' between God and deified humanity: 'there is no limit to the outpouring of the Father's love: man becomes identical with God – the same by content, not by primordial Self-Being'.[43]

Bound up with this are many of the, perhaps surprising, emphases in Fr Sophrony's theology. Like Bulgakov, he believes that there is *kenosis*, self-emptying, *within the Godhead Itself*, among the Persons of the Trinity. In their unity of love, each of the Persons yields, empties himself, before the others. *Kenosis* is an aspect of the love each divine Person has for the others. From this follow two corollaries: first, that in emptying himself in the Incarnation and death of the cross, Christ, as Son of God, is not *veiling* the nature of God, appearing as less than God, as it were, but precisely *revealing* what it is to be God: *kenosis* constitutes God, *kenosis* reveals God's love. And this leads to the other, ascetic, corollary: that our *kenosis*, in imitation of Christ, our experience of emptiness and dereliction, is part of our following of Christ, not a worrying symptom of our erring from the way of discipleship. The 'dark night', associated especially with St John of the Cross, is something with analogies in Fr Sophrony's ascetic teaching, not an example of the way in which the Western Church has lost its way, as Vladimir Lossky sometimes seemed to suggest.[44]

Seeing God as he is

Seeing God as he is: what does this mean? Fr Sophrony was convinced that we should take these words quite literally: we shall see God *as he is*. The idea that in encountering God we enter into darkness, the darkness of apophatic theology, is something that Fr Sophrony was reluctant to accept. For it seems to suggest that we do *not* come to know God as he is; he remains forever hidden from us. In several places Fr Sophrony speaks very critically of such an interpretation of the Byzantine mystical tradition.[45]

---

[43] Sophrony, *We Shall See Him*, 172.

[44] On this, see the chapter on Godforsakenness in Sakharov, *I Love, Therefore I Am*, 171–97.

[45] See, for instance, Archimandrite Sofrony, *Dukhovnye Besedy* [Spiritual Conversations], I (Essex–Moscow: Izdatel'stvo Palomnik, 2003), *Beseda* 2, 40, where he complains about 'some people in Paris' who have objected to his talking about 'seeing God as he is', instead of restricting himself to knowing only what God is not; or *Rozhdenie v Tsarstvo Nepokolebimoe* [Birth in the Kingdom That Cannot Be Moved] (Moscow: Izdatel'stvo Palomnik, 2000), 74, where he expresses his disapproval of the Cappadocian notion of 'divine darkness'.

* * *

These are just a few themes, I hope central ones, in the teaching of Fr Sophrony, the witness to which, in his spiritual conversations with his monks and nuns, and in his letters, is as yet only partially available. The influence of Fr Sophrony and the teaching of his spiritual mentor, St Silouan, in the Orthodox world and beyond is only just beginning.

20

Theology in Russia under communism: Fr Aleksandr Men'

Fr Aleksandr was a phenomenon of the last decades of Russian communism and it is impossible to understand him outside this context. This is not an original observation: almost everything written on him either directly or indirectly makes the same point – they either say so (Fr Michael Plekon, for example)[1] or the background seems to take centre-stage (as in Yves Hamart's excellent biography of Fr Aleksandr).[2] It is, however, natural for us to approach him from this context, for what we have done so far has been to explore the way the *Philokalia* led to a rebirth of theology in nineteenth-century Russia which blossomed in the Russian Religious Renaissance. This theology came to an abrupt end with the Bolshevik Revolution, and was transplanted to the West, and especially to Paris, from which virtually all the main strands of modern Orthodox theology have emanated, even in Greece either by seeking to continue the intuitions of the thinkers of the Religious Renaissance, or by engaging with it critically. Our story, then, really started in Russia and then spread throughout the Orthodox world, both in traditionally Orthodox countries and in the diaspora.

What, however, about Russia itself? We have seen a glimpse of this in our discussion of Fr Pavel Florensky, one of the very few intellectuals to stay behind in Russia, avoiding Trotsky's 'ship of the philosophers', essentially because, with his scientific expertise, it was felt he could be of value to the new Soviet state: he played a key role in the grand project of the electrification of the Soviet Union. However, after the Revolution, although his theological and philosophical work – mostly towards his great project 'On the Watershed of Thought' – continued, it remained unpublished.

Indeed, the state of the Church in the Soviet Union made it impossible for any theology to flourish; it was hard enough for the Church to survive. According to Marxist theory, after the Revolution the Church, as a manifestation of religion, was meant to fade away. As it didn't, its disappearance had to be encouraged, and the Church experienced persecution far more severe than ever before. The great persecutions of the early Church under the Roman Empire were haphazard and episodic; with the structures of a modern state,

---

[1] Michael Plekon, *Living Icons: Persons of Faith in the Eastern Church* (Notre Dame, IN: University of Notre Dame Press, 2002), 234–60, at 237.

[2] Yves Hamart, *Alexandre Men* (Montrouge: Nouvelle Cité, 2000).

the persecution of Christians in the Soviet Union could aim at the extermination of the Church, and very nearly succeeded. Hundreds of churches were closed and turned over to other uses; the same went for monasteries – Florensky's attempt to preserve the Trinity-St Sergii Monastery as a cultural monument was doomed to failure. A hierarchy was preserved, but in a diminished way. When Patriarch Tikhon died in 1925, he was replaced with a *locum tenens*, not a patriarch, Metropolitan Sergii, who was forced to collude with the Bolsheviks to the extent of denying the persecution that was destroying the Church. We have seen something of the repercussions of this in the West, with the departure of the exarchate under Metropolitan Evlogy from the Moscow Patriarchate, and his putting the exarchate under the *omophorion* of the Œcumenical Patriarch. During the Second World War – for Russians, the Great Patriotic War – the Orthodox Church supported the Fatherland, and as a result, after the war, some churches were opened and a limited ecclesial life allowed; the spiritual academies in Moscow and St Petersburg were once again allowed to function, though deprived of many resources (the libraries, for example, had been requisitioned, and were not returned until after the fall of communism), and a few monasteries. This proved only to be a respite, for in the 1960s, after the fall of Stalin and the rise of Khrushchev, the Church once again faced persecution; churches were again closed and pressure put upon the hierarchy.

Aleksandr Men'

What survived during this period?[3] Church life continued at a much reduced level: the tradition of church life was passed on, largely through grandmothers. At an academic level, there was no room for theology – or, almost no room. For there were rare birds who managed to preserve some kind of theological dimension within other academic disciplines. I mention three names and will say a little about them, for witness to the continuation of a theological awareness into which Fr Aleksandr entered. The three names are Dmitry Sergeyevich Likhachev, Aleksei Fedorovich Losev and Sergei Sergeyevich Averintsev.

Likhachev

I shall talk least about Likhachev, mainly because he fits less well into what I want to say in this chapter, but he came from a famous St Petersburg family, and was a great authority on Russian literature, especially medieval literature. He retained his faith throughout the Soviet period, and in his literary studies conveys an attitude imbued with the faith he professed. Although he lived a long life – he died in 1999 at the age of 92 – he suffered from poor health; once he remarked that the NKVD tried on several occasions to arrest him: when they came to his house he was saved by being in hospital.[4]

Losev

Aleksei Losev fits almost too well into the pattern I have prepared for him. Born on 23 September 1893 in Novocherkassk, capital of the Don Cossack territory in the south of Russia, he was brought up by his mother, though he inherited from his soon-absent father, Fedor Petrovich, a love of music and mathematics.[5] He and his mother, Natal'ya Alekseevna, lived with her father, Aleksei Polyakov, a priest. After a slow start in his education, he became interested in philosophy and classical philology, and fired with enthusiasm for astronomy, as well as studying the violin, and even considered becoming a professional violinist. At the gymnasium, too, he was presented, as he entered the final year, with an edition of the complete works of Vladimir Solov'ev, for whom he acquired an abiding love; right at the end of his life, he wrote two books on the philosopher, and his concerns were with him throughout his whole life.

In 1911, Losev left the gymnasium and joined Moscow University, studying philosophy and classics; there he became a member of the Vladimir Solov'ev

---

[3] There is an enormous bibliography on this: see, e.g., Dimitry Pospielovsky, *The Russian Church under the Soviet Regime 1917–1982*, 2 vols (Crestwood, NY: St Vladimir's Seminary Press, 1984); Jane Ellis, *The Russian Orthodox Church: A Contemporary History* (London–Sydney: Croom Helm, 1986).

[4] On Likhachev, see his memoir, *Reflections on the Russian Soul: A Memoir* (Budapest: CEU Press, 2000).

[5] For this biography, see the Introduction by the translator, Vladimir Marchenkov, to Aleksei Fyodorovich Losev, *The Dialectics of Myth* (London–New York: Routledge, 2003), 4–12. See also Aza Takho-Godi, *Losev* (Moscow: Molodaya Gvardiya, 1997).

Religious-Philosophical Society and met the cream of the intelligentsia of the Russian Religious Renaissance: Nikolai Berdyaev, Evgeny Trubetskoy, Sem'en Frank, Ivan Il'in, Sergii Bulgakov and Pavel Florensky. His graduation paper, 'The Worldview of Aeschylus', was examined by Vyacheslav Ivanov. In 1914, Losev went to Berlin on a study tour that was cut short by the First World War. In 1916, his first publications appeared, all dedicated to music. After graduation he remained at the Department of Classical Philology.

During the Revolution, Losev studied and wrote feverishly, as if to escape from the events unfolding around him. His department was closed by the Bolsheviks, and he survived by lecturing on music and teaching for a short while, as professor at the newly founded University of Nizhny Novgorod. In 1922 he married Valentina Mikhailovna Sokolova; the ceremony was conducted by Fr Pavel Florensky at Sergiev Posad. Seven years later, in 1929, they jointly took secret monastic vows as monk Andronik and nun Afanasiya; only in 1993, five years after Losev's death, did this secret become publicly known. During this period, Losev continued working at a feverish pace: eight volumes were published between 1927 and 1930, the last of which being *The Dialectics of Myth*. Among this great mass of publication were Losev's reflections on the *imyaslavie* controversy, in which Losev, like Florensky and Bulgakov, defended the Athonite 'worshippers of the Name', who had been expelled from the Holy Mountain in 1913 by Tsarist troops. Losev found himself arrested by the Joint State Political Directive (*Obyedinyonnoye Gosudarstvennoye Politicheskoye Upravleniye*, or OGPU), partly for breaches of censorship, and partly because OGPU suspected the *imyaslavtsy* of being a seditious movement. A 17-month investigation resulted in a sentence of ten years in labour camps. In 1933, by which time Losev was an invalid, the sentence was revoked and he returned to Moscow, where it was made clear that he could neither teach philosophy nor write philosophical works. He supported himself by part-time teaching and continued his research: two large topics, one on ancient mythology, another on ancient aesthetics. In 1943, Losev finally received his doctorate, while he was teaching at the Faculty of Philosophy in Moscow University. He was soon removed on a charge of idealism, and taught at the Moscow State Pedagogical Institute, where he remained for the rest of his life.

In 1953, the year of Stalin's death, Losev once again was able to publish, and in the following years volume after volume of his works were published on ancient mythology, ancient aesthetics, and the concept of the symbol, as well as a posthumous volume on Solov'ev, his first love, together with an edition of his works, not to mention many articles. Just as this avalanche of publications began, his wife died from cancer in 1954, and her place in Losev's life was taken, with her blessing, by a young graduate student whom the Losevs had taken into their house, Aza Takho-Godi, who has been instrumental in preserving Losev's memory and promoting his influence. In his final years, during Gorbachev's *perestroika*, Losev found recognition, in 1985 receiving the USSR State Award for Philosophy. He died in 1988. In his works the concerns of the Russian Religious Renaissance remained alive in Russia, even if buried beneath a mountain of strictly academic work. For our purposes, Losev is symbolic. Entering into detail about his work and its significance is way beyond the scope of this book, but he, with Likhachev, shows how the light of faith remained burning in Russian academe, even in the darkest days of the communist period.

Averintsev

My third figure: Sergei Sergeyevich Averintsev. In the *Short Literary Encyclopedia*, volume 9 (Moscow, 1978), Losev wrote of him:

> A[verintsev]'s work on the history of the literature of the late classical period and of the Middle Ages shows a special interest in the contradictory dynamics of the transition from the ancient [pre-Cretan] period to the Middle Ages, in the mutual interpretation of the cultural traditions of Greece and the Middle East during the Hellenistic and Byzantine epochs, and in the poetics of the 'shifted word' in response to social shifts. Every symbol of ancient and medieval culture is looked at from the perspective of contemporary attitudes of mind and is approached from within the 'dialogical' situation between the scholar and its maker; the literary word is explained as human 'gesture' and style as 'stance'. A. emphasizes that our knowledge of the humanities is conditioned by 'human understanding' which can be reduced neither to subjective aesthetic criteria nor to rationalist deduction (hence the importance for him of A. Losev, M. Bakhtin, and D. Likhachev).[6]

(Bakhtin is another scholar we could have mentioned who smuggled the concerns of Orthodox theology into strictly literary discussion.[7])

That scholarly assessment of Averintsev I have quoted partly to give an example of the rather hermetic diction used by scholars such as Losev and Averintsev to defeat the censor; Averintsev himself can be quite clear, though all of them had to appear to adopt a historical-materialist approach, if they were to be published, or even just not dismissed from their positions. He was born in 1937 of cultured parents, not so much communist or atheist, as Averintsev put it, but rather leaning to that agnosticism and deism of Enlightenment stamp that had marked the previous century; so he came to Christianity, not through some family tradition, however overlaid, but, as he put it, through 'that possibility that the terrible reality of Stalin's dictatorship paradoxically offered of being led back, constrained to confront the primary truth of faith: *Ecclesia Christi*, the Church of Jesus Christ'.[8] He was born, then,

---

[6] Page 2 in a typewritten *curriculum vitae* of Averintsev.
[7] See Charles Lock, 'Review Essay: Re-Viewing Bakhtin', *SVTQ* 43 (1999), 85–90.
[8] This biographical sketch draws on two obituaries: one in *30 Days*, by Pierluca Azzaro (<www.30giorni. it/us/articolo_stampa.asp?id=3668>, retrieved 12 August 2004), and the other by Avril Pyman-Sokolov in *Slavonica* 10 (2004), 195–201.

in the heyday of Stalinism and witnessed the attempts to wipe out the Church. As again he put it, 'Everything of the Christian legacy that it was possible to destroy was scrupulously destroyed before our eyes in a programmed way, in great style . . . The illusion of a "Christian" nation, of an "Orthodox" nation vanished'; what remained was the Church as 'bodiliness, founded by Jesus Christ himself, the physicality of the Word of God and of the people of God, the physicality of the Church despised and persecuted as locus of fidelity, that was demonstrated even physically': this was the possibility, paradoxically offered back. Not that Averintsev embraced Christianity quickly.

A victim of infantile paralysis, Averintsev spent much of his childhood in bed, or confined to his room, reading. This love of books, and allied to that the love of learning languages, sustained him throughout his life. After school, Averintsev entered the philological faculty of Moscow State University, graduating in 1961 and obtaining a higher degree from the Department of Classical Philology in 1967. From 1966 he worked in the Institute of the History and Theory of Art, and from 1969 at the Institute of World Literature of the Academy of Sciences of the USSR, where, in 1981, he became head of the Department of Classical Literature. In that year he was granted a doctorate of philological studies and in 1987 elected a candidate member of the Academy of Sciences. There was a kind of learned naivety about Averintsev: his range of knowledge, and languages, was amazing; in his lectures he seemed to be thinking aloud – there was little clear structure. This learned naivety was manifest in the 'Thaw period' of the late 1960s: when Averintsev gave a course of lectures on 'The Aesthetics of the Early Middle Ages', he announced them as a series of lectures on Byzantine aesthetics, but in reality, in a soft calm way, he spoke about Christianity. Attended by hundreds of students, the lectures were at first tolerated by the Soviet authorities with mute unease; 'the thing was so inconceivable', his wife later recalled, 'that the authorities thought my husband enjoyed special authorization'. Later they prohibited them. Another example of his learned naivety was his dissatisfaction with the religious articles in the *Philosophical Encyclopedia*: he offered, still not a baptized Christian, to take them on himself, and the fairness and learning of his articles, when published, led one Western reviewer to remark on the change of tone in the encyclopedia, to Averintsev's peril.

Avril Pyman remarks that his embrace of Christianity – like that of intellectuals earlier in the century, Ivanov, Bely, Blok, Mandel'shtam – came not so much through the Bible and the commandments, as via Hellenic paganism which 'distinguished ethics from religion'; 'he became a practising Christian some time after he had acknowledged intellectually the validity of the idea of "one Catholic and Apostolic Church"'. When he eventually embraced Christianity through baptism,[9] it was, for a Soviet public figure and teacher, an act of considerable moral courage, 'but also – as he himself insisted – of high aspiration'.

---

[9] Not until 1973: information from his widow, Natasha Averintseva, *via* Avril Pyman-Sokolova.

There was nothing narrow about Averintsev's embrace of Russian Orthodox Christianity: he embraced fully Vyacheslav Ivanov's notion of the 'two lungs of the Church'. His classical background also led him to think easily of Christianity in relation to other religions. The paradoxical possibility, offered by Stalin's attempt to erase the Church, was a matter of 'getting back on the path of the essential, on the fact in itself and of finding again, in that way, the way of lost unity'.

Witness to Orthodoxy in Russia through broadcast homilies: Fr Schmemann and Metropolitan Anthony (Bloom)

Before we eventually come to Fr Aleksandr Men', there is something else we should mention. One of the factors that kept the faith alive in the Soviet period was the broadcast sermons beamed into the Soviet Union by radio stations like Radio Liberty and, less controversially, the Voice of Orthodoxy. Two men, two priests, in particular are associated with these broadcasts, which took place from the 1960s onwards: from the USA, Fr Alexander Schmemann, and from the UK, Bishop (later Metropolitan) Anthony Bloom of Sourozh. Both these priests presented the Christian faith – the Russian Orthodox faith – intelligently and compellingly. What they had to say could not be dismissed as sentimental nonsense; they spoke not just to the heart, but to the intellect. There are many who have testified how much these regular homilies meant for them and their embrace and practice of the faith in the Soviet period.

All this is, in a way, background, but significant background, for Father Aleksandr came out of the experience in Russia of the attempt by the Soviets to destroy the faith, an attempt that was pursued not just directly, but also by creating an atmosphere of fear and suspicion that ate at the very roots of human society, even the society of the Church. Even among those who remained faithful to the Church, there were those infected by such fear: as gradually the Church experienced more and more freedom in the period of *perestroika*, this fear manifested itself in an intense conservatism and an under-standable desire to cling to what was left of the Church so nearly destroyed by the Soviets.

Fr Aleksandr Men': Life

Fr Aleksandr was born, like Sergei Averintsev, in the heyday of Stalinism – in Moscow on 22 January 1935.[10] His parents, Elena Sem'enovna and Vladimir Grigorevich, were both Jews, though his mother had become a Christian. He

---

[10] Most of the biographical details are taken from Ann Shukman's Introduction to *Christianity for the Twenty-First Century: The Prophetic Writings of Alexander Men* (New York: Continuum, 1996).

was secretly baptized in Sergiev Posad (then known as Zagorsk) by Fr Serafim (Sergei Batyukov), a 'catacomb' priest (that is, one of those who refused to accept the authority of Metropolitan Sergii). During the Second World War, Elena and her children (there was a second son, Pavel) moved from Moscow to Sergiev Posad, where they remained safe. Fr Serafim died in 1942, having heard Alik's first confession, and telling Elena and her sister Vera (who had introduced them to Fr Serafim) that Alik would grow up to be a great man. There remained in Sergiev Posad a tiny community of nuns, led by Mother Maria, who became Aleksandr's spiritual mother. Mother Maria and Father Serafim both represented a spiritual tradition stemming from the monastery of Optino, which in the nineteenth century had become a focus for intellectuals such as Solov'ev, Dostoevsky, and even Tolstoy, who had visited Optina Pustyn', about 200 miles south-west of Moscow.

As a child, Aleksandr manifested great intellectual gifts; natural science became a passion; he also came under the influence of a former priest of the catacombs, now attached to the church of St Nicholas on Maroseika Street, Boris Aleksandrovich Vasilev. Boris, who had spent many years in the camps, and his wife became the centre of a small group of thinking Christians attached to the church which included Aleksandr's mother, Elena, his aunt, Vera, as well as himself. The young Aleksandr read voraciously, and ambitiously: reading Kant at 13 and later Solov'ev. Later, he read the Church Fathers and embarked on biblical studies, following on his own a seminary course.

Stalin died in 1953 and the wave of anti-Semitism initiated before this event by the anti-cosmopolitan campaign ('cosmopolitan' being a pseudonym for Jewish) meant that Aleksandr, now about to leave school, was unable to enter university. Instead he enrolled at the Institute of Fur at Moscow, which enabled him to continue his studies in biology. In his own time, he followed the course of reading for the Spiritual Academy, and encountered another proscribed author, Pavel Florensky. In 1955, the institute was transferred to Irkutsk in Siberia, where Aleksandr soon made contact with the cathedral, which was opposite the institute. In the following year, he married a fellow student, Natal'ya Grigorenko. By 1958, the year in which Aleksandr was to sit his final examinations, Khrushchev's wave of persecution of the Church had just begun: in 20 years, Khrushchev predicted, communism would be achieved and the Church destroyed. His attachment to the cathedral was noticed, and he was refused permission to sit his final examinations. Aleksandr's plans to work for a further three years, and then enter seminary with the view to becoming a priest, came to nothing; there were few seminaries left, anyway. Abruptly he returned to Moscow accompanied by his wife, and was ordained deacon. With his wife and new baby daughter, Irina, he found himself in a cold, dilapidated house, working for an elderly and difficult priest in the village of Akulova, south-west of Moscow. Two years later, he was ordained priest, and assigned to Alabino, about 60 miles south-west of Moscow.

...priestly ministry

There Fr Aleksandr began his ministry.[11] Initially, in the terms of Khrushchev's campaign against the Church, he was forbidden to officiate in any way outside the church building. Fr Aleksandr had a way of getting on with people and managed to conduct baptisms at home, give the last rites, and conduct funerals. He also contrived to find ways of preaching and discussing the faith, both with ordinary people and with the educated and despiritualized intelligentsia; all his services became an opportunity to explain and teach the faith. This was the beginning of the distinctive ministry of the one Sergei Averintsev later called 'the man sent from God to be missionary to the wild tribe of the Soviet intelligentsia'. He also wrote: many, many books, most of them published abroad under various pseudonyms.

With the collapse of Krushchev's campaign against the Church in 1964, a group of priests, brought together by Fr Aleksandr, including Fr Gleb Yakunin, Fr Dmitri Dudko and Fr Nikolai Eshliman, met to discuss and share experiences. They felt keenly the lack of support from the hierarchy in the face of the brutalities and illegalities of the Krushchev campaign. An exception was Metropolitan Ermogen, whom Fr Aleksandr invited to be their bishop: an invitation Metropolitan Ermogen accepted. Together they drafted a letter of protest to the patriarch; however, the letter, when finally delivered to the patriarch, was signed by only Fathers Yakunin and Eshliman. The metropolitan thought it inopportune, and Fr Aleksandr presumably agreed with him. In 1966, Fr Aleksandr was moved to the parish of Tarasovka, to the north of Moscow: the third one to which he had been appointed with a dedication to the Protection of the Mother of God.

The Brezhnev years (1964–82) saw little let-up in the oppressive nature of the régime. Solzhenitsyn was harassed and eventually expelled in 1974; Andrei Sakharov, the outspoken defender of human rights, was exiled to Gorky in 1980. Nevertheless, it was during these years that an interest in spiritual matters emerged among the general public: icons became popular, people placed crosses on graves; yoga, astrology, the paranormal all attracted interest. In this context, Fr Aleksandr was found to be just the person to whom people, especially young people, with vaguely defined spiritual awakenings could turn. It was at Tarasovka that Fr Aleksandr met a French woman of Russian descent who was working at the French Embassy, Assia Douroff. Through this meeting, Fr Aleksandr was put in touch with the Foyer Oriental Chrétien in Brussels, a charity with the purpose of supplying Orthodox Christians in communist countries with religious literature, which ran a publishing house called 'La Vie avec Dieu'. It was with this press that Fr Aleksandr's works were published, beginning with *The Son of Man* in 1968, followed by *Heaven on Earth*, on the Orthodox Liturgy, in 1969; the first five

---

[11] For Fr Aleksandr's reflections on his ministry in the 1960s, see his essay, 'The 1960s Remembered', in *Religion, State, and Society* 23 (1995), 125–58.

volumes of *In Search of the Way, the Truth, and the Life*, in 1970–2; the sixth volume, *On the Threshold of the New Testament* in 1983; and a short handbook, *How to Read the Bible* in 1981. These were written under the pseudonyms A. Bogolyubov and E. Svetlov ('Lover of God', 'Light-bearer'). It was also through Assia Douroff that Solzhenitsyn's books reached the West.

In 1970, Fr Aleksandr was moved from Tarasovka to Novaya Derevna (after a denunciation by a jealous superior). At Novaya Derevna there was no house for the priest, so Fr Aleksandr and his wife acquired a wooden *izba* with an extensive garden in the village of Semkhoz. From there it was a short walk to the station where trains ran on the Moscow line towards Pushkino, the stop for Novaya Derevna. At Novaya Derevna, on the old road that led from Moscow to Sergiev Posad, Fr Aleksandr had a simple wooden church with a small parish room, and a tiny office, where he could receive visitors. There Fr Aleksandr created an unusual community embracing the people of the village together with the Moscow intellectuals who sought him out. It was not easy: the Committee for State Security (*Komitet Gosudarstvennoi Bezopanosti*, or KGB) kept him under surveillance, fellow priests denounced him, moved, doubtless by jealousy, anti-Semitic attacks on him continued, but there he fulfilled an extraordinary ministry, both a personal one to those who sought him out, a liturgical one to the community that thus came into being, and alongside this his constant writing.

In the mid-1980s, things began to change: Fr Yakunin was released from prison and Sakharov from exile; in 1988 the celebrations of the thousandth anniversary of the conversion of the Rus' led to much greater freedom for the Church. Unsurprisingly, this freedom brought its own problems. There were those who wanted the Church to return to the 'radiant past', as it had been, they supposed, before the rise of communism. Many of these were critical of the open discussion that Fr Aleksandr and others had promoted. Ecumenism became widely suspect; there was an upsurge of anti-Semitism. The growing availability in Russia of the writings of those who had been expelled in 1922 and their disciples had a mixed reception. This mood has continued: on 5 May 1998, books were burnt with the approval, and quite possibly in the presence of, Bishop Nikon of Ekaterinburg. The books were by Orthodox priest-theologians Nicholas Afanasiev, Alexander Schmemann, John Meyendorff – and Aleksandr Men': they were felt to contain 'Western contaminated ideas', even 'heresy'. Bishop Nikon was shortly after required to resign at the urging of the Russian synod of bishops.

At Easter 1990, Fr Aleksandr baptized 60 adults. On 1 September that year, he celebrated the thirtieth anniversary of his ordination. Just over a week later, on Sunday 9 September, he set off from his home to the station on his way to celebrate the liturgy. It is not clear what happened, but on the way he was stopped by two men, whom he probably knew. Most likely one showed him something to read, for Fr Aleksandr took out his glasses, which were later found by the path. As he bent over, the other man struck him on the back of the head with an axe. The assailants fled. The blow was not immediately fatal: Fr Aleksandr made his way to the station, realized he was bleeding and struggled back along the path to his house. At the garden gate he collapsed and died. There was a brief and perfunctory legal investigation which was quickly abandoned. No one has ever been charged with the murder.

The influence of Fr Aleksandr now continues, mostly through his writings, but also through institutions inspired by him, especially the Aleksandr Men' Open Orthodox University in Moscow. It is clear that, in his lifetime, he inspired and influenced people through his charismatic presence. His honesty and openness made him approachable to many. He preached an Orthodoxy that was open to the world, not afraid, not turned in on itself. Many Orthodox find such an attitude unnerving. Even in the diaspora, there are those who disparage him.[12]

Writings and theology

It is difficult to form a rounded picture of his theology. His great work, *In Search of the Way, the Truth, and the Life*, in seven volumes, is not easy of access in the West; only the final volume (the first to be written), *The Son of Man*, is available in English translation:[13] a few other things are available in English, mostly sermons and interviews, which are mostly addressed to the immediate circumstances of the last decade of communism. There are some other works available in French: the first volume of *In Search of the Way, the Truth, and the Life*,[14] a commentary on the Apocalypse,[15] and a collection of shorter pieces,[16] as well as the biography already mentioned, and a short life by Fr Michel Evdokimov.[17] Sermons, inevitably, lose something when read: they were live communications, not essays to be argued over. Furthermore, there is inevitably something homespun about his learning. He was widely read, but had not gone through a theological course at seminary or spiritual academy. Perhaps, however, that is an advantage; we have already noticed how few of our Orthodox thinkers had a formal theological training. What I propose to do is indicate some of the more general aspects of his theology, and then engage in a more settled discussion of two topics: first, his teaching on prayer, and finally, his work on the Apocalypse (or the book of Revelation).

Influences on Fr Men'

First, some general considerations. Although Fr Aleksandr followed on his own the reading for courses at both seminary and spiritual academy, his reading

---

[12] An example is the half-hearted review of *Christianity for the Twenty-First Century* by Anastasia Heath in *The Forerunner* 27 (Summer 1996), 17–20.

[13] *Son of Man*, trans. Samuel Brown (Torrance, CA: Oakwood, 1995, from the 1992 Russian edition).

[14] *Les Sources de la religion* (Paris: Desclée de Brouwer, 1991).

[15] *Au fil de l'Apocalypse* (Paris: Cerf/Pully: Le Sel de la Terre, 2003).

[16] *Le christianisme ne fait que commencer* (Paris: Cerf/Pully: Le Sel de la Terre, 2010).

[17] *Petite vie du père Men* (Paris: Desclée de Brouwer, 2005; ET Margaret Parry, Leominster: Gracewing, 2011).

was largely determined by what he could lay his hands on. One of his friends later said of him: 'Animals loved him, and plants, and things, and of course books. He used to say that books found their own way to him when they were needed, just like friends and relatives coming to a birthday party.'[18] It is a familiar feeling – finding the right book at the right time – but it can mean that one's reading assumes somewhat eccentric contours. What were the main influences on Fr Aleksandr?

Vladimir Solov'ev was an abiding influence, as well as those who looked back to him, such as Nikolai Berdyaev, Sergii Bulgakov; he had also read Pavel Florensky. Of Berdyaev, Fr Aleksandr himself says that his core concepts are personalism and historicism. By the former he meant his emphasis on personhood, revealed in freedom; by the latter, Berdyaev's concern to make sense of history as a whole, seeing Christianity in relation to the Old Testament, but analogously to the whole human search for meaning in the religions of what Christians call paganism. What is distinctive about Christianity is Christ, 'the one unrepeatable point of contact between the divine and the human ... Through Christ, God became both akin to and close to man'.[19] Christianity is, therefore, the fulfilment of the whole of the human religious quest. Acknowledgement of this entails no syncretism, such as is found in theosophy, for example, for 'the only world religion is the religion of Christianity, real and entire'.[20]

The heart of Christianity is, then, what Solov'ev had called 'Godmanhood', the primordial union of God and man, manifest in the Incarnation. It is the reality of this that finds expression in the history of human striving after God, the history of religion. Solov'ev himself had envisaged a large historical work, covering the history of Israel, that he would have called *The History and Future of Theocracy*, of which he only wrote the first volume. Fr Aleksandr envisaged a vast history of human religious striving after God that he called *In Search of the Way, the Truth, and the Life*, and completed in seven volumes (and which he dedicated to Solov'ev). He gave this global view of history a particular twist through his borrowing a key notion from the German philosopher Karl Jaspers, probably known best in the English-speaking world (when not quite forgotten) by his work, *The Great Philosophers*.[21]

This key notion was Jaspers' idea of the 'axial age': the period from about 800 to 200 BC in which we find a dramatic shift in human religious perceptions, away from a magical view of the world, to one marked by an aspiration towards monotheism, belief in one God, and the emergence of apophatic theology, the sense that this one God is beyond human apprehension. The axial period was the time when the Buddha, Confucius, Zarathustra and the biblical prophets were preaching; when the Upanishads, the books of the

---

[18] Quoted by Shukman, *Christianity*, 9.
[19] Quotations from Berdyaev's *Philosophy of Freedom* in 'Christianity: the Universal Vision', Shukman, *Christianity*, 97.
[20] Quotation from an article by Berdyaev, published in *Put'*, quoted by Men': Shukman, *Christianity*, 98.
[21] Karl Jaspers, *The Great Philosophers* (London: Rupert Hart-Davis, 1962).

Old Testament and the earliest texts of the Avesta and the Mahabharata were written; the time of the ancient Greek philosophers – from the Presocratics to the Stoics – and the ancient Greek tragedians, Aeschylus, Sophocles and Euripides; of the Jains; of the representatives of the six classical systems of Indian philosophy, the *darshanas*. Simply to realize this, to note the strange synchronicity, gives one a profound sense of the axial period as a huge turning point in the development of the human spirit. This notion of the axial age became central to Fr Aleksandr's vast project. He found Karl Jaspers' delimitation of the axial age awkward, however, for it did not include the period of the Incarnation, and suggested stretching it to include the period of Christ's human life. In fact, had he known Jaspers' *Great Philosophers*, he would have discovered that Jaspers himself came to make such a move, for his four 'paradigmatic individuals', who exemplify the turning of the human spirit in the axial age, are Socrates, the Buddha, Confucius and Jesus.[22]

Another influence on his sense of global history might seem surprising, as he is all too little known, even in his native England: the historian Christopher Dawson, of whose *Progress and Religion*[23] Fr Aleksandr made signal use. (In passing, another name that occurs in Fr Aleksandr's writings, occasioning a little surprise, is that of the nineteenth-century French historian Fustel de Coulanges. It is possible that such an odd book might have turned up in Moscow, but he was, in fact, a favourite of Dawson's who quotes him from time to time.)

Christ the centre of history

This global approach to history would have prepared Fr Aleksandr well to deal with the aspirations of those who looked East as they experienced spiritual awakening, but the purpose of the work lies deeper: in Fr Aleksandr's own desire, inherited or inspired to some extent by the Russian tradition to which he felt such kinship, to be able to flesh out his understanding of Christ as the centre of human history, understood as the human search for the ultimate. One gets some sense of how he approached history in this passage from early on in *The Son of Man*, the last volume of his great *œuvre*, though the first to be written. He has followed Pompey into the Jewish Temple after his conquest of Jerusalem, and told us of the amazement Pompey and his soldiers must have felt to find in the Holy of Holies simply ... nothing at all.

> How exactly did this religion [the religion of the Hebrews] differ from the others?
> One can answer this question, but only starting from a long way away. When the light of reason first flared up in man, he sensed the reality of some higher

---

[22] Fr Aleksandr made use of a Russian translation of a more fundamental work of Jaspers' on the axial age: *The Origin and Goal of History*. See Shukman, *Christianity*, 204, n. 1.

[23] Christopher Dawson, *Progress and Religion* (London: Sheed & Ward, 1929). On Christopher Dawson, see *Eternity in Time: Christopher Dawson and the Catholic Idea of History*, ed. Stratford Caldecott and John Morrill (Edinburgh: T&T Clark, 1997), though there is little in this book about what attracted Fr Aleksandr to Dawson.

Power, filling the universe. For the aboriginal hunters it was natural to identify It with what we now call nature. Thus people sought the presence of Divinity everywhere – in the clouds and stars, in rivers and living things.

From the beginning, as a rule, this led to an unrefined idolatry, to the deification of discrete objects and phenomena. Later in India, Greece and China, the cult of nature led to faith in the supposition that the invisible world is the only genuine reality. But such a view was at odds with general human spiritual experience, and was not widely recognized.

On the contrary, with the coming of religious and philosophical maturity, the assertion that the Supreme reality differed in its essence from all things personal and limited was strengthened.

The last word of pre-Christian thought was the doctrine of the Godhead, whose concealed, inscrutable being is found on the other side of the visible. No matter what you called Him – Heaven, Father, Fate – the profundity of His being could never be known by any mortal. This idea not only flowed from the experiences of mystics, but had a logical foundation as well. Truly, what mind is in the position to grasp boundlessness itself?

However, the mysterious surge upward in man was not extinguished. He was always striving to overcome the distance separating him from Heaven, to unite his life with that other world. As a result two closely interwoven faiths continued to exist: faith in the Incomprehensible and faith in elemental deities. The latter, it seemed, were closer to humans, and it was possible to have direct contact with them. It was considered that there were secret magic tricks with the help of which people were able to influence demons and spirits. A similar utilitarian view remained the predominant one for thousands of years. Polytheism and magic tried in vain to fill the chasm separating earth from heaven.

This dichotomy was first removed in the Biblical revelation. It taught of a 'holy' god, Who is incomparably greater than creation, and at the same time of man as his 'likeness and image'. The mysterious kinship of the infinite Spirit and a finite spirit makes possible according to the Bible, a *Covenant* between them.

A covenant, or union, is the path to the unification of man, not with gods, but with the grand Origin existing over the world.[24]

It is this desire to understand and relate, something he shared with his mentors in the Russian Religious Renaissance, that accounts for other general features of his theology: his openness, his desire to hold to both sides of an antinomy, his appreciation of the good anywhere, which made him question the narrowness induced by fear that he found all around him, both in the world subject to communism and in the Orthodox world. In a more specifically religious sphere, it lay behind his lack of antipathy towards Catholicism and appreciation of Catholic spirituality: on his desk, Jean Vanier recalled, there were photographs of St Thérèse of Lisieux and Charles de Foucauld;[25] he also revered the Lutheran martyr to Nazism, Dietrich Bonhoeffer.

---

[24] Men', *Son of Man*, 10–11.
[25] Jean Vanier in his Preface to *Le christianisme ne fait que commencer*, 5.

Teaching on prayer

Let us close by taking a brief look at two very different works by Fr Aleksandr. The first is his *Practical Handbook in Prayer*, especially the initial chapter, published elsewhere as an article, 'An Inner Step'.[26] The handbook is precisely what it says: practical. It contains information on prayer books and how to use them, different forms of prayer, also details about how to breathe and so on. The short chapter, or article, 'An Inner Step', is also directly practical. He begins by laying down four items: 1. six to ten minutes a day using a prayer book; 2. the same amount of time reading the Gospels and the Scriptures; 3. the Eucharist; 4. prayerful fellowship with God. Fr Aleksandr goes on to say, first, that we must not see these as some kind of remedy. The moment we do that, we are regarding them egocentrically: we want God to be something for us, rather than ourselves wanting to be something for him. This involves an inner step, acting on the conviction that the mystery of God is real; it is like a plunge into the unknown.

He goes on to point out that there are three kinds of prayer: supplication ('our favourite', he comments), confession and thanksgiving. He remarks that all are good, but that in the Our Father it is not supplication that comes first, but acceptance and consent. If we can come to that, then we shall discover freedom, freedom from the sense of needing to do this, or that. The way forward is simple: one step after another. We complicate it by our anxieties. This freedom enables us to look at everything 'through the prism of the Divine': and everything appears full of wonder.

The Lord's Prayer begins by invoking God as Father in heaven. What does that mean? That he is in our homeland. Fr Aleksandr goes on to illustrate this with a poem of Lermontov's, 'The Angel', about the soul being brought by angels to earth to be born: there remains within it the singing of the angels. We are guests here; we do not belong; we are bound to find it uncomfortable – 'we collide with the world, and it wounds us'. So we must call on the Spirit, especially when we are together. Fr Aleksandr goes on to recall the disciples' encounter with the risen Lord, and his greeting, 'Peace to you'. This encounter we shall find as we pray; it is for this encounter that we pray. He ends with a prayer introduced by these words:

> So let us pray that we may know He is with us right now. The Word of God will be with us. We will take Him home, and He will live in us. And finally, let us live in the light and in hope. We believers are happy people who do not take advantage of our happiness; we are rich people who neither take possession of nor utilize our treasure. Therefore, today we will wash away everything – our resentments, our disappointments, our worries and

---

[26] I have used *An Inner Step towards God: Writings and Teachings on Prayer by Father Alexander Men*, ed. April French, trans. Christa Belyaeva (Brewster, MA: Paraclete Press, 2014), but the article can also be found in, e.g., Alexander Men, *About Christ and the Church*, trans. Fr Alexis Vinogradoff (Torrance, CA: Oakwood, 1996), 105–11.

expectations, our sins, and our burdens. We bring these things to the Lord so that he might strengthen us, for this is what is most important.[27]

Practical, and moving towards experience – encounter. Fr Aleksandr's words remind me of another wonderful teacher of prayer: the late Metropolitan Anthony Bloom of Sourozh.

Commentary on the Apocalypse

There is another of Fr Aleksandr's works, rather different from the rest. Called *Reading the Apocalypse: Conversations on the Revelation of John the Theologian*, it was published posthumously, and translated into French with the title, *Au fil de l'Apocalypse*. There are several things striking about this work. First of all, the Apocalypse occupies an odd position within Orthodoxy. Although it is part of the New Testament canon, we know that there was controversy about the work as late as the second century: Bishop Dionysios of Alexandria doubted its attribution to the apostle John and accepted its scriptural status only with reservations.[28] There are hardly any patristic commentaries on it, the oldest being by the otherwise unknown sixth-century writer Œcumenius. Furthermore, it is never publicly read in any of the services of the Orthodox Church. Nevertheless, its imagery is well known – the lamb slain from the foundation of the world, the book with the seven seals, the 24 elders, the woman clothed with the sun, Jerusalem descending from heaven – and is used in many Byzantine hymns. It is a work that has been popular in times of unrest; the word 'apocalypse' in many Western languages evokes a sense of horror, with dramatic and cruel images of a final conflict before the end of the world.

The imagery of the Apocalypse was important to Fr Sergii Bulgakov – one only needs to think of the title of his last, and maybe greatest, work, *The Bride of the Lamb*; he also wrote a commentary on the Apocalypse, which was published posthumously.[29] All of this background is relevant to Fr Aleksandr's short commentary. Much of the purpose of his brief and factual commentary seems to have been to counteract the use to which the biblical book was being put in the dark days of Soviet Russia. Nonetheless, his interest in it draws attention to his kinship with Sergii Bulgakov, on whose own commentary he seems to draw.[30] Like Bulgakov, he wants to read the Apocalypse in the mainstream of Christian teaching about eschatology: the attraction of the vivid imagery of angels armed with terrifying swords who lay waste the world he sees as 'a sign of a certain lack of faith or of a particular form

---

[27] Men', *An Inner Step*, 18.

[28] See Eusebius, *Hist. eccl.*, 7. 25.

[29] Published at the YMCA Press in Paris in 1948; a French translation has just been issued: Serge Boulgakov, *L'Apocalypse de Jean*, trans. Anne Kichilov (Paris: Parole et Silence, 2014).

[30] *Pace* Antoine Arjakovsky in his Introduction to Boulgakov, *L'Apocalypse*, 19, as Fr Aleksandr seems to refer to Bulgakov's comments *ad loc.* on several occasions.

of unbelief'.[31] He interprets the words, 'Behold, I make all things new', in terms of the renewal of Creation, not its destruction to be replaced by something else, in this following Bulgakov, to whom he refers.[32] He concludes his 'conversations' in these words:

> One can say that this exalted anticipation of the end of the world is an unhealthy phenomenon in the spiritual life, which contradicts radically the very idea of hope in the Saviour. It goes contrary to the Christian conception of faith, hope, patience, and humility, qualities to which Christ made appeal and which he incarnated himself.
>
> To sum up the essential thesis of Christian eschatology: we must live as if the Last Judgment was going to happen tomorrow and work as if we had eternity before us. We must not put off to later the work of our salvation: 'Watch and pray', the Gospel teaches us. We must not go too far too fast, nor try to impose our will on the Saviour.
>
> Let us do his will with joy and patience.[33]

* * *

Fr Aleksandr Men' was the priest Russia needed in the last days of communism; many people looked to him and saw in him a prophet. I have tried to give some kind of account of what remains of his theological legacy. I have passed over many things, but hope I have given some picture of how he encapsulated the new confidence that came to the Russian Orthodox Church as its freedom came within sight. I want to close with some words from a lecture he gave on the day before he was murdered.

> Christ calls people to bring the divine ideal to reality. Only short-sighted people imagine that Christianity has already happened, that it took place, say, in the thirteenth century, or the fourth, or some other time. I would say that it has only made the first hesitant steps in the history of the human race. Many words of Christ are incomprehensible to us even now, because we are still Neanderthals in spirit and morals; because the arrow of the Gospels is aimed at eternity; because the history of Christianity is only beginning. What has happened already, what we now call the history of Christianity, are the first half-clumsy, unsuccessful attempts to make it a reality.[34]

---

[31] Men', *Au fil*, 172.

[32] Men', *Au fil*, 154.

[33] Men', *Au fil*, 174.

[34] From the lecture, called by the translators 'Christianity for the Twenty-First Century', in Shukman, *Christianity*, 185, quoted by Michael Plekon at the beginning of his chapter on Alexander Men' in *Living Icons*, 234.

21

Metropolitan Kallistos and the theological vision of the *Philokalia*

Devoting the last chapter of this book to Metropolitan Kallistos of Diokleia is, in many ways, an obvious choice, though in other ways problematic. Obvious, it seems to me, because in Orthodox theology in the diaspora in the last half-century he has been a commanding presence; but problematic, because he is too close to us, and in particular to me. We have discussed living Orthodox theologians already in this book – Metropolitan John of Pergamon, Christos Yannaras and Stelios Ramfos – but Metropolitan Kallistos is much closer to me than any of these: he received me into the Orthodox Church 25 years ago, he has been my spiritual father for longer than that; much of my perception of Orthodoxy has been mediated by – or rather been a gift from – him. On the one hand, it is difficult for me to look at his work

Metropolitan Kallistos

With permission of Metropolitan Kallistos

from a distance; on the other hand, as a father to me, there is the danger of my wanting, maybe subconsciously, to put a distance between us, to assert my own identity. Nevertheless, I cannot avoid this challenge: Metropolitan Kallistos' position within English-speaking Orthodoxy is paramount, and what exactly Orthodoxy amounts to, as perceived by Orthodox in the West, owes a very great deal to him.

There is, however, another reason for bringing this book to a close by discussing Metropolitan Kallistos. One theme running through this book is that the publication of the *Philokalia* in 1782 is to be seen as something of a watershed in the history of Orthodoxy. The vision of the *Philokalia* informs, I have suggested, all that is best in Orthodox theology over the last two centuries. The *Philokalia* has been central to the life and work of Metropolitan Kallistos, so it makes sense to end a survey that began with the publication of the *Philokalia* with reflection on the theological work of Metropolitan Kallistos.

An English Orthodox thinker

But who is Metropolitan Kallistos? Despite his rather exotic title, at least to English ears, he is very English, and it is, I think, important to realize this, for his becoming Orthodox, and what he has made of Orthodoxy, have assumed what seem to me 'iconic' (odd to use the word in this sense in this context!) proportions, both for English people, and other English-speakers, who have become Orthodox, and for the way in which Orthodoxy is perceived within the English-speaking world. When Bishop Kallistos (as he is still generally known, though he became a metropolitan in 2007), then Timothy Ware, became Orthodox in 1958, Orthodox services in the UK were either in Greek or Slavonic, with sermons in Greek or Russian (or Serbian); Bishop Kallistos remarks somewhere that the first time he heard an Orthodox priest speaking English – at a meeting – it came as something of a surprise. Nowadays, it is rare to find the Divine Liturgy celebrated in the UK with no use of English at all, and it is quite common to find the liturgy celebrated predominantly in English. Orthodoxy is much less foreign to the British than it was half a century or more ago, when Bishop Kallistos embraced Orthodoxy. This process of making Orthodoxy in some way at home in the English-speaking world is one in which Bishop Kallistos has played a central role. It has been a process of translation – translation involving several dimensions. There is straightforward translation: a laborious task in which Bishop Kallistos has been deeply engaged personally, from the translation of service books such as *The Festal Menaion*[1] and *The Lenten Triodion*[2] to the translation of the *Philokalia*.

There is another kind of translation that is more like interpretation: a great deal of Bishop Kallistos' early work was of this kind – his book, *The Orthodox*

---

[1] *The Festal Menaion*, trans. Mother Maria and Archimandrite Kallistos Ware, with an Introduction by Professor Georges Florovsky (London: Faber & Faber, 1969).
[2] *The Lenten Triodion*, trans. Mother Maria and Archimandrite Kallistos Ware (London: Faber & Faber, 1978).

Church,[3] and later on his book on what it is to be Orthodox, *The Orthodox Way*,[4] but in addition to these a host of lengthy Introductions to the translations of others, particularly from the Slav tradition, which provided clear expositions of, mostly, the spiritual traditions of Orthodoxy – I think particularly of his Introduction to *The Art of Prayer*, an anthology drawn from the letters of (mostly) St Theophan the Recluse,[5] or his Introduction to the Classics of Western Spirituality translation of *The Ladder of Divine Ascent* by St John Climacus.[6]

His various writings on the Jesus Prayer belong to this category, too. Bishop Kallistos is particularly skilled at this because he is so very English. From the 1920s onwards, many writings by Orthodox thinkers had become available in English translation, particularly Russians such as Nikolai Berdyaev, Lev Shestov, Sem'en Frank and Nadejda Gorodetsky. These works attracted much attention, but almost always seemed to have something of a foreign accent, for they came from a self-consciously intellectual tradition; they were writings from those who thought of themselves as belonging to what the Russians call the *intelligentsiya*. To call someone an intellectual in English is never simply a compliment; it can even be an insult! We have already looked at Mother Thekla's attempt at an English acculturation of Orthodoxy through the interpretation of English poets such as Shakespeare, George Herbert and Keats. This was a very un-English thing to do, parallel to the way in which Russians like to express Orthodoxy through interpreting Pushkin or Dostoevsky. Mother Thekla was herself conscious of the parallel – and the paradox: only a Russian like Mother Thekla could ever have attempted such a task.

For all his deep and extensive literary and philosophical culture, and his superb education – public school and a double-first in Mods and Greats at Oxford – Bishop Kallistos manifests his fundamental Englishness in being very shy of being intellectual. He does not deal in ideas (though perfectly capable of subtle interpretation of them); he wants you to *see*, he wants you to know what it means *in practice*. His principal work on Orthodox theology, *The Orthodox Way*, presents Orthodoxy not as a collection of ideas or doctrines, but rather explores the practical working out of fundamental Orthodox beliefs; I suppose it is often regarded as a work of spirituality, rather than doctrine, but it is not the case that Bishop Kallistos sits light to doctrine – not in the least; rather he is always more interested in what it means in practice, what difference it makes to the way we act and engage with others, that we believe this, or profess that.

---

[3] *The Orthodox Church* (Harmondsworth: Penguin, 1963; rev. edn, 1993).

[4] *The Orthodox Way* (London: Mowbrays, 1979; rev. edn, Crestwood, NY: St Vladimir's Seminary Press, 1995).

[5] *The Art of Prayer: An Orthodox Anthology*, compiled by Igumen Chariton of Valamo, trans. E. Kadloubovsky and E. M. Palmer, ed. with Introduction by Timothy Ware (London: Faber & Faber, 1966), 9–38.

[6] John Climacus, *The Ladder of Divine Ascent*, trans. Colm Luibheid and Norman Russell, Classics of Western Spirituality (London: SPCK, 1982), 1–70.

Life

But let us say something about who Bishop Kallistos is in biographical terms.[7] He was born Timothy Ware in Bath, then in Somerset, on 11 September 1934. His father was in the British Army, eventually rising to the rank of brigadier; he had served in India, but returned to England shortly after Timothy's birth, and continued to serve in the army until after the Second World War. Timothy was the second child in the family, with an elder brother and two younger sisters. On his mother's side, he was related by marriage to the great philosopher and ancient historian R. G. Collingwood, to whose college in Oxford – Pembroke – Timothy himself (by then Archimandrite Kallistos) was eventually to belong as a Fellow.

Timothy went to Westminster School, attached to the Abbey, in London. There he was initiated into what he has sometimes described, borrowing C. S. Lewis' phrase, as the education of 'old Western man': that is, he had an elaborate education in Greek and Latin, learning not only to read these classical languages with great facility, but also to compose both prose and verse, as well as acquiring a first-hand acquaintance with the literature, history and philosophy that survives in these languages. It was an essentially literary education, with very little, if any, exposure to any of the sciences (save for some rigorous, but in twentieth-century terms elementary, mathematics).

Already, at school, the young Timothy displayed somewhat precocious philosophical interests. A story told by A. M. ('Donald') Allchin, who was several years senior to Timothy at Westminster and was to become one of his longest-standing friends, relates how, when Donald was supervising prep.[8] one evening, Timothy's hand shot up and he requested that, having finished his prep., he might be given permission to read. 'What are you reading?' asked the prefect. 'Kant's *Critique of Pure Reason*', came the reply. Later, Bishop Kallistos himself would remark that the real philosophical love of his schooldays was for the great English philosophers, Locke, Berkeley and Hume ('English' by language, for Berkeley was an Irishman and Hume a Scot), to whose clarity of expression and elegance of style he doubtless owes some debt. Among these, his favourite was, not surprisingly, Berkeley, whose deep sense of the primary reality of the world of spiritual beings derived in some measure from his knowledge of the Greek Fathers, especially Origen.

But it was not just philosophy that he took a delight in reading while at Westminster; novels and poetry also engrossed him. There were other influences on the young Timothy while he was at Westminster. One was the services of Westminster Abbey itself; the boys were required to attend Matins,

---

[7] This information is based on the biographical sketch that I contributed to Metropolitan Kallistos' Festschrift, *Abba: The Tradition of Orthodoxy in the West*, ed. John Behr, Andrew Louth, Dimitri Conomos (Crestwood, NY: St Vladimir's Seminary Press, 2003), 13–27, which can be consulted for a more detailed account.

[8] 'Prep.': that is, preparation, studies prescribed as preparation for the next day's classes, at boarding schools, like Westminster, done in the evening under the supervision of a prefect.

and the young Timothy also delighted in the ceremonial splendour of the Sung Eucharist, especially that held annually in honour of St Edward the Confessor, the founder of the Abbey. These services made a lasting impression on him; the great tradition of Anglican church music conveyed a sense of what the Caroline divines of the seventeenth century had called 'the beauty of holiness'.

Another, more profound, influence was extra-curricular. Not far from Westminster School was the Russian Church of St Philip's, in Buckingham Palace Road. There, just before he left Westminster School to go up to Oxford, Timothy by chance (though in such matters there is no chance) found himself in the church one Saturday afternoon during the Vigil Service. Bishop Kallistos has himself told of this occasion, in which he was caught up, from the noise and busy-ness of London, into 'a world that was more real – I would almost say more *solid*' by the darkness, the stillness, the sense of overwhelming presence, a glimpse of the 'beauty of holiness', not confected, but there to participate in.[9]

His classical education was completed by university studies at Magdalen College, Oxford, where he read Classical Moderations (i.e. classical literature) and *Literae Humaniores* (i.e. ancient history and philosophy, both classical and modern, with nothing much in between) from 1952 to 1956, gaining first-class honours.

In 1954, Timothy offered himself for ordination in the Church of England. During his time at Magdalen, especially through Brother Peter of the Anglican Society of St Francis, he had come to know and experience much of the best of the Anglican tradition, with its combination of deep devotion, both personal and liturgical, a sense of mission, and an energetic concern for the needs of the poor and underprivileged. By the time he had finished Greats, however, doubts over Anglicanism were beginning to grow, and he chose to stay on at Magdalen to read for the Honour School of Theology, rather than begin his theological studies at an Anglican theological college. For during his time at Oxford his interest in Orthodoxy had deepened and developed. He received little encouragement in his journey to Orthodoxy: far from it, he was very much discouraged, both by his English friends (who warned him of 'lifelong eccentricity'), and by the Orthodox bishop he had approached (Bishop James (Virvos) of Apamaea, of the Greek Cathedral of the Holy Wisdom in London). Nevertheless, Anglicanism itself he came to feel he could no longer embrace. What troubled him was the diversity of Anglican faith, leaving him with the oddness of affirming as an individual preference what he saw as something to be received as tradition.

The pull of Orthodoxy – its unambiguous embrace of tradition, the continuing witness of its martyrs, its profound life of prayer, as well as the bonds

---

[9] See Bishop Kallistos, 'Strange Yet Familiar: My Journey to the Orthodox Church', in *The Inner Kingdom*, vol. 1 of the Collected Works (Crestwood, NY: St Vladimir's Seminary Press, 2000), 1–24, at 3. For the account of his visit to St Philip's: 1–3.

of friendship being forged with such as Nicolas and Militza Zernov, and the influence and theological insights of theologians like Vladimir Lossky, Fr Georges Florovsky and Fr John Romanides – became overwhelming. From Easter 1957, Timothy Ware ceased to receive communion within the Anglican Church, and on 14 April (1 April, Old Style) 1958, Friday in Bright Week, Bishop James received him into the Orthodox Church by chrismation. Despite his strong links with the Russian Orthodox Church (his spiritual father belonged to the Church in Exile), he was received into the Greek Orthodox Church of the Œcumenical Patriarchate.

In the years following 1958, Timothy Ware first taught at a preparatory school and then spent a year as a scholar at Princeton University, wondering at this time if there might be more scope for his Orthodox vocation in the USA. Fortunately for us in England, he resisted this temptation. In 1960, he returned to Oxford, to do research under the supervision of the Anglican priest and expert on early monasticism, Fr Derwas Chitty, which led to the award of a doctorate (DPhil). During this period he travelled widely in the East, visiting the Monastery of St John the Theologian on the island of Patmos, Mount Athos, and Jerusalem, where he spent six months in 1962–3.

Writings

His studies during these years were intense and diverse. In 1963 there appeared the first edition of *The Orthodox Church*, a Pelican Original (in later editions, from 1991 onwards, a Penguin book), which has continued in print ever since. Written by a young convert not yet 30, and with less than five years' experience of being Orthodox, it is an astonishing book, remarkable for its careful scholarship and balanced objectivity. Half a century later, it remains far and away the best introduction in English (probably in any language: it has been translated into many) to the history and doctrine of the Orthodox Church.[10] (Thirty years later, for the 1993 edition, he extensively revised it, rewriting about a third of the text.)

The next year, 1964, saw the publication of a rather different work, though equally scholarly and objective, *Eustratios Argenti: A Study of the Greek Church under Turkish Rule*.[11] This study, written at the request of the Argenti family, is a study of a period in the history of the Greek Orthodox Church about which very little had been written when Timothy Ware was writing (Sir Steven Runciman's Birkbeck Lectures, on which the main part of his *The Great Church in Captivity* was based, were not delivered until 1966). Eustratios Argenti was an eighteenth-century lay theologian, deeply involved in the

---

[10] The original edition was published as one of a series, alongside others on Roman Catholicism (a remarkable book by Sebastian Bullough OP), Anglicanism and Methodism (books remarkable in other ways), and indeed mysticism and Buddhism. Timothy Ware's book is the only one on a Christian theme to stand the test of time (and the only one not to present its subject as an '-ism', or even an '-y'!).

[11] *Eustratios Argenti: A Study of the Greek Church under Turkish Rule* (Oxford: Clarendon Press, 1964).

polemical theology with the Latins, particularly the issue of the validity of Western baptism (and therefore any other sacraments). Timothy Ware's study is a model of clarity and careful judgement, if perhaps a little dry, owing to the need to give a full account of the Argenti papers.

However, alongside this intensive study, both of the Orthodox Church in general and of Eustratios Argenti and his times in particular, Timothy was engaged in research for his doctorate, successfully submitting his thesis in 1965. This was a study of the texts and the ascetic theology of St Mark the Monk (or 'the Ascetic' or 'the Hermit'), a writer of the fifth, or perhaps the sixth, century. It has, alas, never been published, though some of the material from the thesis has found its way into later scholarly articles. Even though the thesis, because unpublished, is less well known than the books he published in 1963 and 1964, it is the thesis of 1965 that foreshadows what was to be most characteristic of Timothy Ware's later academic endeavours. For it was ascetic theology (or 'neptic' theology, the theology of watchfulness or waiting upon God) that was to be central to his research for the rest of his academic career.

Monk as academic: teacher and scholar

That career began in 1966, when he was appointed to succeed Nicolas Zernov as the Spalding Lecturer in Eastern Orthodox Studies, a post which he held until his retirement in 2001: a remarkable example of stability, appropriate in a monk! These years – 1965 and 1966 – were crucial years for Timothy Ware for other reasons. In 1965 he was ordained deacon, and given the name Kallistos by Archbishop Athenagoras of Thyateira and Great Britain, who ordained him. The following year, he was ordained priest and took monastic vows as a hieromonk ('priest-monk') of the Monastery of St John the Theologian on Patmos. He became Father Kallistos (later Archimandrite Kallistos). The name is a Greek superlative meaning 'best' or 'most beautiful' – not chosen by the ordinand, but conferred by his bishop – and was the name borne by an early second-century pope, whose compassion was pilloried as laxness, and by two fourteenth-century patriarchs of Constantinople, both of them hesychasts, the later of whom, Kallistos II Xanthopoulos, was intended as his patron saint. Although now a monk of Patmos, he made his home in Oxford: living with his parents after his father's retirement.

From that base, Father Kallistos pursued what must seem like several full-time careers. He was a lecturer in the University of Oxford for 35 years; in 1970 he became Fellow and Tutor in Theology at Pembroke College, Oxford. As such, he lectured to undergraduates, principally in Greek patristics, on both dogmatic (for many years he gave a course of lectures on Christology from Ephesus to Chalcedon) and ascetic themes (notably a course of lectures on the theology of the human person in Greek theology). He also supervised a growing number of research students in Greek and Byzantine theology (both dogmatic and neptic). For much of his time in Oxford, one of his colleagues was the internationally renowned Syriac scholar, Sebastian Brock, Lecturer (and later Reader) in Syriac and Aramaic. Together they ran for many years a seminar in Eastern Christian studies.

Although Bishop Kallistos can hardly be said to have created a 'school' of Orthodox theology (something he would not have wanted to do), he has exercised enormous influence throughout the Orthodox world through his supervision of research students, many of them Orthodox, including several, since the collapse of the Soviet Union, from Eastern Europe. All speak of his personal concern for them and their work, and his special ability to inspire them with a sense of the importance of the research they were engaged upon. As one of his former students put it, 'I have never left his office without the sense that my work is worthwhile and that it has just received new life; such is his great and special gift as a teacher.' Many others, both colleagues and academics visiting Oxford, speak of having experienced such inspiration and encouragement. Some sense of the extent of this legacy to the Church may be gauged by mentioning that his former research students include at least two metropolitans, two (or three) bishops, many archimandrites, monks, nuns, professors, teachers and theologians (not only Orthodox).

Parish priest and ecumenist

Alongside this academic career, Father Kallistos also played a leading role in the development of the life of the Orthodox community in Oxford. In 1966 he founded the Greek Orthodox parish of the Holy Trinity in Oxford, which from 1973 shared a parish church with the Russian Orthodox parish of the Annunciation, built in the grounds of the House of Sts Gregory and Macrina, an Orthodox and ecumenical centre, established by Nicolas Zernov. In 1982, he was consecrated titular bishop of Diokleia and appointed an assistant bishop in the Orthodox Archdiocese of Thyateira and Great Britain under the Œcumenical Patriarchate; in 2007 Diokleia was raised to the status of a metropolis. He was also involved for many years with Syndesmos, the international Orthodox youth federation, and from its inception has been a member of the Advisory Board of the Orthodox Peace Fellowship. From its beginnings in 1990, Bishop Kallistos has been involved in the Friends of Mount Athos, and led many of the pilgrimages organized by the Friends.

He is well known, too, for his long engagement in the ecumenical movement. From 1973 to 1984 he was a delegate to the Anglican–Orthodox Joint Doctrinal discussions; in 2007 he became the Orthodox Chairman of the Anglican–Orthodox Joint Commission. But perhaps his engagement in the ecumenical movement has been most intense and long-lasting through his involvement in the Fellowship of St Alban and St Sergius, set up largely under the inspiration of Nicolas Zernov in 1928 to promote better understanding among Christians and particularly between the Anglican and Orthodox Churches.

To find and proclaim the truth of the gospel

These three sides to Bishop Kallistos' life – the academic, the pastoral and the ecumenical – all find their coinherence in his life as a priest, a monk and a man of prayer. Although he has not made his home on the island of Patmos, he usually spends some time annually at the monastery; the importance to him of belonging to a monastic community of brothers can hardly be underestimated. The monastic life is a life of prayer in which the truth and reality of God is acknowledged and rejoiced in. This sense of the wonderful, yet mysterious, *truth* of God informs the three aspects of Bishop Kallistos' vocation just mentioned. The academic is very obviously concerned with the patient discovery and exploration of truth; Bishop Kallistos' academic work combines rigorously scholarly methods with a delight in the truth discovered and an enthusiasm for passing such truth on. His pastoral concern follows from this desire to communicate the truths perceived by the saints; truth is not just something to think about, it is the revelation of wonder and mystery, something that transforms the lives of those who come to know it. This truth is communicated through preaching, but also more tacitly in the very celebration of the mysteries. Coming to know the truth is something deeply personal: for Bishop Kallistos, pastoral concern is also expressed in his role, willingly embraced, as spiritual father to many in the UK and beyond. But if the gospel is about the truth, then the fragmented state of those who call themselves Christians is not just unfortunate: it is a disgrace, something that we must work to remove. Here is the inspiration for Bishop Kallistos' tireless engagement in ecumenism, during a half-century in which the goal of ecumenism has seemed to recede almost daily.

Bishop Kallistos' achievement has been honoured in several ways: he has received honorary doctorates from universities in Greece, Romania, Bulgaria, France (from the Institut St-Serge) and the USA, and is a member of the Russian Academy of Sciences, the first Orthodox bishop to be so honoured since 1917, as well as a member of the Academy of Athens.

I have already mentioned the three books Bishop Kallistos has published, and the works of translation he has been involved in, both as a translator and as an interpreter (through Introductions and Forewords). This is, however, only a small proportion of his published output: there are over a hundred published articles; in 2000 a collection of his articles, *The Inner Kingdom*, was published, the first volume of a projected seven- or eight-volume Collected Works (alas, no further volumes have yet been published).[12] These articles vary from talks given to laypeople to papers delivered at academic symposia and contributions to major works of academic reference, such as the *Theologische Realenzyklopädie* and the *Dictionnaire de Spiritualité*.[13] They are all characterized by precision and

---

[12] Bishop Kallistos Ware, *The Inner Kingdom*, vol. 1 of the Collected Works (Crestwood, NY: St Vladimir's Seminary Press, 2000).

[13] 'Diadochus von Photice', 'Gottesdienst: Orthodoxe Kirche', in *Theologische Realenzyklopädie*, VIII (1981), pp. 617–20, XIV (1985), pp. 46–51; 'Philocalie', in *Dictionnaire de Spiritualité*, XII (1984), cols 1336–52.

clarity: Bishop Kallistos' primary concern is always to engage his audience and communicate with them. One is reminded of Patriarch Photios' comments on the homilies of St John Chrysostom: he said that he 'admired that thrice-blessed man, because he always, in every sermon, made it his aim to benefit his audience'.[14]

This, however, does not help someone, like me, trying to write on his theology, for he has written something, somewhere, on almost everything, and what he has to say is lucid and balanced. One can find articles, or chapters in his books, on almost every aspect of Orthodox teaching; on prayer, both liturgical prayer and the Jesus Prayer; on ecumenical issues; on questions of ascetical theology, not least on questions to do with the make-up of the human person; on contentious issues, such as the ordination of women to the priesthood (on which Bishop Kallistos' position has changed significantly); on various aspects of church history. Of particular importance are the obituaries he has written over the years (published mostly in *Sobornost* and *The Forerunner*) of significant figures in the history of Orthodoxy in the West (mostly) in the twentieth century, some prominent, some more hidden. Such diversity poses problems for an interpreter of his thought. I shall simplify by focusing on the *Philokalia*, and his role in the translation and interpretation of it, for it seems to me that this leads us to the heart of the bishop's understanding of theology, while at the same time bringing out his central role in the world of Orthodox theology today.

Engagement with the *Philokalia*

The *Philokalia* is an anthology of ascetical texts that were preserved and valued by the monastic communities of Mount Athos, though some remarks by Nikodimos in his Preface to the *Philokalia* suggest that not even there had they been thoroughly appreciated; for he says of the works gathered in the *Philokalia* that they 'have never in earlier times been published, or if they have, lie in obscurity, in darkness, in a corner, uncherished and moth-eaten, and from there dispersed and squandered'.[15] So perhaps we should start with the Holy Mountain, for not only did the *Philokalia* originate there, but the decision by Gerald Palmer, Philip Sherrard and (then) Archimandrite Kallistos to embark on an English translation of the *Philokalia* grew out of Bishop Kallistos' visits to the Holy Mountain with Gerald Palmer in the 1960s and 1970s. Speaking of what he had learnt from Gerald Palmer during these visits to Athos, Bishop Kallistos once had this to say:

> First, he greatly enhanced my sense of the Athonite environment, of the *physical reality* of the Holy Mountain. He made me aware – far more than I had been previously – of the Holy Mountain as in itself a sacrament of the divine presence. Athos is not only a mountain of holy monks, of holy monasteries,

---

[14] Photios, *Bibliotheca*, cod. 174; ET: Photius, *The Bibliotheca*, trans. N. G. Wilson (London: Duckworth, 1994), 157.

[15] *Philokalia* (Venice, 1782), 6.

and holy icons. It is itself a *Holy Mountain.* The monks, the monasteries, and the icons are enfolded and contained within a wider framework, within an all-embracing context of sacred space. Walking with Gerald on the paths of Athos, I felt as he did that the very rocks and earth of the Mountain, with all its flowers, shrubs, and trees, possess an intrinsic sacredness. In Fr Nikon's words, which Gerald used to quote, 'Here every stone breathes prayers.' ... Gerald valued the monastic buildings, the icons, the human presence of the monks, the ever-renewed sequence of liturgical prayer. But all of this acquired its full meaning in his eyes because of the sacredness of the very Mountain itself.[16]

Bishop Kallistos continued:

A second thing that Gerald taught me to feel and know more directly was the stillness of the Holy Mountain, its creative silence. By 'stillness' (*hesychia*) I do not mean a total absence of sound, for of course there are always many sounds on the Mountain: of the wind and the sea, of the birds and the insects, of the simantron, the bells, and the chanting. But all these sounds stand out from an omnipresent background of silence – of a silence that is not an emptiness but a fullness, not an absence but a personal presence: 'Be still, and know that I am God' (Psalm 46:10).[17]

The decision to translate the *Philokalia* grew out of the spiritual experience of being on the Holy Mountain. Gerald Palmer had already embarked on the venture of translating the *Philokalia.* Twenty years or so earlier, in 1948, Palmer had visited the Holy Mountain and met Fr Nikon of Karoulia – the Fr Nikon mentioned in the first of these passages – and as a result of this encounter had translated, with Madame Evgeniya Kadloubovsky, two volumes of selections from the Russian translation of the *Philokalia*, the *Dobrotolyubiye*, made by St Theophan the Recluse in the nineteenth century.[18]

One can trace back still further Fr Nikon's influence on making the *Philokalia* available in English, for Mme Kadloubovsky was the personal secretary of P. D. Ouspensky, one of the most famous disciples of G. I. Gurdjieff. A couple of decades earlier, Ouspensky had himself visited the Holy Mountain and come to know Fr Nikon; it may have been then that the idea of making a translation of the *Philokalia* into English was first mentioned. Gerald Palmer was a friend of Ouspensky and, like him, a disciple of Gurdjieff, so the origin of the English *Philokalia* could well be traced back to the esoteric strivings of the early part of the twentieth century. I mention this, not to muddy the spring from which the need for an English version of the *Philokalia* arose, but to suggest that the gestation of the English *Philokalia* was lengthy and

---

[16] Bishop Kallistos of Diokleia, 'Gerald Palmer, the *Philokalia*, and the Holy Mountain', *Annual Report of the Friends of Mount Athos* (1994), 26–7.

[17] Kallistos, 'Gerald Palmer, the *Philokalia*, and the Holy Mountain', 27–8. Both these passages are quoted in Graham Speake's contribution to the Festschrift for Bishop Kallistos, 'A Friend of Mount Athos', *Abba*, 29–40.

[18] *Writings from the Philokalia on Prayer of the Heart; Early Fathers from the Philokalia*, both trans. G. E. H. Palmer and E. Kadloubovsky (London: Faber & Faber, 1951, 1954).

fulfilled a deeply rooted longing for spiritual wisdom.[19] One might recall the roots of some strands of modern Orthodox theology in the realm of the esoteric and the occult (e.g. Solov'ev and aspects of his heritage, or even Olivier Clément, and in another way Philip Sherrard). Gavrilyuk's presentation of the quarrel over Sophia between Florovsky and Bulgakov suggests that distaste for and anxiety about the esoteric roots of sophiology affected Fr Florovsky's attitude.[20] Florovsky's anxiety about getting entangled with the esoteric is understandable, but so, too, is a sensitivity to the ways that have led some to Orthodoxy.

Hesychia

But the experience itself: a sense of the sacredness of the Holy Mountain linked to an experience of stillness, *hesychia*. These give us two themes, or two pathways, to pursue as we seek to explore the place of the *Philokalia* in the theology of Bishop Kallistos. Let us start with the latter pathway: that of *hesychia*. It is from that word, *hesychia*, stillness, that the term hesychasm is derived. The term can be used generally to describe any way of silent prayer, but it has a more specific connotation, referring to the movement on Mount Athos among monks called hesychasts, who through use of the Jesus Prayer claimed to come to a vision of the uncreated light of the Godhead. These claims became the focus for controversy in the fourteenth century, in which the hesychast monks were defended by St Gregory Palamas, and vindicated in local synods held in Constantinople in the 1340s and 1350s. Though the *Philokalia* contains far more texts from the period before the hesychast controversy, it is not unreasonable to see it as a hesychast anthology: its chronological approach means that the explicitly hesychast texts come at the end of the work, so that the collection can be seen as tracing the history of Byzantine asceticism from the perspective of hesychasm.

The meaning of *hesychia* has exercised Bishop Kallistos throughout his life: there is a long section on the hesychast controversy in his first book, *The Orthodox Church*, which also contains a brief, though significant, discussion of the Jesus Prayer;[21] many articles on different aspects of hesychasm and the Jesus Prayer followed, including a series of important articles on Palamism in the *Eastern Churches Review*;[22] and an article on the meaning of *hesychia*, which

---

[19] All this is based on hints revealed in a rather curious book, *The Globalization of Hesychasm and the Jesus Prayer*, by Christopher D. L. Johnson (London: Continuum, 2010): see pages 84ff. and 98ff. He, in turn, refers to Robin Amis, *A Different Christianity: Early Christian Esotericism and Modern Thought* (Albany, NY: State University of New York Press, 1995).

[20] Paul L. Gavrilyuk, *Georges Florovsky and the Russian Religious Renaissance* (Oxford: Oxford University Press, 2013), 132–58.

[21] Ware, *The Orthodox Church* (1st edn, 1963), 72–80, 312–14.

[22] 'Scholasticism and Orthodoxy: Theological Method as a Factor in the Schism', *ECR* 5:1 (1973), 16–27; 'God Hidden and Revealed: The Apophatic Way and the Essence–Energies Distinction', *ECR* 7:2 (1975), 125–36; 'The Debate about Palamism', *ECR* 9:1–2 (1977), 45–63.

was included in volume 1 of his Collected Works,[23] to which one must add his pamphlet, *The Power of the Name*.[24] As with all his articles, one is struck by the range of sources on which he draws and the clarity and vividness of what he has to say. Furthermore, although he is clear in his opinions, he is always respectful of the opinions of others, and writes in a constructive way – something not at all characteristic of writing on hesychasm, for despite the fact that the root from which the term is derived means 'quietness' or 'stillness', controversy over hesychasm is more often noisy and acerbic!

... and what it is to be human

What is particularly interesting about the bishop's thought on hesychasm and prayer is the way in which it is both practical and yet at the same time informs his thought on what it is to be human: what the make-up of the human is. The practical side can be illustrated in a lecture given in Athens in 1998, and published in a splendid edition in 2004, *The Inner Unity of the Philokalia and Its Influence in East and West*.[25] After his opening words in which he speaks of the influence of the *Philokalia*, and the way in which 'it has become customary to speak of a characteristically "Philokalic" approach to theology and prayer, and many regard this "Philokalic" standpoint as the most creative element in contemporary Orthodoxy',[26] he goes on to identify what he calls the 'inner unity' of the *Philokalia*. First, it is concerned with 'inner action', that is, 'the guarding of the intellect', which leads to the discovery of the 'kingdom within us', which is characterized by two virtues: 'by *nepsis*, a term denoting sobriety, temperance, lucidity, and above all vigilance and watchfulness; and by *hesychia*, which signifies not so much exterior silence as inner stillness of heart'.[27] The aim of this inner action is deification: '[t]his ideal of *theosis*, of direct, transforming union with the living God, constitutes a unifying thread throughout the *Philokalia* as a whole'.[28] The means to reach this goal is continual invocation of the Name. Such invocation of the name of Jesus in prayer will 'enable us to "return to the perfect grace of the Spirit that was bestowed upon us in the beginning through Baptism"'.[29] This method Nikodimos, in his introduction to the *Philokalia*, even ventures to

---

[23] 'Silence in Prayer: The Meaning of Hesychia', in *Theology and Prayer*, ed. A. M. Allchin, SSTS 3 (1975), 8–28; also in *One Yet Two: Monastic Tradition East and West*, ed. M. Basil Pennington, Cistercian Studies 29 (Kalamazoo, MI: Cistercian Publications, 1976), 22–47; and in Ware, *The Inner Kingdom*, 89–110.

[24] *The Power of the Name*, Fairacres Publication 43 (Oxford: SLG Press, 1974; rev. edn, 1977). Much translated and reprinted in, for instance, Elisabeth Behr-Sigel, *The Place of the Heart: An Introduction to Orthodox Spirituality*, trans. Stephen Bigham (Torrance, CA: Oakwood, 1992), 133–73.

[25] *The Inner Unity of the Philokalia and Its Influence in East and West* (Athens: Onassis Foundation, 2004).

[26] Kallistos, *Inner Unity*, 41.

[27] Kallistos, *Inner Unity*, 49.

[28] Kallistos, *Inner Unity*, 50.

[29] Kallistos, *Inner Unity*, 51.

call 'scientific', and it can be spelt out in these terms: to pray *without ceasing*, in the *depths of the heart, excluding all images and thoughts*, invoking the *Holy Name of Jesus*, and using, if desired, *physical technique* (head bowed on chest; control of breathing; inner exploration).[30] The lecture continues with some brief discussion of its intellectual provenance, which the bishop argues, surely correctly, is Evagrian–Maximian, with some influence from Palamism (though Bishop Kallistos is very cautious over the nature and extent of this influence), and some brief discussion of the influence of the *Philokalia*.[31] The bishop's account of the *Philokalia* emphasizes its practical nature, and in this way finds in the *Philokalia* a dimension that is never far from his own theological approach.

However, there is a series of articles in which Bishop Kallistos explores the terminology of the *Philokalia* in order to deepen our understanding of the nature of the human.[32] It is particularly striking that the very same sources are used this time to advance our understanding of what it is to be human. This is, maybe, not very surprising, as what it is to be human – how we are constituted – is bound up with the purpose for which we were created, which is union with God, deification, which is effected through prayer, most fundamentally. A good deal of what these articles explore can be found in the Glossary of Terms, which forms an appendix to each of the volumes of the English translation of the *Philokalia*; the articles spell out what is present there in summary form.

The mystery of the human

One point Bishop Kallistos frequently makes when considering the nature of the human person is that the human person is a mystery: one article begins by quoting various Fathers on the unknowability of the human person and concludes by quoting Carl Gustav Jung, who said that the psyche is 'a foreign, almost unexplored country'.[33] The human is created in the image of God, and stress is laid on the unity of the human person, created in God's image. Within this unity, there can be discerned different parts; many of the Fathers

---

[30] Cf. Kallistos, *Inner Unity*, 52.

[31] Kallistos, *Inner Unity*, 53–61. For a longer discussion of the influence of the *Philokalia*, see my 'The Influence of the *Philokalia* in the Orthodox World', in *The* Philokalia: *A Classic Text of Orthodox Spirituality*, ed. Brock Bingaman and Bradley Nassif (New York: Oxford University Press, 2012), 50–60, 286–7 (notes); or, in a more polished version: 'The Influence of the *Philokalia* in the Orthodox World', *Annual Report 2010* (Athos: Friends of Mount Athos, 2010), 37–52.

[32] I have in mind articles such as: 'The Mystery of the Human Person', *Sobornost/ECR* 3:1 (1981), 62–9; 'Nous and Noesis in Plato, Aristotle and Evagrius of Pontus', *Diotima* 13 [Proceedings of the Second International Week on the Philosophy of Greek Culture, Kalamata 1982, Part II] (1985), 158–63; 'The Soul in Greek Christianity', in *From Soul to Self*, ed. M. James C. Crabbe, (London–New York: Routledge, 1999), 49–69; *O Anthropos os «Mysterion»: I Enotita tou Prosopou kata tous Ellenes Pateres* (Athens: Akadimia Athinon, 2008): Bishop Kallistos' inaugural lecture as member of the Academy of Athens.

[33] Kallistos, 'The Soul', 49.

adopt the Platonic threefold division of the soul into the rational part and two irrational parts, the desiring and the spirited or incensive (to use the translation adopted in the English *Philokalia*); others, or sometimes the same, also make use of the Aristotelian distinction between the rational, animal and vegetable 'soul' (or principle of life). The unity of the soul is often to be found in the heart, *kardia*, or the intellect, *nous*. In these articles, Bishop Kallistos explores the different valencies of these two terms – heart and intellect – arguing that they represent ways of understanding the innermost nature of the human in which the human comes to knowledge of God by some form of direct participation. The article in *Diotima* explores the notion of *nous* and *noesis*, arguing that this is a faculty transcending discursive reason, a faculty that knows by a form of immediate participation. In his article on 'The Soul in Greek Christianity' (a contribution of a symposium, *From Self to Soul*, that gathered together papers exploring various ways of approaching the notion of what it is to be human), Bishop Kallistos sums up his conclusion in these terms:

> First, there is the notion of the heart as the unifying centre of our personhood, open on the [one] side to the abyss of the unconscious, open on the other to the abyss of divine grace. Second, there is the understanding of the *nous* or intellect as a faculty far higher than the reasoning brain – a visionary power, creative and self-transcending, that reaches out beyond time into eternity, beyond words into silence.[34]

It is interesting to note Bishop Kallistos' openness to the insights of modern psychology, not least to the notion of the unconscious.

The human and the cosmos

Alongside these explorations of the constituents, as it were, of the human, the bishop also underlines the way in which the human, in virtue of being in the image of God, exercises a role in the cosmos: he or she is a microcosm, or better a *megalocosmos*, since the human comprehends the cosmos, whereas the reverse is not the case.[35]

This cosmic dimension of the human bears a very direct relevance to what we call the 'environmental crisis', although this very way of conceiving it is, the bishop argues, a misconception:

> The present crisis is not really outside us, a crisis in our physical surroundings, but it is a crisis within us, a crisis in the way we humans think and feel. The fundamental problem lies not in the ecosystem, but in the human heart. It has rightly been said that we are suffering from ecological heart failure.[36]

---

34 Kallistos, 'The Soul', 66.
35 Kallistos, *Anthropos*, 38–44.
36 *Ecological Crisis, Ecological Hope: Our Orthodox Vision of Creation*, Orthodoxy in America Lecture Series (Bronx, NY: Fordham University Press, 2005), 10.

There have been several lectures given by the bishop concerned with human responsibility for the cosmos: one of the earliest was his lecture to the 'Friends of the Centre', given in 1997, 'Through the Creation to the Creator';[37] since then there has been his Orthodoxy in America Lecture in 2005, and another lecture, 'The Beginning of the Day: The Orthodox Vision of Creation', given in 2007.[38] In these lectures, Bishop Kallistos draws on the Greek patristic understanding of the human as reflecting the cosmos in his or her own nature, an understanding that entails human responsibility for the cosmos, and relates this to other expressions of a similar insight, from a philosophical notion such as panentheism to the ideas of poets, such as Robert Frost, Katherine Raine and William Blake. Human misuse of the created order is a sin – sin is not to be limited to human relationships – and calls for what Bishop Kallistos calls 'cosmic repentance', cosmic *metanoia*, no mere expression of regret, but entailing a radical turnabout in our ways of life.

This concern for the cosmos relates directly to the place of the *Philokalia* in Bishop Kallistos' understanding of theology. In his account of the visits he made to the Holy Mountain with Gerald Palmer already cited, it is his sense of the *sacredness* of the Holy Mountain that he mentions first. This sense of the sacredness of God's Creation – that 'everything that lives is holy', in Blake's words – is something that becomes tangible on the Holy Mountain, the bishop seems to suggest. Bishop Kallistos is fond of recalling in this context the words of Fr Amphilochios, an elder or geronta on the island of Patmos, whom he knew when he first visited there (he died in 1970): 'Do you know – he used to say – that God gave us one more commandment, which is not recorded in Scripture? It is the commandment *Love the trees* . . . When you plant a tree, you plant hope, you plant peace, you plant love, and you will receive God's blessing.'[39]

The meaning of personhood

Let us close by looking briefly at a lecture Metropolitan Kallistos gave in Volos in 2004, issued as the first publication in a series sponsored by the Ecclesiastical Academy of Volos and the World Council of Churches. The series is called Doxa and Praxis: Exploring Orthodox Theology, and Metropolitan Kallistos' lecture, 'Orthodox Theology in the Twenty-First Century'.[40] In this lecture he argues that, whereas in the last century, Orthodoxy was primarily exercised by questions of ecclesiology, in this century the attention needs to shift to the question of what it means to be a human person, to questions of Christian anthropology. The bishop lists four reasons why the meaning of the human

---

[37] *Through the Creation to the Creator* (London: Friends of the Centre, 1997).
[38] *The Beginning of the Day: The Orthodox Vision of Creation* [in Greek and English] (Ioannina: Shrine of Neomartyr George of Ioannina, 2007).
[39] Cf., e.g., *Through the Creation*, 5.
[40] *Orthodox Theology in the Twenty-First Century* (Geneva: WCC Publications, 2012).

person has become pressing: first, on the social and political level, the threats posed by ever-advancing urbanization and globalization; second, the advance of technology, leading to a life dominated by machines, not least computers; third, on an ethical level, problems posed by genetical engineering and the widespread rejection of traditional sexual morality; and finally, the ecological tragedy, ultimately to be traced back to a failure to understand what it is to be human in relation to the cosmos.

Bishop Kallistos then goes on to sketch out some fundamental affirmations about a Christian understanding of personhood: first, the human person is a mystery; second, the human person is a living icon of the living God; and finally, the human is priest of Creation. Although brief, the bishop's lecture sets before us a theological task we dare not neglect. One might argue that the shift in emphasis is not as great as Bishop Kallistos suggests. Worries about urbanization go back at least to the beginning of the nineteenth century; the Romantic Movement can be seen as a response to that. Orthodox concern with ecclesiology in the last century was intimately bound up with the nature of the human person: the notion of *sobornost'* entailed an understanding of the person as freely existing in symbiosis with community. Bishop Kallistos' point could perhaps be put differently. A concern for ecclesiology, the nature of the Church, could be seen as inward-looking; a concern for the nature of personhood, to understand what it is, to enable persons to flourish in a rapidly changing world, and to grasp the cosmic implications of being human – all of this is not at all inward-looking, and will only be pursued with real seriousness if we are prepared to listen to others – scientists, poets, thinkers – and learn to incorporate in the inherited wisdom of the Church the discoveries and insights of the modern world. Not long ago, the Dominican theologian Fr Antoine Lévy said that he dreamt of 'an Orthodox Church which would be so convinced of the *absolute truth* of her own heritage, so *proud* of it, that nothing would hinder her from fathoming the riches of other traditions and welcoming them with sisterly joy'[41] – but it was only a dream! Metropolitan Kallistos' lecture is a clarion call to Orthodox theology to transform that dream into reality.

---

[41] Antoine Lévy, 'The Woes of Originality: Discussing David Bradshaw's Aristotelian Journey into Neo-Palamism', in *Divine Essence and Divine Energies: Ecumenical Reflections on the Presence of God in Eastern Orthodoxy*, ed. C. Athanasopoulos and C. Schneider (Cambridge: James Clarke, 2013), 96–121, at 121.

Further reading

Rather than providing a consolidated Bibliography in alphabetical order of author, which would give an entirely false impression of completeness and comprehensiveness, I have decided to give a guide to further reading, chapter by chapter.

For further details, see the footnotes to the individual chapters. There are many articles on these figures in journals such as *Contacts, St Vladimir's Theological Quarterly* and *Sobornost*. I have noted those I have used, but not made a systematic search.

1 The *Philokalia* and its influence

English translation of the *Philokalia*, first published Venice, 1782:

> *The Philokalia: The Complete Text Compiled by St Nikodimos of the Holy Mountain and St Makarios of Corinth*, translated from the Greek by G. E. H. Palmer, Philip Sherrard, Kallistos Ware, 4 vols (so far, out of 5) (London: Faber & Faber, 1979–95).

On the Philokalia

Deseille, Placide, *La Spiritualité orthodoxe et la Philocalie* (Paris: Albin Michel, 2011).
The Philokalia: *A Classic Text of Orthodox Spirituality*, ed. Brock Bingaman and Bradley Nassif (New York: Oxford University Press, 2012).

On the background of philosophy in Russia in the nineteenth century

Copleston, Frederick C., *Philosophy in Russia: From Herzen to Lenin and Berdyaev* (Tunbridge Wells: Search Press/Notre Dame, IN: University of Notre Dame Press, 1986).
Young, George M., *The Russian Cosmists* (Oxford: Oxford University Press, 2012).
Zenkovsky, V. V., *A History of Russian Philosophy*, trans. George Kline, 2 vols (London: Routledge & Kegan Paul, 1953).

On the history of Orthodox theology in the modern period

Destivelle, Hyacinthe, *Les Sciences théologiques en Russie* (Paris: Cerf, 2010).
Spiteris, Yannis, *La teologia ortodossa neo-greca* (Bologna: Edizione Dehoniane, 1992).

(Both these books discuss the kind of nineteenth-century Russian and modern Greek Orthodox theology that I am largely ignoring.)
Also relevant:

Špidlík, Tomáš, *Die russische Idee: Eine andere Sicht des Menschen* (Würzburg: Der Christliche Osten, 2002).

Histories of modern Orthodox theology by Orthodox themselves

Florovsky, G., *Ways of Russian Theology*, 2 vols (Belmont, MA: Nordland, 1979; Vaduz: Büchervertriebsanstalt, 1987).

Yannaras, Christos, *Orthodoxy and the West*, trans. Peter Chamberis and Norman Russell (Brookline, MA: Holy Cross Orthodox Press, 2006; from the Greek, Athens: Domos, 1992).

On Optina Pustyn' and the Slavophils

On Spiritual Unity: A Slavophile Reader, ed. and trans. Boris Jakim and Robert Bird (Hudson, NY: Lindisfarne Press, 1998).

Paert, Irina, *Spiritual Elders: Charisma and Tradition in Russian Orthodoxy* (DeKalb, IL: Northern Illinois University Press, 2010).

From a slightly different geographical perspective:

Kenworthy, Scott M., *The Heart of Russia: Trinity-Sergius, Monasticism and Society after 1825* (New York: Oxford University Press, 2010).

Walicki, Andrzej, *The Slavophile Controversy* (Oxford: Clarendon Press, 1975).

On Dostoevsky

Williams, Rowan, *Dostoevsky: Language, Faith and Fiction* (London: Continuum, 2008).

On the pilgrim

The Pilgrim's Tale, trans. with important Introduction by Aleksei Pentkovsky (Mahwah, NJ: Paulist Press, 1999).

The Way of a Pilgrim and *The Pilgrim Continues His Way*, trans. R. M. French (London: SPCK, 1954).

On the Russian emigration and Russians in exile

Arjakovsky, Antoine, *La Génération des penseurs religieux de l'émigration russe: La revue La Voie (Put')*, *1925–1940* (Kiev–Paris: L'Esprit et la Lettre, 2002); ET: Jerry Ryan, *The Way: Religious Thinkers of the Russian Emigration in Paris and Their Journal, 1925–1940* (Notre Dame, IN: University of Notre Dame Press, 2013).

Raeff, Marc, *Russia Abroad: A Cultural History of the Russian Emigration, 1919–1939* (Oxford: Oxford University Press, 1990).

See also:

Les Pères de l'Église aux sources de l'Europe, ed. Dominique Gonnet and Michel Stavrou (Paris: Cerf, 2014). This has essays on Lot-Borodine, Lossky, Kern, Florovsky, Krivochéine, Meyendorff, as well as Roman Catholic participants in the patristic renewal of the twentieth century.

Also entertaining, if not exactly useful:

Ponfilly, Raymond de, *Guide des Russes en France* (Paris: Éditions Horay, 1990).

2 Vladimir Solov'ev and Sophia

There are two recent collections of translations of works by Solov'ev with important introductions:

The Heart of Reality: Essays on Beauty, Love and Ethics by V. S. Soloviev, ed. and trans. Vladimir Wozniuk (Notre Dame, IN: University of Notre Dame Press, 2003).

Kornblatt, Judith Deutsch, *Divine Sophia: The Wisdom Writings of Vladimir Solovyov* (Ithaca–London: Cornell University Press, 2009). Kornblatt's Introduction, nearly 100 pages long, is one of the best recent essays on Solov'ev's notion of Sophia.

A Solovyov Anthology, ed. S. L. Frank, trans. Natalie Duddington (London: SCM Press, 1950).

There are some older selections, as well.

Many of Solov'ev's works are available in English, French and German (a complete collection in German); many of his works in English have been republished recently in slightly revised translations, mostly by Boris Jakim.

For the cultural background, I would recommend:

Pyman, Avril, *A History of Russian Symbolism* (Cambridge–New York: Cambridge University Press, 1994).

About Solov'ev

Cioran, Samuel D., *Vladimir Solov'ev and the Knighthood of the Divine Sophia* (Waterloo, ON: Wilfrid Laurier University Press, 1977).

Smith, Oliver, *Vladimir Soloviev and the Spiritualization of Matter* (Boston, MA: Academic Studies Press, 2011).

Strémooukhoff, D., *Vladimir Soloviev and His Messianic Work* (Belmont, MA: Nordland, 1980).

3 Fr Pavel Florensky and the nature of reason

Works by Florensky referred to (in English translation)

Florensky, Pavel, *Iconostasis*; ET: Donald Sheehan and Olga Andrejev (Crestwood, NY: St Vladimir's Seminary Press, 1996).

Florensky, Pavel, *The Pillar and Ground of the Truth*; ET: Boris Jakim (Princeton, NJ: Princeton University Press, 1997).

'Reverse Perspective', in Pavel Florensky, *Beyond Vision: Essays on the Perception of Art*, ed. Nicoletta Misler, trans. Wendy Salmond (London: Reaktion, 2002), 197–272.

About Florensky

Bychkov, Victor, *The Aesthetic Face of Being: Art in the Theology of Pavel Florensky* (Crestwood, NY: St Vladimir's Seminary Press, 1993).

Lock, Charles, 'What Is Reverse Perspective and Who Was Oskar Wulff?' *Sobornost/ Eastern Churches Review* 33:1 (2011), 60–89.

Misler, Nicoletta, Introduction in Pavel Florensky, *Beyond Vision*.

Pyman, Avril, *Pavel Florensky: A Quiet Genius: The Tragic and Extraordinary Life of Russia's Unknown da Vinci* (London: Continuum, 2010).

Slesinski, Robert, *Pavel Florensky: A Metaphysics of Love* (Crestwood, NY: St Vladimir's Seminary Press, 1984).

Žust, Milan, *À la recherche de la Vérité vivante: L'expérience religieuse de Pavel A. Florensky (1882–1937)* (Rome: Lipa, 2002).

4 Fr Sergii Bulgakov and the nature of theology

Most of Bulgakov's works are now available in English, mostly translated by Boris Jakim or Thomas Allan Smith. The most important are:

Philosophy of Economy: The World as Household, trans. Catherine Evtuhov (New Haven–London: Yale University Press, 2000).
Unfading Light, trans. Thomas Allan Smith (Grand Rapids, MI: Eerdmans, 2012).

The 'great trilogy':
The Bride of the Lamb, trans. Boris Jakim (Grand Rapids, MI: Eerdmans, 2002).
The Comforter, trans. Boris Jakim (Grand Rapids, MI: Eerdmans, 2004).
The Lamb of God, trans. Boris Jakim (Grand Rapids, MI: Eerdmans, 2008).

The 'little trilogy':
The Burning Bush: On the Orthodox Veneration of the Mother of God, trans. Thomas Allan Smith (Grand Rapids, MI: Eerdmans, 2009).
The Friend of the Bridegroom, trans. Boris Jakim (Grand Rapids, MI: Eerdmans, 2003).
Jacob's Ladder: On Angels, trans. Thomas Allan Smith (Grand Rapids, MI: Eerdmans, 2010).

Also:

Avtobiograficheskie Zametki (Paris: YMCA Press, 1991; originally published 1946); ET: *A Bulgakov Anthology: Sergius Bulgakov 1871–1944* (London: SPCK, 1976).
Boulgakov, Serge, *L'Apocalypse de Jean*, trans. Anne Kichilov, with Introduction by Antoine Arjakovsky (Paris: Parole et Silence, 2014).
Boulgakov, Serge, *Sous les remparts de Chersonèse*, French translation with Introduction and notes by Bernard Marchadier (Geneva: Ad Solem, 1999).
Churchly Joy, trans. Boris Jakim (Grand Rapids, MI: Eerdmans, 2008).
'Dogma and dogmatic theology', trans. Peter Bouteneff, in *Tradition Alive*, ed. Michael Plekon (Lanham, MD: Rowman & Littlefield, 2003), 67–80.
The Holy Grail and the Eucharist, trans. Boris Jakim (Hudson, NY: Lindisfarne Books, 1997).
Icons and the Name of God, trans. Boris Jakim (Grand Rapids, MI: Eerdmans, 2012).
The Orthodox Church, ed. Donald A. Lowrie, trans. Elizabeth S. Cram (London: The Centenary Press, 1935).
Relics and Miracles, trans. Boris Jakim (Grand Rapids, MI: Eerdmans, 2011).
Schmemann, Alexander, 'Trois Images', *Le Messager orthodoxe* 57 (1972), 2–21.
Sergius Bulgakov: Apocatastasis and Transfiguration, trans. Boris Jakim, Variable Readings in Russian Philosophy 2 (New Haven, CT: Variable Press, 1995).

See also:

A Bulgakov Anthology: Sergius Bulgakov 1871–1944 (London: SPCK, 1976).

About Bulgakov

Evtuhov, Catherine, *The Cross and the Sickle: Sergei Bulgakov and the Fate of Russian Religious Philosophy, 1890–1920* (Ithaca–London: Cornell University Press, 1997).

Gallaher, Brandon, 'Graced Creatureliness: Ontological Tension in the Uncreated/ Created Distinction in the Sophiologies of Solov'ev, Bulgakov and Milbank', *Logos: A Journal of Eastern Christian Studies* 47 (2006), 163–90.

Louth, Andrew, 'Sergei Bulgakov', in *Moderne teologi: Tradisjon og nytenkning hos det 20. århundrets teologer*, ed. Ståle Johannes Kristiansen and Svein Rise (Kristiansand: Høyskoleforlaget, 2008), 353–65; now available in English: *Key Theological Thinkers: From Modern to Postmodern* (Farnham: Ashgate, 2013), 341–51.

Louth, Andrew, 'Sergii Bulgakov and the Task of the Theologian', *Irish Theological Quarterly* 74 (2009), 243–57.

Louth, Andrew, 'Wisdom and the Russians: The Sophiology of Fr Sergei Bulgakov', in *Where Shall Wisdom Be Found?*, ed. Stephen C. Barton (Edinburgh: T&T Clark, 1999), 169–81.

Williams, Rowan, *Sergii Bulgakov: Towards a Russian Political Theology* (Edinburgh: T&T Clark, 1999).

Also of great interest for the history of the Exarchate in Western Europe, to which the Institut St-Serge belonged, are the memoirs of Metropolitan Evlogy, who guided most of the Russian Orthodox Church in Europe from the Bolshevik Revolution until his death in 1946:

My Life's Journey: The Memoirs of Metropolitan Evlogy, trans. Alexander Lisenko, 2 vols (Yonkers, NY: St Vladimir's Seminary Press, 2014).

5 Nikolai Berdyaev – creativity, freedom and the person

Berdyaev was very prolific, and many of his works were early translated into English. I have based my exposition on the following:

The Destiny of Man, trans. Natalie Duddington (London: SCM Press, 1938).
Dostoevsky, trans. Donald Attwater (London: Sheed & Ward, 1934).
Dream and Reality, trans. Katherine Lampert (London: Geoffrey Bles, 1950).
The Meaning of the Creative Act, trans. Donald A. Lowrie (New York: Harper Brothers, 1954).
Solitude and Society, trans. George Reavey (London: Geoffrey Bles, 1938).

About Berdyaev

I have not found the older secondary literature much help. More recently see:

Segundo, Jean-Louis, *Berdiaeff: Une réflexion chrétienne sur la personne* (Paris: Aubier, 1963).

And very recently:

Zwahlen, Regula M., *Das revolutionäre Ebenbild Gottes: Anthropologien der Menschenwürde bei Nikolaj A. Berdjaev und Sergej N. Bulgakov* (Berlin: LIT, 2010).

6 Fr Georges Florovsky and the neo-patristic synthesis

Works

Not very satisfactory:

Collected Works of Father Georges Florovsky, 14 vols.Vols 1–5, Belmont, MA: Nordland, 1972–9; vols 6–14,Vaduz: Büchervertriebsanstalt, 1987–9.

Also used:

Florovsky, G., *Puti Russkogo Bogosloviya* (Paris: YMCA Press, 1981; reprint of 1937).

Florovsky, G. V., *Vostochnye Ottsy IV-go Veka* (reprint: Gregg International Publishers Ltd, 1972; original: Paris, 1931).

Foreword to Archimandrite Sophrony, *The Undistorted Image: Staretz Silouan 1866–1938* (London: Faith Press, 1958).

About Florovsky

Gallaher, Anastassy Brandon, 'Georges Florovsky on Reading the Life of St Seraphim', *Sobornost* 27:1 (2005), 58–70.

Gavrilyuk, Paul, 'Harnack's Hellenized Christianity or Florovsky's "Sacred Hellenism": Questioning Two Metanarratives of Early Christian Engagement with Late Antique Culture', *St Vladimir's Theological Quarterly* 54 (2010), 323–44.

'Georges Florovsky (1893–1979)', obituary by E. L. Mascall and Rowan Williams, *Sobornost/Eastern Churches Review* 2:1 (1980), 69–72.

Georges Florovsky: Russian Intellectual and Orthodox Churchman, ed. Andrew Blane (Crestwood, NY: St Vladimir's Seminary Press, 1993).

Golitzin, Alexander, '"A Contemplative and a Liturgist": Father Georges Florovsky on the *Corpus Dionysiacum*', *St Vladimir's Theological Quarterly* 43 (1999), 131–61.

Klimoff, Alexis, 'Georges Florovsky and the Sophiological Controversy', *St Vladimir's Theological Quarterly* 49 (2005), 67–100.

But now see:

Gavrilyuk, Paul L., *Georges Florovsky and the Russian Religious Renaissance* (Oxford: Oxford University Press, 2013).

7 Apophatic theology and deification: Myrrha Lot-Borodine and Vladimir Lossky

Lot-Borodine

De l'Amour profane à l'amour sacré: Études de psychologie sentimentale au Moyen Âge (Paris: Nizet, 1961).

La Déification de l'homme selon la doctrine des Pères grecs (Paris: Cerf, 1970).

Un maître de la spiritualité byzantine au XIVe siècle: Nicolas Cabasilas (Paris: Éditions de l'Orante, 1958).

About Lot-Borodine

Mahn-Lot, Marianne, 'Ma mère, Myrrha Lot-Borodine (1882–1954): Esquisse d'itinéraire spirituel', *Revue des sciences philosophiques et théologiques* (2004), 745–54.

Zorgdrager, Heleen, 'A Practice of Love: Myrrha Lot-Borodine (1882–1954) and the Modern Revival of the Doctrine of Deification', *Journal of Eastern Christian Studies* 64 (2012), 285–305.

Lossky

À l'Image et à la ressemblance de Dieu (Paris: Aubier-Montaigne, 1967); ET: *In the Image and Likeness of God* (Crestwood, NY: St Vladimir's Seminary Press, 1974).

Essai sur la théologie mystique de l'Église d'Orient (Paris: Aubier, 1944; republished with an Introduction by Saulias Rumšas OP, Paris, 2005, with the same pagination as the original); ET: *The Mystical Theology of the Eastern Church* (London: James Clarke, 1957).

Sept jours sur les routes de France: Juin 1940 (Paris: Cerf, 1998); ET: *Seven Days on the Roads of France: June 1940* (Crestwood, NY: St Vladimir's Seminary Press, 2012).

Der Sinn der Ikonen (Bern–Olten: Urs Graf-Verlag, 1952); ET: *The Meaning of Icons* (Boston, MA: Boston Book and Art Shop, 1969).

Spor o Sofii – Stat'i Raznyx Let [Controversy over Sophia – Articles from Various Years] (Moscow: Izdatel'stvo Svyato-Vladimirskogo Bratstva, 1996).

Théologie dogmatique, ed. Olivier Clément and Michel Stavrou (Paris: Cerf, 2012); ET: *Orthodox Theology: An Introduction*, trans. Ian and Ihita Kesarcodi-Watson (Crestwood, NY: St Vladimir's Seminary Press, 1989).

Théologie negative et connaissance de Dieu chez Maître Eckhart (Paris: Vrin, 1960).

Vision de Dieu (Neuchâtel: Delachaux et Niestlé, 1962; ET, London: Faith Press, 1963).

About Lossky

Clément, Olivier, *Orient–Occident: Deux passeurs: Vladimir Lossky et Paul Evdokimov* (Geneva: Labor et Fides, 1985).

Louth, Andrew, 'French *Ressourcement* Theology and Orthodoxy: A Living Mutual Relationship?', in *Ressourcement: A Movement for Renewal in Twentieth-Century Catholic Theology*, ed. Gabriel Flynn and Paul D. Murray (Oxford: Oxford University Press, 2012), 495–507.

Williams, Rowan, 'Lossky, the *Via Negativa* and the Foundations of Theology', in *Wrestling with Angels: Conversations in Modern Theology*, ed. Mike Higton (London: SCM Press, 2007), 1–24.

8 St Maria of Paris (Mother Maria Skobtsova) and Orthodoxy in the modern world

Marie de Paris, Sainte (Mère Marie Skobtsova, 1891–1945), *Le Jour du Saint-Esprit* (Paris: Cerf, 2011).

Skobtsova, Maria, *Essential Writings*, with an Introduction by Jim Forest (Maryknoll, NY: Orbis Books, 2003).

Skobtsova, Marie, *Le Sacrement de frère* (Paris: Cerf, new edn, 2001).

About St Maria

Hackel, Sergei, *One, of Great Price* (London: Darton, Longman & Todd, 1965); published in a revised version as *Pearl of Great Price* (Crestwood, NY: St Vladimir's Seminary Press, 1982). This is a brief, compelling biography.

Krivochéine, Xenia, *La Beauté salvatrice: Mère Marie (Skobtsov): Peintures – Dessins – Broderies* (Paris: Cerf, 2012). This is even briefer, but with lots of pictures, illustrations, and a detailed timeline – which draws particular attention to her cultural involvement.

There have been various articles with material on or by St Maria. I have found the following useful (or, it might be more accurate to say, I have found the following):

Ladouceur, Paul, 'The Experience and the Understanding of Death in St Maria of Paris', *Sobornost/Eastern Churches Review* 28:1 (2006), 21–40.

Ladouceur, Paul, 'The Saint as Artist: The Art of Saint Maria of Paris (Mother Maria Skobtsova): The Making of a Poet-Artist', *Sobornost* 36:1 (2014), 48–72.

Marie Skobtsov, Sainte, 'Poèmes', *Le Messager orthodoxe* 140 (2004): *Les Nouveaux Saints orthodoxes de France*, 35–7.

Marie Skobtsov, Sainte, 'Le Présent et l'avenir de l'Église', *Le Messager orthodoxe* 140 (2004): *Les Nouveaux Saints orthodoxes de France*, 38–46.

Skobtsov, Elisabeth, '«Terre Sainte»', *Le Messager orthodoxe* 146 (2008), 4–21.

Victoroff, Tatiana, 'Mère Marie, poète', *Le Messager orthodoxe* 140 (2004): *Les Nouveaux Saints orthodoxes de France*, 29–34.

9 Modern Orthodox dogmatic theology: 1 Fr Dumitru Stăniloae

Eternity and Time (Oxford: SLG Press, 2001).

Iisus Hristos sau Restaurarea Omului (Craiova: Editura Omniscop, 1993; first published: Sibiu, 1943).

Ortodoxie şi Românism (Bucharest: Editura Albatros, 1998). This is a collection of articles from *Telegraful Român*, originally published in 1939.

Spiritualitatea Ortodoxă: Ascetica şi Mistica (Bucharest: Editura Institutului Biblic şi de Misiune al Bisericii Ortodoxe Române, 1992; anastatic reprint of original edition: *Theologia Morală Ortodoxă*, vol. 3: *Spiritualitatea Orthodoxă*, Bucharest, 1981); ET: *Orthodox Spirituality*, trans. Archimandrite Jerome (Newville) and Otilia Kloos (South Canaan, PA: St Tikhon's Seminary Press, 2002).

Theology and Church, trans. Robert Barringer (Crestwood, NY: St Vladimir's Seminary Press, 1980). This is a collection of essays.

Teologia Dogmatică Ortodoxă, 3 vols (Bucharest: Editura Institutului Biblic şi de Misiune al Bisericii Ortodoxe Române, 1978; 2nd edn, 1996–7). ET: *The Experience of God*, trans. Ioan Ioniţă and, for some volumes, Robert Barringer (Brookline, MA: Holy Cross Orthodox Press, 1994–2013). The first volume has no subtitle; the remaining volumes have subtitles: II: *The World: Creation and Deification*; III: *The Person of Jesus Christ as God and Saviour*; IV: *The Church: Communion in the Holy Spirit*; V: *The Sanctifying Mysteries*; VI: *The Fulfilment of Creation*. German trans.: *Orthodoxe Dogmatik*, trans. Hermann Pitters, 3 vols (Zürich: Benziger Verlag/Gütersloh: Gütersloher Verlagshaus Gerd Mohn, 1984–95).

The Victory of the Cross, Fairacres Pamphlet 16 (Oxford: SLG Press, no date).

Details of other works, both in Romanian and in translation, including all his translations can be found in *Persoană şi Comuniune: Prinos de Cinstire* or in *Father Dumitru Stăniloae: A Worthy Disciple of the Classical Patristics* (see below).

About Stăniloae

Allchin, A. M., obituary for Fr Dumitru, *Sobornost* 16:1 (1994), 38–44.

Anghelescu, Gheorgh F., and Cristian Untea, *Father Dumitru Stăniloae: A Worthy Disciple of the Classical Patristics (Bio-Bibliography)* (Bucharest: Editura Enciclopedică, 2009).

Bartos, Emil, *Deification in Eastern Orthodox Theology: An Evaluation and Critique of the Theology of Dumitru Stăniloae* (Carlisle: Paternoster Press, 1999).

Bielawski, Maciej, *The Philokalical Vision of the World in the Theology of Dumitru Stăniloae* (Bydgoszcz: Wydawnictwo *Homini*, 1997).

Costa de Beauregard, Marc-Antoine, *Dumitru Stăniloae: «Ose comprendre que Je t'aime»* (Paris: Cerf, 2009; 1st edn, 1983).

Dumitru Stăniloae: Tradition and Modernity in Theology, ed. Lucian Turcescu (Iaşi: Center of Romanian Studies, 2002).

Giosanu, Joachim, *La Déification de l'homme d'après la pensée du père Dumitru Staniloaë* (Iassy: Trinitas, 2003).

Miller, Charles, *The Gift of the World: An Introduction to the Theology of Dumitru Stăniloae* (Edinburgh: T&T Clark, 2000).

Persoană şi Comuniune: Prinos de Cinstire: Preotului Profesor Academician Dumitru Stăniloae 1903–1993, ed. Mircea Păcurariu and Ioan I. Ică Jr (Sibiu: Editura şi tiparul Arhiepiscopiei ortodoxe Sibiu, 1993).

10: Modern Orthodox dogmatic theology: 2 St Justin Popović

Popovich, Justin, *Orthodox Faith and Life in Christ*, trans. etc. by Asterios Gerostergios et al. (Belmont, MA: Institute for Byzantine and Modern Greek Studies, 1994). This contains various short works translated from Greek into English, though I suspect Mother Maria Rule's translation of 'The Theory of Knowledge of St Isaac the Syrian' was translated from Serbian.

Popovits, Ioustinos, *Odos Theognosias* (Athens: Ekdoseis Grigori, 1992). This contains the doctoral thesis on the Macarian Homilies, and the essay on St Isaac, as well as a (composed) century of extracts.

Various works of St Justin have been translated into French, published in the series *La Lumière de Thabor*, notably:

Popovitch, Justin, *L'Homme et le Dieu-Homme* (Lausanne: L'Âge d'Homme, 1989).

Popovitch, Justin, *Philosophie orthodoxe de la Verité: Dogmatique de l'Église orthodoxe*, trans. Jean-Louis Palierne, 5 vols (Lausanne: L'Âge d'Homme, 1992–7).

About Popović

Obituary by Dame Elizabeth Hill in *Sobornost/Eastern Churches Review* 2:1 (1980), 73–9. (There was also an obituary by Fr John Meyendorff in *St Vladimir's Theological Quarterly* 23 (1979), 118–19, but I have not had access to it.)

There is little secondary literature, save in Serbian and Bulgarian, but see:

Cvetković, Vladimir, 'St Justin the New on Integral Knowledge', *Teologikon* (Veliko Trnovo), tom. 1 (2012), 149–58.

11 Paul Evdokimov and the love and beauty of God

Les Âges de la vie spirituelle: Des pères du desert à nos jours (Paris: Desclée de Brouwer, 1964; reissued 1980); ET: Sister Gertrude SP, rev. Michael Plekon and Alexis Vinogradoff (Crestwood, NY: St Vladimir's Seminary Press, 1998).

L'Amour fou de Dieu (Paris: Seuil, 1973).

L'Art de l'icône: Théologie de la beauté (Paris: Desclée de Brouwer, 1970).

Le Christ dans la pensée russe (Paris: Cerf, 1970).

La Connaissance de Dieu selon la tradition orientale (Lyon: Xavier Mappus, 1968).

Dostoïevski et le problème du mal (Lyon: Éditions du Livre Français, 1942; reissued Paris: Desclée de Brouwer, 1978).

L'Esprit-Saint dans la tradition orthodoxe (Paris: Cerf, 1969; reissued 2011).

La Femme et le salut de monde (Paris–Tournai: Desclée de Brouwer, 1958; reissued 1978).

Gogol et Dostoïevski ou la descente aux enfers (Paris: Desclée de Brouwer, 1961; reissued Paris: Éditions de Corlevour, 2011).

Le Mariage, sacrement de l'amour (Lyon: Éditions du Livre Français, 1944).

L'Orthodoxie (Neuchâtel: Delachaux et Niestlé, 1959; ET, London: New City, 2011).

Le Sacrement de l'amour: Le mystère conjugal à la lumière de la tradition orthodoxe (Paris: Éditions de l'Épi, 1962; reissued 1980).

And in English translation (in addition to several of his books, which have been translated):

In the World, Of the Church: A Paul Evdokimov Reader, ed. Michael Plekon and Alexis Vinogradoff (Crestwood, NY: St Vladimir's Seminary Press, 2001).

About Paul Evdokimov

Not much:

Clément, Olivier, *Orient–Occident: Deux passeurs: Vladimir Lossky et Paul Evdokimov* (Geneva: Labor et Fides, 1985), 105–210.

Contacts 73–4 (2001); 235–6 (2011). These are two double editions.

12 Neo-Palamism: Fr John Meyendorff and some Greek neo-Palamites

Meyendorff

Byzantine Hesychasm: Historical, Theological, and Social Problems (Aldershot: Variorum, 1974).

Byzantine Theology (Bronx, NY: Fordham University Press/London: Mowbrays, 1974).

Byzantium and the Rise of Russia (New York: Cambridge University Press, 1981).

Le Christ dans la théologie byzantine (Paris: Cerf, 1969); ET: *Christ in Eastern Christian Thought* (Crestwood, NY: St Vladimir's Seminary Press, 1969).

L'Église orthodoxe: Hier et aujourd'hui (Paris: Seuil, 1960); ET: *The Orthodox Church: Its Past and Its Role in the World Today* (London: Darton, Longman & Todd, 1962).

Imperial Unity and Christian Divisions: The Church 450–680 AD, vol. 2 of *The Church in History* (Crestwood, NY: St Vladimir's Seminary Press, 1989).

Introduction à l'étude de Grégoire Palamas, Patristica Sorbonensia 3 (Paris: Seuil, 1959); ET (with abridged footnotes and lacking the Appendices and Bibliography, but with minor updating): *A Study of Gregory Palamas*, trans. George Lawrence (London: Faith Press, 1964; now published by St Vladimir's Seminary Press).

Marriage – An Orthodox Perspective (Crestwood, NY: St Vladimir's Seminary Press, 1970; rev. edn, 1975).

Palamas, Grégoire, *Défense des saints hésychastes* (Leuven-Louvain, Spicilegium Sacrum Lovaniense: Études et documents, fascicule 30–1, 1959, rev. edn, 1973); very partial ET: Gregory Palamas, *The Triads*, trans. Nicholas Gendle (London: SPCK, 1983).

St Grégoire Palamas et la mystique orthodoxe, Maîtres spirituels 20 (Paris: Seuil, 1959; ET, Crestwood, NY: St Vladimir's Seminary Press, 1980).

With Aristeides Papadakis:

The Christian East and the Rise of the Papacy: The Church 1071–1453 AD, vol. 4 of *The Church in History* (Crestwood, NY: St Vladimir's Seminary Press, 1994).

About Meyendorff

Obituary by Dimitri Obolensky in *Sobornost/Eastern Churches Review* 15:2 (1993), 44–51.

New Perspectives on Historical Theology: Essays in Memory of John Meyendorff, ed. Bradley Nassif (Grand Rapids, MI: Eerdmans, 1995).

Shaw, Lewis, 'John Meyendorff and the Heritage of the Russian Theological Tradition', in *New Perspectives on Historical Theology*, ed. Nassif, 10–42.

For Palamas and the hesychast controversy, see:

Sinkewicz, R. E., 'Gregory Palamas', in *La Théologie byzantine et sa tradition*, II, ed. Carmelo Giuseppe Conticello and Vassa Conticello (Turnhout: Brepols, 2002), 31–188.

For Romanides' criticisms:

Romanides, John S., 'Notes on the Palamite Controversy and Related Topics', *Greek Orthodox Theological Review*, I: 6 (1960–1), 186–205; II: 9 (1963–4), 225–70.

The Greek neo-Palamites

Mantzaridis, George, *The Deification of Man*, trans. Liadain Sherrard (Crestwood, NY: St Vladimir's Seminary Press, 1984).

Nellas, Panayiotis, *Deification in Christ*, trans. Norman Russell (Crestwood, NY: St Vladimir's Seminary Press, 1987).

13 Liturgical theology: Fr Alexander Schmemann and the Greeks Ioannis Foundoulis and Fr Vasileios

Schmemann

Celebration of Faith, vol. I: *I Believe*; vol. II: *The Church Year*; vol. III: *The Virgin Mary* (Crestwood, NY: St Vladimir's Seminary Press, 1990–5).

Church, World, Mission: Reflections on Orthodoxy in the West (Crestwood, NY: St Vladimir's Seminary Press, 1979).

The Eucharist: Sacrament of the Kingdom (Crestwood, NY: St Vladimir's Seminary Press, 1988).

For the Life of the World: Sacraments and Orthodoxy (Crestwood, NY: St Vladimir's Seminary Press, 1963; 2nd rev. and expanded edn, 1973); UK edn: *The World as Sacrament* (London: Darton, Longman & Todd, 1966).

Great Lent: The Journey to Pascha (Crestwood, NY: St Vladimir's Seminary Press, 1969).

The Historical Road of Eastern Orthodoxy (London: Harvill Press, 1963).

Introduction to Liturgical Theology (London: Faith Press, 1966).

The Journals of Father Alexander Schmemann, 1973–1983 (Crestwood, NY: St Vladimir's Seminary Press, 2000); complete original, mostly in Russian: *Dnevniki 1973–1983* (Moscow: Russkii Put', 2007).

Liturgy and Tradition, ed. Thomas Fitch (Crestwood, NY: St Vladimir's Seminary Press, 1990).

Of Water and the Spirit (Crestwood, NY: St Vladimir's Seminary Press, 1974).

Ultimate Questions: An Anthology of Modern Russian Religious Thought (Crestwood, NY: St Vladimir's Seminary Press, 1977; originally published in 1965).

About Schmemann

Afterword by John Meyendorff to *Journals*, 343–51; originally published as 'A Life Worth Living', *St Vladimir's Theological Quarterly* 28 (1984), 3–10; also in *Liturgy and Tradition*, 145–54.

Basioudis, George, *I dynami tis latreias: I symboli tou p. Alexandrou Schmemann sti Leitourgiki Theologia* [The power of worship: The contribution of Fr Alexander Schmemann to liturgical theology] (Athens: En Plo, 2008).

Mills, William C., *Church, World, Kingdom: The Eucharistic Foundations of Alexander Schmemann's Pastoral Theology* (Chicago–Mundelein, IL: Hillenbrand, 2012).

Obituary by Peter Scorer in *Sobornost/Eastern Churches Review* 6:2 (1984), 64–8.

See also:

St Vladimir's Theological Quarterly 53, numbers 2–3 (2009). This is a special issue with articles by Taft, Fagerberg, Aune, Spinks, Getcha, Alexopoulos, Larin, Meyendorff, Hopko, Vinogradov, Meerson.

The Greeks

Foundouli, Ioannou M., *Apantiseis eis Leitourgikas Aporias*, 5 vols (Athens: Apostoliki Diakonia, 1967–2003).

Vasileios, *Hymn of Entry* (Crestwood, NY: St Vladimir's Seminary Press, 1997); original version: *Eisodikon: Stoicheia leitourgikis vioseos tou mystiriou tis enotitos mesa stin Orthodoxi Ekklisia* [Entry hymn: Elements of liturgical life of the mystery of unity within the Orthodox Church] (Holy Mountain: Iera Moni Stavronikita, 1974).

14 Theology of patristic renewal: Metropolitan John of Pergamon (Zizioulas) and Fr John Romanides

Zizioulas

Being as Communion: Studies in Personhood and the Church (Crestwood, NY: St Vladimir's Seminary Press, 1985; 2nd edn, 2004).

Communion and Otherness: Further Studies in Personhood and the Church (Crestwood, NY: St Vladimir's Seminary Press, 2006).

Eucharist, Bishop, Church: The Unity of the Church in the Divine Eucharist and the Bishop during the First Three Centuries (Brookline, MA: Holy Cross Orthodox Press, 1965).

The One and the Many: Studies on God, Man, the Church, and the World Today (Alhambra, CA: Sebastian Press, 2010).

About Zizioulas

Knight, Douglas H., ed., *The Theology of John Zizioulas: Personhood and the Church* (Farnham: Ashgate, 2007).

Koutloumousianos, Chrysostomos, *The One and the Three: Triadic Monarchy in the Byzantine and Irish Patristic Tradition and Its Anthropological Repercussions* (London: Lutterworth, due in 2015) − though it is more than simply secondary literature on Zizioulas.

Kristiansen, Ståle Johannes and Svein Rise, eds, *Key Theological Thinkers: From Modern to Postmodern* (Farnham: Ashgate, 2013), 435−47 (Lars Erik Rikheim).

McPartland, Paul, *The Eucharist Makes the Church: Henri de Lubac and John Zizioulas in Dialogue* (Edinburgh: T&T Clark, 1993).

Papanikolaou, Aristotle, *Being with God: Trinity, Apophaticism, and Divine−Human Communion* (Notre Dame, IN: University of Notre Dame Press, 2006).

Afanasiev

Afanassieff, Nicolas, 'L'Église qui preside dans l'Amour', in *La Primauté de Pierre dans l'Église orthodoxe* (Neuchâtel: Delachaux et Niestlé, 1960), 7−62; ET in *The Primacy of Peter in the Orthodox Church* (Leighton Buzzard: Faith Press, 1963), 57−110.

The Church of the Holy Spirit, trans. Vitaly Permiakov (Notre Dame, IN: University of Notre Dame Press, 2007).

Romanides

Dogmatiki kai Symboliki Theologia tis Orthodoxou Katholikis Ekklesias [Dogmatic and Symbolic Theology of the Orthodox Catholic Church], 2 vols (Thessaloniki: Ekdoseis Pournara, 4th edn, 1999; original edn, 1973).

'The Ecclesiology of St Ignatius of Antioch', *Greek Orthodox Theological Review* 7 (1961−2), 53−77.

Encheiridion: Allilographia p. I. S. Romanidou kai kath. P. N. Trembela [Dossier {also means: Dagger}: Correspondence between Fr J. S. Romanides and Prof. P. N. Trembelas] (Athens: Ekdoseis Armos, 2009).

Franks, Romans, Feudalism, and Doctrine: An Interplay between Theology and Society (Brookline, MA: Holy Cross Orthodox Press, 1982).

Romiosyni, Romania, Roumeli (Thessaloniki: Ekdoseis Pournara, 1975).

To Propatorikon Amartima [Ancestral Sin] (Thessaloniki: Ekdoseis Pournara, 3rd edn, 2010; original edn, 1957).

Secondary literature

Sopko, Andrew J., *Prophet of Roman Orthodoxy: The Theology of John Romanides* (Dewdney, BC: Synaxis Press, 1998).

15 Lay theologians: 1 Philip Sherrard

Greek literature: studies and translations

Angelos Sikelianos: Selected Poems (Princeton, NJ: Princeton University Press, 1979; reprinted in the Romiosyni Series, Limni, Evia, Greece: Denise Harvey & Co., 1996).

C. P. Cavafy: Collected Poems (London: Chatto & Windus, 1975).

Four Greek Poets (Harmondsworth: Penguin, 1966).

George Seferis: Collected Poems (London: Anvil Press, 1967).
The Marble Threshing Floor (London: Vallentine, Mitchell & Co., 1956; reprinted in the Romiosyni Series, 1981).
Odysseus Elytis: Selected Poems (London: Anvil Press, 1981).
Six Poets of Modern Greece (New York: Alfred A. Knopf, 1961).
The Wound of Greece: Studies in Neo-Hellenism (London: Rex Collings, 1978).

Verse

In the Sign of the Rainbow: Selected Poems 1940–89 (London: Anvil Press, 1994).

On Greece

Athos: The Holy Mountain (London: Sidgwick & Jackson, 1982); originally published in German in 1959, and then as *Athos: The Mountain of Silence* the following year.
Constantinople: The Iconography of a Sacred City (London: Oxford University Press, 1965).
Edward Lear: The Corfu Years (Limni: Denise Harvey & Co., 1988).

Theological

Christianity: Lineaments of a Sacred Tradition (Brookline, MA: Holy Cross Orthodox Press, 1998).
Christianity and Eros (London: SPCK, 1976; reprinted in the Romiosyni Series, 1995).
Church, Papacy and Schism (London: SPCK, 1978; reprinted in the Romiosyni Series, 1996).
The Greek East and the Latin West (London: Oxford University Press, 1959; reprinted in the Romiosyni Series, 1992).
The Philokalia: The Complete Text Compiled by St Nikodimos of the Holy Mountain and St Makarios of Corinth, trans. G. E. H. Palmer, Philip Sherrard, Kallistos Ware, 5 vols (so far only 1–4) (London: Faber & Faber, 1979–95). Philip Sherrard completed his draft translation of vol. 5 before his death in 1995.

On ecology

Human Image: World Image: The Death and Resurrection of Sacred Cosmology (Ipswich: Golgonooza Press, 1992).
The Rape of Man and Nature (Ipswich: Golgonooza Press, 1987).
The Sacred in Life and Art (Ipswich: Golgonooza Press, 1990).

There are many articles scattered over various journals. I have made no systematic search, but mention the following:

'Kathleen Raine and the Symbolic Art', *Temenos Academy Review* 11 (2008), 180–208.
'Yeats, Homer and the Heroic', *Temenos* 12 (1991), 76–93.

About Sherrard

Kallistos, obituary for Sherrard, *Sobornost/Eastern Churches Review* 17:2 (1995), 45–52.
Raine, Kathleen, *Philip Sherrard (1922–1995): A Tribute* (Birmingham: The Delos Press/ Clun: The Redlake Press, 1996).

There are also further studies by Metropolitan Kallistos:

Introduction to *Christianity: Lineaments of a Sacred Tradition*, ix–xlv.

Philip Sherrard: A Prophet for Our Time, First Annual Sherrard Lecture 2003 (Athos: Friends of Mount Athos, 2008).

16 Lay theologians: 2 Dimitris Koutroubis, Christos Yannaras, Stelios Ramfos

Koutroubis

I Charis tis Theologias (Athens: Domos, 1995).

For biographical material, see:

'*In Memoriam Demetrios Koutroubis*', *Sobornost/Eastern Churches Review* 6:1 (1984), 67–77. This is a collection of tributes to him by (then) Bishop Kallistos of Diokleia, Elias Mastroiannopoulos, Christos Yannaras, and A. M. Allchin.

Yannaras

Autobiographical:

Katafygio ideon: Martyria (Athens: Ikaros, 5th rev. edn, 2000; originally published by Domos, 1987).
Ta kath' eauton (Athens: Ikaros, 1995).

Yannaras has written far too many books for them to be listed here. I've referred to:

Heidegger kai Areopagitis (first published as a thesis, Athens, 1967; Athens: Ekdoseis Dodoni, 1972; 2nd rev. edn, Athens: Domos, 1988); ET: *On the Absence and Unknowability of God: Heidegger and the Areopagite* (London: T&T Clark, 2005).
I eleftheria tou ithous (Athens: Ekdoseis Domos; 2nd expanded edn, 1979; original edn, 1970); ET: *The Freedom of Morality*, trans. Elizabeth Brière (Crestwood, NY: St Vladimir's Seminary Press, 1984).
I metafysiki tou somatos: Spoudi ston Ioanni tis Klimakos (Athens: Ekdoseis Dodoni, 1971).
Orthodoxy and the West, trans. Peter Chamberas and Norman Russell (Brookline, MA: Holy Cross Orthodox Press, 2006); trans. of *Orthodoxia kai Dysi sti Neoteri Ellada* (Athens: Domos, 1992).
Peina kai Dipsa (Athens: Ekdoseis Grigori, 1969; though there was an earlier version as a pamphlet in 1961).
To prosopo kai o eros (Athens: Ekdoseis Domos, 4th edn, 1987); ET: *Person and Eros*, trans. Norman Russell (Brookline, MA: Holy Cross Orthodox Press, 2007).
And I should have discussed what is, I think, the best of his works:

Scholio sto Asma Asmaton (Athens: Ekdoseis Domos, 1990); ET: *Variations on the Song of Songs*, trans. Norman Russell (Brookline, MA: Holy Cross Orthodox Press, 2005).

About Yannaras

Mitralexis, Sotiris, 'Person, Eros, Critical Ontology: An Attempt to Recapitulate Christos Yannaras' Philosophy', *Sobornost/Eastern Churches Review* 34:1 (2012), 33–40.

Ramfos

His works are too many to mention; the following are available in English:

I kaimos tou enos (Athens: Ekdoseis Armos, 2000); abridged ET: *Yearning for the One: Chapters in the Inner Life of the Greeks*, trans. Norman Russell (Brookline, MA: Holy Cross Orthodox Press, 2011).

Pelikanoi erimikoi (Athens: Ekdoseis Armos, 1994); abridged ET: *Like a Pelican in the Wilderness*, trans. Norman Russell (Brookline, MA: Holy Cross Orthodox Press, 2000).

About the Greek Church after the Second World War, and Greek theology

Hammond, Peter, *The Waters of Marah: The Present State of the Greek Church* (London: Rockliff, 1956).

Kalaïtzidis, P., Th. N. Papathanasiou, Th. Ampatzidis, eds, *Anataraxeis sti Metapolemiki Theologia: I «Theologia tou '60»* (Athens: Indiktos, 2009).

Other works mentioned

Macmurray, John, *Persons in Relation* (London: Faber & Faber, 1961).

Macmurray, John, *The Self as Agent* (London: Faber & Faber, 1957).

Spaemann, Robert, *Persons: The Difference between 'Someone' and 'Something'*, trans. Oliver O'Donovan (Oxford: Oxford University Press, 2006).

Tournier, Paul, *The Meaning of Persons* (London: SCM Press, 1957).

17 Lay theologians: 3 Elisabeth Behr-Sigel, Olivier Clément

Behr-Sigel

Alexandre Boukharev: Un théologien de l'Église orthodoxe russe en dialogue avec le monde moderne (Paris: Éditions Beauchesne, 1977). (See also on Bukharev: Paul Evdokimov, *Le Christ dans la pensée russe* (Paris: Cerf, 1970), 85–9; Paul Valliere, *Modern Russian Theology: Bukharev, Soloviev, Bulgakov: Orthodox Theology in a New Key* (Edinburgh: T&T Clark, 2000), 19–106; also, Nadejda Gorodetzky, *The Humiliated Christ in Modern Russian Thought* (London: SPCK, 1938), esp. 116–26.)

Discerner les signes du temps (Paris: Cerf, 2002); originally in English: *Discerning the Signs of the Times: The Vision of Elisabeth Behr-Sigel*, ed. Michael Plekon and Sarah E. Hinlicky (Crestwood, NY: St Vladimir's Seminary Press, 2001).

Lev Gillet, «un moine de l'Église d'Orient» (Paris: Cerf, 1993); ET: *Lev Gillet, 'A Monk of the Eastern Church'*, trans. Helen Wright (Oxford: Fellowship of St Alban and St Sergius, 1999).

Le Lieu du cœur: Initiation à la spiritualité de l'Église orthodoxe (Paris: Cerf, 1989); ET: *The Place of the Heart: Introduction to Orthodox Spirituality*, trans. Stephen Bigham (Torrance, CA: Oakwood, 1992).

Le Ministère de la femme dans l'Église (Paris: Cerf, 1987); ET: *The Ministry of Women in the Church*, trans. Stephen Bigham (Redondo Beach, CA: Oakwood, 1991).

L'Ordination de femmes dans l'Église orthodoxe (Paris: Cerf, 1998); ET: *The Ordination of Women in the Orthodox Church* (Geneva: WCC Publications, 2000).

Prière et sainteté dans l'Église russe (Paris: Cerf, 1950); reissued: Spiritualité Orientale 33 (Bégrolles-en-Mauge: Abbaye de la Bellefontaine, 1982).

For an extensive (surely complete) bibliography of Elisabeth's works, see:

Hinlicky Wilson, Sarah, *Woman, Women, and the Priesthood in the Trinitarian Theology of Elisabeth Behr-Sigel* (London: Bloomsbury T&T Clark, 2013), 167–82.

About Behr-Sigel

Lossky, Olga, *Vers le jour sans déclin: Une vie d'Élisabeth Behr-Sigel (1907–2005)* (Paris: Cerf, 2007); there is an abridged ET published by the Fellowship of St Alban and St Sergius.

See also:

Contacts 220 (October–December 2007). This includes gathered tributes. Obituary by Marcus Plested in *Sobornost/Eastern Churches Review* 27:2 (2005), 62–4.

For her theology, see:

Hinlicky Wilson, Sarah, *Woman, Women, and the Priesthood in the Trinitarian Theology of Elisabeth Behr-Sigel* (London: Bloomsbury T&T Clark, 2013).

Olivier Clément

Clément was immensely prolific. Mentioned here is only a selection.

L'Autre Soleil (Paris: Stock, 1975).
Corps de mort et de gloire: Petite introduction à une théopoétique de corps (Paris: Desclée de Brouwer, 1995).
Dialogues avec le patriarche Athénagoras (Paris: Fayard, 1969; 2nd augmented edn, 1976; ET, Crestwood, NY: St Vladimir's Seminary Press).
L'Œil de feu (Clichy (Hauts-de-Seine): Éditions de Corlevour, 2012).
Petite boussole spirituelle pour notre temps (Paris: Desclée de Brouwer, 2008).
Rome, autrement (Paris: Desclée de Brouwer, 1997).
Sources: Les mystiques chrétiens des origines: Textes et commentaire (Paris: Stock, 1982); ET: Theodore Berkeley, rev. Jeremy Hummerstone, *The Roots of Christian Mysticism* (London: New City, 1993).
The Spirit of Solzhenitsyn (London: Search Press, 1976; French original, Paris: Stock, 1974). The English version has an additional chapter.
La vérité vous rendra libre: Entretiens avec le patriarche œcuménique Bartholomée Ier (Paris: Desclée de Brouwer, 1996; Crestwood, NY: St Vladimir's Seminary Press).
Le Visage intérieur (Paris: Stock, 1978).

With Mohamed Talbi:

Un respect têtu (Paris: Nouvelle Cité, 1989).

About Clément

Lossky, Nicholas, obituary for Clément, *Sobornost/Eastern Churches Review* 31:1 (2009), 61–3.
Contacts 228 (October–December 2009). This issue was a tribute to him; apart from the tributes at his funeral and messages *in memoriam* (383–406), it contains Clément's own 'Notes autobiographiques', and what is described as a 'bibliographie succincte' (not at all complete); the rest of it consists of pieces by Clément himself.

More recently another issue of *Contacts* has been devoted to Clément:

Contacts 247 (July–September 2014).

18 Spiritual elders: 1 Mother Thekla (Sharf) and the English acculturation of Orthodoxy

Mother Maria

Gysi, Lydia, *Platonism and Cartesianism in the Philosophy of Ralph Cudworth* (Bern: Herbert Lang, 1962); other works in The Library of Orthodox Thinking.
Mother Maria: Her Life in Letters, ed. Sister Thekla (London: Darton, Longman & Todd, 1979).

Mother Thekla

The Dark Glass: Meditations in Orthodox Spirituality (London: Fount, 1996).
Eternity Now: An Introduction to Orthodox Spirituality (Norwich: Canterbury Press, 1997).
George Herbert: Idea and Image (Newport Pagnell: Library of Orthodox Thinking, 1974).
Hamlet: The Noble Mind (Newport Pagnell: Library of Orthodox Thinking, 1972).
John Keats: The Disinterested Heart (Newport Pagnell: Library of Orthodox Thinking, 1973).
A Story of Babylon (Newport Pagnell: Library of Orthodox Thinking, 1973).

With John Tavener:

Ikons: Meditations in Words and Music (London: Fount, 1994).

About Mother Thekla

Mother Thekla, *The Monastery of the Assumption: A History*, Pamphlet 8 (Normanby, Whitby: Library of Orthodox Thinking, 1984).

See also her:

Introduction to *Mother Maria: Her Life in Letters*, ed. Sister Thekla (London: Darton, Longman & Todd, 1979), xiii–xlviii.
Obituary in *The Times*, 27 August 2011.

There is an entry on her life forthcoming in the *Oxford Dictionary of National Biography*.

19 Spiritual elders: 2 St Silouan and Fr Sophrony: seeing God as he is

St Silouan

Life and teachings of Archimandrite Sophrony:
Prepodobny Siluan Afonsky (Paris, 1952; facsimile published with additional texts by the monastery, 1990). ET: *The Undistorted Image: Staretz Silouan 1866–1938* (London: Faith Press, 1958); republished in two volumes with some additional material as *The Monk from Mount Athos*, with a brief Foreword by Metropolitan Anthony of Sourozh, and *Wisdom from Mount Athos*, with a Foreword by Archimandrite Sophrony (London: Mowbrays, 1973–4); fullest version: *Saint Silouan the Athonite*

(Essex: Stavropegic Monastery of St John the Baptist, 1991; Crestwood, NY: St Vladimir's Seminary Press, 1998); French trans.: *Starets Silouane, moine du Mont-Athos: Vie – Doctrine – Écrits* (Sisteron: Éditions Présence, 1973; there are doubtless later editions called *Saint Silouane . . .*). There are translations into several other languages: Greek, Serbian, Romanian, etc.

Fr Sophrony

His Life Is Mine, with an Introduction by Rosemary Edmonds (London and Oxford: Mowbrays, 1977; now in print with Crestwood, NY: St Vladimir's Seminary Press, 2001); French trans.: *Sa vie est la mienne* (Paris: Cerf, 1981).

On Prayer (Crestwood, NY: St Vladimir's Seminary Press, 1998; Essex: Stavropegic Monastery of St John the Baptist, 1996).

Videt' Bog kak On est' (Sergiev Posad: Trinity-St Sergii Lavra/Essex: Stavropegic Monastery of St John the Baptist, 2006; *We Shall See Him as He Is* (Essex: Stavropegic Monastery of St John the Baptist, 1988); *Voir Dieu tel qu'il est* (Geneva: Labor et Fides, 1984); *La Félicité de connaître la voie* (Geneva: Labor et Fides, 1988)).

The Stavropegic Monastery of St John the Baptist is publishing conversations, letters, articles, etc. in Russian.

English translations are by Rosemary Edmonds; French translations by Hieromonk Symeon. As I mentioned in the chapter, the correspondence between the various volumes in different languages (or even in the same language) is confusing, to say the least.

About Fr Sophrony

Gerontas Sophronios: O Theologos tou Aktistou Photos, ed. George I. Mantzaridis (Holy Mountain: Iera Megisti Moni Vatopaidiou, 2008) – proceedings of a conference in Athens, 2007.

Sakharov, Nicholas V. (Fr Nikolai), *I Love, Therefore I Am: The Theological Legacy of Archimandrite Sophrony* (Crestwood, NY: St Vladimir's Seminary Press, 2002).

Zacharou, Zacharias, *Christ, Our Way and Our Life: A Presentation of the Theology of Archimandrite Sophrony*, trans. from the Greek by Sister Magdalen (South Canaan, PA: St Tikhon's Seminary Press, 2003).

Zacharou, Zacharias, *The Enlargement of the Heart* (South Canaan, PA: Mount Thabor, 2006).

Zacharou, Zacharias, *The Hidden Man of the Heart* (Essex: Stavropegic Monastery of St John the Baptist, 2007).

Zacharou, Zacharias, *Remember Thy First Love* (Essex: Stavropegic Monastery of St John the Baptist, 2010).

20 Theology in Russia under communism: Fr Aleksandr Men'

Works by Fr Aleksandr Men' in English

'The 1960s Remembered', *Religion, State, and Society* 23 (1995), 125–58.

About Christ and the Church, trans. Fr Alexis Vinogradoff (Torrance, CA: Oakwood, 1996).

Awake to Life! The Easter Cycle, trans. Marita Sapiets (London: Bowerdean Press, 1992).

Christianity for the Twenty-First Century: The Prophetic Writings of Alexander Men, ed. Elizabeth Roberts and Ann Shukman (New York: Continuum, 1996) – selected translations.

An Inner Step towards God: Writings and Teachings on Prayer by Father Alexander Men, ed. April French, trans. Christa Belyaeva (Brewster, MA: Paraclete Press, 2014).
Son of Man, trans. Samuel Brown (Torrance, CA: Oakwood, 1998).

In French

Au fil de l'Apocalypse (Paris: Cerf/Pully: Le Sel de la Terre, 2003).
Le christianisme ne fait que commencer (Paris: Cerf/Pully: Le Sel de la Terre, 2010).
Les Sources de la religion (Paris: Desclée de Brouwer, 1991).

About Fr Men'

Christianity for the Twenty-First Century: The Prophetic Writings of Alexander Men, ed. Elizabeth Roberts and Ann Shukman (New York: Continuum, 1996), Introduction.
Hamart, Yves, *Alexandre Men* (Montrouge: Nouvelle Cité, 2000; originally, Paris: Mame, 1993; ET, Torrance, CA: Oakwood, 1995).
Havriljukova, Lida, 'Fr Aleksandr Men' (1935–90): Perceptions of Him as a Spiritual Elder', *Sobornost/Eastern Churches Review* 32:1 (2010), 36–52.
Plekon, Michael, *Living Icons* (Notre Dame, IN: University of Notre Dame Press, 2002), 234–60.

21 Metropolitan Kallistos and the theological vision of the *Philokalia*

Eustratios Argenti: A Study of the Greek Church under Turkish Rule (Oxford: Clarendon Press, 1964).
The Inner Kingdom, volume 1 of the Collected Works (Crestwood, NY: St Vladimir's Seminary Press, 2000).
The Orthodox Church (Harmondsworth: Penguin, 1963; rev. edn, 1993).
The Orthodox Way (London: Mowbrays, 1979; rev. edn, Crestwood, NY: St Vladimir's Seminary Press, 1995).
The Power of the Name, Fairacres Publication 43 (Oxford: SLG Press, 1974; rev. edn, 1977): much translated and reprinted in, for instance, Elisabeth Behr-Sigel, *The Place of the Heart: An Introduction to Orthodox Spirituality*, trans. Fr Stephen Bigham (Torrance, CA: Oakwood, 1992), 133–73.

Selected articles (those I have referred to)

The Beginning of the Day: The Orthodox Vision of Creation [in Greek and English] (Ioannina: Shrine of Neomartyr George of Ioannina, 2007).
'The Debate about Palamism', *Eastern Churches Review* 9:1–2 (1977), 45–63.
'Diadochus von Photice', in *Theologische Realenzyklopädie* VIII (1981), 617–20.
Ecological Crisis, Ecological Hope: Our Orthodox Vision of Creation, Orthodoxy in America Lecture Series, 5 April 2005, Fordham University.
'Gerald Palmer, the *Philokalia*, and the Holy Mountain', *Annual Report of the Friends of Mount Athos* (1994), 26–7.
'God Hidden and Revealed: The Apophatic Way and the Essence–Energies Distinction', *Eastern Churches Review* 7:2 (1975), 125–36.
'Gottesdienst: Orthodoxe Kirche', in *Theologische Realenzyklopädie* XIV (1985), 46–51.
The Inner Unity of the Philokalia *and Its Influence in East and West* [in Greek and English] (Athens: Onassis Foundation, 2004).

'The Mystery of the Human Person', *Sobornost/Eastern Churches Review* 3:1 (1981), 62–9.

'Nous and Noesis in Plato, Aristotle and Evagrius of Pontus', *Diotima* 13 [Proceedings of the Second International Week on the Philosophy of Greek Culture, Kalamata 1982, Part II], 1985, 158–63.

O Anthropos os «Mysterion»: I Enotita tou Prosopou kata tous Ellines Pateres, Bishop Kallistos' inaugural lecture as member of the Academy of Athens, 5 February 2008, Athens.

Orthodox Theology in the Twenty-First Century (Geneva: WCC Publications, 2012).

'Philocalie', in *Dictionnaire de Spiritualité* XII (1984), cols 1336–52.

'Scholasticism and Orthodoxy: Theological Method as a Factor in the Schism', *Eastern Churches Review* 5:1 (1973), 16–27.

'Silence in Prayer: The Meaning of Hesychia', in *Theology and Prayer*, ed. A. M. Allchin, Studies Supplementary to *Sobornost* 3 (1975), 8–28; also in *One Yet Two: Monastic Tradition East and West*, ed. M. Basil Pennington, Cistercian Studies 29 (Kalamazoo, MI: Cistercian Publications, 1976), 22–47; and in *The Inner Kingdom*, 89–110.

'The Soul in Greek Christianity', in *From Soul to Self*, ed. M. James C. Crabbe (London–New York: Routledge, 1999), 49–69.

Through the Creation to the Creator (London: Friends of the Centre, 1997).

About Metropolitan Kallistos

Abba: The Tradition of Orthodoxy in the West, Festschrift for Bishop Kallistos, ed. John Behr, Andrew Louth, Dimitri Conomos (Crestwood, NY: St Vladimir's Seminary Press, 2003). This includes a biographical sketch by Andrew Louth and Graham Speake: 13–40; also a bibliography of his works up to 2002: 363–76.

Index

Andrew Louth is Professor Emeritus of Patristic and Byzantine Studies, Durham University, and was Visiting Professor of Eastern Orthodox Theology at the Amsterdam Centre of Eastern Orthodox Theology (ACEOT), Vrije Universiteit, Amsterdam, from 2010 to 2014. He is an archpriest of the Russian Orthodox Diocese of Sourozh (Moscow Patriarchate), serving the parish in Durham. Educated at the universities of Cambridge and Edinburgh, he has taught at the universities of Oxford (where he holds a degree of DD) and London (Goldsmiths' College), and finally Durham, retiring in 2010, in which year he was elected a Fellow of the British Academy.

He is the author of several books, including *The Origins of the Christian Mystical Tradition: From Plato to Denys* (1981; revised second edition, 2007), *Discerning the Mystery* (1983), *Denys the Areopagite* (London, 1989), *Maximus the Confessor* (1996), *St John Damascene: Tradition and Originality in Byzantine Theology* (2002), *Greek East and Latin West: The Church 681–1071* (2007), and *Introducing Eastern Orthodox Theology* (2013), as well as many articles.